Newspaper Story

Newspaper Story

One Hundred Years of

The Boston Globe

LOUIS M. LYONS

The Belknap Press of Harvard University Press

Cambridge, Massachusetts, 1971

The Author

Louis M. Lyons, journalist and television news commentator, served on the Boston Globe from 1919 to 1946. For 25 years he was curator of the Nieman Fellowships for newspapermen at Harvard University, until retiring in 1964. He edited the book *Reporting the News* and wrote its introduction about the background of the Nieman Fellowships.

For Laurence L. Winship

the linchpin of this history

and W. Davis Taylor

"Dave took the lid off and the Globe took off"

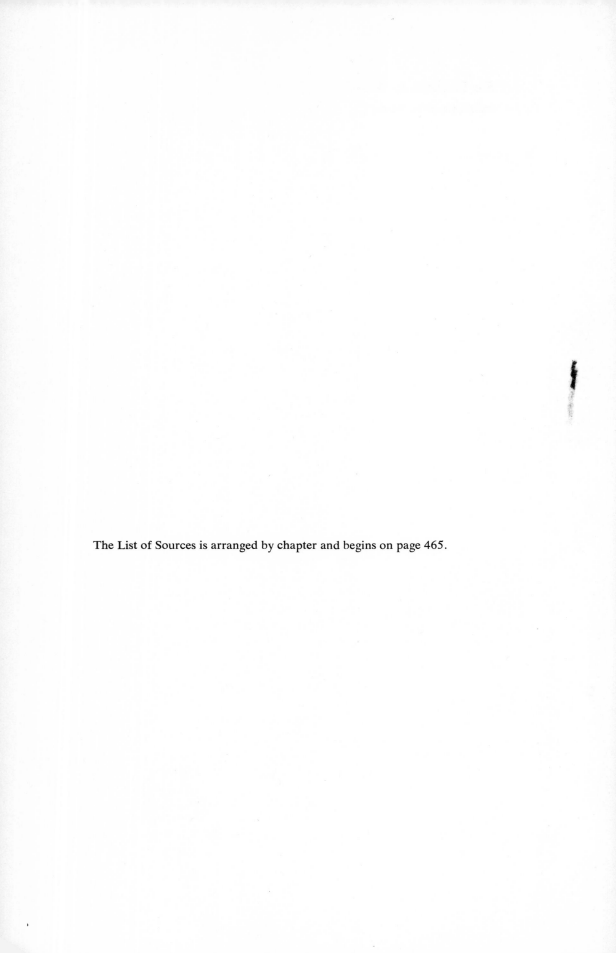

The List of Sources is arranged by chapter and begins on page 465.

Foreword

The institutions men live by come to have lives of their own, vitalized by the individuals who created them and conduct them. Sometimes an institution is the projection of the character of a single individual or, with good fortune, of a succession of men whose life work has been entwined in its continuity.

The Boston Globe is completing its first century as an institution rooted in New England, whose pages have mirrored the life of its region and have both influenced and reflected its condition through these hundred years.

Through all but the first year of its century, the Globe has been under the management of one family. Three generations of Taylors have published the paper; the fourth generation is represented now in the general manager. After the first floundering half dozen years just four editors, two Taylors then two Winships, have spanned the whole epoch. One man, James Morgan, was in effect editorial director and adviser to three successive publishers, serving the Globe from 1884 to 1955. Two of his editorial writers, Lucien Price and James Powers, were colleagues through more than 40 years.

Such continuity is unmatched in American journalism. It largely accounts for the character of the paper and its place as a community institution. One man, A. A. Fowle, was managing editor for 42 years. One man, William D. Sullivan, was city editor 37 years. One man, Harry Poor, as night editor, presided over the organization of the morning paper for more than a third of its century. One man, Francis X. ("Doc") Rooney, decisively influenced its typographical appearance, as composing room superintendent, for more than 50 years. Such Globe bylines as M. E. Hennessy, Frank A. Sibley, A. J. Philpott, James O'Leary, Willard DeLue became household names in the region. Andrew Dazzi ran "Classified" from the days when he opened all the "want ad" envelopes himself to his retirement at the end of 1969 from a department that handles 17 million lines a year.

Such extraordinary tenure has resulted in both pluses and minuses. The Globe, like other human institutions, has had its ups and downs. Its opening years were total failure. Nearly all the 11 other Boston newspapers were moribund when the Globe was launched in a city that had known little distinction in journalism since Benjamin Franklin left town. This newest newspaper was lapsing into the same condition when Charles H. Taylor was brought in, at 27, to solve its insolvency. He created a new newspaper on a broader basis, to bring women and children into the circle of readers and to reach to the interests of the new immigrant generation, till then ignored by the daily press.

His innovations achieved within a decade one of the great success stories in American journalism. He brought the Globe to the leading position in New England and held it there through the half century of his personal management. His sons, who joined the Globe right out of college, carried on, then his grandsons, with their sons. After the founder, the second generation faced a struggle for survival, through depression and war restrictions and under drastic competition in the most over-newspapered city in America.

But in good times and bad, the Globe throughout its history has maintained an unmatched reputation for fairness, to readers, advertisers, and employees. The reliability of its election returns became renowned in the region after its unique performance in 1916, holding to its own correct calculation that the election was uncertain through three days of agonizing suspense.

The Globe was built on Charles Taylor's instinctive interest in people. It has always had in rare degree a personality of its own. Its "Uncle Dudley" editorials, famous for 75 years, reflected this; and their liberal, humane spirit inspired sermons in countless New England pulpits. The wit and whimsy of its "Editorial Points" and "Weather Ears," its household recipes, and its remarkable club of women letter-writers in "Confidential Chat" have made it a household familiar down the years.

The Globe is such a human institution that I have felt it not only appropriate but essential to entwine into its history glimpses at least of the lives of many individuals whose own personality and character have become woven into its collective individuality. Many more should be included, would space and time allow.

This is not a biography of the Taylor family, but their family traits have been built into the newspaper. Unconnected with the Establishment or with established churches, they worked and learned and lived by their own standards, which proved a sound foundation for an enduring institution.

James Morgan's character and wisdom infused the spirit of the Globe staff through two generations, and his judgment guided Globe policy. In his steps, Laurence Winship combined instincts for human relations and for the human side of the news. Their strategic roles in editorial direction covered three-fourths of the century. They had the confidence of the publishers and the affection of the staff. In the last 15 years, Davis Taylor has opened the paper to a strong sense of civic responsibility, which editor Thomas Winship has applied with fresh vitality and enthusiasm through a "youth movement" that has developed an exceptionally resourceful and able staff.

This story of the Globe comes largely from its own files, supported by a few memoirs and many long memories — including my own, which covered the third quarter of the Globe's century. Other staff memories, more informed and longer, have reached back through more than half the century. Indispensable has been the generous help of Davis Taylor, covering the long era of his father's management, and of Laurence Winship's own experience and his memories of working with James Morgan and other early Globe figures.

But the judgments and criticisms are mine alone, and some are such that the Globe management would doubtless wish to disclaim with the kind of note that adorned early columns: "the views expressed here do not necessarily represent those of the Boston Globe." Where these views sound negative, they are doubtless weighted by the fact that my own years on the Globe, before 1946, covered its dimmest period. "My father was a great man," Davis Taylor has told me, lest I not appreciate it. "He didn't have the resources we have now and we don't have the incredible competitive situation he had. He instilled principles in me and they are the principles the Globe stands for." John F. Reid, advertising manager who served under both generations, says, "William O. Taylor held things together. Davis opened up and the Globe took off." The rising tempo of the later chapters reflects the rising curve of journalistic quality and civic vitality of the Globe's latest decades.

The whole first third of the story is based in part on a comprehensive record that

Willard DeLue compiled through many years of historical research. DeLue's own Globe service goes back to 1907. He devoted the final decade of his Globe career to chronicling the paper from its beginning; the manuscript covers the first 30 years and adds many later episodes. Beyond his written record, DeLue has helped me with innumerable details, so that this book is in the fullest sense a collaboration.

Other major sources are a manuscript by A. A. Fowle, "Fifty Years with the Boston Globe," drawn on primarily for its account of the seventies and eighties; James Morgan's biography of General Charles H. Taylor; Florence Finch's vivid recollections of her years on the Globe, 1881–1884, in her book, *Flowing Stream;* the reminiscences of William H. Hills, which cover the primeval days; Lucien Price's memorial essay on James Morgan; and Lucien Thayer's comprehensive account of the Globe's election system and its working through several decades. Robert Healy, executive editor, contributed to the chapter about the Morrissey case investigation that he headed, which won the Globe the Pulitzer gold medal for 1965.

The rest comes either from the paper itself or from its editors and staff. Editor Tom Winship, editorial page editor Charles Whipple, managing editors Ian Menzies and Joseph Dinneen, Jr., Sunday editor John Harris, and book editor Herbert Kenny have patiently described their operations, policies, points of view. Jack Driscoll, assistant to the editor, and Bill Cash of the city staff have dug out innumerable details. Victor Jones's memory spanned sports, night desk, war correspondence, and managing editorship. W. O. Taylor II has helped with computers, typography, and labor contracts.

President John I. Taylor, circulation manager Fred O'Neal, planning director Robert Ahern, production director David Stanger, and the long-time directors of advertising just retired, Jack Reid and Andrew Dazzi, have initiated me into their mysteries, explored their records, and refreshed their memories. Many members of the staff have filled in dates, facts, and details and reconstructed episodes and adventures that make the story of the Globe.

Gene Brackley, a Globe picture editor, and his colleagues Paul Maguire and Edward Fitzgerald, have lent professional hands to the illustrations.

Frank Freidel, professor of history at Harvard, and Max Hall, of the Harvard University Press, gave invaluable suggestions on the organization of the book, which owes much to the professional editing of Meryl Moscatelli and to Gretchen Wang's design.

My wife has typed, retyped, indexed, criticized, and lived through this book.

I hope they and others find it a good story. It was worth reporting.

L.M.L.

Contents

Illustrations

Newspaper Story

1 Another Newspaper

Ballou's Globe: Venture in Bankruptcy

By the hindsight of a century, it is strange that the Boston Globe was ever started. Not one of the little group of rich men who committed jointly $150,000 to incorporate it had ever run a newspaper. Boston then, as for most of the century ahead, already had more newspapers than it could support. The wise money in Boston was going into railroads and western real estate. Had any of the half dozen prominent businessmen who gathered with Lewis Rice in his handsome new American House on the evening of February 7, 1872, consulted his State Street broker, he would surely have been advised against so precarious a venture.

Bankers would remember, if these merchants did not, the fiasco of the last ambitious venture in Boston newspapering. Fifteen years earlier Boston bankers had merged several weak papers with the old Boston Traveller — two l's in those days — and inveigled Samuel Bowles away from his Springfield Republican with a promise to create the city's leading journal. But the project was undercapitalized, and Bowles's thorny independence did not mix with Boston banking. In four months he returned to Springfield to make his provincial paper the most distinguished journal in New England. The Traveller slid back into being just another struggling Boston newspaper.

But Stephen Niles, the pioneer advertising man who had brought the group together at the American House, knew that Boston journalism was rated as undistinguished among the big cities and that half or more of the existing papers were moribund. Niles's literary friend Maturin Ballou had convinced him that there was a place for a superior newspaper. Boston's port and commerce were flourishing. The city had grown 40 percent in its last decade to a population of 250,000 in a metropolitan area of half a million.

None of Niles's converts noted that most of this population growth was of Irish immigrants, not yet doing much reading of the sedately dull journals of the time. None of them had a crystal ball to tell him that a great depression was just around the corner. What they did know as businessmen was that the existing ten papers counted a total of less than 170,000 circulation, and that more than half of that belonged to the Herald, morning and evening, a newsier paper than the rest; not more than two of the ten papers were making any money. But they knew that the late Col. Charles O. Rogers had proved that money could be made in newspapering, for less than three years earlier he had died a millionaire from 30 years of publishing the Boston Journal.

The Journal had built a great pre-Civil War reputation for enterprise, largely on the full stenographic reports of trials and political speeches by its outstanding reporter Stephen N. Stockwell, who had become its editor. Stockwell's stenographic report of a campaign speech by Daniel Webster for Zachary Taylor in 1848 was a sensation when the Journal put out an extra on it the next day. The Journal had gained prestige in the Civil War from the brilliant work of its war correspondent Charles Carleton Coffin, who gave New England its first full report of Bull Run and hardly missed a major battle in the whole four years; but Coffin had left the paper for lecturing and travel books. The Journal's great days were behind it.

The old Advertiser, long known as "the respectable paper of Boston," had developed hardening of the editorial arteries from such rigid faithfulness to finance that it never heard a discouraging word about State Street, Beacon Hill, or the Harvard Corporation. This had turned even most Beacon Hill families to the more independent Transcript — literary, carefully edited, of neat typography, circumspect, and welcome at Brahmin tea tables.

The Advertiser had become a daily in 1813, most of the other papers in the 1830's, the Herald in 1846. They had begun as evening papers, as had most American newspapers, but competition had pushed their editions back ever earlier until they became morning papers. By the Civil War most leading papers were morning. But the war had whet the public appetite for news, and without waiting. The telegraph by then moved distant dispatches rapidly, so the morning papers began issuing extras with war news in the afternoon. These by 1872 had become regular evening editions, though they still carried the label "Extra" — a tradition continued in the evening Globe right down to 1968.

Four Boston papers by 1872 had morning and evening editions. Only the Post was Democratic, and it had sagged into decline that deepened until the paper was rejuvenated in 1891 by a new type of journalist, Edwin A. Grozier. Otherwise the Boston newspapers were Republican after their earlier Whig period, varying in the degree of their partisanship. The Journal was the most die-hard party organ. Nearly all of them in 1872 were ready to bolt the party ticket, repelled by the corruption of the Grant administration.

The national political stagnation of Grant's period was paralleled in journalism. Horace Greeley, founder of the New York Tribune, had died only that year; James Gordon Bennett, founder of the New York Herald, and Henry Raymond, first editor of the New York Times, had died two years before. Leadership and innovation were at a standstill. The new breed had not yet arrived to change the face and dimensions of the newspaper. Joseph Pulitzer was still editing a German newspaper in St. Louis. In Boston 26-year-old Charles H. Taylor was struggling to get on his feet as publisher of a new monthly magazine.

Rising commercialism dominated the city's life. The literary lights who had given Boston its claim as the Athens of America had had little enough contact with the counting room journalism of the period. They had contributed their talents to the Atlantic Monthly, now 15 years along in sustaining the cultural tradition.

Most of the Boston papers sold for four cents. The Herald was two cents; it had tried a penny paper, but Civil War costs had stopped the penny press. The four-cent papers were the bigger blanket-size sheets or had more pages. The reader got about what he paid for in volume. What he had to cope with in type was the tiny nonpareil on crowded pages. If he didn't wear glasses when he became a newspaper reader, he was forced to it soon after.

The newspapers were pretty well bunched up around what later became known as Newspaper Row, on Washington Street between State and Milk Streets. The Journal and Herald were on opposite sides of Washington near the Water Street corner. The Transcript had just left its old location between Water and State to move into a new building next to the corner of Milk Street. The Post was on Water Street at Devonshire. The Daily News, morning and evening, was in Province Court. This most sensational of the local papers soon merged into the Post, as the Daily Times had recently been absorbed by the Herald. The Times, at 12 School Street, retained its identity only as a Sunday paper. The old Advertiser was in Court Street at Franklin Avenue. The Traveller, which had begun in the old State House, still clung to State Street at the corner of Congress. State Street had been the first Newspaper Row, and the Traveller was the last paper to leave it. The Traveller had been the first Boston newspaper sold on the streets by newsboys, in the 1840's, at about the time the Journal was the first to put out a bulletin board to be read from the sidewalk — both innovations that shocked the more conventional editors. The Traveller had been the first two-cent paper in town. It considered itself "a family paper free from immoral tendencies." It would not then, or long after, accept advertising for liquor or theaters.

The notion that Boston needed a new newspaper was Maturin Ballou's. Son and grandson of noted New England clergymen, at 51 he was a man of letters and a man of affairs who had published several books of travel and history, a monthly magazine, and the first substantial illustrated weekly. He was also in real estate and had built a fine modern hotel, the St. James, in fashionable Franklin Square, that later became the Franklin Square House, a sedate rooming house for working girls.

His son, Murray, was already, at 31, president of the new Boston Stock Exchange. Both men were in the group at the American House that February evening. With them was Stephen Niles, who had begun vigorously promoting the planned newspaper. The others were men of substance who had put up $10,000 or $15,000 apiece of the original $100,000 capital for the project. Within a week this was found to be insufficient and they raised it to $150,000. Considering the capitalization of the other papers, $150,000 looked like a lot. But it wasn't. It was all gone within a year; a deep depression then set in to erode the rest. The contributors might as well have given twice as much, for within months fire and panic had depleted their fortunes and wiped some out. But all looked rosy that evening — a timely moment to glance at these entrepreneurs of a new newspaper because none of them would be aboard by the time it turned the corner from bankruptcy to success under a quite different concept than theirs of what a new Boston newspaper should be.

The only one of the original incorporators to stay the course was a man not present that night: Eben D. Jordan, from Maine, self-made merchant prince of Boston as the founder of Jordan and Marsh.* Mr. Jordan was to bail out this newspaper enterprise a few years later, seeing it through to a great estate for his heirs. One other founder absent from the gathering was Cyrus Wakefield, for whom the town of Wakefield had just changed its name (from South Reading) in recognition of his flourishing rattan factory there and his local benefactions. Mr. Wakefield lived only another year and a half but long enough for his fortune, rated at $4,000,000, to be wiped out in the panic of 1873, leaving his estate insolvent.

---

* Eben D. Jordan was born in Danville, Maine, came to Boston at 14, worked as a store errand boy, and at 19 started his own dry goods business. In 1851 with Benjamin L. Marsh he started Jordan and Marsh, a dry goods store, which became Jordan, Marsh and Company in 1852 and Jordan Marsh Company in 1901. By then Jordan had taken over the company entirely from the Marsh family. On his death in 1895, his son of the same name headed the company, which became the leading department store in New England, and succeeded his father as trustee and director of the Boston Globe. A talented musician, the second Eben Jordan was president of the New England Conservatory of Music and principal donor of the Boston Opera Company, which opened in 1909. On his death in 1916 his son, Robert, became a Globe trustee and director until his death in 1932.

The Boston Daily Globe.

VOL. I....NO. 1.   BOSTON, MONDAY MORNING, MARCH 4, 1872.   PRICE FOUR CENTS.

NEW PUBLICATIONS.

BOOKS RECEIVED.

THE SUNDAY PULPIT.

CENTRAL CHURCH.

YOUNG MEN'S CHRISTIAN UNION.

HORTICULTURAL HALL.

CURRENT NOTES.

First issue of the Boston Globe: March 4, 1872.

Those present that night besides Niles and the Ballous were: Lewis Rice, affable hotel man with not only the finest hostelry in Boston but in it the first passenger elevator in the city; Seman Klous, wealthy furrier and real estate man; Samuel A. Carlton, leading manufacturer of matches and president of the National Security Bank; Dr. Henry E. Townsend, Harvard College and Harvard Medical School graduate who had turned to business and become president of the Shoe Machinery Manufacturing Company, a familiar and popular figure in Boston clubs and society.

These men and Jordan and Wakefield, having become incorporators of the Globe Publishing Company, met to discuss plans for the new newspaper, already announced to appear within a month, on March 4. They intended to produce a better newspaper for Boston and expected it to be profitable; they were to prove wrong on both counts. But there is nothing unique about that. Men more experienced in publishing have found it easy to drop fortunes in failing to launch a newspaper.

Their affair with journalism was progressing. Niles had started a circular to prospective advertisers emphasizing that the new Globe would have "abundant capital," that its backers were "names synonymous with enterprise and progress." The extensive advertising he had placed in papers throughout the region announced "New Departure — Something New in Journalism." This was to be "a commercial and business journal of the first class" and "of plain and outspoken independence." It was to sell at the price of the quality papers, four cents. The Herald was printing more news than any of them at two cents, but the Globe offered eight pages to the others' four, to claim "double the reading matter of any other New England daily."

It had been arranged that three of the five floors in the building the Transcript had just vacated would be taken over; then numbered 90–92 Washington Street, it was renumbered two years later as 238–240. This, with successive expansions, was to be the home of the Boston Globe for 86 years. Not Maturin Ballou's Globe, though — that faded faster than the pale daguerreotypes of the period.

Niles assured advertisers that the new Globe would quickly achieve a circulation matched by few other newspapers. The Herald then had nearly 90,000, the Traveller and the Advertiser about 17,000 each, the Journal something in between. Ballou's Globe never got much over 5,000.

But Ballou, in his "salutatory" editorial, March 4, promised that the Globe would be "devoted to the intelligent and dignified discussion of political and social ethics and current events at home and abroad," and that literature and all the arts were to receive "ample and judicious attention from experienced individuals" who would render the Globe's editions "second to none in the country."

He had indeed brought together a notable cast. For literary editor he had secured Percy Whipple, then 53, a noted lyceum lecturer who published essays in the Atlantic Monthly and lectured in the Lowell Institute. One of his more remembered pronouncements was on Walt Whitman: "the author of 'Leaves of Grass' had every leaf but a fig leaf." As music and drama critic, Benjamin Edward Woolf at 30 brought to the paper the prestige of his success as composer of plays and light opera. After a year on the Globe he became critic of the influential Saturday Evening Gazette. For foreign editor Ballou picked a brilliant young writer, Charles E. Pascoe, not long out of England, where he soon returned for a long, notable literary career.

Ballou enrolled a specialist to write on legal matters, Benjamin F. Burnham, later a municipal judge and law book editor. As editorial writers he hired Dr. William M. F. Round from the Daily Times and Andrew J. Lawson from the Traveller.

The original Globe building.

Clarence S. Wason, publisher of the weekly Charlestown Saturday Chronicle, was appointed city editor. An "assistant editor" was Warren Spalding, later renowned as the founder of the Massachusetts prison system. As night editor M. Almy Aldrich, colorful man about town, brought to the post the flair of his military cloak.

This was the cultural cadre of what Ballou described as a "semi-literary" newspaper. A quite select crew. The news was definitely secondary and recruiting a handful of reporters a simpler matter. One was 18-year-old Stephen O'Meara, a Charlestown boy hired to cover the Charlestown district. He came on the staff in time to help report the great Boston fire of November 1872. O'Meara went on to become editor of the Journal and later police commissioner of Boston. He started working for $6 a week; but $8 was the more usual base pay of reporters then, and it ranged up to $12 or $15. This was for a seven-day week, but it soon changed to allow one day off out of 14.

More mature reporters were Frederick Pierce Bacon, a graduate of Boston's Brimmer School, then 30, who had done some newspaper work and was soon to share the music criticism; and 34-year-old David Baker, a Cape Codder, who came from five years on the Journal. The most experienced man on the staff was Samuel Miles, 48, a graduate of Concord Academy who had worked on the Herald and the old Boston Courier, a veteran fireman and an artist who conducted his own art school. He often turned in sketches to illustrate his stories, and years later he served the Globe as art editor. But in 1872 he became the "night local" to cover the police beat.

One of the first staff was a woman, a rarity of that period when women hadn't even got into offices as stenographers. The typewriter was still 20 years off. Georgia Hamlen, a Charlestown girl, presumably started as the girl Friday of the editorial staff, doing miscellaneous chores deemed fitting for a woman. But she was soon assisting Whipple with book reviews and took over reviewing when Whipple left, soon after the first year. She stayed five years before leaving for the Boston Pilot under John Boyle O'Reilly. Then there was a gap of four years with no woman on the paper and a quite definite bias against having any, a bias widely shared in newspapers then and long after. One explanation is to be found in the memoirs of A. A. Fowle, who joined the paper in its third year. After going to work by 2 P.M., covering a police beat through the evening, then returning to the office to write and edit copy till 1 A.M., it was often Fowle's task to escort Miss Hamlen home on nights when her work kept her late at the office. As she lived in Charlestown, he had to retrace his way to his home in the West End. That, he candidly recalled, was tedious. By that time of night the horsecars would have stopped running, and reporters couldn't afford herdics.* Of course Miss Hamlen protested that no one need see her home. But of course someone always did.

Ballou also arranged for correspondents at strategic points throughout New England and beyond, mostly people doing local news work or in touch with public affairs who would contribute regularly or when called upon to see that the paper was "covered" on any important event. This was vitally important to a new newspaper, for the older papers were members of the Associated Press, which had a monopoly of news gathering beyond the local area. The Globe for the next decade and a half

---

* A herdic was a then popular form of horse-drawn hack invented by the American carriage maker Peter Herdic. It was entered from the back and had seats on the sides.

was obliged to build its own system of regional correspondents. This ultimately proved a source of strength; but in the early years it was a severe handicap that had to be overcome by ingenuity and stratagems, and a little later by combining with similarly deprived papers elsewhere for exchanges.

Ballou's Globe made its first appearance Monday morning, March 4, 1872, in the genteel form of the "semi-literary" newspaper he had described. Eight pages of seven-column width at four cents. The front page was all literary if one counts three columns of sermons headed "The Sunday Pulpit"; this became standard fare and a major Monday feature for a long time. Percy Whipple had a column and a turn on books headed "New Publications." A column of miscellany was headed "Current Notes." Three columns were advertising, including an art exhibit and theater openings.

Inside, page two carried "Letters" from far places — London, Havana, Aden, Buenos Aires — some of them frankly dated three or four weeks earlier. These were pleasantly interesting accounts of affairs in foreign parts much in the manner of the New Yorker's "Letters" from Paris, London, Rome of a later day.

Financial and commercial news had its page. There were briefs from around New England and local notes from Roxbury, Cambridge, Charlestown, Chelsea. "Police Notes," "Fires," "Accidents" headed collected items that were the work of the night local man.

The editorial page supported General Grant for re-election, discussed British politics and commerce with Asia, and opposed federal extravagance.

Joseph Chamberlin, who later became editor of the Transcript, said of Ballou's Globe that it was a weekly paper published every day. The Globe looked, in short, what in effect it was, a sort of morning edition of the evening Transcript. But even Brahmin Beacon Hill couldn't use more than one Transcript a day. The new paper made so little impact, A. A. Fowle recalls, that even after two years the manager of a local public event, when called upon for news by a Globe reporter, asked, "The Globe? What's that?"

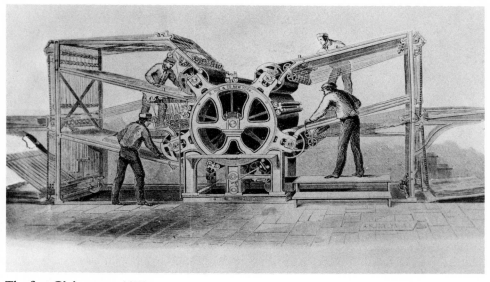

The first Globe press, 1872.

One more paper wasn't enough different to matter, and the city was so oversupplied with newspapers seeking advertising support that the new paper had a thin time. Even after several years it was managing to attract only 15 columns of advertising in a 56-column paper. But the Ballou management didn't last several years; it began falling apart almost at once. Between March and October its $150,000 capital shrank to $30,000 and was draining away every week. At that point Lewis Rice resigned as treasurer. Seman Klous was persuaded to take on that problem. But his business was wiped out the next month in the great fire that spared the Globe and Eben Jordan's store but destroyed the new Transcript building in its vast devastation.

"Devastation" was the one-word headline over the tragic fire story that the Globe staff gathered between Saturday night and Monday morning. The burnt-out Transcript moved in on the Globe to share its presses for two months. This hospitality was less a problem for the Globe than it would have been if Stephen Niles's glowing prospectus about Globe circulation had worked out. But the Globe was printing only about 5,000 copies. There was room for the Transcript's 17,000.

By the following June Maturin Ballou gave up the task of trying to make the Globe go. In September he and his son and Klous sold their Globe shares. Even before the editor resigned it had become evident that a business manager would be needed if the paper was to be saved.

The proprietors turned to young Charles H. Taylor, then struggling to restore his American Homes Magazine, whose plant and equipment, stock and manuscripts had all been wiped out in the great fire. Taylor declined. His excuse was that the legislature was in session and he had been elected its clerk, a position that paid three times as much as he had been paid as a representative; but the incorporators must have realized that the young publisher considered Ballou's Globe a hopeless proposition.

When in June Ballou resigned they tried Taylor again, and this time he agreed, tentatively, to try it. Ballou's departure had brought a sharp sea change in the Globe, so sharp as to suggest that internal conflict preceded his going. The Globe front page looked distinctly different. The news was outside. The sermons and art and book notes were inside. City editor Wason was made managing editor, and he began at once to make a livelier newspaper. Chas. H. Taylor (he never used Charles) came aboard in August "for a few weeks" and never left. The brief tryout he allowed himself led to his election as a director of the company in November. In the next two weeks he was elected clerk of the corporation, acquired 20 shares of Globe stock ($100 a share at the start), and on December 6, 1873, signed a contract as "general manager of the Globe" for two years.

On the same day a new editor was appointed, Edwin Munroe Bacon, at 29 just two years older than Taylor but already a newspaperman of ten years' experience. He was then New England correspondent of the New York Times, as Taylor had been of the New York Tribune. Well acquainted, each appreciated the other's quality and agreed that together they could make a team to pull the Globe up.

They had practically to start over. Ballou's star cast had mostly left. Whipple, Round, and Pascoe had gone, Wason was leaving, and Woolf soon followed. Without capital but with youth and energy and confidence, Taylor and Bacon combined editorial and publishing experience. Veterans already, in their twenties, they were thorough pros — and they needed it all in the rough time ahead, for one month after young Taylor moved into the Globe office the financial house of Jay Cooke & Co. crashed with a thunder that echoed through the financial world. The panic of 1873 was on and its depression was due to last pretty much through the decade of the 1870's.

This was the spot that Charles H. Taylor stepped into on the Globe. Born in 1846, the eldest of seven children of John Ingalls Taylor and Abigail Russell Hapgood, a Marlboro girl, he had grown up in the shadow of Bunker Hill Monument. The family lived close by the Charlestown Navy Yard, where John Ingalls Taylor was employed. His father, John Taylor, a Salem man, had served on a privateer in the War of 1812. Charles Taylor went through the Winthrop Grammar School and one year of Charlestown High School.

At 15 he found himself a job in a Boston print shop and in a few months was able to shift to the Boston Traveller as printer's devil. But it was 1862, and young Taylor enlisted. As a private in Co. F, 38th Massachusetts Volunteer Regiment, he served under Gen. Nathaniel Banks in the Army of the Gulf and took part in that army's disastrous assaults on Port Hudson. Wounded, he was mustered out in the fall of 1863 and returned, a 17-year-old veteran, to resume his printer's apprenticeship on the Traveller at $5 a week. He became a journeyman printer and by volunteering for extra reporting made himself at 19 a regular staff member. Five months before his twenty-first birthday he married Georgiana Olivia Davis, the girl he had left behind when he went off to war. They set up housekeeping with his family in Charlestown.

Chas. H. Taylor at 18: Civil War veteran, apprentice printer.

Needing added income, he obtained the position of Boston correspondent for Horace Greeley's New York Tribune. He had qualified for the job by his own initiative: sent by the Traveller to report the annual meeting of the Massachusetts Anti-Slavery Society, he heard its president, William Lloyd Garrison, surprise the meeting by announcing that with emancipation he considered his life work and that of the society completed. Garrison then gave a valedictory that Taylor got down in full with the shorthand he had picked up by himself. The Traveller didn't see much in it, but Taylor thought Greeley might and sent it on. Back came a $15 check, and soon after appointment as correspondent, a post worth $1,200 a year to Taylor, a good deal more than the Traveller was paying him.

The Tribune job meant covering all major news events in New England. The Tribune correspondent became acquainted with the public men of Boston and Massachusetts. At 23 he was recognized as one of the top newspapermen in Boston. Spurred then by the added responsibility of his first child, Taylor applied for the job of secretary to Gov. William Claflin in 1869 and got it.

Chas. H. Taylor at 23: the Governor's
secretary. Photographed in 1869.

With the added security of this State House job, he bought a house in Somerville; it cost $6,600, and he was able from his savings to pay down $5,000. His new post brought large experience with the legislature and the public. Governor Claflin was chairman of the Republican National Committee and fresh from managing the successful 1868 campaign that elected General Grant president. With this inside track to practical politics, Taylor ran for the legislature in Somerville the next year and was elected. Somerville was a Republican town and Taylor was elected as a Republican. He left the governor's office with the title of colonel, which went with the job of military secretary; the title stuck for 20 years until another governor made him General Taylor.

He continued his newspaper work and added a further dimension to it by starting a monthly ten-cent magazine that he called American Homes. In partnership with a printer and wood engraver named A. M. Lunt, he began publishing in summer 1871. This magazine, aimed at the family, had fiction, poetry, travel stories, departments for boys and girls, and a special "Household" department with fashions, recipes, health notes, and "Sabbath Thoughts." It was illustrated, and to stimulate circulation its publisher offered an "elegant steel engraving" with each year's subscription. The magazine found a place. It had a circulation of 10,000 in May 1872 and its October issue announced that it would start its second year with 25,000. To meet its increased business American Homes had just moved into new quarters with new printing presses when the great Boston fire of November 1872 wiped out everything in the shop.

In this crisis Charles Taylor had a chance to profit from the extensive legislative acquaintance he had gained as secretary to the governor. The clerkship of the House became vacant. He went after it and in November 1872, at 25, was elected clerk, a post that paid $2,500 a year. Undoubtedly a reluctance to walk out from the place his friends had given him was a factor in his first refusal of the Globe offer.

So it was that a year after his election as clerk, with a new legislature coming in, Colonel Taylor came to the Globe to tackle the uphill task of saving a losing enterprise. A slight, erect figure at 27, only five feet seven inches tall with steady dark-brown eyes under black eyebrows set off by black-rimmed nose glasses, Taylor wore a full black mustache that was amplified in his thirties to a beard framing an impressive countenance. He was already experienced as soldier, printer, journalist, publisher, politician; to this he now added businessman. He was not without influential friends, for two years earlier he had organized the Middlesex Club, which had grown rapidly in a membership that included political leaders and their supporters in business.

Perhaps the least difficult problem for manager and editor was recruiting a largely new staff. Besides the critics and editorial writers, several reporters had left. Steve O'Meara, Fred Bacon, Daniel Baker, and Sam Miles remained, and Georgia Hamlen was literary editor.

For city editor they brought in Edwin S. Sears from the Journal, a South Boston man who had worked on the Post and Traveller. One new reporter was Charles W. Dyar, 22-year-old graduate of Trinity College, who became a mainstay of the Globe, going on to be city editor, dramatic critic, and chief editorial writer. John J. McNally, 19, had followed Steve O'Meara as Charlestown district man, adding Somerville, and he came on the staff to cover the night local beat. Edwin Walter Gould, another South Boston man, came on from the city editorship of the Boston Times; in a few years he became music critic. Lewis G. Farmer, a young law student, was the first of a long series of students to combine a newspaper job with studies; he later became an eminent member of the bar. In contrast, Sam Miles stayed almost to his death at 84, in 1908, when he was called the dean of Boston journalists.

Present for a short time was George Fred Williams, barely 20, who had taught school one winter at Brewster after graduation with the Dartmouth 1872 class. Three years later he was law partner of Lewis Farmer, then congressman and several times Democratic nominee for governor. But George Fred Williams' forte was reform. He became a thorny crusader, a maverick to the regular party organization, an impatient critic of the Globe's failure to respond to his crusades. His is a recurring role in the Globe's history.

Another new staffer was Irish-born Michael P. Curran, 24-year-old graduate of Fordham who had served New York papers and the Boston Pilot. He had been district man for Lynn and Salem till brought in to the staff in autumn 1873. An all-round newspaperman, Curran was to serve as night editor, Sunday editor, chief editorial writer and in later life to become a Boston police commissioner.

This was a fairly representative sample of the varied talents that journalism has always commanded: men who would make it a career and men to whom it proved a creative opening to other professions. It was typical, too, that several of these young reporters developed as critics. Journalism develops its own specialists as men's particular bents sort themselves out in the common ground of the city room.

In 1873 the total editorial force on the Globe from editor Bacon down was 14 or 15. The composing room force numbered 20. The printers had had their own typographical union since 1850, and their pay was somewhat higher than that of reporters; in 1872 it was nearly $20 a week.

But filling out staff was a far simpler matter than taking charge of a nonexistent business office. The books showed the company losing $60,000 a year. The original capital was practically gone. Two months earlier the directors had had to authorize a loan to meet current demands. Colonel Taylor shouldered the task of meeting the payroll and bills.

Much the largest demand was for paper. Boston's big paper merchant, Samuel D. Warren, accepted the Globe's promissory notes, which soon accumulated to $40,000. Taylor long remembered a brief exchange with Warren:

"That's fine paper you're giving us."

"A damn sight better than the paper you're giving us," was Warren's gruff response.

This about described the Colonel's problem. He took charge of advertising himself and engaged the paper's first advertising solicitor. But it was thin pickings as the depression deepened. The small Globe building had no telephone, no electricity, no typewriters. It had one ten-cylinder press, an early Hoe, whose utmost limit was 10,000 papers a day, for it had to be fed single sheets, dampened by hand, fed into the press by hand, taken off, folded, and counted. Eight men fed the press, four on a side, and one other started and stopped it.

The paper was printed direct from type, set by hand. The Herald was then the only Boston paper equipped for stereotyping that took an impression from the metal type so that the printing could be duplicated on several presses at once. The type wore out every two or three years and had to be renewed when the printing grew too illegible. Then every printer had to refill his type case, a tedious business.

The counting room occupied the first floor, a counter running two-thirds of its length, with two desks behind it for the cashier and clerk. Colonel Taylor had a 12- by 16-foot office off to the right, with the only carpet in the building. Two steep flights of stairs reached the editorial rooms on the third floor. Editor Bacon's room, 12 by 14 feet, was in front and looked out on a larger room with the "news desk" in its center. This was a flat-topped table with a chair at either end for the two copy editors. A dictionary and a gazetteer between them constituted the library.

The building ran through from Washington to Devonshire Street. At the Devonshire Street end a small news room held the city editor and such of his half dozen reporters as were not on the street. Fowle remembers its chief item of furniture as a green leather-covered lounge that offered welcome respite for weary reporters in their 12-hour days.

The composing room was on the floor above, reached by narrow, winding stairs from Devonshire Street, under a mansard roof that created a ceiling slanting up from ten feet at either end to 14 feet at the center. Its hot gas lights dropped down to within 16 inches of the compositors' heads as they worked at the cases. The Globe had in 1873 about 30 compositors working in a crowded, loft-like space up under the roof; and it was misery in summer.

Without telephones or pneumatic tubes, communication between the news floor and the composing room floor was by way of wooden boxes of 12 by 6 inches, attached to a cord that ran over a small pulley on wooden chutes. A tin tube with a wooden whistle mouthpiece signalled when copy was to go up or proof to come down. Fowle remembered frequent contention as to which department should man the pulley.

Finally, the mail and delivery room projected out over the basement press room. Here Charles Wadleigh could order his extras, with two mailers to help him prepare them for delivery around town in horse-drawn wagons. Wadleigh, like Fowle, stayed on his job over 50 years.

Each department ran independently, its chief supreme in his domain — a fact particularly asserted in the composing room, which ran under its own rules of typography (then and long after), to the frustration of editors. The foreman held to a one-column width of headline and insisted that a story running beyond one column should start the second column at the top, alongside the headline. Such rigidity inhibited innovation in makeup or the achievement of a balanced page. The tyranny of composing room rules persisted, one of the curious internal drawbacks to creative newspaper making.

By Foot and Horsecar

A new hand on the Globe staff that year has given an account of the local news gathering in Boston as Chas. Taylor moved in to the Globe.

The itch to be a newspaperman got hold of 26-year-old Arthur Fowle, working in a tannery in the manufacturing suburb of Woburn, and in the summer of 1873 he applied to Globe city editor Edward S. Sears, who told him in the hardboiled tone of city editors: "Take my advice and keep out of it." But Sears promised to remember him if the Woburn district job fell vacant. It did that fall, with the death of the elderly correspondent. Sears kept his promise and Fowle soon had a chance to prove his news sense.

The Boston & Lowell Railroad erected gates in its Boston trainshed, and commuters had to show their tickets before boarding trains. They rebelled at the loss of the easy, casual way of just getting on the train. Indignation meetings were held in towns along the line and protests published in the local papers. Fowle wrapped up the whole rumpus in a lively story of commuter revolt. The night local man, Emory H. Talbot, left for the Hartford Times, and Sears put young Fowle on the city staff for night locals at $8 a week on January 1, 1874. Fowle stayed more than 50 years, the last 42 as managing editor.

The principal work of the night local was covering the police stations. To get around all of them in an evening in those horsecar days was next to impossible. The cars ran to radial points only hourly at night and herdics cost too much. The alternative was to walk; "leg man" meant what it said in those days. But the reporters for the five morning papers divided the stations up, two or three to each, and met at the end of the evening at Station 2 in City Hall Square to exchange notes — a practical process for survival that became institutionalized on local beats almost universally. The other newspaper managements insisted on barring the Globe man from this pooling because the Globe was outside AP membership, but the exclusion lasted only a fortnight when Fowle had to make all the police rounds, a five-mile jaunt, somehow for himself. The human instincts of fellow reporters soon ended his ordeal by ignoring the fiat of the office.

Fowle's early memories are largely of second-guessing police detectives or coroners to smoke out news on murder cases. He followed one such case diligently for a year, the sensational murder of a choirgirl, Mabel Young, whose body was found in the church belfry, which of course made it the "Belfry Murder." Suspicion fell on the sexton, named Piper, a young man of church background whose arrest brought sharp protest and bitter division among church people that was not abated by a hung jury at the trial nor by conviction after new evidence in a second trial. Playing a hunch, Fowle called on the defense lawyer on a rainy Sunday night to learn that Piper had confessed, not only to the murder of Mabel Young but to an earlier unsolved murder of a girl.

This was a big scoop, and Fowle begged the office to protect their exclusive. But the Globe night editor, M. P. Curran, was correspondent of the New York Times and wanted to send the story to New York. The Western Union telegrapher was sworn to secrecy, but the secret was too big to keep. A Boston Herald pressman in a night lunchroom heard another telegrapher talking about it. The Herald just waited to get hold of one of the first Globes off the press to break out an extra edition at 2 A.M. and sold four times as many copies on Fowle's scoop as the Globe's one-press capacity of 10,000 could print. Fowle remembers an extra two dollars in his weekly paycheck in appreciation, but 50 years later he had not forgotten his chagrin at the collapse of his first scoop.

The Globe's difficulties increased. By March 1874 its books showed assets of $23,636 against liabilities of $73,624. In July the stockholders voted to increase capital by $50,000. In November Dr. Townsend resigned as treasurer and that office was added to Colonel Taylor's responsibilities. He brought in an old Charlestown neighbor, Edward Prescott, as cashier and accountant to take some of the detail off his hands. Prescott, "Uncle Ned" to the staff, stayed on for 30 years and served on the board of directors half that time.

The Colonel cut the price of the paper from four cents to three cents "in recognition of the demand of the times for retrenchment." But it was vital to stimulate circulation, or even to keep what they had, for business failures were multiplying and unemployment was spreading. The three-cent price was also practical recognition of the new three-cent pieces being minted to supply a popular, convenient coin equivalent to what the nickel was later and later still the dime.

The Globe did increase its advertising. On May 1, 1874, there were 20.5 columns of ads in a 56-column paper. Next day, a Saturday, there was enough advertising to warrant a 12-page paper and an even half of it was advertising, including all but one column of the front page. The ads were small, an inch or two deep for real estate, board and room, and miscellaneous, with a few for merchandise in four to six inches; all were of course limited to one-column width.

But it took a lot of ads to meet a paper bill of $675 a week. For the fiscal year ended March 1875 the paper cost was $35,000. Sam Warren was now demanding cash on the barrel. The Colonel lopped one column off the width of the paper, reducing it to six columns, and sliced something off the depth of the page for a material saving in paper costs.

The Globe circulation had almost imperceptibly increased but was still under

10,000. The Herald claimed 115,000. The limited Globe news staff was working hard to compete. On December 18, 1874, they got in details of a South End fire up to 5:30 A.M. A heavy black Gothic "Extra" half an inch high on the front page called attention to the enterprise.

On the last day of the year the Globe published a review of French literature entirely in French. The Colonel liked such a stunt and the complimentary comment it brought and said it would be done every week, as it was for a while. That must have been Georgia Hamlen's assignment.

To get the paper talked about was a prime consideration for the Colonel, a born promoter. Novelty appealed to him. It took some doing to introduce novelty to the Globe, for Bacon, able editor of his time but a man of little originality, was wholly committed to conventional ways, and he had been appointed editor-in-chief, in complete charge of the editorial and news side. Taylor as business manager was also an experienced newsman, of much livelier mind than his editor; he had also to be persuasive to jog Bacon to innovation.

The Globe, since Ballou, had exploited crime news for all there was in it. This is about the easiest news to come by, as it comes off the police blotter; but they also reached for it. Through exchanges they picked up the more sensational crimes from all over. The front page sometimes looked pretty gruesome. On May 1, 1874, the top righthand headline on the front page was "Terrible Crimes," followed by a collection of them. The Colonel nudged the news side to feature interesting trials. He added a court reporter to the staff, William P. Fowler, later a Boston lawyer, to turn in full stenographic reports.

But the Globe was much more than a crime sheet. It featured every kind of local and regional event. In September 1875 a series on the cities of New England started in the lead position with two whole pages inside on Portland, "The Forest City." The article was illustrated with woodcuts, one of the city hall on page one, five scenic cuts on page two, and five more on page six.

The staff exploited all the Revolutionary anniversaries of 1875, April 19, June 17, July 4. On April 19 their first illustrations made for a news story were printed, primitive woodcuts of a Minute Man and representations of Sam Adams and John Hancock on the front page, and inside maps of Concord and Lexington as they were in 1775.

The response to this innovation led the Globe to splurge with a 16-page edition June 17 for Bunker Hill day. The front page had the Globe's first cartoon-type illustration, a four-column cut of Uncle Sam bearing a chain representing the unity of all the states, with arms open, one extended toward Bunker Hill and the other toward Fort Sumter. The caption read "The North to the South. Greeting: Brethren let us dwell together in unity." This was to be a favorite theme of Union Army veteran Taylor, who in a later year headed a Massachusetts commission to erect a monument at Baton Rouge to the Federal soldiers who fell at Port Hudson. He happily fraternized there with Confederate veterans and arranged for an annual dinner at his expense in the Baton Rouge Soldiers Home.

The 16-page issue was loaded with ads. The Jordan and Marsh store had a full page, as did the Mason & Hamlin Organ Company of Cambridgeport. The Globe made no claim to "firsts" with these full-page ads and probably was unaware of any historical significance; and the innovation in this failing Boston newspaper escapes the attention of the historians of journalism, who credit Wanamaker's of Philadel-

The Boston Daily Globe : Thursday Morning, June 21, 1825....Quadruple Sheet.   2

120 doz. Black and White Striped Skirts at 75 cts. each.

100 doz. Black and White Two-Ruffle Skirts at $1 each.

Embroidered Wash Poplin Skirts at $1 50, $2 and $2 25 each.

This is something entirely new, and a very stylish and superior garment.

Large variety of White Skirts at One Dollar each.

Side-Plaiting Skirts at One Dollar and Twenty-five Cents each.

25 doz. White Walking Skirts, handsomely Trimmed, at $1 50 each (fully worth $3 00).

50 doz. French Percale Knife-Plaited Skirts, at $2 50 each, in Navy Blue and White, Brown and White, and Black and White Percale—a very handsome skirt for Country or Watering-places, and sold much below cost of importation.

50 doz. Chemises at 75 cts. each.

50 doz. Chemises at 87½ cts. each.

These are very cheap, as the seams are all felled, and the bands around sleeves and neck and down the front are finely corded.

A full line of Chemises, from $1 to $16 each.

Drawers at 67 cts. to $3 each.

Night Dresses at $1 17 to $13 each.

Together with a complete assortment of Corset Covers, Dressing Sacks, etc., etc.

CORSETS.

50 doz. White and Colored Corsets at 62½c.

75 doz. Corsets at 87 1-2c.

50 doz. Corsets at $1 and $1 25 each.

The Boston Comfort Corset, Ladies', $2 50.

Children's Waists, $1.

50 doz. Corsets at $3 50 each.

These Corsets were sold, last season, for $5 each.

A Small Lot of Very Fine French Corsets at $4 each, reduced from $6.

A Full Line of Hoop Skirts, Paniers and Bustles.

Infants' Department.

Double Cloaks from $4 upwards.

Infants' Robes from $1 75 upwards.

Infants' Lace Hats from 75c. upwards.

Infants' Lace Bonnets, 75c. upwards.

Embroidered Shawls, Short Dresses, in both Nainsook and Pique, Embroidered Waists, Yokes, Bibs, and a full assortment of Infants' Underwear.

JORDAN, MARSH & CO.,
Washington & Avon Sts.

General View.

The Last Rounds of the Ladder.

The Number of Visitors.

The Reason Why.

The Third Story—Carpets.

---

100 PIECES

Broche Striped Grenadines

At 50 Cents.

This is one of the best bargains we have offered, this season; the goods are Silk Finish and are assorted in a great number of different and elegant designs.

50 PIECES

White Ground, Black Stripes,

At 75 cents.

50 PIECES

Steel Ground, Black Stripes,

At 75 cents.

100 PIECES

Black Ground, White Stripes,

At 87 1-2 cents, extra quality.

100 PIECES

Black Ground, White Stripes,

At $1 00 per yard.

100 PIECES

Steel and White Glace Stripes

At $1 00 per yard.

50 PIECES

White Ground, Black Stripes,

At $1 00 per yard.

50 PIECES

Steel Ground, Black Stripes,

At $1 00 per yard.

25 PIECES

STEEL GLACE CHECKS

At $1 00 per yard.

The last-named five lots of Silks, which are offered at $1 00, are of the best quality and fully worth $1 25.

PLAIN COLORED SILKS

In all the most desirable shades, at $1 25, $1 50, $1 87 1-2, $2 00, $2 50 and $3 50.

ALSO, A SMALL LOT OF

Striped Silks

At 50 cts. and 60 cts. per yard.

JORDAN, MARSH & CO.,
Washington & Avon Sts.

100 PIECES

STRIPED HERNANI

At 75c., former price $1 00.

25 PIECES

TWO-YARD WIDE HERNANI

At $1 25 per yard.

These Hernanis are all wool, and have been found to give much greater satisfaction than much higher priced Goods.

A FULL LINE OF

BLACK DRAPS D'ETE,

AT

FOR SACKS, ETC.,

From $1 50 to $5 00 per yard,

IN ADDITION TO

A COMPLETE ASSORTMENT OF

TANISE,

HENRIETTA

AND

BOMBAZINE

CLOTHS,

And other Useful and Elegant Mourning Fabrics, especially adapted to Summer Wear.

JORDAN, MARSH & CO.,
Washington & Avon Sts.

First full-page ad: June 17, 1875.

phia with the first full-page ads, in the Philadelphia papers in December 1879 on the occasion of a visit to the city by General Grant.*

On a six-column page, the Jordan and Marsh ad used three columns for a photograph of the store and a long article about it. The other three columns were headed "Silks for Mid-Summer," "Summer Black Goods," and "Parasols." The Mason & Hamlin ad used the center four columns at the top for a picture of a collection of "Gold and silver medals at industrial expositions in Europe and America"; below was a photograph of the company plant with four columns of type about it. The other two columns were headed "Three Highest Medals" and "Testimony of Eminent Musicians." The Crawford House had a half-page ad, largely occupied by a photograph of the hotel.

Beecher Trial

What pulled the Globe temporarily out of its doldrums that year was the Beecher-Tilton case, the most titillating scandal in years. It provided sensational copy for almost a year, the first five months with charges and countercharges, then six months of trial that ended with a hung jury and with public opinion equally suspended as to whether the most famous preacher in America had been guilty of adultery with a parishioner, wife of a former close associate.

The locale was New York, where Henry Ward Beecher's sermons attracted 2,500 people a Sunday to Plymouth Church; there he also edited major church publications, the Independent and the Christian Union, in which he espoused liberal causes. Theodore Tilton had been a junior associate in editing these publications, but he became an eccentric radical and a sensationalist, associated with Victoria Woodhull in her sensational free love crusading. His character was often impugned, and he was dropped from the church publications. Beecher, at his wife's prompting, advised Mrs. Tilton to separate from Tilton.

Tilton had for several years circulated charges about Beecher's relations with Mrs. Tilton. Finally Victoria Woodhull, in her Woodhull & Claflin's Weekly, aired them. Beecher made a public denial. His church, at his insistence, investigated and wholly exonerated him. Tilton then, on August 20, 1874, made an explicit charge of adultery against Beecher and sued him for $100,000. The case did not come to trial until January 1875. But the pretrial charges and published statements left little unrevealed. This was headline news everywhere, but the conservative editing of the Globe failed to exploit it.

Charles H. Taylor, watching the red ink spread at the rate of $1,200 a week on

---

* Russell H. Conwell in his biography of John Wanamaker, *The Romantic Rise of a Great American,* Harper & Bros., 1924, places the first full-page ad in the Philadelphia Record in December 1879. H. A. Gibbons in his biography of Wanamaker, *John Wanamaker* (2 vols.), Harper & Bros., 1926, places the ad only in 1879. But Gibbons notes that Wanamaker placed "the first half-page ad ever published in a newspaper" on September 26, 1874, in the Philadelphia papers; he does not name them.

his books, exerted his authority as business manager to insist on full coverage of the Beecher case and employed nationally noted reporter Joseph Howard, Jr., to cover it for the Globe.

By September 1, 1874, "The Scandal" had become approximately a stock head on the front page. It led the paper that day, even though the report began: "There is a lull in the Beecher-Tilton scandal today and the attitude of the public is one of suspense, waiting for the revelations of Francis Moulton's forthcoming additional 'thunderbolt' that his friends assert will be a crusher for Dr. Beecher and Plymouth Church." Moulton was a confidant of Tilton and claimed to have been of Beecher. He became a strategic witness.

The headline September 2 was:

>   The Brooklyn Sensation

On September 4:

>   The Unburied Scandal

September 8:

>   The Everlasting Scandal

September 9:

>   Will it Never End?
>   The Brooklyn Imbroglio Again

September 12:

>   Reopened
>   Moulton Makes his Third Statement
>   The matter still a question of veracity between Beecher and Moulton
>   [This runs to three columns.]

On September 12 the Globe editorialized on "Moulton's Plea." In view of the front page sensationalism, the editorial tone may have raised some eyebrows: "We are sorry that we feel compelled this morning to print another chapter in the sad story of the Brooklyn scandal. The third statement of Mr. Moulton will be sought so eagerly on a matter in which the public has had an almost morbid interest, that we have no alternative but to give it to our readers."

Editor Bacon's disgust at the Beecher scandal was expressed in preachy editorials, while the front page played up the prurient interest. To the reader it must have looked like hypocrisy. Actually it meant inner conflict, between an editor clinging to sedate convention and a manager desperately trying to popularize a newspaper facing bankruptcy. For ten months the Beecher case sold papers, and the Globe's circulation rose from under 10,000 to 30,000.*

The foreshadowed trial was practically a daily front page feature all fall. It became so familiar that the headline writers seemed to make a game of varying it: "The Brooklyn Nuisance" on September 18, "The Brooklyn Plague" September 21. The trial opened in January, and Tilton took the stand January 29. On February 9 the headline was:

>   Tilton Still on Stand
>   25th Day of Scandal Suit

---

* That the 1875 circulation bulge resulted from the sensational Beecher trial is evident from the fact that circulation dropped back to 8,000 for 1877, the bottom of the long depression, as of the Globe's fortunes. It was 1880 before it returned to 30,000. Thereafter it climbed steadily, to 40,000 in 1882 and 60,000 in 1884.

The days are counted off in the headlines. February 25:

> The Defense
> 35th Day of the Scandal Trial
> Gen. Tracy Begins the Opening Plea for Beecher
> History of the Entire Case

April 2, the sixtieth day of the trial, brings:

> Beecher's Defense
> The Great Preacher Tells His Story at Last
> His Acquaintance with Mrs. Tilton Explained

The story ran four columns and did so again the next day:

> Tremendous Crowd
> Dr. Beecher Makes Sweeping and Explicit Denials

On Dr. Beecher's seventh day on the stand the story ran five and a half columns. His ninth day:

> Beecher Testimony
> 69th Day of Endless Trial
> Cross Examination Begins at Last
> Relations Between Beecher and Mrs. Tilton Fully Sifted
> Beecher Admits He Was in the Habit of Calling on
>   and Kissing Elizabeth in her Husband's Absence

The evidence closed May 14, but it was June 10 before defense counsel finished their arguments. Plaintiff counsel then continued ten days more. On June 15 the Globe headline was:

> The Endless Agony
> 106th Regular Day of the Scandal Suit
> Mr. Beach Continues to Sum up for Mr. Tilton

On June 24 the case went to the jury. The June 25 top head read:

> Guilty or Not Guilty
> That is What Everybody Wants to Know
> And That is What the Brooklyn Jury Has Not Decided

On the sixth day the judge refused to discharge the jury when they told him their disagreement was over the facts, not the law. But next day, July 2, the judge let the divided jury go. The July 3d headline:

> Stepped Down and Out
> Wearied by Importunities, Judge Nielson Discharges the Jury
> Grace, Mercy and Peace After Six Months Misery

History records the jury as divided nine to three for Dr. Beecher. The Globe, July 3, editorially regretted the lack of a decisive conclusion, saying it would leave the public divided. "The plaintiff has not made out his case. Mr. Beecher has not established his innocence." The Globe editorial is no less indefinite than the jury: "If innocent, Mr. Beecher ought to be able to vindicate himself. If not, nothing should stand in the way of the exact truth."

The trial cost Beecher $118,000 and left him a poor man. This spurred him to increased activity as a public lecturer. He continued the popular preacher of Plymouth Church until his death in 1887.

First Telephone Story

The year 1877 yielded a historic episode for the Globe: what it proclaimed as the first news dispatch ever sent by telephone.

Alexander Graham Bell had transmitted the first telephone message the year before to his young assistant in the next room: "Mr. Watson, come here. I want you." On February 12, 1877, Bell lectured on his invention to a distinguished audience of the Essex Institute at Lyceum Hall in Salem. He demonstrated a two-way telephone conversation, conducted over a telegraph wire, between there and a room at 5 Exeter Place, Boston, off Chauncy Street.

The Globe had a lively young correspondent in Salem, Henry Batchelder. At the end of the meeting he arranged with Bell to transmit his report of the meeting over the telephone to Exeter Street, where the Globe's representative was a young Boston University law student, Austin Barclay Fletcher.* Next morning the Globe headlined the story:

Sent By Telephone

The First Newspaper Dispatch Sent By Human Voice Over the Wires

The year 1877 also brought to Boston a religious revival by the historic team of Moody and Sanky, Dwight Moody the evangelical preacher and Ira D. Sanky, organist and singer. A great tabernacle to seat 6,000 was built at Tremont Street and Warren Avenue and a huge choir organized for the meetings. All New England was alerted for a ten-week revival that actually lasted for three months. Weeks in advance the Globe announced it would print full reports, to be mailed anywhere for 75 cents a month.

The Globe opened January 26 with columns of description of the dedication of the tabernacle and woodcut illustrations of it. "We never sold 25,000 copies of the Globe quicker than we did yesterday," an editorial chortled the next day. Day after day the newspaper printed verbatim Moody's sermons and all the incidents and excitement of the revival. The Globe arranged with a New York publisher to supply the stenographic texts for Moody's sermons for $25 a week. He supplied books of the sermons to sell at $1 apiece, the Globe to keep 60 cents.

So this was a profitable venture besides one that added circulation. But the vast space used for the sermons, five or six or seven columns a day, kept news out of the paper. The staff had a problem to recover lost ground on general news once the religious fervor was over.

* It was Austin Barclay Fletcher's bequest to Tufts University 46 years later that established the Fletcher School of Law and Diplomacy.

Eben Jordan Saves the Globe

In spite of Beecher and the Moody-Sanky revival, the annual directors meeting in 1877 had another gloomy report. Three years of hard work had reduced the annual deficit from $60,000 to $10,000. But $200,000 had been sunk in the enterprise, and assets stood at only $83,000, of which $47,000 represented equipment. The corporation owed $78,000, close to $50,000 of this on "notes payable." Cashier Prescott's cash balance showed $632.47, about enough for one week's paper supply.

The cut in the annual deficit had come in part from increased circulation, but more largely from cutting down on staff, telegraph tolls, and payments to correspondents, all of which meant cutting the quality of the paper.

Colonel Taylor had exhausted his own resources and raised a mortgage on his house that took all the $5,000 he had put into it. His accruing debt to the paper manufacturers had reached its limit, and nothing was ahead but bankruptcy. His uphill struggle to keep the paper going became painfully evident to the staff.

Some weeks the staff were paid in rolls of three-cent pieces turned in by the news distributors. A few times a payday was skipped, though it was always caught up the next week. Pencils were scarce in the office and paper scarcer. Charles Dyar was writing editorials in his copper-plate penmanship on the backs of old envelopes. The Herald was printing rumors that the Globe was about to suspend. Members of the staff were casting about for other places, some drifting away to other jobs.

What saved the situation was a notion Colonel Taylor picked up in Martha's Vineyard while he was soliciting summer resort advertising. The new Martha's Vineyard Narrow Gauge Railroad had run into unexpected construction costs, had exhausted its capital, and faced bankruptcy or reorganization. Taylor met the railroad manager, who described the answer the railroad had found. The creditors accepted two-thirds of their bills, with the balance in new stock put up by the original stockholders. Thus cleared of floating debt and interest, the railroad was beginning to show a profit.

Why not such a plan for the Globe, Colonel Taylor wondered. He consulted Eben Jordan, by then almost the only surviving stockholder. Jordan had taken up the paper of those who opted to get out and sell their shares; he had given Taylor constant support and encouragement; now he promised to back a new financial arrangement to save the Globe.

The Colonel at first meant to copy the Martha's Vineyard plan, to reduce the Globe's 2,000 shares of stock to 1,000 and issue 1,000 new shares, presumably to clear off debts and provide new operating capital. But he was unable to get this plan accepted. With Jordan he devised another plan, for a new company to buy out the old one for an amount sufficient to pay off its indebtedness, which by then reached $100,000. The reorganization was worked out in late 1877.

Eben D. Jordan put up the money. On February 5, 1878, the Globe Publishing Co. became the Globe Newspaper Co. and 1,250 shares of $100 stock were issued, 1,243 of them to Colonel Taylor, two to Ned Prescott, and five to Mr. Jordan's lawyer, Francis A. Nichols, evidently to pay for the law work on the reorganization. Colonel Taylor transferred 330 shares to the Samuel D. Warren

Paper Company and 910 shares to Eben Jordan, keeping only three for himself, probably to reimburse funds of his own advanced to the paper. Mr. Jordan also took on other outstanding debts.

So Colonel Taylor was nominal owner of the Globe, without any capital in it; Eben Jordan, nominally only a creditor, was in effect the owner. From that deal to salvage the paper, the joint Taylor-Jordan ownership resulted that continued ever after, through the heirs of Charles Taylor and the estate of Eben Jordan.

Ten years later Colonel Taylor was able to buy back some of the $100 shares at $575, and later still more at $1,000. Jordan had redeemed the shares held by the Warren Company. Taylor was evidently deterred by sentiment from trying to buy out his sponsor and friend Eben Jordan. But on Jordan's death in 1895, Taylor by agreement purchased enough shares from the Jordan estate to give him exactly one-half ownership of the Globe. Ever since, the Taylor-Jordan equal sharing has continued. But throughout the Globe has remained entirely under Taylor management, now in its fourth generation.*

Now a wholly new newspaper came into being, a new kind of newspaper. With the reorganization assured, Colonel Taylor had already launched a Sunday paper. The Herald had had a Sunday edition since 1862, when eagerness for war news broke down the Puritan prejudice against a Sabbath publication. The Herald had a Sunday circulation of more than 65,000 when the Sunday Globe was started on October 14, 1877.

A Sunday paper meant only a seventh issue of the daily, the same eight-page size; but it sold from the start at five cents. To the staff it meant an extra day's work. A. A. Fowle, by that time city editor, remembered that it cost him $5 a week, the amount he had earned working Saturday night for the Sunday Courier, a weekly paper. But staff work was soon staggered so that the men had one day off in 14.

With new plans, Colonel Taylor invited editor Bacon to continue with the new paper. But Bacon doubtless realized that he was out of tune with the radical changes Taylor had in mind. He was reportedly miffed also at not being taken into the new corporation. Bacon resigned to become the Boston correspondent of the Springfield Republican and very soon to join the staff of the Advertiser, where he became editor-in-chief in 1883. Three years later he became editor of the Post and continued to direct that paper through five languishing years until E. A. Grozier bought it to rejuvenate it in 1891. Bacon then turned to literary work and local history. He died in 1916, a distinguished editor of the old school. But in 1878 the time had come for a new school.

---

* A Taylor family legend is that Eben Jordan was first impressed by Charles Taylor's work as a newspaperman five years before the Globe was started. As Davis Taylor tells it: "The General came to Eben D. Jordan's attention by covering for the Traveler Charles Dickens' lecture in Boston 1867 and then setting in type single-handedly the whole of his talk. Its accuracy so startled Mr. Dickens that he asked Mr. Jordan if he could meet the *men* who had covered his performance and when Charles Taylor showed up alone, he was amazed that it had been done by one man, and old man Jordan never forgot it."

James Morgan's biography of General Taylor has him covering the Dickens appearance for the New York Tribune, whose correspondent he had become. But he might well have covered it for both his old paper and his new one.

The Boston Daily Globe.

VOL. XIII....NO 66.   BOSTON, THURSDAY MORNING, MARCH 7, 1878.

NEW HAMPSHIRE ELECTION.

Democratic Prospects Flattering.

REPUBLICANS DEJECTED.

Favorable Reports from Concord.

Legislative Gains Predicted.

RUSSIA AND TURKEY.

A Synopsis of the Terms of the Treaty.

ENGLAND'S DESIGNS ON EGYPT.

A Congress of Powers Considered Probable.

WHAT RUSSIA NEXT PROPOSES.

Free Navigation of the Danube to be Restored.

Chas. H. Taylor's new Globe: March 7, 1878.

II A Different Newspaper

Chas. Taylor's New Globe

Chas. H. Taylor had been running the Globe for five years. Now, though he owned none of it, he was in full control. It was his to make or break. In 1878, at 31, with five children and a mortgage on his house, he was about to make a radical breakthrough in newspaper methods. He turned a losing morning paper into an all-day newspaper, and turned it from Republican to Democratic; he inaugurated at the same time a new policy for the times to deal impartially with political news, as with all other kinds, and to add a broad family dimension to his newspaper's appeal. Newspapers till then had dealt with the interests of men. Colonel Taylor introduced material aimed at women and children, too. He cut the price of the Globe to two cents, to bring it within reach of more people.

He began doing all these things at once and with such effect that in less than three years the Globe circulation went from 8,000 to 30,000. Within ten years it became the dominant paper of the region, its publisher hailed as "the wizard of journalism" and his Globe as one of the most exciting newspapers in the country.

Before launching his new Globe, Colonel Taylor negotiated for an editor to replace Mr. Bacon. The appointment of Edward C. Bailey was a dramatic stroke that made its own strong impact on the community. Bailey, then 58, had been editor and owner of the Boston Herald until he sold it in 1869, postmaster of Boston, and Democratic candidate for governor; he was the brother of a United States senator from New Hampshire where Bailey had retired a few years earlier and where he was publishing the Concord Patriot. Bailey was one of the best-known newspaper names in the region and a leading Democrat. To lure him back to Boston to edit the Globe was a ten-strike. To reinforce Bailey on the editorial page, the Colonel added Frederick E. Goodrich, who had been editor of the Democratic Boston Post. The Post had fallen upon evil times; it had come under control of a stockjobber who ruined its stockholders so that it was soon forced into reorganization, making Goodrich available.

The Colonel had already enlivened and improved the appearance of the paper. Inside pages as well as the front page now exhibited a more attractive balance in makeup. The editorial page had been cleared of all but editorial matter. A new feature, "All Around the Hub," had been added. Charles M. Vincent, Martha's Vineyard publisher, had been taken on to develop, among other things, a new column of "Table Gossip" that was the forerunner of "Society" news. Frank Nichols, a literary lawyer, and Tom Maguire, Boston correspondent of the New York Herald, strengthened the local staff. There had been a lot of changes in the uncertain previous years. But Charles Dyar held on, now city editor. Michael Curran was in charge of editorials. Sam Miles, Andrew Lawson, William Downes, and James Frost remained. Now, significantly, there were two new staffers. Mike Meehan, Irish-born Civil War veteran, politician, and contractor, joined the Globe. He was secretary of the Democratic Central Committee, a strategic liaison that suggests the influence of Bailey and Goodrich. Another significant relation is indicated by the emergence of a Globe printer, George Perry, to reporting. Perry had become secretary of the newly organized Boston Central Labor Union. Without title, he was in effect the first labor editor of the Globe. An addition that brought some éclat to the paper was Howard Malcolm Ticknor as music critic. Son of William D. Ticknor of the distinguished publishing firm of Ticknor & Fields, he was a former assistant editor of the Atlantic Monthly and was returning from ten years' music study in Italy to a chair at Harvard College. He wrote music for the Globe for ten years.

To strengthen his business office the Colonel brought in a man who knew Boston transportation from ten years in the shipping room at Jordan and Marsh department store. Thomas R. Downey, then 32, like the Colonel a Civil War veteran and a Charlestown man, took charge of circulation. He became one of the great circulation managers, a post he held on the Globe for nearly 50 years. His handling of distribution got the paper to the right place at the right time and was a big factor in its rapid rise in circulation.

Perhaps the least noticed new employee that year was a 14-year-old Charlestown boy, Edward F. Dunbar. He did not long remain unnoticed. The Colonel soon made him his own office boy, a spot from which Dunbar quickly became an advertising solicitor and then the advertising manager, paralleling Downey's half century in the other key business post under the publisher.

It was wholly characteristic of Chas. Taylor that he picked two Charlestowners for places closest to him in the office, as he had earlier picked his old Somerville neighbor Ned Prescott to handle the Globe's books. He kept his close touch with Charlestown and Somerville; this was his background, where his roots were. It was no accident that he chose to run a people's newspaper and to seek his circulation and his close associates among the common run of people such as he had grown up with.

All his life he chose to promote men from within his staff and to fill top posts with the men next in line. In later years he used to tell of a businessman who asked his advice about filling a key vacancy in his organization.

"Why, your man is right in your own office," Taylor told him.

"What do you mean?"

"The man at the next desk. He knows the job."

Colonel Taylor chose to launch his reorganized paper on the anniversary of the first issue of Maturin Ballou's Globe. On Monday, March 4, 1878, the Globe announced that "on Thursday, March 7, the Globe will issue morning and evening editions in folio form* and the price will be reduced to two cents a copy."

"A live progressive Democratic newspaper" the headline proclaimed in larger than the normal body type. "The Globe will advocate all liberal measures which will advance the interests of the masses in their social and financial condition, and will endeavor to promote their moral and intellectual welfare . . . The Hon. E. C. Bailey has accepted the position of editor and the business management will be under the control of Chas. H. Taylor, who has been manager of the Globe for nearly five years past."

So on Thursday, March 7, the first evening edition of the Globe appeared. It carried over most of the morning edition and added two columns of later material on the front page and more late news on the back page. Its three top heads on

---

* "In folio form" was an elegant way of describing a four-page paper. Folio, a term most commonly used of books, is a folded sheet printed on both sides to make four pages of print.

page one: "Morning Edition," "Globe Extra — Three O'Clock," and "Globe Extra — Five O'Clock."

The two two-cent papers had in size only divided the former three-cent paper, for instead of one eight-page paper the Globe was now two four-page papers. But it went back to its original seven-column page from the six columns to which penury had reduced it.

The lead editorial on March 7 was headed "The Globe."

> The Democratic Party has long needed a daily to advocate Democratic principles at a low price . . . within the means of the masses . . . This need the Globe will undertake to fill.
>
> The Globe will aim to give the public a paper that will not offend the sensibilities of an intelligent public which will be a proper journal for circulation in the family circle.
>
> With the kindest sentiments toward all . . . we ask a widespread circulation and a liberal advertising patronage which we have no doubt will be accorded.

The page one heads are blacker and the stories more exciting. Crime evidently pays. Murders thicken. The lead headline March 8 is "The Murder." This one is in Marlboro, but others are farther afield. In that month Keene, New Hampshire, and Camden, New Jersey, provided murders for one day; Wheeling, West Virginia, turned up "An Awful Crime" one day and on the next there was a "Horrible Murder in Montreal," followed the day after that by "More Bloody Work," "Frightful Double Tragedy in West Columbus, Ohio."

A combination head March 27 read "Murder Arson Suicide Tried by a Waltham Man." The Globe had said it would not offend, but this steady diet of crime news did offend the more refined, making it strikingly plain that Chas. Taylor's Globe would depart 180 degrees from Maturin Ballou's original Globe plan to compete with the Transcript for Beacon Hill tastes.

The Sunday Globe, with several months' run behind it, continued six-column width, eight pages, at five cents. It presented a clean front page, clear of advertising as the daily paper was not, with neatly balanced heads of two or three banks. The Sunday edition avoided crime news to present articles of general interest. It carried the same title as the weekday editions, Boston Daily Globe. Its headlines were of the same type as the daily and the same one-column width. But the topics began to suggest the later Sunday feature: The Religious World — The State of Today — Gossip for Women — Mark Twain on Cats (a reprint from the Atlantic Monthly) — Bric-a-Brac (odd items from other papers).

The first Sunday under the new regime, March 10, the editorial page carried an editorial "The Sunday Globe," announcing the intention "to make the Sunday Globe a live paper and fully up to the times . . . not a namby-pamby paper — not devoted to interests of cliques or cabals. We shall not hesitate to attack public men . . . and to denounce class legislation. We shall pay our respects to the Prohibitionists and to the advocates of Commissions."

The little old Hoe press in the Globe basement clanked overtime to keep up with the demand for the first day's new Globe. "A day of unparalleled success," the Globe

Eben D. Jordan.

boasted next day. "More than 50,000 copies of the different editions sold before 6 o'clock."

This novelty sale of course did not keep up, but a much increased circulation did. The single press could print only 4,000 papers an hour. But the Colonel had a bit of luck in that the bankrupt Post had ordered a new Hoe press of the latest type, which had won for the Hoe company a gold medal at the great Centennial Exposition of 1878 in Philadelphia, and couldn't pay for it. Colonel Taylor offered to take the press for a bargain price of $15,000 and on terms of $1,000 down and $500 a month. The new press could turn out 12,000 papers an hour.

This was a perfecting press, so-called, which printed papers from curved metal plates cast from molds of the type — stereotypes. This reduced wear on the types. Also, it was fed paper from a roll instead of in sheets that had to be inserted singly, and it received impressions on both sides as the paper rolled through the cylinders. But type still had to be hand-set. The linotype did not come in till 1886.

The Democratic allegiance was clearly a factor in the circulation growth, for on May 20 the Boston Democratic Committee declared formally that it was "the duty of every Democrat in Massachusetts to aid personally in increasing the Globe's circulation and influence." The Post's circulation and influence had fallen away. The Democrats had no place else to go. Democratic interest in the Globe was further evidenced with stock purchased in the paper by the chairman of the Democratic State Committee, Jonas H. French. French was president of the Cape Ann Granite Company and a political ally of Gen. Benjamin Butler, whose political campaigns for governor the Globe supported over the next several years.

French's stock acquisition led to charges by Butler's political opponents that he had acquired part ownership in the Globe. Butler's name never appeared as a stockholder, but his friend French first bought ten shares and then 250, perhaps a gesture to buy favor for Butler or to hold stock for him.

Colonel Taylor conducted a personal stock-selling campaign among friends and people of influence, and also put up Globe shares as collateral for bills or loans. He obtained the shares from Eben Jordan and, as he was able to redeem them, thus reduced Jordan's ownership and gradually built up his own. French soon disposed of his 250 shares, perhaps because of the talk that Butler was buying into the Globe.

Others who bought Globe shares at that time included A. Shuman, Boston merchant; Louis Ober, proprietor of what later became the Locke-Ober restaurant; and James S. Whitney, steamship company president and former Collector of the Port, a Democrat. His son Henry M. Whitney became a big real-estate developer of the Back Bay and of the West End Street Railway Company, which became deeply involved in political controversy that found the Globe supporting Whitney's street railway operations when its former reporter George Fred Williams was leading a campaign charging Whitney with corrupting legislators. Whitney made himself politically vulnerable in the struggle for transit control and expansion, and this dogged his political career over a long period. Transit was to be a recurring political issue through most of the Globe's first 100 years.

Attacks on Whitney, as on Butler, involved the Globe as their supporter and also in the whispered suspicion that they owned some of the Globe. This, if it ever was true, could only have been true in minuscule portions and soon would have ceased to be true as the Colonel and Eben Jordan gradually acquired control of all Globe shares. But the Colonel's indiscriminate stock-selling campaign in 1878 let him in for this kind of suspicion at a time when just being Democratic was a black enough mark with Proper Bostonians.

The Advertiser and the Post were languishing. The Journal too was in decline. It was described as going gaudy and sensational in its old age, with boxes and lurid headlines, possibly to meet the new Globe competition. But this was out of character, and the paper declined till finally absorbed in the Herald in 1917. The Traveller was still a lively paper in the 1880's but limited in its appeal, as it continued to be until annexed by the Herald in 1912.

Colonel Taylor was in the van of new trends and a new dynamism in journalism. New inventions and improvements were facilitating larger papers and rapid printing for mass circulation. The Associated Press monopoly was soon to break down, freeing the dissemination of news. In New York, Pulitzer was about to parallel Taylor's innovations with spectacular success and national impact. Sunday newspapers were increasing in number. Evening papers were rising in one city after another to challenge the dominance of the morning papers.

The very special case of the evening Globe was that it was an extension of the morning paper and was always to remain so, to carry the same editorials, features, and advertising all day, to be in reality an all-day newspaper with only the news columns changing to keep pace with the developing news.

This was very different from the old Advertiser's evening paper, the Record, started in 1884, which was as different from the Advertiser as could be; and that was the aim, to catch the readers who found no appeal in the Advertiser's Toryism. The Record was breezy, witty, light, and politically independent of the rigors of the Advertiser. It soon had a 32,000 circulation, more than that of its parent. But for economy the Record was soon being edited and published by the Advertiser, which severely limited its development.

The Colonel, in launching the evening paper, made it a cardinal point not to force a second paper on the reader. "I want it to fit the reader's own time," he would say. Carrying out this principle, the morning and evening paper were never offered at a combined rate as other morning-evening papers were. The morning paper has its own weekly rate for subscription or delivery and the evening is a separate account. The advertiser can buy the morning or evening separately; if he buys both he does get a reduced combination rate.

The newness of the Globe was all Taylor. The paper announced and practiced impartiality in its news, rare enough in that day of partisan journalism. Years later Chas. Taylor emphasized this as the first change he made, to alter the spirit of the party newspaper. "My theory was that the news columns should be entirely independent and give impartially the news of all parties. Both parties were entitled to a full share of the columns of any enterprising daily newspaper whatever its political bias on the editorial page."

Editorially the Globe stated on March 7, 1878, that "while the Globe will advocate Democratic measures and support all Democratic nominations, it will be entirely free from all personal abuse of political opponents. It will not admit into its columns any scurrility and will refrain from anything bordering on blackguardism." It would be "a proper journal for circulation in the family circle."

The family circle was the new Globe's broad target. Colonel Taylor approached it with the same methods that had won friends for his little American Home magazine seven years before. He did not overlook the women or the children in planning departments and proposing features. The tone of the paper in particular he sought to make one that would fit into the home. He wanted it pleasant, friendly, informal, homey, with human interest, and a neighborly interest too — to report on all local matters big and little, to include the names of all on a local committee, to bring in everybody who was doing anything. The Globe soon had a reputation of printing more names than any other Boston newspaper. The Colonel was playing on a very human trait: people like to see their names or the names of others they know, and they talk about it. To get the Globe talked about was ever a key aim of its publisher. He moved away from the clichés of what made news: anything of fresh interest was news.

The kinds of features used by the Colonel in his earlier magazine lent themselves especially to weekend reading of the Sunday paper. From the start he gave special attention to the Sunday paper, building its circulation until it soon passed the daily and in not many years doubled it. He urged its special advantage on advertisers and with his solicitations created much new advertising for Sunday.

He faced tough competition. The Herald had had a Sunday paper for 15 years when the Globe's began. But at that time the Sunday Herald was less than half the daily circulation, which had reached 100,000. The Herald, prosperous, had built a fine new building right across the street from the Globe, at 241 Washington Street — "the finest newspaper building in the country," the Herald said.

But the Globe caught up with the Herald in its first few years, and on Sunday went way ahead until on its tenth anniversary Chas. Taylor could say that the impetus of the Sunday Globe had immensely strengthened both Globe and Herald. Both in size of paper and in volume of advertising and circulation their growth was enormous.

The Sunday paper had wrought a business revolution, Taylor said. Saturday had been the big shopping day and Monday the poorest day of the week in the stores, blue Monday. But the Sunday paper advertising started Monday off in high gear and its momentum carried through the week.

The Sunday Globe started the first newspaper serial in a metropolitan daily newspaper on Sunday, November 17, 1879:

After Dark in Boston

or

The Faith and Fate of a Working Girl.

The signature was Mrs. Abigail Perkins, but the story was the work of a Globe reporter, J. O. Kaler, who was to produce many more; the serial became a Globe fixture, starting on Sunday and continuing through the weekday editions. It was a matter of business ethic with Chas. Taylor never to start a new feature in a two-cent paper that would force the reader to pay more for the Sunday paper to continue the series.

The Sunday paper proved a natural occasion for special articles of all sorts, and especially for women's affairs, poems, songs with music, illustrations, special correspondence, and presently cartoons, the forerunners of the comics.

Circulation brought in advertising. The first issue of the new Globe carried an ad of a Jordan sale of ladies' linen, cambric, and lawn suits at prices from $1.50 to $10.00, and an R. H. White ad for Lyons black silk at $1.50 a yard. By May 26 the Sunday paper had a whole back page ad for Carboline, "a wonderful discovery, the only article that will restore hair on bald heads."

Advertising was developing nationally. Total advertising doubled between 1870 and 1880 and nearly doubled again by 1890. Among the early lavish users of newspaper space were such nostrums as hair restorers and soaps. Some of the earliest advertised products continued as familiar household names over a long period, among them "Ivory Soap — It Floats — 99 44/100 Per Cent Pure," and "Have You Used Pear's Soap?" Castoria, Purina, Scott's Emulsion were not far behind, and along with these pioneers Lydia Pinkham's compound; soon after came Mellen's Baby Foods and Royal Baking Powder, which by 1890 had the largest national advertising budget of any, $600,000. That would buy a lot of advertising space at early rates. By 1886 the Boston rate was 11 cents a line, just half of New York's; that was about $1.50 an inch, or $30 a column, some $200 a page. Of more importance in the long run than individual products was the increased use of advertising by local department stores, which soon became the mainstay of newspaper revenue.

The Globe's front page on March 7 had three columns of advertising and on subsequent days as much as the Colonel could get, some days almost none, other days almost the whole front page. Years later he gave as his philosophy that an eight-column front page, which by then the Globe had, should have three columns of advertising to represent the proportion of ads to news throughout the paper. He thoroughly believed that ads were news, at least to the woman. The Globe clung to front page advertising longer than almost any other paper in the country. Taylor immediately took ads off the editorial page, which on that March day had five columns of editorials, one on books, and one for drama.

Sports was always lively news in the Globe, often on the front page. Sports has traditionally been important news in all newspapers. Even Maturin Ballou's first edition had an inconspicuous item predicting that "the Boston Red Stockings will have the strongest nine in the country next season." The top center headline in the Globe May 2, 1878, was "That Pennant," followed by "The Boston Nine going for it once more."

From police, Arthur Fowle had been made editor of sports, which, next to crime, made the most exciting news of the late seventies and early eighties. Walking matches were in terrific vogue and called for as detached and professional coverage as latter-day track meets. The public interest was such that the completion of one walking match brought a sale of 30,000 extra Globes when the regular run was less than half that.

Baseball, trotting, cricket, rifle shooting would add up to some three columns a day before there were any designated sports pages. Prizefighting was the big thing, and it had a special cachet because it was illegal and had to be managed by con-trivance. Sports reporters had to be "inside" on the arrangements. They were often drafted as referees. One notable Globe sports writer, Eugene Buckley, graduated to be state boxing commissioner.

Mr. Fowle had the title of sports editor but for a long time no staff; that is, he had to find staffers to take on his events. These were popular assignments. Half the staff became proficient at sports reporting, and the sports editor post proved a step-ping stone to the posts of city editor and managing editor throughout the Globe's first 70 years.

The Globe published eight pages daily through the 1870's. By November 1880 it was putting out a 10-page Sunday paper. The Advertiser's 20-page issue to observe its move to a new building in 1883 was the largest newspaper ever put out in Boston to that time. Another Boston record was an entire page of classified ads in the Boston Sunday Globe in October 1880.

Instead of increasing the size of the daily, the Globe printed a two-page supple-ment on special occasions. By 1880 this was a regular Wednesday and Saturday addition.

Mechanical improvements came gradually. In 1875 machinery for folding and trimming the pages was introduced. It was 1887 before the Globe with a new build-ing installed its first double perfecting press, pioneer of the sextuple and web presses. It could print 25,000 papers of eight pages. The first linotype machine came in 1894. The Globe was then installing typewriters and trying to get veteran newsmen to use them.

Colonel Taylor appears to have left the organization of the news and editorial departments to Colonel Bailey, who after all had been editor and publisher of the Herald. Bailey brought an assistant from his Concord, New Hampshire, paper, Leonard B. Brown, and between them they managed the news with neither city editor nor managing editor. This didn't go so well. Mr. Fowle, who under editor Bacon had served as city editor, suggested to Colonel Taylor that they needed a managing editor and city editor.

Benjamin Palmer was hired from the Herald as managing editor. At 38 he had had experience on several New England papers, and at the Globe he soon built a shipshape news organization that moved rapidly ahead of the competition. Palmer served as managing editor for five years, a period of solid progress, and in later years returned to write obituaries and remained till his death at 76 in 1916.

More men were added to the staff, and the composing room grew from 30 to 40. Nathaniel Morton joined the Globe in 1880 from the New Bedford Mercury to become New England editor. By 1883 he was doing a lively column called "Young Man About Town," which continued until he was lost with many others in January 1884 in the wreck of the *City of Columbus,* a long remembered sea disaster off Cape

Cod. Charles Howard Montague came onto the staff in 1880 after a brief period on the Traveller. Only 22, he had been a printer and court stenographer; he now became Palmer's secretary. He soon developed into a brilliant reporter and became a great city editor.

Edward Bailey retired from Boston journalism for the second time in 1880. Colonel Taylor took the title of editor and publisher, which he held the remaining 41 years of his life, as did his son after him for 34 years more. Bailey's leaving seems to have been just a desire to give up active daily journalism at 60. No conflict is recorded nor any change of editorial policy. Bailey's contribution to the paper in those first years of its Democratic identification must have been chiefly his own presence as a leading Democrat and his extensive political acquaintance.

Frederick Goodrich left the editorial page the same year to become secretary to Mayor Frederick Prince.

Superintendent Robert Boss, up under the gaslights of his stifling loft, abated the Globe's sensationalism with the rigidity of his makeup rules. For so long as headlines were limited to single-column width, crime could not dominate the front page as with later banner heads; the other two top headlines balanced the news diet. "Washington" and "Foreign News" made two front page headlines May 1, 1878. On May 13 "Florida Investigation" and "Electoral Frauds" were front page. Some days there were no front page crimes. Headlines ran "Savings Banks," "The European Situation," "The Dominion," "War Clouds over Europe," "Fenianism," "Suffrage."

The Colonel had supported women's suffrage back in his legislature days. He continued to in the Globe, along with other liberal causes — direct election of senators, a shorter workday, Saturday half holiday, Labor Day holiday, tariff reduction, and the cause of Ireland. By 1880 one-third of the population of Boston was Irish-born, and Boston was soon to have its first Irish-born mayor in Colonel Taylor's good friend Hugh O'Brien.

A New World to Florence Finch

Georgia Hamlen had been nearly four years gone and the Globe had had no other woman on the staff in November 1881. It was only when the Globe had begun to pioneer in special features for women that this lack was noted. By then the office had developed its own legend that Colonel Taylor harbored a prejudice against women reporters.

Ben Palmer, the managing editor, so put it to Miss Florence Finch. But, he conceded, they needed a woman to handle "millinery openings." This was a pretty thin story. They needed a woman for millinery and for art and for reporting women's affairs and for all the other women's touches that were missing. Could she also do a column for women on Sundays? Oh yes, indeed.

So Florence Finch joined the Globe, and the result many years later was a most literate, lively, and illuminating account of the Globe at the end of its first meager decade. She was on the paper from 1881 to 1884. These were years of growth and development, both for the Globe and for Florence Finch. The Globe of her young days and her days on the young Globe combine to make a bright chapter.

But no one could have come into a new job with a more negative view of it. She had come to Boston out of the University of Kansas after working in Chicago just long enough to save train fare to Boston. She had brought introductions to proper Bostonians who tried to put her on the road to making a living writing. But it was hard going. She tried everything but the Globe. Her nice Beacon Hill friends had warned her against the Globe: low, vulgar people, sensational, and Democrats. They even supported that disreputable General Butler for governor. A lot of rowdies.

But at last, in desperate plight, Florence Finch tried the Globe. She had heard they might be going to hire a woman. A new world opened to her. Fifty years later, at the end of a full life, she wrote of it in the afterglow of that bright interlude.

She was hired for ten dollars a week to be reporter, art critic, general assignment reporter, expert on women's wear, and weekly columnist for women. For none of these functions had she any experience whatever; but nobody in the shop knew any more about them. She called her first Sunday column "The Woman's Hour," a phrase taken from a politician's speech she had heard: "The woman's hour has struck."

And it was striking for Florence Finch.

She was sent to report a sermon by Bishop Brooks, whose Gatling gun speed was the terror of reporters. Shorthand men couldn't take him. She couldn't either, but she found him so effective a speaker that she didn't need notes. "It was as easy as unwinding thread from a spool to write rapidly my report of over half a column . . . Finding how successful my method was, I continued to use it and never through my reporting career did I take notes. I listened with concentrated attention and afterwards it was as clear in my memory as a picture of what I had seen." * This, at a time when shorthand reporting was counted one of the prime reporting skills, was a highly individual departure. The newspapers were given to running complete campaign speeches of candidates, whole sermons, and long interviews, verbatim.

Miss Finch tried her hand at feature articles, starting with one about the beauty of the Public Garden, which seemed marvelous to her as set down in the busy heart of the city. This kind of fresh reporting by a naive stranger to the city appealed to Colonel Taylor, and she was encouraged to do more features. She suggested a series on American humor and humorists and researched it thoroughly in the Public Library. Then she wrote to contemporary humorists and received amusing replies that they let her use. The series ran weekly for two months, and she found that the same people who had urged her to stay away from the Globe were clipping the articles.

"This series, which the Boston people I had met seemed to think a surprising thing to find in such a low and vulgar paper as they supposed the Globe to be, was in line with what I found to be General Taylor's policy of developing his journal."

The low opinion her literary friends had of the Globe was doubtless largely based on its support of Democrats, the most conspicuous at that time being General Butler, who was considered a notorious character by Beacon Street and held in such low esteem at Harvard that he was conspicuously omitted from the honorary degree

---

* Florence Finch Kelly's description of her Globe experience is in pages 161–212 of her book *Flowing Stream*, E. P. Dutton, 1939. Her appraisal of General Taylor with Adolph Ochs and William Randolph Hearst — "Three Journalists of Genius" — is in pages 471–516 of *Flowing Stream*.

list that till then always included the governor. But there was no doubt that the Globe was sensational, battening on police news and exploiting the prizefights that had to be conducted surreptitiously.

Miss Finch was soon writing pieces for the Atlantic and editorials for the Globe — so the Globe was not all low brow in the 1880's. The Colonel might have claimed, as McGregor Jenkins did of the Atlantic 40 years later, that it was for people who had one high brow and one low brow.

The Globe sent Miss Finch to report Oscar Wilde when he lectured in Boston as a kind of advance agent for the D'Oyly Carte Company that was coming with their Gilbert and Sullivan repertoire. She found him almost totally lacking the quality of an effective or attractive public speaker and decided that the audiences, largely women, were drawn almost wholly by curiosity. The most distasteful work assigned her was reporting social events that were given extensive coverage. Bored at one event, she tried her hand at elaborate description of the women's costumes, and the managing editor told her that it was the best story of its kind ever in Boston. So she couldn't escape what became the society page. But she found lively interest in an assignment to a party given by Houghton Mifflin for Harriet Ward Beecher Stowe, surrounded at 70 by the literary lights of the time. She listened to catch the flavor of their literary conversation, and William Dean Howells and Thomas Bailey Aldrich paused near her in animated discussion: one was arguing the delights of an obscure North End restaurant he had discovered and the other held forth on special dishes of another dining spot.

But the work she threw herself into was as art critic. Boston was then the art center of the country. Aware of her ignorance, she asked questions and studied art books. She must have added some luster to the Globe's art columns, for they let her go to the big spring and fall exhibits in New York. She argued for open-mindedness toward new art forms and influences and reported with enthusiasm the first exhibition in America of a European collection of what was beginning to be called Impressionism. That the Globe opened its columns to her vigorous defense of the avant garde in art says something for its appreciation either of art or the kind of writing that was bringing the Globe to the attention of those who had the year before looked down their noses at it.

It is interesting that in her memoirs of more than 50 years later, Florence Finch remembers a feature of that first Impressionist art exhibit in 1884: the pictures were better lighted than any before because gas had given way to electricity.

She had hardly got onto her art assignment when the literary editor's desk fell vacant, and books were turned over to her. When Lily Langtry came to Boston, she was given that assignment, too. She had till then seen just one stage play, but after her story of Lily's performance, the dramatic critic called on her for assistance. It was an era of classic drama, and she learned about that on Monday night reviews — Edwin Booth in *Hamlet* and Mme. Modjeska, Maurice Barrymore, and James O'Neill in *The Count of Monte Cristo*.

Soon she found that "any door I wanted to open yielded readily to my touch." In her social notes she scattered editorial paragraphs, humorous, mildly irreverent. These turned up missing, to her disappointment, till she found them moved to the editorial page. Then she was taken off society and put to editorial writing. She found that Colonel Taylor liked freshness and originality in editorials and that he appreciated items of pungency and piquancy on that page that would give the reader a chuckle and lead him to ask, "Did you see so-and-so in the Globe this morning?"

She had grown up in strictly Republican Kansas. The Globe was editorially Democratic, but she found it also liberal and independent. It was of course against the Republican tariff. Having to study about the tariff, she discovered "it was quite as much an ethical as an economic question," and that appealed to her. She was liberal, inclined a little toward radicalism as it was in the 1880's. There were just two editorial writers and the chief was off Sundays. It happened on a Sunday in 1884 that Governor Butler, who was anathema to the respectable but had been supported by the Globe as a Democrat, announced his candidacy for president on the Anti-Monopoly and Greenback ticket. Young Miss Finch had become politically sophisticated enough to know this was a delicate item; it had to be taken seriously, but without in the least committing the Globe to the new heresy. She managed so deftly that the Colonel beamed Monday morning that the editorial was just right.

The times were out of joint, and all sorts of radicalism was in the air: the Knights of Labor, Henry George, the Pullman strike, the Haymarket Square bombing, Eugene Debs, socialists and anarchists.

The Globe's other editorial writer, Benjamin Tucker, called himself an anarchist. He edited a socialist periodical and had translated European radicalism. He came of an affluent family who at the time owned a small amount of stock in the Globe. The office understanding was that that was why Colonel Taylor had given Ben Tucker a job despite his unorthodox views.*

Tucker and Miss Finch discussed freely and fully the ferment of the times. But when they tried to insert expository descriptions of what communism, socialism, anarchy, and such heretical systems were all about, these would always be cut out. Colonel Taylor read the proofs. He was quite willing to have his editorial page enlivened with provocative ideas so long as they weren't explicitly labeled with incriminating ideological names.

Miss Finch's friends continued to deplore the fact that she wasn't on the Transcript and to feel sure that on the Globe she would have to associate with low, rowdy, disreputable men. But she found the Globe staff

> as pleasant and well-bred and agreeable a lot of young and slightly older men as one would be likely to meet in newspaper or business offices anywhere.
>
> Among them were many recent graduates of Harvard and Yale and to these were added a few more every year.
>
> Apparently this was part of Mr. Taylor's scheme of building up his paper, feeding into it steadily young blood with the wider horizons and better trained minds of college youth and trying to identify them with its interests and possibilities. It was an astute policy for most of those I worked with rose to the highest positions on its staff.
>
> During my time the whole fourth floor, both editorial and news staffs, was ebullient with the blithe high spirits of youth. But that did not interfere with the very considerable quantities of work.

Miss Finch's $10 a week had gone up to $15 by 1884. She thought she was worth more, but this was not a popular idea in the Globe of 1884; so she left for New

---

* Sixty-six years after Florence Finch and Benjamin Tucker were trying to get their ideological concepts into Globe editorials, the Globe on July 10, 1969, ran an editorial page piece recalling "Tucker, Forerunner to Today's Anarchists." It related Tucker's anarchism to the alienation of youth in the 1960's and the demands for participatory democracy.

York, which was what other brilliant Boston journalists of that period were doing. There were plenty more where they came from, which was frequently Harvard College, though the Globe was taking on bright boys from the Colonel's boyhood haunts of Charlestown and his early home town of Somerville, and the managing editor then and for 40 years more had come up from district man in Woburn.

One of those blithe young men on the Globe was Allen Kelly, chief editorial writer, who married Florence Finch within a year of her leaving the paper. When she left, her Globe colleagues, those rowdies she'd been worried about, presented her with two beautifully bound volumes of Bartlett's Quotations!

So departed the second woman journalist on the Globe. Many came after her. Soon the Globe was pioneering in special departments for women not yet seen in journalism.

Florence Finch, green girl from Kansas, had proved she could do anything on a newspaper. And on the paper despised by the Brahmins she had had a cultural awakening, a postuniversity education. The girl who had never been to an art exhibit, and just once in her life to the theater, left Boston a matured critic of the arts and theater. This has happened again and again and again. Journalism has proved the university for the questing.

Part of Florence Finch's swift success on the Globe must have been that no one on the paper knew anything about her special fields, art and women's affairs; that's why they hired her. So she could go her own pace, work her own way, develop her own interests. This has proved the recipe for success and even distinction in many another journalistic career. Olin Downes developed as a nationally distinguished music critic on the Boston Post, and Elliot Norton as the outstanding dramatic critic in Boston from the tabloid Record-American, certainly in large measure because they could go it alone. There was no one on the paper to veto their styles or philosophies. They were uninhibited to develop their talents. They escaped the discipline of the news and editorial departments that groove work to an institutional policy and mold. Reporters often observe that the farther they get from the office the more freely they can report, and that's the same thing — get far enough away and the office is no longer capable of directing. The foreign correspondent is much more on his own than the city staff man and has more of a chance to develop individual distinction in his correspondence.

The reporter is the operative man, the editor the directive agent of management who has to exercise caution about the reporter's production. The copy desk is institutionalized caution, the protection against libel, error, indiscretion.

Such caution is of course essential to survival. But as staff men mature in responsibility, the wise office gives them increasing latitude, depends more on their judgment. They are the eyes and ears of the institution. To give them their heads opens the door to exploration and discovery and permits development of individual distinction of style, for the fullest fruits of journalism. The Globe was to learn and apply this in a later generation; but Chas. H. Taylor was moving instinctively on the same path. There was more openness and flexibility in his first decade of the Globe than ever after for 60 years in Boston.

This was the Globe after four years of Colonel Taylor's innovations. It had become an institution to reckon with, its circulation already rivaling the long established Herald, its novelties exciting interest nationally. Many years later Florence Finch put it all in perspective, writing not in the glow of youth but after she had been on the New York Times for 30 years. Her evaluation of Taylor as a jour-

Chas. H. Taylor at 35: successful publisher.

nalistic innovator in his first decade as a publisher, still in his 30's, includes him with Adolph Ochs and William Randolph Hearst as "three journalists of genius."

> The Globe as I remember it in the early 1880's was the most wide-awake, the best all-round newspaper in Boston. His purpose was to set people talking about the Globe and keep them talking about it . . . He depended upon unusual and striking effects, on ventures that would arouse curiosity and interest among intelligent readers. He aimed at a wide comprehensive appeal. He was one of very few publishers whose sympathies leaned toward the interest of the working man. He wanted his paper to have a reputation for fair and square treatment of ideas, events, developments and people and he wanted the spirit throughout to be a spirit of kindness and good humor.

She saw the weakest point in Taylor's vision of the Globe as its provincialism.

> The Globe thoroughly covered New England but did not cover national and foreign news as well as the New York papers. The policy of concentrating on the local region brought big circulation and immediate financial success. But in the long run it relegated the Globe to a provincial and unimportant position in the country's list of great newspapers.
>
> In other respects he was one of the greatest journalists of his period because he so definitely broke with the traditions of the past. He was determined to transmute into his paper his belief in democracy and his faith in human nature. All this showed a new viewpoint in newspapering. He introduced into American journalism a new note of tolerance, of free plain speech and of the objective point of view. He was one of the first newspaper publishers to have an inkling of and to attempt to translate into actuality the 20th century conception of the newspaper as an instrument of social service. He did not see that conception in the fullness to which it later came. But he caught its outlines and glimpses of its possibilities. He made the Globe a prophecy of the newspapers of today.

Chas. Taylor Finds James Morgan

That Florence Finch does not include Joseph Pulitzer, greatest innovator of them all, in her essay must be simply that she never worked on his New York Morning World. Pulitzer and Taylor were contemporaries. Pulitzer put together his Post-Dispatch in St. Louis the year, 1878, that Charles Taylor reorganized the Globe to his own pattern. But Taylor was five years along with his development of the Globe before Pulitzer got into New York.* The two had become friends when Pulitzer visited Taylor in Boston while still shaping his new St. Louis paper. "We stayed together . . . from Friday luncheon till Monday talking about building up newspapers," Taylor later recalled. "From that time on for years we kept in very close touch, often working out each other's ideas on our papers at the same time. When Joe got his World going he tried to get me to go over to New York. He told me if I would go over for three days a week he would give me $100,000 a year." * Pulitzer's first biographer, Don Seitz, cites Pulitzer's regard for Charles Taylor as "the most valued" of all the successful newspapermen from whom he sought advice.

A decade after Florence Finch left, Taylor's older son, Charles Junior, served a brief apprenticeship on Pulitzer's World. Pulitzer turned to Colonel Taylor to help him find a private secretary: E. A. Grozier, a shorthand reporter on the Globe who soon became managing editor of the World. Grozier returned to Boston in 1891 and introduced Pulitzer methods to resurrect the Boston Post to become the Globe's rival in the next generation.

To bracket Taylor and Ochs focuses on basic similarities of outlook and character. Ochs like Taylor aimed at printing the news, objectively, fairly. Both were essentially businessmen who promoted sound ideas for making newspapers. Neither was such a crusader as Pulitzer was. Neither was primarily concerned with causes. Ochs would have preferred no editorials, lest they seem to influence the news columns. Taylor cautiously disinfected his editorials of ideological implications. Both sought the broadest basis of readership through reader service. Unlike Pulitzer, Taylor kept himself detached from the editorial department once he had established it in the hands of trusted lieutenants. In this respect his luck was better than Pulitzer's. For Pulitzer all his life was distrusting, hounding, frustrating, checkmating, and driving his most brilliant editors.

Colonel Taylor, when his new Globe was only five years old, found a young man in whose wisdom, judgment, and creative journalistic instinct he placed so much trust that James Morgan became the philosopher of the Globe and its editorial guide across two generations of Taylor management. Morgan at 22 was a telegrapher, serving the new United Press at the Boston end of a news wire in the Globe building. He had followed the magic of the telegraph keys out of his Kentucky home at 13, already a regular telegraph operator. It took him into news dispatching and all

* Joseph Pulitzer had taken over the German-language Westliche Post in St. Louis from Carl Schurz in 1872. He sold it back to Schurz four years later. In 1878 he bought the bankrupt St. Louis Dispatch and immediately combined it with the year-old Post to form the St. Louis Post-Dispatch. After five years' success with the Post-Dispatch, in 1883 he bought the New York Morning World that was losing money under the ownership of Jay Gould.

* Quotations in this section are from James Morgan, *Charles H. Taylor,* privately printed, 1923.

over the country, as well as to his self-education, for he saw everything with a tourist's fresh interest and pored over his country's history and politics. A stint in Washington fascinated him with the government and acquainted him with its personnel. It occurred to him, when sending a dispatch about the speech of a congressman, to identify the speaker with the (D. Va.) or (R. Pa.) that more than 90 years after is still standard practice.

Morgan was filing a telegraph wire in Washington, at 21, when the United Press was organized in 1882 to serve such papers as the Globe, denied news dispatches by the Associated Press monopoly. There he met Walter Polk Phillips, Washington correspondent of the new United Press who the next year was to become its national manager. Phillips was so impressed with the young telegrapher that he persuaded him to join the UP, and in 1883 Morgan was assigned to its Boston office in the building of one of its best customers, the Globe. Colonel Taylor, incidentally, was soon to become president of the United Press.

But it was a tiff with his good friend Phillips that led James Morgan to the Globe. It was Morgan's practice to get into the office well ahead of the 10 A.M. starting time for the opening of the UP wire to transmit news for the evening papers. One morning, while preparing material to send, Morgan heard Phillips tapping out a message for all operators to get on the line. By the time he had laid down his news copy to respond, Phillips, who had had no response from any point, was impatiently dressing down his operators for not being on the job.

Morgan took this as an unjustified personal affront. It roused his Kentucky ire, and he promptly tapped out his resignation. William Hills, the Globe exchange editor, happened to be in the room, and on learning the situation went to Colonel Taylor to suggest that here was an opportunity to pick up a first-class mind in James Morgan.

So James Morgan joined the Globe as an editor of exchanges January 1, 1884. He came to the paper in its pristine years and in his own ebullient youth. At 22 he went to work for a successful publisher of 32 in a still unformed institution. Morgan had much to do with shaping it, his own work enlarging its dimensions and deepening its quality. He had already ten years behind him of being on his own, and he now found new zest and adventure in newspapering, taking to it like a colt to his Kentucky bluegrass. Colonel Taylor and James Morgan took to each other and the building of the Globe in one of those rarely happy combinations. Taylor quickly learned to give his full confidence to young Morgan. Within months Morgan was through with the exchange room apprenticeship, doing general reporting. He turned to political reporting which, he later said, nobody else seemed to want. It was the area of the Colonel's prime interest, and he doubtless nudged Morgan into it as he saw his natural bent.

Morgan was soon the State House man and two years after joining the paper he became its Washington correspondent. The Colonel said he would sign Morgan's articles and make him famous. Signed articles were rare in those days; even the leading Washington correspondents signed only a last name, or often a pseudonym at the end of the dispatch.

So in 1886 James Morgan went to Washington to begin a career as political journalist that lasted with growing distinction more than 60 years. He began in the first administration of Grover Cleveland and observed every administration to Eisenhower's. But not for long in Washington. After two years the Colonel needed him more in the office, where he was called Sunday editor, then assistant managing editor. That was as high a title as James Morgan ever held in a paper that managed with a minimum of titles and avoided most of the compartments of journalism. But from his twenties to his nineties Morgan was in effect editorial director. He wrote politics and history, features and serials, and was the chief idea man on the Globe all his life.

The Irish

A new Boston newspaper seeking a new readership would find a natural clientele in the new Irish, and in supporting the causes of labor and the underdog element it would naturally form association with Democratic politicians, who were chiefly Irish.

Democratic and Irish were almost synonymous in city politics in 1880 and for a long time after. This was especially so in Boston, the nearest port to Ireland and so the cheapest travel route for Irish immigrants starved out in the great famines. They encountered in Boston a more inhospitable reception than in the always more cosmopolitan New York, partly from their numbers and condition and partly from the intense class feeling of the ruling Brahmin caste of Boston. Isolated in the economic life of the city, the Boston Irish turned naturally to politics. This was the road to becoming a policeman or a civil service clerk, a school janitor or a laborer for a contractor on city work.

The emotions of American Irish were at the time deeply involved with the plight of Ireland under a cruel landlordism and repressive British domination. Henry George was just bringing out his book *The Irish Land Question* and had become the correspondent from Ireland of the Irish World, of New York.

Colonel Taylor's staff on the Globe included vigorous and able Irishmen eager to espouse the Irish cause, and none more so than Michael Curran, who was editor of the Sunday Globe and followed Edward Bailey in charge of the militantly Democratic editorial page. Curran was himself an active Irish Land Leaguer. He is said to have been a strong influence in persuading Colonel Taylor to support the Irish cause, although that would seem to have been the natural if not inevitable road for the Democratic Globe to take.

So when the great Irish leader Charles Stewart Parnell came to Boston January 12, 1880, Colonel Taylor was on the platform with his good friends John Boyle O'Reilly, editor of the Catholic diocesan weekly the Pilot, and P. A. Collins, soon to be a congressman and later mayor, at a great meeting in the Music Hall to welcome Parnell. Collins was president of the American Land League and joined Parnell in his American tour to raise funds for the Irish Nationalist party. Wendell Phillips, the fiery Abolitionist and leader of the Labor Reform party, who had joined Colonel Taylor in support of Ben Butler for governor, introduced Parnell. Phillips, long noted as a flaming orator against privilege anywhere, was then in his seventieth year. He set off the ardent crowd in ecstatic applause when he began:

"I have come here, as you have come, to see the man who has forced John Bull to listen."

That made the Globe's next morning headline: Parnell, "Who Made John Bull Listen." The Globe story filled five columns of page one and two more columns inside.

The Globe was the only paper then championing the Irish in Boston, a monopoly worth something. For that very day Frederick O. Prince, Democrat, had been inaugurated for his third term as mayor. This evidence of the rising Irish political influence the Globe had obliquely noted in a whimsical headline on Prince's first election: "Mayor F. O'Prince."

The Irish issue grew in intensity in the next year as the British Parliament began legislation to crush the Land League. Parnell sent the Globe several articles on the rising crisis. The Globe ran a series on "Rack Rents, a Tale of the Irish West." When the League founder, Michael Davitt, was imprisoned and Irish M.P.'s were ejected from the House of Commons for their tactics to block coercive legislation, Parnell cabled the Globe a colorful dispatch on the tense situation.

So it was a major event in Boston the next spring and a tragic setback to the Irish cause when the British high official in Ireland, Lord Frederick Cavendish, with his deputy, were murdered in Dublin's Phoenix Park. This threatened also a special tragedy for the Globe, still outside the Associated Press. The Herald, with its battery of big Bullock presses, would exploit the biggest story of years from Ireland and the Globe would offer only a conspicuous famine of news for its new Irish readership.

But George Kelly of the mailing room encountered a Herald reporter who was gathering interviews from Boston Irish leaders. All George knew was that the murders happened in Phoenix Park. It was a Saturday night, May 6, 1882. The Colonel had left the office at 11 P.M., happy in the feeling that next day's paper would be the best Sunday edition ever and with the most advertising. It was a short walk to the house in Charles Street where he had moved from Somerville to be near the office. He had no telephone. Kelly ran to the Colonel's house and woke him up. Taylor remembered every detail of that news crisis:

> On getting to the office I found that we still didn't have a word from Dublin. We were not yet in the Associated Press and with other papers were trying to build up an independent service, the United Press. It got its British news from the Central News Association of London. But as there were no Sunday papers in London the Central News used to shut down Saturday noon.
>
> There wasn't a minute to lose as we would have to put our final edition to press in two or three hours. The first thing I thought of was to have a man look up Phoenix Park in a gazetteer. He complained that he couldn't find out much about it, but I said "Never mind, you have seen parks and they all look a good deal alike. Go ahead and give us a description of the scene of the assassination." Then I thought of O'Reilly and Collins. They had no telephones so I sent out a reporter in a herdic to interview them.

The reporter was Edwin Grozier, then a year out of college. Grozier went first to O'Reilly's Charlestown home in Monument Square and got his interview. Then he said he would have to run over to South Boston to see Collins. He didn't see how he could make it in time.

"You can't do it, my boy," O'Reilly told him. "But come back in the house and I'll give you General Collins's interview. I know just what he would say." So Grozier reported in with his O'Reilly interview and the ersatz story from Collins.

But the Globe still had only the trimmings for the main story and nothing of that. Mike Curran was the Boston correspondent of the New York Herald. Curran had long since gone home, but the Colonel decided to sign his name to a wire to the New York Herald offering to share their cable costs for a copy of the story from Dublin. "It was only a flier but it was our one chance. Pretty soon our story began coming over the wire. My heart leaped for joy as I grabbed the first sheet. When the second sheet came I noticed it was addressed to 'Globe and Herald.' Aha, I said, the Herald too has to go fishing around. That made me feel better."

So the crisis was met. The Globe was not scooped on the big story. For its Sunday final edition it had everything anybody had on the Phoenix Park murders.

"Years afterward I was in Dublin," Colonel Taylor ends his story. "Boston friends met me and asked what I wanted to see. 'The first thing I want to see is Phoenix Park,' I told them. 'I want to get a good look at it if I don't see anything else in Dublin.' "

Managing editor's office 1886: A. A. Fowle and Virgil Eaton.

At a time when most newspapers were hostile to organized labor, the Globe gave headline attention to the wage complaints of New Hampshire factory girls and reported unrest among Boston longshoremen; it covered the Boston convention of the Eight Hour League in November 1878, where its reporter heard speakers denounce all the local papers except the Globe for failing to report demonstrations of the unemployed in Fall River.

That month the Globe attacked the Constitutional requirement in Massachusetts that proof of poll tax payment be a prerequisite for voting. It kept hitting at the poll tax until this requirement was removed in a Constitutional change in the nineties.

Another of the Globe's early campaigns, on behalf of new Catholic residents, was toward allowing priests into the local hospitals to administer last rites to dying patients. Incredibly, this was not permitted in Boston hospitals — even the city hospital — down to the 1880's.

The Colonel started the "Help Wanted" advertising, companion to a then larger "Situations Wanted," in the early days when new Irish immigrants were looking for jobs. Tearsheets of the help wanted ads were sent around to the bulletin boards of the numerous employment agencies. "Help Wanted" was to grow into one of the main strengths of the Globe.

A Poem from Dr. Holmes

In 1881 Chas. Taylor was only nine years away from having been a reporter himself, for Horace Greeley's Tribune. The reporter's instinct was still strong in him and he responded like an old fire horse to the biggest story that had broken in his career.

President Garfield was shot by a crazy man, Charles J. Guiteau, on July 2 in the Washington railway station on his way to visit Williams College, his alma mater. Garfield lingered between life and death through a summer of agonized suspense for the nation.

The bulletins on the President's condition dominated the front page all summer.

Gaining (September 10)

No Relapse (September 11)

Critical Again (September 16)

Sinking (September 18)

Dead (September 20)

The one dire word topped a series of 13 decks that ran close to the bottom of the column.

The wires flashed the word a little after 11 o'clock on the night of September 19. The Globe broke out a midnight extra with specially designed mourning rules on every column that the Colonel had ordered as soon as Garfield was shot.

The Colonel stayed in the office all that night. Thousands and thousands of the Globe extra were sold, and he began immediately to plan a special memorial edition for the day of the funeral. He wanted tributes by the leading poets. Emerson

The Boston Daily Globe.

VOL. XX.—NO. 89. BOSTON, TUESDAY, SEPTEMBER 27, 1881—GARFIELD MEMORIAL NUMBER. PRICE TWO CENTS.

HONORED IN VERSE.

The Tributes of a Galaxy of American Poets.

After the Burial.

BY OLIVER WENDELL HOLMES.

Sonnet—James A. Garfield.

BY H. BERNARD CARPENTER.

Midnight.

SEPTEMBER 19, 1881.

BY JOHN BOYLE O'REILLY

The Last Bulletin.

BY MARIE E. BLAKE.

Rejoice.

BY JOAQUIN MILLER.

Laurel—Cypress.

BY LOUISA PARSONS HOPKINS.

Humanitas Regnans.

BY M. J. SAVAGE.

Fatherless.

BY KATE TANNATT WOODS.

"He is Dead, Our President."

BY CHARLES TURNER DAZEY.

J. A. G.

BY JULIA WARD HOWE.

The Sobbing of the Bells.

BY WALT WHITMAN.

Garfield memorial edition: September 27, 1881.

was beyond writing; Lowell was out of the country; Longfellow was sick. The Colonel set his heart on getting Whittier or Dr. Holmes.

He drove first to Danvers to try Whittier, but the old Quaker poet felt that to turn out a special poem on short notice might prove beyond him. Taylor then drove to Beverly to see Holmes. The doctor brushed him off, suggesting he get John Boyle O'Reilly. He already had O'Reilly, so he laid siege to Holmes. Next morning he went to the Harvard Medical School to wait for the little doctor to come from his class. He offered him $600 with the argument that if Holmes waited to do it for the Atlantic Monthly "perhaps 2,000 hair splitters will attempt to decide whether you are up to your standard. If you write it now for me, 100,000 people will be thrilled by your great tribute to the President."

Taylor got his poem from Holmes and led his memorial edition with it. Poems also by Walt Whitman, Julia Ward Howe, Joaquin Miller, John Boyle O'Reilly and a half dozen more were on his front page under the heading "Honored in Verse," "The Tributes of a Galaxy of American Poets."

He did indeed sell more than 100,000 Globes that day. The issue had also the first full biographical sketch any newspaper had published on the death of a public figure. The paper was eight pages instead of four to make room for the tributes and for reports of the funeral procession and of memorial exercises held in many places. Again its columns were framed in black mourning rules. That edition, the Colonel was to recall,

> proved to be the biggest thing the Globe ever did. It waked up all New England to see a Democratic paper come out with a magnificent tribute to a Republican President.
>
> In appealing to the masses as I had done with the Globe, I had to offend some people as everyone has to do; but all had to take off their hats to the Globe's Garfield number. I had calculated it would take me ten years to get into a position to make the kind of paper I wanted to make. But that day, at least, I made the Globe what I wanted it to be and it carried the paper a long way on the road. That memorial edition put up our average daily circulation ten thousand. It was the best idea I ever had.

An interesting point was raised during Garfield's long illness in a Globe editorial September 6, 1881, under the heading "Have We A President?" The question was raised whether the disability of the president did not require the vice president to take over the executive function: "The vice president's duty was and is to quietly assume the duties of the President's office until the disability is removed and then step down. He has neglected it."

That is precisely the duty that was enacted into law after President Eisenhower's illness in 1957.

Mugwumps and Democrats

In the first four years of his new Democratic Globe, Colonel Taylor wandered in a political wilderness with the rest of the Bay State Democrats in support of that extraordinary, eccentric, and controversial politician General Benjamin Butler. Butler was a political maverick to the last degree and forever destructive of party unity.

But Colonel Taylor had both sentimental and practical reasons to support Butler. He was a fellow Grand Army man and he had effectively espoused the cause of labor and cultivated the interests of the Catholic Irish. As a legislator, he had tried in vain to have the State restore the Ursuline convent in Charlestown* that had been burned by a Protestant mob.

Butler was a prewar Democrat, but the war and his conspicuous role in it turned him into a radical Republican. As such he served ten years in Congress, to lose out in a Democratic sweep of 1875. He was anathema to the conservative Republicans of Massachusetts. Butler took up with the radical Greenback party and was elected again to Congress in 1878; he ran for governor the same year on their ticket, to lose.

By 1879, the first political campaign for the new Globe, Butler had won the Democratic nomination. This split the party, and after supporting Butler in the campaign, Colonel Taylor applied himself both editorially and in the party councils to restoring unity, an aim that both occupied him and evaded him in two more Butler campaigns.

But in 1882 Butler was elected, even as his party lost everything else in Massachusetts. The Globe was his sole journalistic support and could crow over the election, breaking out for the first time a two-column headline.

Governor Butler sought all the things the Globe supported, women's suffrage, the secret ballot, the ten-hour day, protection for women and children in industry, and elimination of the poll tax requirement for voting. These all failed against a Republican legislature and council and in 1883 Butler was defeated for re-election. The Democrats also lost the Boston mayoralty.

Butler then launched a national campaign for the presidency under a new banner, the Anti-Monopoly party. The Globe withheld support from this final fling but it did assign a reporter, Charles H. Montague, to accompany Butler on a national politicking tour. It was the only paper in the country to do so, which doubtless was good for circulation among the considerable Butler cult of Massachusetts Democrats.

But when Butler sought to control the 1884 Democratic convention for its nomination, the Globe came out squarely for Grover Cleveland. Butler, with the Greenbacker and Anti-Monopoly nominations, faded into the shadows of also-rans.

The nomination of Cleveland against James G. Blaine brought the Globe into joyous and raucous jousting with the Boston Republican press, for the Republicans were deeply divided over Blaine's nomination. Blaine was tagged as a corruptionist over deals made with western railroads while in Congress from which he profited

* The Ursuline convent was in a section of Charlestown that became part of Somerville but which had not then separated from old Charlestown.

and which he could never satisfactorily explain. "Blaine the Tattooed Man" was a Democratic campaign taunt. The Democratic torchlight parades bellowed: "Blaine, Blaine, James G. Blaine, the continental liar from the State of Maine." "Burn this letter," the postscript Blaine had used on the notorious "Mulligan Letters" about his railroad relations, was a campaign refrain.

The Republican Advertiser and Transcript bolted Blaine and the independent Herald also came out for Cleveland. The Journal held diehard for Blaine and published and exploited the story of Cleveland's paternity of an illegitimate child that made a Republican campaign ditty:

Ma, Ma, Where's My Pa?

Gone to the White House, Ha Ha Ha.

The Globe editorially taunted both the Republican bolters and the nonbolters in their embarrassment over Blaine. It congratulated Massachusetts Republicans on "the nomination of the man most obnoxious to them."

"Planning a Bolt," the Globe headed a June 8 page one story exploiting the action of the Massachusetts Reform Club in repudiating Blaine and organizing the "Independents for Cleveland" on motion of Thomas H. Higginson. Other notables joined the bolters, Charles Francis Adams, Josiah Quincy, President Charles W. Eliot of Harvard, to side for the first time with such old-line Democrats as Leverett Saltonstall and, inescapably, with the new breed of Irish Democrats.

"A combination of Harvard College with the slums of Boston" taunted Republican leader Joseph Walker. "Mugwumps" the regular Republicans called the bolters. Mugwump was from the Indian Mugquomp, meaning a chief, a great man. Satirically, the Blaine supporters twisted this into a designation of a high and mighty fellow, one who felt himself superior.

William Everett, one of the Blaine bolters, accepted the mugwump term and turned it into an accolade. In a speech in Quincy, September 13, Everett declared: "I am an independent — a Mugwump. Mugwump is the best of America. It belongs to the language of the Delaware Indians and it means a great man." Others have held it derived from the Algonquins, a Massachusetts tribe. John Eliot in translating the Bible for the Indians of Massachusetts had used mugwump as a translation for "duke." But the regular Republicans gave it other meanings. "A mugwump is a person educated beyond his intellect," said railroad president Col. Horace Porter. Dana's New York Sun, first to use the word as a political label, said a mugwump was one who couldn't make up his mind: he had his mug on one side of an issue and his wump on the other.

The division cut deep and was lasting. Arthur Stanley Pease, great classicist of Harvard, remembered 50 years later his grandfather saying he'd never send his sons to Harvard "because it made mugwumps of them."

The campaign brought a temporary coalition of Republican reformers and Democrats in Massachusetts which later fell apart over the spoils of federal appointments and the anomaly of reform to a party that needed the jobs. Civil Service had been instituted federally in the final year of the Arthur administration and in Massachusetts in the election year of 1884. The Globe took a dim view of it then and long after, holding that it threatened to fasten a caste system of officeholders on the country. It made it more difficult, of course, for Democratic ward heelers to place hungry Democrats in the security of permanent public jobs.

But it was not, after all, the Brahmin bolters of Massachusetts who accomplished the narrow defeat of Blaine. It was the margin of a few hundred votes in New York, widely believed to have resulted from the provocative charge of a Presbyterian clergyman, the Rev. Samuel D. Burchard, in the last week before election, that the Democrats were the party of "Rum, Romanism and Rebellion." Blaine, on the same platform with Burchard, was reported to have failed to hear the insulting observation, and so failed to repudiate it before it had provided the Democrats with the charge of bigotry. Cleveland's margin of 1047 votes in New York gave him the election. "Victory at Last," proclaimed a two-column headline in the Globe. The Democrats were in for the first time since the Civil War and had carried the House of Representatives too.

Before election Arthur Fowle had become managing editor, and he celebrated the Cleveland victory by breaking out a row of seven woodcut illustrations across the top of the front page, in effect a banner headline (November 16, 1884). This stirred up a revolt by the orthodox composing room chief. When Supt. Boss complained to Colonel Taylor that Fowle was breaking all typographical tradition, the Colonel replied, as Fowle reported it, "Mr. Boss, the Globe has no traditions."

The Globe did, however, start a tradition in that campaign. It created a symbol that it called "the Globe telephone man," to be developed a year later into "the Globe man," a broad-beamed and beaming cartoon figure who proclaimed Globe circulation and advertising gains from a fixed front page position for a long generation. The Globe's first telephone had been installed in the managing editor's office in 1881; in 1884 the telephone was still a novelty to most readers. In the campaign that year "the Globe telephone man" in cartoon carried on telephone conversations with the political opposition, putting them in their place and persistently claiming the coming Democratic victory. He could get in a claim for Globe circulation at the same time. It was a woodcut of the Globe telephone man that Fowle placed at the head of every column of the front page to celebrate the election. The Globe sold 121,000 papers that day, double the average circulation.

Grover Cleveland, elected on a platform that, as the Globe had applauded, "breathed reform in every line," naturally wanted to hold the coalition that had supported him. He had a Republican Senate and needed to keep the anti-Blaine Republicans in his camp. He had had his own headaches with Tammany's chieftains to sustain his reform position. He had little affinity for the Boston Democratic machine, who to George Fred Williams were low spoilsmen. The Massachusetts mugwumps included both distinguished names and able people. They wanted to influence the new reform administration and they had claims. These of course conflicted with those of the regular Democrats. The Globe sourly deplored the passing over of such a deserving Democrat as Boston Congressman P. A. Collins for a cabinet post in favor of a Salem patrician, William Crowninshield Endicott, who was appointed secretary of war. Endicott was a Democrat too, but the mugwumps backed him for the key post over Collins. With similar backing Leverett Saltonstall, another Brahmin Democrat, won the post of collector of the port over organization candidate Peter Butler, whom the Globe supported, as did Boston maritime interests. "If there had been the least spark of either gratitude or appreciation, General Collins would today be a member of the cabinet," complained a Globe editorial.

Colonel Taylor was by now a member of the Democratic Resolutions Committee, which he later chaired, and so was very much personally involved in maintaining party strength. When it came to the 1885 platform, in which the Colonel had a personal hand, the Globe insisted it should not be designed "to suit the whims of a few hundred outsiders." It wanted the state ticket to include "no icebergs, no eminently respectable nonentities, no individuals who consider their membership in the Democratic Party a favor to that organization, no aristocrats who distrust and fear the people."

"The Mugwumpian idea of the day," the Globe sourly opined, "is that any Democrat who ever made a speech for the party, ever paid a dollar for campaign purposes, or even put in an hour's work, is a dangerous man and must not be recognized by the present appointing power. This is the Utopian Mugwump theory. This is the new dispensation."

So pretty obviously mugwump utopianism and the Globe's party regularity didn't mix.

But the currents of difference ran deeper than party politics. Among the Proper Bostonians of the period, reform and high principles in national affairs had become sadly mixed with anti-Catholicism, with anti-immigrants. The old stock were becoming persuaded that American politics was being debased by the ignorance of immigrants and the vulnerability of their politicians to corruption. Leagues to restrict immigration had a fertile seedbed in Boston among the most respectable. The new women's suffrage, limited to school committee voting, was cultivated to get out the women's vote against a Catholic majority on the Boston school committee.

The Globe lit into what it regarded as hypocrisy; the same people had disparaged General Benjamin Butler when he espoused social justice for the new Catholic immigrants and economic justice for the workingman.

The Globe had chosen its side. For the next dozen years it was staunchly for the party of the underdog until the Bryan heresy over money in 1896 changed everything.

Women are People—and Readers

Its energetic political affiliation undoubtedly spurred the Globe's circulation, and vigorous promotion of its circulation rise developed advertising. The paper broke even in 1879, the year after Colonel Taylor had turned it Democratic and cut the price to two cents. It made money the next year and was paying dividends in 1883. Advertising was up that year by 25 percent over 1882. The Globe was gaining on the Herald. In 1883 it had passed all the other papers.

The one-day sale of 121,000 the day after Cleveland's 1884 election was all the presses could print. More papers could have been sold. A second Hoe web perfecting press with a 25,000 paper an hour capacity had been installed and a third ordered. But there was a question of where to put it. On November 1, 1885, the Globe announced plans for a new building, a great edifice with the most modern equipment to handle the Globe's rapid growth. By then daily circulation was averaging 70,000, and the Sunday Globe with 85,000 to 90,000 was claiming to have overtaken the Sunday Herald. Boston's population had grown by 65,000 in 10 years.

From a business point of view a most important thing was the growth of the Sunday paper, which sold for five cents and, with its size increased to 12, then 16 and often 20 pages, had twice the space of the daily for special features and advertising. It was necessary to hire extra printers Saturday nights for the big Sunday paper. One of them, A. J. Philpott, who later became a leading member of the staff, remembered a peak weekend in 1884 when 28 columns of advertising were set; that would have been four pages in probably a 16-page paper.

It was in the Sunday paper that Colonel Taylor's innovations were most conspicuous. New departments started in the Sunday paper. By 1883 its circulation was running some 10,000 ahead of the daily, and this accelerated rate continued.

Women were coming into their own in the Sunday Globe. To Florence Finch's "Woman's Hour" column there was added in spring 1884 a "Housekeepers' Column" of menus and recipes, probably started and certainly carried on by Estelle Hatch, who had come on the paper just before Miss Finch left. Miss Hatch, who wrote under her mother's maiden name, Jean Kincaid, was a quite different type from Florence Finch. A Maine graduate of Wheaton Seminary, she had been a school teacher and was very school teacherish when at about 25 she invaded the stag precincts of the Globe, where she put up "no smoking" signs and tried to insist that the men should not work in their shirtsleeves in the office. Prim as she was, Miss Hatch was also a pioneer. She had introduced the first course in business training while teaching at Hyde Park. She was to become a leader of women's clubs, president of her alumnae association, and a founder of the Cantabrigia Club of Cambridge, a founder and the first secretary of the New England Women's Press Association, and in the mid-nineties editor and publisher of her own magazine, the New England Kitchen Magazine. This must have grown out of her Globe work in putting the kitchen for the first time into a newspaper. But much more than the kitchen went into the Globe.

Soon after Miss Hatch joined the paper, the Globe came out with a supplement to the Sunday paper of August 31, 1884. The four-page item was called "Women's Daily Globe." But it was dated September 1, 2002. This was the kind of stunt the Colonel liked; and he liked this particular one so well that he promoted it in advance and accumulated dealer orders for more than the presses could meet. The Globe presses could tick off only about 100,000 copies of a 20-page Sunday paper; this didn't cover the demand for the Women's Daily Globe, so the supplement was reprinted with the Monday paper.

The hypothetical 2002 newspaper was put up as a whimsical vision of what a women's world would be. An all-woman congress was receiving reports from such agencies as "the department of perfumes." Men were petitioning for the right to vote and an editorial asserted that "they were not yet equipped to exercise that privilege." This satire keyed right into the then intensely active suffrage movement which the Globe heartily supported. A petition to the legislature for women's suffrage that spring had 21,500 signatures, as against only 4,000 the year before. Lucy Stone was agitating for the cause in her Woman's Journal. The Boston Transcript at that time was antisuffrage; this was a chance for the Globe to edge in. The supplement carried an appeal to the ladies that the Globe was "the best Sunday paper for the home circle because it was filled with the choicest and most entertaining reading matter for all members of the family." This was what Colonel Taylor aimed to have. He later said: "When I could get the paper into the homes and the women reading it, I knew it would stay there." *

The Sunday Globe was now carrying not only serialized novels but stories written especially for girls. Its first syndicated commentator had already been introduced: George Alfred Townsend, whose signature "Gath" was nationally known for his "Letter" on public affairs. Townsend's letter was started in the Globe January 6, 1884, and the next year another nationally known correspondent was added when the Globe got Joseph Howard, Jr., away from the Herald. The two were established correspondents and had been even in the Civil War, and had been syndicated by New York newspapers for several years. They dealt with whatever subjects interested them — politics, business, theater, art, books — and brought the larger world of affairs to the local newspaper reader. These men were public personalities, with a role like that of later columnists, but basically reporters, writing feature articles. Howard was to become practically a national correspondent of the Globe and to accept special assignments from Colonel Taylor on big events, as indeed he had already done on the Henry Ward Beecher trial and would do on the execution of the Haymarket bomb anarchists in Chicago. Howard's reporting in 1892 of the Lizzie Borden trial was enough to establish that bizarre affair as a national event.

The Globe also encouraged special Sunday articles by its own growing staff and introduced departments of miscellany which must have derived largely from the exchanges. "Slings and Arrows" was a staff-produced department of pungent paragraphs that had been running for several years. "Table Gossip" was a column of personals that had been started as soon as Colonel Taylor joined the paper and had by the early eighties developed into the society department.

On September 13, 1885, a new column appeared on the editorial page, a column of paragraphs headed "Editorial Points," which became a fixture and characteristic of the Globe, daily and Sunday from then on.

The "Ed Points," as they came to be known in the office, may have been started by Allen Kelly, then an editorial writer and the chief contributor to "Slings and Arrows"; but they were soon to be taken over by exchange editor William D. Hills, whose role as "Ed Pointer" lasted more than a quarter century. In their early days the editorial points probably derived largely from items culled from other papers by the exchange editor. But they gave rein to banter, wit, and pithy comment and came to have a style and character of their own under such talented latter-day Ed Pointers as Frank P. Sibley and Donald B. Willard.

William D. Hills, Billy Hills to the office, became one of the figures of the Globe. He was another of Colonel Taylor's Somerville neighbors and had come on the paper in 1881, a year after his graduation from Harvard, Phi Beta Kappa. In 1882 he had been assigned the exchange room, a strategic post in the days of limited wire service. All newspapers culled from the news of others with which they exchanged. The prevalence of this dependence on exchanges was recognized in the long-familiar editors' habit of adding a line to the obituary of a former resident of another place: "Boston papers please copy."

---

* The General's statement about getting the paper into the home is quoted in James Morgan's biography *Charles H. Taylor.*

The Globe's "Miscellany Page" of items selected from other papers was for many years an interesting Sunday feature. Another feature that Hills created in 1885 out of the exchanges was "Odd Items from Everywhere." A short column called "Bric-a-Brac" had been started in 1877 from exchange items; Hills converted this into a column of verse including his own. "Bric-a-Brac" was a Globe feature until 1959, when the exchange department was absorbed into the Globe library.

Hills had a keen eye for a sound sentence and a telling word. He could turn a quip with the best of them. An accomplished linguist and grammarian, he had the talents of a modern columnist. He had also personal charm and the assurance of his scholarship, fortified by a substantial mustache and later a slight pointed beard. He had the qualities also of a tutor, and it became the habit of the office to assign new hands as a sort of apprenticeship to the exchange room, to learn about news under Billy Hills. His recommendation for graduating the neophytes on to the reporting staff must have been influential.

In 1885 the paper began to make a special editorial page feature of letters to the editor under the title "What People Talk About," which continued under that heading for three-quarters of a century. Two years after the start of the "What People" column the Globe launched a new department, "The People's Lawyer." This was the suggestion of another Somerville man, a lawyer friend of the Colonel, Percy A. Bridgham, who dealt with readers' legal problems in what became a regular Monday morning feature that Bridgham conducted until 1922 and successors until 1935, when an enactment of the Massachusetts legislature banned the giving of such free legal advice.

Harvard Invasion

The blithe young college graduates who impressed Florence Finch as "pleasant, well-bred and agreeable" increased as the Globe expanded. By the fall of 1886 the Globe boasted it had "the largest staff of Harvard graduates in America" and printed "more readable Harvard news than any other paper." "Readable" must have been the key word: the news was mostly sports. Harvard sports featured the Globe's front pages and dominated its sports pages for two generations. The chief instrument of this, as of most else that developed in the Globe news columns for the next 50 years, was a slight, soft-spoken man, William D. Sullivan, who had been the Harvard College correspondent. He was graduated in 1883 into the Globe, to become sports editor in 1884, city editor in 1889, and managing editor on Arthur Fowle's retirement in 1926.

His contagious enthusiasm for both Harvard and the Globe must have been effective even then, for three Harvard classmates came to the Globe that year or the next. One was Charles W. Hooke of Castine, Maine, later known for his short stories under the pen name Howard Fielding. The others were George W. Heilbron, who in his later years became part owner of the Seattle Post-Intelligencer and a leading Seattle banker, and Marshall H. Cushing, later secretary to Senator Henry Cabot Lodge, and the first secretary of the National Association of Manufacturers.

Fred Burton, Harvard '82, came on the same year as Sully, and just afterward came Robert Luce, also '82, later lieutenant governor and congressman. This was the beginning of a Harvard tide that never ceased.

The Harvard nucleus in the 1880's was surrounded with men from other colleges. Edson White of Wakefield was graduated from Dartmouth in 1880, joined the staff the following year, was already assistant day editor in 1883, and the next year became day editor. Other college men were staff veterans: Charles Dyar, Trinity '73, drama editor; Michael Curran, St. John's '64, chief editorial writer; and two young lawyers, Francis A. Nichols, literary editor, and Sam Merrill, in whom Estelle Hatch found a husband as Florence Finch had in Allen Kelly. Marriage did not separate either of these pioneer women journalists from their careers, however.

"The damn college graduates are spoiling the business," growled gruff Dan Saunders, the boxing editor. But Dan was to grow old in contentment, working under Sully. The sports writers of those rough and ready days were mostly not college men, nor were some of the most prominent reporters then and later.

The First 100,000

Eighteen eighty-six was a landmark year for the Globe. Before the end of the year its circulation, both daily and Sunday, had reached 100,000; it claimed an average for the year of more than that for the Sunday paper, which the Globe boasted had the biggest circulation in the country outside New York.

The Sunday was running 16 pages regularly now, and the Colonel defended this against those who felt that Sunday papers were growing too big. The Sunday paper was bound to grow even bigger, he insisted in an editorial April 25, 1886, possibly even to 32 pages.

The new Globe building was going up and it was necessary to move new presses into the basement without waiting for completion, to meet circulation demands. The Globe was overtaking the Herald and boasting that it already had. The Herald derided and denounced the claim. Probably the daily Globe did not pass the Herald for another couple of years. Before 1890 it clearly was the dominant paper, a position it held for several decades.

Meantime the rival claims and counterclaims provoked bitter exchanges and much billingsgate. The Globe in 1884 had acquired as chief editorial writer James W. Clarke, who had fallen out with the Traveller, where he had been editor. Clarke had a sharp pen and sharpened it further in ridicule of his former employer, the Herald's editor, Edwin S. Haskell, who retorted in kind. Haskell called Clarke a mudslinger and charged that the Globe "lives on politics of the lowest type."

"Mr. Haskell is a Grandpa," wrote Clarke, "to whom mere mention of the Globe is gall and bitterness. The Globe's great success has made Mr. Haskell more irritable than at any time since he was bounced off the Journal because he was not worth his hire."

This, in an era of journalistic vituperation, was actually mild stuff compared to New York, where at the same time Dana's Sun was calling Joseph Pulitzer "the Dick Turpin of journalism" and "a contemporary Judas, whose face is repulsive, cunning, stamped with malice, falseness, treachery, dishonesty, greed and venal self abasement." Pulitzer's World was calling Dana "a mendacious blackguard, assaulter of women, an unmitigated scoundrel, actuated by a hatred that amounts to insanity . . . defending his alliance with thieves." All this over a contest for election of a district attorney of New York.

This aura of personal journalism New York style was quite un-Bostonian and had been ever since the end of the colonial theocracy. But the Globe-Herald rivalry was jangling, raucous. It was a battle for high stakes: advertising was becoming a big business. Ads grew bigger, the papers increased in size. The two papers accused each other of padding circulation figures, of undercutting advertising rates, of reckless boasting. There was no check on their claims, as the newspaper bureau of audit did not come into existence for another generation. One thing about their circulation claims is pretty sure: they were announcing press run and not net sales. Returns must have averaged at least ten percent, as they commonly did much later, so each was orbiting its claims.

But Clarke's acid pen was out of character for the Globe even then, and this may have been the principal reason that he soon drifted off to New York, although the surface explanation of his difference with the Globe was that it had been over his heretical views on the rising silver question. Financial orthodoxy was the new theology, shortly to separate even Brown University's great President Andrews from the fiscal fundamentalist trustees. Colonel Taylor, as he had been earlier with Florence Finch, was wary of editorial ideology. But basically his style was more bland than Clarke's militancy. He enjoyed a sly dig more than a bludgeon stroke. And he had more effective weapons than scolding at the opposition.

In 1886 the Colonel introduced staff bylines, a pronounced innovation. Even the big-name national commentators usually signed their syndicated articles at the end only with a pseudonym or surname. News was essentially anonymous. George Alfred Townsend's early letters were signed "Gath"; the Boston Journal's notable Washington correspondent Ben Perley Poore (who became the first president of the new Gridiron Club in 1885) signed his dispatches "Ben:" just as its great Civil War correspondent, Charles Carleton Coffin, had been "Carleton" to Journal readers.

The Sunday Globe had by 1885 been signing the music and art reviews by its critics; they appeared alongside the signed specials of the national commentators Howard and Townsend. But these critics were contributors rather than staffers. The music reviews of Howard Malcolm Ticknor were easily the best in town, and the world of art was handled by Susan Hale, sister of Edward Everett Hale, herself an artist, writer, and lecturer. More important to Globe revenues were the still unsigned theater reviews by Charles Dyar, staff man, which brought in a full page of theater ads every Sunday.

Personalizing the news columns went along with Colonel Taylor's effort to personalize and humanize the whole paper as another way to get the Globe talked about. Let people know who was writing what they read. Make the Globe writers familiar figures, household names.

This was a journalistic breakthrough. It gradually took hold and spread, unevenly and with variations, but eventually as generally standard newspaper practice. Actually the practice was not carried out consistently in the Globe through much of its history. Bylines were most usual in the Sunday paper on feature stories; in the daily they came to be used for a long time only on out-of-town assignments which were ordinarily the big stories — big enough to assign a staff man to go out and take over from the local correspondent or supplant the wire service coverage. But in 1886 and the years immediately following, the Globe made a special point of byline stories.

The times were ripe for this recognition of the reporter. The American reporter had come into his own. The eighties and nineties have been called the great age of reporting; certainly they were the beginning of great reporting. In an earlier period it was the editor himself, Greeley, or Sam Bowles, who made personal travels to explore national trends and contribute his own observations to his paper. Now editors worked through staffs, and the staffs grew larger and attracted men of larger talents as the growth of advertising swelled the size of the newspaper and the development of more modern presses supplemented telegraph and telephone, typewriter and more efficient internal organization of the newspaper to process, publish, and display its wares. The world was not yet pressing manifold affairs and convulsive problems daily upon the reader's attention. There was space for colorful writing of the local story of the moment, and little to distract the reader from what the newspaper offered in a day before movies, radio, or television. Newspaper reading was a major recreation, and such lively papers as the Globe and the New York World were making it more interesting with their introduction of new features.

The city itself was a new excitement to its new, thronging population, coming to it from small towns and farms and with every ship from abroad. City life was a romance to these new residents, to be exploited with news and features — its bustle and change, its confusion and crime, its politics and fashion, police court and high society, stock market binges, panic and boom, newly conscious labor restlessly organizing, women's suffrage making demands, municipal corruption competing with reform, and unsophisticated urban populace beginning to realize the new worlds of art and music and the city theater. The Boston Symphony Orchestra had been organized in 1881; the Museum of Fine Arts, begun in 1870, now had its first building in Copley Square, where work had begun in 1880 on the Italian Renaissance building of the new public library.

All this was grist to the reporter's mill. The American newspaper rose with the city. Boston, whose population had been fairly static to the Civil War, was burgeoning with immigrant and country-to-city tides. From 1870 to 1890 it grew from 250,000 to 448,000, to reach 560,000 in 1900. Illiteracy of the large foreign-born group was declining; more of the growing city population could read.

These conditions, largely unique to America, helped account for the development in this period of great American reporting. There was nothing like it in Europe. Visiting Britishers called American reporting the greatest. British journalism still found its prime force and chief distinction in the "leader writer" of the editorial page. The Times of London, now in its most imperial period, had a handful of brilliant foreign correspondents, authorities on their areas. But their names were known only to the office, and even there the view of the managing director, the great Charles Bell, was that the British public could take only one thing at a time. About the notion of an assistant to the correspondent in the Balkans, then the tinderbox of Europe, he said, "two things in the Balkans would be more than the British public could stand" — quite an un-American view of news.

The Times had to bow to American reporting when it sent its top journalists to cover the Japanese-Russian peace conference in Portsmouth, New Hampshire, in 1905. Their American correspondent, G. W. Smalley, scooped the foreign editors every day and paid no attention at all to their serious concern whether the sources of his news beats might disturb the balance of the Times's diplomatic posture between Japan and Russia.

In the ebullient journalistic climate of 1886 the Globe began printing the bylines of James Morgan on his new assignment in Washington and then such local staff men as Virgil G. Eaton, Henry G. Trickey, David J. McGrath, and Thomas F. Keenan. Young men, in their twenties or early thirties, they were already pros. Trickey and Eaton in particular became known as investigators assigned to murder mysteries that were the surefire top stories; but they were versatile. McGrath was particularly sharp on covering trials under city editor Charles H. Montague, himself a graduate from court stenographer. Keenan had taken on local politics after Morgan.

These men had style, a literary quality in their writing. If today the purple passages strike the eye, they reflected the newspaper taste of the time. Eaton, a lanky, black-bearded Maine man, was called the best writer on the staff and turned his hand to news, editorials, features, and such miscellany as the "Slings and Arrows" column. His natural talents carried him in two years from district reporter to editorial writer, and in another two years he was night editor. Henry Trickey's professional development was even more rapid. He was graduated from Belmont High School on to the Globe in 1884 and within two years was handling major assignments. He was equally effective as a crime reporter, in covering public issues, and in interviews.

The interview, an innovation of James Gordon Bennett and highly developed by Dana and Greeley, still had a freshness of form. In 1859 an interview that Greeley had with Brigham Young was a notable event. One of Henry Trickey's remembered interviews was with Jefferson Davis, who, at 80, had written his Civil War memoirs and refused Mississippi's election to the Senate because it would have required him to ask for a federal pardon.

In 1887 Trickey went to Utah to report on the effects on the Mormons of the new federal Edmunds Act against bigamy. Globe men were getting around. Trickey had written on the fishery troubles with Canada, but his penchant was for crime investigations. Eaton and McGrath too were often on such assignments; there was crime enough to go around. Such investigative reporters worked with the police and became their familiars, but they also worked on their own, and their big stories came when they uncovered the first or essential clues to a crime that had attracted regional attention.

Signed editorials were another innovation of Colonel Taylor's, started in the Sunday paper the year before the news bylines began to appear. The signed editorials, however, were confined to the Sunday paper; in the seven years that this practice was continued it served chiefly to bring on to the page the names of public men discussing public issues. It was clearly another device to get the Globe talked about. At no time were all the Sunday editorials signed — the paper's own positions on politics and affairs remained anonymous. Some staff-signed editorials were included, but these tended to be special pieces on subjects of the writers' special interests. The signed editorials enlivened the Sunday paper. The first batch, November 8, 1885, included Lucy Stone on "Encouraging Signs for Women's Suffrage," John Boyle O'Reilly on "What an Irish Parliament Could Do," a piece by the chief editorial writer James Clarke on the question of Byron's place in English poetry as compared with Browning's, and one by a Yale editorial writer, William E. Decrow, on the problem of raising funds for universities. But it was slightly fudging the issue to call these signed articles editorials. They could as well have appeared as specials anywhere in the Sunday paper.

Their importance is rather as a prelude. On July 31, 1892, the signed editorials were all focused on a single topic, and in this "symposium" form the Globe continued for many years a weekly panel discussion by three to six contributors presenting their several views about a question of public interest. In later years the central place on the Sunday editorial page given to the symposium was pre-empted by a single article, staff written, but the name "symposium" clung to this feature. To the office it was still "the symposium" and the most distinguished spot in the paper.

Just before the signed editorials had been transmuted into the symposium the Globe introduced, on Sunday, January 4, 1891, a new form of lead editorial in between essay and column that carried the signature "Uncle Dudley" — years later introduced also in the daily paper, this signature was a distinguishing mark of the Globe editorial page and of its distinction, through most of its first century. But that is another and bigger story.

New Building

The new Globe building was completed in the spring of 1887. It was the tallest building on Washington Street, a monument to the Globe's success.

"The noblest newspaper home in New England," the Globe exulted editorially May 1, 1887. Next day, at a housewarming, 400 guests from the journalistic fraternity of the region came to inspect and admire the reddish freestone blocks of its seven-story facade, its elevator, which rose five stories and was the only one in a Boston newspaper building, its new Hoe jumbo press, the first double perfecting press in New England, which could turn off 25,000 eight-page Globes an hour, and even a library, or "morgue" as the newspaper word has it, in the charge of a real librarian, Henry M. Jarrett. The nucleus of the library was the collection of clippings that Billy Hills had started filing in long envelopes and keeping in boxes in 1881; he had eight boxes to turn over to the librarian.

The Globe staff expanded from their cramped quarters into larger new rooms occupying the sixth floor. The elevator went up only five floors, which was as high as the new tenants' rented offices went. On the seventh floor the composing room had cases of all new type fonts for the 100 compositors that increased circulation required. The new body type was a little larger, so more readable. At the rear of the composing room the page forms were made up to be sent down by a special elevator to the stereotyping department at the bottom of the building, to be matted and cast into semicylindrical plates for the presses. An opening had been cut through to the old presses in the basement of the old leased building, which was torn down and replaced two years later with a new annex to be occupied on lease like the old one.

To share its celebration with the public, the Globe announced on Sunday, May 2, that a small coupon to be published in the upper righthand corner of the Monday Globe would be good for one five-cent ride on any horsecar running in or out of Boston that day. The Globe paid the horsecar lines for 151,074 five-cent fares. Before the day was over, 294,330 Globes were sold.

The Globe was a 12-page paper, still at two cents. The paper claimed, before the year was out, an average daily circulation of 129,000, which just topped what the Herald claimed. The Globe got one and a quarter cents on each paper; newsboys or dealers got the other three-quarter cent. This was enough, though, with the five-cent Sunday paper, so that on the opening of its new building the Globe declared: "Not more than six daily newspapers in the United States do a business exceeding $1,000,000 per annum. The Globe is one of the six." It announced at the same time that it was carrying 20,000 small want ads a month, or 200,000 a year — which no other New England paper, and no more than six in the world, could match.

That season also saw the end of the long war of the news wire services. The Associated Press absorbed the United Press and ended its news monopoly that had excluded Colonel Taylor and other newer publishers. So the Globe was "in" on any wire service news available to any AP member.* It now had its own correspondent in New York, in the office of Pulitzer's World, to relay any of the World's foreign news service that the office chose to order by wire.

So there was plenty to celebrate. The Boston Cadet Band serenaded the Globe with two concerts in front of the new building that evening. A week later in the Hotel Vendome a testimonial banquet was given for Colonel Taylor with 300 guests, including the governor and mayor and leading American publishers and the most influential businessmen of Boston. Chas. H. Taylor, at 40, heard himself extolled as one of America's journalistic geniuses. It was just ten years since he had reorganized a bankrupt newspaper. In the gathering were his three young sons and his father, who still lived in the house in Charlestown where 15-year-old Charlie Taylor had set out to find his first job 25 years before.

At the close of the year the Globe announced that it would enter upon 1888 "with no debts and a very satisfactory surplus."

But within five years the new building was outgrown. The Globe then purchased the Chandler Building that adjoined it on the rear, on Devonshire Street. The price was $275,000 and the terms were $5,000 cash and a 15-year mortgage at four percent. This was the first building the Globe owned. The first two buildings had been leased.

---

* The Associated Press of that time had been controlled by seven New York publishers who sold its news to other newspapers; the New England Associated Press was a subsidiary. The United Press had been organized in 1882 by a dozen publishers of newspapers outside the Associated Press. In 1887 the New York Associated Press secretly acquired control of the United Press and merged it with the New England Associated Press, bringing the United Press newspapers into Associated Press membership.

A new United Press was started in 1907 by E. W. Scripps and in 1956 was merged with Hearst's International News Service to form the United Press International. The Associated Press in its present cooperative form dates from 1900.

Transit and "Corruption"

Traffic was choking Boston's narrow streets by 1887. How to get public transportation moving had become a major concern. It was the prime issue of the political campaign that year in a controversy that found the Globe on one side and such mugwump reformers as ex-Globe reporter George Fred Williams* vehemently on the other.

No question but that downtown traffic was a mess. The cars of six different horsecar companies crawled through the congested streets. Most had terminals right downtown in Bowdoin Square or neighboring Scollay Square. The Globe published a rush-hour count of 303 cars an hour passing Park Street Church on the corner of Tremont Street. The horsecars were jammed in with carts, wagons, and foot traffic. They stopped to take on or discharge passengers anywhere, with no regular stops. A Globe writer described "a mile an hour pace" of intown transit.

A dramatic solution was offered that year by a new corporation, the West End Street Railway, which was a subsidiary of a West End Land Company — a strongly backed enterprise for the development of new areas beyond the Back Bay, later the Kenmore Square section and then called the West End, extending to Brookline. The company needed effective transit for their land development, and they had been granted a franchise to lay track on what became Massachusetts Avenue and out Beacon Street to the reservoir. But they had a bigger plan. In spring 1887 they applied to the legislature for the right to consolidate all the horsecar companies, having secretly gained stock control of some, to introduce electric cars, and to build tunnels (later called subways) under Boston Common.

Opposition flared on various fronts. Rival transit interests protested. A Save the Common movement sprang up. Charges arose of corrupt lobbying to influence the legislature. The West End Railway interests were identified with the Democrats: Henry M. Whitney, of large steamship interests, who headed the company, was a staunch Democrat. Among the influential bankers and businessmen associated with him was Col. Jonas French, Democratic state chairman; their legislative counsel was the prominent Democrat P. A. Collins. Eben D. Jordan, who had sponsored Colonel Taylor's reorganization of the Globe and was still its principal stockholder, was one of Whitney's backers.

The Globe vigorously supported the transit consolidation plan. It was a public necessity to solve the traffic problem, the Globe declared: "Boston must go forward." It caricatured the opposition with a front page cartoon of a sour-faced Dame Boston with "Beware of Progress" on her skirt, trying to sweep back the city's development with a broom of "Old Fogyism." The lobbying that scandalized George Fred Williams the Globe brushed off. The Republicans controlling the legislature had done nothing about the lobby.

Williams said, "I am aiming at a corporation which has a reputation for em-

* George Fred Williams was born in Dedham, Massachusetts, in 1852, graduated from Dartmouth College in 1872, admitted to the bar in Boston in 1875, and elected to the Massachusetts House of Representatives in 1889; he served in Congress 1891–1893, was the Democratic nominee for governor in 1895, 1896, and 1897, was minister to Greece 1913–1914, and died in 1932.

ploying improper methods in the conduct of its business." But the Globe chose to blame the system and the Republicans. "It has been very distinctly proved," it editorialized,

> that before asking the Massachusetts legislature to pass a certain class of bills it is now assumed, as a matter of course, that a small army of agents must be retained and roundly paid for its services . . .
>
> The Republican Party cannot be congratulated on the demoralized tone that prevails on Beacon Hill . . . It is useless and pointless to inveigh against "the soulless corporations." The West End Company sought legitimate legislation. Its interests and the interests of the people of Boston in this matter of rapid transit are substantially the same . . . Yet it had to face the hard fact that Beacon Hill was held by the lobby . . . that under Republican rule the pathway to perfectly honest and necessary legislation is blocked by a crowd of professional leeches and harpies.

Yet if the West End hadn't employed these "legislative birds of prey," the Globe asserted, they could have killed the bill. "Boston needs transportation," it concluded in another editorial, "The People's Interest is Paramount." The West End proposal was "a well considered plan."

This of course was largely political double-talk. Not everyone proved as insensitive to the transit corruption issue as the Globe, and the Democratic candidates were defeated. But the public need for transit proved paramount. Three days after the November election the West End Street Railway's plan was approved by the State Railroad Commission. The next day it took over 225 miles of track, nearly 1,600 horse cars and 9,000 horses. Thirteen months later the first electric trolley car in Boston made a round trip from Park Square to Allston. The city had to wait some years more for the first subway in America; but that first electric car forecast the end of the horsecar, though it was 11 years later, the day before Christmas of 1900, that the last horsecar in Boston made its final run along Marlboro Street, between Arlington Street at the Public Garden and Massachusetts Avenue.

But the issue that entwined transit with corruption — to be echoed in many another American city — lingered long in Massachusetts politics. It dogged the future of Henry Whitney: when he was nominated for lieutenant governor 15 years later, his nemesis George Fred Williams exhumed the West End lobbying issue to lead a Democratic defection from the ticket, and Whitney was narrowly beaten. Even a generation after that it was a telling issue brought against another leading Democrat, William Gaston, that his firm had been counsel for the successor to the West End Street Railway, then the Boston Elevated Railway, which had inherited the dead horses of its progenitor and the public suspicion of its ways with the legislature. Alvin T. Fuller made transit corruption his winning issue over Gaston in 1926.

The Globe's posture in the West End Street Railway issue was clearly ambiguous and, to such an intransigent reformer as George Fred Williams, equivocal. It fitted strangely into the pattern of the Globe's political stance and that of the Democratic platform for which Colonel Taylor the year before had been the committee chairman. It was for tariff reform, for poll tax reform, for women's suffrage and for all the workingman's issues and it attacked the Republican legislature for choking off such reforms. The Globe attacked the Republican candidate, Gov. Oliver Ames, as a millionaire who had dodged Civil War service by hiring a substitute, and charged that he used a "corruption fund" in his campaign.

But Colonel Taylor was above all else a practical man. Economic development of the city was both important to a publisher as to other businessmen and a natural issue for a journalistic promoter of civic enterprise.

The backers of the street railway scheme included both political associates of Colonel Taylor and businessmen in whose capacity he had confidence. To Williams it would be a suspicious circumstance that Whitney had been an early Globe stockholder and that Colonel French, the Democratic chairman, had not only owned Globe stock but had been publicly charged in 1879 with holding it in the interests of Ben Butler.

Colonel Taylor was enough inured to the barbs of political controversy by now to take such charges and suspicions in stride. But his ability to promote economic reforms and at the same time to support these high binders in devious transit politics suggests his two sides. Out of his own background and character he had a basic sympathy for the aspirations of the ordinary working man, who was also his best customer. But — wholly typical of the rising young man of his time — he admired success. Such successful men as Jordan and Whitney had had confidence in him. "The great god success" that later muckrakers caricatured was practically unchallenged in the eighties. Concentration in business finally weaned the Colonel away from politics. He was later offered nomination for mayor, for governor, and for senator and brushed them all aside, saying the only office he wanted was his Globe office. His everyday association, like any publisher's, was with the downtown businessmen. He got on well with them. They respected his fair dealing and enjoyed his good humor, his penchant for anecdotes. He became a favorite speaker and chairman of business dinners and a founder of the Algonquin Club, the favorite club of the leading businessmen.

If the Globe's political stance in 1887 looks confusing, the political situation in Boston and Massachusetts was more so. The Democratic candidate for governor, Congressman William T. Lovering, a former mayor of Lynn, had the same claim on Colonel Taylor's esteem of a fellow G.A.R. man as General Butler had eight years earlier. Lovering had lost a leg in the Civil War. But to conservative Republicans he was a dangerous radical, for he had had a leading part in putting through the legislature a ten-hour-day for women in industry.

The prohibition movement was in one of its spasms of political activity. The drys had won Republican support, at least nominally. The Globe and Boston Democrats had been engaged in a running battle with the Prohibitionists for some years, particularly ridiculing the ban on public bars that prohibited "vertical drinking." The requirement that liquor be served only at tables and with food had brought in the era of the free lunch, generally in the form of a shopworn sandwich placed on the table and ribaldly disdained. The Globe had ridiculed a Law and Order League for snooping to see that this law was enforced. The Globe charged that the league especially hounded liquor places run by Democratic politicians, who seem to have had a penchant for the liquor business.

As a newspaper controversy the issue was enlivened by the high moral stance of the Boston Traveller, which was Republican and congenitally Dry. The Globe could hit two birds with one crack at the hypocrisy they charged in the Republican paper's "flings at grog shops" and the "rum power." The Globe charged that the Traveller had as tenant "one of the busiest bars in the city."

"Editor Worthington received a round rental from this barroom," the Globe asserted. It thereupon concocted a "Worthington cocktail, a seductive appetizer mixed by our biblical and bibulous contemporary."

Women's suffrage was a lively issue that the Globe had always supported. But this too had become involved in political crosscurrents. Women in Massachusetts had had a limited franchise since 1879: they could vote for the school committee. In Boston, now with an Irish-born mayor, the school committee also had a Catholic majority. A drive to register women to vote for the school committee had truculent anti-Catholic sponsorship. Such a leading suffragette as Alice Stone Blackwell warned against letting the suffrage movement become involved with militant Protestant groups. This grew into the most inflammatory issue in the municipal election of 1888, when the Boston Republican organization endorsed an openly anti-Catholic school committee slate, with a Save the Schools battle cry.

The Globe waxed hot in that campaign. "The public schools are not in danger," it said. "If they have any enemies they are to be found in the ranks of that party, which for the sake of a supposed electioneering advantage is willing and eager to make them the pivot of political strife."

The Globe deplored "the sudden warming up of the cold gray ashes of Know-Nothingism." The Republican candidate against Mayor Hugh O'Brien was a Yankee, Tom Hart. "Candidate Hart," the paper said, "believes that Catholics should have equal rights with others, but at the same time heads a ticket on which the candidates for school committee were nominated because they were anti-Catholic."

A reiterated editorial appeal was "Vote for O'Brien and squelch Know-Nothingism." On election day the Editorial Pointer rhymed:

> Tis the Know Nothings, O,
> Mr. Hart's flags are flyin'.
> But the Know somethings go
> As one man for O'Brien.

But not enough of them did. O'Brien was defeated and the Republican school committee slate won.

The sectarian issue deepened the political division in Boston until in another generation it became a moat between Democratic Boston and its Republican suburbs. It was compounded of class struggle, power struggle, and incompatible differences of background and outlook. The mugwump reformers were the element most immediately affected by it; they were the heirs of the humanitarian and liberal tradition, of Abolition and Reform, whose idealizing of good government had turned them in 1884 against their own party under Blaine. They saw no such concern among the new breed of Irish Democrats taking power in their old city and, in their view, corrupting and demeaning the public service. They had espoused Civil Service to curb the patronage that was easing the less competent and less scrupulous into public office.

The Globe had become anti-reform in the terms that reform was presented by the Boston patricians. It supported the Democratic issues of economic reform, for a better break for the underdog. Civil Service would check a chief avenue of advancement to those who were least acceptable to the Brahmins in their businesses. Such people had found the first opportunity in the police and fire departments, in public works, and in municipal clerkships — all through the channels of politics.

The old stock Bostonian had a philosophical difference with the flooding immigrant tides of Catholics, for the Church had never shared American liberal support of the great revolutionists and libertarians of Europe who were generally anticlerical. Their specific bias was against the alien as failing to share their ingrained tradition of civic virtue and responsibility in public office. They laid all the evils of politics to the ignorance and prejudice and exploitability of these new masses who threatened the old order, eroded civic standards, made a business of politics. Such reform quickly moved into campaigns to curb immigration. The Globe fought literacy tests that were aimed at limiting immigration.

The rise of the parochial school was further occasion for division. Archbishop John J. Williams had promoted Catholic schools in 1880, following parents' complaints that Catholic children were often humiliated by Protestant schoolma'ams in the public schools. This led to a movement for legislation to regulate private school instruction. The legislation failed. The Globe opposed it vigorously, as did such leading libertarians as Thomas Wentworth Higginson, founder of the Boston Symphony, and Charles William Eliot; but other leading Harvard names soon gave an aura of respectability to the anti-alien movement. The turbulence of industrial unrest underscored the nativist claim that "foreign elements" were bringing violence and anarchy to America. A Germanic view of history, with its strong ethnic emphasis, was taking hold of prestigious Harvard scholarship, promoting the view that such immigrants could not be assimilated. Eminent recruits to this view included Nathaniel Shaler, Charles Eliot Norton, Barrett Wendell, Francis Peabody, and Albert Bushnell Hart. Increasingly their students looked with repugnance on a Boston that before the end of the 1880's was two-thirds foreign by birth or parentage and saw in this a danger to American institutions. The Harvard class of 1889 graduated three young Brahmins who felt so strongly that, as their first class reunion approached five years later, Charles Warren, Prescott Hall, and Robert DeCourcy Ward — all scions of the Anglo-Saxon Establishment — organized to halt the alien dilution of their heritage by founding the Immigration Restriction League. There was active response and public expression for their cause among such names as Joseph Lee, Robert Treat Paine, William Dean Howells, Thomas Bailey Aldrich, and John Fiske. Henry Cabot Lodge and President Francis Walker of M.I.T. became early converts in the nineties. Lodge pressed a national literacy bill in 1897 that Cleveland vetoed. In the following decade A. Lawrence Lowell, John F. Moors, Robert A. Woods, Owen Wister, Thomas Nixon Carver, and David Starr Jordan were to add such weight to the movement as decisively influenced President Theodore Roosevelt's commission on immigration to come out for restriction.

The end product of the campaign that started in Boston in the 1880's was the Immigration Act of 1924 that fixed quotas for each ethnic group on its 1890 ratio so as practically to exclude southern and eastern Europeans, with the purpose of perpetuating the earlier ethnic composition of the American population.

On both sides there were of course mixed motives. The restrictionists saw their Puritan heritage jeopardized, their Athens-of-America culture diluted, and, also, their political power undermined. The Globe of 1888 opposed them from a basis of democratic justice and tolerance; but it was also taking up the cause of its own constituency — mostly on the other side of the railroad track — and their Democratic party.

The same natural allegiance was reflected in the Democratic Globe's strong prolabor position throughout the long struggle for minimum hour laws and for union establishment in the industries of the region. The opposition was much the same; civic reform movement leaders tended to be relatives of industrial employers or of capitalists.

These divergences had arisen at the very start of the mugwump and Democratic coalition of 1884 and by 1888 had broken it up. The mugwumps were the forerunners of later independents and ticket-splitters, who came to have a decisive influence in Massachusetts elections.

General Taylor and Uncle Dudley

Politics sold papers better than prizefights in 1888 when Grover Cleveland lost re-election in spite of a majority of the popular vote. New York was again pivotal. The Tammany chiefs had taken their revenge on the stubborn reformer, their treachery as decisive in his defeat as the Reverend Burchard's folly had probably been in his election four years earlier.

But in New England it was the Democratic tariff reduction, slight as it was, that roused the protectionists, the textile moguls and their banking and mercantile allies, to mount such a well-heeled campaign as routed the Democrats. The tariff was a made-to-order issue for the Globe, with its working-class clientele, and it had a consistent record of vigorous assaults on protectionism.

The Globe sold 424,230 papers the day after election, to claim the greatest sale ever in New England. But the Herald next day claimed they'd sold even more, 441,738, and a noisy war of circulation claims was joined again.

The Globe's greatest satisfaction in 1888, and that of Massachusetts Democrats, was the discovery in that campaign of a new and exciting party leader. Thirty-one-year-old William E. Russell, who had already proved an able and constructive mayor of Cambridge for four terms, was beaten for governor in the Republican sweep of 1888 and again in 1889. But the magnetism of his leadership, his eloquence, energy, political intelligence and personal quality, sparked a Democratic revival that elected him in 1890. Three notable terms as governor lifted him to national prominence in the brief brilliance of a career that was cut off with his untimely death at 39.

Russell was all but canonized in the Globe: "A candidate without a flaw." Chas. H. Taylor personally rejoiced in the young leader and developed an almost paternal affection for him. When he became governor in 1890 Russell appointed Taylor an honorary member of his military staff. From this came the title of general, by which Taylor was familiarly and formally known all the rest of his life.

Taylor was not yet a general in 1888, but he had reasons for satisfaction. The Globe overhauled the Herald in circulation by the end of that year, to achieve a dominance in New England that it held for a long time. It announced an average daily circulation for March of 142,000, which rose within four years to 200,000. Advertising was keeping pace.

The office was prosperous. The staff was large, lively, and happy, with a strong loyalty to managing editor Arthur Fowle, who ran the shop with an easy rein and backed up his men. Edwin Grozier, later publisher of the Boston Post, said of his days as a Globe reporter in the eighties: "Perhaps my most vivid recollection of those days was the intense loyalty of the staff to the paper." The publisher was leaving "Upstairs" now largely to his editors. In 1889 William D. Sullivan's ebullient energies were transferred from sports editor to assistant city editor; the next year, on the death of Charles Montague, Sully became city editor for a span of 35 years of never-flagging enthusiasm in pursuit of the news.

A new creative force came into the office when James Morgan was brought back from Washington in 1889 after two sparkling years of making politics interesting. He had been back in the office during recesses of Congress to write politics, contribute political editorials, and produce a fertile flow of ideas for features and special projects. His reporting of both national conventions of 1888 had been the talk of the town.

Morgan had especially distinguished himself in the spring of 1889 in his coverage of the big story of the year — the opening of Oklahoma, then Indian territory, to settlers. Morgan went out to join a horde of 50,000 avid land-seekers and to render in the Globe an epic chronicle of this saga of the American land, still realizing westward.

His reports vividly described the Sooners' excitement and anticipations in the adventure for conquest of the last frontier. But they also grimly recorded the hardship, frustration and tragic disillusion of those who fell victim to the ineptitude and corruption of federal land officials. Their scandalous mismanagement of the historic operation, disclosed in Morgan's reports, created a major problem for Benjamin Harrison's administration, whose subsequent determined move for reform of the shoddy Land Office proved one of the bright spots in Harrison's hapless single term.

The Globe entered heartily into the spirit of the Oklahoma story, greeting the event in an editorial April 22, 1889, that evidently reflected the enthusiasm with which Morgan had proposed the assignment.

The Oklahoma Land Rush

"Today will witness the strangest sight since the Exodus of the Children of Israel . . . and their journey to the Promised Land . . . a swarm of eager adventurers — 60,000 to 70,000 — ready to make a grand rush into Oklahoma as soon as the gate is swung open. The outcome of this savage rush promises to become serious as there isn't land enough for half the hungry boomers . . ."

The headlines that day and ensuing days told of the scenes of chaos that Mr. Morgan reported.

Last Chance
Off for the Land of the Boomers
Scenes on the Eve of the Birth of a Great Commonwealth

His first dateline was Kansas City, where he described the special trains setting out for Indian territory, the soldiers holding the boundary line against any beating of the gun, the marshall's orders against taking liquor into the territory. Next day, dateline Arkansas City, his story was headed

> Awed Indians
> Wonder at the Wild Race
> For the Virgin Soil of Oklahoma
> Mad Stampede Begins at Noon
> Boomers on Fleet Steeds
> Armed with Axes and Arsenals
> Santa Fe Gives its First Train to Newspapermen

Morgan wrote next day from the nebulous town of Guthrie, in the Cherokee Strip.

> 'Twas Looted
> Land Sharks Capture Oklahoma
> Officials Share in the Job
> Corner Lots as Bribes to Soldiers

His report charged that, long before the official hour, the site of Guthrie was laid out with lots staked by insiders who had been sneaked in on four private trains the night before. Settlers arriving at the appointed time found the best lots all occupied by men who had been designated "deputies" and let in early.

Morgan's subsequent reports described conditions: Guthrie the first night without a lantern or a candle, lighted only by campfires, settlers holding down their claims without even blankets. A boomer sitting in a rocking chair in the middle of his lot, gun in hand, without shelter or food.

Three days later the headline was

> Almost Starved
> Morgan Escapes from Oklahoma
> Exodus Greater than Influx
> Guthrie the Most Miserable Town in America

He described the chaos, disillusion, lines standing all day at the few places where food was sold, no well and no water except at the railroad tank, guarded by a soldier — red water sold at five to 25 cents a cup.

Editorially the Globe contemplated the mad land rush. "It means that the American people are land hungry — free land is gone — it suggests the need of better distribution of land to the common people so it will not all be gobbled up by greedy corporations . . ." (April 25, 1889).

Back in the office, Morgan's series on the Sooners brought the appellation "Oklahoma Jim." But the impact of such an experience on the sensitive reporter was reflected in a letter to his elderly father in Kentucky in which he expressed his opinion of "a cheap sort of democracy which suffers cattle barons to squat on Indian lands while keeping out honest but poor and uninfluential farmers with bayonets."

Mr. Morgan returned on the fiftieth anniversary of Oklahoma, to be exclaimed over as "one who got away."

When General Taylor had appointed him to Washington at 25, Morgan had written his father, "I fear that he has some extraordinary illusions about me." Now Taylor called him back to Boston. Morgan turned over the Washington bureau to A. Maurice Low, English-born correspondent of the London Post, who had been assisting him and who now became the Globe's correspondent for the next 23 years. Low became a distinguished British figure on the Washington scene. He was knighted in 1922.

Now at 27 James Morgan had a chance to realize his value to the Globe. He had been back only a few months when he was offered the post of managing editor of the Traveller, which was badly slipping and in need of fresh leadership. The Globe met the offer promptly by naming Morgan assistant managing editor with the handsome salary of $60 a week, exceeded only by the $70 paid managing editor Arthur Fowle and chief editorial writer James Clarke, who had been editor-in-chief of the Traveller.

At this time good reporters got $18 or $20 a week. The starting pay was $10 or $12, and only a few of the top men got $25 or a little more. The city editor was paid $50, the day editor $40, the night editor $36. These were good salaries at a time when only the better white-collar jobs paid over $20 a week, and when union painters got $16.50. Treasurer William Durant of the prosperous Transcript protested the raising of an exceptional staff member there from $20 to $25. "What would he do with the extra $5? Move into a house that cost him that much more rent or buy a piano for his daughter."

Eben Jordan was reputed to have told Charles Taylor he didn't see why reporters should be paid more than his ribbon counter clerks. But the Globe was doing very well indeed, and its publisher, in the speeches and interviews his success increasingly called for, always said that reporters were the most important people on a newspaper and that its editorial content was what sold a newspaper.

Morgan's role in the paper was a new one that eludes definition. He himself was sui generis. Assistant managing editor was as large a title as he ever held and even that was gradually forgotten. Editorial director would have been a realistic description of the role he played over the next half century and more. But he always evaded executive titles and executive desks. He always had a younger assistant who had developed under his tutelage to move into the desk job while Morgan traveled and wrote.

James Morgan in later years.

Now he continued to write politics and contribute editorials. But his chief activity was developing Globe features. For a time he seems to have been called Sunday editor; but from whatever desk, he developed features for both Sunday and daily, and directed feature writers — who by now included half a dozen women to handle the increasing production of special articles and departments to seduce women readers. This undefined range of James Morgan's early activity on the Globe later defined a very broad scope for its Sunday editors, responsible for both daily and Sunday features and the editorial page. But in the 1890's this was all amorphous. Morgan was essentially an "idea man," as colleagues of that time later remembered. But the authority of his ideas and his pervasive influence in the office, on his employer and his colleagues, can only be understood in terms of the extraordinary quality of the man.

All his life a close student of American history, he had developed a sophisticated background in American politics and a mature judgment of affairs that won confident acceptance by the office. He had a journalistic instinct for anything new that was interesting, worth exploring. He brought to New England a tourist's fascination for its rich history and a delight in sharing it with readers. He was all his life a traveler and writer. His writing developed an almost biblical simplicity and strength, a limpid style that could be lyrical when the subject warranted. But his influence in the paper flowed from his own nature. He was soft-spoken and mild and had an old-fashioned Kentucky courtesy, a warm feeling for human relations, an interest always in the human aspect of an issue or a situation, a quiet but sparkling humor that went with a moderation of manner and expression. The affectionate admiration of the office that grew with the years to become almost idolatrous was manifest even in 1892 when he was 31. That year, at the Globe annual dinner which the publisher had instituted, the office poet, Francis J. Douglas, saluted James Morgan: "Tender apostle of the kindlier heart, the more abundant faith, the ampler view . . . to you the grace of the cavalier . . . of the more perfect equal gentleman." *

Thirty years later his lifelong employer General Taylor, in his own last year, addressed Morgan as "Dear boy" in an affectionate note and told him again of his neverending confidence and pride in the man he had taken off a telegraph wire at 23 to become the very soul of his shaping newspaper.

If any colleague was ever jealous of James Morgan it could have been James Clarke, chief editorial writer, whose abrasive feuds with the other papers were quite out of tune with the mood and style of either Taylor or Morgan — and, now that the Globe was in the ascendancy, were superfluous as well. Clarke's leaving for New York in 1892 was reputedly a friendly departure, but contemporaries said he had found his position irksome.

Clarke's leaving followed by a few months a landmark innovation in the Globe editorial page. The "Uncle Dudley" editorials, which were to be a hallmark of the Globe for more than 60 years, were introduced in the Sunday paper of January 4, 1891. Each editorial was an essay-type discussion of events and ideas that was a marked departure from the more staccato, dogmatic, usually partisan editorials of the time. The "Uncle Dudley" signature was taken from a popular aphorism of the

---

* In a book of tributes to Mr. Morgan from the Globe staff on his ninetieth birthday, Laurence Winship wrote: "Whatever you say is so is so to me even if it isn't so."

but that they do find beyond death . . .
what we hope to find."
"Why, you never spoke of this before!"
exclaimed his wife, "not even to me."
"I can hardly speak of it at all," was the
reply. The man of science was in tears.
                        UNCLE DUDLEY.

day, "take it from your Uncle Dudley," which simply meant "if you ask me, this is my opinion." It suggested an affable, informal, philosophical approach of a wise old fellow thinking out loud.

James Morgan would never admit that Uncle Dudley was his creation and that he was the original Uncle. In his biography of General Taylor he says of its start only that the General "put Uncle Dudley in the Sunday Globe as a substitute for the old type of editorial." But it was in tune with the different tone that Morgan had brought into the editorial department and it reflected the mood and character the General wanted the Globe to present. "Uncle Dudley has none of the Olympian aloofness or the airs that went with the royal 'we,'" as Morgan put it. "His attitude is the opposite of that which Whistler struck when he said to someone who questioned a dictum of his: 'My dear fellow, I am not arguing with you, I am telling you.' Uncle Dudley conceives himself an adviser rather than a dictator, more an interpreter than an advocate. His success solved the editorial problem to General Taylor's lasting satisfaction."

More than two decades later the Dudley was made also the lead editorial in the daily paper. "I was just coming out of pneumonia when the thought struck me," Morgan quotes the General. "I was so mad because I hadn't thought of it years before that I couldn't wait another day to start the column running in the daily and I insisted on starting it, regardless of my temperature chart."

The Dudley editorial expressed on the editorial page the spirit of nonpartisanship and fair play that the General had from the start employed in the news columns and that reflected his own temperament. Morgan says that the General had earlier looked upon the editorial page as a necessary evil. "Sometimes he doubted if it was even necessary." Then Morgan reveals his own views, adding "nor did his instincts play him wholly false when they revolted against the editorial page as it still was at that time: its stereotyped stupidities, its assumption of infallibility and omniscience; on the one hand, its damnable reiteration of party cries, and on the other hand, its holier than thou arrogance, 'making virtue repellant,' as Joseph H. Choate said of one of the ablest editorial pages, the New York Evening Post under Godkin."

So the shift of gears from the dogmatic to the philosophical fitted Morgan's temperament equally with the General's, whoever invented Uncle Dudley. "General Taylor was not given to dogmatizing on any subject," Morgan wrote in the biography. "He had none of the doctrinaire in him and was tolerance himself toward every one and everything. He simply could not mount the editorial tripod and become oracular; and for several years he merely sat on the fence editorially."

Morgan's is an uncritical biography of General Taylor, written out of affectionate appreciation of a lifelong friend just after the General's death in 1921. But there is a clue to a shrewder side of the publisher than just a tolerant temperament in this reference to sitting on the fence and to the statement that the changed form of editorial "solved the editorial problem to General Taylor's lasting satisfaction."

The silver issue in 1891 was becoming increasingly bitter and divisive within the Democratic party and tore it apart within five years, when General Taylor withdrew permanently from personal participation in the political wars. The editorial moderation of Uncle Dudley offered escape from the wrangling issue, at least in the big Sunday paper. Further, the Globe was consciously broadening the base of its appeal by moderating its partisanship. It continued to support democratic principles, if with a smaller "d". This was only doing what came naturally with the Republican high tariff unpopular — "a license to practice extortion on the American people," said the Globe — and a Republican legislature thwarting the reforms for labor and suffrage that Governor Russell was pressing. The Democrats for the time had the popular side, and the 1890 elections had brought in a Democratic Congress to presage the presidential victory that followed in 1898, when the Globe headlines could exult "Four More Years of Grover" and in the evening edition "Russell Re-elected."

The Globe was ready for this victory. With an enormous output of energy it distributed on the day after the 1898 election the largest number of papers yet printed in a single day by an American newspaper, 627,270 — topping by 30,000 even the victory edition of Pulitzer's World. The Transcript had lent its presses to supplement the maximum production of the Globe's five jumbo presses and a brand new $45,000 Hoe quadruple, "the largest printing press ever brought into New England," the Globe said (it was believed also to be the first electrically driven press anywhere). The Hoe could deliver 48,000 complete 24-page newspapers an hour. The Globe by now was 24 pages daily, divided between morning and evening, and 28 pages Sunday.

Blizzard Breakthrough

According to the New York Sun, the great storm of March 11–13, 1888, permanently fixed the word "blizzard" in the English language. It left its legends, notably in newspaper work. The great storm began Sunday night. It was bad in Boston, much worse in New York. The wires were down. The Monday night New York train for Boston was stalled before Hartford and had to return next day to New York. In Boston six to eight horses had to be put on the horsecars. For 48 hours no news moved by wire even from Lowell and Worcester. More than half a century before the Weather Bureau began naming hurricanes, the storm of 1888 was known in New England as "the Great White Hurricane."

The Globe had an energetic correspondent in George Dickinson, former night editor, at the New York office in the World building. A long-distance leased telephone line had just been installed. But the telephone lines were down between downtown New York and King's Bridge, a dozen miles out. On Tuesday Dickinson borrowed a lineman from the telephone company and got permission to cut into the wire east of King's Bridge, but the storm blocked them. Dickinson doggedly made the rounds of telegraph offices until, late Tuesday night, he found the United Telegraph Company had just got a line opened to Albany. He persuaded them to send 2,000 words to the Globe, which next morning published this as "the only direct news received in Boston from New York since Monday morning." That day Dickinson with a railroad work train bucked through the drifts and over a bridge to King's Bridge and with his lineman set up communication to the Globe, where a telegraph operator, S. F. Shirley, transcribed with a pen some 16,000 words in a period of just under eight hours. This was all the news of New York and all that had come into New York from the rest of the world, and in the Thursday morning paper it was a conspicuous beat. No other Boston paper had more than news bulletins from New York sent by way of London. The Globe boasted it was the greatest scoop ever in Boston journalism.

Ten years later another great November storm left its legend on New England — "the night the *Portland* went down." This too interrupted communications with New York and provided another occasion for ingenuity and enterprise that the Globe exploited. It occurred to managing editor Fowle that passengers on the Fall River boat from New York might have New York papers. So he sent Globe men to meet the boat in Fall River. The Providence Journal had the same idea. Three New York newspapers were located, and the Providence Journal man bought a Times, the Globe reporters a New York Herald; the other paper was the Sun, but the passenger carrying it cherished it as a souvenir of the great storm and wouldn't part with it. But he agreed to accompany the Globe men to the Globe office and wait while the Sun news was dictated from his paper. So next morning the Globe had two columns of New York news, mostly about the blizzard, over its contemporaries, who had only skeleton dispatches cabled through London.

Mr. Fowle recorded long after that in all his 50 years of newspapering the great blizzard of 1888 presented the hardest news gathering job and its solution gave the most satisfaction. Fowle in his reminiscences has telescoped the two storms. But Willard DeLue disentangled them, to find that the Fall River boat had been unable to make its run in the 1888 storm.

Sending telegraph news from the outlying New England region was unsatisfactory. Most small telegraph offices had local women operators, unaccustomed to rapid filing of long press dispatches. The Globe filled the gap by training a few telegraph operators as reporters or copy editors, and they became emergency operators who were sent out with portable telegraph kits on big fires, storms, or murders.

In the disastrous Lynn fire of November 26, 1889, both local telegraph offices were destroyed. The Globe operator on the assignment, Eugene J. O'Connor, climbed a shed, tapped the outgoing wires, and got out the first news of the extent of the destruction. His stories brought outside aid to control the fire and won him a gold medal, awarded by the city government of Lynn.

News Enterprise, 1890

In 1890 the term "investigative reporting" had not been invented. But top reporters counted investigation part of their role. Eugene Buckley was such a reporter. He was rowing editor, but available for a big story any time. On August 19, 1890, a Boston-bound train from Woods Hole (then Woods Holl) was derailed in Quincy. More than 20 passengers were killed, among them a former editor of the Globe, Edwin C. Bailey.

Railroad officials indicated the cause of the wreck as either a spread rail or a broken flange on a locomotive wheel. But Gene Buckley, on the story, wasn't satisfied. He had been a trainman before he was a reporter. He checked carefully and found no sign that the rails had spread or that any locomotive wheel was damaged. A track gang at work had jumped aside as the train bore down, and their tools were scattered about. Buckley suspected that a track jack might have been left in place. He searched the area and found the jack hidden in high weeds, some distance from the tracks. It bore marks that could have been made by being run over. Buckley got hold of a photographer, had the jack photographed, and left it where he found it. Next morning the Globe reported that the wreck was caused by the abandoned jack and showed its photograph. Later testimony at an investigative hearing was that a railroad official had ordered a workman to hide the jack.

A beat or "scoop" on an important news event is of course always important to a newspaper and especially to a new or struggling one. Even for a newspaper safely established in a leading position a scoop counts in prestige and is a great thing for staff morale. It is something worth exploiting in promotion. The young Globe was never behind hand in tooting its own horn over any scoop; Chas. Taylor counted it good business promotion.

A dozen years after the Globe escaped being scooped over the Phoenix Park murders, another circumstance of the difference in London and Boston edition times enabled it to enjoy a notable beat in Boston. Its own alertness was of course a necessary element.

This scoop was on the death of Alfred, Lord Tennyson, October 6, 1892. The Globe by then had its own correspondent in the office of the New York World, Pulitzer's paper.

Tennyson was known to be dying. All papers had obituaries in type, photographic cuts ready to lock in the forms. British correspondents kept a death watch at the poet's home at Aldworth. But the doctors' evening bulletin indicated he would last the night, so when it came press time for their final editions in London the correspondents laid off their vigil. They were wakened to learn that Tennyson had died in the night. It was too late for European editions, and even with five hours' lead time in New York it was nearly 4 A.M. there before the news cleared through London, 50 miles from Aldworth.

At 4 A.M. in New York morning papers had gone to press. But the Globe had kept the wire open to the World and held the paper open as long as possible. When the brief bulletin ticked off the telegraph keys, Jack Taylor, the night editor who had been a telegrapher, grabbed a pencil and wrote a one-line bulletin as he heard the keys click, then rushed it to the forms. In 12 minutes the presses were rolling with a page one lead:

Tennyson Dead

England's Poet Laureate Fell Into His Last Sleep This Morning

Under it there was a pen and ink sketch of Tennyson, two columns wide, that was already in type; under that his poem "To Sleep," identified as his last published verses. The full story ran a column on the front page and two inside, under the one sentence Jack Taylor had snatched off the wire: "Alfred Tennyson, the poet laureate, died at Aldworth at 1:35, Boston time, this morning."

In its own evening edition the Globe was able to claim it was the only newspaper in the East to have had the story of Tennyson's death that morning.

Some of the reporters' exploits of 1890 have long since become clichés by imitation. But when they were novel they made exciting stories. In 1889 one of the Globe girl reporters — they now had six — managed to get herself arrested as a drunk and confined briefly in jail at Deer Island, to come out with an "exposé" of the jail conditions. Nellie Bly had done this for the New York World at Blackwell's Island, but it was new journalistic territory in Boston. Next season one of the men, Lewis Cushman, whose previous adventures had been chiefly in balloon ascensions, succeeded in feigning insanity twice within a few weeks and becoming successively an inmate of the insane asylums at Northampton and Danvers. On both occasions another Globe man, Sam Merrill, whose extracurricular interests had established him as an authority on libel law and on the moose of Maine, effected Cushman's release as his "brother." This yielded more exposé.

An investigation that looks more legitimate from 70 years' hindsight was Virgil Eaton's camouflage as a tramp to test Maine's antitramp law. Virgil browsed about the state as a vagrant, knocking at farm doors to get handouts and to discover the public attitude toward tramps. He found the Maine folks friendly and hospitable, which may have had some relation to his being a State of Mainer himself and a persuasive and very entertaining character. Nobody called the police. The drastic law didn't seem to be working. Eaton's reports were diverting and gave the Globe occasion for a "Repeal that Law" editorial that denounced it as "atrocious . . . brutally uncharitable and un-Christian."

On the lighter side, Larry Dyar put in a day disguised as a hand organ grinder — then a new occupation — with a monkey and all the trappings. He ended the day with a yield of 57 cents, a bite from the borrowed monkey, and a lame back from the 63-pound hand organ, but an increased respect for organ grinders.

But the Globe energies expended on such sporadic stunts were minor compared to its mobilization of forces against prohibition, a hardy perennial issue of the period. The Globe every season rallied the workingman and Democrats against this invasion of liberty. In April 1889 a special election on a state prohibition amendment turned on all the Globe's batteries, daily and Sunday, front page and editorial page, against prohibition.

No No No No

ran the top headline election morning, April 22, 1889.

The day before the top headline had been just "NO," and under it, in big type three columns across: "Tomorrow the contest between our present high license law, embodying local option, and the Constitutional Prohibition of the manufacture and sale of alcoholic beverages, including cider . . . Vote No." Subheads had

Ιston Daily Globe.

TUESDAY MORNING, APRIL 23. 1889—TEN PAGES.   PRICE TWO CENTS.

IT IS "NO."

With No Mistaken Sound.

Over 42,000 Majority in the State.

In a Total Vote of 220,892.

The Country Towns Do Nobly.

All the Cities in Line but Somerville.

Complete Rout of the Anti-Cider Gang.

Local Option is Fully Good Enough.

Beer and Cold Water for Those Who Like Them.

Every Man Can Act as He Pleases Still.

YESTERDAY'S VOTE.

Total Vote of State,	220,892
For the Amendment,	89,175
Against the Amendment,	131,717
Majority "No,"	42,542

LAST YEAR'S VOTE.
VOTE OF THE STATE ON LICENSE.

Yes,	124,649
No,	107,734

The expected has happened, only the majority against the amendment was larger than even the most ardent opponent of the proposed legislative measure anticipated.

RESULT OF YESTERDAY'S VOTE AT A GLANCE.

CIDER KNOCKS OUT CHAIRMAN HASKELL OF THE PROHIBITORY COMMITTEE IN ONE ROUND.

PAUNCEFOTE LIKE DEPEW.

Says He Comes to America with Most Peaceful Intentions—His Acquaintance with Blaine.

NEW YORK, April 22.—Sir Julian Pauncefote, the new English minister, who arrived on the Etruria Sunday, was as leisurely recovered from the fatigue of his voyage after a night's rest at the Brevoort House to see newspaper men today.

Sir Julian is a typical Englishman. He is over six feet tall, well built, with the appearance of an athlete, and is in striking contrast to his late predecessor, Lord Sackville, who was undersized. His face is clean shaven with the exception of carefully trimmed side whiskers. Its head is partially bald and his hair and whiskers are nearly white. He is just six years of age, which is considered young for a statesman in England.

"I know I shall like America," Sir Julian replied to the usual question. "True, I have had scarcely a chance to see anything but I have met so many Americans in England and heard so much in your country that I don't feel like a stranger."

SIR JULIAN PAUNCEFOTE.

EVEN THE BEAR BURNED.

Furs, Paintings and Draperies Go Up in a Boylston Street Blaze.

About 11:55 last evening a "late-comer" passing by 22 Boylston street, who happened to glance upward, was surprised to see the kindled bear, which adorns the front of A. Arnstein's furrier's establishment, a mass of flames.

Captain Charles Hensen, Skipper of Yacht Brooklyn.

PHILADELPHIA, April 22. — Captain Charles Hensen, skipper of the yacht Brooklyn of the Corinthian Yacht Club, Marblehead, Mass., a passenger on the Danmark, and who materially assisted in transferring passengers, tells a story as follows:

---

listed: "The lawyers against it / The Ministers against it / Business Men Against It," with long lists of names under each heading filling most of the front page.

The lead editorial the day before election was "Tomorrow's Duty," followed by "Stand Up and Be Counted." Others were Facts from Kansas — More Testimony from Maine — Practical Temperance.

The Globe had been building up the opposition throughout the month. On April 3 a page one report was headed

> No Good
> So Say the Editors of Rhode Island
> How the "Dry" System Really Works

On April 7 an editorial picked up a book, *The Tobacco Problem,* to note "a well developed coterie of anti-tobacconists who are ready to put their views in a Constitutional Amendment as soon as they are strong enough . . . It would be just as rational to suppress tobacco by a Constitutional Amendment as it is to suppress drinking."

The morning after election the headline was:

> It is No
> Over 42,000 Majority
> The Country Towns Do Nobly
> Local Option is Fully Good Enough
> Every Man Can Act as He Pleases Still

A rare cartoon two columns wide at the top of page one was labeled "Results of Yesterday's Election at a Glance." It showed a farmer in a barrel marked "cider" knocking out the chairman of the prohibition committee in one round.

The Sunday paper had in autumn 1888 added Frank Carpenter's travel letter to the Howard and Townsend columns; this was a Sunday Globe fixture for 35 years. The earlier casual "Table Gossip" had been formalized in 1887 under the inevitable society editor, Mrs. Caroline H. Washburn, who continued that office until in 1897 she moved to the Herald.

The important area of labor had come under Cyrus Field Willard, who had joined the paper at 28 in 1888, when he became the first man in Boston, if not indeed anywhere, to carry the title of labor editor. Willard had started out as a telegrapher and lost his job for his active role in a disastrous telegraphers' strike in 1883. The next five or six years found him editing a labor paper in Haverhill, where he was probably also corresponding for the Globe. Willard, inspired by the creative socialism of Edward Bellamy's *Looking Backward,* was eventually drawn off into one of the utopian movements of the era; he was followed in 1891 by a more down-to-earth-labor man, John F. O'Sullivan, a fighting labor organizer in the new Federation of Labor, following earlier work in the Knights of Labor. O'Sullivan was already president of the Boston Central Labor Union and led in organizing the Seamen's Union, which he represented at an international meeting in Glasgow during his first year as the voice of labor in the Globe, where he continued until he was killed in a railroad accident in 1902.

Jim Frost, an early city editor, had become financial editor, and John O'Callaghan, who had come on the paper after a few years of publishing the Bunker Hill Times and had just returned from an instructive tour of troubled Ireland, was now the chief writer on Irish affairs.

With the possible exception of labor, there was clearly more expertise in the sports department than in other fields. Sports made big news, and its impact was in no way diminished by the elevation of William D. Sullivan from sports editor to city editor. John N. Taylor was moved from night editor to sports editor. A definite sports staff had begun to shape up.

By 1890 the Globe had much the largest staff in town, large enough so that it now ran on a two-platoon system, with a separate day side and night side so that, except for district men, reporters were no longer on call around the clock.

Edson White had taken over the library; William F. Kenney followed him as day editor, a post he held for 20 years, the last few while he served also as president of the Boston Public Library board.

Sports specialists were added, and some of those who were new then became noted names. The Globe was a strong baseball paper. In 1883, when Boston had a championship team, the entire front page on October 1 was given to that story. The new city editor's inside track with the baseball world gave Sully a big scoop in 1887 when baseball's most popular idol, Joseph King Kelly, was secured for Boston. "The Only Kell," proclaimed the headline February 14. In 1889 the Globe publisher offered $1,000 to the Boston team if it won the pennant; when it lost to Pittsburgh he made the $1,000 award anyway, for effort. "The most generous gift ever made to a baseball club," said their captain.

In 1887 Timothy Murname, who'd been a big league first baseman, joined the staff at 37, to become in the next two decades the best-known name in baseball, noted also for the spectacular inventiveness of his baseball language which the copy desk wrestled into a semblance of English. When the second baseball league arose Tim had to have a baseball colleague; this brought in James O'Leary, a converted telegrapher, a lovable, big, smiling Irishman who followed Tim as the dean of baseball writers.

Even lacrosse, which had a flare in Boston in the eighties, had its expert: J. Allen Lowe was appointed to handle the many lacrosse leagues all over Greater Boston. This often took two columns in the paper. In 1887 the Globe awarded a silver lacrosse stick to the winner of the intermediate league championship, played on the Common. When lacrosse's transient popularity yielded to the bicycle craze of the early 1890's, Lowe moved over to horse-racing.

The Globe's first bicycle editor, Charles S. Howard, had turned to journalism from a job with the leading bicycle manufacturer, the Pope Company. The early high wheel had restricted bicycling in the eighties. But in the early nineties the more manageable bike with wheels of equal dimensions gave rise to bicycle clubs in every neighborhood. Cycling became the popular family event for weekend runs and a racing sport that drew great crowds to Park Square Garden, site of the later Statler Hotel, that featured six-day bike races. Bicycle races at Franklin Park became so popular that there were 780 entries by July 4, 1896. By then one of every seven persons in America owned a bicycle, and the bicycle industry accounted for ten percent of all national advertising. The price of a good bicycle new was nearly $100, but secondhand ones were always available.

The last two decades of the century were a great time, too, for walking matches, rifle matches, yacht racing; even cricket had a sufficient following to give rise to the Longwood Cricket Club, later the host to national tennis. Prizefighting of course held its primacy whenever a big fight was promoted, and Dan Saunders continued to preside as boxing editor. In 1892 he went to New Orleans to report the historic bout that saw Jim Corbett defeat Boston strongman John L. Sullivan. The Globe devoted enthusiastic attention to all these games and did its share of promoting them with prizes.

Rowing was the special province of Eugene Buckley, a leading sculler and organizer of rowing clubs before he began writing about it in the Globe in 1887 and the first president of the New England Amateur Rowing Association of Boston. Boat clubs sprang up all around town. General Taylor's sons Charles, Jr., and William O. took rowing lessons from James Butler, famous oarsman and coach. In 1887 the Globe put up the prize for the New England Rowing Association regatta.

Yachting became a special interest of the Globe and its publisher. With prosperity, Taylor had a summer place at Swampscott on the North Shore by 1887 and acquired a 100-foot steam yacht and joined the socialite yachtsmen in the American Yacht Club. Next year he moved over to Marblehead for a summer place, joined the Corinthian Yacht Club, and took with zest to the Marblehead races. His sons became yachtsmen, Charles, Jr., William O., and John I. each in turn becoming master of a 25-foot racing sloop of his own. So the whole Taylor family shared in the yacht-racing fever built up by three successive years of America's Cup international races, 1885–1887. The cup defenders were all Boston owned, two of them built at Lawley's South Boston shipyard and designed by local naval architect Ed Burgess.

One of Burgess' young student assistants, George A. Stewart, became yachting editor of the Globe in 1886. Stewart headed a Globe staff of seven, including young Charles Taylor, to cover the 1887 cup races off Newport. A fleet of 13 carrier pigeons winged their stories from the Globe's yacht to a telegraph line on the pier. The wire fed the race story to the Globe bulletin board, avidly followed by a crowd that filled Newspaper Row. The Globe in 1889 offered $1,000 in prizes for a Globe Grand Open Regatta under the auspices of the South Boston Yacht Club. The General accompanied the judges on his own yacht. By that year the telephone voice had replaced the telegraph code to flash play-by-play from the Harvard-Yale football game, and an announcer with a megaphone took over from the bulletin board. Competition from both sides of the Row to be first with the bulletin flashes was keen.

Harness-racing made its special demands. Every county fairgrounds was shaped to the curving half-mile track, and in the metropolitan area gentlemen's driving clubs sprang up. At one time there were 18 such driving clubs in Greater Boston, their members owner-riders. The first turf editor in the Globe was Irish-born Tom P. Evans, who issued signed announcements of racing choices in the eighties and inaugurated departments of turf notes, "Hoof Prints" and "Stable Echoes." Allen Lowe shifted from lacrosse to the turf in 1888 to follow Evans for the next ten years. Then in 1896 Frank G. Trott began a 50-year span as a leading national authority on horse-racing.

Charlie Howard's shift from bicycling to help the drama editor in 1888 suggests the contrast between the sports specialization and the casual handling of the fields of criticism. The contrast grew after Howard succeeded Charles Dyar in 1891 to run the drama department for the next 50 years. An explanation for the freer play and more authoritative work of the sports writer might be the relative absence of directly connected advertising, although of course it stimulated the sports equipment business. But the relation of theater advertising to theater reviews was so close that the same editor handled both, an arrangement not calculated to develop independent criticism — and it did not.

Charles Dyar, handling the theater in the 1880's between stints as city editor and chief editorial writer, had developed a rationale that the Globe appears to have been glad to follow. Dyar, a tolerant man, adopted the philosophy that a critic should not impose his judgment on the theatergoer but let him enjoy the play according to his own taste. This would be a natural attitude for a newsman moved into a field where he could claim no special authority; it became a convenient attitude for the office as theater advertising built up, and hardened into commercial policy when Charles Howard switched to drama from his bicycling chores. Plays were not criticized, but simply reported. When, later, the developing movies were added to Howard's department they were included in the same bland treatment, which seldom emitted a disparaging word and so made no difficulty with theater advertisers. This vacuum of criticism lasted into the 1950's.

General Taylor's own special interests in some fields and absence of interest in others must have been an active cause of such variations in Globe operations. The Globe had expert coverage of such special areas as politics, yachting, and baseball and only casual coverage of theater, art, and books. Unlike his friend Joseph Pulitzer, General Taylor's personal interest in the theater was limited to the frequent use of season tickets for Keith's vaudeville emporium. But his enthusiasm for baseball led him to buy the Boston American Club in 1904 — which made a career for his third son, John I., as president of the Boston team. The General was undoubtedly in tune with the tastes of his mass readership. Not much in the Globe of the 1890's was influencing the mass taste.

Some of the new hands on the growing news staff that Sully took over in 1889 figured large after the paper turned the corner into the twentieth century: M. E. Hennessy, who acquired the most extensive political acquaintance of any writer of his period; Harry Poor, long the controlling hand in shaping the morning paper as night editor; William E. Alcott, night city editor, then librarian and a national leader in the new field of special libraries; Charles S. Groves, later Washington correspondent; Lawrence J. Sweeney, who came in as office boy at 14 in 1892, to be a star reporter of later years especially in sports. Sweeney reported the first Boston marathon in 1897, on a bicycle, and later was the first to follow the long race in an automobile. But boxing was his favorite sport, and when it was legalized in 1920 he became one of the first official referees under the State Boxing Commission headed by his brother-in-law Eugene Buckley, the old Globe oarsman. Another early devotee of the prize ring was James T. Sullivan, who came aboard the paper as a lad in 1891 and became automobile editor in a later day.

The Globe and Lizzie Borden

The Globe celebrated its twentieth anniversary year in 1892 with a special issue on May 1 that carried the largest volume of advertising, 183 columns, ever until then in a Boston newspaper. It exulted in the biggest circulation in New England. It had arrived.

But a few months later the Globe was lucky to escape ruination. The paper fell for a false story that purported to disclose the state's complete murder case against Lizzie Borden. It wrapped the double murder of her mother and father right around her neck. The "inside story," exploded by the Globe before Lizzie had been tried or even indicted, was exposed as false as soon as it was printed; it must have been the harried condition of the Borden lawyers, desperately seeking to contrive any plausible defense for Lizzie, that led them to settle for a complete retraction and apology.

But six weeks later the grand jury, in the same presentment that charged Lizzie with murder, indicted Globe reporter Henry Trickey for tampering with a witness. Trickey left town and was killed by a train in Canada two days later. This personal tragedy that resulted from the paper's appetite for solving murder mysteries makes the Lizzie Borden case a dramatic chapter of Globe history.

The Borden family lawyers had not yet in their extremity brought in the noted Boston trial lawyer George Robinson, former governor. Robinson's bill for the three-week trial the following June was $25,000. As governor, Robinson had appointed the trial judge who proved compliant to such vital defense motions as that all that part of the inquest testimony recording the several variants of Lizzie's story should be excluded, on the ground that Lizzie had not been formally arrested until after the inquest. Robinson led the jury also to doubt the existence of the murder weapon. He won Lizzie's acquittal, though the verdict of colloquial history ran otherwise, as in childhood's rhyme:

> Lizzie Borden took an axe
> And gave her mother forty whacks.
> When she saw what she had done
> She gave her father forty-one.

If the State could have proved that axe, it might have been a different story.

Only Lizzie and the Irish maid Bridget were in or about the small Borden house in Fall River when her mother was murdered in her bedroom at about nine in the morning and her father, while napping in the living room, about an hour and a half later. The house was locked. The natural disposition of the Fall River Establishment to suspect Bridget instead of banker Borden's sedate daughter was immediately rendered impossible by Lizzie's own story. Bridget had been outside the house washing windows at the time of the first murder, and Lizzie had sent her up to her room on the third floor before the second murder.

Suspicion momentarily fell on Lizzie's uncle, an unprepossessing horsetrader who had left the house very close to the time of the first murder but was definitely downtown at the time of the second. He was in fact at the bank where he was to have met Mr. and Mrs. Borden to consummate a real estate deal that may have precipitated the murders. He had a horsefarm, where Mr. Borden kept his own driving horses. It became mutually advantageous for Mr. Borden to take ownership of the horsefarm, and he was planning to put it in the name of his wife, Erma. He had made such an arrangement in an earlier real estate deal, which had added to the resentment that Lizzie and her older sister Emma felt toward their stepmother. Lizzie was in her mid-twenties, Emma a dozen years older. The sisters so detested the stepmother that for years they had refused to eat meals with her. Their father, notably miserly with his daughters, maintained this grim household in a little box of a house on the wrong side of the tracks, though he had become one of the richest men in Fall River.

Emma on that August day was away visiting a vacationing friend at the shore. Lizzie was to have joined her but changed her mind and stayed home when the horsetrader uncle arrived for an overnight visit in connection with the land deal. Mr. Borden had left the house early, expecting his wife to meet him at the bank. It was her failure to arrive that led him to break his daily pattern and come home at mid-morning, to Lizzie's surprise; but she said that her mother had indeed gone out. Mr. Borden, since he was already at home, decided to take his usual mid-day nap earlier.

Lizzie's screams brought Bridget downstairs to see her employer, his head smashed in, stretched on the couch. Lizzie sent Bridget out to fetch the doctor across the street and a relative farther off.

When they came, and the neighbors and then the police, all solicitous of Lizzie, she told of having been out in the barn resting in the loft, out of sight of the side door, and returned to find her father murdered. The police lieutenant went out to the barn to find, he later testified, dust undisturbed and the loft so unbearably hot he could not stay there a minute. He looked for an axe and found only several rusty and dusty ones in the cellar. But poking about further he found another axe concealed in a chimney opening that would seem to have been known only to an intimate of the household. It looked dusty too, but appeared instead in his view to have been newly washed and then covered with ashes. Police arriving later tracked up the barn dust and failed to agree about the axe. At the trial two young boys said they'd been in the barn loft that day and it wasn't so hot. Somebody came forward who had seen a tramp over the back fence — though how or why a tramp would have got into a locked house to kill an inoffensive stranger and hide, presumably in the broom closet, an hour and a half to kill her husband and then escape with no attempt to exploit his crime, nobody explained.

When sister Emma, called back, got to her room, she found that Lizzie had changed her dress during the morning and had hidden the first one, swabbed up, in Emma's closet. The sister kept this to herself until a neighbor later reported seeing Lizzie next day, through the kitchen window, burning a dress in the kitchen stove. Then Emma agreed that it was an old dress and had been stained by paint and was always too tight.

The double murder August 4 became of course a great sensation, then a deep mystery. Lizzie was the sole source of pertinent information. Her questioning, at first apologetic, then curious, gradually turned incredulous and then suspicious. The family lawyer, Andrew J. Jennings, had come over promptly out of sympathy. Police were stationed at the house at night. Neighbors and friends stayed with

Lizzie in her room. It was only on the seventh day after the crimes that the mayor and district attorney agreed they would have to act. They informed lawyer Jennings and went to Lizzie, the mayor explaining that she was not under arrest but that they must formally take her testimony. This went on some days, privately, lawyer Jennings shown the transcript each day. Only on September 1 was Lizzie formally arrested and held for the Grand Jury, which didn't come in till November 15. She was indicted December 2 and trial was set for the following June.

The September 14 arrest did not solve anything. Reporters continued to prowl about the mystery. Henry Trickey, whose meat was murder mysteries and who had to his credit a number of exploits in solving them, stayed on the case for the Globe. Like other reporters, he worked closely with the police and shrewdly gave them credit and publicity for their work. One of his police associates on the Borden case was a private detective, E. G. McHenry, who had been employed by the local authorities early in the case but not retained after Lizzie's arrest. One day Detective McHenry asked Trickey if he'd like to have the whole government case against Lizzie — for $1,000? McHenry said the city marshal had assigned him to make copies of affidavits of 25 witnesses who had been turned up since the inquest. He had copies and they made an airtight case.

Trickey gave McHenry the $30 he had on him and went back to Boston to get authority and funds to proceed. But when he returned McHenry had disappeared; he played cat-and-mouse with the reporter for a week, but then did produce a sheaf of papers, received $400, and got Trickey to agree to give him 24 hours' notice, so as to have a chance to cover his tracks, before publishing. But Trickey didn't trust the detective to protect his expensive scoop, and he must have rushed the story to print, for he failed to take elementary precautions to check names and addresses of McHenry's "witnesses" (who didn't exist) — or even their street numbers, as lawyer Jennings was quick to point out as soon as the Globe story appeared.

On Monday morning, October 10, the whole center of the Globe's front page was occupied with Trickey's great scoop.

> Lizzie Borden's Secret
> Mr. Borden Discovered it and Hot Words Followed
> Startling Testimony from 25 New Witnesses
> Erma Was Killed During That Quarrel
> Family Discord and Murder

The story was explicit:

> The Globe is enabled to lay before its readers not only every fact of importance now in the government's possession, but as well to describe how and by whom the information was secured by the patient and unceasing toil of the police . . . The evidence is forthcoming from 25 people, all of whom stand high in the community . . . and who have no motive of speaking maliciously about the defendant. Every statement of importance in the 20-odd affidavits now held by the government, which the Globe today publishes substantially in detail, is corroborated in a most convincing manner . . ."

The affidavits occupied a whole inside page. One neighbor was quoted as saying he saw Mr. Borden enter the house and at the same time saw a blind cautiously opened by a young woman in the bedroom where Mrs. Borden's body was later found. "The window was so situated that she must have been standing over the mutilated remains of her mother at the very time her father was about to enter the house."

Others "heard a scream" and saw Lizzie at the window, identifiable by a particular headdress familiar to her. A neighboring couple were quoted as having visited the Bordens the night before and overheard the father tell Lizzie he would give her one day to "name the man who got you in trouble or take the door on Saturday."

The maid Bridget was quoted as saying that Lizzie told her she could have all the money she wanted if she didn't talk to the police. Others told of Mr. Borden telling them of Lizzie's "secret." A lawyer (a real lawyer) was quoted as saying Lizzie had consulted him about property rights under a will; this bit was probably true. Another testified the father had told him he was cutting Lizzie off in his will.

The story hadn't collapsed before a big play in the evening edition.

> Astounded
> All New England Read the Story
> Globes Were Bought by Thousands
> Lizzie Borden Appears in New Light
> Belief in her Innocence Shaken
> Excitement Runs High in Fall River
> Police Think the Scoop a Corker
> Lawyer Jennings Says Lies Have Been Told
> Doesn't Believe There is any Secret
> Opinions on Spying by Detective McHenry

But it was fraying around the edges. Even in that edition there was a small item, a telegram from police inspector H. C. Harrington: "Statement in today's Globe regarding what I said is false."

Defense attorney Andrew J. Jennings gave the Associated Press a statement: "The matter published in a Boston paper relating to the Borden murders is a tissue of lies . . ." Jennings noted that "as to the purported witnesses, Mr. and Mrs. Fred Chase of 198 4th Street, there is no such number or any within 50 of it." Of another witness, he "can't find him in the directory nor anyone who ever heard of him." The lawyer quoted, a Mr. Morse, said the whole thing was false.

Henry Trickey, back in Fall River, was discovering how dreadfully he had been had. He got hold of Detective McHenry, who claimed that he had used fictitious names but that all else was true.

But back at the Globe it was evident that McHenry's concoction wouldn't stand up. The Borden family doctor stated that Lizzie had no "secret."

Tuesday morning the Globe was backtracking hard. They laid it onto McHenry and printed on the front page "Henry Trickey's Statement" that related all his affair with the detective.

> Detective McHenry Talks
> He furnished the Globe with the Borden Story
> It has been proved wrong in some particulars
> Globe Secures Best Detective Talent Available to Find the Murderer

In this story McHenry was quoted as still asserting that the facts he had given were true but that "the names of witnesses were given wrong for obvious reasons."

Daily Globe.

DAILY GLOBE:
Sept. '92 - - 200,143
Sept. '91 - - - - - 154,178
GAIN - - - 45,965

OCTOBER 10, 1892—TEN PAGES.   PRICE TWO CENTS.

LATEST!

For Other Evening News See Second, Fourth, Fifth and Eighth Pages.

ASTOUNDED.

All New England Read Story.

Globes Were Bought by Thousands.

Lizzie Borden Appears in New Light.

Belief in Her Innocence Sadly Shaken.

Excitement Runs High in Fall River.

Police Think the Scoop is a Corker.

Lawyer Jennings Says Lies Have Been Told.

Doesn't Believe There is Any Secret.

Opinions on That Spying by Detective McHenry.

FALL RIVER, Mass., Oct. 10.—Doubts of Lizzie A. Borden's guilt; hopes that in the government's weakness she might receive exoneration; belief that her past life might be a powerful factor in making the world give assent to her plea, "I am innocent," all were shaken this morning. Facts, appalling in themselves, tremendous in their significance, have thrown Fall River, where the sentiment for and against has been so intense, into a condition of excitement, amazement and horror.

During the entire history of the Borden tragedy a shadow so profound had never fallen across Lizzie Borden's path, and all Fall River saw it. What it meant and what

on Main st., a man rushed out on to the sidewalk, having a GLOBE above his head, and shouted:

"For heaven's sake have you seen THE GLOBE?"

The headlines were soon seen, and then there was a furious rush for the news stand. Men trampled on each other in their eagerness to secure a paper, and in a short time the sidewalk was crowded with an excited mob, reading the startling news.

It fairly electrified the crowd.

Meantime a boy fought his way through the crowd and put a flaming bulletin out upon the sidewalk. The crowd became denser and denser, and excitement raged. Passers by stopped, read and dove into the news depot, some returning with two or three papers. Three men stood behind the counter working to satisfy the demand for GLOBES. Men threw down their money, grabbed the paper and became absorbed in the story without waiting for their change. Some could not contain themselves, and fairly shouted in amazement as they read.

Boys with huge bundles were rushing about Main st., shouting, and together with

The Excited Readers

made the centre of Fall River a regular pandemonium.

Inside of 10 minutes several thousand people were gathered about Main st., from Pleasant to Franklin sts., reading and discussing.

And still the demand for GLOBES had not been half met.

There were corner gatherings and animated discussions, but not the expression of diverse opinions.

Mingling among the crowd THE GLOBE correspondent heard such expressions from many lips as this: "This is a sad day for Lizzie Borden. I had asked myself what could have incited her to do it, if she did it, but there is no doubt about a motive now. It is all explained.

"I had hoped she might be proven innocent, but it looks bad for her now, and her past life—w y great Scott. Fall River never knew her, her intimate friends did not know her."

No story ever caused such a furor, because none ever came with such corroboration or so unexpectedly.

Boys carried GLOBES into the mills, where they were eagerly read by the operatives while they tried to work.

Detective McHenry's spying upon Lizzie in some quarters met with condemnation, but it was quickly supported by many who cry: "If the woman is guilty she deserves conviction; any method to serve the ends of justice is right."

THE GLOBE's story caused an awful cloud to settle over the influential part of the city. On the hill, among Lizzie Borden's friends, and around the Central Congregational church, there was a gloom that was pathetic. In that part of the city hopes in her innocence were centred, hopes that aroused to fervent prayer. The GLOBES went there, they were read, but it was a grave matter for them. No outburst of excitement appeared in this quarter, but there was a poignant grief. Many went for Lizzie Borden, whose hope had buoyed up for weeks. She was their fellow church member, their friend in many cases, life acquaintance, fellow worker in the temperance cause, their respected sister in the church and social world.

At Police Headquarters

the story created a tremendous sensation. Police officers bought copies of THE GLOBE and saw their work minutely outlined. How could THE GLOBE have got it? . Still there it was with many things they thought no one could possibly have been informed of outside the small police circle. All hands not on duty hurried to the station house.

City Marshal Hilliard was not in, having gone to New Bedford to consult with District Attorney Knowlton.

Deputy John Fleet was preparing the morning court docket. Mr. Fleet was handed a copy of THE GLOBE. His eyebrows went up half an inch as he comprehended the force of the headline.

"Great heavens," said he, "what does this mean; what is this, anyway?"

"It comes pretty near telling its own story," said the reporter.

"Does it?" echoed the deputy, "why, my dear man, it is a corker. It is beyond understanding. Say, now, how did you fellows get all this?"

"Read right, isn't it?" was asked.

"You must excuse me; give me time to think this thing over. This is the biggest surprise we have had here for some time. Pretty solid stuff, too."

Mr. Fleet read with astonishment.

"There is liable to be some decided criticism of your department on account of allowing McHenry to spy on the defendant," was suggested.

"Well, I have not read it all yet," said Mr. Fleet, "and can't talk upon that. But this means that we will have to do some tall work now that that story is published. Say, how did THE GLOBE get it?"

Special Officer Medley was one of the first to buy a GLOBE, and a reporter saw him immediately after. Said he: "You fellows have

LIZZIE HAD A SECRET.

Mr. Borden Discovered It, Then a Quarrel.

Startling Testimony of 25 New Witnesses.

Seen in Mother's Room With a Hood on Her Head.

Accused Sister of Treachery and Kicked Her in Anger.

Theft of a Watch---Money Offered to Bridget ---Story of a Will.

FALL RIVER, Mass., Oct. 9.—Besides those who testified for the government in the preliminary examination of Lizzie A. Borden before Judge Blaisdell fully 25 new witnesses will be called by the State at the trial of the defendant for murder in December.

On the afternoon of September 1 Miss Borden was committed to the county jail at Taunton to await the action of the grand jury at its November sitting.

Judge Blaisdell's jurisdiction not being final his action in thus concluding the examination was justified in two ways. He knew that if he dismissed the defendant she would soon be under arrest on a bench warrant issued by a court higher than his own. Moreover, he knew that the government's case against her was much stronger than was indicated by the testimony developed in open court.

He knew that it was the desire of District Attorney Knowlton to submit the least evidence necessary to hold the prisoner, and therefore, when he heard enough from his seat on the bench to partly substantiate his opinion formed elsewhere on other facts, the government's case was closed, and the defence followed with little testimony and able argument.

Judge Blaisdell said in his decision he was satisfied that the government had not produced enough evidence to warrant the conviction, nor perhaps the finding of an indictment, but he felt satisfied that enough had been shown to warrant holding the defendant for the grand jury, which body could deliberately consider the entire case against her and report upon the evidence.

The public, however, not occupying the position of confidence with the State's officials that Judge Blaisdell possessed by virtue of his office was highly indignant at the decision, and from the Atlantic to the Pacific the finding was denounced and termed "a high-handed outrage."

The situation indicated other facts to those who had without prejudice or opinion followed the case along. The ability and characteristic fairness of the attorney-general, Albert E. Pillsbury, precluded the possibility that he was participating in a persecution of Miss Borden.

Mr. Knowlton has for years borne the

one in which he saw Miss Lizzie is so situated that she must have been standing

Over the Mutilated Remains

of her mother at the very time that her father was about to enter the house, between 10.30 and 10.45 o'clock.

The next witness of importance is Mrs. Gustave F. Ronald, whose husband is a well known civil engineer, and whose home during the winter is at Pawtucket, R. I.

She and her husband were guests at the Wilbur House at the time of the murder.

About 9.30 o'clock on the morning of Aug. 4 she went out with her baby in its carriage for a walk.

She wheeled the little one un 2d st. and stopped under the big trees near the Borden house about 20 minutes of 10 o'clock.

A minute later she heard a terrible cry or groan and began looking around to see whence it came.

She looked up at the Borden house and saw in a room through a partially open window a woman whose head was in part covered by a rubber cap or hood, and whose face she saw plainly, as the distance was short.

This window she has designated to the authorities, and it is the one nearest to the murdered woman as she lay in the guest chamber of her home when found by the police.

Mrs. Ronald was almost that minute approached by Mr. Peter Mahany of 103 Pleasant st., Fall River, who is a timekeeper in the Troy mill.

He likewise had heard the groan, seen the woman at the window, who wore the peculiar head covering, and recognized her as the younger daughter of the Borden family, all members of which he knew quite well by sight. The window that he designates as the one in which he saw Miss Lizzie was the same as that pointed out by Mrs. Ronald.

Augustus Gunning, who now resides at 308 Plainfield st., Johnsonville, R. I., near Providence, was at that time a lodger in Mrs. Church's house, and he too, about 10 o'clock on the morning of Aug. 4, saw Lizzie Borden in the window of the guest chamber with a dark-colored garment on and a hood of similar color covering her head. As he looked across she seemed to be engaged in cleaning, but upon seeing

The fiasco on Lizzie Borden: October 10, 1892.

However, the Globe reported that the statement of Dr. Bowen as to Lizzie's physical condition convinced them that "in this respect at least, McHenry was wrong. The story may be wrong in some other minor particulars, but the weight of the evidence favors the main facts to be true."

But this wouldn't stand up either. Lesser headlines told: "Mr. Morse is Very Angry / He has commanded his lawyers to take steps at once to secure legal redress." Another headline was "Can't Find Witnesses / So Jennings is Not Convinced" and another " 'I Can't Believe It' / What Rev. A. E. Buck of Fall River Has To Say of the Case." What the family minister had to say was what everybody was saying by that time.

The Globe said it next edition. The center of the Tuesday evening front page retracted in bold face type under a top headline:

The Lizzie Borden Case

. . . The Globe feels it its duty as an honest newspaper to state that it has been grievously misled in the Lizzie Borden case. It published on Monday a communication that it believed to be true evidence. Some of this remarkably ingenious and cunningly contrived story undoubtedly was based on true facts . . . The Globe believes however that much of it is false and never should have been published. The Globe being thus misled has innocently added to the terrible burdens of Miss Lizzie Borden . . . We hereby tender out heartfelt apology for the inhuman reflection on her honor as a woman and for any injustice the publication reflected on her . . . The same sincere apology applies to Mr. John V. Morse and any other persons to whom the publication did an injustice . . .

This, incredibly enough, seems to have been enough to hold off any damage suits. Next day the Globe had a headline:
"Honest Amend / Globe Apology Pleased Its Readers / Regrets Spread Broadcast at Fall River / McHenry's Acts Condemned by Fair-Minded Citizens." Its leading editorial repeated the apology and alibi.

The Globe of course was lucky to escape ruin from such a witches' broth. Why no suit was brought is perhaps explained by the obvious fact that the Borden attorneys had their hands more than full with the grand jury about to come in and the prospect of trial after that. They would have had their own reasons for not choosing to risk the further exposure of a libel case. And the whole area was full of sensational stories — none such a whopper as the Globe's, but enough to keep defense counsel on edge.

The Globe suffered no setback. Within three weeks of its retraction of the Borden story it published the largest edition ever put out until then by an American newspaper, 627,270 copies the morning after the November election.

But three weeks after that the second blow fell. On December 2 Trickey was indicted for tampering with a witness, presumably Bridget, who may have testified concerning the concoction McHenry had sold Trickey that she had been approached to agree not to deny the story. But this is conjecture, for the case against Trickey for any crime greater than carelessness remains an even more impenetrable mystery than the case against Lizzie. The Trickey indictment was secret, and the Borden influence caused not only the inquest record but the grand jury record to disappear.

Lawyer Jennings took all the defense records home with him after the trial and would never allow them to be seen.

The evening Globe December 2 recorded:

Lizzie Borden Indicted by Grand Jury
Second Indictment Found Was Kept Secret

"There is a second indictment which was kept a secret as the party indicted is not in custody . . . District Attorney Knowlton will neither admit nor deny that it relates to Mr. Trickey, but that is the impression at the courthouse." The indictment story in the Globe next morning, Saturday, December 3, said:

It is reported, on what seems indisputable authority, that Henry G. Trickey was the person named and that he is accused of tampering with a government witness.

Detective McHenry and his wife were heard by the Grand Jury on the conversation between Trickey and McHenry over the purchase of McHenry's story by Trickey. It is reported that another important witness was approached by Mr. Trickey, and that this witness was offered inducements to leave the country.

It was the aim of the State to show, by pressing the case against Mr. Trickey, that the defense was the promoter and originator of the scheme to get at the evidence in McHenry's possession . . ."

That was Saturday. On Monday morning, December 5, the lead story in the Globe was:

Henry G. Trickey Dead
Tried to Board a Moving Train and Fell
Although Only 24 Years Old, His Life Was Most Eventful
The Globe Loses a Most Loyal and Devoted Member of its Staff

The Globe story was a combination report and obituary that eulogized Trickey, without mentioning the indictment. He was killed at Hamilton, Ontario, on Saturday, December 3, "on a business trip in the interests of the Globe. Being late, he attempted to board a western-bound train when he stumbled and fell under the wheels." He was described as a generous nature with an impulsive spirit of tremendous loyalty — "loyalty sometimes overran his caution but he was young and ambitious, enterprising . . . one of the hardest workers on assignment, with tireless energy and a keen appreciation of the values of news . . . No wonder that caution sometimes halted and the man erred. In this line [of crime investigation] he of course made mistakes and was sometimes the victim of those whose only purpose it was to mislead . . ."

Trickey's death opened the grand jury door enough for another story from Fall River next day, December 6:

With the news of the death of Trickey several facts have come to the surface which put a different aspect on the circumstances surrounding the unreported indictment . . . Members of the grand jury admit that although he was nominally the person named as having been guilty of a breach of the law, he was not the central figure in this chapter of the Borden case. Government officials now admit that he was the victim of circumstances and that a trap that was set for him was intended to catch bigger game.

The district attorney has been anxious to have all the facts related to Trickey's indictment kept from the public since the news of his death . . . But they are known . . . The local papers devote considerable space to Trickey's connection with the case and his death . . . The Fall River Globe this evening states editorially that "all who knew him ask that the public suspend judgment . . . He had his faults but his mistakes were generally those of his judgment, not of the heart. They were the errors of one over zealous to do his entire duty. It is more than likely time will vindicate him. He proved himself to be impetuous to a fault, but while his methods of work may not have been wholly commendable, his cheery disposition and his fund of good nature made him generally popular with his fellow workers . . ."

The Globe's blooper was one of the few stories hostile to Lizzie published at the time. The Fall River Establishment quickly closed ranks to support the banker's daughter. Their influence was pervasive with the police and authorities, in the jail, at the court house, with the local newspapers. Lizzie was portrayed as a tragic victim of circumstances. Her arrest was resented. Women's organizations all over the country expressed sentiments of consolation for her ordeal. Ministers prayed over her sad predicament. The prosecution became so unpopular that Attorney General Albert E. Pillsbury backed out of his role to lead in prosecution of a notable capital case. He assigned the Borden case to his assistant, William Moody, later U.S. attorney general and a Supreme Court justice. Most reporters appear to have been either pro-Lizzie or skeptical of the state's evidence. Joseph Howard, whose national syndicated column naturally moved to Fall River for the trial, was so partisan to Lizzie that she thanked him personally at her reception for the press when the trial ended. The Globe assigned a staff man, John Carberry, to the trial but of course featured Howard's articles.

The Lizzie Borden trial in June 1893 must have been a bonanza to newspapers, as it became to whodunit writers ever after. It opened June 5 to the Globe headline

>Life and Honor at Stake
>Trial of Lizzie Borden for Double Murder Begins
>at New Bedford Today

"Demoniac Deed" was the front page head on Joseph Howard's opener while the jury was being selected.

On some days the testimony occupied seven pages of a 12-page Globe. It repeatedly took over the entire front page. Sketches sometimes eight columns wide portrayed the courtroom drama and identified all the personnel. One day a four-column sketch of Lizzie leaving the court took half the top of the front page; the paper then had seven columns to a page. One day the trial took 35 columns, another day 33.

The vertical headlines in those days were so detailed in their narrative as may well have saved all with weak eyes from the vast bulk of the minuscule type of the trial report.

June 7:

>Bridget Tells
>Her Doings on Day of Murder

June 8:

> Under Fire
> Bridget Sullivan on Stand
> Her Story Occupies Several Hours

June 8, evening:

> Lizzie's Mind Clouded
> By Dosing with Morphine Before the Inquest
> Alice Russell Tells of the Dress Burning
> No Blood Stains Seen on Her

June 9:

> Even Fight
> Lizzie Borden is not Cast Down
> Marshall Fleet and His Tale of a Hatchet
> Found it in Tool Chest in Cellar

Thirty-six columns that day, on Lizzie's change of clothing, later burning of a dress, the police detective's finding of "the murder weapon" hidden inside the locked house, and the controversy over it. That's a continuing story.

June 9:

> Snarls in their Yarns
> Police Contradict Former Sayings
> One Didn't Think the Broken Hatchet Important
> Officer Admits Inspection of the House was Careless

The defense clouded the issue of the hatchet enough so that the June 11 headline tells:

> Defense in Good Humor
> Contradictions by Officers Brighten Lizzie Borden's Chances

A new week opened Monday, June 12:

> Day of Days
> Mighty Question to be Decided
> Shall Inquest Testimony be Admitted?

The answer came next day:

> Her Testimony Shut Out
> Lizzie's Statements at the Inquest Cannot Be Used
> Immensely Important Ruling
> Prosecution is Finally Baffled in Attempt to Introduce the Record
> Court's Reason That Defendant Spoke as One in Custody
> Therefore Her Statement Was not Considered Voluntary
> Damaging Statements Are Thus Excluded

There was hardly any other news in the 12-page paper that day.

June 14:

> No Blood
> Experts Yield No Clue to Crime
> Spots on Axes Were Rust
> Lizzie's Garments Pass the Ordeal

Joe Howard's story that day indicates the way things were going: "Howard Convinced that Guilt is Not Established."

But there was still damaging testimony to come even after Lizzie's own contradictions of the inquest had been kept out.

ston Daily Globe.

UESDAY MORNING, JUNE 13. 1893.—TWELVE PAGES.

PRICE TWO CENTS.

O'BRIEN HAS TWO BAD WOUNDS.

Lewis Cohen is Charged With Stabbing Him on Hanover St, Seeking Revenge for Some Harmless Guying.

James J. O'Brien, a resident of the North end, is at the Massachusetts general hospital with a knife wound three inches long on the left side of his neck and a similar wound on his left cheek.

He alleged assailant, a Hebrew, Lewis Cohen, is in a cell at station 1.

A party of Hebrews, among whom was Cohen, chartered a herdic last night, and about 12.30 o'clock this morning were landed in front of hotel Ludwig, on Hanover st.

When the party got upon the sidewalk, the Hebrews began to argue with the driver about the price of their ride, and a crowd gathered about them, members of the throng guying the Hebrews, and telling them to "pay the man his money."

Cohen, it is alleged, became infuriated and pulling out a knife or some other coordinate instrument made an onslaught on the crowd and cut O'Brien twice before he could get beyond reach.

The police of division 1 were quickly on the scene and the wounded man and his alleged assailant were taken into the station close at hand.

Dr Dunn, after dressing O'Brien's wound, ordered his immediate removal to the hospital in the police ambulance. Cohen was locked up on the charge of assault and battery with some sharp instrument.

LOCAL FORECAST.

For New England Tuesday and Wednesday:

Fair weather; cooler Tuesday morning; warmer Wednesday; variable winds.

Synopsis: Fair weather generally prevails throughout the country, rain having fallen at only a few stations, the heaviest being at Galveston, Tex.

The Temperature Yesterday

as indicated by the thermometer at Thompson's Spa: 3 a m, 67 ; 6 a m, 66°; 9 a m, 66 ; 12 m, 64 ; 3 p m, 64 ; 6 p m, 63°; 9 p m, 63 ; 12 mid, 58 . Average temperature yesterday, 63¾.

Epistle from Syria.

PORTLAND, June 12—At the afternoon meeting of Friends an epistle was read from the missionary station at Ramallah, Syria. Most of the session was taken up with reading a summary of answers to queries from quarterly meetings and a discussion. Tonight was the meeting of the Woman's foreign missionary society, with addresses by Isaac Sharp of London, Mrs Ella Hartley of Oregon and Phebe S. Aydelotte of Fall River, who gave an account of the woman's congress in Chicago.

Chicago Hotels Begin Assignments.

CHICAGO, June 12—A receiver was appointed this morning for the Harvey World's fair hotel and the Harvey home improvement company. Col Walter Thomas Mills is the principal creditor. The assets of the home improvement company are scheduled at $141,500, and the liabilities at $99,000, and the assets of the hotel com-

---

LIZZIE WEPT

But Her Tears Were Those of Joy.

Signal Victory Won by the Defense.

Inquest Testimony Ruled Out by the Court.

Damaging Statements Are Thus Excluded.

Prisoner Breaks Down at Announcement.

Dr Dolan Tells About the Autopsies.

His Opinion of How the Wounds Were Inflicted.

Atty Gen Pillsbury Goes to New Bedford.

Another Bombshell in Waiting for Prosecution.

NEW BEDFORD, June 12—And then she broke down and cried.

Who?

Miss Lizzie Borden, accused of the brutal murder of her father and stepmother—she's the one who broke down and cried.

What for?

For joy, pure, unadulterated joy, and I will tell you about it.

It will be remembered that when court adjourned on Saturday night last an agreement as to facts connected with Miss Borden's condition and the circumstances attending her testimony, at the time of the Fall River inquest, had been agreed and filed with the court, the understanding being that arguments should be held today pro and con the admissibility of the evidence given by her at the time of monumental distress, chagrin and mental suffering.

Knowledge that the arguments were to be held today attracted an unusual crowd to the court house doors. Thoughtful minds had removed the now historic cow, and officers were stationed to compel teams to move along the road as quietly and considerately as possible.

Chief Justice Mason and his associate, Judge Blodgett, were cordially and courteously welcomed by their left-over associate, Judge Dewey, upon whom the burden of the care of an exceedingly uncomfortable and physically depressed jury had been no

---

CAUGHT BY A GLOBE CAMERA.

THE BORDEN JURY MARCHING THROUGH THE STREETS.

most, and extra camp chairs were placed in some of the aisles, while the enclosure ordinarily reserved for members of the bar was largely filled with experts of high and low degree.

Armed with a perfect library of law books, Dist Atty Knowlton, whose impassive countenance grows

More and More Sphinx-Like

as the days roll on, and Dist Atty Moody, who was evidently impressed with the responsibility placed upon him on this occasion, waited the pleasure of the court, while ex Gov Robinson, with his front locks as smooth as those of Jonathan Slick; counselor Jennings, nervously watching every motion, and counselor Adams, the best-groomed man of all the lot, alertly listened for the court's order concerning the jury.

This, mind you, was at 9 o'clock in the morning, eight hours before an adjournment for the day was possible, so it seemed rather unnecessary to have gone to the trouble of bringing the jury all the way to court, when it was seen that the sheriffs were directed to conduct them from the room during the argument which was then about to begin. However, like so many kings of France, they first marched up the steps and then marched down again, chewing the cud of reflection as, singly and concertedly, they wondered why, if they were really a coordinate branch of the court, they must be excluded at the very time when the excitement was expected to begin.

Order being restored, Mr Moody, upon whom down to this time the public burden of the prosecution has been laid, began his plea for the presentation, by the notes of the official stenographer, Miss White, of

It was in order that the state might benefit by these damaging contradictions that Mr Moody made his plea. He began by stating the statute law, and showing therefrom that all that was done by the police, the district attorney and the sitting magistrate was done in obedience to the explicit statutory direction. He argued that because Miss Borden responded to the subpena her testimony was voluntary, ignoring altogether the fact that she was taken by the city marshal, and that she had no adviser to warn her that she need not go unless she so chose, and ignoring the furthermost pregnant fact that the

Warrant for Her Arrest

was quietly reposing in the commonwealth's pocket ready for just that emergency.

Mr Moody made the ingenious plea that, as Miss Borden's testimony was in the nature of a denial, rather than confession, the law bearing upon the admission of confession was not applicable to this case. I was interested in following the peculiar bent of the young man's mind, shown not only in the argument immediately referred to, but in this, namely, that many rules in respect to criminal law were made at a time when the accused had not the right to testify in his own behalf. He insisted that if the present question were to arise in the state of New York the evidence offered would be admitted, and argued strenuously that the only question which occurred to his mind for the serious consideration was whether the testimony given by Miss Borden was voluntary or compulsory.

Gov Robinson replied at considerable length, covering the precise ground so far as Miss Borden's condition is concerned, taken by me in my dispatches printed Sun-

went, had no protection, save that afforded by the constitution of the commonwealth and the amended constitution of the United States itself.

"If this," said he, "is freedom, God save the commonwealth of Massachusetts. If this be freedom, compulsory must here-after be known as voluntary."

DR DOLAN EXAMINING THE SPREAD.

It pears by the evidence that although the city marshal had a warrant for

Miss Borden's Arrest

in his pocket during the entire inquest procedure, the literal arrest was made by virtue of a subsequent warrant, on which Mr Robinson made a well directed thrust.

"They have," said he, "under oath sworn she had done the murders, but rather than serve it they said, 'We will hold the paper in our pockets and get what we can from her, and later if we decide to arrest her we will put away that paper,' worse than the burning of a dress, and literally arrest her on another warrant."

The profound sensation created by this characteristic point, admirably made by

Continued on the Second Page.

DIST ATTY MOODY—GOV ROBINSON'S ARGUMENT IS MAGNIFICENT, BUT IT ISN'T LAW.

End of the Borden trial: June 13, 1893.

June 14:

> "You've Given Me Away"
> Lizzie's Strange Words to her Sister in Police Station —
>   Matron Testifies
> For Two Hours Lizzie Would Not Talk Any More to Emma

June 15:

> Even So
> What if Lizzie Did Ask for Acid?
> Defense Claims That Proves Nothing
> State Says it Shows Murderous Intent

A druggist was prepared to testify that Lizzie had tried to buy prussic acid the day before the murders. But the defense persuaded the court to exclude this from the jury as irrelevant. The afternoon headline ended that move:

> Prussic Acid Shut Out
> Prosecutor Ends Case
> Lawyer Jennings Opens Defense
> Her Life History is Answer to Charge
> Mysterious Stranger Now Recalled

Next day:

> Borden Defense Rests
> Emma Testifies She Advised Lizzie to Burn Dress
> Paint-Soiled — Was Too Tight

June 17:

> Hopeful
> Lizzie's Counsel Sustained
> Arguments Probably be Heard Monday

Sunday was a between day:

> Guilty or Not?
> Fate of Lizzie Borden in the Balance
> Wherein Case Against Her is Weak

Tuesday, June 20, brought:

> Last Words in the Great Trial
> Ex-Gov. Robinson's Denial of Lizzie's Guilt Answered
>   by Dist. Atty. Knowlton's Able Argument

The last words took 35 columns. But the end was near.

Wednesday, June 21:

> Not Guilty
> Decision Reached on First Ballot
> Last Scene in the Great Borden Trial

Only some fringe advertising shared eight pages with the finale.

That afternoon the anti-climax:

> Jurors Say
> The Borden Case
> Broke Down of Itself
> Evidence of Defense Wasn't Needed

Next morning's paper concluded:

> Her Old Home
> Lizzie Borden Returns to its Refuge

Her Future Uncertain
Church and Charity May Claim Her
Loyal Friends Firm in their Support
Search for the Guilty Will be Resumed

It never was.

Globe circulation averaged 198,000 for that year.

Color, Contests, and Comics

The Globe by 1892 had direct telephone communication with its New York correspondent, officed in the World building. It had the first soundproof telephone booth in a Boston newspaper. It claimed to have reached 200,000 circulation that fall; whatever the figure was, it topped all Boston circulations and hit a peak not attained again until the end of that decade, when the Spanish-American War brought a temporary bulge in all newspaper circulations.

Intervening was the long depression of the 1890's. The price of newsprint fell with all other prices, from $40 to $35 a ton, to rise again with the war demand at the end of the decade. Cheaper newsprint and bigger presses sustained fatter newspapers as advertising grew apace and with it the need for more features, larger staffs, more space, and more elaborate distribution systems.

To meet the space need the Globe acquired the Chandler Building, adjacent to the rear on Devonshire Street, in 1892. This second annex, described in a full-page article September 10, 1893, permitted enlargement of all facilities, to include a new telegraph room with space for ten telegraphers to receive the ceaseless stream of news flow.

The new building allowed space to introduce the first linotype machines, which speeded typesetting for the bigger papers. Some of the other papers had had them already for two years. The Globe put in ten early in 1894 and had 30 by the end of the year. Typewriters for reporters came in at the same time. Soon a notice to contributors on the letters column advised: "Typewritten copy will always have the preference." The old-time reporters continued to fist out their copy by pencil. But new hands were required to use the new typewriters. This did more than provide legible copy; it made it possible for the desk to determine quickly and with reasonable accuracy what the volume of copy was that they would have to accommodate or cut.

For distribution, fleets of horse-drawn trucks fanned out to all the railroad terminals and on direct hauls out to the further suburbs. The seven morning and nine evening editions were scheduled to meet train departures for the more distant areas and to stagger the load on the presses. But every new deadline gave a chance to replate with any new story or, in the absence of one, to rearrange the front page to look new.

In those horse and wagon days 30 to 35 wagons distributed the papers within Greater Boston. Stables were located at strategic points. A dozen to 15 wagons would leave a stable on Dorchester Avenue for the Globe's Devonshire Street side to carry bundles of papers to the post office, the railroad stations, and the narrow-gauge ferry for East Boston and Revere. The main stable was in the South End at Tremont and Northampton Streets, others were in Charlestown, Somerville, East Boston, and Cambridge. The Wilson, Tisdale Company, an autonomous organization that manned its own paint and body shops and did the horseshoeing and harness work, operated this system. They began changing over to trucks just before the first world war, at first mounting their wagon bodies on truck chassis. By 1922 they were completely motorized. The farther wagon deliveries were handled by the Hotel & Railroad News Company, which also distributed the other newspapers. It was merged with the Wilson, Tisdale Company in 1953; the Globe then established its own delivery system.

Streetcars were also used, and wagons picked up the paper bundles at the end of the car lines. Streetcars were loaded at night, originally in Post Office Square, later at Dock Square, then on Hanover and Portland Streets, with the morning papers. But streetcars had no room for newspapers in the day time, so the evening papers were distributed by train to points where wagons picked them up. With the decline of railroads, trucks have taken over most of the delivery. The same delivery organization now supplies nearly 100 trucks to carry Globes all over New England.

Achieving circulation supremacy was only part of the battle. It was necessary also to convince advertisers that this Johnny-come-lately paper had as much to offer as the older papers. The Herald remained a strong competitor. The Journal, still the staunch Republican organ, had a considerable renaissance now that Stephen O'Meara, who'd begun as a young reporter with the beginning of the Globe, was its able editor. The moribund Advertiser had salvaged its continuance by launching a sprightly evening paper, the Record, whose one-cent price and lively style forced the ailing Traveller into a change of ownership in 1894 and drove it down to one cent. Between them enough was added to the competitive situation to offset the rapid population rise of the metropolitan area. A new competitor loomed in the morning. In 1891, E. A. Grozier, who had had his prentice years on the Globe and then served Joseph Pulitzer, first as secretary and then as one of his rising editors, had come back to Boston and bought the Post. That paper had become almost defunct, ruined and looted by a stockjobbing promoter. Grozier introduced a Boston variant of New York's yellow journalism, set an undercutting price of one cent with a cheap advertising rate, and took a political stance more militantly Democratic than the Globe. The new Post was only a marginal factor for the first few years but in five years had picked up 125,000 circulation, a base from which it was to zoom two decades later to the biggest circulation of any morning paper in the country.

Grozier now moved the Post from Milk Street onto Washington, next door to the Herald and Traveller, opposite the Globe. So in the early 1890's Newspaper Row was completed — on one side the Globe, Advertiser-Record, Journal, and Transcript and opposite the Herald, Post, and Traveller.

The sedate Transcript, a little further up on the corner of Milk Street, was hardly a factor in the struggle for mass circulation. It was solidly established with its cultivated Proper Bostonian clientele, and now under George Mandell, who inherited the control from his father in 1890, it grew in prosperity and distinction. This even though Mandell held off using photographs so as not to outrage the sensibilities of the aging treasurer, William Durant, until Durant departed the scene at 87 in 1903;

Durant felt strongly that esteem for the Transcript was due largely to the fact that it did not print pictures. But the Transcript's affluent circulation, at this time about 20,000 and never to go much above 30,000, was self-limiting. This was not one of General Taylor's problems, nor Tom Downey's, now in charge of a consolidated counting room, as they exploited every avenue of promotion for the Globe. They were spending $15,000 to $20,000 a year advertising in other papers, which was exceptional at that time. They constantly published the Globe's circulation on the "ears" of the upper corners of the front page and ran big bold face office ads within the paper every month or so to show their gains over the other papers both in circulation and advertising linage. On January 16, 1893, the top of the editorial page featured an announcement that for the year 1892 the Globe had carried 5,924,-000 lines of advertising, 458,000 more than the Herald.

The Globe especially advertised the bigger and bigger Sunday paper, with its ever-increasing variety of features. The Sunday paper was 36 pages by 1894. It had a fully developed household department, which in 1895 was carried over into the daily paper. It ran the syndicated humor of Bill Nye, M. Quad's Mr. Bowser, and Peter Finley Dunne's Mr. Dooley, which General Taylor had enthusiastically encouraged Dunne to syndicate.

Color came to the Sunday Globe in 1894 with the fourth big Hoe quadruple press, which had a color cylinder. Big ads in November announced "The Sunday Globe in Color." The first color supplement, November 25, 1894, was of four pages, featuring color photographs. From it quickly developed a Sunday magazine, usually eight pages in that period with the first two or four in color, the others with fiction, fashions, popular music, words and notes. Halftones came in at the same time. That spring O'Meara's Journal achieved a first in Boston by publishing 21 halftone pictures on May 6.

A novelty in the new color for the Sunday Globe was an insert of cut-out dolls: a doll and three dresses and a hat, lithographed on light-weight cardboard. The dresses one Sunday were a summer dress, a lawn dress, and a little girl's dress. "The Hit of the Season," a Globe ad claimed in 1895. "A new doll every Sunday — 200 combinations of costumes."

Color soon brought the color comic supplement on Sunday. In 1897 Rudolph Dirks started his strip "The Katzenjammer Kids," which soon appeared in the Globe as "The Captain and the Kids." Two years later a staff artist, Ed Payne, created a set of characters, "Kitty and Danny," "Billy the Boy Artist," and "Prof. O. How Wise," who peopled the Sunday Globe's color comics pages until Payne's death in 1955.

The Sunday circulation soared phenomenally right through the depression of the nineties. From 123,000 in 1887 it reached 246,000 in 1896. Its price held to five cents and the daily's, morning and evening, to two. What supported all this was the modern industry of advertising.

The growing size of the newspapers was an index to the rise of advertising. In 1880 advertising had accounted for 44 percent of the Globe's revenue; by 1889 it made 54 percent. Part of this changed ratio was because the larger-sized papers were still sold at the old price, 12 pages now instead of eight daily, 36 Sunday instead of 12–16. The more flexible makeup permitted ads of more than one-column width. Probably it would be more realistic to say that the demands of advertising pushed out the column lines. Instead of the earlier "notices" of an inch or two,

THE BOSTON SUNDAY GLOBE—JANUARY 19, 1930

local stores now took whole half pages or sometimes whole pages. On April 1, 1892, an ad for hats made a strip all across the bottom of page one, with pictures of six men wearing hats of different styles. A clothing ad thrust up a third of the page, four columns wide. The top lefthand four columns was an ad for Sarsaparilla. This presents a makeup horror but evidence of the new strength of advertising.

National advertising was expanding and introducing new products. The biggest ads of the eighties were largely for patent medicines, hair restorers, and such bromides. On April 1, 1889, the back page was dominated by two big ads:

> Debility
> Paine's Vegetable Compound

and

> Rogers Royal Herbs
> The Wonderful New Remedy

But the nineties brought the names of packaged breakfast foods into such daily prominence as to make them household words: Postum — Grape Nuts — Force — Aunt Jemima's Pancakes. By 1902, Sunny Jim was a million-dollar advertising account.

Uneeda Biscuit early became a familiar of the ads, and Eastman Kodak. Probably the best-known dog in America by the close of the 1890's was the one that appeared in the Victor phonograph ads, ear cocked to "His Master's Voice."

This was fast changing the economy of journalism. Newspapers from small enterprises became big business and brought into being such ancillary enterprises as syndicates to provide features for their hungry columns. Journalism was becoming an industry. Its work was becoming regularized. In 1894 Globe reporters, already on a two-platoon system separating morning and evening paper staffs, went on a six-day week. This the staff credited to the humane instincts and persuasiveness of the city editor, and they presented Sully with a pair of field glasses inscribed "One Day a Week."

Circulation areas extended from the city deep into the countryside with the passage in 1897 of Rural Free Delivery. The daily paper could now reach the farm and soon displaced the weekly edition. The Globe discontinued its weekly in 1892.*

The climate of challenge in Boston's overnewspapered competition was ready-made for General Chas. H. Taylor. He was a natural promoter, and he promoted every kind of thing in the Globe. Sports lent themselves particularly to promotion, with prizes; in the next decade the Globe promoted the beginning of aviation with a $10,000 prize for the first flight down to Boston Light and back. All these promotions promoted Globe circulation. Years later General Taylor said he didn't think highly of contests — which the Globe in its maturity dropped — they "caused people to run from paper to paper" and "disappointed more people than they could please," he said. But in the nineties he was up to his neck in contests.

The first one arose in 1889 out of a joint project of two Globe writers, city editor Montague and drama critic Dyar, to do a mystery novel for a Globe serial, "Written in Red." It occurred to somebody to omit the last chapter and offer a $200 prize to the reader who contributed the most fitting finale. There were 12,000 responses.

This seems to have whetted the office appetite for contests. Next season the G.A.R. was holding its annual encampment in Boston. The General, a great G.A.R. man, launched a contest for "the most popular G.A.R. man in the country" and offered a $1,000 gold sword to the winner. Voting was by coupons printed in the Globe. The idea sold like hotcakes and sold Globes all over the region. The Traveller came in lamely with a companion contest for the most popular member of the Women's Relief Corps. Midway in the seven-week contest, the Traveller charged that police were coercing liquor establishments to collect Globe votes for a Capt. Martin L. White, of Station 5. Investigation prompted by Mayor Matthews pointed higher up than the Captain. Police Commissioner William M. Osborne was himself a contestant. Matthews had him up before the governor and council on charges of permitting police pressure to collect votes for him. The hearings showed that police were indeed evidencing active interest in the G.A.R. contest, which the Globe reported with enthusiasm. The state-appointed police commissioner was a bête noire of the Globe's home rule principles, anyway. They couldn't lose on this one.

> Busy Police
> Cut Out the Coupons in Station Two
> Globes Were Plenty at Headquarters
> But Some Were Not for Osborne

In fact more were for Fire Commissioner Richard F. Tobin, a senior vice commander of the G.A.R. who won the gold sword.

Commissioner Osborne was acquitted of any impropriety. His counsel, ex-Gov. George Robinson, produced good copy for the Globe in his argument: "The Globe contest precipitated public excitement. Papers were full of it. Streets were alive

---

* Daily newspapers usually had developed from weeklies and usually continued their weekly editions to mail subscribers. This was profitable, for the weekly content was made up from type already set for the daily. The Globe started a weekly edition of eight pages at five cents a copy or $2 a year in January 1873. An energetic selling campaign was put on in 1877 that brought its circulation to 10,000, more than the daily. The books showed revenues from weekly sales of $16,820, and expenses assigned were $12,718; so it made its contribution in that year of overall deficit. The Sunday Globe, started October 1877, and the rapid rise of local weekly newspapers in that period must have steadily diminished the weekly edition.

The Globe Man.

about it. Men, women and children were at work about it, and it was not an unusual sight, as you probably know, to see people in the streets carrying scissors in their pockets by which they could cut coupons from the Globe which some friend would let them have for that purpose . . . Why, it would seem as if people for the time being had gone daft trying to find out the most popular Grand Army man." The Globe reported that 5,000,000 vote coupons were submitted in that contest.

Then came a Christmas contest with a whole series of categories, for the most popular saleswoman, teacher, mechanic, fireman, lettercarrier, etc. A saleslady at Jordan Marsh won a $3,500 house. A teacher won a 70-day all-expenses-paid trip to Europe.

In the 1892 election the Globe offered a guessing contest over the number of votes to be cast in New York State for Cleveland and Harrison. The prize was $5 a week for life. It was won by a young Boston bookkeeper, Lewis M. Woodbridge, who submitted 10,000 entries ($200 worth of Globes for the coupons). When he died in 1948 in Bath, Maine, he had received $14,560 prize money.

Then came the great 1893 World's Fair in Chicago. The contest for the most coupons to win a trip to the fair brought in 7,000,000 votes that took a special force of 50 people to handle and brought the Globe an announced circulation rise of· 29,000. Forty-eight winners were sent to the fair.

Contests were also used to stimulate advertising. The Sunday Globe of December 27, 1891, offered a gold watch for the want ad drawing the largest response. The winner, announced the following Sunday, drew more than 500 replies.

The Herald that year offered a ten-volume set of the *Americanized Encyclopaedia Britannica* for a year's subscription and an additional payment of $2 a month for 12 months. The Globe responded with an offer of the full ninth (1891) edition (25 volumes) for 15 coupons from the Globe plus $1.50 a volume, and denounced the Herald's "Americanized" edition as a fake.

In 1893 the Globe had a composing room force of 110 days and 98 nights. The contract with the typographical union was still based on piece rates, 45 cents to set 1,000 ems; but when called for hourly work, compositors were guaranteed 1,200 ems or 54 cents an hour, with the rate half again as much for matter set in half measure and double rate for setting stock tables and more demanding composition. "Waiting time" was paid 40 cents an hour.

Piece rates continued to appear in contracts up to 1938. But by 1898 the primary basis of pay was an hourly rate at a minimum of $23.10 for a week of 42 hours for the morning paper, $21 for the evening paper, and overtime at 75 cents an hour.

By 1899 the work week was figured as 40 hours for $24 for the morning paper, with overtime still at 75 cents an hour. In 1902 the rate had changed only slightly, $24.36 and 80 cents. The work week had returned to 42 hours. It was still 42 hours in the 1911 contract at an hourly rate of 63 cents for day work and 67 cents for nights, for a weekly base pay of $26.46 and $28.14; overtime was 82 cents an hour days and 87 cents nights.

The stability of these rates over a period of 18 years reflects the long depression of the 1890's and the stable price level of the first decade of the 1900's, indeed, up to the first world war.

Total weekly earnings obviously depended on the amount of overtime work, which was always a factor, usually a substantial factor, in total earnings. The stipulated hours a week (40 or 42) was not so much a limit to the week's work as a guarantee of that much work and the point at which overtime began.

The 1897–98 contract says: "Not less than 36 nor more than 42 hours shall constitute a week's work and when practicable a week's work shall consist of six days of seven hours each . . . all hours over ten in any one day and 42 in one week shall be counted as overtime." In 1902 all hours over nine a day were counted as overtime and in 1911 all hours over eight. In 1969 it was all hours over seven and a quarter in a five-day week of 36¼ hours.

The early contracts dealt almost entirely with hours and pay scales for journeymen and apprentices. An arbitration clause was introduced in 1898. The whole contract was printed in 32 inches of column-wide newspaper body type in 1893 and had grown only to 34 inches in 1911. Contracts became increasingly detailed and complex after 1946 and by 1968 took 315 inches of type, ten times the length of 1893. The 1968–69 contract, printed in a pocket-size book four by five inches, had 70 pages, two of which were taken up with the index of 59 sections or subjects covered. This was just for the one compositors' union contract.

Globe Wins on Elections

Governor Russell's elections — 1890, 1891, 1892 — were all close. Any election that the Democrats were going to win would be close in those days and for a long time after. The third Russell election, in 1892, a Republican year, was so close that some Boston papers didn't concede it till Thursday. But the Globe felt secure late Tuesday night. Its figures next morning were only 50 off the official returns. Russell squeaked in by 3,000.

General Taylor had his own Globe system on elections that early became one of the strengths of the paper that built prestige for it even among the sedate who considered it sensational. The politicians themselves came to rely on the Globe on election night, and it saved them from many a premature celebration. In 1911 all papers but the Globe issued election night figures electing Republican Louis Frothingham governor. The Republican headquarters was gearing up for a victory celebration when George Holden Tinkham, Back Bay congressman, arrived with the word that the Globe had Governor Foss re-elected. Foss was re-elected.

It remained for the Wilson-Hughes election of 1916 to establish Globe election returns beyond cavil: it was the only paper in the country that reported the election as in doubt and continued to for three days until the last precinct in California elected Wilson. What saved the Globe from the common error in such a national election was General Taylor's bump of caution and his political experience, combined with James Morgan's realistic appraisal of the situation in the doubtful states.

But on Massachusetts state elections the Globe system was based on science and organization.

The vote count is never completed between the closing of the polls and the deadlines of morning newspapers. They project an estimate from the returns that are in and what they know or believe about the part that is still out. This works well enough in a sweep but can go way off in a close one.

The Globe system in brief was based on percentages. Chas. Taylor had worked it out by 1883, and from then on he presided every election night for the rest of his life over the Globe's vote compilation. But the preparation had started long before election day. It took close work for a small corps of people for weeks, even months, and then the mobilization of the whole office and all its friends to operate it on election night.

The Globe system was to find a base line in the previous election, the vote for governor or senator, and prepare a full set of books that put down his vote in every precinct. Then the new figures could be compared with the old, precinct by precinct. The election count would come in unevenly. The cumulative vote would mean nothing. It might all be coming from Democratic cities or from Republican towns. What did mean something was a precise comparison of what was in with what the same precincts did last time.

If the Republican candidate won last time when he ran four percent ahead in the reported precincts and now was five percent ahead, clearly he would be in if he kept up this pace; keeping tally on every new set of returns would tell if he was. If he lost last time when he ran even in the towns that were in, and was now doing less than even, clearly he was in trouble unless the trend changed.

Keeping close tabs would show if it changed and where, and show at all times what areas were unreported. Telephone calls could nudge correspondents to try to speed up the returns or find out what was holding them up. More important, the system showed whether the missing territory was Republican or Democratic. If half a town's precincts were in, that gave a pretty fair line on that town; the local correspondent could tell the political complexion of the part not in — which side of the railroad tracks was still to come.

If, finally, certain late-reporting cities or suburbs had made no reports by edition time, the system told their performance in the previous election and so about what to expect from them. If a candidate led by 50,000, were there any areas unreported that could make that up?

That roughly was the system. The General and Mr. Morgan, their accountants and bookkeepers from the business office — the slide-rule men as the office called them — huddled in a quiet office, usually with a few of the General's business friends, to receive copies of all bulletins and keep up a continuous estimate and surveillance. Word would come out to call Springfield with a question, or check the Worcester third ward figures again.

The rest of the office would be organized around tables, each provided with a complete book of the last election figures by precincts. Each table had one segment of the operation. The state was divided into three parts, Boston, outside cities, and towns, the general complexion of which was fairly well known. If a Democrat didn't carry Boston by 30,000 or 40,000 (in later years 100,000) he was going to be in trouble upstate. If a Republican was not piling up a comfortable lead in the towns he would be swamped in Boston.

A further subdivision assigned separate election crews at tables for governor, senator, and congress and for legislature, executive council, and so on. So everybody had his particular part, and the table captains, from previous experience, became expert on their segments.

The political writers hovered about to follow the night's trend. But they also could be called upon to give a judgment on some riddle in the returns. What caused the bulge in Fall River? Had the governor done anything to alienate Berkshire? The figures, localized, told the political specialist as much as a chart tells a navigator.

The processed vote as it accumulated was dispatched to strategic desks on multi-duplicated slips, white, green, blue, yellow, the color telling whether they went to the copy desk, composing room, political editor, bulletin board or, in later years, radio or television announcer. Everything prepared, prearranged, precise, to be fitted finally into its appropriate table in the paper.

The system worked. It was ultimately very generally adopted. The Globe held to the same process, refined by improved machines and adapted to a larger vote, a later count, and changing political patterns in the state. Long after General Taylor election night was institutionalized. The publisher and the editor and "the slide-rule boys" in their back room stayed up with the vote tally till the paper had gone to bed. The rule was that if by midnight a candidate was leading by three percent it was safe to call him elected. For less than that the headline was "leading."

With such ritualistic precision came conditioning in caution. The Globe didn't hesitate to say for the first edition headline only "Republican Leading" if there was any uncertainty that the lead might not hold up through the night. Even in 1944 when the New Deal was winning its fourth straight election, Mr. Morgan, at 83, was to say at first edition time, "let's wait for Minnesota."

The community knew that the Globe waited to be sure. In 1920, with Republican leaders gathered in confidence of Harding's victory, old Senator Lodge unloosed the jubilee with the word: "General Taylor's election figures are the best in the United States. He says Harding has won." Two years later Lodge's own last election was in such doubt that many believed the Democrat, Col. William Gaston, had won. The Globe said Lodge had squeaked by with a bare 7,000 margin, and so he had.

In 1940, a presidential year when the Democrats swept the state for president and senator, the Globe system early detected that Governor Saltonstall was breaking the pattern, running far ahead of his ticket. It called Saltonstall elected even though large areas of Democratic strength in the cities were still unreported. The Post all night had been electing the Democrat, Paul F. Dever, by radio and in print. At press time, Dever was making unexpected gains in the tide of late city returns where the Democrats had put on a big registration drive. The Globe made an arbitrary cut in the lead assigned Saltonstall but stuck with its basic calculation that he had won. He proved the one Republican survivor of a Democratic sweep.

This was the one time that Lucien Thayer, in charge of the election crew, remembers going home worried about the Globe results. His anxiety woke him after an hour's fitful sleep and he called the office at 7 A.M. "Go back to bed," said Al Monahan, who'd taken over the relief from Thayer. "That bulge for Dever was because the AP put 10,000 Brockton votes for Saltonstall in the Dever column."

The extrordinary care and prudence of the Globe's election coverage provided sinews of strength in public confidence through all its history. It had also side effects. It gave credibility to General Taylor's profession of wanting his news columns to be unbiased, and it must always have had an influence on the staff that the organization from top to bottom turned on such immense effort for accuracy and fairness in this fundamental matter of the people's vote.

A generation after the General, a young reporter on the Globe was impressed to hear friends on the Transcript say that the Transcript exempted the Globe from its rule that any news picked up from another newspaper must be checked before using. "We know the Globe has checked it."

Family Business

Eben D. Jordan died November 15, 1895. He still owned the larger part of Globe stock, but by earlier agreement General Taylor purchased from the Jordan estate enough shares to give him an exact half. The General himself was a trustee of the Jordan estate, so the relation between the two halves of ownership continued the intimate one that had existed between Charles Taylor and Eben Jordan.

Both men in their wills appointed three trustees and both stipulated that on the death of one the other two could select his successor. This created self-perpetuating trusts, a protection from outside influence.

In the two-column editorial that he signed, "The Death of Eben D. Jordan,"

General Taylor explicitly acknowledged his debt to the merchant who had supported his newspaper enterprise.

> When I took charge of the Boston Globe in 1873, it had sunk $100,000 and was losing $60,000 a year. A second hundred thousand was raised and sunk. Then followed a third $100,000 and the turning point of money-making had not been reached. These dollars were buried in the Globe between 1873 and 1878. Every one of the original stockholders whom I found here in 1873 dropped out during this trying period except Eben D. Jordan. He alone believed that I would win and stood by me even when the battle seemed almost hopeless. No amount of debt or trouble could shake his confidence. In the darkest hours his nerve was strongest . . . It was not so much the material aid which he furnished me from time to time, but his encouraging words, his undaunted spirit and his infusion of courage . . . Now that he has passed away I feel impelled publicly to express my lasting obligation to him for his priceless service to me. I know that he did it without any mere sordid motive. He became interested in and believed in me by an accidental business association and wanted me to succeed in the profession I had chosen. I say he did not do it for any hope of pecuniary reward, for he was a rich man at the time and I never knew a man who cared less for money for money's sake or for what it would secure . . . He helped me as he did others from a sympathetic quality that led him to aid those who came across his path . . .

By now the continuity of Taylor management, which was to be so strong a characteristic of the Globe, was already visible in the office. All three of the General's sons had gone to work at the Globe, as their sons were to do after them.

They had been in the office as boys, summers and after school. Charles, Jr., had taken a year off at Harvard in 1888 because of illness. His health restored, he decided against going back to college and instead worked a season on the New York World, then came back to apply his Pulitzer journalism lessons at the Globe. By January 1890 he was being called assistant managing editor, but when that title was needed for James Morgan four months later, Charles went downstairs as assistant business manager. The second son, William O., completed Harvard in 1893 and joined the business office. The year before, John I. had come on in the city room; but he soon went downstairs to work on want ads, which the Globe was pushing to rapid expansion. John's interests proved less journalistic than his older brothers. So when in 1904 the General bought the Boston Red Sox, John became president of the baseball club.

The younger Taylors joined the management team with Tom Downey, who headed the whole counting room operation but concerned himself especially with the vast and complex circulation. Edward Dunbar was advertising manager. As things shaped up, William O. was to have the title of business manager, Charles of treasurer and manager. Charles's interests were general, his talents versatile. He quickly became expert in typography and designed a type font for the paper known as Taylor Gothic. He took a special interest in developing the embryonic engraving department. Among other things he took on labor relations, for which his hearty nature, ready laugh, good fellowship, and democratic spirit seemed to qualify him. In a few years he led in organizing the New England Arbitration Association, whose aim was good labor relations.

The Globe's were good, as was manifest early and often. The General had instituted an annual staff dinner with the opening of the new building in 1887. Everybody was invited and as many came as could get away from work. In 1889, with a total organization of 991 there were 555 at dinner. These were convivial occasions. The staff provided their own entertainment, with quips and jokes and poems and speeches. At the first Globe dinner the head of the typographical union was moved to make a speech about General Taylor as a good employer, noting that one way the General had celebrated the new building was to give a raise all around. Such encomiums continued through the years until the Taylor homes must have been cluttered with gifts from one department of the paper or the other, appreciatively inscribed.

"The Boston Globe is the best paper on the continent to work for if light work, human treatment and an always open door to the managing editor's office count for anything," commented The Journalist, a trade paper in New York, December 24, 1892.

With prosperity the General had moved his family to Beacon Street, and in 1896 he acquired a summer home with a generous shoreline on Buzzards Bay under the shoulder of Cape Cod. All sailors, the Taylors took to the Cape and its ways. Charles, Jr., particularly soon counted himself an authority on the Cape as on ships and maritime affairs. He was all his life insistent on the Globe's accuracy in all maritime and Cape Cod matters.

Harry Poor, night editor for the first third of the twentieth century, always remembered a tart note from CH Jr to the effect that the Thachers of Cape Cod spelled their name with only one T. Charles was always the most acute critic of the paper. He kept the typography under daily surveillance and shot off memos every morning to the department responsible for typos and errors in spelling and proper names or any other bugs or boners that caught his critical eye. When his brother William O. joined the business office in 1893, Mr. Fowle observed that that would give Charles more time to dispatch his daily cryptic notes around the office to point out trespasses. William O., strictly business, always left such vagaries to Charles. If a staffer sought approval of a piece of copy that concerned the business department, William O. would say: "Show it to my brother Charles. He's the journalist."

Technically the Globe was moving ahead. When in 1893 the New York World announced that it had instituted the first photo-engraving plant of any newspaper, Charles Taylor, Jr., vigorously protested. The Globe that year had spent $30,000 on its engraving department, which Charles had had under his direction in his brief period as assistant managing editor in 1890. His interest in its development had continued when he moved into the business office and was in a position to provide for it. He insisted that the Globe in 1886 had set up the first photo-engraving plant in the country. It remained outside the Globe building, for lack of space, until the new building in 1887 could accommodate it.

The Globe's pioneering photo-engraving was located in Chatham Row, in the market district. Messengers carried engravings and copy to the paper. Morgan J. Sweeney, who had been a commercial artist and engraver, was in charge from the start. Sweeney was probably the creator of the first Globe cartoons, signed Boz, as far back as 1876. The Globe Man was his creation. In 1885 Sweeney was joined by a 20-year-old snapshot photographer, John W. Butters, Jr., who in later years developed and headed the department. Butters made pictures and also processed and engraved them.

Purchase of the Chandler Building in 1892 allowed the engraving department to move into this adjacent building. Engravings were then delivered to the composing room over an especially constructed connector walk between the buildings. When the old Advertiser Building was acquired the engraving department was moved there, in 1903. Now on the Washington Street side, with no gap between abutting buildings, it was in a better geographical position to serve the composing room and remained there until the Globe moved from Newspaper Row in 1958.

The photo-engraving department's equipment and quarters remained limited and awkward until, in 1923, John F. Maguire, who had grown up as an apprentice in the department, introduced modern equipment for both photographers and engravers and a retraining program to catch up with advances in the craft.

The composing room members had organized in 1884 the Globe Relief Association, with the superintendent, Robert P. Boss, as president. They chipped in 25 cents a week to a fund to aid members in illness or their families in deaths. In 1888 the editorial department members established the Globe Mutual Aid Association, which was incorporated in 1892 with Charles H. Taylor, Jr., managing editor Arthur Fowle, and city editor William D. Sullivan among the incorporators. Charles

The stereotype department in 1903.

Junior had joined both these office organizations as soon as he joined the paper — a characteristic Taylor gesture, to belong to whatever was important to the staff. Office marriages further enhanced the "Globe family" spirit. Charles's marriage to Marguerite Falck, a niece of managing editor Fowle, in 1890 occasioned a big Globe party, as did other weddings, notably William O.'s to Mary Moseley soon after he had joined the paper. The marriages of Allen Kelly to Florence Finch and Sam Merrill to Estelle Hatch of the Household Department were only the first of interstaff weddings. There was a good deal of conniving to get James Morgan married. His editorial assistant, Ned Burns, finally pulled it off by introducing Morgan to the right girl. In October 1894 James Morgan and Helen Daily of Cambridge were married; he was 32, she 19. This proved one of the most enduring and satisfying of marriages. Until his death 60 years later, Helen and James Morgan weren't separated a night of their married life. She became in effect James's secretary, accompanying him to political conventions and on assignments that carried them over much of the world, to translate his scrawl into legible script or typed copy.

General Taylor, with his editorial department in confident hands and his sons sharing the business work, relaxed. He was much in demand outside the office as an after-dinner speaker or toastmaster. The elite Algonquin Club was "a monument to his sagacity and enthusiasm and above all to his infinite capacity for friendship,"

The composing room in 1900.

William D. Sullivan.

said the club resolution on his retirement from 20 years of its presidency. His luncheon table at Young's Hotel, where he was surrounded by a group of business friends, soon had the name of the Taylor Club. Wherever the General sat was the head of the table. He now wore a full beard, black, and eyeglasses with a black ribbon that added distinction to a sharp eye and a serene countenance. He had the mien of the man in charge and a happy facility to share the enjoyment of good food and good talk.

An institution takes its tone and character from the men who make it; particularly is this true of a newspaper, whose personality is revealed every day. The Globe very definitely reflected its founder. A man of simple tastes and a friendly nature, a practical man, shrewd in his business judgments, the General believed in and literally applied the homilies that honesty is the best policy and that human nature will respond to confidence and kindness.

Now that he could shunt off the pressures of the office and give himself freedom for friendships and outside associations, General Taylor had occasion in talks and interviews to express his philosophy about journalism and human nature, and habitually he wove these together.* He was wholly aware, as he once put it, that "the natural temperament of the editor determines the tone of the newspaper he controls."

"My aim has been to make the Globe a cheerful, attractive and useful newspaper that would enter the home as a kindly, helpful friend of the family. My temperament has led me to dwell on the virtues of men and institutions rather than upon their faults and limitations. My disposition has been always to build up rather than

---

* General Taylor's journalistic principles and his aims for the Globe, voiced in numerous speeches and interviews, are quoted in pages 151–152 of James Morgan's biography, *Charles H. Taylor,* in a chapter entitled "The Creed of the Globe"; also in an article, "General Taylor's Views on a Newspaper's Duty," in the Globe June 22, 1921, the day of the General's death.

The General's emphasis on women readers is quoted in Morgan's biography and in *Addison Archer's Interviews,* a brochure of 1899 that describes the Boston newspapers at the turn of the century.

The introduction of the Uncle Dudley editorial, and the General's views on editorials, are described in Morgan's *Charles H. Taylor,* pp. 142–143.

to join in tearing down. My ideal for the Globe has been that it should help men, women and children to get some of the sunshine of life, to be perhaps a little better and happier because of the Globe."

This statement his sons and his staff accepted so wholly as the core of the General's philosophy that they printed it on every anniversary of his death, and when they built the present Globe building in 1958 they inscribed it in bronze in the entrance lobby. It was applied in the paper in all sorts of ways.

The General's rule for reporting elections was to say who won, not who was beaten. A cartoon of a public man, he said, should be one that his own wife would laugh at. "Never drag in the family of a man who has gone wrong; they are suffering enough as it is," he admonished his editors.

> Try never to print a piece of news that would injure an innocent person . . . There are two sides to every story; get both sides . . . We should never say that a man has refused to be interviewed. He has a right to refuse if he does not care to talk. Always treat a man fairly in the Globe so that you may meet him again and look him in the eye . . . A reporter must never break his word. If a man tells him something and stipulates it is not for publication, his wishes must be respected scrupulously. Never mind if the Globe does get scooped in such a case; honesty and fair dealing will win in the long run.

But he didn't claim to have all the answers, or to have built a perfect newspaper. "The ideal newspaper never has been published and never will be since all men in all walks of life seem to have about the average of virtues and faults. I fear that the people who sit down in idle despair over the modern newspaper will have to wait for a paper that is published only for angels and edited by archangels . . . The best way to get readers and the only way to hold them is to give them plenty of good reading matter."

His naturally cheerful disposition sought expression in the paper. "Let's lighten it up. I'd like to run a joke at the head of every column." He did get a daily story instituted as a feature of the editorial page. For a long time the daily anecdote or saying was tucked in to any corner of the page; on August 16, 1901, it was given a fixed place at the head of the first editorial column. On May 1, 1917, it was given a title, "Original and Stolen Thoughts," which on July 1, 1919, was changed to "Original and Stolen Stories." The first appearance of its lasting title, "Globe Man's Daily Story," was Saturday, July 12, 1919.

What William E. Brigham, long-time Washington correspondent of the Transcript, was to recall of the early years of the Globe was "its bright breezy conversational style." This breeziness was carried into editorials too. Even in its early partisan days the Globe's jousts with the Republicans were carried on often in a lighthearted badinage. General Taylor's view on editorials, which James Morgan translated to a later generation, was: never berate and never take a negative position. If you can't find a constructive approach to an issue, let that subject wait till you can.

The General's visits to the office now seldom went above the first floor, the business office. He had assumed the title editor and publisher when Colonel Bailey left the editorship in 1880. But he was rarely on the editorial floor after he had his editorial team established there. He dealt through the managing editor — a policy

The Boston Globe

Published by GLOBE NEWSPAPER COMPANY
242 Washington St. Boston. Mass,
(Established March 4, 1872. Evening edition first issued March 7, 1878. Sunday edition first issued Oct 14. 1877.)

MONDAY, NOVEMBER 2, 1936

SUBSCRIPTION RATES

	Daily		Sunday	
	Per Mo.	Per Yr.	Per Mo.	Per Yr.
Boston Postal Zone		9.00	.55	6.50
Zones 1. 2. 3 (including New York city and all New England except Northern Maine)	.50	6.00	50	6.00
Elsewhere in U. S. and Canada	80	9 60	70	8.40

(Please do not send cash. Use money orders or checks.)

BACK NUMBERS (Per Copy)

	Daily	Sunday
Under three months old	5c	15c
Three to six months old	10c	20c
Six to nine months old	15c	25c
Nine months to one year	25c	50c
More than one year old	Out of Print	

The Associated Press is exclusively entitled to the use for publication of all news dispatches credited to it or not otherwise credited in this paper and also the local news published herein. All rights of republication of special dispatches herein are also reserved.

Globe Man's Daily Story

Now they are saying that it was at the Union League Club in New York where two members sat next to each other and read for two hours without exchanging a word until one of them folded up his paper and remarked:

"Looks like rain."

An hour later the other member finished his paper and turned to his companion, now deep in pleasant somnolence, and replied:

"Sunny."

Be Prepared

Every two years thousands and t sands Massachusetts citizens emerg polling places feeling rather asham selves. It is not that they regret, at least, having voted for this or th for one of the more important offices places they were fully decided in ad their marks should be made. But opened the official paper they were ap number of preferences they were record. They saw positions of whi never heard and the nominees for were utterly strange to them. As th "X" marks through the list they were not measuring up to their obligations

Such a state of mind may be avc taining advance information. The M ballot was devised for independent vot states it is possible by making a sir vote an entire party ticket, but that is in this Commonwealth.

Most of those eligible to vote ton received at least one sample ballot. be examined with care. The person w decide the elective officials of his state tricts should be at sufficient pains to mind which candidates should be s down the line. By checking his deci sample ballot and taking it with hin sure of doing what he intends to do in

---

of restraint, of keeping Upstairs and Downstairs, editorial and business, separate entities and a policy of nonintervention that became Globe management tradition. But with it went editorial restraint through editors who had become imbued with the General's moderation and caution for keeping an even course.

The Sunday paper was 40 pages by spring 1895, and critics were writing about the oversized Sunday paper. On May 12 the Globe's lead editorial, two columns in that Sunday edition, was "The Size of the Sunday Paper," a defense of expansion of the paper to five times its orginal 1878 size. It recounted all the new features and new reader services.

That issue had a full page of "Scenes on the Subway" as work progressed on the first subway in America. A feature was headed "Society on the Wheel," with sketches of "approved costumes for fair riders" showing bloomers worn under short, flaring skirts. A feature on women's bathing suits was headed "New Smart Set Water Dresses for Fair Bathers." The illustrations showed pleated skirts, leg-o'-mutton sleeves, and long black stockings. A feature on "Boston Papers in Foreign Languages" was illustrated by the logotypes of half a dozen German and Swedish papers, mostly weeklies with the only daily the German Der Telegraph. The Sunday Globe circulation was 200,000, representing a gain of 17,000 in a year. The daily was 12 pages.

"No Free Puffs" — CHT Jr.

As business manager, Charles, Jr., quickly proved a vigilant protector of the Globe's financial interest. On March 31, 1893, less than three years after joining the office, he issued a confidential set of rules for the Globe staff that began:

> The columns of the Globe have of late contained evidence of a disposition on the part of many individuals and business concerns to secure free advertising under the pretense of furnishing news.
>
> This tendency is most marked in the case of persons who are not in the habit of patronizing the regular advertising columns of the paper.
>
> In order to obviate this evil and to protect the interests of the Globe's regular advertisers, the following rules have been adopted, and will be enforced in this office from this date.

There followed ten rules with many subdivisions:

> 1. Notices of an advertising nature must not appear in the news columns unless ordered by CHT or CHT Jr., whether they refer to Globe advertisers or not.
>
> Any item is a puff which is of more interest to the firm or person mentioned than to the general public.
>
> 2. All notices which would serve to advertise merchandise of any sort are to be treated as puffs. [This rule had 11 subdivisions.]
>
> 3. All notices which would serve to advertise individuals in respect to their trades or professions are to be treated as puffs . . .
>
> 4. All notices which would serve to advertise companies . . . are to be treated as puffs. [Seven subdivisions of this one, covering caterers, bands, hotels, entertainments, steamship and insurance companies, exhibitions, and prizes with a commercial tinge.]
>
> 5. Commendation or criticism of other papers in political speeches, interviews, etc., should not be used in news reports.
>
> 6. Libel suits against other newspapers must not be mentioned except by special orders.
>
> 7. Labor troubles of other Boston newspapers must not be mentioned unless the paper in question uses the matter as news.
>
> 8. Editorial courtesy should always be shown in referring to individuals connected with the staffs of other papers.
>
> 9. Mention of Globe employees and of members of their families should not be made in the paper except when of absolute news value.

Rules 5, 6, 7, and 8 are clearly of a different nature from the taboos on free advertising. They recognize newspapers' mutuality of interest in avoiding publicity to each other's troubles. Rule 9 was applied with special rigor to the Taylor family, and it required particular vigilance toward Charles himself, as his activities extended into the public domain. A lifelong cardinal rule of CH Jr was no puffs for Taylors. All the family supported this rule.

More than a quarter century later CH was still policing his rules against free advertising. Victor O. Jones, who later became executive editor, recalled one of his early experiences after joining the paper in 1929. As one of the corps of writers sent to the Harvard-Yale boat race, Jones's assignment was "crowds and color." To indicate the amount of celebrating the night before the race, he reported that next day all the New London drug stores were sold out of bromo seltzer. A memo from CH remonstrated that this was a trade name and Jones could have made his point by using "head ache remedy."

It was Jones who discovered the 1893 book of CH's rules, back in a drawer of a desk he inherited from Walter Barnes in 1933 on succeeding him as sports editor. He tendered it as a memo to Davis Taylor in 1968. The Globe publisher laughed: "Uncle Charles would certainly be having the shivers if he saw the trade names used by almost all newspapers today."

Confidential Chat

Of all the habit-forming features that hold readers to a newspaper, perhaps the most extraordinary is that department of the Boston Globe that carries the headline "Confidential Chat." It is an institution within an institution, a women's correspondence club. It has been running almost as long as the Globe.

"Confidential Chat" evolved from the first "Housekeepers' Column" of 1884, which a decade later Estelle Hatch had expanded into the first regular column about women's affairs in any newspaper. "New Recipe Feature" was the heading on the new department, which appealed to women readers to send in "true and tried recipes," started Sunday, October 28, 1894. "By this system of exchange the woman who sends in one recipe gets the benefit of all the others." Two days later appeared the first letter: "Mrs. E. A. B." sent her recipe for chocolate cream pie.

By the next spring the department had developed to include a letter on "Feeding the Baby," and contributors had begun to use pseudonyms — Dorchester, Dottie, A Young Housekeeper. The next year other subjects came in, "Crocheting, Knitting and Fancy Work," "Hints on Care of Flowers." The letters increased and the topics expanded. Readers discussed clothes, children, husbands, in-laws, neighbors, interior decorating. The letters spread over a page in the Sunday paper, then more than one page, and required several columns in the daily paper. "General Correspondence" was the heading until in January 1922 it was changed to "Confidential Chat" — which indeed it had become. The department had become a club in which women exchanged letters about their domestic problems and private lives. They wrote under such names as Chatters, Fireman's Wife, Aunt Chovis, Chere Julie. Decade after decade this anonymous correspondence went on. Some letters revealed that their grandmothers had been "chatters."

Sophisticated Globe reporters regarded the Confidential Chat department with amused disdain when they were not chafing at the space it took out of the news hole. Latter-day psychiatrists would doubtless have seen it as affording psychological release for limited lives. But as a newspaper feature it was not to be sneezed at. By 1955 some office calculator figured that Chat files contained 1,750,000 letters. By 1965 they were coming in at the rate of 2,000 a month. That summer "Confidential Chat" became a problem that required its editor to write a confidential letter to his contributors.

On Sunday, July 25, 1965, ten letters appeared all addressed to the same letter-writer, who had signed herself "Thank God Instead." They all rebuked her for having urged chat writers to stop whining about their troubles. The Globe reprinted the original letter and right away one could see why they had had to: it was dated February 14. The backlog was more than five months.

The department editor took a box on the page to explain and apologize:

> Dear Tarnished Halves and so many others — Indeed, that epistle by The Master ("Wife Loathes American Women") did bring in a swarm of letters! At long last they've been read and are moving toward print.
>
> A good number of the letters will be used, but many others, even though worthy of publication, will go through the mail to The Master (address, please). There were altogether too many LONG letters, which made the chore of selection more difficult. O, for the short, bright, pleasure-to-read letters!
>
> Likewise now read and soon to start on their way are many excellent letters to Kiddily ("No Real Solution to Days of Chaos"), Shiny Piggies (regarding clothes dryers), Troubled Stepmother (who asked for guidance in facing up to several problems with her stepchildren), and to Ann ("Let's Grow Up BEFORE Marriage!").
>
> In line, after the above letters make print within the next month or so, are excellent letters to I'm So Stupid (the grandmother who asked: "What Kind of Fool Am I?") and a barrage of letters addressed to Mrs. Apple Pie ("Clinging Vine Homebodies Strike Me as Irresponsible").
>
> And then I'll take a look at the more than 500 letters containing requests for advice and information from Chat readers — letters that we have deliberately held back in a drive to clear up a big backlog of letters answering earlier requests.
>
> Then some 1200 recipes are awaiting a reading after which many will start the journey into type.
>
> For sure, there's enough on hand right now to keep the Chat pot boiling for weeks to come!

Some higher-up must have spotted this about 500 letters and 1,200 recipes waiting to be printed, for a few weeks later the Sunday Globe included a special 24-page magazine supplement of Chat letters. Next season they had to do it again, to catch up.

One of the most explosive episodes in "Confidential Chat" was set off by a letter under the unlikely pseudonym of Urbancic Ert. On Sunday, July 26, 1964, she had six letters on the same page answering queries and challenges from Simmering Sue, Roller Coaster, Willing Spirit, Very Fine Grind, Well Fed, and Complaining Husbands. This was evidently a continuing story: a backward look at the files showed that Urbancic Ert had written no fewer than 20 letters that month. They all developed from a letter of hers the month before in which she told how she fed a family of five on $13.50 a week. They weren't undernourished and they

CONFIDENTIAL CHAT

Tell mom her bigger boys are bullying your son, 4

Dear **Domestic Engineer** —Regarding your problem with older children bullying your 4-year-old son, I wouldn't hesitate to ap- school to the point that he will be afraid of any child his age or otherwise, and of any new circumstance that he may have to en-

weren't sorry for themselves, she said. Indeed, a reason for this strict economy was that she and her husband, a college teacher, planned a trip to Europe.

She told how she managed, buying the cheaper cuts of meat, getting things only in season, making stews and casseroles and soups from leftovers, doing all her own cooking and baking and making minimum use of a canopener. She trained her children to clean up their plates, not to eat before mealtime, and so on.

This letter brought down a deluge on Urbancic Ert. Women protested it couldn't be done. Some denounced her for spending money on a trip to Europe that she was squeezing out of her children's proper food. To the contributors she was a traitor to her sex, a phoney, or just a plain liar.

Urbanic calmly answered them all. She explained that to a professor a trip to Europe would be of professional importance and to her culture was part of life; she didn't live by bread alone. She included little preachments on tolerance to some, and homilies on bringing up children so that they won't come to the table half full of candy and cokes saying they aren't hungry or "there's that rice pudding again."

Another dimension of "Confidential Chat" was revealed much later, by the murder of Martin Luther King. A letter was featured in a box in the department, Sunday, April 21, 1968. "What More Can We Do?" was its headline. "Today I carry a big burden of guilt," wrote Green Acres. "What can I do realistically? Changing people's attitudes is more necessary than changing laws. Who has some good practical ideas?"

Responses dominated the pages in subsequent weeks. On May 12 a letter began: "This is wonderful. Just to get some of these ideas out into the open. I too feel there is a sort of 'sin of omission' here . . . I am encouraged by these recent Chat eye-openers." The writer asked how to invite a Negro child for two summer weeks with her children.

Another letter that day began: "I am a colored mother who has shared your dreams, thoughts, recipes, problems and prayers for many years. I have never written but feel now that it is my duty to write . . . There are many things that can be done . . . Work on a person to person basis . . . We can all get along if we all really try. I've seen wonderful things come from the Chat pages. I give you my hand and heart. Will you do the same for me and mine?"

Opposite the Chat page that day, the Books Department started by featuring an article on "Literature Relevant to Black Children," its position and content quite evidently suggested by the women's letters. "Confidential Chat" had come out of the kitchen.

A touching episode from Chat annals was recounted by Maine author Louise Dickinson Rich in the Women's Home Companion in 1943, under the title "Grandma and the Sea Gull." The Globe obtained permission to reprint the article and published it in 1944 in a pocket-size booklet under the title "Arbutus and the Sea Gull." The essentials of the story in Miss Rich's words were:

> My grandmother had an enemy named Mrs. Wilcox. Grandma and Mrs. Wilcox moved as brides into next-door houses on the sleepy elm-roofed Main st. of the tiny town in which they were to live out their lives. I don't know what started the war — that was long before my day — and I don't think that by the time I came along, over 30 years later, they remembered themselves what started it. But it was still being waged bitterly . . .
>
> I don't know how Grandma could have borne her troubles if it hadn't been for the household page of her daily Boston newspaper.
>
> This household page was a wonderful institution. Besides the usual cooking hints and cleaning advice, it had a department composed of letters from readers to each other. The idea was that if you had a problem — or even only some steam to blow off — you wrote a letter to the paper, signing some fancy name like Arbutus. That was Grandma's pen name. Then some of the other ladies who had had the same problem wrote back . . .
>
> That's what happened to Grandma. She and a woman called Sea Gull corresponded for a quarter of a century, and Grandma told Sea Gull things that she never breathed to another soul — things like the time she hoped that she was going to have another baby but didn't, and the time my uncle Steve got you-know-what in his hair in school and how humiliated she was, although she got rid of them before anyone in town guessed. Sea Gull was Grandma's true bosom friend.
>
> When I was about 16, Mrs. Wilcox died. In a small town, no matter how much you have hated your next-door neighbor, it is only common decency to run over and see what practical service you can do the bereaved.
>
> Grandma, neat in a percale apron to show that she meant what she said about being put to work, crossed the two lawns to the Wilcox house . . . And there on the parlor table in the place of honor was a huge scrapbook, and in the scrapbook, pasted neatly in parallel columns, were her letters to Sea Gull over the years and Sea Gull's letters to her. Grandma's worst enemy had been her best friend.
>
> That was the only time I remembered seeing my grandmother cry.

"Confidential Chat" was always part of the Household Department, but in 1957 it was given its individual editor, Richard Elson, who presided over its letters until his death in 1967 — which brought the Globe a host of letters grieving as over a personal friend. Robert Allen then became its editor.

Bryan Upsets Gold Bugs — and the Globe

The Bryan campaign of 1896 was a landmark for the Globe as for eastern Democrats generally. Deep in depression, the privations of debtors, chiefly western farmers, had given rise to radical populism. Politically the issue had precipitated into an attack on the gold standard as the primary cause of deflation. "Free silver" was the cry of the western plains that urged coinage of silver on a 16 to one par with gold. Silver was also a western product. The free silver movement captured the Democrats of the west, encountered the resistance of business and conservatives of the east. Cleveland, a Democrat, was president and followed a conservative gold policy. The eastern gold bugs faced a crisis in the approaching Democratic convention in Chicago in July.

The gold men were dominant in the party in Massachusetts. The brilliant young party leader William Russell had withdrawn from politics in 1893, at 36, after having served four terms as mayor of Cambridge on a nonpartisan ticket and three terms as Democratic governor. At the personal urging of President Cleveland, Russell now re-entered the political arena to rally gold forces in the east. His national reputation made him a possible presidential nominee of the Cleveland Democrats. The Globe, the strong Democratic paper in New England, was all out for Russell and for gold; it actively promoted him as presidential timber. But on the eve of the convention a break came in the solidarity. Ex-congressman George Fred Williams came out for free silver.

In 1893, as chairman of the state platform committee, Williams had led in a plank renouncing free silver. But three years of depression changed his mind, as it had many another. He was a jealous rival of Russell for state party leadership, and the rivalry had grown bitter. Williams was now regarded as a maverick by the party orthodox. A zealous reformer but an abrasive personality, an irritant in party conclaves, he was persona non grata to General Taylor and the Democratic organization men. But he immediately became a hero of the silver men and he became prime news. His break with the gold bugs was the lead story in the Globe — as it brought the western populist movement right into the center of Massachusetts politics — and his course at the convention became a major thread of the Globe's voluminous reporting of that historic event. Russell became a leading participant in the great debate in which Bryan's famous "cross of gold" speech clinched the nomination for Bryan.

James Morgan led the Globe convention contingent, ably supplemented by the paper's distinguished Washington correspondent A. Maurice Low. John D. Merrill, state political editor, went from the State House to cover the activity of Russell and the state delegation. The Globe also had the columns of Joseph Howard. The convention, its prelude, and its aftermath dominated the front page and occupied several entire inside pages for a month that summer and intermittently through to November with its explosive political effects.

On July 2 the Globe editorially expressed "confidence there will be enough thinking delegates in Chicago . . . to refuse to be stampeded. The most dangerous men in the Democratic Party today are the men who would revolutionize its time-honored policy, defy the sentiments of the business public and make democracy sectional not national."

But that day's front page had an interview by M. E. Hennessy with George Fred Williams headed

> Popular Uprising
> And I Propose to be in it
> Said George Fred Williams
> Massachusetts Democrat Maverick
> Defies State Leadership
> Ostracism in Massachusetts

The preconvention headlines had no mention of Bryan. Richard Bland of Missouri, affectionately known as "Silver Dick," was the intellectual leader of the silver cause from his long leadership in Congress for silver coinage. But he lacked sufficient demagogic appeal to match the emotionalism of the silver crusade.

On July 2 the top head was "Democratic Dark Horses / Being Secretly Groomed for the Chicago Crisis." On July 3, "Bland Leads the List"; and on July 4, "Fight Begins / Gold Men Will Try to Save the Party."

"Uncle Dudley's Notions" that Sunday offered an essay for the status quo against "upsetting the financial regime."

July 6 the top head was "Bland Will Lead / Nothing Can Head Him Off." James Morgan wrote that day that "if a dark horse could be discovered, his fortune would instantly be made. Some people keep in mind William J. Bryan, the boy orator of the Platte. He has repeatedly offered his life for 16 to one. But there were no takers." and Bryan was taken in this light, slightly derisive tone by the eastern Democrats. But they were aware of him as a threat.

Next day Mr. Morgan was writing: "Convention day dawns with uncertainties denser than ever before in the memory of convention goers." He was already a veteran of conventions since 1884, and he covered them till 1944.

July 8, after the first session, the Globe head noted "Silver Men in Control"; July 9, "Bland and a 16–1 Plank / That is the Outlook at Chicago / Conservatives Ruthlessly Ridden Down."

But the score changed on that day, the day of the great debate on the platform. Next morning, July 10:

> Bland and Bryan the Favorites

Their two portraits occupied the top half-page. The Globe editorially noted: "The special feature [of the day before] was the enthusiasm displayed for William Jennings Bryan of Nebraska, whose speech for the free coinage plank made such a stir in the convention hall."

That evening edition told the story:

> Bryan the Convention Candidate.

Curiously, none of the Globe's star correspondents quoted a line of Bryan's famous speech. James Morgan quoted "Pitchfork" Ben Tillman, who played a character role, and Russell of Massachusetts, whose speech was concededly the most brilliant and effective on the gold side, and parts of others. He described the tremendous effect of Bryan's speech, sweeping all before him. But its eloquence evidently melted the pencils of the reporters. That evening partial texts of Bryan, Russell, and Hill were carried inside the Globe. Their headlines were labels: "Ex-Cong.

Bryan's Speech." A historian erodes his eyesight through the tiny type to the final sentence for the golden words that shook the Democratic party from its roots.

It was not until Monday, July 13, when Mr. Morgan had had time to get home and read the Chicago papers, that the Globe ran the full text of Bryan's speech under glowing headlines:

Won the Nomination
Speech Which Created a Candidate for the Presidency
William J. Bryan's Flow of Words Winding Up With the Metaphor of the Crown of Thorns and the Cross of Gold

The speech created a crisis for the Democratic Globe and proved a turning point in its history.

The General wired his political correspondent, who was also in effect his editorial director: "What do we say now?" Morgan replied: "Don't say anything." Morgan returned, as he told it in later years, "to hold onto the General's coat-tails all summer to keep him from going over to the other side of the street" — that is, to the Herald's Republican side.

Editorially the Globe immediately stated that it could not support Bryan. The lead Globe editorial July 11, 1896 was headed: "The Nomination of Bryan."

> The majority has chosen as nominee for President one of the ablest representatives of the young free silver democracy of the West. He has had a brilliant and notable career. Against his personal character no word has ever been spoken . . .
>
> The Globe is not however prepared at this time to support candidate Bryan. It does not approve of the platform and fully believes . . . all classes of people will see that the greatest good of the greatest number will best be promoted by the gold standard . . . It may prove the wisest course for the Democratic Party to hold its organization in the different states, especially in the East, and conduct its state and congressional campaigns upon sound money platforms. By this method Congress can be constituted in a way which should be for the best interests of the country . . .

The Globe, till now a thick and thin Democratic paper, thence took an independent stance that it maintained long after the unpleasantness of 1896; not till 1967 did it again formally endorse a candidate. It must have been a time of perplexity and anxiety, but it was also less of a strain on the Globe and created less loss of clientele from the years of the Taylor policy of keeping the news columns nonpartisan, printing both sides, and moderating its editorial partisanship.

Immediately the Washington correspondent was assigned to follow Bryan back to a hometown triumph and on into his campaign. Photographs of Bryan's family featured the news columns — his profile and western background, his elderly parents and all the human interest about the new political star so suddenly risen. The Globe similarly gave the full treatment to a homecoming day in Boston for that silver maverick George Fred Williams, headlining the speculation whether he would seek the nomination for governor.

The Globe exploited a chance to give some comfort to its silver constituents with a neighborly laudatory editorial to the vice presidential nominee, Arthur Sewall, of Bath, Maine, a successful businessman who supported the silver issue as an economic answer to deflation. A staff man was sent to Bath to report a big celebration for that town's favorite son.

As the dust of the convention settled, the Democrats fully expected to sweep the election, and most people accepted the prospect. The day after the nomination a Globe headline reported:

> Always Loyal
> Bay State Democrats Will Support Nominee
> Rank and File of Party Are Not Bolters

A week later a headline told of Republican anxiety:

> Sen. Sherman Alarmed at Silver Sentiment
> Urges Active Measures to be Taken at Once

They were. A July 27 headline notes:

> With Hanna
> Maj. McKinley Retires to Cleveland

Mark Hanna, political mahout of Ohio industrialists, had moved in.

The Globe began running a series on gold that proved predictive, for a new cyanide process of refining gold ore, along with discovery of new gold mines in Africa, was already abating the gold scarcity that was the basis of the free silver campaign.

Frank Carpenter, who by now shared national distinction as a syndicated writer with Joe Howard, began a series on gold mining in the United States. The Globe immediately featured it, with an announcement that it had secured Carpenter to do the series "no expense spared . . . The letters will be non-partisan without bias toward gold or silver."

The first article was wholly technical, but it explored the "new process of gold reduction that opens new fields of prospecting . . . the cyanide process extracts low grade ores" (revolutionizes gold mining and refining). This must have been reassuring to those who had been worried by the silver agitation. By October 3 the Globe was saying in an editorial: "There never was so large a stock of gold in the world as now." It reported the figures by countries.

On July 15 the Globe front page was perfectly balanced between the Democratic and Republican state rallies, with a three-column head to each. The evening Globe on July 18 led with an interview by Maurice Low, the Washington correspondent following Bryan, with Mrs. Bryan: "Mrs. Bryan to the Globe / She Gives First Interview Since her Husband's Nomination."

The upsets and confusion of the eastern Democrats were reflected in the news through the summer. The top headline July 27 was:

> Cleveland to Bolt
> Said to be preparing document to repudiate the Democratic convention

Joe Howard's letter the day before had given an indication of the Republican campaign to come under Mark Hanna's sponsorship of the effort for McKinley: "Campaign of Education Sorely Needed / Financial Question the Most Befogged of any age."

The Globe by no means gave over its Democratic sentiments while it sat out the Bryan campaign. It found ways to needle Republicans that avoided the gold issue. A fortnight after the Bryan nomination, the Globe editorially (July 28) derided the stance of the Republican candidate:

> What Could McKinley Say?

"In face of the foreign trade increase under the Democratic tariff . . . it is no wonder McKinley announced he will hardly get further East than Ohio during the campaign. If he has nothing but the tariff to talk about, how can he explain to New England the gains in exports under what he calls 'the present suicidal system?' "

Their discomfiture with the silver Democrats did not deter the Globe's Democratic editorialists from satirizing the Republicans. "Uncle Dudley's Notions" July 26 is a political review and appreciation of President Cleveland, but it quickly takes after the Republicans, claiming

> pained surprise at Republican friends affecting to be merry over the great exhibition of whiskers at St. Louis [the Populist convention which had also nominated Bryan despite his repudiation].
>
> Certainly the Populists did not introduce whiskers to the political arena. That distinction belongs indisputably to the Republican Party. It is responsible for all the whiskers in the Presidential line. No other party ever nominated a bewhiskered man. Until this year with McKinley the Republicans never nominated any other kind. [The list is enumerated: Fremont, Lincoln, Grant, Hayes, Garfield, Harrison.] Thus we see that Populism in respect to its whiskers, as well as in respect to many of its principles, is only Republicanism, carried to extremes.

Nor did the Globe let its discontent with the Bryan nomination eclipse its basic concern with the social issues it had persistently espoused. Within a few days of the Bryan nomination its lead editorial, "A Wail of Discontent," agreed with John Russell Young of the New York Herald on

> one idea that is worthy of consideration of all classes, however much men may differ over the financial question . . . that the West is swept with a wave of discontent. It has taken the form of silver. This discontent is based upon the indifference of Washington to any interest but those of monopolies . . . Neither party takes a proper interest in the measures of vital interest to the people. The result is rebellion, expressed in the nomination of Mr. Bryan. He suggests that after the financial question has been settled, it will be well for both parties to put their houses in order and bring themselves nearer in touch with the people.

And a week later, July 24, an editorial entitled "Socialism in Europe" says that "every accession to the ranks of an ill-assorted and jumbled socialism is a call to congresses and parliaments to put justice before all things."

The conclusion of the Bryan convention struck a double blow to Charles Taylor. William Russell returned from the convention exhausted and died three days later, at 39. General Taylor was personally devoted to Russell, his "candidate without a flaw." A brilliant and dedicated public servant Russell might have been on the presidential ticket in 1896, had the political tides flowed differently.

The Globe turned its columns in mourning and for several days was literally filled with eulogy and tributes to Russell. The General himself signed the editorial: "If ever there was a favorite son of a State, Governor Russell was the man. None knew him but to love him."

On July 16 the entire front page was given up to Russell's sudden death. Another page was given to his last speech, at the convention, and another to a biography. Next day again nothing else was on the front page:

>Statesman's Bright Career
>
>Blow to the Old Bay State

Four full pages printed tributes to Russell, with all rules turned as they were again on the editorial page.

Still on the third day the three-column center of page one was headlined:

>Slept Into the Fulness of Light
>
>Death Came to the State's Beloved Without a Pang or a Tear

After four days, the Sunday paper had a two-thirds page photograph of Russell among party leaders.

Something went out of Charles Taylor and out of the Globe with the death of Russell. The General never again idolized a politician, and he withdrew from a personal role in party affairs. He left politics to his political writers and devoted himself singly to business.

Massachusetts Democracy did not see Russell's like again until John F. Kennedy. Two decades after Russell, David I. Walsh as governor administered a bright short period of reform and innovation before he went to the Senate and turned conservative. Democratic politics in Boston bogged down in Curleyism for a long, dismal epoch while the Globe glumly made no comment.

By 1896 the Globe had gone to an eight-column width. The paper averaged ten pages daily, selling for two cents. A table of contents was carried on page one in the morning edition, summarizing the main items on each page. This practice was continued for years until the size of the paper prevented it. Then for many more years there was no attempt at a news index until the 1960's.

Harvard and Other Sports

Football was regularly the big fall story in the 1890's and long after. It took a good murder or an election to compete with it. Harvard was the local protagonist, and the Globe staff was overwhelmingly Harvard. Harvard and Yale was the classic rivalry. But Princeton made it the big three, and the Princeton Tiger enlivened the football cartoons with their stock characters of the Yale bulldog and John Harvard in his Puritan hat.

Harvard built the first football stadium, on the lines of the Roman coliseum. The gladiatorial combats there required a whole platoon of the Globe to cover them. Besides photographers, cartoonist, and telegraphers to wire the play-by-play for the Saturday football extra there was the city editor, Sully, to write the lead story, the sports editor, and two or three of his staff, including Melvin Webb, the baseball writer who converted to football in the fall, and John D. Merrill, the elegant mustached political editor who was also editor of the Harvard Alumni Bulletin and had been the Globe's undergraduate correspondent in Cambridge until his graduation in 1889. To balance things up, a Yale point of view was obtained from Samuel

J. Elder, prominent Boston lawyer and a Yale Club man who joined the Globe-Harvard contingent.

Joseph Smith, another Yale man and assistant Sunday editor, contributed a statistical chart of the game, a Globe invention. With straight lines and curved lines, dotted lines and broken lines, it indicated the movement of the ball throughout the game and the manner of its propulsion, whether by punt, run, pass, or kick. Fumbles, interceptions, and runbacks had their individual symbols. The chart ran across five or six columns in the Sunday paper. Joe Smith had a bent for statistics. He was in charge of the Boston newspaper pool at City Hall that processed the Boston vote as it came from the police precincts every election night. He edited the miscellaneous material that fitted into the Sunday pages, crosswords, cartoons, panels, short pieces, all of which he handled meticulously with the assurance from Mr. Morgan that small things were just as important as the big ones. Joe Smith was a fine figure of a man and imposing in the dinner coat which he wore frequently as the Globe publisher's favorite substitute at such public dinners as required only sitting at the head table, with no speaking part.

The Globe on a Sunday after one of the big Harvard football games would have six to ten separate stories which, with action photographs and cartoons and statistics, would flow through three to five pages. Eight signed stories ran on the 1894 game. The first color supplement featured the Harvard and Yale 1894 football squads. This was before all the other colleges developed football; there were just a few powers in the 1890's and early 1900's and Harvard was one of them.

If Yale or Princeton should win — or even Penn or Rutgers, which improbability did happen at times — there was still eloquent writing to be done about the great spirit of the Harvard eleven and its game struggle. Even Sam Elder's contribution of the Yale point of view conceded that Yale's 1894 victory came after "a great contest in which too much credit cannot be given the Harvard team." But when Mel Webb was assigned to write the lead, he sometimes became so wound up in the terrific struggle Harvard put up that he wouldn't get to the score until the story had run off the front page, inside somewhere. When Sully wrote the lead, on the really big ones, he found so much color and excitement to pack into his lead sentence that it would travel many lines of type before a period. And you wouldn't want it to stop; it sparkled and crackled.

Webb, a heavy-set man of serious mien, was a walking encyclopedia of sports information. He concentrated meticulously on detail, which made for a rather pedestrian story. But after one big game Mel lost his notes and had to write the story out of his vivid impressions of the dramatic points of the game. James Morgan wrote him a note that it was the best story he had ever done. "A good joke on James" said Mel. "He didn't know I'd lost my notes."

The same or a variant of the Globe forces mobilized in June for the great Harvard-Yale rowing classic. Eight to a dozen Globe men would go down to Red Top on the Thames to occupy a Globe cottage hard by the Harvard crew and coaching staff for the week before the race. Thus they became fully acquainted with every oarsman, his strengths and background, and even had time to visit the Yale crew quarters. John D. Merrill was always at the Red Top headquarters too, a natural liaison between the journalists and the collegians. He covered every Harvard-Yale crew race from 1889 through 1939. A charming man, gay, with a sweet disposition and a tenor voice from his Glee Club days, he was the life of the party, and such a fixture of Harvard rowing that on his death after 50 years of the annual Red Top stay, the Harvard crew erected a memorial bench to him there.

The Globe sports department was practically an adjunct of the Harvard coaching staff, or maybe vice versa. For it was a Globe man, George Stewart, the pioneer yachting editor, who organized the first formal football coaching at Harvard. Stewart as coach of the 1892 team also contributed a Globe story on the game. The Globe's intimate relations with Harvard athletics carried over into the days of more organized athletic activity. Sully was himself a member of the Harvard Athletic Committee, as was of course John Merrill. All through the great Percy Haughton era of 1908–1916 the Monday morning quarterbacking was regularly done in Sully's city editor office at the Globe.

As Lucien Thayer, Harvard 1910, remembers from the vantage point of the city room, Percy Haughton would stomp in early Monday, all six feet four of him, and demand of the nearest listener: "Where's Sully?" The city editor would appear with all the Globe photographs of the Saturday game especially saved for him in an envelope. Merrill and Webb would gather from the sports department. Several old Harvards would drift in, the graduate athletics treasurer, one or another old football grad, and one of Haughton's assistant coaches.

They would examine the Globe prints and hold a post mortem on the game. Then Haughton would develop plans for the next week's plays. According to Thayer, one of the strategies hatched in the Monday morning city room conference was what soon became nationally famous as "the hidden ball play," which Harvard's President Eliot disapproved of as a deception. They would excuse Sully's secretary and close the door to contain secrets and exclude any interfering business. Mary Gallagher, who was Sully's secretary through the Haughton epoch, used to say it was foolish of her to come in Mondays; she never had a chance to get any work done.

The Globe intimacy with the Harvard athletics department didn't necessarily produce inside stories, for the Globe wouldn't have given away any Harvard strategies. On one notable boat race, Bill Cunningham of the Post, covering the event single-handed and without a Red Top prelude, scooped the whole Globe contingent. That year Yale had a very powerful crew; its victory was anticipated. The Yale crew finished seven or eight lengths in the lead and in their exuberance kept right on rowing to their boathouse without stopping for the conventional cheer for Harvard. Their coach had to bring them back. This, the only unforeseen development in the race, Cunningham had all alone in the Post. The Globe task force were evidently too dispirited to notice it.

The Taylors took the Harvard atmosphere in the news room good naturedly, took it quite for granted. One day Charles, Jr., looked in at the library to check a point about Harvard, saw a Globe staff man there, and asked the question of him. "I'm sorry, Mr. Taylor. We'll have to ask one of the Harvard men," came the reply.

"What? Aren't you Harvard? How did you ever get in here?"

Dewey's War

The bristling issue of free silver of the 1896 campaign was soon overshadowed by planks in the conventions of that year that received minor attention at the time but became war cries early in the McKinley administration. The Democrats in 1896 had a plank expressing sympathy for the Cuban rebels against Spain. The Republicans had come out flatly for Cuban independence, a stand that the Globe briefly applauded.

The Globe was no warmonger, but it did not share the all-out peace position of editor Edward Clement of the Transcript, who put his paper as solidly against war with Spain as it had been half a century earlier against war with Mexico.

The Globe shared the popular repugnance to Spanish treatment of the Cuban rebels, and after the battleship *Maine* was blown up February 15, 1898, it expressed the general impatience to push Spain out of Cuba. Its headlines were more hawkish than its editorial position because it had the New York World news service, and Pulitzer was competing with Hearst in inflammatory reports out of Cuba. Their widespread news services to other papers undoubtedly infected public opinion. But it was the moral indignation of church groups that put President McKinley under irresistible pressure. Congress was getting the same pressure and prodding the reluctant President. Interestingly, the business community was more dovish than the church groups. When the Boston Board of Trade telegraphed the President their "most emphatic approval of the conservative course you are pursuing in the endeavor to adjust peaceably the relations of this country with Spain," the Globe demurred with an editorial April 3, 1898: "If nine-tenths of Congress members vote for Cuban independence who shall say . . . that they do not represent the people in this matter."

Nine days later the Globe reminded the President of the Republican plank of 1896, as plenty of others were doing. The war came a fortnight later.

It was 9:45 the night of February 15 when the *Maine* was blown up. Most of the officers were ashore, for the Spanish diplomatic and military community at Havana had received the visit of the battleship with a round of cordial receptions and dinners. It was not until after midnight that the report of the disaster reached the Navy Department. So the news in the 8 o'clock morning Globe extra consisted of sketchy bulletins. But the headlines were black and deep. "Treachery Suspected" was the top head. The Globe report was by the New York World correspondent, Sylvester Scovell: "The battleship Maine was blown up in plain sight of Havana at 9:45 tonight. Captain Sigsbee says one quarter of his crew of 600 are dead. He says he is not able officially to state the cause until he has made an investigation. Five minutes after the explosion the Spanish warship Alphonso Doce had lowered her boats and was picking up those who were swimming. U.S. Consul-General Lee is at the palace conferring with Capt. General Blanco."

An AP dispatch followed, practically the same. Dispatches from Washington speculated on the possible accidental cause. Secretary Long said Captain Sigsbee did not assign any cause: "The whole thing is still a mystery to me." Sigsbee said, however: "Public opinion should be suspended until further report." Secretary Long admitted that the explosion was suspicious though he professed to believe it an accident.

Next morning's headline:

>Floating Torpedo
>Sigsbee's Opinion is that such caused the loss of the Maine
>Divers' Investigations Will Determine the Question of Peace or War

Editorially on February 17 the Globe saw an accident the probable cause but said that a thorough inquiry was urgent. But the World correspondent did not wait upon an inquiry. "It Was No Accident" was the Globe head over Scovell's dispatch that evening. "Spanish fanaticism might have done it — Cuban intrigues might have caused it — There was no fire from physical causes — On this depends war with Spain."

Next morning the headline over his dispatch was

>Spain's Responsibility
>Question of her liability is raised in Washington

A subhead: "Truth May Never be Known." Captain Sigsbee's temperate and judicious dispatches could not counter the sensational headlines.

War fires were fanned. It was March 20 when the Naval Court of Inquiry reported that the *Maine* was blown up by an external explosion, evidently a submarine mine. By now any external explosion was interpreted as Spanish guilt by the war hawks. War came one month later, April 21.

But the Army was totally unprepared for war, and the only plans General Miles had were for coastal defense. Admiral Sampson's orders were limited to a blockade of Cuba. The public was depressed by inaction, and when word came that Spanish Admiral Cervera had set sail from the Cape Verde Islands, fear of attack spread among the Atlantic Coast cities.

The public followed with fascinated concern sketchy reports of the progress of the battleship *Oregon,* under Capt. Charles E. Clark, ordered from San Francisco March 19 to join the Atlantic squadron. On the two-month voyage around the Horn, she was out of communication when war was declared. May 1 brought great public relief at the report that the *Oregon* had safely reached Rio de Janeiro, where she would learn the country was at war and be alerted to the danger of a Spanish fleet. Captain Clark joined the Atlantic squadron May 25 and took a vigorous part in defeating the Spanish fleet at Santiago July 3.

But long before either the Army or the Navy was ready to move on Cuba the nation was electrified by Dewey's victory at Manila. Ordered from Hongkong to prepare for possible hostilities, he was on his way to the Philippines when the war opened.

On Sunday, May 1, the headlines exploded:

>Dewey the Conqueror
>He Sails into Manila with Spanish Fleet in Hiding

The news was sketchy and vague and all from Spanish sources, for the United States had no Pacific cable and the only telegraph connection with the Philippines was Hongkong, 600 miles across the China Sea.

Next morning:

>Dewey Destroys Fleet
>Wins a Great Victory at Manila

But all the news was still via Madrid, and though it admitted Spanish losses it had the American squadron retiring severely damaged. This Spanish error was natural enough — Dewey had retired for breakfast.

Next day further details were confirmed from London. But Dewey was not heard from. Tuesday evening the headline was

Manila Ours

Dewey Has Captured It

— over a half dozen lines from Hongkong, copyrighted by the New York Journal. Below it was a New York World report that "the Manila cable is cut; that leads to the belief Manila has yielded."

Next morning:

Cable Silent

Country Anxious to Hear from the Hero of Manila

The lead: "The fate of Manila is still in doubt . . . no reliable information . . ."

But the Globe hadn't waited to celebrate. The editorial May 3, "Our Far Flung Battle Line," had flags spotted down the column. Five columns of the center of the editorial page were given to a sketch of the battle and under it four stanzas by Edward F. Burns: "They Remembered the Maine." Editorially the Globe observed that "the Maine has been remembered 10,000 miles from Havana harbor."

But it was Saturday before details arrived, and it was a Globe scoop in Boston. The New York World correspondent, E. W. Harden, had joined Dewey's fleet at Hongkong on the dispatch cutter *McCullough* and was one of two correspondents to witness the battle. The other was Joseph Stickney of the New York Herald, a favorite of Dewey's, who stood with the Commodore on the flagship *Olympia* throughout the battle and reported the laconic order: "You may fire when ready, Gridley." But Harden beat Stickney in a rickshaw race to the Hongkong telegraph, to file a succinct paragraph that beat Dewey's own official dispatch and commanded the headlines alone on Saturday morning, followed by a full, colorful account Sunday. Dewey had cut the Manila cable himself and held back the *McCullough* three days to complete his conquest before letting any dispatches out.

So the Globe in Boston, with the World in New York, had the big scoop of the war that Saturday, May 7. The front page was filled with black headlines over Harden's four-line dispatch.

No American Killed

At Battle of Manila

Only Six Men on U.S. Warships Wounded

Spanish Loss, 300 Killed Wounded 400 — 11 Battleships Destroyed

USS McCullough Arrives With Dispatches at Hongkong

Harden's entire dispatch Saturday was: "I have just arrived here on the U.S. revenue cutter McCullough with my report of the great American victory at Manila. Commodore Dewey destroyed the entire Spanish fleet of 11 vessels. Three hundred Spaniards were killed and 400 wounded. Our loss was none killed and but six slightly wounded. Not an American ship was injured." That was all for that day. The AP report was only three lines: "The navy department has received a cable from Hongkong of the arrival of the McCullough. Full details are expected within a few hours in regard to the battle of Manila."

Sunday's front page had Dewey's own dispatch; inside was Harden's full account of the battle.

Globe readers may have been a little confused by a headline May 2, just as the great news was filling in from Manila, "Where is that Fleet?" It was asking about Spain's Atlantic fleet. "The destination of the Spanish fleet is unknown. It may be

The Boston · Daily Globe.

VOL LIII NO 127.   BOSTON, SATURDAY MORNING, MAY 7, 1898 TWELVE PAGES.   PRICE TWO CENTS.

GLOBE EXTRA---10 O'CLOCK.

NO AMERICAN KILLED

AT BATTLE OF MANILA

Spanish Loss.

Killed - - 300
Wounded - 400

Eleven Warships Destroyed.

U S S McCULLOCH ARRIVES WITH DISPATCHES AT HONGKONG.

(By E. W. HARDEN.)

HONGKONG, May 7--I have just arrived here on the U S revenue cutter Hugh McCulloch with my report of the great American victory at Manila. Com Dewey destroyed the entire Spanish fleet of 11 vessels. Three hundred Spaniards were killed and 400 wounded.

Our loss was none killed and but six slightly wounded. Not an American ship was injured.

Copyright, 1898, New York World.

(By Associated Press.)

WASHINGTON, May 7--The navy department has received a cable dispatch from Hongkong announcing the arrival of the revenue cutter McCulloch.

This is all that the dispatch contains, but full details are expected within a few hours in regard to the battle of Manila.

Dewey's victory: May 7, 1898.

plowing its way toward the New England coast or the shores of Cuba . . . There is absolutely no information in the possession of the government as to the ultimate intention of the Spanish admiral. In this uncertainty, plans for the invasion of Cuba have come to a halt." This from Maurice Low in Washington.

But three days later, May 5, the headline was "Off for Battle — Sampson and his Ships Seek the New Armada"; and that afternoon, "Victorious — Two U.S. Expeditions Land" (in Cuba).

Next day the Globe had an editorial, "The Late War Scare": "Was there ever a more flimsy bugbear than the war scare that so recently seized upon some of our bankers and business men . . . and cast a shadow of fear over our seaside resorts." And indeed, it was bad for business.

The Globe soon had its own Washington correspondents in Cuba. Maurice Low had gone with the 9th Massachusetts from their Florida training camp and was at the battles of El Caney and San Juan Hill. When Low returned to Washington, the center of the larger war news, big Jim O'Leary left his baseball beat to join the 9th and 2d Massachusetts in Cuba.

But the first Globe war assignment was with the Navy. Boston, like other coastal cities, was nervous about the location of Spain's ancient warships, which actually were seeking hiding places in Cuban harbors. "Bombardment insurance" was advertised on the front page the week war was declared. The first Bay State unit activated was the Naval Brigade, commanded by a young Annapolis graduate, John W. Weeks, later senator. With the brigade went Globe reporter Edward J. Kenney, of Charlestown, a familiar of the Navy Yard from boyhood. He cruised for some weeks with a hastily organized auxiliary naval flotilla which included two converted Boston ferryboats.

The military editor, J. Harry Hartley, was with the state's infantry units at their Framingham training camp. Winfield Thompson and John Carberry of the Globe staff covered many war stories on the home front. But the most distressing war news was of conditions in the Florida training camps, of the rotten beef and malaria. Maurice Low was among the first to expose the ineptness of the Army in providing adequate shelter and rations for the troops and care for the wounded. Later O'Leary continued such reporting. But the most devastating reports came to the Globe in letters from a soldier experiencing the wretched conditions, James Brendan Connolly, later renowned for his sea stories "Out of Gloucester." Connolly, serving with the 9th, wrote a friend in Boston, James Shields Murphy, vivid descriptive letters. Murphy took them to the Globe, which published them prominently, and they were sensational.

John Carberry and Winfield Thompson reported on the return of the sick and wounded from Cuba. Then Thompson was assigned to Havana for five months to cover the reconstruction to peace. Jim O'Leary stayed with the 2d and 9th until their last units came home. Then he returned, wearing a broad-brimmed, faun-colored regulation infantry hat, and he kept on wearing it and successors of the same style the remaining 50 years of his active life with the Globe sports department.

Jack Taylor of the staff had gone to training camp with the 2d Massachusetts and later with the 6th Massachusetts landed in Puerto Rico. After the peace he was sent to the Philippines to report the Filipino insurrection for six months. The Globe in placards to news dealers proclaimed itself "the only New England newspaper having a special staff correspondent with our army in the Philippines."

This must have been a disappointing venture. The Globe and its readers, with all other newspaper readers, were soon to know why. Soon after Taylor's return, the evening Globe of July 17, 1899, exploded in a three-column front page headline:

Are "Gagged"

Manila Correspondents Break Silence

Protest to General Otis

"Ultra-Optimistic View" of Gen. Otis is "Not Shared by the General Officers in the Field"

Ten leading correspondents signed the sensational disclosure that began: "The people of the United States have not received a correct impression . . . The dispatches err in the declaration that the situation is well in hand and in the assumption that the insurrection can be speedily ended without a greatly increased force."

The next morning's headline on Maurice Low's report of the Washington reaction was:

Almost Dazed

Report of the Correspondents at Manila

Surprises All

Army Men and Cabinet Officers

Alike Stricken Dumb

Low's dispatch described "consternation" in the administration and told "how thoroughly the War Department is demoralized . . . Secretary Alger should go because his absolute unfitness for the position has been so thoroughly demonstrated. Adj. Gen. Corbin should go because he is Secretary Alger's other self." Secretary Alger did go, and the result was to bring Elihu Root into the cabinet.

Low reported "What the correspondents have now told has been known to a certain number of persons in Washington for some time. The War Department has been charged with altering or suppressing Gen. Otis's dispatches. There is no doubt this is true. There is no doubt the half has not been told of the condition of affairs in the Philippines."

The Globe editorially July 18 said that General Otis has "proved not of commanding caliber . . . He has made the foolish and fatuous mistake of mingling prophecies and party politics with his function as commanding general." Gen. Elwell S. Otis was relieved the following May by Gen. Arthur McArthur, but a month later Judge William Howard Taft was appointed to take the Philippine administration out of the hands of the generals — whose successors half a century later in Korea and Vietnam were to prove equally obtuse about the role of the press in an open society.

Journalistically, the most creative development of the war, and the greatest boon to the Globe, was Peter Finley Dunne's Mister Dooley. Dunne in 1898 was managing editor of the Chicago Journal. He had for several years contributed occasional humorous pieces in Irish dialect, which were already appearing in papers outside Chicago, expressing the practical philosophy of his character Mister Dooley. The war gave him a larger scope. Theodore Roosevelt's ebullience was a natural target. "Alone in Cuby," Mister Dooley interpreted T.R.'s war memoirs. General Taylor, an early convert to the Dunne humor, quickly introduced Mister Dooley into the Sunday Globe and urged Dunne to syndicate his offerings. This soon made Dunne's fortune. The first collection of his columns, "Mr. Dooley in Peace and War," in 1898, was an immediate best-seller that established Dunne solidly among American humorists. A 1901 collection of "Mr. Dooley's Opinions" included the imperishable observation that "the Supreme Coort follows th' iliction returns." Mr. Dooley continued a Globe feature for as long as Dunne produced him, until 1915.

But the Spanish War was only a matter of a few months in its active military phase. Dewey destroyed the Spanish fleet in Manila in the first fortnight. Two months later the Spanish commander in Cuba surrendered Santiago. It was too short and limited a war to disrupt the normal tempo of American life. The Filipino insurrection lasted another two years but it was remote and involved small forces.

The larger impact of the war was on American psychology and politics. The scandals of the training camps with their rotten beef, graft, and tropical disease came at the end of a long period of the crassest commercialism and an era of laissez-faire government. The wartime exposures roused the American people and opened the way for the following years of muckraking reform, of pure food laws and organized medical attack on the scourges of malaria and yellow fever.

The takeover of the Philippines made America a Pacific power, with a new relation to Asia. It made Americans conscious of becoming a world power. The immediate effect in politics was to raise the issue of anti-imperialism with a hard core of support among the erstwhile mugwumps of Massachusetts, to divide Republicans again and enlarge the "independent vote."

Editor Clement in the Transcript voiced the conscience of the anti-imperialists. The Globe was sufficiently infected with the mood of "manifest destiny" to support the keeping of the Philippines.

The Spanish-American War brought Globe circulation for April 1898 to a record peak for a Boston newspaper, 278,000 daily and 295,600 Sunday. An editorial May 2 celebrated "all records broken in April." The daily was 12 pages, the Sunday 40 pages, still at five cents.

Advertisers and Contemporaries, 1899

In 1899 Addison Archer, a Boston advertising man, published a brochure for advertisers of 150 pages on the Boston newspapers called *Addison Archer's Interviews: regarding the character, circulation, and advertising value of the leading newspapers of Boston.*

Besides a business analysis, he included extensive interviews with the newspaper managers; he was particularly interested to interview General Taylor even after he had had a full discussion of the business of the Globe with Charles, Jr., as business manager. For, Archer said, "General Taylor has been so widely quoted and is so widely recognized as one of the two or three most successful editors and publishers in the United States."

Archer's interview was rather elementary, but it brought out some points. "Who are the most important people in making a newspaper?" The General's reply: "The reporters. To have local matters well written is of more importance than anything else."

The Globe by 1899 had full Associated Press service. But General Taylor still valued the special news services he had built for the Globe. "The AP is of course of great value to all newspapers, but less so to the strong papers," he told Archer. "The AP gives the weak paper that pays a small sum the same service it gives the large paper that pays a large sum. We have our own news bureau at all principal New England points and cover the news there, we think, better than the local AP papers . . . The Globe is read by more women in each thousand of its circulation than any other popular paper in the country . . . Why? Because we have catered directly to them for 25 years."

"Which paper do women read most?"

"The Sunday most, next to that the evening paper . . . The women find more in the Sunday paper of interest to them than in all of the rest of the papers put together during the week. They read the advertising as much as they do the news. Advertising addressed to women is news to them and enables them to save money. The paper that pleases the women is more profitable than any other kind."

Archer's pamphlet, despite its obvious commercial nature, is a compendium of information on the Boston newspapers at the close of the nineteenth century. He has more detail on the Globe than any other paper, for the reason, as he explains, that Charles Taylor, Jr., opened his books and explored with him every cranny of plant and equipment.

Archer wrote: "There is nothing problematical about the Boston Globe. It has the largest circulation in New England. The circulation of the Globe is proven by every kind of evidence to be exactly what the Globe says it is, namely:

The daily Globe actual average, 1898 — 230,413.

The Sunday Globe, actual average, 1898 — 269,645."

This is the press run, Charles told him; returns averaged eight to ten percent. The Globe's paper bill, Archer reported, ran about $440,000 a year. They used 85 to 95 tons every Sunday.

"Did the war [of 1898] prove a good thing for the Globe?" Archer asked Taylor, Jr.

"No, I don't believe it proved a good thing financially for any newspaper in the country. While we gained in circulation, we lost in advertising and the expense of getting the news was enormous. Our present advertising rates are based on a circulation of 150,000 and have not since advanced from our rate of 20 cents a line."

The Globe's circulation was 70,000 more than any other daily in Boston and on Sunday more than double the second Sunday paper, Taylor told Archer. The Globe press capacity was put at 170,000 eight-page papers an hour. The presses were listed as "a sextuple with a color deck, a double color press, a triple press and four quads." The Globe then ran three morning and seven evening editions, a considerable consolidation from the number a decade earlier.

"We usually set 130 to 170 columns of advertising for Sunday and have set as high as 225 columns," Taylor said. "We can set a column of ordinary advertising in 25 minutes, a page in three hours and a half. All the advertising for the Sunday paper is set between Friday night and 10 o'clock Saturday night."

The editorial staff then numbered 110, of whom 20 were desk editors. The Globe had 200 correspondents through New England, 150 more scattered over the country. The library or "morgue" had obituaries, sketches, and pictures on 120,000 individuals, classified by Taylor as "100,000 respectable people and 20,000 criminals."

Archer found the Globe's chief strength in its policy to give the news impartially. Taylor said, "We are not making a party paper. The day of party organs has passed."

Archer was particularly enthusiastic about the Globe's type book, a service to advertisers. He says the Globe was the first newspaper in the country to get out such a type book, some ten years before his pamphlet, showing advertisers what sizes and varieties of display type were available in "Taylor Gothic." Archer explains the name: "When the American Type Founders' Company brought out the Quentall type, Charles Taylor, Jr., said it was beautiful but should be made more practical and worked it over with the type manufacturers to evolve what they called 'Taylor Gothic.' "

Then Archer asks a question that critics on and off the Globe were to ask for the next 50 years: "If you are so particular about typographical appearance why do you run ads on the first page?"

"Because advertisers pay for it."

"Do they pay enough difference to make it pay you?"

Yes. Do you want my idea of an ideal front page? I would have three columns of advertising on it. I would run that advertising down the left hand side. The front page would have 8 columns and the only advertising on it would be those 3 columns. The first page is the show window of a newspaper where it puts out its display stuff and the stuff that sells papers on the news stand. The papers that do not print advertising on the first page find it mighty hard to get enough good matter to make a good show window out of their front page. So they put matter on it that ought to go to the back of the store or down in the basement. Take any paper that does not print first page ads and you will find that it has a weak first page five days out of seven.

Some advertisers had a bone to pick with the Globe because it made an extra charge for breaking over column rules and also for the use of photographic cuts in an ad or for a decorative border. But Charles Taylor, Jr., was firm on his rate card. "Broken column rules and cuts and display make advertising worth more," he insisted. "Put in a column of plain type and put in beside it a one-quarter column with a cut and display type and you get more effect in the one-quarter column than you do in the full column. Take the ad that is run across two or three columns instead of down a single column and you get more display than you do with twice that space in a single column."

Archer interviewed all the important advertisers in Boston. They agreed that the Globe was the great popular newspaper of New England and that General Taylor's was the big success story in journalism. But the big stores generally joined the Herald with the Globe as "the leading newspapers." The Herald's lesser circulation was balanced up by the high standard of its editorial page and its readers "of high intelligence and more than average buying capacity," and it got the same advertising rate from department stores as the Globe with its larger circulation. Jordan Marsh, the biggest store, divided its advertising evenly between Globe and Herald, a page and a half or two pages to each every Sunday.

"The Herald is the best advertising medium for representative houses," said the advertising manager of Leopold Morse, a leading clothing house. "The Herald reaches the solid people. Its financial article is widely read by nearly all the large investors. The Globe is equally good as an advertising medium but I think it is more adapted to large department stores and establishments dealing in cheaper and medium class goods."

All acclaimed the Transcript as the family paper of Boston and the finest newspaper. Its circulation was only 21,000, but it "reaches the people of means and refinement." Businessmen counted the Transcript an ornament to Boston, its limited circulation very valuable. The Transcript business manager, George Mandell, told Archer: "We run no prize fights, no scandals, no divorce cases and no debasing sensational matter of any kind. We mention only the weddings and deaths of prominent people. We exclude objectional advertising. We always investigate any advertising that is doubtful."

The Journal, now publishing Sunday as well as morning and evening, was highly regarded and called much improved under the editorship of Stephen O'Meara. It was the leading Republican newspaper, owned by the Draper textile mill family and other wealthy families. Its circulation, put at 70,000–80,000, was only half the Herald's, but it stood very high with the merchants as a staunch New England institution. The Advertiser, whose circulation by now was even under the Transcript's, still had status with the conservative financial community.

The Record, the one-cent evening edition of the Advertiser, was called sprightly, crisp, and popular; it had brought its circulation to 50,000 and then 70,000; and the Traveler, by now spelled with one "l," after coming down to one cent had made notable gains. The Post, at one cent, had worked up a circulation of 124,000 for 1898; it had "a very low advertising rate." Some of the merchants were beginning to include it in their advertising budgets. One said that the Traveler "is a resurrected newspaper advancing on sensational and aggressive lines"; another described it as "a racy newspaper" with "a similar constituency in the evening to the Post in the morning but the Post is the better paper."

A real estate man found the Globe and Herald "both distinctly first class mediums for the general run of real estate advertising. Several years ago the Herald carried higher grade advertising in our line than the Globe, but within the last few years the Globe has been marching up to a par with the Herald.

"Some time ago I don't think the Republicans read a Democratic newspaper, but I am satisfied that in recent years thousands of Republicans are reading the Globe every day."

When Mr. Archer reached out beyond the advertisers to interview some leading citizens, he drew a sharply contrasting picture of the Boston press from a leading Republican lawyer, Jesse H. Gove, and reform Democrat George Fred Williams. Mr. Gove, who had been in public life, said he did not believe there is "a city in the country where public men are treated so fairly, kindly and honestly as in Boston. The Boston newspapers are editorially honest and just . . . the one side advocating, the other side opposing; we can come very close to getting all the facts. I have always found Boston reporters bright honest gentlemen, always to be depended upon. I never asked a Boston reporter to refrain from mentioning anything that afterward appeared in the paper."

George Fred Williams had a very different view. A maverick Democrat on the silver issue but twice his party's candidate for governor, he had been vigorous for reform and had criticized the Boston papers for failing to support reform, particularly the Globe for its complacency over the traction deals. He said:

The Boston papers are run as a body from the counting room with little pretense at disguise.

The Herald has been professedly independent because an assumption of independence seemed to be the most profitable policy. Its business end of late has been taking a cant toward Republicanism and this shift is likely to increase until it becomes a fair Republican organ under a veil of modesty.

The Globe is not a Democratic newspaper. I do not understand that it wants to be a party organ. It is simply a fine business property which Gen. Charles H. Taylor is shrewdly and conservatively conducting with a trustee's care for its preservation and increase. He does not think that his property will be advanced by antagonizing anybody or anything of consequence editorially. This view naturally leads to the publication of an exceedingly good-natured paper with a colorless editorial page. . . .

. . . I think that the Transcript is on the whole the best newspaper in Boston. It is well proportioned and well rounded out . . . The Transcript has become a remarkably complete newspaper. It prints the news and faces the facts more unflinchingly than any other paper without any attempt to distort or suppress them. This is especially notable in its views of the industrial situation. When there is no boom the Transcript will not stoop to compose one.

The Post has the best opening for remarkable expansion in circulation and influence of any morning paper in Boston. It is the most nearly and truly Democratic of any.

Williams was prophetic about the Herald, which did become a Republican newspaper, absorbing the Journal, and about the Post, which became a militantly Democratic paper and attained a vast circulation before the new century was far advanced.

The Post publisher, E. A. Grozier, described to Archer the campaigns the Post had pushed in the 1890's: "The Post has almost unaided and alone advocated and achieved $1 gas in Boston, reduced the subway lease from 50 to 20 years, reduced the guaranteed dividend to the West End road under the lease to the Elevated road from 8 to 7 percent; brought about the large and growing system of free transfers."

III New Century — No Change

1900

As the year 1900 approached, the Globe was playing a numbers game. An editorial December 28, "The Coming Century," explained that the twentieth century would not begin until 1901 because every century goes from one through 100. This evidently was a conversational gambit of the time.

On January 1, 1900, the Globe editorially hailed "The Year of Grace," still insisting that the new century was a year away, but that 1900 was the year to prepare for it.

Whatever the arithmetic, the psychology of the turn of the century was overwhelming. The Globe wasn't letting its editorial quibbling influence the news columns, which on December 31 announced "the approaching end of the century."

December 24, 1899, had recorded the final run of the last horsecar in Boston. The last day of 1899 was a Sunday and the Sunday symposium was on "Who Is the Greatest Man the Century Has Produced?" Of the five distinguished contributors, two voted for Lincoln, one for Herbert Spencer, one for Charles Darwin, and one divided his vote among Darwin, Emerson, and William Lloyd Garrison. That impartial one was Thomas Wentworth Higginson, a leading civic force in Boston, who eliminated Lincoln by quoting him as saying he owed his career to Garrison.

That day the Dudley editorial, "In the Mirror of Time," reviewed other centuries as well as the nineteenth and concluded that one should be modest about his own times. A full-page Globe calendar for 1900 had the Globe man occupying the center, announcing "largest circulation in New England."

Circulation was actually down, as was every other paper's after the Spanish War, which had increased it by more than 20 percent — up 40,000 for 1898. The daily paper did not again pass 200,000 till the first world war began. It was about 180,000 in 1900. But the Sunday paper, whose growth had been steady and not much bulged by the war, continued its climb toward 300,000. Now a 48-page paper, its price remained five cents; the daily, a 12-page paper, was two cents morning and evening. The department stores, Houghton-Dutton, R. H. White, Shepard Norwell, Jordan Marsh and Filene's, ran big ads Sundays.

The Globe rejoiced in the 1900 census reports as they came out piecemeal to show a 25-percent population gain for Massachusetts in the decade. This was a larger rate of growth than Rhode Island with 24 percent and Connecticut with 21. But the three northern New England states had fallen off the pace. Vermont grew only three percent, Maine five, New Hampshire nine.

The Spanish War had been over for more than a year. But in the Philippines the Aguinaldo insurrection was to go on another two years and overlap the Boer War and the Boxer Rebellion. The war of the admirals, Sampson and Schley, over the Battle of Santiago was to continue through the headlines for a year longer. War headlines were black through late 1899 and 1900.

On December 28 the Globe led with a war dispatch via the London Post by Winston Churchill: "As Seen by Churchill / Boers' Position one of strength, he writes." The Globe had three editorials on the Boer War within four days: "A Good Time for Mediation," "An Empire at Stake," and "A Classic War."

The Globe had been critical of the administration's handling of the Spanish War but joined in the national plaudits for Admiral Dewey, who returned to the United States that fall to unprecedented public acclaim. After New York's celebration he came to Boston for a banquet tendered by the Commonwealth. In the Globe of October 15, 1899, the design of the banquet table, with the names of guests at each seat, took a full page. A facsimile of the menu and the speeches took another page.

Dewey's name was on every lip and a spontaneous presidential boom for him arose. The American people presented him a home in Washington; but a fortnight later he married, a second time, and deeded the gift house to his new wife. This took much of the gilt off the Admiral's braid with the public. He proved further inept in a statement about the talk of the presidency. "If the American people want me for this high office, I shall be only too willing to serve them," he announced in a public interview April 4, 1900. "Since studying this subject, I am convinced that the office of President is not such a difficult one to fill." That finished Dewey as presidential timber. Neither party considered him at its convention.

A headline of November 1, 1901, recalls a case that excited the country for many months:

> Schley's Case
> Counsel for Admiral Schley Told Court of Inquiry
>   Their Case Was Closed

The board of inquiry found against Admiral Schley in his long controversy with Admiral Sampson over the Battle of Santiago, which raged for three years after the war in Cuba. Their assignments were such as to breed confusion. Schley had an independent mobile force but under certain circumstances was to join Sampson's fleet. When ordered to Santiago in May 1898 to bottle up Cervera's fleet till Sampson could reach the scene, Schley responded that he was unable to carry out the order — "obliged to return to Key West for coal."

Sampson's fleet came up while Schley was still there. As Cervera's ships tried to escape, their two forces combined to destroy the Spanish fleet. Each American officer believed, or later claimed, he was in command. A tactic of Schley's early in the action caused confusion, later righted; but Sampson's severe criticism of Schley's action in the battle became a cause célèbre that led Schley to ask for the board of inquiry. He lost. The board found that his conduct before the battle was "characterized by vacillation, dilatoriness, and lack of enterprise." But Schley continued a popular favorite for his amiable, bluff old seadog ways, over Sampson's cold, demanding precision.

Some other November 1901 headlines:

November 1

> Test a Success
> New Electric System for Steam Railways

November 2, evening

> Canal Treaty Ready
> Expect Reciprocity Will Be Granted British West Indies

> In 100 Hours
> Routes from New York to London Planned
> Railroads Would Make New York a Way Station

The "Sunday Symposium" November 3 was "What is Secret of the Power of a Boss?"

November 6 (Wednesday)
>Tammany Overthrown
>
>Seth Low elected
>
>New York mayor on Fusion ticket
>
>William Travers Jerome, district attorney

Jerome had campaigned against Tammany on the theme: "The Ten Commandments Have Not Been Repealed."

November 9 had a headline "New Horticultural Hall Dedicated," with the three-quarter century of the Horticultural Society reviewed; also

>No Tariff Revision
>
>"No Change for two Years at Least"
>
>President Roosevelt is against it. Believes to Open the Question
>>Would Unsettle Business
>
>Surplus Will Be Reduced by Abolishing War Taxes

An editorial:

>Reciprocity Will Not Down

"Protectionists oppose reciprocity. But McKinley left it 'as legacy to his party.' How can President Roosevelt fail to support it in his message? Roosevelt is protectionist but not of the 'hide-bound' order. The people expect Mr. Roosevelt to support reciprocity."

But T.R. didn't. That ebullient Massachusetts politician Eugene Noble Foss, an ardent apostle of reciprocity with Canada — then a lively issue, popular in the industrial northeast but not with western farmers — urged Roosevelt to take up the reciprocity issue. But as Foss recounted it to James Morgan, T.R. responded: "No, Gene. I'm going for the railroads; there's more in it." T.R. thus voiced a politician's sure sense of economy of force. A British prime minister of a later day, Harold Macmillan, acknowledged that a prime minister can influence events only about five percent, and this against all the factors of inertia, complexities, divided support, and the limits of his political credit. Roosevelt wasn't going to squander his strength over too many fights at once.

"That Mad Man" President

By the 1900 presidential election the Globe had forgiven Bryan his silver heresy of 1896. Silver was only one issue, it pointed out. Indeed, silver had faded as a key issue. Without ever formally endorsing Bryan, the Globe clobbered the Republicans on the tariff, the unpopular Philippine War, imperialism, and trusts. Under the cartoonist's pencil of Frederick Opper, trusts had become the most familiar political symbol in America, gross figures with inflated stomachs and greedy countenances. The cartoonist had come into play in the 1896 campaign, with Opper in the new Hearst press and John T. McCutcheon on the Republican side. Mark Hanna, as Opper saw him, was the impressario of the trusts, their stand-in with the party of McKinley.

On the day before election the Globe ran an Opper cartoon from the New York

Journal titled "The McKinley Minstrels" — a blackface chorus of trusts, 11 of them, all labeled, from oil to crackers, beef to sugar. An editorial, "All Trusts Look Alike," derided Mark Hanna, who denied the existence of trusts.

Moorfield Storey, a Boston civic leader, carried the mugwump banner of anti-imperialism in Massachusetts as an independent after failing to win the Democratic nomination for Congress in the elite suburban Newton-Brookline district. Anti-imperialism was not especially the Globe's cup of tea; it was the Transcript's forte. But running Storey's attacks on the administration added an extra lick. When three soldiers returned to Waukegan, Illinois, objecting to the administration policy in the Philippines, that story was worth carrying halfway across the country.

Bryan was hailed editorially by the Globe as a great campaigner who had struck fear into the GOP in Indiana and Ohio; "Labor in the Cabinet" acclaimed him as the first presidential candidate ever to come out squarely for a federal labor department, which the paper envisioned as providing instruments to settle industrial disputes and avoid strikes. It cited the New Zealand compulsory arbitration law: "There has not been a strike or lockout for five years under it."

A confident tone ran through the campaign period. "Ohio Sure" was a November 1 headline. On November 3 an editorial "For Mr. Bryan" listed 70 names of "representative men in Massachusetts for Bryan . . . A good many surprises are in store for the overconfident Republicans of Massachusetts."

The Uncle Dudley editorial Sunday before election, "The Final Review," said Bryan had waged an effective campaign. "The Republicans seemed to have no plan of campaign. They counted on an assumption of success and band wagon momentum. The greatest advantage the Republicans had was control of the machinery of public opinion — almost a monopoly of the customary sources of public opinion — every Republican prediction, every wager on McKinley, every dire forecast of results to follow a Bryan election, every threat of employer or banker, anything to disparage, discourage or demoralize the common enemy — has been eagerly caught up and heralded forth in the roar of thousands of presses."

This sounds like Adlai Stevenson's complaint of a one-party press 52 years later, when he had much more occasion to complain. For in 1900 the Globe had the largest circulation in Boston, and the Post, growing all the time, was more militantly Democratic. In New York the World, Democratic, was the dominant paper and Hearst, flamboyantly anti-McKinley, second. St. Louis, Cincinnati, and other midwestern cities had strong Democratic voices.

The morning before election the Globe's lead headline was

> The Battle's Won
> Coercion and Money Have Failed, says Bryan
> Democratic Managers Claim 308 Electoral Votes

They only got half that many. McKinley widened his 1896 margin over Bryan. But New England did register strong Democratic gains, and the McKinley margin in Massachusetts fell from 163,000 in 1896 to 82,000 in 1900.

Editorially the Globe accounted for the Republican sweep as due to "good times." Bryan was "defeated by prosperity." But the Republican Party was "on trial." "The Winners have the responsibility to carry out their platform, including regulation of trusts. Republicans will dodge that issue at their peril."

A page one box on election day reminded readers: "Get the Globe Extras for the most impartial returns tonight. The Globe's famous stereoptican will furnish the best bulletin service — bright, breezy and accurate."

The election brought to the center of the national stage Vice President Theodore Roosevelt, whose teeth and glasses, initials and expletives were a boon to cartoonists for the years ahead. The Globe was soon observing that:

> The vice presidency is a place where the occupant, barring accidents, is supposed to be buried. Vice President Roosevelt may prove the rule by being an exception. At least
> such is the opinion of your

> Uncle Dudley

Six months after President McKinley's inaugural, the nation was stunned by his assassination at the hands of a mad anarchist. The President was shot September 6 while holding a public reception at the Pan American Exposition in Buffalo; he died eight days later in Buffalo, just 20 years after the assassination of President Garfield. Within 35 years three American presidents had become the victims of assassination.

General Taylor personally wrote and signed two double-column editorials, one a sorrowing tribute to "The Dead President," the other a confident appraisal of the capabilities of "The Living President," the ebullient Theodore Roosevelt. The Globe published a full page of obituary, its columns turned in black borders, and pages of tributes by public men.

Roosevelt had been summoned back from a hunting vacation in the Adirondack forest and only reached Buffalo to be sworn in as president 13 hours after McKinley's death. That was a Saturday, the 14th. The evening Globe had a six-column sketch of Roosevelt taking the oath, and a biographical piece about him headed

> President the Youngest of All
> T.R. is 42

Monday evening's paper reported Roosevelt in charge in Washington:

> His Policy
> Roosevelt Outlines it to the Cabinet
> Not Divergent from that of late President

For its McKinley memorial edition, the day of the President's funeral, September 19, the Globe must have reached back in the files to its tributes to President Garfield. This was a repeat performance, embellished by the typographical advances of 20 years. The front page was draped in black with a border of laurel wreathes. Five memorial poems and four prose tributes filled the page. Across the top center was spread a poem by James Whitcomb Riley, under it other verses by Julia Ward Howe, Richard Henry Stoddard, Will Carleton, and Edward F. Burns, the Globe's own staff poet and editorial writer. There followed prose pieces by Samuel L. Clemens, Joseph Jefferson, George W. Cable, and Winston Churchill the American author.

That was the first page. What followed inside was more of an innovation. Pages two through four carried tributes by women addressed in sympathy to Mrs. McKinley. There were 91 separate signed messages, most by the wives of mayors of New England cities and the others by women of special distinction in their own right, Mary A. Livermore, Mrs. Sarah White Lee, Elizabeth Stuart Phelps Ward, Mary Boyle O'Reilly.

The center of one page carried the musical scores and words of McKinley's favorite hymns, Nearer My God To Thee and Lead Kindly Light. The center of the page opposite had a sketch of Mrs. McKinley and of a black-draped vacant chair. The streamer headline was

>   Women of the New England States
>   Send Through the Boston Globe on the Funeral Day
>   of the Lamented President
>   Sweet Messages of Sympathy to Mrs. McKinley

The rules were turned to black borders throughout the paper that day.

A few days later a special article introduced the new occupants of the White House under the headline "An Interesting Family." There were photographs of Mrs. Roosevelt, Alice, then 18, Theodore, Jr., and Kermit.

America was about to enter upon a new chapter of The Strenuous Life under T.R.

This was less than a total surprise, for T.R.'s reputation for exuberance reached back to his zeal for reform in his Albany legislative days at age 24, through his attacks on the spoilsmen of politics as federal Civil Service commissioner, his battles with corruption as police commissioner of New York, his pronounced jingoism before the war with Spain, and his campaigning for governor of New York with a troop of Rough Riders.

The Globe, viewing the turbulence of his career in New York, had observed long before Teddy reached Washington that if he ever became president "the people of the United States would have insomnia for four years." But when he had been vice president only three months, Uncle Dudley reappraised Roosevelt to say that "he was the only person in the administration who had seen the need of preparing for war and as assistant secretary of the navy went ahead to prepare the Navy. In the war he showed courage, enthusiasm and general abilities. He served as governor of New York with ability and with discretion. His reputation for courage, ability and honesty stood the test of the battlefield and of a position of prominence and power. Power makes the most strenuous and impetuous more or less conservative and brings out the best qualities of a brave man."

In this reappraisal, undoubtedly by James Morgan, Uncle Dudley said, "I want to withdraw that conclusion about insomnia. Not that the American people would be likely to go to sleep for four years if he were President, but we need no longer 'view with alarm' his possible promotion to that exalted position."

That was June 2, 1901. Fifteen weeks later Theodore Roosevelt was President. "That mad man is President," groaned Mark Hanna. "That damned cowboy in the White House," mourned other GOP stalwarts.

But General Taylor, Democrat, declared editorially that it was no time for unhappy predictions. Roosevelt had had "one of the most striking careers that has ever been known in the history of this republic." As governor, Roosevelt

> showed plainly that he was his own man . . . the impetuous and strenuous features of his nature were chastened and tempered by great responsibilities . . . That discretion and conservatism will be still further developed by the responsibilities that now devolve upon him. He is an educated and well

equipped man in the prime of manhood. He is naturally a hard worker . . . He is entitled to begin his career as President with the good wishes of every lover of the republic. Let us all hope he will make a record worthy of his day and generation and one which will reflect credit on his country.

Seventy years after, such an attitude strikes one as simply the journalistic norm — to accept the democratic process, to respect the president, to give the new man a chance. But the appreciative letters on his editorial that came to the General from leading public men suggest that it was not the norm of his times. The tone of other partisan papers, the New York World, Hearst's New York Journal, the Boston Post, was quite different. The General was running a frankly partisan paper. But his humanity surmounted his partisanship. From his early twenties he had been deeply involved in politics in an era of bitter partisanship, and it was in his character to moderate this. After him, for a generation of the Globe, his policy became a formula for neutrality. But General Taylor was not neutral; he was humane.

The Auto Arrives

"Campaign by Auto" was a front page headline in the Globe November 1, 1903. The Democratic candidate for governor, William Gaston, had covered 20 miles to speak in ten Boston wards the evening before. "It was the first trip of its kind ever attempted in this State and very successful. Mr. Gaston said the auto assisted him to cover a much larger territory than if an ordinary carriage had been employed. Both machines used were of the French pattern and high speed. Hon. W. T. A. Fitzgerald, chairman of the city committee, planned the trip."

The Republicans were vulnerable. Governor Bates had proved a weak executive. The Republican legislature had turned down labor bills, the income tax, women's suffrage. But on November 4 the Globe editorially conceded that "Governor Bates's strength was underestimated." He won by a narrow 35,000. "Col. Gaston made a gallant fight . . . a signal service in pointing to needed reforms in State government."

William Gaston, despite the Globe's support and hopes for him, never won an election although he was a figure in Democratic politics for more than 25 years. Member of a conservative law firm, he was tagged as a corporation man and was miscast to lead the rising labor movement of the early 1900's against the Republican Establishment. But he could finance his own campaigns. The Democrats turned to Gaston again in 1922 when Senator Henry Cabot Lodge had to face his first popular election for the Senate. Lodge had proved unbeatable for 30 years, and the Democrats probably felt they owed Colonel Gaston the chance to make a sacrifice run. But it proved one of he closest elections ever: Lodge 414,000 Gaston 406,000. Unquestionably a more contemporary candidate could have beaten Lodge. Gaston made one more foray in 1926 against Gov. Alvin Fuller, who disposed of him by attacking his connection with the Boston Elevated, which in bankruptcy had wrung from a complacent legislature a guarantee of six-percent dividends for 30 years.

This dead horse became a big factor in the deficit of the El — passed on to tax-payers — which frightened the metropolitan community over the next 40 years from making needed extensions of transit to meet suburban expansion.

But Gaston refused the nomination in 1904 and it went to William O. Douglas, a Brockton shoe manufacturer who believed in good pay and unions and in advertising. The constant advertising of the Douglas shoe carried his photograph so that his face was as well known as Lydia Pinkham's. Douglas defeated Governor Bates for the first Democratic victory in the state in a dozen years. It came while President Roosevelt was sweeping Massachusetts, a notable early instance of the capacity of Bay State independents to split tickets. "Roosevelt's election was expected," the Globe commented. "Douglas's election is the greatest surprise in the history of Massachusetts. There is no parallel for it. His phenomenal success is the more marked because it is the first time he has been a gubernatorial candidate. His novel advertising caught and held attention and proved again that 'advertising pays.' " But the Globe analysis proved there was more to it than that. "Citizens of every calling were dissatisfied with conditions . . . Mr. Douglas's addresses were simple, direct and business-like. Businessmen believed in his reciprocity and tariff views. Wage earners welcomed his frank statements. That he will make a strong and popular governor is the sincere belief of the Globe."

But he didn't. He was miscast in politics, impatient with legislative frustrations and, after a colorless one-year term, refused renomination. The Democrats were in limbo again for four years, which ended in 1910 only when a maverick Republican, Eugene Foss, turned Democrat and exploited the Republicans' persistent veto of labor bills. Foss won three times; this was a transitional period until David I. Walsh's election in 1913 brought a forthright reform administration to initiate progressive legislation across the board.

End of Innovation

The period of innovation in the Globe was approximately over with the turn of the century. The new appeals, to women, to children, to the new classes, to labor, had established a new constituency. From here on the growth of the newspaper followed the growth of the community. Proven practices were continued. Successful methods became traditional policy.

The Globe settled down and took on an institutional character that deepened with the years that moved it, almost changeless, from one generation of management into the next. The same men were at the helm in the editorial department. They had learned General Taylor's ways and applied the formulas that had worked well.

The times were fairly easy for a static journalism from the Spanish War to the first world war, a period that historians have generally counted as an overlap of the nineteenth century, ending in 1914. The American community wasn't demanding much more change than came naturally to the energetic Theodore Roosevelt. Radio and television were still far in the future, but the new automobile was creating a whole new field of advertising. The Globe's chief challenge came from two newer newspapers that in their turn were innovators.

Edwin Grozier's Post had a 13-year start when Hearst launched the Boston American in 1904. Each in turn cultivated new elements of readership at the bottom of the cultural ladder, as the Globe had at its start. Each exploited new dimensions of sensationalism. Each in this period was militantly Democratic, although a generation later they both became conservative, leaving the Globe the one liberal paper in the city.

But in the early 1900's the rise of these two new mass circulation papers left the Globe in a middle position. It had been for a quarter century the popular mass circulation paper of the region. It now occupied a moderate position, with the conservative Herald, paper of the businessman, and the sedate Transcript at one end of the journalistic spectrum, the Post and American at the other.

This new middle ground in which it found itself had a psychological effect on the Globe. The change was gradual, perhaps imperceptible even to the management. But the Globe was becoming a more conventional newspaper, its headlines less exciting, its editorial positions moderated. The new sensationalism repelled both the Taylor management and the Globe editors. They had no appetite for such a war of yellow journalism as New York had been through.

The newspaper situation in Boston at this period gave the Taylors occasion to share the sensibilities ascribed to Adolph Ochs when he began publishing the New York Times during the Hearst-Pulitzer newspaper war. Ochs's biographer, Gerald Johnson, says Ochs built the Times on the conviction that there were enough people who wanted the news but liked a quiet life. The Taylors had a particular aversion to Hearst methods and to Hearst's personal publicity. This brought stringent insistence on keeping the Taylor family out of the paper. As Charles, Jr., was a very active man, involved with charitable, institutional, and publisher's affairs, careful surveillance on the copy desk was called for. The Globe reaction to bizarre and frenetic Hearst campaigns was to avoid campaigns. The Globe wasn't rocking the boat, which had a moderating effect on journalistic enterprise. It became less sensitive to being scooped by the Post. The Post scoop was suspect to begin with and would turn out not to matter much. Globe circulation was stable. But the paper developed the feature side, adding columns, specialties, new departments. It featured the human side of the news. Its coverage of events, large and small, was the most comprehensive of any, its staff the largest.

It excelled in coverage of anything that responded to organization — fire, flood, election, convention, parade. Whenever planning, preparation, organization, completeness came into play, the Globe could not be beaten. The great fires, Chelsea and Salem, the *Titanic* disaster, the great Vermont flood — on all such overriding events the Globe was ever on top of the story. It had the largest sports staff and the most sports pages, and included schoolboy games, even sandlot leagues. It could be reasonably described as a paper for all the family. Typical Globe features had their big innings in the Sunday paper, long dominant but now double the circulation of any other Sunday paper in the region. The Globe subscribed to every syndicated feature it could lay hold of. The personalities of journalism appeared in the Globe: Mr. Dooley and George Ade, later Walter Lippmann, Dorothy Thompson, and a whole galaxy of columnists.

Within its own staff, descriptive writing brightened the pages. Before the first world war, absence of pressure of world news gave liberal space for colorful detail, for the dramatic recital of shipwreck or flood and for all the tragicomic kaleidoscope of the passing scene.

M. E. Hennessy.   John D. Merrill.

The Globe had sensitive writers with an ear for the quality of words. Frank P. Sibley was noted for his photographic eye for the detail of an event, and equally as the maestro of the courtroom drama. He became distinguished as the Globe's correspondent in World War I with the Yankee Division. A. J. Philpott, self-educated as a printer, was equally at home interviewing Mark Twain or pursuing a psychological trail to Mexico, to a missing man, investigating spiritualist seances, or appreciating the Museum of Fine Arts's newest acquisition. He was the first New England reporter to go up in an airplane, the first newspaperman elected to the American Academy of Arts and Sciences; Boston College conferred a doctorate on him; Bashka Paeff sculptured his classic head in bronze for the museum. Winfield Thompson was a take-charge reporter who could manage the news of shipwreck or election. John Carberry for 20 years moved about the country wherever the action was, to meet Peary's return from the North Pole, to cover the McNamara brothers' trial for bombing in Los Angeles, the Baltimore convention that nominated Woodrow Wilson, the 1914 investigation of the New Haven Railroad. Lawrence J. Sweeney had progressed from office boy to top-rank reporter by a versatility as wide-ranging as the day's news grist. M. E. Hennessy knew everyone in politics. John D. Merrill's aplomb was equal to any occasion on State Street, at Harvard, on Beacon Hill, or in sports. James Morgan, besides finding features for everyone else, undertook the largest himself. He followed the path of Napoleon 20,000 miles for a year-long feature and the footsteps of Lincoln for another historical series and at every election illuminated political history for Globe readers.

On his long writing absences, and also to guide the editorial page after Charles Dyar ended his long regime as chief editorial writer in 1904, Morgan left his associate Edward Burns, poet and scholar, in charge of the Sunday paper and features generally. Burns had as editorial associate Henry Appleton, who had studied abroad and taught modern languages before he joined the paper. He followed labor and economics and the Irish land troubles.

The Globe was a big, sprawling paper for its time, 14 pages daily, 60 Sunday in 1904. What it lacked in form and coherence and in typographical appearance it made up for in reader interest. Its content was as miscellaneous as a variety show, and there was everything in it.

The reader was drawn inside the paper by the practice of continuing lead stories to inner pages and also by putting important and interesting stories inside. Whether from a business motive to lead the reader through the ads or from a journalistic concern to spread interest throughout the paper, the Globe always opened up to a sense of anticipation. Whatever the front page featured, there would be more worth seeing inside, stimulating "cover to cover" reading. This led Globe editors to an assurance that the reader would find a good story wherever it was. The confidence was justified, but it resulted in hodge-podge. Critics of typography would say for three-quarters of its first century that the Globe was put together with a shovel. Staff critics were blunter: the Globe wasn't edited, it just leaked out.

But an institution comes to have a life of its own. Those in control may modify it, but to reverse it or change it radically is to risk losing the identity that has established it and won its clientele. In a newspaper this is highly visible. A publisher is reluctant to change the appearance of a paper that has become familiar. The Globe long held to old-fashioned typography and makeup, with the ads on the front page and on the tops of inside pages that had become characteristic.

With its emphasis on features and lively reporting, the Globe was broadening its base, practically and politically. Its appeal was to average readers who lived on the side streets of the city and in the modest houses of new suburban developments. They included the large and growing group of independent voters who would elect such bland and nearly nonpartisan politicians as David I. Walsh, Democrat, and Leverett Saltonstall, Republican, with little concern for party labels.

The Globe's gradual withdrawal from any particular concern with Democratic politics coincided with a sharp change in the Boston political scene. The early Irish mayors, Hugh O'Brien for four terms in the middle 1880's and Patrick Collins in 1901 and 1903, were the ablest and most respected men their minority party could put up. As minority men they could succeed only by personal quality in competition with the Gastons, Quincys and Saltonstalls. This era ended in City Hall when Patrick Collins was followed in 1905 by John F. Fitzgerald; the politics of the machine and the ward heeler took over. Fitzgerald was followed by James M. Curley, whose intermittent administrations at City Hall covered a span of 40 years.

But the Boston-bound politicians of the Fitzgerald-Curley period never won in state elections save for the one time that Curley rode in on the coat-tails of Franklin Roosevelt in the depth of depression in 1934. The Globe by then was totally nonpartisan, conspicuously neutral in the widening gap between Democratic city and Republican suburb.

T.R. and Hearst

Through the early 1900's the Globe like the rest of America operated within the dramatic orbit of Theodore Roosevelt, who was constantly in the headlines with his trust-busting campaigns, his forays against standpatism, his rhetorical Armageddons, his strenuous nationalism, his whimsy for simplified spelling. Roosevelt was the first public man to discover the Monday morning news vacuum and to fill it with timely pronouncements and actions. His initials T.R. fitted any headline.

The Globe found much to applaud and much to caricature in the athletic President. It frequently contrived to turn cheers for his progressive policies into a foil to attack the standpat Republicans in the State House or in Congress.

Roosevelt's 1904 victory over his conservative Democratic opponent, Alton B. Parker, the Globe hailed as a personal triumph, his popularity "from his bold fighting quality — a belief he is honest in his convictions . . . Seldom has a President had such a great opportunity to work for the public good," the paper editorialized. "Seldom have the people expected so much of one. Having declined another term, T.R. has nothing to fear from exerting himself against the powerful influence of the trusts — but everything to gain."

Roosevelt had announced upon his election: "Under no circumstances will I be a candidate or accept another nomination. On the 4th of March I shall have served three and a half years and this constitutes my first term. The wise custom which limits the President to two terms regards the substance but not the form."

T.R. later regretted this but in 1908 was stuck with it. It was a much more downright statement than Calvin Coolidge's later "I do not choose to run."

In an editorial October 6, 1906, the Globe supported Roosevelt's view that "there must be an extension of the power of the Federal government — an inherent power where the object is beyond the power of the several states which he holds are wholly powerless to deal with corporate wealth. The President is still striving to turn his party out of the path of conservatism into its original road of radicalism."

Roosevelt's Nobel Peace Prize in 1905 for mediating the Russo-Japanese War at Portsmouth gave a lift to the national pride and tended to obliterate earlier concern over his questionable coup that acquired the Panama Canal site. The whole seamy side of that deal had not then been exposed.

Globe headlines of November 1903 had reported the swift sequence of the movement for Panama's independence:

November 4

Independence of the Isthmus is Proclaimed

U.S. Hurrying Warships to Scene

November 5

Perfect Order in New Republic of Panama

Bluejackets Landed

Revolutionists Ask Recognition

Colombian Troops May Go Away

Expect Canal Will Now be Built

November 6

Colombian Troops Leave the Isthmus

Recognition Today is Probable

November 6 evening

> Is Recognized
> Panama is Nation
> Action Taken by Cabinet
> De Facto Government Can Now Do Business

November 9

> Colombia Sends Protest to U.S.

The Globe in a naive editorial November 6, "A Canal in Sight," said: "If people of the Isthmus, without our aid, succeed in detaching themselves from Colombia and establishing a stable government, we would, of course, be ready to recognize the new government. Then we could properly propose to make a treaty whereby the Panama Canal may be speedily constructed. But we must keep our hands clean."

But three days later, after the Colombian protest had raised some questions, another editorial, "The Isthmian Troubles," suggested there was no need for haste. "A great power in relation with a small one should act with dignity." But T.R. acted with speed to get a canal treaty.

On June 22, 1906, a Globe headline:

> "Dig" the Order on Canal
> Senate Approves Lock Plan
> President Will Order Work to be Pushed

In the 1906 election campaign, the Globe gave generous front page space to a Roosevelt attack on William Randolph Hearst, candidate against Charles Evans Hughes for governor of New York. The November 2 headline was: "Root Flays Hearst for the President / Secretary Says He is not Guiltless of the Murder of McKinley / Branded Him as a Violent and Unworthy Demagog / Bitter Denunciation Delivered in Address at Utica Mass Meeting." Root was quoted, "I say to you with the President's authority that he regards Mr. Hearst as wholly unfit to be governor, as an insincere self-seeking demagog."

Root quoted T.R. in his first message to Congress, when he spoke of the assassin of President McKinley as

> inflamed by the reckless utterances of those who, on the stump and in the public press, appeal to the dark and evil spirits of malice and greed, envy and sullen hatred. The wind is sowed by the men who preach such doctrine, and they cannot escape the responsibility for the whirlwind that is reaped.

> I say, by the President's authority, that in penning those words, with the horror of President McKinley's assassination fresh before him, he had Mr. Hearst specifically in mind. And I say by his authority that what he thought of Mr. Hearst then, he thinks of Mr. Hearst now.

Hearst lost to Hughes while the Democrats were winning every other office in New York. In an editorial on the election results, November 7, the Globe observed: "The whole country eagerly watched returns from New York. Mr. Hughes defeated Mr. Hearst after perhaps the bitterest campaign on record. The outcome was so problematical that President Roosevelt came to the rescue of his party, allowing his secretary of state [Root] to inform voters what he thought of Mr. Hearst. His opinion was so condemnatory that it must have had much to do with the defeat of Mr. Hearst."

Hearst was intensely active in Massachusetts politics also. He had started the Boston American in 1904. His chief editorial writer, Granville McFarland, was his spokesman in Democratic councils; in 1907, failing to win the Democratic nomination for the Hearst candidate, McFarland organized the Independence League that nominated Thomas L. Hisgen, a labor man, for governor. This was widely regarded as a buildup for a Hearst move for the presidential nomination in 1908. George Fred Williams led in blocking the move and swung the Massachusetts Democratic organization once more to Bryan's support.

Hisgen divided the Democratic vote with Henry Whitney, the steamship and street railway magnate who had the Globe's support as able to supply businesslike government. But Whitney's involvement in the old street railway franchise issue of the 1880's was brought up against him again, as in 1905 when he had been defeated for lieutenant governor, and again proved his albatross. Now he added a handicap of railroad interests for a proposed merger of the New Haven and the Boston & Maine that alienated many Democrats.

Theodore Roosevelt's back-to-the-land movement found journalistic response. The Sunday Symposium in the November 3, 1907, Globe asked: "What chance is there for a man from the city to support himself and family on a farm?" Leaders of the agricultural colleges of New England contributed, saying it depended on the man, chances had never been better for those who took to it, but cautioning about the problems to be met.

The President's gospel of the strenuous life had its echoes, too. Edward Payson Weston, a great advocate of walking, created such interest that the Globe assigned a top reporter, Edward J. Park, to cover his walking tour in Connecticut. The headline November 5, 1907: "Fresh as at Start / Weston Covers 16 miles in four hours."

Another Sunday Symposium, October 7, 1906, raised the question, "Are Winter Sports Neglected by Americans?" Dr. Dudley A. Sargent deplored that Americans had lost their enthusiasm for bicycling. Professor Robert J. Roberts saw winter exercise neglected.

A light note of raillery containing a seed of seriousness ran through occasional Globe editorials and editorial points of the T.R. era, to the effect that Roosevelt had stolen the clothes of the Democrats, who stole them in turn from the Populists. When Bryan returned in autumn 1906 from a European trip, the Globe took occasion to compare him with Roosevelt in a long Uncle Dudley editorial (September 6), "The New Bryan's Resemblance to the Old." The Republicans

> must give adequate guarantees that Mr. Roosevelt's successor will be equally alert to keep up with the Democrats. There can't be any backward steps, for the American people, when they are on the march, never walk like a crab . . .
>
> Mr. Roosevelt only read the plain signs of the times when he set about to seize the advance ground of the Democrats and he crowded them out so successfully that they retreated to conservatism in 1904. By that bold stroke he renewed his party's lease of power with the most general approval ever won at the polls.

But the acceptance shown Bryan on his return from Europe showed there would be no turning back to conservatism. "Cleveland and McKinley brought that long siege to its climax."

There followed a eulogy of Bryan: "Whether Bryan is destined to go on to the end as a John the Baptist in our politics — preparing the way for others . . . he does not have to win elections to serve his country.

"Without office, without the prestige of electoral victories, he has exerted for 10 years more power than many a President . . . His campaigns undeniably made the present Roosevelt policies politically possible and politically necessary."

Two years later the Globe welcomed Bryan to the 1908 presidential campaign and found occasion to hail him as an innovator in American politics.

Jubilee

The Globe observed a Jubilee Week in 1903 which was the thirtieth year of General Taylor's management. It celebrated particularly "the leap from horsecars to electrics, from the dimness of a world lighted by gas to the blazing illumination of electricity."

Three years later it gave equal emphasis to the newness of the automobile. Announcing a 1906 auto contest, it hailed the auto as "at once the great convenience and the great pleasure vehicle of the day. Nowhere else in this country can it be enjoyed as on the beautiful and unequalled roads of New England. The Globe herewith makes an offer to bring this superb modern invention within reach of its readers."

Ten autos were offered as prizes, $1,000 touring cars, $800 runabouts. Every contestant was allowed one assistant to collect Globe coupons who, if his principal won an auto, qualified for a pony cart or bicycle.

In 1906 a bicycle was the dream of a ten-year-old boy in a quiet Boston suburb. Almost all the older kids had bikes. The automobile hadn't yet taken over the roads. Trolleys ran on tracks that kept to their place. The roads were safe enough so that police seldom interfered with coasting on them in winter, sometimes protecting the best coasting hill. All it took was a cop at the bottom to blow a warning whistle if a coal wagon were starting up.

An unexpected chance for one lad's bicycle came when Mr. Fred Hasty, the locomotive engineer next door, entered the Boston Globe auto contest and needed an assistant. Mr. Hasty thought they had a chance. The Highlands was a friendly section of moderate home developments, on the edge of the five-cent trolley fare to Boston. The boy rang doorbells assiduously to get neighbors to save their Globe coupons for Mr. Hasty. The 17,562 Globe coupons this effort yielded brought the engineer just outside the prize list. But he saw that the boy got his bicycle. With impartial enterprise the boy set out on the bicycle to build a Saturday Evening Post route. The Post was five cents, weekly, and two cents of the nickel went to the boy who sold it. The Post gave prizes too, for the greatest increase in sales each week — magic lanterns, flashlights, baseball mitts, hockey sticks. But building a magazine route proved tougher going than collecting coupons. The first woman to answer a doorbell said she'd have to ask her husband and the boys whether they'd rather have the Saturday Evening Post or the Sunday Globe. Each was five cents. A difficult decision.

That was the competition. People who could afford both a magazine and a Sunday paper bought the Sunday Herald. People who didn't even think about a magazine bought the Sunday Post.

But the Sunday Globe kept up with all such competition. It claimed twice the circulation of any other Sunday paper in New England and as much advertising as the next two Boston papers. The Globe Man, a beaming roly-poly in a front page cartoon, proclaimed the ever-escalating figures of the Globe on his expansive vest.

The Globe was a family item from childhood in a neighborhood like the Highlands. Mutt and Jeff were familiar figures from earliest memory, and on Sundays there were colored comics, Kitty and Danny, Professor O How Wise, and the Captain and the Kids. And Mr. Bowser and Mr. Dooley. And lots of baseball with the features of the day's game graphically told in a cartoon that might take half the top of a sports page. Cy Young and Ty Cobb were household names. The Globe described the Red Sox outfield as the finest in baseball — Tris Speaker, Duffy Lewis, and Harry Hooper. A daily feature by a patriarch of the game named Tim Murnane spelled out the rules and its fine points for sandlot devotees.

In its 1903 Jubilee Week the Globe had not neglected to celebrate the revolution on the newspaper in those 30 years. The Dudley editorial of Sunday, November 8, 1903, was "A Jubilee Reflection: The Sunday Newspaper," and it had a good story to tell.

> In 1873 the Herald was the only Sunday paper in Boston. But it was only a daily paper on Sunday. It was four pages. Today's 56 page Sunday Globe is 14 times the size of the Sunday paper of 1873. The 1873 paper had 11½ columns of advertising. Today's Sunday Globe has 237 columns of advertising. The news content of the 1873 paper was almost all general news. It had only 300 words from Europe. There was no sharp departure from the makeup of the daily paper, no signed contributions by representative thinkers — no letters of travel or comment — no poetry or fiction or household subject or social news or sporting departments — not a line for the young — not a picture for the eye. The Sunday paper has broadened the scope of the press — for all the family."

The editorial went on to recite the growth of the Globe and of Boston. Daily circulation had gone from the 5,000 of 1873 to 195,000. The Sunday circulation was 297,000. Boston had grown in population from 292,000 to 613,000 and in valuation from $694 millions to $1,220 millions.

Next day's Jubilee editorial was on "New England Influence." It refuted "the pessimists who prefer to believe that New England influence has declined in the last 30 years."

A full page of articles on "the advance of New England" was published each day during the week's observance.

Other advances were right around the corner. The November 3, 1904, paper announced "Handsomest banking house in the United States — New Quarters of Kidder, Peabody Company on Devonshire Street Just Completed." A photograph showed the two-and-a-half-story Greek temple structure of the bank, its low classical facade conspicuous between taller buildings of commercial appearance. A later generation commented that it was also conspicuous for its wasteful use of high land values, squatting in disdain of utilizing even the normal building height of the area.

News of November 1909 welcomed Boston's own opera and a new art museum.

The Opera House opened November 8 with "a magnificent audience in the new house" and "curtain calls following each act" with an "ovation to Eben Jordan," president of the opera company. The Globe of November 9 gave six columns on page one to a sketch of the interior of the Opera House and two whole pages inside to "La Gioconda," and published the full list of subscribers.

That was a day of cultural celebration. The opening of the new building of the Museum of Fine Arts had a whole page for its "priceless collections — magnificently housed," a six-column spread of interior photographs, and a story of the "problem of effective display solved by patient study by experts."

With the opening of the Opera House the Globe blossomed out with a music critic, Arthur Wilson. It had been a long time since it had had one, so long that Wilson thought he was the first and so told his latest successor, Michael Steinberg, in an interview on his ninetieth birthday in the Globe of May 10, 1970. It was the second Eben Jordan, a devotee of music and chief contributor to building the Opera House, who persuaded the Globe to take on a music critic. Jordan, however, was

The night copy desk in 1903. Harry Poor is in the slot (fifth figure from left).

soon unhappy over Wilson's music criticism and, according to Wilson, tried to get him fired. But, as Wilson recalled it, General Taylor said they had never wanted a music critic in the first place but now they had one were going to keep him. Wilson stayed with the Globe ten years, then in 1919 returned to his earlier profession of music teaching.

A young M.I.T. instructor, Penfield Roberts, then took on the music criticism for a dozen years. Roberts, only three years out of Harvard, was teaching English at Tech, where he now added a course in music appreciation. His initials, P R, at the end of Globe symphony reviews through the 1920's signalled a cool detachment that resisted the raptures of Boston concert audiences over the romanticism of Koussevitzky. In 1932 Roberts, by then associate professor of history and a collaborator with William L. Langer in the *Encyclopedia of World History,* gave up reviewing. Cyrus Durgin then started a 30-years' stint of distinction in covering both music and theater.

On September 1, 1909, the New York Central ran an ad in the Globe:

Overnight to Chicago
20th Century Limited
The 20½ Hour Train — Boston-Chicago

The lead editorial that day was "Waste Not, Want Not." Edward Hyatt, superintendent of education in California, had warned of the need to educate young people to the importance of conserving our natural resources. The Globe picked this up: "Our natural resources are not inexhaustible. Future citizens need to learn to protect their birthright in land and water." It endorsed Gifford Pinchot and his conservation movement.

A September 16 headline:

Taft Sustains Secretary Ballinger
Approves Interior Dept. Acts in Alaska Coal Lands Case
Orders Removal of [L.R.] Glavis for Disloyalty to Superior

and on September 18: "Taft Reads Rebels Out / Boldly Defends Payne Tariff." September 17, from Nairobi:

Killed Bull Elephant
Col. Roosevelt Secured a Good Tusker

Debut of James M. Curley

The day before the 1904 elections Boston newspaper readers became sharply aware of the name Curley. James M. Curley, age 30, former state representative and now alderman, was running for re-election. Another Curley, Thomas F., no relation, was a state representative running for re-election from the same Roxbury district.

But it was not the election that brought them onto the Globe front page November 7, 1904.

Curleys' Friends
Big Turnout in Roxbury
Men Who Go to Jail Say They were Betrayed

Election bulletin, November 1907.

"One of the most remarkable political meetings ever held in Roxbury was that of the Tammany Club of Ward 17 last night — a reception to Alderman James M. Curley and Repr. Thomas F. Curley who will begin 60 day sentences in Charles Street jail at noon today." The evening edition headline was

> Curleys Castigated
> Judge Lowell is Severe
> Calls Taking Office Effrontery
> Constituency Shares in the Shame
> Sentence of Two Months Reaffirmed

The two headlines aptly describe the divided verdict of Boston on James M. Curley, who dominated political headlines in Boston for most of the next 40 years.

Some 300 Tammany Club members and friends filled the court corridors as the Curleys faced Judge Lowell. The evening Globe summarized the two-year-old case:

> Briefly the history of the case is this:
> On Dec. 4, 1902, an exam was made by Civil Service officials to obtain eligibles for post office clerks and letter carriers.

Bartholomew Vahey and James J. Hughes (of Ward 17) were among the applicants.

Within a few days, there were rumors that some unnamed politicians had represented some of the applicants. Examination of the writing in application blanks with the exams confirmed the suspicion that some one else took the exams for two applicants.

On Feb. 25, 1903, the Curleys surrendered to U.S. authorities. They were held in $2500 each for the U.S. grand jury.

On April 3, 1903, they were indicted for impersonating others at a civil service exam — Vahey and Hughes were indicted for conspiracy to violate the law. After trial in the U.S. district court they were convicted Oct. 2, 1903. Sentence was two months in jail. They appealed to the U.S. circuit court in January which denied their appeal March 4, 1904. An appeal to the U.S. Supreme Court was denied November 2. The U.S. Appeals Court issued an order to the circuit court to enforce its March 1 decree for sentencing.

When the offense was committed Thomas Curley was a deputy collector of the city and James M. Curley a State representative.

Subsequent to conviction Thomas Curley ran for State representative and James Curley for alderman. Both were elected.

Both campaigns were bitterly fought. The Good Government Association and Republicans denounced the Curleys and their supporters in unmeasured terms.

The Democrats replied that the cases were not concluded and the men should not resign under fire.

The Tammany Club stood by both.

In court today, H. W. Dunn, counsel for the Curleys, argued for a fine, not jail — that they had been humiliated enough.

A Street Commissioner, a Representative, an ex-Senator, spoke for the Curleys.

Judge Lowell said he could not conceive of such effrontery as was exhibited by the Curleys in acting in office and running for office after conviction. He considered their constituency shared in the shame of their actions.

Both Curleys said they expected to be elected tomorrow and to serve.

They were.

Patent Medicines and Other Ads

On March 15, 1905, the Massachusetts House of Representatives devoted the whole afternoon to debate on a bill requiring that patent medicine bottles carry labels of their contents. Some 20 members participated in the debate, which described the contents of "cancer cures" and other nostrums as including morphine, cocaine, and often 20–40 percent alcohol.

Nothing of this appeared in the next day's Boston newspapers, or indeed in any newspaper in the state except the Springfield Republican. The patent medicine business was enjoying more than $100 millions of annual sales and spending some $40 millions a year on advertising. The Massachusetts bill was beaten. The newspapers lobbied against it; they had to under an ingenious contract which the Proprietary Association of America had contrived. The advertising contract would be cancelled if legislation hostile to proprietary medicines was enacted by the state legislature. All the patent medicine industry had to do when such legislation appeared was put the newspapers on notice about their advertising contracts.

Mark Sullivan exposed this in Collier's of November 4, 1905. It was one of the notable instances of the muckraking of that era and was followed up by Mark Sullivan and Samuel Hopkins Adams in the campaign for a national pure food and drug act. The newspapers of the period had abandoned reform to the magazines, and Sullivan's exposure explains why. They were enormously dependent on this advertising. In the Globe of March 16, 1905, patent medicine ads totaled ten percent of all ads. Ten years before on the same date it had been 20 percent. Only as advertising expanded and diversified were the papers freed of this corrupt incubus.

The self-cancelling advertising contract was the invention of F. C. Cheney, manufacturer of a catarrh cure, who as president of the Proprietary Association of America in 1905 divulged his system to his association, which adopted it. Cheney made the point that this contract "throws the responsibility on the newspapers." He had signed such contracts, he reported, with some 16,000 newspapers and had had no refusals. When a newspaper got out of line it was dealt with. The Cleveland Press, a Scripps-McCrae paper, launched a campaign against the "patent medicine trust." A boycott was promptly clamped on the proprietary medicine advertising of the entire Scripps-McCrae group of papers, lifted only when M. A. McCrae gave assurance that he was suppressing the crusade of the Cleveland Press. This action was reported to the nineteenth annual meeting of the Proprietary Association.

Among the earliest and most pervasive of the patent medicine advertisers were Peruna, Paine's Celery Compound, Lydia Pinkham's Compound, Greene's Nervura, and Smith's Revivifier and Blood Purifier.

Edward Bok opened the campaign against the nostrum peddlers in 1892 when he banned all such advertising from the Ladies' Home Journal. It was Bok who persuaded Mark Sullivan to give up his law practice and devote himself to investigations of patent medicines and then to other reforms. Colliers' and Everybody's magazines pulled the laboring oars for the Pure Food Act of 1906.

The muckrakers had less effect in reform of advertising than did its own growth. The twentieth century brought advertising to a maturity required by its own immense development. In the nineteenth century it had been a supplemental revenue; but by 1914 advertising revenue had become nearly double circulation revenue. Advertising had become professional: the age of mass production required mass merchandising and the rise of manufacturers demanding markets legitimatized advertising. Led by the new automobile, national product advertising squeezed out the patent medicines and elixirs of the more primitive earlier period. The newspaper was the prime merchandising medium.

The Associated Advertising Clubs of America in 1912 produced a "Truth in Advertising" code. The same year a postal regulation required all advertising to be labeled "advt."

Total daily newspaper advertising in the United States was $275 million in 1915, but $650 million in 1920. Twenty percent of it was national advertising in 1915, 30 percent by 1920. The competition of broadcasting still lay in the future.

In August 1914, the Globe advertised the advertising linage of the first seven months:

Globe First in Boston
1st seven months

Advertising

Globe	5,049,000 lines
Post	4,440,000 lines
American	3,521,000 lines
Herald	2,602,000 lines

General Taylor's early maxim that advertising is news found interesting confirmation. When the Model A Ford came out in 1928, the newsboys in front of the Globe office followed their merchandising instinct instead of the judgment of the day editor. They ignored the front page headlines and opened the paper to the two-page spread of the Ford ad, hawking it with "Read about the new Ford car." It seemed to pay off.

Steffens' Boston

The Good Government Association, the reform movement that had fought the Curleys in 1903, had been organized that year. Their prime activity in 1903 was to support Louis A. Frothingham, Republican speaker of the Massachusetts House, for mayor of Boston. He lost to the able, highly respected Mayor Patrick A. Collins. But Collins died before his term finished, and in 1905 John F. Fitzgerald, political leader of the North End, won election with the support of Martin Lomasney's potent Ward Eight organization, despite the opposition of Curley's Tammany Club. Fitzgerald had won three terms in the Congress where in his first term he had been the only Catholic in the House. His election introduced machine politics to City Hall. Hungry ward heelers filled the municipal departments with a legion of new employees. New contracts burdened the city's taxes. Proper Bostonians were alarmed. The Republican legislature created a finance commission as a watchdog on City Hall, but its operations proved largely futile.

The impetus to reform brought a new city charter in 1908 aimed at ending boss rule and the log-rolling of the huge City Council of 75 members elected by wards. It made elections nonpartisan, with a small City Council elected at large. It was called a "strong mayor" charter. The prospective strong mayor for 1909 was James J. Storrow, counted Boston's leading citizen. But John F. Fitzgerald, after a defeat in 1907, put together for the first time a combination of the several city machines, uniting Martin Lomasney's West End, James M. Curley's South End, and Patrick Joseph Kennedy's East Boston organizations with his own North End support. Fitzgerald beat Storrow, a shocking blow to the old Boston Establishment. The strong mayor setup fell into the hands of the enemy. Fitzgerald was the target of the Good Government Association until Curley beat him out in 1913 to create a more permanent target.

But reform was in the air in 1908, and it occurred to Edward A. Filene, the inventive, socially minded president of Filene's, to bring Lincoln Steffens to Boston to help plan a different kind of "bigger, better, busier Boston" than Honey Fitz's campaign slogan had in mind.

Steffens was famous for his investigations of municipal corruption published in muckraking magazines and brought together in his striking book of 1905, *The Shame of the Cities*. Steffens had found a consistent pattern of graft which had by then developed his philosophy that where there is a politician bribe-taker, there is a business man bribe-giver to obtain franchises or special privileges. Steffens had become an evangelist to convert "the good people" to his conviction that "it is good business men who corrupt our bad politicians." Filene agreed with Steffens to raise a fund to pay him for a year's study in Boston, to leave him a free hand, to report to a committee of leading citizens his recommendations for building a united and aspiring community.

Filene aimed at a two-year program. Steffens wanted to project it long-range, a dozen years ahead. They compromised on the "Boston 1915 Movement," which never came off. Boston balked Steffens. Filene's group failed to enlist decisive support of the most influential people. Filene lacked leadership — though he had created the famous automatic bargain basement of Filene's and employees' credit unions, initiated the first organization of chambers of commerce, and crusaded for consumers' cooperatives. The one monument to his work with Steffens was the Boston City Club, dedicated to community betterment and nondiscriminatory membership. But Filene was considered a maverick by other businessmen and was soon ousted even from the management of Filene's over his plan to turn over control to an employees' cooperative.

The 1915 movement failed to get off the ground. Steffens' difficulties in Boston were so complex that it was years before he could complete his report; and the committee could then do nothing with it, couldn't even find a publisher for it. The completeness of his frustration was only disclosed in his autobiography in 1931. Then Steffens said that he had found Boston more corrupt than any other city because unconscious of its own corruption, which was more subtly concealed. "Boston has carried the practice of hypocrisy to the nth degree of refinement, grace and failure."

But Steffens' findings on Boston did have an outlet in Metropolitan Magazine, which on February 20, 1914, and ensuing days that week took a two-column ad, half a page deep, in the Globe to announce:

> Lincoln Steffens
> Begins the Boston Book in the March Metropolitan on the news stands today
> It cost the Boston 1915 Committee from $10,000 to $20,000
> Buy it for 15 Cents

On encountering this announcement, a historian looks hard to see how the Globe dealt with the promised exposure of the Hub.

And he has to look hard. The editorial page had nothing on it, although it had space that day for an editorial on bird feeding and another on egg substitutes. No editorial comment on Steffens' report any day that week. Muckraking Boston was not a popular subject.

Nothing in the news columns that day either. But next day, on page eight under a one-column head, Steffens was quoted for a few paragraphs. That day Mayor

Curley made the front page twice. One story was a plea for feeding the birds. The other urged more politeness, especially on subways. The Globe goes for that to find

Chivalry Not Dead in Boston

Trolley Etiquette Observed by Men

The page eight space given to Steffens quotes him that "Boston is the case of a failure of government by good people. Boston is paved with good intentions. So is Hell . . . Boston is a common city of superior people. It has all the good things that other cities think, if they had them, would make impossible political corruption. Yet Boston has always had the good things and has always had political corruption."

The Globe's attitude on the Boston condition was to change 180 degrees, but not for a long generation. By the 1960's it was often engaged in two investigations at once, demanding reform. But that was a different era.

Actually, a candid discussion of Steffens' Boston report would have found strong defenses against his charge that Boston was more corrupt than other cities and that scandals were concealed. Steffens' penchant for self-dramatizing led him to theatrical generalizations. Scandals had been frequently aired in Boston, whose own ardent reformer George Fred Williams had made such an issue of street railway franchises in the 1880's as reverberated through elections for 40 years.

Before Steffens' publication in 1914 the scandal of the Morgan-Mellon exploitation of the New Haven Railroad and control of the Boston-Maine had brought legislative investigation that exposed a policy of corrupting legislators and newspapermen. Indeed, it led the Globe, with other papers, to reorganize their State House coverage. For future security the Globe shifted the incorruptible John D. Merrill from financial editor to the State House, where he became the trusted confidant of public men for a quarter century. He produced few headline stories, but Globe management evidently slept easier for having him there. They were content to let him write his own ticket. He was in effect the Globe's ambassador to politics and as a symbol of integrity was valued more than news.

Three generations intervened between the Boston of Boss Patrick Joseph Kennedy and his great-grandson President John Fitzgerald Kennedy. It was a long interval of retarded civic development. The same citizenry who elected Honey Fitz and Jim Curley made the core constituency of the Globe. It is no coincidence that the same long static period had its parallel in the retarding of the Globe's maturity to its full civic role.

Chelsea Fire

William Alcott, night city editor, was starting to church on Palm Sunday, April 12, 1908, a bright, sunny spring day with a brisk wind, when he noticed a column of smoke blowing over from next-door Chelsea. "My Gorry," said Alcott, using his strongest expletive. His Sunday School class would have to wait. He phoned the Globe. Stephen Holland, clerk to the city editor, was on the city desk, tiding over on Sunday morning from the late-night "lobster watch" man until the earliest arrival of the night city staff.

"Steve, there's a bad fire in Chelsea," said Alcott. "The second alarm has just come in. You'd better get hold of Denny."

Dennis J. Kelleher, the Chelsea-East Boston district man, had gone to church. But Mrs. Kelleher knew how to reach him — call the rectory. Denny had an arrangement with the pastor to call him out of church in an emergency.

By now a third alarm. Alcott was back on the phone: he was going to Chelsea. Send all the men you can. In half an hour the fire was completely out of control. In 40 minutes it had become a great conflagration. By noon the whole city was threatened. A third of Chelsea burned down that day.

Alcott phoned again that he had established headquarters in the Chelsea telephone exchange. Holland called up reporters to send to Alcott, then called city editor William D. Sullivan at his home in Winchester. W.D. phoned the General, who directed, "Get ready for an extra." This meant mobilizing a whole corps of off-duty crewmen on a Sunday morning, reporters, editors, compositors, stereotypers, pressmen, mailers, and wagon drivers. Steve got a crew of messenger boys and sent them off in herdics with addresses, to raise forces. By now W.D. had come in to take charge. What about newsboys? Steve rushed out to the Newsboys Reading Room, found a couple of lads there, and told them to spread the word: the Globe was getting out an extra.

Alcott phoned that the fire was coming his way. The Chelsea telephone exchange would soon be going, so he was retreating to the Everett exchange. There he arranged for two lines to the Globe. A dozen reporters were bringing him their fragments of the story. He had 15 reporters and three or four photographers deployed by noon. But the Everett exchange was swamped. The telephone company asked the Globe to give up one line and said they could keep the other only if it was in continuous use. That was another chore for Steve Holland, who between the news calls kept the line in use, talked and talked, recited poetry, told stories, sang songs over and over.

By a bit of luck the man whose job it was to shut off the steam to the stereotypers' tables had forgotten to do it that morning. So when the stereotypers came in, the steam tables were hot to dry the paper molds for the press plates and much time was saved. The first extra was on the street at 3:12, a second more complete one at 4:00, and a final one after the fire had burned itself out about 6:00.

The Globe activity had brought Acting Governor Eben S. Draper into the office, and he used the Globe phones to call out militiamen to patrol the fire and to order cots and blankets for the homeless of Chelsea. The Governor later moved his headquarters to Boston City Hall. The Globe newsboys and such wagons as could be mustered distributed 125,000 extras that afternoon and evening. There was no profit in it but enhanced prestige for enterprise, and it was stimulating to office morale that the paper could rally to an emergency and beat the town. Young Steve Holland was ranked with the boy who held the dike. He served many more years as assistant to the city editor, but that Palm Sunday remained his red-letter day. Newspaper work is like that.

Two for the North Pole

In September 1909 the North Pole burst upon the American consciousness in a raging controversy between two claimants for its discovery — Dr. Frederick A. Cook and Commander Robert Peary — that filled the front pages and most of the rest of the newspapers all month. Their acrid contention for the honor of discovery rocked on for five years.

The evening Globe of September 1 exploded with the world-shaking news for which no one was prepared:

America First at North Pole

Honor Won by Dr. F. A. Cook

The black headlines, three columns wide and nine lines deep, brought the story from Copenhagen. The first message came from the Shetland Islands to the Danish Colonial Office: "Dr. Cook, the American explorer, reached the North Pole April 21, 1908, according to a telegram received from Lerwick, Shetland Islands. Dr. Cook is on board the Danish government steamer, *Harsegede,* which passed Lerwick at noon today en route to Denmark."

The last line of the Globe headline foreshadowed what was to come:

Shackleton Delighted But Melville Doubts Report

Rear Admiral George W. Melville, retired, had conducted several Arctic expeditions. "I did not know that Dr. Cook had an outpost available for that purpose. I do not think the report can be true," he said.

But from London Lieut. Ernest H. Shackleton, Royal Navy, recently back from an expedition that had come close to the South Pole, was reported "more than pleased. If the news is correct it is a very remarkable achievement."

Next day some details began to come in. "Cook Reaches Pole by intrepid dash of picked men and dogs." The Paris Herald carried a signed statement from Cook: "Made 500 Mile Dash in 37 Days." From New York: "Cook's Friends Puzzled / Plans Kept Secret, Were Perfected When He Left Gloucester."

The Globe on September 2 had two pages on the history of polar exploration, a map of Cook's route, quotations of other explorers. General Adolph Greeley, commander of a polar expedition of the 1880's, called it a "remarkable achievement." But from Washington came the headline: "Scientists in Doubt / Await More Definite Reports." From London, Capt. Robert A. Scott, commander of a British antarctic expedition: "Must Have Had Luck." But Scott accepted it; Cook was well fitted, he said.

The Globe quoted the New York newspapers that day. The Times saw the news "not yet confirmed but thrilling mankind." The New York Herald accepted it without question: "The dream of the ages realized." The Tribune saw the world "longing for more authentic information" but recognized the improbability of positive proof. "If he reached the Pole there is little probability that conditions permitted him to deposit any record, and if he did where and by whom is it to be verified?" The New York World hailed Cook, "yesterday scarcely known among Arctic explorers," but added: "Until yesterday the furthest north of record was Peary's. He is still in the North. It may be another year or more before he hears of Cook's achievement. He may never hear of it, or we of him."

But it was only another four days. Peary had sailed from New York July 6, 1908, provisioned for three years.

September 3 the Globe's top head was:

> Officially Confirmed
> Discovery by Dr. Cook Vouched For
> Copenhagen Plans Royal Welcome

The "official confirmation" was a wire to the State Department from the American minister in Copenhagen that the Danish government had been advised by the inspector for North Greenland that Cook had returned and reported the discovery of the North Pole, "presenting the necessary confirmatory data with record of his observations."

"No Doubt in Denmark" was an evening headline. The Globe published a list of Washington scientists, all believers. But Prof. W. H. Pickering of Harvard observed, "It will be a very difficult matter for the sole participant in a one-man expedition to prove that the pole has been reached."

Two days later this proved a perspicacious judgment. Dr. George W. Barton of Boston said bluntly, "I don't believe it." Admiral Melville said, "I am more than ever convinced it is a fake. Yet no one can positively deny it."

Dr. L. O. Wolfe, who'd been with Peary as surgeon, said, "Cook violated the ethics of polar exploration by using part of the route Peary had been working out."

Percival Lowell, not yet the discoverer of the planet Pluto, commented from the Harvard Observatory: "Scientifically the discovery of the North Pole is of just the same significance as a new record in the 100 yard dash."

Mrs. Peary said, "If Dr. Cook has discovered the Pole, I most certainly extend my heartiest congratulations." She said she expected a message from Commander Peary by the middle of the next month.

The Globe's editorial September 3, "The North Pole," noted that no story of discovery had been more picked to pieces than Dr. Cook's. "The wise will wait judicially for the facts . . . But it has been the fate of explorers to be doubted. Stanley came in for doubt and dissection but in no measure as great as this. The world was caught unawares . . . Cook's critics will demand proof as positive as Holy Writ. Let us hope he is fortified with scientific proof to silence the scoffers when he walks down the gangplank at Copenhagen."

He did next day and the Danes, convinced, went all out in royal honors. "Dr. Cook Given Seat at Right Hand of King."

Then the bomb: While Denmark was heaping honors on Dr. Cook, the morning papers of September 7 broke out with:

> Pole Found by Peary April 6, 1909
> No Trace of Dr. Cook Discovered
> Bare Message from Labrador Coast
> More Details Promised Today
> Scientists Have No Doubt of Peary's Success

Peary's own messages came through: to the AP from Indian Harbor "Stars and Stripes Nailed to the Pole — Peary." To the New York Times "I have the Pole, April 6. Expect Arrive Chateau Bay September 7." To his wife "Have made good at last. I have the old pole. Am Well. Love."

The Globe had two pages on Peary, photographs, maps. The evening paper headline:

Commander Peary Says He Reached the Pole First
He Discredits the Reported Success of Dr. Cook
London Believes Peary

Next day's news had Peary delayed by weather, Cook declining controversy, and the National Geographic Society planning to honor both. A page one Globe cartoon was entitled "Ours in any case." Peary and Cook were pictured grasping at the Pole: "It's mine," "I saw it first." Uncle Sam was saying, "Never mind, my brave boys. It's all in the family."

September 8 Peary wired his wife, "Don't let Cook's story worry you. I have him nailed." The headlines the next day reported: "Peary's Charge Arouses World / Cook's Supporters Loyal." The Globe's John Carberry, off to meet Peary, reached Sydney, Nova Scotia, that day; the morning paper September 10 carried his byline on a report that Peary's slow steamer, refueling at Indian Harbor, was expected off Sydney Harbor two days later. The Canadian government was meeting it with tugs. Carberry was with Herbert Bridgman of the Peary Arctic Club. Cook was reported hurrying home to combat Peary. "Danish Papers Back Cook / No New Evidence."

But the day before Carberry's first report the Boston Post broke out an exclusive, "Peary's Own Story." It was copyrighted by the New York Times and the Boston Post — a skimpy few lines, relayed, for Peary himself had not yet reached the end of a telegraph line, but a first. Next evening's Globe reported the second installment of Peary's story as carried by the Post that morning. The Globe continued to suffer this lag behind the Post for days while Carberry gnawed his fingernails in frustration at Sydney, for Peary's battered ship was held up for extensive repairs. A party of 30 including his family waited at Sydney. On September 12 Carberry reported, "Mrs. Peary impatient . . . Declares the delay a shame."

Peary's skeleton dispatches in the Post described spending 30 hours at the Pole, where the ocean was "very deep," and recalled his exultation that "the prize of three centuries was mine," but mostly denounced Cook's story as "a gold brick . . . He has not been at the Pole at any time." Peary declared he could prove it. The Globe had to pick up the morning Post story, the only news from Peary, each afternoon. This went on from September 9 to 13, when Carberry captured the lead headline with the report of a plan of an international committee to settle the Cook-Peary controversy. This was reported as Peary's own suggestion in a message from Indian Harbor.

This splurge of enterprise by the Post in sharing the Times's exclusive was no accident; indeed, it cast a shadow that overcast the Boston journalistic scene for the following two decades. E. A. Grozier had now been in control 18 years. He was at his own peak of energy and innovation. His young managing editor, Clifton Carberry, had begun to establish himself as a driving force in the news department. Charles Wingate was developing the Sunday paper. Olin Downes and Kenneth Roberts were new on the staff, joined later by Bill Cunningham and Elliot Norton.

The September 12 Uncle Dudley editorial saw in the Pole's discovery by both Cook and Peary within a week "another coincidence" that recalled Darwin and Wallace in evolution and Morton and Jackson in anesthesia. It recalled Darwin's generosity to Wallace in giving priority to Wallace's notes before publishing his own. It admonished both explorers that they could do no better than emulate Darwin's magnanimity. "No one can bluff or bluster his way into the hall of fame."

Two days later the Globe editorially noted that "a change has set in. Feeling in

Daily Globe.

TEMBER 20. 1909—FOURTEEN PAGES. COPYRIGHT, 1909, BY THE GLOBE NEWSPAPER CO. PRICE TWO CENTS.

N—7:30 O'CLOCK

COOK'S SHIP DETAINED OUTSIDE SANDY HOOK

GRAPHIC STORY OF PEARY'S TRIP

Globe Man Interviews the Explorer and Crew.

HARRY WHITNEY,
New Haven Man Who Met Both Cook and Peary In the Far North and
Upon Whom Peary is Said to Rely for Proof in Part of His
Charges. On the Other Hand, Dr Cook Says Whitney, With Whom
He Left Some of His Records, Will Support Him.

(By John W. Carberry.)
NORTH SYDNEY, N S, Sept 19—Commander Robert E. Peary and all the members of his expedition who are presumed to know any of the facts part of what occurred during the two days Dr Cook remained in the Peary camp is still a mystery. Sifting the statements of all the Peary party, from the chief down to seamen, the only de-

Ordered to Remain There Until Morning.

Object Not to Disarrange Plans for Reception.

Peary's Ship Being Pushed to Reach Sydney Tonight.

She is Making 10 Knots an Hour Under Steam and Sail From Battle Harbor.

Cook, in Wireless Message, Says Whitney Will Tell Truth About Him.

(By Edwin J. Park.)
NEW YORK, Sept 20—Somewhere between here and the eastern end of Long Island the Scandinavian liner Oscar II, explorer, aboard, is heading along toward Sandy Hook, with the design of not getting in until tomorrow morning. The Oscar II could have docked tonight, and her commander, Capt Hempel, was driving her yesterday, as he had driven her ever since he left the port of Christiansand, in the hope of landing Dr Cook today, one day ahead of the steamship's scheduled time of reaching New York.

Capt Hempel sent a wireless message Sunday saying he expected to make port today. Yesterday, when the members of the Arctic club of America, heard about it, they started to see what they could do to have the vessel held off the coast until tomorrow morning. The Arctic club of America had laid itself out pretty extensively in arranging for a formal reception to the explorer, and it never would do, in the judgment of its members, to have the program disarranged by the premature arrival of the steamship. The Arctic club had among other

things, chartered the steamer Grand Republic to go down to quarantine tomorrow morning and take Dr Cook off for a brass band and oratorical reception, and having him come into port late this afternoon or this evening wasn't desirable, from many points of view.

In the first place it costs a neat sum of money to hire a big steamboat for even one day, and the holders of several hundreds of tickets sold at $2.50 each by the club, and for upward of that sum by ticket speculators, named Sept 21 as the date, therefore it had to be Sept 21.

A committee of the Arctic club went to see agent A. L. Johnson of the Scandinavian line, at 1 Broadway, and explained things to him. Agent Johnson was willing to oblige, and he sent a wireless to Capt Hempell telling him

Continued on the Fourth Page.

The North Pole controversy: September 20, 1909.

favor of Dr. Cook is on the increase. If Peary is to prevent further damage to his reputation, he must prove his assertions at once. If he has any evidence the world is entitled to hear it without further delay." The Globe printed the first installment of Dr. Cook's own story the next day.

John Carberry's assignment finally paid off. His week's frustrating wait at North Sydney was shared by Mrs. Peary and associates of Peary, while the world awaited the explorer's return. Pressures built up. Finally the Canadian government steamer *Tyrian* took the waiting Sydney group to Indian Harbor. On September 17 Carberry led the paper:

Globe Man Interviews Peary on Cook's Claim

Carberry was able to report that "the Globe correspondent had the distinction of being the first New Englander personally to greet Admiral Peary since his return from the Far North."

Carberry had all day with Peary and his companions. But he could clear only half a dozen paragraphs through the sketchy communications of Labrador. He got off a second brief story, then shrewdly took a ship back to Sydney, where he could wire freely. On September 20, the Globe had the full fruit of Carberry's success — four full pages of Peary's own story, double-column, large type, "that may fairly be called," the Globe trumpeted, "the first complete story of the Peary expedition."

Dr. Cook's articles were still running in the Globe — "The Conquest of the Pole." On September 18 Cook, on ship from Denmark, had issued a rejoinder to Peary:

Roused by Peary's Charges, Cook Reaffirms his Claims

Gives Interview on Board Steamer

Cook was back first, for a New York banquet September 22.

"Tears in His Eyes at the Warm Welcome"

On the other side of the front page:

Says He'll Soon Discredit Cook

Peary Welcomed at Sydney

His Man Henson Talks

Henson says he was at Pole with Peary

The Globe Sunday Symposium September 19 had half a dozen geographers and meteorologists discussing

"What Use is the North Pole?"

The bitter controversy between Peary and Cook raged on for years. Indeed, only the start of the world war five years later broke it off. Cook then dropped his appeal for a congressional investigation. The rivals contended on the lecture platform, in books, even in Congress. Cook, an engaging popular lecturer, generally won public acceptance. Peary, embittered, roused public resentment by his testy, contemptuous treatment of Cook. "Peary is no gentleman," my grandmother said.

But Peary won the contest in official and scientific circles. A committee appointed by the National Geographic Society unanimously accepted his records. Cook, after his initial acceptance in Denmark, never achieved scientific confirmation. In 1911 Congress, after two years' importuning by Peary's Navy friends, promoted the Commander to Rear Admiral and retired him with the thanks of Congress. Peary earned later distinction as he turned his attention to aviation in the war. He died in 1922. Cook's name was later clouded by his exploitation of oil stocks. He founded a Texas company, was convicted for mail fraud in its promotion. The oil stock was reported later to have paid off, but Cook was sentenced to Leavenworth in 1925; paroled in 1929, he received a presidential pardon in 1940, shortly before his death.

1910—Airplanes and Democrats

By 1910 the automobile was adding a new dimension to the American economy, smoothing and widening the roads, and creating a whole new area of advertising that was increasing the size of the newspaper. Although Henry Ford's electrifying announcement of a five-dollar day for Ford workmen was still some years off, the glamor of the gasoline engine was already replacing the fascination the telegrapher's key had held for young James Morgan and printers' type for A. J. Philpott. An index of the auto's impact was conversion of the Globe's bicycle editor, James T. Sullivan, to automobile editor.

With the rapid development of the automobile industry and its advertising, James Sullivan became an important figure on the Globe and a familiar to the early leaders of the motor industry. He was the Globe's ambassador to the industry and its ardent promoter. He had a special claim to appreciation by both his publisher and his advertising customers, for he claimed to have invented the kind of "reader" that was legitimate despite the law against unidentified advertising because he contrived to include enough information in his promotional pieces to qualify them as "news." This in its pristine day, around 1915, was counted as ingenious a stroke as the latter-day transmuting of press agentry into "the engineering of consent."

But the novelty and the news of 1910 was captured by the airplane. The French aviator Bleriot had flown the English Channel in 1909. The Globe put up a purse of $10,000 for the fastest flight from Squantum Field in Quincy to Boston Light and return. Claude Graham White, an Englishman, won the prize for the 33-mile round trip, acclaimed "the longest flight over salt water in the United States." Patrol boats had been stationed along the harbor to pluck the flier out of the water if he splashed down, as almost everyone expected he would.

The next year the Globe sponsored what was hailed as "the first airplane flight over land," Boston to Nashua to Worcester to Providence and back to Boston, 160 miles. Earl Ovington won it. "Millions in New England saw their first airplane flight that day," the Globe reported September 4, 1911. A. J. Philpott went up with Graham White, one of the first newspapermen to fly, on a trip from Waltham to Concord. A headline of November 1, 1910, records

> Johnstone Rises to Height of 8714 Feet
> American in a Wright Climber Captures World Altitude Record

A week later there was a landmark national election. "Democratic Tidal Wave," the Globe headline of November 9 reported. The Democrats captured control of Congress for the first time since 1892. Woodrow Wilson was elected governor of New Jersey. A Globe editorial titled "1912" noted that "election returns indicate that to the list of prospective Democratic candidates for the Presidency in 1912 must be added the name of Woodrow Wilson, with Governor Harmon, Governor Dix and Mayor Gaynor. The country's dissent from the Payne-Aldrich tariff . . . makes the Democratic nomination a prize such as it has not been since 1892."

The Globe was soon running a Sunday special by M. E. Hennessy on "Woodrow Wilson at Close Range" that described the New Jersey governor as "southerner in hospitality, engaging in conversation, broad-minded and charitable, but immovable."

The Globe of November 1, 1910, reported that 1,423,429 people lived within half an hour of downtown Boston and that the Boston Elevated planned to extend rapid transit to Dorchester by way of South Station. The El did extend rapid transit over the next few years through Dorchester on one side and out to Cambridge on the other, giving a temporary illusion of an expanding transportation system to tie in the rapidly extending suburbs. But it proved an illusion.

One year later Boston and Hyde Park, a close-by suburb of 15,000, prepared to vote on Hyde Park's annexation. The Globe editorially welcomed this as "the first step toward welding of the towns in the Metropolitan district. Our business organizations have long argued that our neighbors should in fact as well as name become a part of New England's metropolis and help place this community in trade and commerce and universal importance where it rightfully belongs."

Hyde Park voted to join, but it was the last annexation. Unlike other metropolitan cities, Boston was to remain cramped in its core limits, hemmed in between the ocean, the Mystic River, and the Charles, its westernmost boundary the Brookline and Dedham lines. This made all the difference in the suburban out-thrust of the decades ahead. As stronger elements moved outside the machine politics of the city, Boston's valuations shrank and its civic leadership diminished, and gradually the more progressive new industries followed the population to the suburbs. The El, limited in its franchise and later burdened by deficits, failed to follow its passengers out; the automobile took over commuter transportation to clog the narrow city streets with traffic and parking congestion. 1911 proved a watershed year in Great Anticipations.

The Globe's election system scored another triumph in 1911, and on November 8 the paper crowed: "Not Fooled by Early Returns." The Globe's contemporaries were selling extras in early evening along Newspaper Row announcing the election of Frothingham (Republican candidate) by 20,000–40,000. The Globe gave out nothing founded on guesswork, and by 9 P.M. clearly indicated "the election of Foss by 4,000 to 5,000." He won by a narrow 8,300, while the rest of the Republican ticket squeaked through.

Headlines that same week included the retirement of Buffalo Bill; the indictment of the Reverend Clarence V. T. Richeson for the murder of a young choir singer, Avis Linnell of Hyannis, that rocked Richeson's fashionable Cambridge congregation; and the opening of the trial of the McNamara brothers for bombing the Los Angeles Times, a trial that marked the violence of labor-management relations.

John Carberry was covering the McNamara trial. The Globe on November 3 questioned whether the trial was impartial. "When a prospective juryman frankly declares, as has happened twice, that his antipathy toward the accused is such that no evidence could change his belief in their guilt, and the judge announces that the talesman's prejudice does not disqualify him from sitting on the jury, one begins to wonder whether the presumption of innocent until proved guilty has been reversed in this instance."

The Sunday Globe in 1911 was still five cents, up to 82 pages, its circulation 328,000 to the daily's 195,000. Andrew Carnegie received the Nobel Peace Prize. Charlie Brickley kicked four field goals as a Harvard freshman to beat the Princeton freshman 12–0. Americans were fleeing Mexico City as a truce ended in the Mexican Revolution; "President Taft firm for neutrality."

Speaker Champ Clark demanded annexation of Canada during the Congress debate on reciprocity. This defeated Premier Laurier's campaign for reciprocity, which the Globe had long supported, and defeated Laurier. It was to be a factor in defeating Champ Clark the next year for the Democratic nomination for president.

A Globe editorial on Lloyd George's pension and unemployment program was headed "The War on Poverty." It asked "Can the United States avoid it?"

James Morgan's Hero, Wilson

The eight-column banner head on the evening Globe of July 2, 1912, was
>Wilson Named on 46th Ballot

A four-column front page photograph went with it, with the caption "The beautiful daughters of Woodrow Wilson."

The Globe entered into the nomination of Wilson with enthusiasm. The headline over James Morgan's story next morning was
>Public Opinion Wins
>Wilson's Victory a Triumph for Common Sense
>Feeling Among Delegates He is Absolutely Certain of Election

Morgan reported it as "a dramatic victory for common sense — an astounding triumph, really without parallel, a political revolution."

Morgan was now 53, and at the peak of his powers. He had been charting political currents for the Globe now for almost 30 years. At last he saw the democratic process in prospect of fulfillment. He wrote with the assurance of a master student of American politics and with the complete confidence of his publisher. The editorial that day Morgan had certainly written or outlined to the office:

> Woodrow Wilson fits the era. No better choice could have been made. The Democratic party has proved itself worthy of the confidence given it by the voters in 1910 and verified the predictions made by the Globe when the present House of Representatives was organized.
>
> The Democratic convention has given the independent voters of the Nation an opportunity to mark for a Democrat who always considers public questions dispassionately and broadly, yet acts with firmness . . . The Administration of Gov. Wilson is probably the most notable of recent years throughout the Union . . . With Gov. Wilson in the field the Roosevelt 3d party movement cannot be very formidable in the coming election."

Theodore Roosevelt had already split the Republican party with his dramatic walkout from their standpat convention in Chicago and was preparing to launch his Progressive Party — the Bull Moose party — for an evangelical campaign.

Morgan led a Globe corps to both Chicago and Baltimore with Maurice Low, Washington correspondent, M. E. Hennessy, John D. Merrill, and John Carberry. It had been a political season of rising drama and it culminated in Baltimore with a week-long bitter contest through 46 ballots. William Jennings Bryan ran interference for Wilson and dominated the convention with such masterful strategies as held the public in suspense. Bryan had forgiven Wilson his "devout wish" that the

Nebraskan be "knocked into a cocked hat." He was committed with his Nebraska delegation to Champ Clark of Missouri. But Bryan scented collusion between the conservative forces of Clark and Gov. Judson Harmon of Ohio to defeat the progressive principles represented by Wilson. He could not attack Clark while pledged to him. But New York was supporting Harmon. Bryan's political instinct picked Tammany for attack; breathing the old fire of 1896, he offered a motion that the convention regretted the presence of two Wall Street promoters, August Belmont and Thomas F. Ryan. Wall Street had picked Harmon as its candidate in a move to sell the Democratic party to the predatory interests of the country, Bryan thundered. His resolution passed 899–196. Clark led on the first ballot with 440 to Wilson's 324 and Harmon's 148. All three hung on, ballot after ballot, with little change. But on the tenth ballot New York shifted from Harmon to Clark, pushing Clark up to 550 to Wilson's 400. Bryan had expected this. On the fourteenth ballot he announced he could no longer feel bound to Clark, whose acceptance of Tammany support showed he was no progressive. This checked the trend to Clark. The convention stood stalemated for days, time enough for the public to react to Bryan's charges, to understand his tactics, and to let the delegates hear from home. On the twenty-fifth ballot Wilson passed Clark and 21 ballots later won the magic number of 725. A great national drama, and James Morgan knew what it meant and how to tell it.

Morgan came back from Baltimore to indite another editorial, July 5: "Wilson a Well Rounded Man . . . whose popularity we predict will grow as people become acquainted with him and better appreciate his purposes." The Globe ran a cartoon from the New York World, "New Recruits for the Democratic Zoo," a dilapidated elephant and a dejected bull moose.

Next day's editorial was on "Wilson's Chances in New England." Taft had carried the whole region in 1908, but the Globe saw Maine, Massachusetts, and Connecticut all doubtful now.

The Olympics in Stockholm made front page news in July, and the Globe editorially celebrated American success: Meredith in the 440 and 880, Lippincott in the 100 (10 and 3/5 seconds), Craig in the 220, Jim Thorp in the pentathlon, McDonald in the shotput. But an Englishman, Jackson, took the metric mile.

An editorial July 9 hailed the Norris bill for the presidential primary "a step in the right direction." A July 10 headline, "Imperialism in U.S.," recorded a "vigorous protest from Latin America." On July 11 a Globe headline asked, "if the Red Sox outfield isn't the best in the game, which is?" Tris Speaker, Harry Hooper, and Duffy Lewis were posed in a photograph. The Red Sox were leading the American League despite Ty Cobb of Detroit, who led in batting, but Speaker was just behind.

The growth of the motorcar industry was evidenced by more cars registered in Massachusetts the first half of 1912 than in all of 1911 — 46,883 new cars in the six months. James T. Sullivan, the automobile editor, had an article July 14 on "Safe and Sane Motoring . . . Drivers when at fault should not blame their cars . . . How speed maniacs can be put off the highways . . ."

July 15 headlines recorded that the United Shoe Machinery Company was to be dissolved in an antitrust suit and the 16 Massachusetts congressional districts reapportioned. The Globe started a book-lovers' contest.

History Day by Day

A landmark daily series in the Globe, "The War Day-by-Day," started in 1911 and ran four years. It began with a short series by Winfield Thompson, top reporter of his time, on the fiftieth anniversary of Lincoln's leaving Springfield for his inauguration. Mr. Morgan liked it so much he suggested it be kept going right through the Civil War. Winfield needed help and chose a lad who had been resourceful in finding things as library clerk. Willard DeLue, then 21, thus started writing history in and about the Globe that wove through the next 50 years while he held a round dozen editing positions but always managed to get back to writing.

Willard DeLue.

DeLue, Dorchester born, had started to work as office boy in a law office for five dollars a week after finishing the Christopher Gibson Grammar School in 1905. But he had a feeling for newspapering. With another future Boston journalist, Joe Toye, he got out a little Dorchester weekly when he was 17. In 1907 he secured a job on the Globe as library clerk. Next year he was moved into the Exchange Room, to work under William Hills, who appointed him New England exchange editor — still at five dollars a week. Mornings, DeLue clipped the New England papers and sorted the clippings for appropriate members of the staff. In the afternoon he put together a column called "Odd Items from Everywhere."

He might be through with that by 4 or 5 o'clock, but then Hills came in to dictate his Editorial Points. DeLue had to come back in the evening to read proof on the points. So his day stretched from 9:30 A.M. to 10:30 P.M. or later. This meant he had to have supper in town or use carfare home and back, ten cents a day extra, which cut his wages down to $4.40 net. He spoke to Mr. Hills about it several times, to be put off until one day the boy blew up and denounced the injustice of it. The result was that he went back to the library, but soon emerged as West Roxbury district man until Thompson chose him to work on the war series.

His job was to dig up suitable illustrations and then, as the series was syndicated, to make up and lay out pages. But soon he shared in the writing. Thompson took the war in the east, DeLue in the west. He visited the battlefields but lived mostly in the public library, where he learned research. He learned to write, too, and now turned his hand to Sunday features. From office boy and library clerk DeLue at 23 had a solid stint of historical research and writing under his belt.

Over the following half century he contributed even more history to Globe pages than James Morgan, who by now was finishing his most ambitious series, "In the Path of Napoleon," that ran for a year in the paper and became a book. By happy chance Morgan's story of the rise and fall of the Napoleonic empire backed right up to the opening of the world war in Europe. It intrigued General Taylor that the first battles were fought over the roads to Waterloo.

DeLue had a surcease from serials in 1916 when Harry Poor persuaded him to take a year's stint on the night desk. This was welcome, for the desk minimum of $30 a week was better than a young reporter's wage and DeLue wanted to get married.

The war took Winfield Thompson off to the War Shipping Board, and he stayed in the shipping industry. The next big historical event was the Pilgrim anniversary in 1920, A. J. Philpott's big story. The Plymouth story unearthed the old rivalry with Provincetown as the first landing, and all this erupted in the Globe as backdrop for the final grand pageant in Plymouth.

The Plymouth tercentenary was observed in July 1921 instead of in winter 1920. George Pierce Baker, then conducting Harvard's famous 47 Workshop for budding playwrights, wrote the pageant. President Harding came to Plymouth for an anniversary address.

But Plymouth was not Boston, whose tercentenary was years off. 1922 offered the hundredth anniversary of the Hub's becoming a city, and DeLue embarked on a series, "Tales of the Old Town," that ran for 100 days. Then came the hundred fiftieth anniversary of Lexington and Concord in 1925. DeLue with Donald Willard produced a series, "Thrills of 1775," that rehearsed the beginnings of the American Revolution.

The Globe ran a four-page special 150th Anniversary Section April 20, 1925, "How a Nation was born at Concord and Lexington." DeLue and Willard wrote the lead articles; others were by Carlyle Holt, Joseph Dinneen, Louis Lyons, and M. J. Canavan, with a special by an antiquarian, Charles A. Lawrence, on "The American Rifle that Won the War." One whole page was given to Lawrence's sketches of the varieties of uniforms worn by the Revolutionary forces.

Globe readers had history coming out of their ears. In a little more than a decade they had been exposed to every engagement of the Civil War, to the Napoleonic Wars, and to the birth of America and the start of the Revolution. This to James Morgan was the essence of journalism. Eager tourist and student of history, he insisted on sharing it all with readers. As the readership was still very largely second-generation American, these ventures in history were undoubtedly more instructive than all the self-conscious government-sponsored "Americanization" programs rife in that period.

When 1930 brought on Boston's own tercentenary, part of the Globe's treatment was to bracket pictures of the Puritan settlement leaders with their descendants of ten generations later — Winthrops, Endicotts, Saltonstalls. Resemblances were striking, most notably so in the persistence of Sir Richard Saltonstall's long, narrow face in Leverett Saltonstall, then speaker of the Massachusetts House. The attention this attracted proved a political help to Saltonstall. When he entered his first campaign for governor in 1938 against James M. Curley, Bob Washburn's column in the Transcript quipped that it was a political asset for a Back Bay Republican to have "a South Boston face." Curley snorted that if Saltonstall took that face to South Boston he would be mobbed. Saltonstall demanded that Curley apologize to South Boston for this imputation of violence to its residents. He took up Curley's challenge to walk through South Boston, introducing himself to Irish bartenders and longshoremen. As Curley's crack had much wider currency than Washburn's original whimsy, Saltonstall was able to say: "My opponent says I have a South Boston face. It will be the same face after election as before." His vote in South Boston was the largest any Republican ever received there as he beat Curley for governor by 130,000. The "South Boston face" appellation stuck to Saltonstall. "It has always helped me when I am introduced with that quip," he said 30 years later.

DeLue's contributions tended toward travel and history but were varied. Some of the earliest were tailored to the six daily papers of one week and known in the office as "the sixes" — "Six Great Forgeries," "Six Great Orators," and so on. They ran at the top center of the editorial page.

In February 1932 he had a series on "New Englanders in the Orient"; in 1933 a biography of James B. Conant, "the Dorchester boy who will be president of Harvard at 40." In March 1939 "Going Places with Willard DeLue" followed the Santa Fe Trail, byproduct of his trip to the San Francisco World's Fair. In 1939, the hundred fiftieth anniversary of the inauguration of the United States government, he did a month-long series on "the birth of the Federal government, told in the modern newspaper manner." Under a headline of antique type, "News of the Nation," each day's story carried the dateline of 1789. In 1947 DeLue contributed "Autumn Rambles in New England," then "November Rambles in New Hampshire," continuing to "Winter Wanderings in New England."

Uncle Dudley Joins the Globe

Of all New England institutions, the Globe was doubtless the only one to derive a lasting benefit from the great Lawrence strike. The strike brought a year of revolutionary violence to an explosive point that made 1912 a watershed year in New England's dominant but lowest-paid industry. The long, bitter strike was repressed and its IWW leaders convicted. But eruptions followed repeatedly in that and other textile centers until a culminating strike in 1922 started migration of the cotton industry south.

The near revolution in Lawrence frightened conservatives into repression. But in others it awakened a social conscience. One of these was a young editorial writer on the Boston Transcript, Lucien Price, then five years out of Harvard. The Transcript sent him to Lawrence, and what he found there gave him his first realization of the conditions of the mill workers. But that was not the story the Transcript wanted. They didn't use it. This was Price's second awakening to the conditions of his own job. He turned to the Atlantic Monthly and published there, July 1914, under the pen name Seymour Deming, "A Message to the Middle Class" warning them of the dangers of their social attitude. This brought his relations with the Transcript to the point of no return, with the result that in 1914 Lucien Price joined the Globe, which for the next 50 years published the work of the most superb essayist and penetrating social philosopher in New England journalism.

Lucien Price.

Soon after, William S. Packer came to the Globe from essentially the same cause. An Episcopal minister in East Boston, Packer had worked with the victims of strikes and poverty until he found his social mission incompatible with the church Establishment. He had then taken up journalism, as an editorial writer on the old Advertiser-Record in its last days. There Roger Babson discovered him to do labor reports for his Institute. Packer joined Price on the Globe editorial page during the first world war. The end of the war brought to join them James H. Powers, a dynamic spirit and brilliant young writer who had learned all the reporter's trade could teach in a few sparkling years out of Boston University.

These three men, under James Morgan, constituted the editorial staff of the Globe for an average of just under 50 years each that coincided with the second half of Mr. Morgan's 93 years. It was one of the most extraordinary teams in the history of journalism. Its members expressed the mind and conscience of the Globe for a full half its first century.

As their talents sorted themselves out, Powers became in effect the foreign editor. Packer dealt with the practical from taxes to tennis. Price's work ranged over the whole social and cultural scene, biography, music, education, history. From the passing scene he took his text for essays that a multitude of New England ministers learned to look to for their own sermons.

By a historic coincidence, the Globe only the year before had opened its editorial page to a new form that gave its new editorial cast a broader forum. Powers, Packer, and Price became the composite personality of Uncle Dudley.

On April 28, 1913, the Uncle Dudley essay form of editorial that had run in the Sunday paper for more than 20 years was introduced in the daily. This proved a landmark change. It provided a flexible vehicle and elbowroom for the kind of thoughtful discussion of affairs for which Price, Powers, and Packer were especially qualified. The Sunday paper, April 27, had announced that "Uncle Dudley's ideas will appear in the daily Globe, beginning Monday."

At the start the daily Dudley was precisely what the Sunday Dudley was, but one column instead of two. It was a thoughtful essay unrelated to the day's news. For some time the week's essays were prescheduled, a week at a time, and the first week's repertory was announced that Sunday, April 27:

Monday	Woodrow Wilson's Wisdom
Tuesday	Saved by a Bank (history of the Bank of England)
Wednesday	The Newspaper and the War (refuting the charge that the press fomented the war)
Thursday	The Bravest Act of a President (Jackson and the Bank)
Friday	The Tariff and the Income Tax (suggests new tax may replace tariff revenues)
Saturday	Trade and Civilization

This preplanned schedule continued to be announced for several Sundays, then ceased. For the daily Dudleys were gradually relating to the background of the news. Eventually the Dudley shaped up as the lead editorial, indistinguishable from others save for the signature. But this made all the difference. It allowed a departure from the news on days when nothing compelled attention. It was the special opportunity for Price to discuss some social, cultural, philosophical topic. He always had a folder of "spare Dudleys" on tap, timeless essays. Often he had worked them over many times as his thought developed; for he was ceaselessly writing, ever perfecting his style and refining his thought. Even on a routine day the form and full length of the Dudley would give Powers a chance to put foreign policy in perspective or Packer to treat a civic issue in its full dimensions. Between them they also wrote the shorter daily editorials and the longer Sunday Dudley, and often the Sunday Symposium or some other major Sunday article.

An introduction to the three men calls for a visit to their editorial cubicle, on the fourth floor of the old Globe building, that has just room for their three desks and a bookcase. But they don't need much space. They use the desks mornings to spread out the newspapers and winnow them for topics worth writing about. Then after they have gone up to the fifth floor for the midday editorial conference with Mr. Morgan or in his absence Sunday editor Thaddeus Defrieze, whose jurisdiction includes also daily features and editorials, they return to type out the thoughts that they have been cogitating and refining all day. They aren't in their tiny office much of the time. Price has almost certainly written his piece among his books in his Beacon Hill bachelor's apartment, in his tiny precise penmanship, that he will now type out. Powers, a big handsome man who exudes vitality, may have been out lecturing to a foreign affairs institute or doing his own research at the Athenaeum, just up on Beacon Street — and hospitable to Globe people, for assistant Sunday editor Joe Smith's aunt left him a quarter of a share in it. Packer will have been smoking his black pipe on some reporter's desk in the city room, getting at the vitals of a City Hall story. Or else he has been seeing to the tennis courts in Winchester, where he's chairman of the recreation committee, building the finest set of suburban courts around and producing, with Mrs. Hazel Wightman, the greatest crop of junior tennis players.

Price, his white cuffs rolled up over the sleeves of his sports jacket, his French beret on his desk, is undoubtedly laughing uproariously at a crack of Jim Powers about some political stupidity in the news; Packer, chuckling silently, takes out his pipe to describe a lugubrious evening of trying to extract an adequate playgrounds budget from his local finance committee.

They generally lunch together at a hidden little restaurant with red-checked table-cloths down in the market district. But they've been "discovered" there, Price says, and he wants to try some other place of more secure privacy. His own loud laughter makes discovery almost inevitable.

Price grew up in a rigorous intellectual climate in an Ohio family that lived with music and books. He was a student at Western Reserve Academy, which implanted in him a lifelong addiction to learning, a special admiration for the Greek civilization, and a love of music. He resisted appointment as a tutor at Harvard after he was graduated with high honors in 1907. But he kept up his intimacy with the academic community and in later life was a companion of Alfred North Whitehead and ultimately the great philosopher's Boswell — in *Dialogues of Alfred North Whitehead.*

In his early Globe days Price was a convinced socialist. Later, perhaps in reaction to the communist revolution in Russia, he applied his social conscience less ideologically; in later years his primary concern was with the intellectual growth of the individual as the first requisite for a good society. Price was a pacifist in the first world war. The death in the war of a dear friend, Fritz Demmler, had a profound influence on his own life. This dedication was given particular visibility in the Uncle Dudley he wrote for the Globe each year on All Souls' Day, the anniversary of Demmler's death on a Belgian battlefield — a piece in memoriam that was ever Price's most beautiful writing and most profound insight into the human condition.

A collection of these Dudleys, entitled *Immortal Youth: A Litany of All Souls,* was published in 1945 by the Beacon Press. Price wrote: "What Demmler's death meant to me was that society kills off its men of genius." Later he wrote of the effect on himself: "I have considered the rest of my life [from the war on] a free gift which it has never been possible to regard as belonging to me."

In 1936 Price's All Souls' Day editorial opened: "Was it poetic instinct that set All Souls' Day on November 2d? For autumn is a season of reflection, the year draws to its death, and yet although October's brilliant orchestration of foliage color is tuned down to November's muffled drums, still the funeral march of the year moves to noble music."

Price took instant interest in any new member of the staff, and his own instinct for perfection rubbed off in some degree on many. His influence and later his worldwide intellectual acquaintance brought to the Sunday Globe some of the writing of Romain Rolland and Gilbert Murray.

Price lived in monkish self-containment and purposeful dedication in a third-floor study and bedroom in an old brick house on Beacon Hill where he had a fireplace, books, and privacy to work and think. From it he made walking trips to explore the country around, starting systematically within the metropolitan area, then to the seacoast towns, Gloucester, Marblehead; later into the Connecticut Valley towns and the Berkshires for spring sojourns in Amherst in the 1920's, Williamstown in the thirties, and then farther to Vermont and Newfoundland. Summers he lived by the sea and rowed a dory in all weather till he was 70, thereafter content to seek the quiet beach and salt air and sand, conducive to thought. Life, he said at 70, is a quest for good schoolmasters. "Plato is my man and Beethoven."

But Price in 1914 as revealed in his Atlantic Monthly article looked upon middle class America, imposing drastic antistrike regulations, as being blind to the wretchedness of industrial labor. He urged that only the growth of a social conscience could avert a revolution. He deplored the absence of freedom to speak out. The newspapers were not to be trusted: they were edited out of the timidities and prejudices of their middle class readers. "You are not getting the news. Editors see no demand

ALL SOULS' DAY

Was it poetic instinct that set All Souls' Day on November second? For Autumn is a season of reflection, the year draws to its death, and yet although October's brilliant orchestration of foliage color is toned down to November's muffled drums still the funeral march of the year moves to noble music.

On such nights as these of clear skies and bustling winds which set leaves swirling and surf resounding on the granite shores of the seagirt headland, those glittering stars are eyes that, as they peer and sparkle, say ever more clearly on this Feast Day of the Dead: "Eternal beings that we are, we ask you, mortal: What do you make of your mortality?"

A reflective mind, in advancing years, questions less what is to come after death than what has been made of life thus far and what can still be made of that which remains.

for news of the rumblings of the industrial revolution. Colleges don't teach it. Ministers don't preach it. Their polite congregations dislike having their sensibilities harrowed. A reformer is a dangerous person. The middle class does not understand. It will not listen. It can only intensely resent."

Bill Packer had come to much the same impression of the comfortable who occupied his Episcopal Church pews on Sunday. He had been up against the human condition in its direst straits along the East Boston waterfront with its derelicts and alcoholics. Over this problem he had come into association with Dr. Elwood Worcester, Episcopal pastor of Emmanuel Church, who developed a practical psychotherapy using both medical and religious elements that became known as the Emmanuel Movement. It proved particularly efficacious in such problems as alcoholism and divorce. But Packer had a catholic concern for all human affairs. He devoted his energies particularly to young people, with the playgrounds his practical ministry.

He was some years older than Price and had the appearance of a country parson, rather untidy, a little tweedy, with pipe ashes on his vest and pockets bulging with tennis balls or the president's budget message as the case might be. Packer's writing was as practical down-to-earth as Price's was elegant and Powers' critical. Their composite Uncle Dudley was an editor of all the talents.

His two colleagues always looked upon Price as the master craftsman. The three were equals in discussion; but for the power of Lucien's prose and the dimensions of his thought they put him on an eminence.

The daily creation of the Uncle Dudley in that pristine decade beginning in 1914 was described by Lucien Price years later in a reminiscence of the editorial conference with James Morgan that took the form of a memorial essay in the Globe at Morgan's death in 1955.

> The three of us would go up (at 4 p.m. during the war, at 2 p.m. in the decades that followed 1922), armed with sheaves of notes and memoranda; everything would be tossed into the common fund; actually, anyone of us was expected to be able to handle whichsoever topic, or topics, were decided upon — politics, economics, humanism, history, local affairs, the arts, science, letters and music — the whole run-of-the-mill; actually, however, though with due regard not to overload one writer too many days in succession, the one best suited to a subject duly congenial was generally assigned. These discussions lasted an hour, sometimes two. Everything was threshed out, and by the time the session ended it was well understood what and what not was to be said.
>
> These discussions could get very spirited. Even heated; but never on James's side. *He had taken over a maxim of Napoleon's: "Never let your choler get above your collar." The blood above his neckband was always cool.* The rest of us were not invariably so wise. There would be days when we would come out of the conference-room sputtering mad. But James? Imperturbably calm and urbane. And, after all, it was true; he was the one who had to act as shock-absorber, and stop the bricks, if any.
>
> *He had only one or two rules, but they were very good ones. They had been picked up gradually, somewhere along the way. One was: "No negatives." The ideas must be positive and constructive; otherwise, leave the subject alone until we had something helpful to suggest.* This itself can sound negative or sterile, and often did so seem, but in the long term it was good sense; for out of it came the other rule: "Never berate." As a young man he had been turned loose once or twice on a justly unpopular figure, only to discover how fatally easy it was. *What has to be avoided if you expect to stay in the arena of public discussion for a long while is the peril of deteriorating into a common scold.*
>
> These contests — they went on five days a week, and Sunday afternoons by telephone — were called "putting on the gloves with James." He fought fair, but often with very fancy foot-work, both in, and sometimes afterward, outside the editorial conference-room. Of course there would be intervals, sometimes longish ones, when the conferences were Moravian love feasts, all sweetness and light; or again, there would come an occasion known as "blue Monday," when James himself was negatively-minded. No idea was any good. A dozen, fifteen of them might be put up, only to be knocked down. Finally the question would be, "Well, James, what would you suggest?" James would pick up the afternoon paper and absently turn its pages. It was probably from sessions like this that the decision came to use general topics of permanent interest, often having nothing to do with the news at all. These proved unexpectedly popular. It even came to be said, "Thank heaven, there is no news. Now we can write about something worth while!" And evidently a good many readers felt the same way, for they became a permanent feature of what is known as "the Dudley column."

This liberal attitude was, and is, owing to Mr. Morgan. *His own mind was so spacious, his own temper so tolerant, his own spirit so genial and gracious, that it came naturally to him to let others develop whatever talents they possessed in their own way.* This, accidental though it may seem, was a sheer master-stroke. It resulted in richness, variety, versatility, and depth. Everything was grist which came to that editorial mill, and as time went on, those columns were filled with the great ideas which have animated Western man for the past thirty centuries. And the people heard them gladly.

A roving dialectic such as this is much rarer than it sounds. Almost the last lesson which any responsible executive learns is the fine art of letting things alone; of picking the man and the task, then trusting him to go ahead and do it on his own. Once the topic had been discussed and decided upon, the man assigned was left alone to write it, his competency was not questioned, and his copy was not tampered with; the presumption being that he knew his business or he would not have been there . . . The man assigned to write a given editorial had a mandate; he knew the limits within which it had to be written and how far he could go; he could not exceed that mandate without a breach of faith.

It was this procedure which Mr. Morgan developed during the ten years from 1914 to 1924. After that, he could go away to Europe and leave it running for months.

L. L. Winship Starts a Newspaper Career

Just before the opening of World War I the Globe news staff was reinforced by three young Harvard graduates who rapidly acquired a variety of experience in the expanding areas of reporting that war conditions impose. Lucien Thayer and Charles A. Merrill, 1910 classmates of Walter Lippmann, and Laurence L. Winship,* of the 1911 class, were to become key editors in the coming decades.

Thayer taught high school French for a year before moving to the Globe. Winship worked first for his father's Journal of Education at $6 a week. Merrill's uncle was an executive on the Baltimore & Ohio Railroad, and he found a job there but didn't like it. Winship had grown up with Merrill in Somerville. He saw an ad in the Globe: "Chance for a young college graduate to learn the newspaper business." He sent it to Merrill, who was taken on to serve an apprenticeship under Billy Hills in the Exchange Room at $8 a week. For a year Winship looked over his friend's shoulder at this glamorous world of journalism. At the end of a year Merrill was

---

* Laurence Winship was the son of Albert E. Winship, founder of the Journal of Education and its editor for 47 years. A. E. Winship was a leader in establishing the National Education Association. In 1891 he was editor-in-chief of the Boston Traveller. His older son, George Parker Winship, librarian and bibliographer, was librarian of the Widener collection at Harvard University 1915–1926.

Laurence L. Winship.

promoted to the news staff at $12 a week. Winship applied to Billy Hills and let him know that he felt well enough acquainted with the job Merrill was leaving to take it on where Merrill left off. He got the job but it was still at $8. He eked out a living by keeping up his $6 a week chores for the Journal.

They all took to newspapering with enthusiasm. Thayer soon became a feature writer, then assistant to the city editor. For many years he organized the Globe's election coverage. When the pictorial side of journalism received belated recognition on the Globe 25 years later, Thayer became the paper's first picture editor and an assistant managing editor.

Merrill developed into one of the most thorough reporters and covered major stories throughout the country and abroad until he became night city editor in 1926, then in 1937 city editor and assistant managing editor. He was a frequent contributor to the editorial page both in his reporting and editing days until his death in 1951.

Winship's rise in the paper was most rapid. In three years his salary had risen to $25, and he married on that. He early evinced a keen sense of news values and a direct simplicity of writing that brought out the inherent interest of the story in clear, succinct style. He had also an extraordinary instinct for human relations that gave him an ever widening acquaintance among people in public affairs who learned to give him their complete confidence.

His stories of a great Billy Sunday revival in Boston in 1916 won recognition for him and the Globe that increased with his coverage of the National Guard mobilization in 1916 and of Camp Devens in the first world war. The Globe's major casualty of the war was Thaddeus Defrieze, who had become James Morgan's brilliant junior in running the Sunday paper and the editorial page. To fill this strategic gap in 1918 Winship was appointed Sunday editor. In 1926 he became assistant managing editor and in 1937 managing editor; finally in 1955 he became the first outside the Taylor family to hold the title of editor, which eight years later passed to his son Thomas.

Winship's desk became the vital center of the Globe while he was Sunday editor, and continued so for more than 50 years. Under his editorship for 19 years the Sunday paper was the pace-setter. It grew steadily in circulation in response to his instinctive sense of the public interest in a situation. His personal quality and natural leadership brought out the best work of the staff. He was soon directing the features for daily as well as Sunday editions, selecting the columns, taking charge of the editorial page, exercising a quiet but pervasive influence over the whole shape and tone of the newspaper.

Winship's appointment as Sunday editor solved Mr. Morgan's problem permanently. After Charles Dyar retired as chief editorial writer in 1904, he had turned over the direction of the editorial page, the Sunday department, and the daily features first to Edward Burns, then on his death in 1914 to Thaddeus Defrieze. But Winship was to last, to absorb Morgan's editorial role and with it Morgan's methods and philosophy. So doing, he inherited the complete confidence that the publishing family had reposed in Morgan.

Morgan habitually freed himself from an executive role, was free to write, to preside over the editorial conference when in town, to make suggestions, have ideas; but his just being there, or at the end of a telephone line, was the big thing. Winship spent all the time he could with him, and his most frequent suggestion to a writer was, "Why don't you give James a ring? He'll have something on it."

Billy Sunday cut a wide swath across the nation with his athletic evangelism in the fall of 1916. In Boston church people mobilized for his coming. A huge tabernacle went up on Huntington Avenue. The magnitude of the event required even Mr. Morgan's personal attention. A fortnight in advance the Globe advertised that "James Morgan will analyze Billy Sunday in a remarkable series. Billy Sunday is coming in a week. James Morgan has spent many hours with the famous evangelist." Laurence Winship had been sent to report Sunday in other cities as a prelude to his Boston meetings. Normally the big assignment to cover Billy Sunday in Boston would have gone to one of the older men. But Winship had caught Sunday's flavor, and his own stories caught on; so when Sunday launched his Boston revival the assignment stayed with Winship. November 13 the headline was

> Billy Sunday in Boston
> 55,000 Gathered To Hear Him
> 15,000 Had To Be Turned Away

Sunday's sermons were emotional orgies that brought melodramatic response. He claimed wholesale conversions. Many of the most despaired-of pronounced themselves saved. People "hit the sawdust trail" to Billy Sunday's invitation. Some of the journalism stimulated by his meetings was even more lurid than his own exhortations. One day after reading a tearjerker in the Post, Winship said to the Post reporter: "I didn't see that happen." "It could have," replied his imaginative competitor.

The end of the war brought in another new crop of reporters whose bylines became familiar in the Globe through the next generation: Carlyle Holt, Gardner Jackson, Louis Lyons, John Barry, Henry Harris, Joseph Dinneen.

"Evening" One Cent

"The Evening Globe" first appeared as a separate identification February 1, 1914. Until then it had been simply "Daily Globe" afternoon as morning. No other change was made in appearance or content.

But on the same date the price of the evening paper was reduced to one cent. Next month the Globe announced that daily circulation had risen by nearly 100,000 in February. But this did not last. Average circulation for the year was given as 175,000 in 1913 and 209,000 in 1914. It rose with the war to 242,000 for 1916. But 1913 was a low year. The daily circulation had fallen from a peak of 196,000 in 1902 to the 175,000 of 1913. The Sunday also, after a continuing rise from its beginning, dropped in 1913 from its peak of 321,000 to 311,000. It was still five cents, although its size had increased tenfold with no price change over 35 years. World War I with its general price rise was shortly to push the Sunday price to ten cents and bring a slight dip in circulation, soon recovered.

1913 was a year of hard times, relieved only by the opening of the war in Europe. But a primary cause of the circulation dip in 1913 and the cut to one cent for the evening paper must have been the rising competition of the new Boston American and the fast-growing Post under Grozier. The Post was one cent.

By 1914 the Globe had accepted the permanence of Republican ascendancy in the congressional delegation to the point of naming as Washington correspondent the recently retired secretary of the Republican State Committee. Charles S. Groves had earlier been a Globe political reporter but for five years had been Senator Lodge's righthand man in managing party affairs. Senator Lodge was regarded as the primary source of Washington news for a Boston paper; for the remaining decade of his life the Globe's Washington coverage consisted mainly of keeping in touch with the senior Senator.

Groves was to serve in Washington two decades after Lodge, but he made slight concession to political change. He explained to a reporter sent down to explore wartime programs in the 1940's: "I never expected the New Deal to be permanent." The Globe's lapse in failing to tune into changing times in its national reporting was a factor in its falling behind in the thirties and forties, or perhaps an index of it. The best that managing editor Winship could do in this era, against the Globe statics, was to buy every political column he could lay hands on — and he got most of them — to reinforce the Washington reporting. This so filled the paper with "fixtures" that reporters complained chronically about the limits of the "news hole."

But one highly individual resource the Globe had through this whole epoch was M. E. Hennessy (he used only initials), who had known all the politicians within memory and had written about them all. His stock in trade was an anecdotal treasury about the great and near-great which he put into a Sunday column filled with personality notes entitled "Round and About With M. E. Hennessy." Mike Hennessy's figure was a memorable journalistic asset. He was often mistaken for Irvin Cobb, with the same surplus of chins and stomachs and an almost perpetual chuckle that would ripple up and down his front. He traveled incessantly, even till he was 80, to Washington, off to conventions, or wherever some notable political event brought out national figures. He was acquainted with them all, and once they'd met him they never forgot him.

Boston Evening Globe

VOL XC—NO. 130   BOSTON, TUESDAY EVENING, NOVEMBER 7, 1916—FOURTEEN PAGES   COPYRIGHT, 1916, BY THE GLOBE NEWSPAPER CO.   PRICE ONE CENT

EVENING EDITION—7:30 O'CLOCK—LATEST

ACUSHNET GIVES WILSON BIG GAIN

"FIGHTING NINTH" REACHES HOME, IS CHEERED BY MANY THOUSANDS

A large crowd greeted the first section of the 9th Regiment at the South Station. One of the happiest couples on the arrival of the train was Sergt C. W. Clark of H Company and Miss Gertrude C. Murphy, who are shown in the picture.

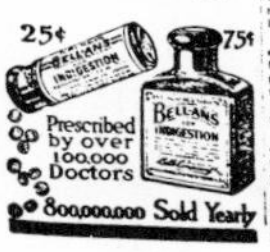

VOTE ALL OVER NATION IS HEAVY

NEW YORK, Nov 7—The opening of the polls in the National election was attended by heavy voting throughout the country, according to reports received in this city today.

Gratification was expressed today at both Republican and Democratic National headquarters here at the fair weather for election, as it was expected that it would bring out a great number of voters. It has been confidently asserted by both of the leading parties that the outcome of election would be greatly influenced by the so-called "silent vote," and it was believed that good weather would bring this class out in particularly strong numbers.

Chairman William R. Willcox of the Republican National Committee was at his desk early, receiving telegraphic reports from throughout the country relative to the early action of the electorate in coming out to vote. He said he was gratified at the reports he had received.

Democratic National Committee was at his home at Harrisburg, Penn, where he had gone to cast his vote. He expected to be at his desk at National headquarters here later in the day, it was said.

Size of New York Plurality in Doubt

At the last Presidential election more than three votes were cast in New York city. The city, party leaders concede, will result in National election as Democratic, and the question at issue between the two parties is the size of plurality. The Democrats claim a lead of 50,000, while the Republicans declare the Democratic plurality will not exceed 25,000.

Long before the polls were open in some portions of the city men were in line, waiting to cast their ballots, and predictions were that the greater part of the vote would be cast before noon.

State Vote Heaviest Ever Cast

The Republican and Democratic State chairmen both predicted early today that New York State probably would cast the heaviest vote ever polled in a Presidential election. Both of the chairmen said in statements given out today that the weather was everywhere fine and that, particularly in the rural sections, the voters were early at the polls. Indications were that by noon the

latest part of the vote would be cast. New York State in the last National election cast a total of 1,586,761 ballots for the Presidential candidates. It was believed that these figures would be exceeded.

About 60 percent of the New York city vote had been cast at 11 a.m, it was estimated by the Election Board.

"Fight is Won," Willcox Thinks

"This fight is won. We have Republican weather and it's all over but the shouting," said Chairman Willcox of the Republican National Committee, when he stepped into the press room, after hearing reports of the progress of the voting from all over the country. He declared the result of the returns at New Ashford, Mass, were "indicative of the whole country."

"Chairman McCormick of the Democratic Committee had it all that hour for the Presidential result," continued Chairman Willcox. "Ordinarily we shouldn't pay any attention to such small towns, but New Ashford voted, Vance, Emory and Commanding upon the New Ashford vote, Henry Morgenthau, chairman of the finance committee, said: "We don't bother by pin-pricks. We expect an upheaval of the masses throughout the country."

Mr Morgenthau announced today that the total expenditures of the Democratic campaign amounted to approximately $1,500,000. This money, he said, had all been collected except about $200,000, most of the committees not yet worrying about that.

Political observers are no doubt just when the National election results will become known. They are so near it as to give opinion that it will be close to a real result because of the complete election returns resulting from the rival number of women who will vote and whose votes.

WILSON AND REPUBLICAN GOVERNOR PLEASE WICHITA

WICHITA, Kan, Nov 7—The vote count here today, under the double election board system, ran the bill precincts of the 3d Ward, a downtown district, giving William M. Hughes, Republican, for Governor, approved by the downtown wards cast, obtained 42, and the political results have in past years shown more variance than in any other borough of the city.

Long before the polls were open about 30 men of the city men were in line, waiting to cast their ballots. Business observations it is the Republican Governor for the next four years, Chairman McCormick will return us to

NEW ASHFORD REPORTED FIRST

Smallest Town in State Gives Hughes 16, Wilson 7

PITTSFIELD, Mass, Nov 7—New Ashford, the smallest town in the State, had the distinction of being the first to make its election returns today. The polls closed at 12 a m, and the count showed: Hughes, 16; Wilson, 7.

In 1912 New Ashford gave Wilson 4 votes, Taft 7 and Roosevelt 6.

REPORTERS AIDED TOWN TO BREAK ALL RECORDS

NEW ASHFORD, Nov 7—New Ashford, the smallest town in Massachusetts, believes that it is the first town in the United States to report the Presidential election returns. It will be a matter of much pride that, in its race for publicity, for by being the first town in the whole Nation to report the biggest news of the day. New Ashford hopes to take that place in its own. New Ashford has cuddled down under the brow of Greylock, to the west, the plainest sort of a New England hamlet. In 1916 it had a population of 87, and its registered voters number 28. It is the most isolated town in Northern Berkshire, without a State highway, a trolley line, having no railroad or telegraph and with a single telephone, and that in a distant country house.

This effort of the town to achieve fame was conceived when the Pittsfield press sought some way of getting the vote of New Ashford in means. It has been necessary for the press associations and correspondents to send messengers to New Ashford to carry the vote to Pittsfield, often getting the returns to Pittsfield at a late hour.

Automobiles for Voters

The newspapers agreed to assist in getting out the voters of New Ashford by automobile, providing the Selectmen of the town would open the polls at 6 a m and close them at 10. The town Clerk, Town Clerk Charles E. Baker, Selectman Elmer P. Beach, Emory Baker and Henry M. Wilson, consented. And for the past week New Ashford's attempt to break the point has been carried to a high degree in the smallest town in the State.

Besides the town officers mentioned the registered voters are William Baker, Henry B. Baxter, Warren M. Harrison, Alfred G. Beach, Charles Goodell, Walter Goodell, Aimee D. Ingraham, Fred Ingraham, Bernard Mackay, Harry F. Phelps, Matthew G. Smith, Charles Sherman, Frank Thompson, Guy Wade, Joseph

Continued on the Second Page.

KANSAS CITY, KAN, FAVORS HUGHES

KANSAS CITY, Kan, Nov 7—Incomplete returns given out here early today by election judges for nine of the 108 precincts of Wyandotte County, Kan, including Kansas City, Kan, gives Hughes 378, Wilson 328.

RETURNS FROM 16 OUT OF 26 WICHITA PRECINCTS

WICHITA, Kan, Nov 7—Incomplete returns from 16 out of 26 precincts of this city, as given out by election judges, show 600 votes for Wilson and 651 for Hughes. For Governor, Capper, Republican incumbent, 665.

The Congressional race in the 5th district shows Wilson (R), 316, and Ayers (D) incumbent, 302.

HUGHES GETS 651 TO WILSON'S 551 IN TOPEKA

TOPEKA, Kan, Nov 7—The first available election returns in Kansas today were reported from 16 precincts out of 62 in the city of Topeka, the incomplete count giving Hughes 651 and Wilson 551.

A double election board system used made it possible for the returns to be given out before noon.

The count for Governor in the 16 incomplete precincts reported give Gov Capper (Republican) 604 and W. C. Lansdon (Democratic) 365.

The election returns from 16 out of 62 precincts in Topeka compiled at noon today show the following results: Hughes, 990; Wilson, 804.

In 23 precincts the incomplete vote for Governor given today: Capper, 1201; Lansdon, 706.

The population of Topeka in 1910 was 42,400.

HOW THE GLOBE WILL GIVE ELECTION RETURNS

Searchlight Flash and Lights on Customhouse Tower

WILSON ELECTED	ONE Sweep Across the Sky (Repeated Every 30 Seconds)
HUGHES ELECTED	TWO Flashes Across the Sky (Repeated Every 30 Seconds)

LIGHTS ON FOUR CORNERS OF TOWER

McCall Elected	Red Light
Mansfield Elected	Green Light
Lodge Elected	White Light
Fitzgerald Elected	Yellow Light

Double Stereopticon Service In Newspaper Row In Front of Globe Office and in Scollay Square

Globe Extras Throughout the Evening

In Boston Watch the Globe Stereopticons Outside of Boston Watch for the Globe Flash and Lights on the Customhouse Tower

GET THE GLOBE EXTRAS
FOR LATEST RETURNS AND ALL THE DETAILS

BOSTON'S VOTING RECORD BROKEN

Forty Percent of Total Cast Before 10 O'Clock

It was a storm of ballots in Boston today, and when the votes are counted tonight all indications point to a larger vote than has ever been polled in this city.

It was the same story in almost every town morning—waiting lines. Had the booths been four or five times as large as they are they could not have accommodated the rush of voters.

In many precincts more than 50 percent of the voters had cast their ballots within two hours after the polls opened at 6 o'clock. All forenoon the stream of voters kept up, diminishing as the morning wore on. But there came another rush at noon in sections where workingmen go home to dinner. During the afternoon the balloting was light.

With an approximate vote of 40 percent cast before 11 o'clock all records were broken in this city. In the prevailing official returns have not been received by noon. Fully 80 percent, under the ideal weather conditions, were at the polls, whereupon more than three-quarters of the vote had been polled by noon.

The intense interest in the election and the unusually heavy vote created incentives to get people to vote early. And there were many evidences that the motor cars, taxis and carriages at many precincts was kept busy after the dinner hour in early days.

In the polling booths the party workers who checked off the names as the voters had a hard job to keep up with them. Because many of them had not cast ballots at the primary election they had to vestibule to fill their polling booths this morning, and to get them through the registration books having previously been out voting on their fight to cast of their names were cancelled.

John F. Fitzgerald, candidate for United States Senator, cast his vote at 8.30 this morning in the basement of the Henry L. Pierce School, Washington st and Welles av, Dorchester. He went to automobile, was greeted by the clerks, poll officers and friends and then called for his ballot. He was pleased with the Democratic activity manifested everywhere in Dorchester and said today that he expressed no opinion as to the result.

Big East Boston Vote

Wards 1 and 2 polled more than half the total vote at noon. In every precinct of both wards the vote was running away ahead of the Presidential year, four years ago and of last year's vote. There was a strong Wilson sentiment throughout the island, and it is said President will go out of East Boston with a big plurality.

As Hon Frederick W. Mansfield, Democratic candidate for Governor, is an East Boston man, his local supporters were active to see his favor. Much interest is focused on the fight for Representative in both wards as well.

Heavy in Charlestown

The vote in Wards 3 and 4, Charlestown, was the heaviest up to noon that

has been cast in many years. At that time it was shown that a little more than 50 percent of the vote had been cast.

The Republicans showed up at the polls in good numbers and the ideal weather promised to bring out the total Republican vote of Charlestown. Many old Hughes men were on the job early for him and on election, registered their votes.

The Democratic vote in the south heavily has a large counter rooting their boys to the jobs. Up in Ward 3, Charlestown, the dinner hour it was reported that more than three-quarters of the vote had been cast.

In Ward 9 the noon vote was estimated at this, in Ward 3, 1462.

In North and South Ends

In Ward 3, formerly Wards 6 and 8, there was a heavy Wilson and Fitzgerald vote early. Before 8 o'clock in the North End wards of this precinct flocked more than 40 percent, in the West End about 35 percent, and the South End section nearly as heavy. Voters went early to the polls this morning. In Ward 3 the noon vote was indicated in every precinct more than 300 votes were cast before 10 o'clock. In Ward 7, precinct 3, more than three-quarters of the vote had been cast before noon.

Large South Boston Vote

Judging from the vote cast in the South Boston wards, 5, 10 and 11, up to noon, as compared with the voting at primaries and elections in the last three years, it was expected that seven-eighths of the total registered vote of the precincts would be cast.

The average in the 34 precincts of the district at noon was between 250 votes, and it was shown that an extraordinary vote was being polled. In Ward 5, there was 65 ballots had been cast at noon. In Precinct 8, Ward 10 there were 88 votes at noon.

The polls opened at 6 this morning, and during the forenoon large numbers went to the polls. The closing time of

Continued on the Fourth Page.

HUGHES LOST 27 T. R.-TAFT VOTES

Wilson Gained 19 of These— Many Voted "Scattering"

GOV McCALL ABOUT TO ENTER POLLING BOOTH — DEMOCRATIC CANDIDATE ABOUT TO CAST HIS BALLOT

GOV SAMUEL W. McCALL, Photographed as he entered the polls in Winchester This Morning.

HON FREDERICK W. MANSFIELD, Photographed as he voted in Ward 1 this Morning.

The town of Acushnet, reporting its vote at 1.30 this afternoon, showed the following count:

For President—Benson, 4; Hanly, 3; Hughes, 127; Reimer, 1; Wilson, 26; Chafin, 1.

The vote in 1912 was: Chafin, 2; Debs, 2; Reimer, 1; Roosevelt, 34; Taft, 104; Wilson, 29.

The town of Acushnet in its four years, while it gave Wilson 26, caused a loss of 27 votes for a Democratic candidate to the belief of Chairman John J. O'Connor of the Democratic City Committee from a section of the city. Melrose experienced in all parts of the city.

Melrose is one of the Republican strongholds in the State, but Wilson will lead

Continued on the Second Page.

NORWELL GIVES HUGHES 179, WILSON 107

The town of Norwell reported the following result: Hughes, 179; Wilson, 107.

In the vote for Governor in the today's election Norwell gave Mansfield, 79; McCall, 202; and for United States Senator, McCall, 70; Taft, 82; Roosevelt, 104.

NEW BEDFORD PRECINCT, HUGHES 260, WILSON 106

NEW BEDFORD, Nov 7—Ward 6 Precinct 14, of this city gave Hughes 260, Wilson 106.

RECORD VOTE MAY BE POLLED AT WINTHROP

WINTHROP, Nov 7—At noon it looked as though Winthrop was headed toward a record vote. There was heavy voting in all of the four precincts from early morning, and at 1 o'clock more than 100 votes had been cast. Winthrop's total vote is 2928.

The Hughes sentiment is very strong, and it is believed he will leave town with a big plurality, as will Gov McCall and the rest of the Republican ticket. A big vote was expected, however for Hon Fred W. Mansfield, Democratic candidate for Governor, for Hon Fred Melrose is one of the Republican strongholds close until 6 o'clock tonight.

REPUBLICANS GETTING OUT OLD VOTERS AT MELROSE

MELROSE, Nov 7—Because of the heavy vote cast during the forenoon the Republican party was out in full strength in all the seven wards with the Republicans doing most of the work. Automobiles were used to get out the old voters and the Republican City Committee officials had conducted an active campaign predicted that Hughes and the other Republican candidates would carry the city by an unusually large vote. There was a big Wilson vote this morning and during the forenoon large numbers went to the polls. The closing time of

Continued on the Second Page.

Read Globe Election Extras Tonight

It was perhaps an index of its prewar parochialism that the Globe should settle for national news through a Lodge-Groves interpretation, even as it was applauding the Democratic reforms of Gov. David I. Walsh. Or perhaps it was somebody's idea of impartiality. When Walsh won the governorship in 1913 for the fourth Democratic state victory in a row, the Globe congratulated him for the high level of his campaign and called his election "salutary" and "significant for the growth of religious tolerance in Massachusetts." He was the first Catholic governor. The Globe ran on the front page a letter from Walsh congratulating it on having proved "true to its reputation for fairness. So long as there are powerful and impartial newspapers like the Globe, the people of New England will be well and intelligently served and the public rights safeguarded."

When Walsh was re-elected in 1914 the Globe applauded the "endorsement he merited for his personal and efficient conduct at the State House and in the campaign."

He had extended savings bank life insurance, established state forests, reformed workingmen's compensation, and organized new departments of health, a commission on economy and efficiency, and the directors of the Port of Boston.

Walsh won against a Republican tide in 1914 that saw the party gain four congressional seats in Massachusetts and elect all three of the New England senators chosen in the first direct senatorial election — in New Hampshire, Connecticut, and Vermont.

The November 2, 1914, front page recorded the indictment of 20 New Haven Railroad directors, who "sought to monopolize New England Railroad Transportation . . . The first step to determine if the Sherman Act can be enforced . . . Never were so many prominent men indicted": William Rockefeller, George F. Baker, Theodore Vail. Not indicted but listed as conspirators were Charles Mellen, the late J. P. Morgan, Chauncey Depew, Charles F. Choate, and President Lucius Tuttle of the Boston & Maine.

The suffrage cause took a bad beating in the 1914 national election, and the Progressive party, born in 1912, declined "from a split to a splinter," as the Globe described it editorially. The party had received under three percent of the vote and consequently was dropped off the Massachusetts ballot in the next election.

Calvin Coolidge moved up a first rung on the political ladder, as it was then constructed in the Republican-controlled legislature, in 1914. He became president of the state Senate, an opening that had come when the 1913 election saw the suffragists "Get President Greenwood," as the Globe headline reported November 5. Senator Greenwood had been one of the most adamant opponents of women's suffrage. Within hours of Greenwood's defeat Coolidge, with the help of his Boston merchant admirer Frank Stearns, had corralled by telephone the votes to fill the Senate presidency.

The same week that brought disaster to Senator Greenwood the evening Globe, November 1, 1913, carried the conclusion to a bizarre case of a long-missing heir that had run through the newspapers for several years. The master's findings took six columns in the Globe that night to discredit the claim of "Dakota Dan" and accept "Fresno Dan" as the son of the late Daniel Russell of Melrose. His younger son, Daniel Russell, had left home at 13 in 1885. His older son, William, had continued to live in Melrose. The father died in 1907, leaving a substantial estate to the two sons. In 1909 a man turned up from North Dakota claiming to be the missing Daniel Blake Russell. William didn't believe it and made a search of his own that turned up in 1910 a Daniel Blake Russell in Fresno. The court battle between "Dakota Dan" and "Fresno Dan" fascinated newspaper readers as Dakota Dan produced 58 witnesses and Fresno Dan 35, all equally positive in their identifications of a man who had left home as a boy 25 years earlier. The master had finally interviewed 168 persons before discrediting Dakota Dan on physical scars, handwriting, and especially such illiteracy and lack of cultivation for the son of the Russell family as made his witnesses' stories "incredible." The judge had carried his investigation then into the background of Dakota Dan to discover his real identity as a French Canadian named James Rusaw. Brother William was happy at the recognition of Fresno Dan.

That November 3 a headline reported the Massachusetts corporation tax as upheld by the Supreme Court.

A Dudley editorial November 1 had asked: "Should Doctors Be Paid by the State?" Bernard Shaw proposed it. The Globe said "it would remove suspicion from a noble profession. It would raise taxes but would be health insurance . . . We should pay doctors to keep us well and not make them dependent on the prevalence of disease."

The Sunday Globe was running Theodore Roosevelt's autobiography from the McClure syndicate, a whole page. Two other full pages were taken by literary series: one of O. Henry's Masterpieces and another "a literary classic" that ranged from passages in Samuel Richardson's *Pamela* to Thackeray's *Vanity Fair*. Roald Amundsen contributed "How I Discovered the South Pole"; Mr. Dooley the same day was on slang. A whole page was given to district notes — Roxbury-Dorchester-Woburn — a dozen to 20 of them. These district notes appeared also in the daily paper, as they would for another 20 years, product of a staff of district reporters who had their own "district room" that made up in effect a substratum of the city staff.

The daily paper was 12–16 pages, three of them sports pages. One of these was made up with the Braves baseball game on the right and the Red Sox on the left, each with a two-column head, and in the space between a four-column cartoon on the day's game by Wallace Goldsmith. Headlines in June, 1913, reported "Prices Highest in 30 Years," "Coal Strike on Again," and "New Boston College Building Dedicated in Newton."

The daily paper introduced a farm page February 16, 1914. The lead story of the morning paper that day was "Need of More Farmers — Also Knowledge to Improve Unproductive Lands." A popular interest had developed to restore the abandoned farms of New England. This was not unrelated to Teddy Roosevelt's back-to-the-land movement. Both had some relation to a series of recessions that made the farm look like a secure place to unemployed city people. Legislators became more liberal in support of their agricultural colleges, which were introducing courses in rural sociology, agricultural economics, and farm cooperatives. Nothing came of the movement to resuscitate abandoned farms, which had been abandoned for the sound economic reason that they wouldn't yield a living. Many were later reforested, although nature took care of that anyway. But the Wilson administration had launched the agricultural extension service with its county agents, farm demonstrations, farmers' weeks, and farmers' bulletins, to carry the agricultural college work to the farm. This was a permanent and productive development. One effect of it was to stimulate farm pages in many newspapers. They had real news for the farmer, such as the message of Professor Ralph Reeves, brought from Oregon to the Massachusetts Agricultural College, that New England could compete with the northwest in apples, saving 40 cents a box on freight, but that orchards must be systematically pruned, sprayed, cultivated and the crop graded and stored and marketed efficiently.

The evening paper that day, February 16, had a six-column picture of "some of the 500 women who appeared at the suffrage hearing at the State House."

The Dudley editorial February 19 was on "The Office Woman — A Pioneer of her Sex." The next Sunday, February 22, the Symposium was "Are We Becoming More or Less Democratic?" A. J. Philpott was signing art exhibition reviews. Mr. Dooley was on dancing. James Montgomery Flagg's series of sketches, "A Girl You Know," presented its nineteenth picture for a half page.

The daily paper had three comic strips: Keeping Up with the Joneses, Day by Day with the Days, and Knobs. Saturday, February 8, an editorial "Fair Warning" reminded readers of the first income tax. On February 27 a front page headline:

> Victims Smile at Income Tax
> More than 14,000 file returns in Boston

Legends to Live By

Legends attach to the life of an institution like ivy on college halls. Some legends are myth, some reality. A real legend of the Globe grew out of the sinking of the *Titanic* April 14, 1912. That White Star liner, the greatest ship in the world, struck an iceberg in the North Atlantic on her maiden voyage and sank within four hours, taking with her 1,513 persons, among them some of the most notable names in New York society. It was a Sunday midnight, April 14, that this greatest of sea tragedies occurred. Confused reports came through the limited wireless waves for the Monday morning papers. The *Titanic* was believed still afloat, though sinking, but several ships were steaming to the rescue.

Monday afternoon the word through the Marconi station at Cape Race, Newfoundland, was that the Cunard liner *Carpathia,* eastbound, had reached the scene in time to pick up many survivors. How many was unknown. The range of wireless at that time would not reach the *Carpathia,* 1,000 miles at sea. But about midnight Monday the White Star officials disclosed a message relayed from the steamer *Olympic* that the *Carpathia* had picked up only 675 of the 2,200 passengers and crew. Smaller ships with only short-range wireless might have rescued some. Reports of survivors varied that night between 655 and 866. That is where the news stood for Tuesday morning papers.

On the copy desk, confronted with confused reports, someone said, "If we could only get contact with the *Carpathia.*" Someone else recalled that the *Franconia,* a sister Cunard ship, was sailing next morning for England. In 24 hours it would be within wireless range of the *Carpathia* and still within shore range. "If we had a man on the *Franconia* . . ."

Why not? Winfield Thompson, yachting editor, a seasoned reporter who knew all the shipping people, was on special assignment doing the "War Day-by-Day" historic serial of the Civil War. A 2:30 A.M. telephone call waked him with the word that he was sailing on the *Franconia* at 9:00. Nobody had access to the cashier's safe at that time of night, but Young's Hotel was almost across the street and they always had money in the safe. General Taylor had a luncheon table at Young's, where Globe editors were familiar guests. Thompson needed $1,200 and Young's had it.

Thompson's instructions were brief: "Get in touch with Captain Rostron on the *Carpathia* and find out exactly how many survivors there are." This was easier said than done, for the *Carpathia* was of course bombarded with wireless messages from other vessels and her operator had more than he could handle. But she was a sister Cunard ship, and the *Franconia* officers knew Thompson and wanted to help. The *Franconia* established contact with the *Carpathia* 500 miles out, at 6:10 Wednesday morning. The Wednesday evening Globe had a 50-word dispatch that was picked up by the wire services for the press of the world. The *Carpathia* had 705 survivors on board and would reach New York Thursday about 8 P.M. The official figure later was 706. That was Thompson's whole assignment. He had a round-trip to England, where he spent some days as guest of his old yachting friend Sir Thomas Lipton.

In the hindsight of half a century, one may ask what difference whether they knew Wednesday or Friday that the number of survivors was not 866 or 655 but 706? Half a century later it made no difference. But it set the Globe vibrating that afternoon of April 17, 1912, to see Thompson's wireless message and to realize that the press around the world would be carrying the story "by Winfield M. Thompson, Boston Globe reporter on board Cunard Liner *Franconia* — special wireless dispatch to the Globe." This was their message to Garcia. The journalistic instinct was to go get the story. This was "news enterprise," the essence of journalism.

Thompson, a Maine man, was then 43, had been 18 years on the Globe, had covered major assignments all over the country, and had been made yachting editor in 1907 and covered America's Cup races, Marblehead Race Week, and maritime events national and international. In 1920 he would leave the paper to go into the steamship business. But first he shared with Frank P. Sibley a long, arduous assignment, in 1916, to the Mexican Border with the Massachusetts National Guard when for months the danger of war with Mexico seemed close.

Legends that are myth may become equally real in effect if they symbolize a core of truth. A generation of Globe men stood in awe of Harry Poor, until his death in 1934 night editor of the Globe for 45 years, a man who seemed to express in his every glance and movement the tension and verve of his nightly plotting against the clock to ready his paper for the midnight deadlines. His lithe, lean form moved down the hall on quick step if he needed a word with the city editor, or leaped up stairs two steps at a time to catch a makeup crisis in the forms. His warm brown eyes swept lightly around the news room to light up in quick recognition or to brood darkly over some problem unresolved as press time rolled around. In smile or scowl, his face muscles flexed with the mood of the night and his expression told the story of how the night was going.

Harry Poor's hair was prematurely white. The legend of the office was that his hair turned white overnight, under the strain of sifting out the news the night the battleship *Maine* was blown up. This wasn't true, yet a shorthand for truth of all the nights of strain that had whitened his hair and etched those lines in his plastic countenance.

Harry Poor.

But the drama of that night when the *Maine* was blown up remained with John Coyne, then the copy boy on the night desk, all his life. "I remember Harry Poor taking copy from the telegrapher's typewriter a line at a time, scanning it, sending it up to the composing room, and writing the headlines as he watched the copy. We were on the street a few minutes after the news came in." Of such stuff is legend made.

In his day, Harry Poor sat in the slot at the center of the desk and fed out the copy to the desk editors around its rim, first absorbing its relative importance. He picked out all the pictures for the morning paper, laid out the front page dummy, chose the stories for page one, and ordered the size of heads for them. Then he went upstairs to make up the paper. Rules of the printers' union forbid an editor's touching type, but the rule never applied to Harry Poor. He picked up galleys of type and placed them beside the chases where they were to go. He had time to dummy only the front page. The inside pages were laid out "by ear."

Now these chores are divided among several men. The slot man gives out the copy, the night editor lays out each page on dummies, the picture editor handles the photographic cuts, and there's a makeup editor for each of half a dozen departments. But Harry Poor carried all this in his head, as night after night he created a newspaper from little piles of copy paper. His imagination envisioned the front page from the first urgent bulletin handed him from the wire, set his plans in motion, started the long night's shaping and changing.

The copy desk had of course its negative function, to avoid libel and errors. It had to cut the copy to fit the space. Its function made it traditionally at war with reporters, always agonized at any cuts in their copy. But its function was essentially creative, to see to the coherent organization of the story. The copy desk had prime influence on the tone of the paper.

The Globe's editor emeritus, Laurence Winship, long remembered how Harry Poor "saved" him on his first big story, coverage of the 1916 Billy Sunday revival.

I was so carried away with the prominence given my first few stories that I started the fourth day's with: "I have seen many things but nothing like the drama of the tabernacle last night." Harry Poor killed my grandiloquent lead and substituted a matter of fact sentence. I was properly outraged and it was some time before I realized he had saved me from looking like a prima donna. The desk saved me many times but it didn't save me once when I had a brief hitch on the day desk. My first day, Bill Kenney, the day editor, tossed me the story of Harry Thaw's arrest. I wrote the head: "Harry Thaw Held in $1,000,-000 Bail." It went along to the composing room and they called me back to ask if I didn't have an extra 0 in my head.

This writer remembers vividly the only journalism instruction he ever had. It came from Harry Poor. As a cub, he had been handed the monthly report of the Boston Elevated, which then, as ever, was in constant deficit. But the month of January 1920 had been very stormy. People had to ride and their fares wiped out the red ink that month. The reporter's story started, "The Boston Elevated had a remarkable record for January." The night editor brought the copy around to the news room himself to say, " 'Remarkable' is an editorial word, not a news word. The thing is to write it so that the *reader* will say, 'Isn't that remarkable.' " This was delivered with a smile and a friendly pat. The lesson stuck.

That same winter brought an extraordinary display of northern lights, spectacular to see but the cause of extensive interference with radio and telephone communication throughout the region. The city editor assigned the reporter to look up Aurora Borealis in the encyclopedia for a box item. Then he suggested the reporter go up on the Common and get a good description. The lights streaked a colorful pattern across the heavens. The reporter had a dim memory of Indian legends about the aurora that he thought Hawthorne had told. He knew the Parker House library would be open at night, so he stopped by and found the stories in *Twice Told Tales*. Back at the office, more dispatches had piled up on his desk from all over, reporting the strange effects of the northern lights. This accumulation, he realized, disappointed, wouldn't leave any space for his Indian myths. Writing was slow. But he got off a take to the desk to let them know the story was coming. He'd have to hold it down.

Soon a copy boy came by to say, "Mr. Poor says let that story run." This was a thrill that sent the blood tingling. It uncorked all the reporter's excitement. It sped his fingers over the keys as the story, that had now attained a life of its own, ran on and on. It led the paper next morning. But even that meant less than that Mr. Poor had seen the story through a reporter's eyes. He'd said, "Let the story run."

Years later, when the reporter had wired in a report of the funeral of President Coolidge's father on a bleak winter day in Plymouth, Vermont, a message came back from Harry Poor: " 'Stark' was just the right word to start your story."

To War with Richard Harding Davis

The R.F.D. man stopped at the end of a winding dirt road to stuff the papers and letters into the mailboxes, six of them in a row by the corner of a stone wall and hedgerow. He was barely in sight from a field where a boy was hoeing corn, just tasseling; but if you didn't happen to catch sight of him, the clank of the tin covers of the mailboxes and the scrape of his wagon wheels as he pulled back into the highway from the gravel shoulder signalled his daily visit. It was a welcome break from the hoeing to go fetch the mail.

The newspaper was on top, the morning Globe, and the headlines heavily black. It was August 14, 1914. The boy sat on the stone wall to scan the front page. One story invited, held, fascinated. Richard Harding Davis, in his first dispatch from the war, was reporting the advance of the German army through Brussels. The boy read on, turned the page inside, devoured it all.

> The entrance of the German army into Brussels quickly lost the human quality. It was lost as soon as three soldiers who led the army bicycled into the Boulevard Duregent and asked the way to Gare du Nord.
>
> When they passed, the human note passed with them. What came after them and which 24 hours later is still coming, is not men marching but a force of nature, like a tidal wave, an avalanche, a river flooding its banks . . .
>
> When for three hours they had passed in one unbroken steel gray column and there was no halt, no breathing time, no open spaces in the ranks, the thing became uncanny, inhuman . . . It held the mystery and menace of a fog rolling towards you from the sea. The gray of the uniforms helped this air of mystery. Only the sharpest eye could detect among the thousands that passed, the slighest difference . . . All moved under a cloak of invisibility.
>
> It is a gray green . . . the gray of the hour just before daybreak, the gray of unpolished steel and of mist among green trees. You saw only a fog that melted into the stones and blended with ancient house fronts . . . Like a river of steel it flowed, gray and ghostlike . . . Now for 26 hours the gray army has rumbled by with the mystery of a fog and the pertinacity of a steam roller . . .

A box told that Davis' story had been rushed by special courier to London, for the wires were down to Antwerp and Ostend. He had sent the dispatch by a young Englishman named E. A. Dalton, who made his way by road to Ostend and by refugee boat to Folkestone, then up to London.

The boy put the mail on the back porch and returned to his hoeing. He'd have to lay off at noon and get in some more licks at studying for the four examinations he still had ahead of him in September for admission to the agricultural college. Farming seemed pretty tame after reading Richard Harding Davis. The war was a long way off — a romantic assignment for a war correspondent. But the war came nearer, and when it was over the boy went looking for a newspaper job. Incredibly enough he found one, with the Boston Globe that printed Richard Harding Davis.

The world war had captured the headlines and the world was not to let them go, ever again, to lapse back to localism. The Globe had already started as a front page fixture its "Chronology of the War," and the Sunday paper had a full-page map showing "disposition of troops in the great European War."

Concern for adequate news of the war had been voiced in a Globe editorial of August 8: "All sides of the story wanted." It observed that Germany was isolated, that all war dispatches were from French or British sources. "Most welcome would be the Teuton side."

The Globe had announced on August 3, the day Germany declared war on Russia and the French mobilized, that Richard Harding Davis, "most famous American war correspondent," would represent the Globe. That day Uncle Dudley described "the line-up of the powers . . . There is something almost grotesque in the political alliances that have existed between the nations of Europe the past 50 years as they prepared for the great contest that is now underway with colossal velocity . . . Behind it the European stage was being set for a great tragedy . . . Of the two, Germany is the more to blame."

Next day's editorial closed: "It is the business of the United States to remain neutral . . . and that she will no sane individual can doubt."

With Britain's entry, the Dudley August 5 was "The Last Hope Gone: Now no great power remains at peace to bring the warring factions to their senses."

While Europe exploded through the news pages, the editorials sought to keep a reasoned perspective. Uncle Dudley August 7 said, "The Germans have done themselves much harm. But we must be warned against allowing prejudice to color our opinions. All the news dispatches from Europe are seasoned in London to suit British and Anglo-Saxon tastes."

The President, August 11, urged "taking no sides." He feared "distress and disaster if partisanship begins." The Globe that day had an editorial on "the duties and dangers of a neutral nation."

But already the propaganda battle was militantly joined in the American press. An article in the Globe by H. G. Wells on August 20, "Wells Appeals to America," asked that no exports be sent to Holland, for the Germans could get them. Even before that, August 9, the Globe had a Sunday article by F. Lothrop Stoddard, stridently pro-German, "Is there a Slav Peril? The answer is Yes. All the Slav peoples are united against western civilization. The Germans had no choice but to fight them." It was Britain's mistake to enter the war against Germany.

On August 17 Harvard's German psychology professor, Hugo Munsterberg, entered the lists: "Kaiser's status in war defended." He warned that the war news came from only one side, with Germany cut off from the cables. "England's King Edward VII, feeling the commercial rivalry of the Germans, united the French and Russians to encircle Germany."

The Uncle Dudley editorial that day was "Taking the Glory Out of War," and on August 18, "How Belgium Became Neutral." August 14 it was on "Aspects of the German Character" — "docility to authority, submission to verboten decrees and to the arrogance of the military caste — a malady that must be drastically treated if an approach to democratic principles is to come in Germany."

Concern about Allied control of war news continued to preoccupy editorials through the early months of the war. By March the Globe was carrying a daily box of "official statements" from all the war camps, that soon became the familiar war "communiqués," putting an official gloss on claims of all sides.

The German submarine war increased the difficulty of keeping a neutral mind. When the U.S. cargo ship *Frye* was sunk, a Globe editorial March 12, 1915, noted: "Fortunately no lives were lost . . . A blunder by the Germans . . . a bill for damages should be sent to Berlin." Even this stance could not last long as the submarine sinkings of neutral shipping disregarded human life. March 15 brought "British Embargo on all Commerce to Germany." The tempo of the submarine war increased. Secretary of State Bryan's efforts at evenhanded diplomacy became more tenuous against the German provocations until his pacifism was no longer tenable. The sinking of the *Lusitania* May 7 passed the point of national tolerance of Bryan's pacifism in the face of German "frightfulness." He resigned.

But even as the submarine warfare brought the world war closer to America, a new concern nearer home diverted national attention to Mexico: Its revolution had dissolved into anarchy and guerilla warfare. A bandit leader, Villa, had begun harassing President Huerta's forces and raiding the Texas border to involve Huerta with the United States. March 10, 1915, brought a front page headline: "Bryan Warns Americans to Quit Mexico City." Then on March 12, the same day as the Globe editorial on the sinking of the *Frye,* the paper was arguing against intervention in Mexico. The Dudley editorial was headed "Wishing 'Kultur' on Mexico."

A week earlier, February 26, the Globe had announced an arrangement to receive the reports of ten correspondents in Mexico. Four were New York World men. "Every night the writings of these correspondents are sifted by Globe editors, and the Globe is thus able to present the most accurate and complete reports of the Mexican situation."

Sibley to the Border

Mexican troubles were in the headlines through 1914–1915 as relations worsened under provocation of anarchy, violence, and confiscation of American property. Globe editorials constantly expressed concern over pressures for intervention and urged moderation.

The tension reached the brink of war in April 1916, when President Wilson responded to a raid by the bandit Villa on Columbus, New Mexico, with an order to General Pershing to take his cavalry across the border in pursuit of Villa. Through the next two months Villa eluded Pershing. President Carranza then demanded the withdrawal of American forces.

Wilson refused and Carranza moved his federal troops into the northern zone, where in June they came into conflict in two skirmishes with units of Pershing's cavalry. In one encounter a large Mexican force overpowered a troop of 60 of Pershing's men and took most of them prisoners.

President Wilson's response to Carranza's ultimatum was to order mobilization of the National Guard that brought 100,000 militiamen to state camps overnight. The first units ready were sent immediately to the border and kept there the rest of that year.

To the Globe's Uncle Dudley, June 19, the mobilization came "as a shock . . .

If the government intends to keep Pershing on foreign soil, it has embarked, it would seem, on a risky and expensive measure . . . We could still withdraw without serious loss of face. We could more easily have withdrawn last week. The chance of extricating ourselves gracefully, when the news of our mobilization reaches Mexico City, are manifestly slight."

Five days later, June 24, the whole top of the front page in the evening paper was given to black headlines of

Pershing's Report on the Carrizel Fight — 14 killed, 43 prisoners
Break Between U.S. and Mexico Draws Nearer
President May Decide to Occupy Northern Mexico with Regular Troops

That was Saturday. Monday's headlines told that

Bay State Troops Will Start Today

The Globe's top reporters, Winfield Thompson and Frank P. Sibley, went with them. Wednesday the headline was

Secretary Lansing Again Rejects Mediation

In that atmosphere the Globe's Uncle Dudley, titled "Measuring Swords with Mexico," saw "the comparison of a great athlete with a sickly dwarf . . . The United States can afford to be magnanimous even under extreme provocation."

Next day the Globe supported a proposal of Henry L. Stimson that the United States pause for deliberation. He urged recall of Pershing from Mexico and then a decision of whether to hold at the border or occupy the zone where border raids originated. Uncle Dudley warned against the notion that "this will be a short war."

The day after, Carranza released the American cavalry prisoners but was silent on the Mexican attitude toward Pershing's presence. The Globe editorial that day was on "our next move in Mexico . . . Carranza's release of the prisoners has eased the tension. Now it is our turn." The editorial urged holding back from war. A blockade would bring Mexico to terms. We should seek an international border patrol. Every day that week Uncle Dudley was discussing the Mexican crisis — urging acceptance of mediation, which several South American governments proffered; appraising the Carranza rule; describing the plight of ordinary Mexicans; considering the problems of the families the guardsmen had left at home.

On Saturday the theme was "Our larger stake in the Mexican crisis — South America was beginning to trust us. But now judgment is suspended . . . We must listen to any offer of mediation from Latin America . . . even at this 11th hour." Announcement of Sunday Globe articles featured one by James Morgan, "Easy to Get into Mexico but Hard to Get Out."

What saved the situation was that both presidents had other, greater crises to occupy them — Carranza with a nation in disorder, Wilson with the war clouds of Europe reaching ever closer. Eventually mediation by Argentina, Brazil, and Chile was accepted. Wilson expressed relief at this out. The guard, held for many months at the border, had some practice at war maneuvers for the war they were to be plunged into the next year. And Frank Sibley of the Globe, with his six-foot-three string-bean figure, thin mustache, distinctive Windsor tie, and cavalry hat, became a familiar of the men of the Massachusetts Guard whose war correspondent he became when they fought in France as the Yankee Division — a name that had its origin in one of Sibley's stories.

The Globe through 1916 devoted a great share of its space and staff energies to keeping in touch with the New England outfits at the border and equally with the

Frank P. Sibley.

home front. A page one box the first week told "how to get letters and gifts to Bay State troops."

Sibley and Thompson both carried cameras, an innovation for American reporters at the time, and their snapshots of hometown boys enlivened their stories. The Globe undertook a novel service to the troops too, by wiring a daily summary of New England news to the El Paso Herald, which printed it under a Boston Globe-El Paso Herald Edition overline.

During the week of mobilization for the Mexican border the critical Battle of Verdun was on page one. An eyewitness account of the battle of Jutland was a Sunday feature June 25. Roger Casement, sentenced to death, pleaded for a free Ireland June 29. The same week "Roosevelt Comes Out for Hughes" to close the gap on the 1912 split. The Republicans were reunited against Wilson.

Long Count of 1916

The historic election of 1916 established the stature of the Globe for dependability. It was almost the only newspaper in the country that did not elect Hughes on the face of Tuesday night's returns, that stuck through three suspenseful days to the unsatisfying report that the election remained in doubt. Ever after in elections people of all parties in Boston looked to the Globe to be sure.

Philosophically, too, 1916 was a peak year for the paper as it took a confident stance with the progressive policies of Woodrow Wilson. Both in the state under Governor Walsh and in the nation in Wilson's first term most of the things the Globe had stood for all its years had come to pass.

The ardor with which James Morgan had greeted Wilson's 1912 nomination had increased with his record in office and deepened with his firm determination to keep America out of the war in Europe. Wilson had become his own secretary of state after Bryan and had sought to balance a neutral diplomacy against allied embargo demands and German submarine warfare. His ordeal had grown increasingly difficult as every new instance of German "frightfulness" brought fiercer cries from the war hawks, led by the belligerent Theodore Roosevelt. Wilson's statement that there was such a thing as being "too proud to fight" brought him ridicule in Republican newspapers, which caricatured the somewhat pedantic style of his notes — "May I not point out . . . ."

But to James Morgan, born into a Kentucky family divided by the Civil War, any peace was better than any war. When Wilson was renominated by acclamation, Uncle Dudley for June 16, 1916, declared: "That he has kept us out of war will be his greatest campaign asset . . . We want none of Europe and its whirlpool of blood. In comparison with the fact that the country is at peace, all other issues are small sideshows."

At the Democratic convention, Morgan emphasized the fervor for peace "that transcends politics and personalities and is more nearly a religion. It is this alone which stirs the hearts of the assembly."

Three days later a Globe editorial said that "the Democratic candidates appeal powerfully to those who voted for Mr. Roosevelt in 1912 . . . The support of the President will be reinforced by many who see a service to humanity in Mr. Wilson's success in the submarine controversy."

The Globe's support of Wilson's peace policy held right up to the election. On November 2, the Uncle Dudley was on Hughes's foreign policy. It picked up his campaign argument that peace can be had with glory and honor by simply "putting up a front . . . He will bluff for America's rights to the last jot and tittle. The safety and prosperity of the United States will be in the hands of one who plans to keep us out of war by placing a chip on his shoulder and daring the effete governments of Europe to knock it off . . . Mr. Hughes seems to think that the nations of Europe are too proud to fight."

On November 1 Uncle Dudley compared "Wilson and Hughes as Leaders." It saw Wilson's concept of the presidency as national leadership, which was what the country needed. "But Hughes says 'I look upon the President as the administrative head of the government.' Mr. Hughes has made it plain he does not intend to lead his party in law making. He will leave legislation to the members of congress. This means putting legislation into the hands of the Old Guard. The Old Guard has neither died nor surrendered, but is eager to take a chance on bringing back the good old goldbrick days."

On November 4 the Dudley foresaw "the closest national election in years." One had to go back to Cleveland to find a contest like 1916. "For the first time the election of senators has coincided with a Presidential campaign." (They had been elected by legislatures, usually in the spring.)

The Globe announced that it would flash the election result from a great searchlight in the Custom House Tower where it could be seen for 25 miles around: for Wilson's election one sweep repeated every 30 seconds, for Hughes two flashes.

On election day the Globe analyzed its own straw vote, which gave Wilson a popular majority but Hughes more electoral votes, "although a shift of 30 electoral votes in some very close states could elect Wilson." "The Globe applied its percentages state by state and was not influenced by the popular vote *much as it would have liked to announce Mr. Wilson a winner.*"

But the searchlight beam went unused election night, November 7.

"Race Close, Hughes Leads" was the Globe's November 8 headline. Hughes carried Massachusetts by a narrow 20,000. A box told why the searchlight had not flashed: "No guessing on the election by the Globe . . . Nine states with 59 votes in doubt." The Dudley editorial, "Hanging in the Balance," explained the uncertainty that led the Globe to hold back from a definite result. "The indications are that Mr. Hughes has won but the lack of definite news from the West makes it uncertain. When it was announced in early evening that New York and Illinois had chosen Mr. Hughes, it seemed a clear indication. But Mr. Wilson showed unexpected strength in states which were expected to give safe pluralties to Mr. Hughes."

That evening's headline:

> Wilson Needs 13
> Hughes Lacks 24
> Close Race for California's 13 Votes, Minnesota's 12, Nevada's 3, New
>   Mexico's 3, Oregon's 5

A box urged "Watch Custom House Tower again tonight. Three flashes will mean contest still in doubt."

The signal that night was three flashes.

Thursday, November 9, the headline:

> California Favoring Wilson
> Minnesota Leans to Hughes
> Either State, with one other, would give election to President

An editorial that day, "The Globe Does Not Guess," said the New York papers had called it for Hughes and were copied all over the country. It described the Globe's election system.

The Dudley November 9 on "This Prodigious Election" sensed the full dimensions of the national drama:

> A great nation is standing stock still with fascinated eyes fixed on a row of cold figures — figures big with destiny.
>
> Whence comes this about? It comes from West of the Mississippi. Westward the course of decision takes its way . . . The decision has leaped from Hell Gate to Golden Gate.
>
> We found ourselves submissively awaiting the judgment of the Yon Yonsons and the Ole Olesens of the great North West. It is their innings . . .
>
> These huge throngs before the bulletin boards are abiding the case of a mental conflict in the mind of a nation at conflict with itself. Not blows but figures will decide. A Nation has staked its head or its headship on those figures. It is the knowledge that the figures will be true which prevents the passion coming to blows.
>
> So the sun goes down and comes up and goes down again until watchers begin to feel a sense of something tremendous happening . . . The Old World fights. The New World votes. We stand at one of civilization's crossroads. In the dead of night there is a sound as of the trampling of many feet. Democracy is marching on.

That evening the headline was "Wilson Is In Lead," followed by: "Again tonight the Globe searchlight will flash from the tower."

The Boston Daily Globe   EXTRA

VOL XC—NO. 131   BOSTON, WEDNESDAY MORNING, NOVEMBER 8, 1916—TWENTY PAGES   COPYRIGHT 1916, BY THE GLOBE NEWSPAPER CO   PRICE TWO CENTS

RACE CLOSE, HUGHES LEADS

No Win — Yet: the 1916 election, November 8.

Friday morning November 10:

      Election of Wilson Shown on Face of Returns

      Republican Chairman Concedes California

      New Hampshire for Wilson by 74 Votes, According to Globe's Count

The Globe editorially says the election shows the American people doing their own political thinking. "The voters are thinking independently upon the new issues which the war change in the world has brought. Men now do not vote blindly on a partisan basis. They allow no party to think for them."

The next day Uncle Dudley sees America as endorsing Wilson's foreign policy, "thankful he is not sending men into the flaming jaws of the European Moloch. In endorsing such a policy Democracy endorses itself . . . The larger part of Wilson's support comes from the West where the people are not so excited and not so prejudiced about the war . . . The country has endorsed Mr. Wilson's domestic policy of social and remedial laws unparalleled in half a century . . . A great nation has the steadfast faith in Democracy to go ahead."

On Sunday, November 12, Uncle Dudley told the Globe's own election story, and it held high drama — "Those 54 Hours in the Globe Office."

From sunset Tuesday until 11 P.M. Thursday the Globe went through an acid test . . .

With the world watching this result of the first great plebiscite since the European War began . . . with great masses of the American people watching to see whether Democracy or the party of special interests would triumph, with newspapers of the highest character announcing decisions first one way and then the other, the Globe would not be swerved . . . The strain was tense and exhausting.

When the early returns came in from rural Massachusetts it was evident that the average expectations were going to be upset. Mr. Wilson's gain in small Bay State communities made the most astute of our observers prophesy the President's reelection, although it was not known then that the men on Cape Cod had seen the same vision as the cowboy on the Western plains.

Instead of the confirmation of the early returns came the avalanche of the East, and before the polls had closed in California, New York newspapers were announcing the election of Mr. Hughes.

New York had overwhelmingly championed the Republican leader. Illinois and Indiana confirmed the decision. By all political precedents the Democrats were beaten throughout the whole East. By bulletin board and extra editions, the newspapers gave the result as final.

But the Globe refused to guess with the rest. Its first edition stated only what the returns indicated. Other papers talked of Republican sweeps . . . They forgot the change of the times. They had not seen the light in the eyes of those Western delegates to the Democratic convention last June . . . The Globe office seethed with anxious men. They accused us of refusing to concede a manifest victory, of holding back the truth because of our political complexion . . . We saw only two columns of figures. We flashed no signal . . . We telephoned to special correspondents in the Middle West. Telegrams were sent to the capital of every doubtful State. Telephone calls were put in for Minneapolis and San Francisco.

Daylight came without any thought of sleep. All through the day the Globe was receiving the latest estimates and figures. The same men who kept the tables for the morning paper did so for all evening editions. The time was too vital, the test too severe to warrant any thought of rest.

The second night was a repetition of the day. All Thursday the truth was gradually filtering into the office. Headlines were made stronger. When it was seen that New Hampshire was doubtful, the Globe rushed its own men to Concord and retabulated the State.

At last the final hour came when the actual returns told only one message. The light on the Custom House Tower was flashed. The cheers of waiting crowds could be heard inside the building. The test was over.

Lucien Price remembered all his life the luminous moment when the long suspense of that 1916 election was over. "Mr. Morgan burst out of his office with his sheaf of copy to send up to the composing room, and being asked what had happened, said, as much to himself as to his questioner: 'It is the first time the just ever elected anybody.' "

Sibley to France

World War I deepened the Globe's relation to its region as a family newspaper through the extraordinarily intimate identification of its war correspondent, Frank P. Sibley, with the Yankee Division. This relationship of Sib with the YD men lasted throughout his life.

But he had a long, frustrating experience to be allowed to join the New England unit. By the time the 26th Division went overseas in the summer of 1917, General Pershing felt overrun by correspondents and had pressed the War Department to accredit no more. Sibley made a personal appeal to Secretary Baker that the Globe's interest was only to be allowed to accompany its New England men. He wouldn't add to Pershing's headquarters' congestion. But Baker was adamant. Nevertheless, Sibley got him to say that if Pershing would accredit him the War Secretary would not object. On that, Sibley sailed for France in September. In Paris the A.E.F. press officers refused him accreditation. But French officers were hospitable and arranged a trip to the front. Sib said he was always treated by the French Army like a gentleman but by the American military as a suspicious character. Months of waiting yielded no accreditation. Out of funds, and fearful he would be recalled if he cabled for more money, Sib got himself a job with the Paris edition of the Chicago Tribune. There he cultivated military acquaintance and finally in January won a favorable response from General Harbord, Pershing's chief of staff, to join the 26th Division.

But this concession to his limited special arrangement still left him without official accreditation. When his letters to the Globe renewed demands on the War Department from the other Boston papers, Washington informed Pershing's headquarters that Sibley's status was an embarrassment. He was ordered home. But his friends in the division didn't want to see him go. His dispatches to the home front had echoed back in the division and were good for morale. YD officers connived to keep Sib with them, often playing a hide-and-seek game with headquarters' inspectors. The division commander, Gen. Clarence R. Edwards, wrote after the war that Sib became "part of the soul of the division." These National Guard officers thoroughly shared with Sib a sense of animosity from the Pershing regulars. Their informalities brought them their own troubles with headquarters rigidities, and General Edwards had a reputation for bluntly indiscreet references to the top brass. This friction grew to feud between regulars and local Guard officers by the end of the war, with General Edwards and Col. Edward L. Logan, of Boston's 101st Division, local heroes and Sibley both their frequent defender and a personal counsellor to tone down their public indignation. Colonel Logan was a popular South Boston judge, but local resentment at West Pointers' criticism of him was a larger factor in naming Boston's Logan Airport for him.

Sibley wrote the history of the Yankee Division in France that the Globe ran in a series April–June 1919 and Little, Brown then published as a book. Before that, even Pershing had come to appreciate the role of the hometown correspondent with his regional divisions, and he wrote Sibley on March 19, 1919, a gracious letter of thanks for his services: "You had the responsibility of keeping the people at home adequately and accurately informed and you performed those duties so that it may be said that in no war has an army been supported by such a well-informed intelligent public opinion."

The Globe won further status for reliability when it stood alone among Boston newspapers and was one of very few in the country in not printing the false armistice report on November 7. The UP wire brought Jack Howard's erroneous scoop about noon, that the armistice had been signed at 11:00 Paris time and hostilities had ended at 2:00 there. A story from Chicago told of confirmation in a private message to a big financial house. But day editor George Gavin was skeptical, as were some of his colleagues. He held up the dispatch. Headlines of the other evening papers screamed Peace, and emotions went wild. Globe newsboys, discouraged, sent a delegation to ask Mr. Gavin what the Globe was going to do; wait for real news, he told them. The Globe did more than wait. Its Washington correspondent reported he could get no confirmation. London knew nothing. Globe newsboys began to exploit its silence with "no official news of armistice." The Dean of St. Paul's Cathedral sent to the Globe to inquire and then canceled a celebration planned at the cathedral. Finally at 2:15 Secretary of State Lansing issued a denial of any armistice. This was in time for the Globe's final evening edition: "Armistice Not Signed." Next day the Globe purred editorially over its caution: "When the war is really over, the Globe hopes to be the first to publish the news."

IV Struggle and Survival

Police Strike

Before he had had much rest from his war coverage, Frank Sibley, now the recognized star reporter of New England, was covering the Boston police strike and in the years immediately following became deeply, personally involved in the Sacco-Vanzetti case. These two historic episodes were climactic to his career, and deeply disillusioning to him.

Sib was a Yankee born and bred, out of a Chelsea boyhood and residence on the Hingham shore, Harvard man, natural newspaperman with an all but photographic talent for explicit detail, as objective and unideological a reporter as could be found and with an ever appreciative sense of the human aspect of a story.

The police strike called up his wartime friends of the National Guard. They became pawns in the melodrama that created a president and brought tragedy to the families of 1,100 policemen. Knowing the Guard officers gave Sib an inside track in reporting it and a sense of personal involvement; also, he had long acquaintance with all the political participants in the drama.

The Sacco-Vanzetti trial, which he reported, outraged his sense of justice. For one time in his life he stepped out of his reporter's role to testify his protest. This clouded his personal and public relations and diminished his role on the Globe, which also diminished the Globe.

The sharp inflation that followed the war, leaving wages behind, brought a wave of strikes in 1919. Widespread industrial unrest made fertile ground for revolutionary developments. Invasion of the labor movement by the IWW in certain centers, notably Seattle and Minneapolis, frightened industry and brought reaction in the form of suppression, as by tough Mayor Ole Hansen of Seattle.

Strikes and threats of strikes rocked the country. In Boston the police, underpaid and overworked, had organized and affiliated with the American Federation of Labor. The Police Commissioner, a stiff-necked conservative and a martinet of a disciplinarian, had tried their leaders for violating department rules. He made clear his position that affiliation with the AF of L would not be tolerated. The police threatened to strike if action were taken against their union leaders.

Mayor Andrew Peters of Boston had no control over the Commissioner, who was appointed by the Governor. But the Mayor was responsible for the safety of the city. Mayor Peters was a Democrat, Gov. Calvin Coolidge and Police Commissioner Edwin U. Curtis Republicans.

With the police crisis coming to a head, the Mayor on August 27 appointed a Citizens Committee of 34 representative citizens, headed by James J. Storrow, perhaps the leading citizen of Boston. He had been chairman of the school committee, chairman of the wartime Massachusetts Committee of Safety, and was the next year to be appointed state fuel commissioner to deal wtih a fuel shortage. A partner in the prestigious banking firm of Lee, Higginson, Storrow represented an element with a solid stake in Boston. He was also a concerned citizen.

Storrow's committee said the police should not affiliate with the AF of L; but they saw no objection to joining their own independent union. The Storrow committee was anxious to avoid open rupture with the police. They proposed that the issue be arbitrated. But the Police Commissioner was adamant that the issue of "a divided allegiance" could not be arbitrated, and the other issues were not relevant to the problem of discipline. The Storrow committee worked intensely at conferences with the police, then on September 1 conferred with the Commissioner. But to no effect. On September 3 Storrow wrote Curtis asking delay in sentencing the police leaders. But the Commissioner's counsel, Herbert Parker, former attorney general, refused even to pass the letter on to Curtis. Parker, a thorough conservative, saw the issue as demanding a showdown on police unionism.

That day Storrow and his associates appealed to Governor Coolidge to intervene with the Commissioner. Coolidge told them bluntly that "it is not my duty" to interfere with the Commissioner. In his autobiography Coolidge was to say that he regarded the unionized police as mutineers, that their issue could not be arbitrated.

Next day the Mayor asked Curtis to postpone his sentencing. Curtis put it off to September 8, a Monday. The Storrow committee met continually the fourth, fifth, sixth — on Saturday the sixth making their report to the mayor — for compromise, no firing of the 19 leaders, no strike, arbitration. The Mayor recommended this to Curtis. The committee report was published Sunday, September 7. The committee had sought the support of all the newspapers and got most of it. The Globe on Monday declared the Storrow report "a very workable solution. The public will recognize the fairness of the Citizens Committee plan . . . For either commissioner or police to refuse this would be a very grave mistake."

Governor Coolidge was at home in Northampton Saturday and Sunday preparing for several scheduled speeches. He telephoned Senator Murray Crane and William Whiting, Holyoke manufacturer, two of his senior advisers. Both supported Curtis as had two other influential advisers, textile manufacturer William M. Butler and Boston merchant Frank Stearns.

Coolidge had a speech Monday to the state AF of L in Greenfield. He didn't mention the police situation. He had planned to spend several days visiting state institutions; but Stearns telephoned urging him to return, for Curtis had rejected the Mayor's recommendation of the Storrow report.

The Transcript had held out against the report. "No Time to Surrender," their Monday editorial was headed. "Now is the time and this is the place for a finish fight, if Boston police make their membership in the AF of L the price of peace."

This expressed the attitude of the police commissioner, of his stern old adviser Herbert Parker, of the conservative mill executive William Butler, of Frank Stearns and the men around the Governor. Curtis suspended the 19 police leaders.

That afternoon Storrow and the Mayor saw the Governor. He again declined to interfere. They urged him to mobilize 3,000–4,000 of the state Guard. But Coolidge said that could be left to Curtis. Curtis was convinced the men would not strike.

But Monday night they voted 1,134–2 to strike Tuesday afternoon. The Boston Herald in a Tuesday editorial reflected the hardening position of the business community and the Republican politicians: "A police strike would be far less disastrous than complacent surrender of the city's government to an outside authority."

The Globe made no further editorial comment. Its top headline that morning was explicit:

> Expect Police Strike Late This Afternoon
> Volunteer Force Ready to Act

The volunteer force, as other stories described, was under active recruitment. "About 100 business and professional men assembled at the Chamber of Commerce in secret and were told by Police Superintendent William H. Pierce to be ready for instant service as police. Each was instructed where to report if notified by phone of emergency . . ."

The eight-column banner head that afternoon was:

> Harvard Organizing Force for Police Duty in Boston
> Call Issued by President Lowell

and a six-column head under that:

> Nearly Unanimous Strike Vote by Policemen
> Gov. Coolidge Refuses to Remove Curtis

So the stage was set.

Tuesday afternoon the Mayor asked Curtis what preparations he had made to protect the city in case of a police strike. Curtis said he had the matter in hand. At five o'clock the Mayor succeeded in getting the Police Commissioner and Governor into a final session. Coolidge refused to call up troops. He had "no authority" to interfere with the Commissioner.

At the appointed time, 5:45, 1,117 of the 1,544 police walked out of the stations. Riots and looting swept the city that unprotected night. The Governor had gone to bed at ten and was unaware till next morning of a night of terror. He said in his autobiography that he always felt he should have called out the state Guard when the police left their posts but that the Commissioner had not felt it necessary.

The Commissioner hadn't believed it would happen. He had made no prepara-ration. On Wednesday morning the Mayor took over. He called out the state Guard units in the city and removed Commissioner Curtis, who an hour later advised the Mayor that a threat of riot required his emergency action. Curtis protested to the Governor over his removal.

Wednesday morning's front page was black with the headlines of mob looting in the wild night of an unprotected city. But the Globe editorial tried to cool it, ap-pealing against pressing the panic button. "Keep your shirt on. We can rely on our-selves . . . Most of us love peace and order. Don't exaggerate the chaos. Until the strike is settled we must manage on common sense and common decency."

Wednesday night saw more serious rioting and a number of persons shot to death by guards dealing with mobs. But "by Thursday morning order had generally been restored," according to the Citizens Committee.

Thursday morning the Governor acted to call out the entire state Guard, under his command. He restored Curtis to charge of the Boston police. This action coun-tered the Mayor, who had said Wednesday that his Citizens Committee had re-ceived no cooperation from Commissioner Curtis and no help or practical sugges-tions from the Governor. Bridling at this, the Governor took charge and didn't notify the Mayor. To suggestions of advisers that it would be tactful to do so he said, "Let him find it out in the papers."

The Globe with the other newspapers played down or eliminated these behind-the-scene frictions. But the Globe rather wryly noted the change of command, observing that it was nice to know who was in charge anyway. "Yesterday the police situation was in the hands of Mayor Peters. Today it is in sole charge of Governor Coolidge. What is the background of these sudden shifts?" The editorial

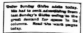

The Boston Daily Globe   EXTRA

VOL. XCVI—NO. 72   BOSTON, WEDNESDAY MORNING, SEPTEMBER 10, 1919—EIGHTEEN PAGES   PRICE TWO CENTS

MOBS SMASH WINDOWS, LOOT STORES
WILD NIGHT FOLLOWS STRIKE OF POLICE

WASHINGTON ST STORES SACKED

Lawless Throngs Surge Through Unprotected City, Demolishing Property—Members of Union Quit Stations at 5:45 in Afternoon, Leaving Only 30 Out of Usual 420 Patrolmen On Duty—Metropolitan Police Rushed to Quell Trouble in South Boston

Goods Worth Thousands of Dollars Are Stolen

Plundering Everywhere, Hoodlums Roam South Boston Streets

STRIKING POLICEMEN MEET AT FAY HALL

Officers From Other Greater Boston Cities Attend

Union Officers Report 1400 Patrolmen Are Out

FIFTY STUDENTS AT HARVARD ENROLLED

Will Help Protect Life and Property in Boston

Action Urged by Pres Lowell and Emergency Committee

SUMMARY OF THE STRIKE SITUATION

Peters Calls on Citizens to Aid Officials of the City in Preserving Order

Volunteers to Begin Duties at 8 This Morning—Coolidge Won't Oust Curtis

RIOT STRIKE
AND
CIVIL COMMOTION
INSURANCE

NORTH BRITISH & MERCANTILE INSURANCE CO.
of London and Edinburgh

PENNSYLVANIA FIRE INSURANCE CO.
of Philadelphia

KIMBALL & GILMAN, Managers

PROTECT YOURSELF
Strike—Riot—Civil Commotion and Burglary

INSURANCE
R. S. Hoffman & Co.

DON'T RISK
LOSING YOUR VALUABLES

Fidelity Trust Company

Sure Relief

TUDOR TEA

BELL-ANS
FOR INDIGESTION

The Accountancy Trained Man His Post War Value
LECTURE BY Horatio N. Drury

PACE INSTITUTE

Volunteer Police

BRYAN TODAY

SCORES VOLUNTEER FOR POLICE DUTY
Harvard Athletes Among Those Ready to Serve

BURNS HOLDS CROWD BACK WITH REVOLVER
Saves Employer's Goods as 5000 Threaten

BYSTANDERS MUST ASSIST OFFICERS

Now Is The Time For Peaches

CAN YOU HELP US?

See Next Sunday's Globe

Cobb, Bates & Yerxa Co.

VOLUNTEERS REPORT AS CITIZENS, SAYS LOWELL

Let's Go BROCKTON FAIR
"The Show Wonderful"
Sept. 30, Oct. 1-2-3

Boston's the Style for New England

SEN. JAMES A. REED OF MISSOURI
And Other Speakers

WILL ANSWER PRESIDENT WILSON
AT
ANTI-LEAGUE OF NATIONS

MASS MEETING
SYMPHONY HALL TONIGHT

Admission Free   Music By Teel's Band

Speaking Begins Promptly at 8 o'clock

FOR PROTECTION —TO— MERCHANTS and OTHERS Exchange Trust Co.

WATERPROOF YOUR FORD TODAY
DRY-FORD

GLOBE DISPLAY ADVTS READ THEM TODAY

Police strike: September 10, 1919.

recited the division of powers over police, between City Hall and State House: the mayor responsible for safety, a governor's appointee over discipline. But "the real point is, the Governor is now in charge. It is at least a gain to know exactly where to look for responsibility in leadership in the crisis."

That night the Central Labor Union voted: "the time is not now appropriate for the ordering of a general strike."

So labor had got the message. This believed danger of a general strike had deeply concerned the business and political community. In the anxiety the Globe had refrained from alienating labor over the police strike; but it now came down hard against a general strike. Its editorial September 11 on "The Strike" warned: "The whole country would be aroused the moment the policemen's strike grew into a strike of other crafts. Every man would have to settle for himself where he stood in a crisis involving organized society. Do those who are advocating sympathetic strikes doubt for a moment where the overwhelming majority of citizens stand on that question? Soberly, in kindly spirit, the Globe asks the men and women of the ranks of organized labor to weigh that question."

Notably this editorial says no word against the police strike — the "crisis" would come "if the strike should grow into anything bigger." Then "the whole situation would change its aspect."

The fear of a general strike did not disappear with the CLU vote. The next day, September 12, the Globe took the exceptional step of a front page editorial occupying a central three-column space. It was entitled only "Editorial." "Why does a general strike fail? . . . By its very nature it is a challenge to the whole community, and so leaves nothing for the community to do but to vindicate its supremacy."

This second-day editorial with its abnormal front page emphasis suggests the clue to the Globe's editorial restraint in the preceding days, while the Transcript and Herald fulminated. The community seethed in class bitterness, labor versus antilabor, and business shivered in fear of a general strike. The editorial writers were clearly under wraps not to add any provocative note to the flammable situation. The Globe stayed its hand for the greater crisis behind the police strike.

The CLU called for the Commissioner to let the men return to duty under the status quo ante, as Samuel Gompers had proposed in a telegram to Coolidge. Coolidge rejected the proposal. The strike was "desertion of duty," he said. The Boston Herald lauded the Governor for his position. The Globe didn't mention it editorially.

Finally on September 13 the Globe passed judgment on the police strike. The day before, President Wilson had called it a crime against civilization. The Globe editorial says:

> President Wilson pronounced the judgment of the public on the issue that precipitated the police strike. Public opinion says policemen should not join a labor union . . . The policeman is an employe of all of us. He should be above the suspicion of bias or partiality, or divided allegiance.
>
> [But] since the public claims a special duty from the policeman, it owes a special duty to him. We have been careless of our public employes . . .
>
> But above all the public has to demand of its policemen an obligation which the President describes as "sacred and decent."

That day, a Saturday, Gompers sent the Governor a second telegram saying the disorder was due to the Commissioner's denial of the men's "right which has heretofore never been questioned" to affiliate with the AFL.

This brought Coolidge's reply in the Monday morning papers, containing the statement "there is no right to strike against the public by anybody anywhere any time." The Transcript saw in Coolidge's reply "a state paper certain to enhance the high traditions of the great office so worthily filled today."

But the Globe didn't mention it editorially. In the Globe, this Coolidge reply that was to become historic did not lead the paper, nor were the words that caught the public ear quoted in the headline or the lead of the story. They came at about the middle of the 400-word statement, headed only "Coolidge Reply to Gompers." The lead headline was

> No General Strike in Boston Says a Gompers Lieutenant

Curtis announced that day that no striking policeman would be taken back, and started recruiting a new force. He had finished bringing it back to strength, 1,574, the following January 10. The Herald on September 15 said, "No striker should under any circumstances ever again be a policeman." The Globe said nothing about it.

The September 17 Dudley was on "Everybody's Business," saying the ordinary citizen had not paid any attention to the public business; he resented a snarl like the police strike, but it was time he learned about his government, and so on. It made no reference to Coolidge's reply to Gompers and took no position on the strike or on the refusal to reinstate strikers. The lead headline that afternoon: "Phone Operators Vote Strike."

Sibley's story that day reported: "The 8th day of the strike passed calmly everywhere. The guards on the streets had little to do. The guardsmen are beginning to believe their tour of duty will be a long one. Cooking and bathing installations have been put in the armory."

On Saturday, September 20, the top headline:

> Big Steel Plants Closed
> Marking Start of Strike

and on Sunday, the lead:

> Carmen Fail to Vote on Sympathy Strike
> Walkout Would not Help Police and Could Hurt Carmen

That is what the Globe had been waiting for. The city still feared a general strike. The September 22 editorial was

> The Decision

"With a certain sense of relief, the city learns today that local labor delegates have agreed upon the inadvisability of a general strike . . . The issue of the policemen's strike had to be driven home by the community. It might have been more bitter, but bitterness is the last thing Boston wants to leave as the mark of its struggle with the issue of a policemen's union."

That afternoon the lead was "Great Steel Strike is On." (The strike failed and ended January 8, 1920.

The afternoon of September 22: "300 Candidates Wait to Enroll in the Police / Recruiting Begins / Many of Applicants Are Ex-Service Men."

The September 25th lead: "Striking Policemen Flayed by Coolidge / They

'Dispossessed Themselves' / To Reinstate Them Would be 'to Flout Sovereignty of the Laws.' " Coolidge's proclamation opened: "There seems to be a misapprehension as to the position of the police of Boston . . . They deserted. They stand as though they never had been appointed . . . Every attempt to prevent the formation of a new police department is a blow at the government. That way treason lies. This is the cause of all the people . . ."

Saturday, September 27, the headline: "Storrow Committee Won't Report Now / Members Discuss Draft Written by Chairman / Recounts Attempts to Avert Police Strike." The story said "the desire not to complicate matters decided the committee" not to file a report "at present."

On October 4:

> Storrow Report is Made Public
> Shows Efforts to Avert Police Walkout
> Committee Believed Compromise Possible
> Curtis Refused Plea

October 9:

> 700 Men of State Guard Sent Home

But it was January before Commissioner Curtis had brought his wholly new police force up to strength.

The city settled the riot and looting damage for a total of $34,000, though the damage reported the first night of the strike was set at $200,000.

On September 23 the Republican primary renominated Coolidge by a larger margin than in 1918.

All Souls

The Globe continued to reflect Wilson idealism through the war and the treaty and the fight for the League. James Morgan covered the Paris peace conference and wrote in the spirit of Wilson's vision of the peace.

Even in the crisis of the police strike, Morgan was preoccupied with Wilson's fight for the treaty. The Uncle Dudley, September 6, 1919, earnestly supported the treaty. The spirit of its critics was "national selfishness — echoes of an old time policy of 'splendid isolation.' Its rebuke is written in blood. What has become of all those high hopes and solemn promises with which we entered the war?" The editorial appealed in an emotional note for "the higher flag of the ideal."

A week later in the Sunday Symposium Morgan discusses "What the Treaty Aims and Reservations Mean." He doubts the wisdom of the Senate reservations. "The judgment of the people is that we must have a treaty to prevent wars that we cannot keep out of . . . The people are strongly favorable to the principles of the league. They must leave the details to the President and Senate. All they ask is that they act in the spirit of the popular judgment."

Even after Wilson's collapse, Morgan carried his Wilsonian convictions right into the Republican camp in the 1920 convention to break a lance against the foes of the treaty. Dourly he wrote of that smoke-filled room nomination:

Harding was the first choice of the professionals in the party all over the country. The business interests whom the politicians represent, also wanted Harding. The standpatters had the chance fairly thrust upon them. For this convention has been extremely conservative. The Bull Moose was strong at the primaries. But the delegates were of a different sort and the party control remains where it was in 1912 with a standpatter of the standpatters for the standard bearer — a man who compared T.R. with Aaron Burr . . . Calvin Coolidge may prove to be the ticket's main strength with the country . . ."

The front page that Sunday, June 13, carried a pithy editorial that echoed Morgan's tone and may have been dictated by him from Chicago: "If the Republican party can win in November, the victory will be with conservatism. The nomination is one more achieved by that redoubtable group known to the popular imagination as the Old Guard. Senator Harding is a conservative candidate with a conservative platform. The platform suffers from a predominantly negative tone . . . Once more the Old Guard has got what it wanted. It now remains to be seen whether the voters will want what they have got."

Morgan's negative view of the business-as-usual candidate outraged the Globe business office. But General Taylor, hearing about it, wrote Morgan a letter of affectionate and complete confidence. The General, who was starting on the last year of his life, wrote in longhand from his Buzzards Bay home:

June 20, 1920

My dear Boy:

I spend so much time in trying to correct faults in many men I sometimes forget to mention my appreciation of the few who register 100 per cent every time which is your usual habit. I read your pictures of the Chicago Convention every day with increasing pleasure and admiration. As your experience widens your power seems to increase though that has hardly seemed possible.

The nearest approach to your fine work that I can recall is that of the late John Russell Young. I think you saw him in one or two Conventions and will recall his brilliancy.

If I do not always write you please remember that I always have these sentiments and cannot make any suggestions for improvement.

With kind regards to Mrs. Morgan I am as ever

Your friend
Chas. H. Taylor

Whatever "Downstairs" thought about it, Morgan kept the Wilsonian flame alight in the Globe through the Democratic convention. A week after the General's letter, as the Democrats gathered in San Francisco, the Globe hailed "The Democratic Opportunity."

"The Democrats have a great strategic opportunity — to anoint as their leader a man who will be backed as a representative leader. American voters are more open-minded than they have ever been. The enormous liberal sentiment of the nation is a powerful voice."

Morgan's own story next day, June 29, carried the headline "Convention Wildly Cheers the President." He reported: "There has been no anti-Wilson talk here at any time . . . The opening session was wholly Wilsonian . . . Neither would an anti-administration candidate on the plank stand any chance."

But this buoyancy about Democratic chances and liberal sentiment was soon deflated. Already such an administration insider as Secretary of the Interior Franklin Lane was writing in his diary that the Wilson administration was frayed out and washed up. What Lane realized, Morgan must have felt in his bones.

As the convention season opened with the Republicans, a Globe box advertised Morgan's coverage — "a political writer second to none." An eight-column strip at the bottom of the editorial page had photographs of "The Globe's Big Seven at the Convention." The center and largest picture was Morgan, flanked by Groves, Hennessy, Merrill, Ring Lardner, Dorothy Dix, and James Montague, the last three syndicate stars. The Globe Dudley that day was on the nineteenth amendment, saying the Republican party was trying to avoid the issue. "But in 30 states women will vote this year"; two days before, a front page headline, "Wets Set Back, Suffragettes Win by Supreme Court Ruling — Drys See Decision as Legalizing 18th Amendment." On the same page, "Senate Against Mandate, 52 to 23." Wilson

Part of the Globe truck fleet on Devonshire Street, about 1927.

had asked a mandate on Armenia. Inside on page seven, "Food Administration Control of Wheat Ends." This completed Herbert Hoover's wartime job.

The Globe balanced Morgan's dim view of candidate Harding with a Sunday feature June 20 by Charles Groves, "Marion, Ohio, Folks Know Why Harding Won — Because Everyone Likes Him Personally."

Coolidge's nomination for vice president in a convention surge induced a Sunday story on Massachusetts' three earlier vice presidents, Elbridge Gerry, John Adams, and Henry Wilson, by Katherine Bartlett. She was new, one of the few women on Boston news staffs, whose byline was to be familiar for three decades. The same Sunday another new name, Marjorie Adams, movie critic, the first journalism school graduate on the paper where her name became a fixture for 50 years, had a story "Breaking Into the Movies — the Story of a Day on a Hollywood Set."

Coolidge occasioned three Editorial Points June 17:

"The Thoughtful New York Sun wonders how many inquiries Governor Coolidge's landlord has made relative to a lease for March 4 of that $32 a month dwelling.

" 'Accept my sincerest sympathy,' reads a telegram received by Governor Coolidge from Vice President Thomas Marshall, who despite the dignity of his high office, will have his little joke.

"What University will be first now to make Governor Coolidge an LLD?" Wesleyan did a week later.

Mr. Morgan's new young Sunday editor, Laurence Winship, joined the Globe team at the Democratic convention. He was to have a reporting role every convention season thereafter through 1968.

The 1920 census news came out piecemeal during the June conventions. It was not encouraging: "Detroit and Cleveland Pass St. Louis and Boston — St. Louis Increases Lead." Boston population had grown 77,000, up 11.5 percent to 748,000. But St. Louis was 773,000. Detroit had grown by 113 percent to 994,000, fourth largest city; Cleveland by 42 percent to 797,000.

A June 22 headline, "Prices at New High for May," showed a 14-percent price rise. Next day "Vanzetti on Trial in Bridgewater Holdup — Jury Impanelled" was an inside story, a two-column head on page 2 and only two paragraphs. The trial was for the December 24 Bridgewater holdup that preceded the Braintree holdup. This casually reported Plymouth trial convicted Vanzetti half a year before the Sacco-Vanzetti case opened.

June 24 the lead headline was

>   Five Sinn Feiners Killed in Riot
>   Mowed Down in Londonderry

The same front page reported:

>   Judge Anderson Orders 14 "Reds" Freed —
>   Communist Membership Not Cause for Deportation —
>   Judge Scores Federal "Spies" and Officials' "Lawless" Actions

This had arisen from the Palmer red raids and brought Massachusetts Judge George Anderson into bitter-worded controversy with Attorney General Palmer. On June 25 the Globe gave a whole page to the names of Boston elementary school graduates. In 55 of the 77 schools, tercentenary exercises were held.

There was a sugar shortage. The editorial page June 25 had a two-column head, "Preserve Fruit Without Sugar — Prof. Chenoweth Shows Housewives the Way." The story assigns the Massachusetts Agricultural College horticulturist to Amherst

College, a typical mistake of the Boston papers that irked the alumni of MAC, which later became the University of Massachusetts. Others made the same mistake; both colleges are in Amherst. Governor McCall, having to address both alumni the same night, mixed them up, misnaming President Butterfield as Meiklejohn. Butterfield said it ought to be easy to identify his name with the agricultural college.

Governor Coolidge vetoed a movie censorship bill that June. Harvard beat Yale by seven lengths at crew for an eight-column banner head, the front page story by city editor William D. Sullivan with five others inside, four bylined by John D. Merrill, Eugene Buckley, Mel Webb, and Albert Barclay, the latter a Yale grad contributing the viewpoint of the vanquished.

Through the June conventions, the Globe editorial page carried a daily series by Mr. Morgan, "Five Minutes a Day with Our Presidents." It grew into his book *Our Presidents,* later several times revised to carry through the New Deal.

The 1920 election was a landmark in Boston. For the first time the Democratic city went Republican. "Avalanche to Harding" was the Globe headline day after the election. "Bay State Gives Harding 407,420 Lead, Boston 30,000."

Next day the Globe noted how close the figures had come on their incomplete returns. Final returns showed Harding with a margin of 403,000.

The Globe had anticipated a Republican victory, which took no prophet. "Betting Odds Ten to One on Harding" was the Globe's election morning headline. But its news columns were so impartial as to run a final day parallel column windup: "League Big Issue Say Candidates." A cartoon showed Uncle Sam tossing a coin between Cox and Harding, "Putting It Up to the Voter."

It was the League issue of course that put the Irish Democratic voter of Boston into the Republican column, for article ten was felt to sustain such status quo as Britain's control of Ireland.

What caught the eye of the Globe's editorial director about that election was that it broke the Solid South. Maryland, Tennessee, Missouri, and Oklahoma abandoned their traditional Democratic stand to vote for Harding. Morgan wrote for the Sunday editorial page, November 7, "How the Solid South is Slowly Going to Pieces." He hailed it as progress along the long slow road to reunion, away from the sectionalism that has been "a curse to both parties and to the politics of the country."

That Sunday paper was 84 pages, at ten cents. The lead story was of Harvard Battling Princeton to a tie before 44,000 in the stadium. It took both city editor Sullivan, and sports writer Mel Webb to do justice to the crucial struggle in two front page stories, more inside.

Uncle Dudley escaped from the aftermath of election to write of "The Thinking Class . . . There's a great deal of talk about 'the working class' and 'the owning class' — but the thinking class is open to everyone."

That week saw an innovation on the editorial page that continued as an annual for nearly 40 years. November 1, 1920, "The Eve of All Souls" was dedicated "to an artist killed in battle" and signed only with initials L.P.

In 1920 a newspaper union was formed in Boston, affiliated with the AF of L. It was short-lived and failed to achieve a representative membership of local newspapermen. But at the time it created a flurry in city rooms, from the practice of some other local unions of refusing to give news to any nonunion reporter. This was highly annoying to the night city editor of the Globe, William Alcott, who, though he had been a member of the printers' union, was adamant that no union was going to dictate Globe assignments. The Globe would do without their news, which on occasion it did, with nobody noticing the difference.

The union, however, did establish a $38 minimum for reporters. This affected only the most unappreciated or overlooked staffers, for the going rate for a good reporter was around $50 a week. But starting pay on the Globe was $17, and it was within the discretion of the city editor how gradually it moved upward in individual cases. A reporter who showed competence would be at $25 in six months and probably $30 in a year or so. It was another 15 years before the American Newspaper Guild, started by Heywood Broun, took permanent hold, to add editorial staffs to the dozen mechanical unions in the newspaper industry.

Night Side

The way to a newspaper job half a century ago was mysterious to many who yearned for the glamor — or the vagrancy — of journalism. Some lads almost by chance, right out of school, got on as office boys. This was a chance to learn the ropes gradually to be given small chores and, if they proved proficient, eventually to become reporters. To go directly onto the staff was a chance largely limited to those who had formed an earlier connection as college correspondents or had gained experience on smaller papers. More occasionally, an opening came from knowing someone in a position to "speak to" the managing editor. In 1919 a youth who had been graduated into the war, then briefly tried schoolteaching, found a way to the Globe by this route. But not directly. An old family friend had made him an offer: if he won a commission the friend would give him his first officer's leather puttees. The commission and puttees were realized; this led to several letters from Army camps to the donor. He showed them to his good friend William D. Sullivan, city editor of the Globe, who evinced polite interest. Thus emboldened, the youth applied for a job. But it was too soon. The city editor very kindly said there might be a job; but the Globe must keep open the places for its men who had gone to war and not yet returned. Perhaps in six months, and meantime the youth's sponsor, who was in advertising, might give him some apprentice training. So he learned to write news items, small bits for trade publications, for six months.

Then he went on the night side, where cubs began at $17 but in view of his pretraining the Globe would make it $18. It was six months before the neophyte saw the city editor again. It took that long for him to write a story that anybody noticed. Thus reminded of his existence, the city editor raised his pay to $25.

The city editor had gone home before the night staff came to work. The night side trick would vary, 4–11, 5–12, 6–1, 7–2. Much of the time it was like a fireman's job of just being there, in case. The night side men sat at desks in a barracks-plain room that was occupied by the district men in the daytime. In the first hour or so they rewrote for morning the major stories in the evening paper, telescoping them to short pieces which might get into the paper if there was room. Then there was rewriting of "releases" sent in that might have germs of news in them. Some items would require checking by telephone. Staff would be assigned to such dinners or evening meetings as promised news. More often a new hand was called upon to take telephone calls off the city desk and type out the phoned reports of correspondents around the region. The night side tided over to mop up loose ends and handle incidents that came up after the day side went home — and of course any real news break that occurred in the evening.

The Globe then operated substantially with a single staff. All the top editors and senior staff worked days, for both papers. All the planning and big stories were done by the day side. The night staff was definitely second string, of new hands breaking in and an odd lot of those who could best be spared from the major assignments of the day. Some were consigned to jobs of the night side that were normally inside, to guard against their weakness for liquor, the bane of journalists of that era.

The night city editor, William Alcott, a straitlaced man who taught a Sunday school class, had less then patience with alcoholic members. A meticulous man, he was inclined to be short also with new hands who were careless about middle initials or adequate addresses. He would point to the city directory or the office dictionary as the case required. He was in constant war with the sprawling, casually organized sports department, which never manned its telephones to take the miscellaneous schoolboys' sports items phoned in from all over the area all evening. Their calls spilled over to clog his city desk phones, where they had to be siphoned off among his sparse staff. The night copy desk, already burdened with a great grist of copy from the day staff, was necessarily selective and ruthless in handling whatever unscheduled stories the night city desk developed. It was a nagging job. Mr. Alcott wanted everything to be neat and tidy. He wanted to clean up all loose ends and have nothing left over, an impossibility in the helter-skelter of news. Consequently, when a big story broke in on his precise pattern of work, he was apt to be resistant to its demands until precious time had passed. Then he would have a less than adequate choice for the assignment. So the night desk was often impatient with Mr. Alcott, who was chewed up with his frustrating job. He had been night city editor then for 15 years, after as many earlier years on the staff. A thorough, conscientious, and responsible newspaperman, his high competence had been shown on the great Chelsea fire of 1908. It was he who had alerted the office that Sunday morning, then gone to the scene to take charge of its reporting and to organize coverage and transmission of the story. But that was 11 years earlier, when he was 40. Eleven years of nightly tension to get ulcers. He had begun life as a printer, which had sharpened his eye for detail and started his self-education. But his nervous temperament was miscast in that nightly barrage of harassing telephones. A year later he was out during three months of crisis with ulcers. When he returned he was persuaded to take on the library, which Willard DeLue had been reorganizing. Here his instinct for order, organization, detail, and completeness just fitted the job. He developed one of the most adequate newspaper libraries anywhere. Within a year he had led in organizing newspaper librarians and in a few years was recognized in his new profession by election as national president of the Special Libraries Association. Starting at 54, Mr. Alcott was Globe librarian till 81, when he retired in 1950.

But this was 1919. When the Boston police walked off their jobs at 5:45 one night, just as the night side was taking over, of course the strategic coverage had been assigned. But the police strike broke over all anticipations; its chaos spilled into the city room to wreck all schedules, to impose sudden new demands, create new angles. As crisis and confusion built up, the night city editor, faced with an immense amount of copy, realized there would have to be a lead story, knitting it all up. Instead of assigning a reporter for this rewrite, he decided to do it himself. He started to type on the little old-fashioned verticle Oliver beside his desk, used for staff assignment memos. But his phone kept interrupting, so he decided to dictate the story. He summoned the $18-a-week neophyte, who shuddered — he was just learning to use a typewriter, and not this antique contraption. He was still very slow. Now he would be found out. The night city editor started to dictate and the cub started to type. He fell way behind. But then Mr. Alcott stopped — no, start over. He began again. Another false start. Then his telephone rang. Then "Where were we?" "Oh, yes. Well, start over." Then he had to read his notes over again and the typist had a breather. Then the phone again. But soon Mr. Alcott saw how useless it was and called in a reporter to turn the job over to him. The cub had a reprieve. Next day he practiced like anything at typing so as not to be caught again.

That same fall the Massachusetts legislature passed the first daylight saving bill, an issue of sharp contention between farmers and city dwellers. On arriving at the office ahead of others on the night trick, the cub received an abrupt assignment from the night city editor: "Call up Governor Coolidge to see if he is going to sign it."

Strangely enough, the Governor answered the phone at the Adams House. He said curtly that he hadn't seen the bill yet, so he couldn't say. Then he asked, "Who writes the Globe Editorial Points?" The neophyte didn't know; "why?" he asked. "I thought one today was rather vicarious." The reporter looked up "vicarious," then looked up the Editorial Points. The first one ran: "Which holds the most votes for a possible Presidential candidate — daylight saving or no daylight saving?"

When he reported his failure, the night city editor rasped: "Well, I'd say you came out about even. He hadn't read the bill and you hadn't read the Globe." Reporters were expected to have read the paper before they came to work.

Night side work had the advantage of more time than was ever possible for the succession of afternoon editions. Its handicaps included the most obvious condition that public and business activity had closed down. It was hard to reach important people. If you did reach them, they would be somewhat less responsive than to the familiar State House or financial reporter and were unlikely to yield more than the bare bones of the situation. But one of the satisfactions of night work was that when you were through you were all through. There were no distractions. The city was quiet, the phone didn't ring, you could relax. For men with families night side work wiped out normal family and social life. And one had to live within the area of all-night transit service. But for a cub still fascinated by the atmosphere of the city room, there was no hurry about going home when the night trick was done. For by that time the debate had been launched in the city room. It was never ending. It was on the League of Nations: article ten of the covenant was anathema to the older generation of Irish in Boston, for it implied guarantee of the status quo of member nations. To the Irish this meant the permanence of Britain's hold on Ireland.

Jim O'Leary.

One of the most intransigent British-haters around was old Jim O'Leary, the Globe's veteran baseball writer. One of the most convinced Wilsonians and League supporters was Willie Alcott.

Jim O'Leary was a big, hearty man of the most open disposition who fitted easily into the relaxed trade of the baseball writer. His affability and good fellowship had won him the affection of the office and the world of baseball. Politics touched the simple pattern of his life hardly at all. Perhaps that explained his becoming so passionately obsessed with what he regarded as the injustice of the League.

When Jim had finished his story for the morning paper he'd come around to bait Alcott, who by midnight would have cleared from the city desk everything that had any chance for the morning paper. And they'd go at it to raise a din that soon brought the late staffers drifting in to sit on the edges of desks and enjoy the show.

Jim would have spread his bulky figure over a desk opposite Alcott's, and his ruddy face would glow bright red under a heavy thatch of white hair as he tilted back the cavalry hat he'd worn since the Spanish-American War and leveled a stubby forefinger at the sputtering night city editor. Alcott had all the arguments and details of the League at his fingertips, undoubtedly from panels and discussions in church. The church people were the core of League support, as they had been for Wilson in his long-held "keep us out of war" policy. Jim had vehement answers to all Alcott's chapter and verse. It was always a bang-bang affair, spiced with the racy insults that two intensely intolerant, inflexible men can exchange only with equals in taking it and dishing it out. They wrangled with the intimate awareness of each other's weak points and indulged in delicious recollections of each other's failures of judgment in the past. It was an irreconcilable contest of a pair who had known and respected each other for years on every other subject but this one. The argument was joined practically every night. One might marvel at Alcott letting himself in for this night after night; though, stuck at his city desk, he could hardly have escaped the free-wheeling baseball writer. But the explosive arguing must have provided a release of tensions. Doubtless it was homeopathic psychiatry for a nerve-wracked city editor.

General Chas. H. Taylor.

Death of General

General Taylor died June 22, 1921, at age 74. The only public notice of his final illness had been seven lines on the front page the day before: "General Taylor of the Globe very ill." The columns were turned to black borders on June 22, and two pages were given to a biography and tributes; his favorite poem on friendship and death, Arthur Macy's "In Remembrance"; and his favorite hymn, "Ten Thousand Times Ten Thousand." One article recited "General Taylor's Views on a Newspaper's Duty." The Uncle Dudley was headed simply "Charles H. Taylor." This is what it said:

> He was the originator of this column and its unfailing inspiration. The last day he sat at his desk he outlined an editorial for it.
>
> That editorial, that appeared last Wednesday, was an appeal for courage and leadership in the present business situation which he faced without a doubt of a prosperous future for the country . . .
>
> The whole argument rested on his philosophy of life. For he believed that men are leaders, not necessarily because they know more, but because they have faith in themselves . . . He had a quiet pride in his self reliance . . . His success really was the triumph of very simple and very human qualities.
>
> When he became the editor-in-chief of the Globe, he merely put himself into the paper and made it a human thing . . . He addressed himself straight to the homely problems and interests of our every day life . . . He knew his New England as a pilot knows his harbor.
>
> He found the American newspaper a onesided partisan political organ for men only, and he broadened it to include both sides of every question under discussion and to include in its scope the women and even the children.
>
> His virtues were the simple native kind that begin at home . . . He was

as scrupulous in keeping faith with the readers and the public as in his personal relations. His idealism was only realism to him.

A remarkably clear, sane and vigorous mind that was positive and creative, rather than negative and critical . . . flowing with sympathy and rippling with humor — an extraordinary energy put forth from a slight and apparently frail body . . . these proved the natural equipment of the man for the successful, useful, helpful, happy life that he lived to the full.

The editorial that the General had written a week before he died was titled "Leaders and Leaners." The nation was in a brief postwar recession which had hit New England with its flagging textile industry harder than most sections. The editorial was a buoyant assertion that the business leadership of the country had the capacity to meet their problems. The General divided businessmen into those who led and those who leaned on others and appealed for leaders. "In the present business situation there is little room for men who sit around waiting for something to turn up. We are in the midst of a worldwide condition and all business is on the casualty list of the war . . . The leaders are taking care of themselves and to a considerable extent of the leaners . . . Commerical prosperity is the result of courage and brains and sweat."

The Globe published on June 22 and thereafter on every anniversary of the General's death, at the top of the editorial column, a quotation of his philosophy* under the heading:

Chas. H. Taylor
The Corner Stone of the Globe

After General Taylor died in 1921, Morgan, now 60, wanted to retire. The Taylors persuaded him instead to take a couple of years off and do a biography of the General — a labor of love. Then they got him to come back on his own terms, to write what he liked and be counsel and Dutch uncle to editors and staff.

Almost to the end of his long life he would come in Fridays, if no other day, for luncheon with the staff members closest to him. The group over much of the period would include Winship, Welch, Merrill, Holt, Lyons. He always laid one of his special wedge-shaped cigars by each place, or, for a man who didn't smoke cigars, a package of cigarettes. After dessert he would light up and start the best talk in town, then go back to the office for the editorial conference that opened with his passing the cigars around again. At 85 he had to stop smoking. To the commiseration of one of the staff he chuckled: "It's all right, the doctor didn't say anything about whisky."

* This quotation of General Taylor's philosophy is given on pages 111–112 above.

Transition: CH Jr. and W.O.

General Taylor's death, occurring almost exactly halfway in the Globe's first century, of course made a watershed in that history. The period of the founder's personal identity with the institution was over; yet the change was almost imperceptible. This complete continuity was itself a projection of the General's management. The instrument of continuity was his second son, William O. Taylor, to whom the father chose to turn over control.

This passing over of the elder son, Charles, Jr., came as a surprise, inside and outside the paper. Charles was better known, within the office, within the newspaper industry, within the outside community. Charles was the more dynamic personality, a more assertive temperament, a man of many interests and of positive opinions, a man who made an impression in any group, to be remembered. Charles had joined the paper five years ahead of his younger brother and had already become business manager before W.O. was through college. He took so naturally to newspapering that as a boy in Boston Latin School he spent most of his out of school hours at the Globe, taking a hand in all departments and asking questions. At Harvard he was correspondent of the New York Herald. He broke off college before his senior year to go into the newspaper business. He put in a four-month learning period on the New York World, then in its most vital period of innovation. He had been at least nominally assistant managing editor before concentrating on the business side. He had kept up his personal association with the editorial side, was indeed its often caustic daily critic. Everybody knew Charles. His laugh was loud in the corridor. He had a quip for everyone; it might have a bite to it, but it generally ended in a laugh. William O. was the quiet, behind-the-scenes manager, absorbed in the business his father had increasingly turned over to him, not yet as familiar a figure to the staff nor in the city. Charles's very name had long identified him as the evident heir of General Taylor. He had been president of the American Newspaper Publishers Association by 1902.

The strengths of William O. were to become apparent in his leadership of the paper through the following 35 years. But in 1921 the "story" to all concerned was the passing over of Charles. It was a situation that invited speculation, rumors of family quarrels, of a clash of personalities, of the General's lack of confidence in Charles's judgment. People recalled occasions of the General's apparently having been irked at Charles's explosions of outrage at some staff stupidity, at his impetuosity. An office legend was that in the 1896 crisis of Bryan's nomination, that caused Saltonstalls and Endicotts to shift their political allegiance from the Democrats, Charles pressed the General that the Globe take that course. But that was not the General's way; rather, he sat out that election. "Some say we've been doing the same ever since," James Morgan chuckled 30 years after. But that was not really so, as long as the General lived. Short of formal endorsement, the Globe had continued to put its weight behind Democratic reform, with Wilson and David I. Walsh, and with T.R. when he stood against "the interests." But in the considered judgment of the senior editors who best knew the father and his sons, the General's choice meant simply that he felt William O. the sounder businessman. Nobody after ever questioned that judgment.

Chas. H. Taylor, Jr.

The brothers continued to occupy the same office and share the management, their two wide, high, folding-top desks backed against each other. Charles, so far as appeared, continued his various supervisory roles as business manager. Labor relations were a primary concern of his, and relations with the publishing industry, and many of the editorial details that concerned the business office.

The anecdotes and "human interest" in the office centered on Charles. He was full of crotchets and eccentricities, but also of warmth which, even in explosion, held the affection if also amusement of the staff. His manifold interests gave him a natural relation with staffers writing on special subjects. He was a collector and connoisseur, a specialist in typography, on sailing ships, on Cape Cod, and was himself involved with the industries and charities of the area. He was for years president of the Industrial School for Crippled Children. He was a fellow of the American Academy of Arts and Sciences and of the council of the American Antiquarian Society, president of the Club of Odd Volumes, member of various historical societies.

He was the first president of the Business Historical Society, a close friend of the then new Harvard Business School, to which he gave many items of business history. He served in the twenties and thirties on three Harvard visiting committees, for the library and the departments of history and English. Harvard gave him an honorary degree in 1937, as William and Mary had in 1933. He was to leave collections to the Fogg Art Museum and the Harvard Library.

If he counted himself the authority on every one of his interests, he undoubtedly did know more about it than others in the office. He was a bear for accuracy, spellings, middle initials. This of course was a good quality for an editor, and he had come into the business when journalism was sloppy with no small amount of fakery. He policed the paper and pounced on error.

His morning confrontations with the superintendent of the composing room over typographical lapses were loud and sharp. Then he would call the city editor down from upstairs, not once, but often several times in a morning. William D. Sullivan, who had been running the news department when CH was in short pants, would sigh, change from his alpaca coat, and take the down elevator once more to see what was the matter this time.

CH had on his desk a red and a blue pencil, blunted with vigorous use. His first chore on reaching his desk would be to ring all the typographical "bugs" in the paper with a red mark and then the editorial lapses in blue. Then he would indite a flock of brief and pungent memos to the perpetrators of these sins. This, if often irksome, was of course healthy admonition. But these virtues of an editor could be added up as a negative influence for a publisher and evidently were by General Taylor. William O., without such diversions of energy, held to the central direction of an institution of ever growing size and complexity in what had become the most intensely competitive newspaper field of any in the country. That was to be his problem from 1921 to 1955, years of difficulty, depression, and change. Charles was much of that time a kind of informal if unconscious liaison with the staff, and withal a moderating influence.

It was Charles's habit, when getting his hair cut in the Globe barber shop, to pay for anyone else in the shop at the time. On one occasion the other customer was a reporter, back from an arduous trip, having the full treatment. As he paid the bill, CH glanced disdainfully at such a sybarite with "gosh, what did he have?" When he happened into a tobacco shop while a Globe reporter was ordering a box of cigars sent to a man who had been helpful on a story, CH insisted characteristically, "send the bill to me."

The family rule of keeping Taylor names out of the paper appeared to the staff as a revulsion against the egregious self-publicizing of William Randolph Hearst. Charles carried this penchant for anonymity to such a point that when, as one of the survivors of a shipwreck in 1924, he gave the Globe a graphic and certainly the most technically accurate account, two columns long, it was ascribed only to "a Boston passenger." New York newspapers, uninhibited, quoted Charles H. Taylor, Jr., of the Boston Globe.

An enthusiastic sailor, an expert on navigation and ship architecture, CH could be a terror to anyone on the Globe who had to treat of ships. Even after his retirement in 1937 he followed such subjects in the Globe like a hawk. A reporter had a telephone call one morning before breakfast. "This is CH. On that story of yours about the Clipper ship, don't you know if you had a ship of those dimensions, it would break in two?" It sent the reporter looking up his file of CH memos.

One after an interview with Bishop William Lawrence, whose son was the Reverend William A. Lawrence, addressed to city editor, night city editor, day editor, night editor and L. M. Lyons, Esq: "When we observe Bishop Lawrence's birthday Sunday, I trust we will not give him a middle initial that he does not possess. Yrs, C.H.T."

And another, after a column "Signs of Fall" had mentioned it was "time to blanche celery": "That was a splendid column this morning, but 'blanch,' as with celery, is spelled without a final 'e' as you will find by consulting Webster. Yrs, C.H.T."

But he had another side.

The same reporter had been given an unusual assignment, at the height of the boom in the twenties, to look up a report that a Wall Street operator was trying to corner the Cape Cod cranberry crop — most of the national production for Thanksgiving sauce. Fantastically, it was true. The reporter got hold of a Cape real estate agent who showed him a list of scores of cranberry growers who had sold options on their bogs to this man. The Globe had run the first of two articles that morning.

The Taylors summered at Buzzards Bay and felt a proprietary interest in the Cape. CH called the reporter "Downstairs" to launch at him: "People are saying you've been had with this cranberry story." But that night the head of a Boston real estate firm called on the reporter to beg him to stop his cranberry series. He had $250,000 at stake in commissions, he said. The reporter told him the articles were done, were the property of the Globe. He'd have to see the publisher.

"You mean Charles Taylor. That man practically threw me out of his office today."

Next morning the city editor reassured the reporter: "I guess CH is straightened out. His complaint today is that we put your byline in smaller type than another on a story he says was not so important."

CH never mentioned the episode again. But that Christmas the reporter had a handsome print of a ship model, inscribed "To a damn good newspaperman from his boss. C.H."

The same reporter recalls a somewhat parallel experience with William O. Taylor, publisher. The reporter had been exploring one of the recurring milk wars between dairymen and dealers. Returning to the office, he was confronted at the city desk with "W.O. says no milk strike story."

"But we can't duck such a story. I've got telegrams from all the dairy organizations in my pocket. These farmers read the Globe. They *are* going to withhold their milk."

"OK," said the assistant city editor. "You can go Downstairs and get your head batted in. I've had it."

So Downstairs. "Mr. Taylor, I don't see how the Globe can hold out this milk story."

"Damn it. Of course we'll print it. I said, 'Don't use milk *strike*.' People will think it's the milk wagon drivers."

A publisher is made aware of the sensitive stories. On another milk series, the reporter had a call from the advertising manager. "How long is your milk series going to run?" "I can't tell yet, why?" "The Hood Company has ordered 65 copies of the paper as long as your series runs." So you know somebody's looking over your shoulder. When a bill to regulate the cosmetics industry was up in legislative hearings, the big advertisers were alert. A memo to the reporter from the publisher was characteristic: "On the cosmetics hearings, give both sides. W.O."

William O. Taylor.

Trustee Publisher

Cartoonists rejoice in those public figures whose features lend themselves to caricature and despair of others whose personalities offer no salient targets. William O. Taylor, in contrast to his brother Charles, would be a problem for cartoonist or biographer. His life seems to have been wholly contained between the Globe and his family. He achieved approximate anonymity as he directed the paper through his business and editorial associates.

Only the senior editors had much of any direct contact with him, but they didn't even know how much he read his own paper. They knew he never went anywhere and often walked to his home from the office. Legend was that he never put on a dinner coat from one end of the year to the other. He always had a substitute to send to ceremonial dinners where the Globe needed to be represented. He was never known to make a speech. He read mysteries and westerns. The office story was that he had his secretary read the fiction offered for Globe serials, let her taste determine what to use. He also bought various radical publications. "Wanted to see what they were doing."

He sat quietly in his corner of a big office with the door always open, listening to all kinds of people but saying very little. In what seemed to others an urgent problem, he would sit through an office conference and then decide to think it over a night or a week. But his associates learned that if the matter seemed critical to him he gave an instant yes or no. If the heads of the business departments came to him in agitation over a situation, he might reach for one of the printed cards in his desk and pass it around. It was from the Bible, Romans 9:18: "For I reckon that the sufferings of this present time are not worthy to be compared with the glory that shall be revealed to us." He kept a Bible in the bottom drawer of his desk and had a habit, when confronting an editor or staffer with a sticky problem, of reading him one of his favorite texts. This tended to put the situation in a ludicrous light and dissolved the tension. An inbred conservative, he often had occasion to resort to his biblical texts during the long era of the New Deal to demonstrate the absurdity, in his view, of its philosophy. His orthodoxy he would habitually defend by reminding any editorial romanticist that he had studied economics with Professor Ely. That had been in 1890, but he counted it as unchanging as the laws of the Medes and Persians. It was his conventional wisdom, and he fell back on it to refute any of FDR's economic experiments. But he would end such confrontations with a laugh as if he didn't expect the staff of a liberal newspaper to pay that much attention to his crotchets. It was amazing that so orthodox a publisher presided on the whole so amicably over a liberal newspaper. He did not impose his views, not even with such generalizations as Charles's occasional admonishments to "no Bolshevism" (even that was left to editorial interpretation).

The influence of the business office on editorial policy was obviously negative, but it was never explicit — more an atmosphere than a policy. The editors were buffers between liberal staff and conservative management. The Taylors had confidence in their editors, who in W.O.'s time remembered the General. W. D. Sullivan as city editor, hiring a reporter, responding to the man's expressed concern that he might prove too radical for the Globe, reassured him: "O, we have lots of radicals on the Globe. They have lively minds." He didn't add that the Globe knew how to contain them. Winship, responsible for the editorial page through more than 40 years, knew the limit of undefined policy. He had absorbed it from James Morgan; and how much Morgan's philosophy derived from the General, how much was adjustment to it nobody knew. Morgan himself had an old-fashioned aversion to socialism that he once described as selfishness. This was much like James B. Conant's suspicion of alien philosophies.* American radicalism was something else — native to the American dream. So it was with Morgan. W.O. would not have sorted things out that way. But he had absorbed the General as much in his way as Morgan had. He had not been poor; nor had he had the enlarging experience of the politician and the journalist that shaped the General's start, nor had he launched a newspaper of appeal to the wage-earner and the underdog. But W.O. had a strong sense of his trusteeship, his obligation to the institution he had inherited. When in 1928 the International Paper & Power Company was acquiring a hold on newspapers and bought a half interest in the Herald, W.O. had occasion to make a public statement that the Globe was not for sale. "The Globe is a New England institution," he said. "My father left it in trust to me and I shall keep that trust for my heirs."

It was much like the feeling of a trustee of a college, that his responsibility to the institution is something apart from his own business interests or views. This deep sense of responsibility was a quality concealed by W.O. under a curt mask of matter-of-factness. He was puritanical to a degree that embarrassed him to have to repeat a vulgar expression. But his profanity on occasion was explosive. His personal modesty was innate; Winship remembers his saying one day, "Lucien Price was down here with one of his damn fool ideas. He says I should have a portrait painted by Charles Hopkinson. Who the hell is Charles Hopkinson?" Bostonians thought Hopkinson the leading portraitist of the period. "Price is crazy," W.O. concluded. There was no portrait. But next day W.O., with no context for the remark, observed to Winship, "Price is about the best writer we have, isn't he?"

If W.O.'s attitude and policy seemed to the staff negative, there was character in it, too. The Globe, almost alone among big northern newspapers, never joined the

---

* James B. Conant, "Wanted: American Radicals," Atlantic Monthly, May 1943.

anti-Roosevelt chorus which even the Democratic Post took up. When the Ford Company withdrew its advertising for many months over a lapse in reporting Henry Ford's Sudbury activities, nobody on the staff was blamed for it. Winship learned only by accident and long afterward of a Globe Sunday story that cost the Globe $10,000 for libel. When all the influence of Joseph P. Kennedy was brought to bear on the Globe to fire a reporter for an interview in 1940 that cost Kennedy his ambassadorship, W.O. took no action; he never mentioned it to the reporter, who only knew of it years later.

Insiders to the financial operations of the Boston newspapers often expressed amazement at the extent to which the Globe under W.O. was plowing resources back into the paper instead of raising dividends to stockholders. He had, so far as could be seen, as complete control as though the paper was wholly instead of half Taylor-owned. Only once, at the bottom of depression, salaries were cut ten percent. There had been more than one cut before that on most newspapers as in other lines. But next year the cut was restored although the depression had not notably lifted. The Post at that time was drawing on its building reserve fund to keep up salaries. The Transcript failed to survive the depression.

Among the radical writers W.O. read was his classmate Oswald Garrison Villard, editor of the Nation, whose own newspaper, the old New York Evening Post, had passed away. Villard wrote a discouraging and disparaging book in 1943, *The Disappearing Daily,* whose chapter on Boston was entitled "Journalistic Poor Farm." In Villard's caustic description, the Globe, as a matter of fact, came off better than its contemporaries, with consideration for its fairness and decency. But Villard said the Globe was "without a vestige of social policy." W.O. asked one of his editors, "What does he mean by that?"

As Villard was the harshest critic on the journalistic scene, a telescoped glance at his references to W.O. and the Globe is worthwhile:

> Generous and worthy, William O. Taylor inherited his father's kindly heart and has been politically and socially content to move on in the same old highly successful groove. As the years pass the Globe changes little. Why should its owners care if it is entirely conventional and typographically cheap and ugly . . . Curiously enough it does do something worth while. It contributes the best editorials printed in any Boston newspaper. "Uncle Dudley" has often found pleasure in dwelling on fundamentals, in dealing with the basic ideals of spiritual and moral liberties, usually in generalities, but none the less valuable. In its news columns the Globe has often done yeoman service by giving the only accurate, unbiased reporting of labor troubles or important trials. The accounts of the famous Lawrence strike by the veteran reporter, Frank P. Sibley, were the best reporting done in New England in years. Similarly in the . . . Sacco-Vanzetti case Mr. Sibley distinguished himself and his newspaper . . . Since the Taylors have done so much along these lines, it has always seemed a great cause for regret that their ambition could not have carried them further. The present head knows that he has continued to hold for the Globe the respect of a large section of the public which believes in the essential integrity of the paper. Like his father, William O. Taylor has been a model employer and has the merited confidence of his employees to a rare

degree, as he has the confidence of his readers. Yet the Globe has been sadly subservient to the great advertisers. Editorial puffs of them and their doings appear in its columns and never unfavorable comment.*

On his eighty-first birthday, W.O. received a more appreciative and intimate summing up of the 30 years he had published the Globe from James Morgan, who had served both father and son then for 67 years:

"As you majored in Biblical literature at Harvard," wrote Morgan, who well knew what a twinkle that would bring to W.O.'s eye,

> you may have missed the stern resolve that Seneca's boatman took in the face of a gale: "O, Neptune, you may save me if you will; you may sink me if you will; but, whatever happens, I will hold my rudder true."
>
> That is what you, William O., have done with the Globe and for all of us on board since you were called to the helm at the onset of a thirty-year storm, in the course of which you have not had a normal, quiet day . . .
>
> It has been no holiday cruise, but you have held the rudder of our craft true while we have watched newspapers all around us going down. Pulitzer's World, Dana's Sun, Bennett's Herald, are metropolitan examples of a nation-wide wreckage which we of the Globe have escaped under your weather-wise, steady, panic-proof steering.
>
> All the Globe family owe their gallant, modest leader an unpayable debt. But if they brought their I.O.U's to you on your birthday, that would only add to the paper shortage and give another boost to the price you have to meet for newsprint.

That mention of newsprint, like the Bible course, was another little play on one of W.O.'s whimsies. If the Washington correspondent bearded him with a grievous recital of the high cost of living in Washington, W.O., scenting what was coming, would launch into his burden of meeting the unconscionable price of newsprint. The cost of newsprint was an office joke.

Among other things about the Globe that W.O. would never change was his own title of editor and publisher, which he counted part of his inheritance.

When Winship was 65 he felt it time to retire as managing editor. W.O., then in the last year of his life, was leaving the Globe management to his son Davis, who reported to Winship that he had showed the retirement letter to his father. W.O. had said: "I didn't know Laurence had that much sense. Tell him to appoint anyone he likes managing editor, Sunday editor, and stay where he likes, just so long as he has a telephone and everyone knows he has the final say. Tell him there'll be no change in his salary."

Davis Taylor thought Winship should have some title and suggested executive editor, then having a vogue. But Winship didn't like the vogue. "How about plain editor?" Davis phoned next morning to report, "I told Dad you said you would just call yourself editor. He said, 'I'll be God damned if he will. I am editor and publisher of this paper and always will be.'" The day his father died, Davis phoned to say, "Now you can call yourself editor."

* Oswald Garrison Villard, *The Disappearing Daily*, Alfred A. Knopf, 1944, pp. 178–179.

On May 1, 1922, the Globe announced its average circulation figures for the six months ending April 1 for the years 1914 — 1918 — 1922.

	daily	Sunday
1914	156,000	276,000
1918	277,000	317,000
1922	284,000	323,000

Sacco-Vanzetti

Intense interest in the case of Sacco and Vanzetti had developed before their trial opened, and an extensive campaign had raised funds for their defense. The Globe headline May 29, 1921:

Sacco and Vanzetti Go On Trial May 31

Nation-wide Interest Being Shown in Case

The story said "it is believed the trial will rank in interest with the famous Mooney case in California. For months eminent lawyers have been working night and day in the interest of the accused men. Fred H. Moore of Los Angeles, one of the leading lawyers in the Mooney case, is chief counsel . . . The League for Democratic Control has raised thousands of dollars for the defense . . . Interest has spread as far as Italy where depositions have been taken."

And an item that was not elaborated: "Counsel for defense has already filed a motion to vacate the finding of the jury which found Vanzetti guilty of the Bridgewater crime," referring to the other payroll robbery for which Vanzetti had been convicted in Plymouth court. This circumstance of Vanzetti's earlier conviction received little attention then or later, although when the second trial opened Frank P. Sibley reported in the Globe that Vanzetti was brought from Charlestown State Prison where "he has been serving a term for another offense."

At the time of the Braintree factory holdup with its killing of a paymaster and guard, April 15, 1920, police were already investigating a similar crime in Bridgewater. Eyewitnesses had described several "Italians" who made their getaway in a car which the Bridgewater police chief, James Stewart, had located and identified in a garage outside Brockton. Stewart's theory was that the two crimes were committed by the same gang; Braintree and Bridgewater are only 18 miles apart. He'd had the garage watched. When three Italians called for the car, they became suspicious of a trap and fled. The police were notified and took Sacco and Vanzetti off a trolleycar for Brockton. The two lied about knowing the owner of the suspect auto, who had escaped, and later claimed that they did so to protect him, believing he was sought as a radical. They claimed they had planned to join him in using his car to warn radical friends of danger because associates had already been arrested in New York in the Palmer red raids.

Sacco and Vanzetti were indicted in September. Witnesses of the Bridgewater crime identified Vanzetti with it. He was tried in December with a perfunctory defense by a local lawyer who was in the habit of taking cases for usually illiterate local Italians and depending on their equally illiterate alibi witnesses. Vanzetti was found guilty of the Bridgewater holdup.

The new Sacco-Vanzetti defense team were obviously concerned over the implications of this involvement of Vanzetti with the earlier crime — that it would have had its effect on the climate surrounding the Sacco-Vanzetti case.

Describing the Dedham courtroom scene the opening day, Sibley noted, "Neither of the defendants looks a desperate criminal."

News of the first five days of the trial was of the extraordinary problem of selecting a jury. A panel of 175 talesmen had been mustered the opening day, when only three jurors were selected. The second day proved no more productive. The third day a panel of 160 more came to court but only three more were chosen. The effort to avoid service on the Sacco-Vanzetti jury was obvious. Many claimed a strong aversion to capital punishment. Others claimed physical ailments, and indeed many of the Norfolk County townsmen were deaf or infirm.

Judge Webster Thayer, an imperious authoritarian who had asked to be assigned the case, expressed his impatience both with those who claimed strong feeling against capital punishment and about the local officials who sent in such inept jurymen. On the third day he appealed to the newspapers to call attention to this "negligence" by the local authorities.

Sibley reported "The men who didn't believe in capital punishment had to stand a scorching and scornful inquiry by the judge."

"Do you set your opinion above the law?" the Judge had asked one. The man answered that it would disorganize his nerves for the rest of his life to send a man to the electric chair.

"Not lack of courage, is it?" Judge Thayer had asked.

"No."

"Excused."

To another the judge had said: "Let me suggest that since you feel so strongly about it, you begin work at once to have the law changed."

June 4 the jury was completed. That day the Globe's Uncle Dudley made its only comment on the Sacco-Vanzetti case. "Twelve Good Men" was its title. The editorial commented on the unusual action to secure a jury from "bystanders" but said that once selected juries "work amazingly well. Human nature has a way of rising to unavoidable responsibilities."

June 6 the headline reported: "Jury Goes to Scene of Crime / Walter H. Ripley Made Foreman." This Quincy storekeeper was the oldest man on the jury; he died before the final review of the case.

The first report of testimony brought the June 9 headline:

> Witness Fails to Identify Sacco
> Louis Wade Has Changed His Opinion
> Felt Sure of Identification at Time of Arrest

Next day the headline told of a positive witness:

> Woman Testifies Sacco Was in Car
> Mary E. Splaine Tells of Seeing Speeding Car after South Braintree Killings

But under cross-examination Mary Splaine was confronted with the record of her first police examination, in which she said she couldn't be sure of the man she had seen. Now she denied the earlier record at first, then said she was sure after police had shown her a photograph of Sacco.

The prosecution used all of June with its case. Sacco and then Vanzetti took the stand July 6 and 7. Each denied being at Braintree the day of the crime. Each admitted lying to police on arrest. They claimed to believe their arrest had been because they were radicals, associated with others then caught in the red raids of Attorney General Palmer.

The case went to the jury the afternoon of July 14. They brought in a verdict that evening after having been out five hours. The July 15 headline:

Sacco and Vanzetti Both Found Guilty of Murder

Sibley had the verdict and Judge Thayer's charge to report in the same story. He devoted only a short paragraph to the charge, of which so much was later made in appeals. He said it took two hours to read. He noted that the Judge had told the jury the real issue was one of identity. "He spent considerable time on a thorough treatise on the subject of consciousness of guilt."

Except for that paragraph, and his description at the opening of the Judge's scornful treatment of those professing objection to capital punishment, Sibley's trial reports make no reference to the conduct or attitude of the Judge. Sibley later volunteered testimony to the Review Committee that largely concerned statements and conversation of Judge Thayer outside the courtroom to which others also testified.

Lois Rantoul, who observed the trial as representative of the Council of Churches, reported to the Review Committee a conversation with Judge Thayer in the court lobby during the trial. She told the judge she had not heard sufficient evidence to convince her of the defendants' guilt. "Judge Thayer expressed dissatisfaction with this, both by word, gesture, tone of voice and manner," she said.

Robert Benchley made affidavit of a conversation in which Judge Thayer referred to the defendants as "Bolsheviks" who were "trying to intimidate me."

The Review Committee was to report, six years later, that the Judge had been indiscreet in his conversation with outsiders during the trial and that this was "a grave breach of judicial decorum." Nevertheless the committee reported their "impression that the judge tried to be scrupulously fair."

But nothing of this got into the reports of the trial, nor did State Police Captain Proctor's prearrangement with the District Attorney that he could testify about the fatal bullet only that it "was consistent with" being fired from Sacco's pistol. Captain Proctor later made affidavit that he was unconvinced about the bullet and had told the District Attorney that he could not testify it was from Sacco's gun. Sibley quoted Proctor verbatim in the evening paper June 21:

"Have you an opinion as to whether bullet No. 3 was fired from the Colt automatic, here in evidence?"

"I have."

"What is it?"

"That the appearance of it is consistent with having been fired from that gun."

Cross-examination was detailed, technical, on all the bullets. But Proctor was not asked to explain or develop his consistency statement. The other ballistics expert, Captain Von Ambergh of the Remington Arms Company, who followed Proctor, was sure of the bullet from the Colt. Police testified they took the Colt off Sacco.

The reporters of course were unaware of the subtlety of the prosecutor's examination of Captain Proctor. So also, evidently, was Judge Thayer, who cited to the jury Captain Proctor's testimony as identifying the bullet with Sacco's gun. Yet six years later the Review Committee said: "It must be assumed that the jury understood the meaning of plain English and that if Captain Proctor was of the opinion that the bullet had not been fired from Sacco's gun he would have said so." But the District Attorney had set up his questioning to avoid just that. Proctor by then was dead.

Not only was none of this in the news of the trial, the witnesses were never called who later came forward to say they had seen the murder gang, five young men all clean-shaven. This description would not fit Vanzetti.

The Sacco-Vanzetti case was in and out of the news from 1921 to 1927 as the defense sought a new trial, brought forward new evidence, and obtained a new chief counsel, the able William G. Thompson. Judge Thayer turned down an appeal for a new trial and the State Supreme Court upheld him. Later, when a convict named Madeiros confessed the Braintree crime, another motion for retrial was rejected. Agitation over the case spread worldwide. It became, indeed, as noted as the Mooney case.

When finally in the summer of 1927 Governor Fuller was persuaded to form a committee to review the case, he appointed A. Lawrence Lowell, president of Harvard, Samuel Stratton, president of M.I.T., and Judge Robert Grant. They met for ten days in July 1927, heard witnesses, called some of their own. District Attorney Katzman and William G. Thompson attended and could cross-examine witnesses. The hearings were private; news consisted chiefly of what could be adduced from the identity of the witnesses, who had been abjured from discussing their testimony and, evidently wanting not to jeopardize the review, practically all did abstain from public statements.

On the opening day of the Review Committee sessions, the Globe reported that "Frank P. Sibley and Elizabeth Bernkopf, newspaper reporters, were next interviewed." Later, when a Transcript editorial writer testified, the Globe identified him only as "James E. King of Wellesley." If the reading public had any curiosity about what these veteran newspapermen had to tell the committee, it went unsatisfied.

Through the years of agitated controversy, the Globe contributed nothing to public discussion of the Sacco-Vanzetti case. It reported developments, item by item, but stopped there, editorially silent. The Herald received a Pulitzer Prize in 1927 for its editorial proposal of a review board. Felix Frankfurter contributed his disturbing analysis of the case to the March 1927 Atlantic Monthly. Dean John H. Wigmore, replying to Frankfurter, published in the Transcript. Frankfurter's rejoinder was in the Herald. The Globe was a nonparticipating bystander to this ferment in the community.

The Sunday paper, August 7, 1927, carried the Review Committee report that the two men were guilty "beyond a reasonable doubt," that the trial was fair, that Judge Thayer was indiscreet in talking outside the court but *not* prejudicial in court. The District Attorney was not in any way guilty of unprofessional behavior, the jury were capable, impartial, and unprejudiced. The Committee's own hearings were private because they had no power to summon witnesses; they felt people more likely to come and speak freely if statements were not to be published. Each juror felt sure that the defendants' being radicals and foreigners had no effect on his opinion.

The Committee said: "There has been much propaganda in this case by adherents of the defense committee, to which neither courts nor prosecution could properly reply in the public press." It reported it "gives no credence to the confession of Celestine Madeiros."

Vanzetti's alibi was "decidedly weak . . . The committee does not believe Sacco was in Boston that day. Their lies on arrest are not all explained by their fear as radicals of deportation. Why should Sacco not have said he was in Boston seeking a passport, if innocent [instead of saying he worked at the factory all that day] . . . This crime and the one at Bridgewater do not seem to the committee to bear the marks of professionals but of men inexpert in such crimes."

The committee did not believe prosecution had withheld evidence it believed valuable to the defense.

Judge Thayer had counseled defense that bringing out radicalism might prejudice the jury, but defense counsel thought danger of conviction so great that they put Sacco and Vanzetti on the stand to explain their behavior on arrest as fear of deportation for themselves and friends.

The jury perceived no bias in the Judge. The committee talked to ten available jurors; the foreman was dead and one was in Florida.

Guard Berardelli's pistol disappeared; one like it was found on Vanzetti. Sacco had in his pocket bullets of the same obsolete type, no longer manufactured.

One of Vanzetti's witnesses had sworn to an alibi for him in the Bridgewater case. Another was shown by cross-examination to be lying at the trial. Two others did not seem certain of the date till they'd talked it over.

The full text was carried (six columns) in the Globe of August 7, 1927.

Intensive efforts to stay the executions filled the remaining fortnight with a sequence of frustrations. Globe headlines sketch the last days.

August 19, afternoon:
> Sacco and Vanzetti Lose in Supreme Court [Mass.]
> Decision Made by Full Bench
> Exceptions Overruled
> "No error of law"

Sunday, August 21:
> Judge Holmes Refuses to "Meddle"
> Appeal Today to Brandeis Planned
> Defense Asks President and Governor to Grant Stays Till Court Can Act

Holmes said he had absolutely no authority as a U.S. judge to "meddle with it."

August 22, afternoon:
> Sacco and Vanzetti Denied Stay of Death
> Every Justice Declines to Act
> Taft, Stone, Sisk Appealed to, Failed to Intervene
> 107 Pickets Arrested at State House
> Demonstration in Sacco Case
> Several Hundred Police to Guard State Prison

August 23:
> Madeiros, Sacco and Vanzetti Died in Chair This Morning
> Men reiterated their innocence
> Seven year battle in Courts failure
> Vanzetti Forgives. Sacco Says Goodbye

> Prison is Guarded by Veritable Army
> Last Minute Pleas Bombard Governor
> Paraders Dispersed at Charlestown
> Police Take 156 of "Death Watch" in Front of State House

All of page one was on Sacco and Vanzetti.

August 23, afternoon:

> Bodies of Three Men Claimed by Relatives

After the execution the Commonwealth of Massachusetts was not yet through with the Sacco-Vanzetti case. On Sunday, August 28, a funeral cortege carried their bodies from the North End eight miles to Forest Hills. Seventy mounted police and 500 patrolmen were assigned to the route. Beacon Hill was blockaded to prevent the procession passing the State House. The Globe reported that police had turned the North End into an armed camp.

Monday, August 29:

> 200,000 See Huge Parade
> Force Used to Drive Back Line of Sacco-Vanzetti Marchers at Forest
>   Hills

The unsigned story reported: "The reason for police action at that point was not stated. No report of the trouble was carried at the station. According to police, no clubs were used.

"What started the trouble, Sergeant?"

"That I couldn't tell you."

On August 28, 40 years later, the Globe recalled it all in an article by Alexander J. Cella: "Few could have imagined that 40 years later the very mention of the names of Sacco and Vanzetti could still inflame such raw emotional wounds in Massachusetts . . ." His article concludes:

> In the Sacco-Vanzetti case, pride and prejudice, deceit and ambition, ignorance and fear, intolerance and hostility, suspicion and distrust, all the base alloys of human conduct, were present. But there was nobility and grandeur, too, in the quality and character of the two men and in the spirit of those who consecrated themselves to the struggle for vindication.
>
> They are gone now, most of them. Fred Moore and William Thompson, the tireless lawyers; Aldino Felicani and Gardner "Pat" Jackson, organizers and intrepid directors of the work of the defense committee; Prof. Arthur M. Schlesinger of Harvard and Mrs. Helen Rotch, president of the Massachusetts League of Women Voters, both of whom were among the 26 signers of a protest statement which sought to place the legal issues of the case in their proper social context; Felix Frankfurter, whose Atlantic Monthly article of March, 1927, did much to arouse the conscience of the world: Frank Sibley, veteran courtroom reporter for the Boston Globe who was outraged by the conduct of the Dedham trial and officially protested to state authorities; Tom O'Connor, former State House reporter who was to devote most of his life up to the time of his recent death to the continuing struggle for vindication. All of these and thousands more.
>
> They were not wild-eyed dreamers. But they rallied to the defense of Sacco and Vanzetti in the belief that when the freedom of the lowest and most despised was threatened, there could be no real freedom for anyone.

Frank P. Sibley, Reporter

Frank Sibley was 56 in 1927. His health had always been frail. His reporting thereafter was less active. During his long involvement with the Sacco-Vanzetti case, the big stories had gone to younger members of the staff, Charles Merrill, Willard DeLue, John Barry, Louis Lyons, Carlyle Holt. Merrill covered the Scopes trial in 1926. Lyons had the Lindbergh stories of 1927. They all did Sunday features. Merrill, Holt, and Lyons also filled in on editorials.

Sib had a serious illness in 1934 and after it was assigned the Editorial Points, which he could do at home. These pithy paragraphs reflected Sib's risible and pungent comment until his retirement in 1944, when his inevitable successor was Donald B. Willard, long recognized as the office wit.

Sib's passing from the city room marked the close of a romantic era of reporting of which he was a supreme symbol. The Globe had a no-star system, but Sib's very personality contradicted this. The striking length of him was punctuated by his flowing Windsor tie and cavalryman's hat, and his long Yankee face by its clipped mustache. A twinkling eye suggested an apt story coming up, but behind the twinkle was a benign shrewdness. He had been a reporter since 1891, on the Globe since 1902. Reporting was his trade and he was proud of it and full of small conceits about it. One day in a momentary respite from a tedious year-long trial of financial interests — the Willett-Sears case — Sib was standing in the Globe front doorway when William O. Taylor stopped to say, "Well, Sib, you're having a long siege." W.O. was both his employer and his classmate. Sib beamed as the boss passed. "That means he likes my stories."

Sib had in large degree what he once told a student group was the essential quality of the journalist: perennial curiosity. This was quite different from Sir Philip Gibbs' insistence on, "an ear for the quality of words." Sib had the ear too, but his Yankee concern for the facts over the style expressed a difference in national traits. Sib was rarely dragooned into making such a talk. His predilection ran, rather, with Gluyas Williams, whose cartoons brightened the Globe's editorial page in the thirties and forties. Gluyas told the Newton Women's Club that a cartoonist speaking to a women's club would make a good subject for a cartoon.

Sib was always prepared for the frequent stretches of waiting for juries or district attorneys with a pocket chess game, although his conversation made the best interim entertainment.

The first time this writer saw Sib he was making out an expense account on return from a Vermont bearhunt. His system was simple. He dumped out his pockets of coins and small bills onto a piece of copy paper, added it up, and deducted it from his $100 advance. "And if they want that red mackinaw they can have it."

Expense accounts were not a problem with the Globe. For years CH as treasurer approved every week with a chuckle the item a State House reporter put in for daily travel to the State House. There was no way to go from the Globe to the State House by public transportation, but CH always approved this minor larceny of $1.20 a week.

After one late election night Lucien Thayer took his election staff to Young's for a late meal and celebrated with wine. Old Mr. Fowle came by the reporters' table

EDITORIAL POINTS

Just as soon as the election is over we can get excited over the Simpson-King Edward affair again.

———o———

On his 50th birthday Chinese friends of Generalissimo Chiang Kai-shek presented him with 50 fighting airplanes. Now all he needs is 50 aviators.

———o———

Betting odds quoted in New York on Saturday were 3 to 1 on Roosevelt, in case you are interested in a last-minute wager.

———o———

When Oxford gave an honorary degree to President Conant of Harvard he was hailed as a "mighty sleuth of atoms" and all last week Harvard alumni were saying that they wished he would dig up an atom who could kick, pass and run. And then see what happened!

———o———

Mayor George J. Bates and Mrs Bates of Salem celebrated their silver wedding anniversary at a great banquet and ball and a pleasant time was had by all, even by Mr and Mrs Bates.

and when Thayer's expense account went in returned it with a notation that the Globe didn't pay for reporters' wine. But when Thayer turned to his immediate boss, city editor William D. Sullivan said they did indeed on such occasions and OK'd it.

When Donald B. Willard joined the Globe staff in 1923 with an M.A. from Tufts, he was and remained through ensuing decades the only Globe man with an advanced degree. Honorary degrees came to some members of the staff, but they had not done graduate work. The journalist is a generalist. He has an opportunity to become a specialist through his own work. Even Walter Lippmann, a distinguished scholar of journalism, had only the undergraduate degree. Unlike New York, where Columbia University had a graduate program in journalism, Boston newspapers did not recruit journalism students. The first journalism studies in Boston were in the undergraduate business school at Boston University. Later journalism there was combined in a separate school with public relations. When Harvard built a new graduate school of business administration in the 1920's reporter Lyons, doing a story on it, asked a dean if it would include journalism. "Good God no," the dean exploded. "Journalism is nothing but the gift of gab." Some journalism at that time could be so described. But it was already taking itself more seriously. The science writer was coming into his own and by Harvard's tercentenary in 1936 had reached a stature that brought Pulitzer Prizes to the five recognized science writers who reported the tercentenary lectures.

The Boston papers continued to draw on graduates of the liberal arts colleges. This might have been different had President Eliot accepted Joseph Pulitzer's original intent, to establish his school of journalism at Harvard. But they disagreed on what journalism education should be, so Pulitzer's program and money went to Columbia. But in the late twenties the Globe did rather tentatively recognize the local journalism school products, employing two Boston University men, Alexander Haviland and Lafayette Marchant. Haviland within a few years became night city editor, later city editor, and finally in 1963 executive editor until his retirement in 1969. Marchant became one of the able members of the reporting staff, later a desk editor. But the Globe's investment in journalism graduates did not for several decades go much beyond that first step. When a college student in the thirties asked Bill Packer what course he should follow for newspaper work, Bill laughed. "Well, I'm an ex-parson. Doc Haven is an ex-dentist; Joe Ward is an ex-engineer; Henry Harris escaped from his family's investment house; Louis Lyons went to an agricultural college; Jim Powers majored in romance languages." Going to lunch that day, Packer briefly joined the sidewalk superintendents looking down at a construction gang at work. "I imagine those fellows would run about six journalists to the dozen," he said.

This self-deprecation failed to reflect the intellectual capacity of the staff. Books by James Morgan and Lucien Price came to fill a shelf. Many another member of the staff produced a topical book out of his work, contributed magazine articles, and lectured on public affairs. When the Nieman Fellowships at Harvard opened a chance for selected newspapermen to go on leave for a year of background studies, the response of the Globe staff, with the encouragement of the office, was such that by the late 1960's Nieman Fellows on the Globe included the executive editor, managing editor, two Washington correspondents, a state political writer, science writer, education writer, natural resources editor, medical writer, editorial writer, assistant city editor, and a columnist who had been executive editor. But for all of them this was in the nature of the self-education that journalism imposes on its responsible members.

The Globe's appreciation of the Nieman Fellowship program was evidenced in 1965 by the willingness of publisher Davis Taylor to take on the national leadership of a fund-raising of $2,200,000 to recapitalize the program. It was Davis Taylor's standing among publishers and the dedicated energy he put into it that raised half this money from newspapers to match the other half from the Ford Foundation. Taylor had no sooner completed this two-year campaign when the Globe staff had a chance to cheer for the recognition of his quality on the part of his fellow alumni in electing him to the Harvard Board of Overseers.

City Editor

A modest item in the New York Times one day in 1963 announced staff changes. City editor Frank Adams was moving to the editorial page and Abe Rosenthal, foreign correspondent, was returning from Asia to be "metropolitan news editor." Development of the metropolitan area, the Times explained, required replacement of city editor with metropolitan editor. That inconspicuous statement marked a transition and the passing of a tradition of the city editor with all the legend that had grown up around his local suzerainty. Of course there was more to it than the enlargement of locality.

News had become more fluid and required more attention to what was going on outside conventional news "beats," which had been conventional too long. Abe Rosenthal was soon developing stories that had no locality except that their manpower was in the city staff. Other newspapers, without any formal change of titles, had had similarly to adapt to changing conditions.

A change of titles would never have occurred to the Boston Globe at any time in its first 60 years, when it had the barest minimum of titles and when its most important editor, James Morgan, had none.

But the title of city editor had been outgrown on the Globe almost from the time William D. Sullivan moved his ebullient energies to the city desk in 1889; by 1926, when he became managing editor, the only visible change was in title. Sully had been managing the news from the city desk; old Mr. Fowle, as managing editor, had found enough to do in handling the regional correspondents. Sully sent his reporters wherever the news developed, anywhere in the country and on occasion abroad. The Sunday paper, editorials, and features were the domain of Morgan and Winship. But the news was Sully's and nobody tried to partition it. Not that Sully was at all an empire-builder. He just covered all the news there was, filled in all the gaps. As news enlarged in all its dimensions, it was all handled by the one city room staff, and Sully as city editor directed that staff. He'd hired most of the men himself; he knew them, had confidence in them, picked them for the assignments he found them best at. Even for Sunday features, throughout this period, writers were borrowed from the city staff, a day or two at a time. The consequent variety of staff work made the Globe an interesting place to work. A reporter might be on a local story today, on a Sunday feature tomorrow, then sent to Washington to cover an inauguration or out across the country on a political campaign; and on completing an important assignment, he might be asked to write an editorial on the subject. Further, the Globe had no separate "rewrite" staff as other papers had started. If a reporter could not get back to the office for the evening edition, he telephoned his story to another reporter. If a story with several angles required someone in the office to pull it together, a reporter was assigned to that. He might be out on a story today and in the office tomorrow linking up other reporters' stories. And Sully presided over all this.

A good city editor knows both his city and his staff and fits the man to the assignment. He has his men catalogued in his mind, the descriptive writer, the hard-digging investigator, the man sharp on technical details, the effective interviewer, the man who did a good job on the public utility hearings last time. Of course, continuity of events indicates much. One thing leads to another and reporters become identified with certain kinds of news.

An assignment from Sully was often a conference, a seminar, a social event. He would stroll around to the reporter's room, a cubbyhole shared with two to four others, announce himself with a cheery greeting — or if the man was back to, at his typewriter, tap him lightly on the shoulder — to say, "I think I have a very interesting story for you. You remember so-and-so." Then he would recite what he knew of the situation, recall anecdotes, perhaps sit down and draw a little diagram, suggest that so-and-so may be worth talking to about it; then, looking at his watch, "You can get a train, I think, in about half an hour." Finally, turning on his way out, "Say hello to old Mr. Pease, our correspondent. That was a good story he gave us last week."

Sully's enthusiasm was infectious. He never got over the excitement of a good story. Every day was a new day with fresh possibilities of interest. He was coach and mentor to his staff. When a reporter came off a long, arduous assignment, Sully was apt to say, "Now you go roll your hoop for a few days, see your family, get a rest."

Sully kept the tone of the small shop of half a dozen men he'd started with long after the Globe had become one of the largest papers in the country. His role had expanded imperceptibly with the scope of the paper.

The city desk is where the action is. The city editor deploys his troops from the city staff. His telephone, or a battery of them, alerts the office to the situations that call for assignments. His assignment book is a log of the day's events. The reporters take off at his bidding to discover what news there is in the alerts that flow in to his desk. They return to report to him, or to the night city editor, who takes over at the end of the day. The reporter is instructed approximately the space to give his story. When he has written it, he turns it in to the city editor or one of his assistants, who reads it for a check of the facts before sending it around to the copy desk for final editing.

On a modern metropolitan paper the operation becomes somewhat more complex and more informal than in Sully's day. The city editor may want the science editor or political editor to have a look at the story to see if it has further possibilities of development. More likely he has talked to them before making the assignment. Or these specialists, self-starters in the fields of their responsibility, will tell the city desk what they are up to. One may need to tell the desk that two meetings in his field that day look worth covering; can the city desk assign one of them?

The city desk is the focal point. The city editor is responsible for seeing that all details are carried out. Much of the legend of journalism is about city editors. The great city editors had as prototype O. K. Bovard of the St. Louis Post-Dispatch, who conducted his staff like an orchestra leader to bring out the full value of every note in the rhythm of the tingling life of his city.

Another familiar type was the mean city editor, a martinet in ruling his staff, like Charles Chapin of the old New York World. Irvin Cobb told one day that Chapin was out sick, said, "I hope it's nothing trivial." * The Boston Post in the twenties and thirties was under the discipline of city editor Eddie Dunn, whose practice was to give a man a sealed envelope marked to be opened at six o'clock in Copley Square, or five o'clock in Bridgewater. The reporter then had his assignment cold. No chance to background himself by consulting the office files or a colleague who might have an angle on it. He was a messenger of the city editor, his role precisely prescribed — and so limited.

Joe Herzberg of the Herald Tribune in the forties knew his city like the back of his hand, could direct and inform his staff as fully as a village postmistress. His predecessor, Stanley Walker, had made literature out of the beat and tempo of the city in his books *Mrs. Astor's Horse* and *City Editor*.

But the city editor is at the mercy of his staff. They are his eyes and ears. Only through them can his staccato list of assignments turn into a living record of what goes on.

Globe editors by the 1920's were pretty safe with their staffs, either college-

---

* Irvin Cobb on Charles Chapin is quoted in James W. Barrett, *Joseph Pulitzer and His World,* Vanguard Press, 1941, p. 277.

trained younger men or tested veterans. George Dimond, assistant city editor, would recall with a grim shake of his head the fakery of his earlier days at the turn of the century. George, out of Vermont, was a church deacon. He believed in honesty and knew when he was getting it.

Nobody on the Globe in that era could have conceived of abstracting from the Atlantic Monthly's printing plant the proofs of Al Smith's answer to the challenge to his religion in 1928. The Boston Post eventually paid thousands of dollars in a damage suit for that offense. But it was a priceless scoop the morning they exploded the headline on the presidential candidate's answer to the issue of the hour.

As the Globe did not have star reporters except for Sibley, sui generis, Sib's stardom was a luminous exception, though for less than a decade. It was a democratic system. No one escaped a share of the routine stories unless he could think up special stories faster than the editors, which sometimes happened. Other papers did use the star system. The Boston American would pick out a lively and personable girl reporter and assign her to any kind of story that lent itself to special promotion. The Herald assigned a girl reporter in the second world war and promoted her stories over the more important general war news. The Post would single out one reporter to take most of the big stories. Bill Cunningham on the Post developed from sports writer to sports columnist to reporter and columnist of things in general, his copy set in extra large type, with special spacing, often given an entire page. The Herald hired him away for a salary more akin to that of a Hollywood star than a reporter.

The Globe went in for none of this; the staff were all more or less on the same level. Of course the abler men were given the more important assignments, but in pay and office treatment all were nearly on a level within a narrow range. In the 1920's, before the Newspaper Guild began classifying jobs and pay, experienced reporters on the Globe ranged from $50 to $100; maybe a few got $125. The managing editor's pay was $12,000; city editor, Sunday editor, day and night editor around $10,000. Globe reporters were, at Globe rates, as well paid as on any paper. But top editors had higher salaries on other papers.

These pay scales held through the 1930's, for the depression prevented raises, even brought one pay cut. For the younger men, in their twenties and thirties and not yet at their top range of pay, to go for a decade without a pay raise just as their families were becoming more expensive was a hardship. It helped account for the rise of the Newspaper Guild in 1935.

Of course all the mechanical departments of the paper had long been unionized, among the strongest unions. Pay there could not be cut. Only in the news and editorial departments was this possible, creating a strong incentive to join the guild.

Gardner Jackson

Of the various ways that men fall into careers, sheer accident brought Gardner Jackson to the Globe and so to the Sacco-Vanzetti defense committee on which he became a vital force. On a visit to a relative in Boston in autumn 1920, Jackson happened to drop in for lunch at Thompson's Spa, to find himself beside Lucien Price, the Globe's leading editorial writer. They fell into conversation, hit it off, and Price persuaded the Globe to hire Jackson.

Jackson had been back from World War I a year; he had not returned to finish his course at Amherst College, but instead went to New York to try to write plays. Then his father, Denver banker and railroad president, persuaded him to try business for a year. The father died and Jackson joined the Denver Times; he had been there just long enough to play a part in an investigation of vice rackets.

Soon to be married, he was casting about for something more satisfying to do. As his father had been one of the wealthiest men in Denver, he had no problem about earning a living. He chose the Globe because of the outlook he had discovered in Lucien Price. The editorial page was shorthanded, and Price's idea was to have Jackson fill the gap. As it worked out he did editorials about two days a week, reporting and Sunday features the rest of the time — a regimen several of us shared.

Within a few months the trial of Sacco and Vanzetti began. Almost immediately Jackson's wife, from reading the newspaper reports, became concerned that the two were not getting a fair trial. She asked Gardner to find out. He looked up Frank P. Sibley, who said he thought Mrs. Jackson was very perceptive.

Jackson then explored the background of the two men and met the extraordinary Aldino Felicani, a gentle anarchist who was the linotype operator for La Notizio, an Italian newspaper in Boston. Felicani was Vanzetti's best friend and within the limits of his resources and acquaintance was doing all he could to interest people in the case.

Jackson offered help, both financial and journalistic. He wrote material for Felicani and, as his own interest in the case grew, sought to interest others. A dynamic character who threw himself into things with terrific intensity, Jackson also captivated with an engagingly uninhibited approach to people and issues. He was credited with interesting Felix Frankfurter in the case, which led to raising the issue of the judicial process at the highest intellectual level.

Jackson was drawn ever deeper into the Sacco-Vanzetti defense until finally he resigned from the Globe to give it his full energy. But he had in a few years made an enlivening contribution to the paper. The impact of psychology and psychiatry was then new and news. Jackson had become deeply interested, at first through the psychological problems of relatives. A brother was a suicide. A sister, a psychologist, studied under Freud in Vienna where the Jacksons visited her. Jackson through these personal involvements became closely acquainted with Dr. Stanley Cobb, neuropsychiatrist at Harvard Medical School, McFie Campbell, chief of the State Hospital for Mental Diseases in Boston, and others. He was constantly discovering material for special articles on psychology or suggested by psychology. He brought a psychological approach to subjects and to people that gave a particular tone to his articles. He came to have a special appreciation of the bizarre and to seek to discover the motivation and psychological implications of actions. He wrote with special relish about anything that struck him as fantastic.

When Boston University in December 1925 appointed as new president a Methodist minister of Pittsburgh named Daniel Lane Marsh, Jackson was sent to do an interview article for the Sunday paper. While waiting for his appointment in Dr. Marsh's reception room, he idly picked up a book on phrenology and was turning its pages when Marsh entered. "The best thing I can do for you is refer you to that book, which has a full phrenological description of me in it," Marsh told him. Sure enough, it had a color photograph of Dr. Marsh and a map of his skull, locating his traits of character.

Dr. Marsh went through it in detail with the reporter, explaining the bumps that indicated qualities of heart and mind, judgment, decisiveness, humanity, imagination, leadership, and so on. With mixed incredulity and glee Jackson pounced on his story as the new university president psychoanalyzed himself by the bumps on his head. Happily he got it all down, gave his story the full treatment, and wired it back to the Sunday paper. But none of it appeared on Sunday.

"What happened?" Gardner demanded of Winship.

"Come off it," Winship said. "We knew you must have been drunk."

"But I've got my full notes to prove it." He convinced the editor, and the story of Dr. Marsh's phrenological qualifications ran the following Sunday, January 3, 1926. Not a riffle of protest reached the Globe, to the disappointment of the reporter that such fantasy could be accepted without question.

Another Jackson effort that aroused skepticism in the office had a positive response. Herbert Hoover, as Secretary of Commerce, appointed Dr. Julius Klein chief of a new bureau of domestic commerce. Klein came to Boston for a speech, which Jackson reported. Klein described the power of advertising as a panacea for the economy. Used to its optimum, advertising could create and sustain such dimensions of consumer demand as would guarantee a permanent and ever rising prosperity. This in 1922 was heady stuff, and in what seemed to Jackson the hyperbole of Dr. Klein's exuberant vocabulary it struck him as an item to be as prized as a phrenological interview. He wrote it with gusto, selecting Klein's most ecstatic sentences to quote.

The city editor said: "Come now, Gardner. This is too fantastic." Gardner raised his right hand and asked that a Bible be sent for. "Well, the copy desk will throw it out," the city editor shrugged, and passed it. Out came the day editor. "Gardner, what's this nonsense?" "I swear, and here are my notes." The day editor shrugged and printed it.

A few days later the publisher sent for Gardner Jackson.

"This is it," Jackson groaned. "I suppose Klein has reneged after seeing how foolish he looked."

"Mr. Jackson, you wrote the story of Dr. Klein's speech to the Chamber of Commerce?"

"Yes, sir." Before he could add, "I'll show you my notes," Mr. Taylor said: "Congratulations. Dr. Klein writes me that it is the most faithful and intelligent report of a speech he's ever had."

Jackson's experiences with Globe editorials were something else. The editorial writers—Lucien Price, William Packer, James H. Powers — he thought "a remarkable bunch of fellows whose quality of mind and outlook greatly influenced me." And James Morgan, who presided over them, was "a terrific factor in our development, one of the great journalists in the country, and one of the best historians — a wonderful man."

But it was a mixed impression. "We editorial writers found we were able to be very honest intellectually on subject matter far removed from the immediate concerns of Boston or Massachusetts. We could be wonderful on international or abstract things. But when it got right down to the economic problems of our own area, there was always a prohibition."

This is a crusader's criticism of an editorial policy that certainly did not crusade, as indeed only a very exceptional few newspapers did at that time. But it is a judgment that needs to be balanced. For at the very time of which Jackson was writing, when the Globe was sitting out in silence the local Sacco-Vanzetti ferment, James Morgan expressed in a Sunday Symposium of July 17, 1921, the nub of his philosophy which over many years he had made the philosophy of the Globe. "Who Beat Bolshevism?" was his subject. And if this sounds international and abstract, it will be seen that he brought it home as a moral for America:

> The defeat of Bolshevism is not a victory of capitalism over communism, or individualism over Socialism. Rather it is a victory of social evolution over social revolution. The hope of the former is what beat the latter.
>
> Our political and social system has not by any means received a clean bill of health. It has received an opportunity to remedy its many defects in accordance with our formula. And the opportunity must be improved to vindicate the formula . . . A revolution never happens by the bottom of society rising up, but by the top of society falling down. Keep the channels of progress open to change and all is well.

Jackson never did finish his college course. When nearly 30 and deep in the Sacco-Vanzetti case, he left the Globe to resume his studies as a special student at Harvard, where Arthur M. Schlesinger was close friend and adviser. But Schlesinger urged Jackson to put all his energy into the Sacco-Vanzetti defense. "You can be making history instead of studying it." So for the second time Jackson abandoned pursuit of a college degree.

After his traumatic experience with the Sacco-Vanzetti defense, Jackson went to Washington, secured appointment as correspondent of the Montreal Star and characteristically became on such intimate terms with members of the Canadian government that they gave him their confidence about the difficulties President Hoover had raised over a St. Lawrence Seaway agreement. Jackson shared this information with Gov. Franklin D. Roosevelt and thus became a charter member of the New Deal — a protégé of Mrs. Roosevelt also — and throughout its course a provocative and often controversial force. His interest in sharecroppers led him then to join John L. Lewis's efforts to organize them and other groups on the thin fringes of the American economy.

The 800-page reminiscence Jackson was persuaded to confide to the files of the Oral History Library at Columbia University in 1959 is a catalogue of biographical briefs and evaluations of practically everyone who was a factor on the political, economic, or social scene in America through three decades. It is not wholly reliable as a record, for his memory was erratic. But it is immensely perceptive in characterization and evaluation of persons and movements and is an eloquent Odyssey of the spirit of a man of his times.

Cooling with Coolidge

The Coolidge era cooled it through the 1920's, a decade of easy feeling, riding the boom. Coolidge stories became as numerous as Ford jokes had been. The times made it easy for publishers to follow Coolidge's negative attitude toward government, glad to have it relegated to a quiet secondary role. It was an era of the human interest story, of exploring the region for features, when most journalism could be described by the title Gerald Johnson later gave his column in the New Republic, "The Superficial Aspect."

A 1924 visit of the Prince of Wales to hunt with the North Shore Myopia Club was a big story, heightened in anticipation by the Prince's penchant for falling off his horse. The Globe staff of six assigned to it included three strategically posted photographers. But the Prince held to his horse that day. The old chestnut about the Beacon Hill butler announcing "two reporters and a gentleman from the Transcript" came true with that assignment. Bayard Tuckerman, a noted horseman and a less noted Boston insurance man, was host. When besieged by the press, he wouldn't deal with anybody but the Transcript. William McDonald, the paper's leading reporter, acted as spokesman, mediator, and regulator of the press arrangements; he was fully professional and Tuckerman accepted all his proposals.

Lindbergh's solo flight across the Atlantic was the sensational story of the decade and Lindbergh such a popular hero as was hardly to be raised up again. The nation tingled to the crackle of the dim radio of 1927 with the reports through a Saturday afternoon that he was in sight of Ireland, now over England, had reached the coast of France. Correspondents were hours bogged down that night in a vast traffic jam getting into Paris from the airport with their stories of the lone flier stepping out of his plane to explain "I am Charles Lindbergh." He carried in his pocket the most superfluous baggage in the whole history of impedimenta, a letter of introduction from Theodore Roosevelt, Jr. Lyons had the assigment to cover Lindbergh's return for a delirious welcome in Washington and presentation by a President who revealed a hitherto unseen Coolidge grin, then to New York for the prototype of all tickertape receptions as the metropolis engulfed Lindbergh.

An eclipse of the sun in 1924, the first in living memory, had its totality belt across Nantucket, where Boston reporters clustered in a small white church steeple to hear cocks crow at midday. The whole populace was equipped with smoked glasses to witness the sun's corona. The newspapers published astronomy lessons. The Harvard Observatory under Harlow Shapley gladly took on the role of instructor to the public at large — a role most effectively sustained in the dawn of the space age. A second eclipse only eight years later, with its totality belt across the White Mountains, proved more journalistically productive. It brought fresh distinction to Meyer Berger, of the New York Times, for his remarkable roundup of reports from scores of astronomical teams at their isolated observation posts through the mountains. But a passing cloud at the strategic moment balked photography at the Globe's mountain post, and the best photographs published were taken from the roof of the Globe building.

It was Charles A. Merrill who first caught the full drama of Coolidge's father administering the presidential oath to his son in the farmhouse living room. It happened too late — 2:45 A.M. — for the morning paper August 3, whose headlines

The Boston Sunday Globe

THE BOSTON SUNDAY GLOBE—MAY 22, 1927—110 PAGES   READ THE SUNDAY GLOBE MAGAZINE AND EDITORIAL SECTION   (5)   **PRICE 10 CENTS**

CAPT LINDBERGH LANDS PLANE SAFELY AT PARIS AFTER CROSSING ATLANTIC ALONE IN 33 1-2 HOURS

SIRENS AND GONGS SPREAD GLAD NEWS

"Let 'er Go!" Comes in Second as Word of Landing Is Flashed to Fire Department by Globe

HARVARD VICTOR IN THREE RACES

Wins Varsity, Junior and the Freshman

Coach Brown's Crews Make Fine Showing on the Charles

Eli Class Eight Wins, Penn Takes the "150"

HOW THE CREWS FINISHED

NATION'S HEAD SENDS PRAISE

President Speaks for American People

Cable to Lindbergh Tells of His Joy at Successful Flight

Governor Fuller Sends Congratulations

WASHINGTON, May 21 (A.P.)—President Coolidge, in a congratulatory cablegram to be delivered to Charles A. Lindbergh in Paris, told the transatlantic flyer that the "American people rejoice with me at the brilliant termination of your heroic flight."

25,000 Madly Cheering Frenchmen Take Tired Young American To Their Hearts—America Goes Wild at News, Raising Deafening Din From One Coast to the Other

"Well, Here We Are," Is Only Speech of Flyer—Mother In Detroit, Sobs Happily

Youth, Asleep on Feet, Thinks Until Last of Ship—Feat Marks Epoch of Air

LINDBERGH'S TIMETABLE

FRIDAY

*7:51 A. M.—Took off from Roosevelt Field, Long Island, vanishing a moment later over Westbury, bound for Paris, 3640 miles away.
9:40 A. M.—Sighted at Halifax, Mass.
12:25 P. M.—First observed over Nova Scotia, at Cape St Mary, 10 miles from Meteghan, Digby County.
3:30 P. M.—Sighted over St Pierre, Miquelon.
7:15 P. M.—Passed St John's N.F, and headed over the Atlantic.

SATURDAY

Lindbergh lands: May 22, 1927.

were all of Harding's death. Just a brief front page item under a one-column head, "Unable to Reach Coolidge by Wire," reported that telephone and telegraph offices had closed down early in the Plymouth district.

Next morning Merrill took the first description of the oath-taking by telephone from the country correspondent. "What kind of light did they have?" he asked. "A kerosene lamp." So Merrill brought the oil lamp into his lead for the early afternoon edition, which carried the headline:

> President Coolidge Given Oath by Father
> Old Fashioned Oil Lamp Lit Scene in Living Room of Vermont Farm
>   House

The Globe always believed that Merrill's question elicited the first published reference to the oil lamp in the oath-taking scene. A check of the Boston and New York papers and the Associated Press story for August 3, both morning and evening, shows no other reference to the oil lamp. Next day it was a featured detail in the press of the nation.

Charles Merrill was the complete newspaperman of his period, a rare combination of reporter, editorial writer, and executive. He had become a first-class reporter in his first five years, before serving in World War I. It was his own idea, after the war, to return for a series on postwar Europe in 1921, then in 1923 to go to Ireland to report the birth of the Irish Free State. The only Boston reporter in Ireland, Merrill managed to obtain a rare interview with Michael Collins, leader of the Irish Republican Army.

Merrill covered top stories in the 1920's, the Scopes trial in Tennessee and the Hall-Mills murder case, and he made a national political tour in 1924. He was writing editorials and Sunday features. In 1928 he covered the Hoover-Al Smith presidential campaign. In 1930 he made another productive trip to Ireland. In 1937 he became city editor and assistant managing editor, but he continued to contribute to the editorial page and to undertake major foreign assignments. At the end of the second world war he went to Germany to report on the new German Occupation Government. In 1948 he went to Rome to cover the critical Italian election. The next year he was in Israel to report the beginnings of that new state. His sudden death at 62 in 1951 left a big hole in the Globe organization. Winship lost his right-hand man.

Coolidge stories that abounded in those days mostly had to do with his legendary silences or laconic utterance, like the one of the lady seated next to him at a state dinner who said, "I have a bet I can get you to say three words"; Coolidge's reply, "You lose." His response to a question about a biography of George Washington done in the debunking fashion then having a vogue: looking out the window at the Washington Monument, he observed, "Seems to be still there." Democrats liked a story in 1924 that Coolidge sounded out Borah, the strident lion of Idaho, on going on the presidential ticket that year. Borah's alleged query was: Which end? A story more acceptable to Republicans had someone telling Coolidge he'd just seen Borah horseback riding and Coolidge asking: Was he going the same way as the horse?

This was the era of western insurgency that finally alienated the farm bloc from an unresponsive Republican party. "Sons of the Wild Jackass" New Hampshire's conservative Senator George Moses called the Farmer-Labor and Non-Partisan League secessionists from the GOP who had temporarily captured Minnesota and North Dakota. Coolidge was content to let Moses say it.

The Globe had its own early Coolidge story, right out of his 1920 nomination for vice president. When the surprise news came over the wire from Chicago of this anticlimax to Harding that stampeded the convention, Leverett Bentley, State House reporter, was sent to the Adams House to inform Governor Coolidge and report the result. Coolidge poured Bentley a cooling drink. Soon Bob Brady of the Post and Tom Carens of the Herald arrived. Mrs. Coolidge came in as the Governor was pouring their libations. Mrs. Coolidge noted Bentley's now empty glass and said, "And Mr. Bentley, Calvin." "Bent's had his," said the Governor. That was Bent's own story and thought to be a good one.

Arthur Krock, who came to know Coolidge well in Washington, had his own explanation of such occurrences: Coolidge was a tease, rather than stingy. There is evidence for that. People didn't know how to take him. Keeping himself a riddle was good politics, and of course what a politician doesn't say doesn't hurt him. Coolidge's 1928 decision, "I do not choose to run," proved a national riddle. Its various interpretations filled columns of newspaper space elaborating on the possible options of its seeming indefiniteness. It raised less question in New England, closer to the Yankee idiom, where "do not choose" carried a negative finality that implied also "I could if I wanted to but I won't."

In 1928 Al Smith came to Boston and into the hearts of the multitude, who turned out the vastest crowd ever until then on the sidewalks and the Common. Massachusetts with Rhode Island proved the only island of northern support for Al in that election; but here the feeling for this man of the sidewalks of New York went deeper than politics and beyond his religious affiliation. It was an affection for his human quality, for all he stood for — his openness, his unabashed Brooklynese in accents and mannerisms, his naturalness, his ability to speak to the people as one of them who knew the score. "Let's look at the record."

The easy decade closed in the great crash of October 1929. But the vast shadow it cast before was unapprehended; and the dire effects of depression still lay some years ahead. The momentary excitement of the stock market collapse was a Sunday feature assignment to Lyons. The Sunday editor, to relieve the grimness of it, added a sentence: "Next day the market rose again — five points." This of course was a mere reflex action, for the market soon found lower and lower levels. But the impact at the time, even on newspapermen if not financial writers, was so brief that the same reporter, two months later interviewing Mr. Coolidge back in Northampton, assumed that Coolidge's greeting — "How's business?" — was just a casual opener. The reporter hadn't the slightest idea how business was; it was an alien world to him. But not to Coolidge. He had ridden the boom of the twenties and escaped the crash. Depression was to be Hoover's cross.

In 1926, when Arthur Fowle retired and W. D. Sullivan became managing editor, Winship's becoming assistant managing editor marked a recognition of the dynamic center. The long-time assistant city editor, George Dimond, was moved up to city editor in accord with Taylor policy. But new vitality was brought into news coverage for the morning paper by making Charles Merrill night city editor with, for the first time, a separately oriented night staff, theretofore just a stopgap carryover from the day staff.

The search for a new water supply for Boston was a continuing issue through the 1920's. An extraordinary bureaucrat, Xanthus H. Goodnough, chief sanitary engineer, made it his cause to block inadequate makeshift sources and strike out for the western Swift River of clear, pure water in endless volume. He had to block off water power interests eyeing the Swift Valley. The Globe kept Goodnough's quest in the headlines. It became one of Lyons' pursuits. Another was electric light rates, over which he was able to attach to Henry Shattuck's campaign to use the lower rates of the local municipal light departments as a yardstick.

Shattuck's exposure of the exploitation of local electric companies by the huge holding company systems of that wide-open period gave support to the resistance of an able Public Utilities Commission chairman, Henry Attwill, who insisted, counter to Supreme Court dogma, on basing Massachusetts rates on "book value" rather than "reproduction value." Between them they saved Massachusetts from the fate of Maine, which became an Insull satrapy that collapsed with Insull.

Shattuck, a rich trustee of property, was a Republican of rare independence but bypassed by the Republican organization because of that independence. He became Republican leader of the House but never governor. He could have been Republican candidate for mayor but realistically chose to support instead a young reform Democrat, Maurice Tobin, who in 1938 defeated and ended Curley's reign, to go on to be governor and secretary of labor. Shattuck gave the city a park to be named for Tobin's parents. Shattuck had consciously divided his plans for public service into three parts, to serve ten years each in city council, in state legislature, and at Harvard. He did all three, for more than one decade each. As Harvard's treasurer, with his legislative experience, he helped President Conant when at the end of the war Conant was asked by Governor Tobin to plan for the education of returning veterans. Conant's planning with Shattuck's legislative steering brought about the evolution of the State College to the University of Massachusetts.

A Coolidge Era entrant to the journalistic scene was Will Rogers, cowboy comedian. Adolph Ochs of the New York Times persuaded Rogers to contribute a daily commentary that took the form of a single, terse paragraph bringing a comic flick of shrewd observation to the day's news. The Globe was the first paper outside the Times to use it, for Laurence Winship had met Rogers at political conventions, subscribed to his humorous articles on politics, and become an early convert to his puckish horse sense that was soon appearing in 350 newspapers. The paragraph, "Will Rogers Says," was a front page fixture in the daily Globe from 1926 until Rogers' untimely death in a plane crash in 1935. Such Rogers quips as "America never lost a war or won a conference" and "it's funnier to be a Democrat" became as much a part of daily conversation as Mr. Dooley's observations had been a generation earlier.

A Gene Mack sports cartoon: July 22, 1929.

Banned in Boston

The redoubtable Henry Mencken provided a hilarious story for the Boston press on April 5, 1926, when he came to Boston to invite arrest by selling a copy of his banned Mercury magazine to J. Frank Chase, the Comstockian agent of the Watch and Ward Society. Mencken performed this operation on Boston Common before all the news photographers in town and a ribald crowd of several thousand. On receiving Chase's 50-cent piece, he bit it hard, rang it on the pavement, and only then handed over the magazine that Chase's Pecksniffian sensibilities had rendered contraband in Boston.

But next day an old Yankee judge, James Parmenter, refused to find Mencken guilty, even under the obsolete obscenity laws of Massachusetts that had made "banned in Boston" already a burlesque line. Mencken had delivered a scathing attack on Chase, the Boston authorities, and the prudery that had brought Boston's cultural reputation to a nadir. Chase had his revenge in preventing the distribution in Boston of the March 1926 Mercury for Herbert Asbury's story "Hatrack." After his acquittal, Mencken was escorted through a cheering multitude by Professors Zechariah Chafee and Felix Frankfurter to be lionized at Harvard and dined by the literati of Boston.

But the book banning went on another four years before the community was enough aroused to emancipate itself from Watch and Ward censorship by changing the law. The Watch and Ward Society had for 50 years focused its energies against commercial vice and corrupt politics and the frequent combination of the two. As late as 1923 its board had included Bishop Lawrence, Charles William Eliot, Francis J. Moors, Julian Coolidge, John H. Storer. But after J. Frank Chase, a fundamentalist clergyman, became its secretary, its attention shifted to a censorious concern for the contemporary culture. His most vocal and nagging supporters were the fundamentalist preachers of the Park Street Church ("Brimstone Corner") and Tremont Temple, later joined by the Catholic hierarchy.

Boston booksellers had set up a protective device, a secret gentleman's agreement with the Watch and Ward Society and the authorities. Richard Fuller of the Old Corner Book Store contrived and led this enterprise, which he described to the American Booksellers Convention in 1923:[*]

> Authorities agreed not to make an arrest until a book complained of had been read by the Committee of the Watch and Ward Society, and the Booksellers of Boston. Later the State of Massachusetts agreed to abide by the decision of that committee. Whenever a book was found to be of the class that was not fit to sell, the booksellers were notified and they immediately stopped the sale of it. The dealers were given 48 hours to stop the sale after the decision had been made known to them, and then if they did not comply with the rule, they were proceeded against. For the first few years all worked well. But the last two years we have had Hell from so much work. During the past year we have suppressed 14 books.

[*] In Richard F. Fuller, "How Boston Handles Problem," Publishers' Weekly, 103, May 26, 1923, pp. 1624–1625.
Also Paul S. Boyer, *Purity in Print*, Charles Scribner's Sons, 1968, pp. 171–173.

Burton Rascoe asked Fuller to name the suppressed books but Fuller refused. "It would only give publicity to those books. When the notice goes out, there is no publicity whatever. The newspapers are cooperating with us. They refuse ads of those books. The literary editors refuse to review them. The booksellers won't sell it. In two weeks nobody is talking about it. We have had a few black sheep. If the Watch and Ward Society catches them it means going to court and in every case the courts have imposed a fine."

J. Frank Chase died in 1927 and the cozy booksellers protective system died with him. The Suffolk County district attorney, William Foley, abrogated the agreement. Thereafter police acted on their own literary judgments. Books in Boston took their chances with the courts. Such books as Dreiser's *American Tragedy* and Sinclair Lewis' *Elmer Gantry* were outlawed. Even Upton Sinclair's novel *Oil* was banned over a reference to birth control. When challenged in the courts these bans were generally upheld as falling under the obscenity law.

Every new suppression divided the community and the press and raised fresh efforts to change the obscenity law so that a single word offensive to the censorious could not condemn a book. The Transcript was at once a supporter of Mencken's crusade for freedom to print. The Post supported police censorship. The Herald at first accepted the commercial policy of the booksellers but came out against the later police censorship. The Globe was silent through the opening seasons of agitation, but as the community grew more restive it was saying by spring 1927, "censorship of books by public officials is a dangerous business as well as, generally, a stupid one."

By then even the business community was disturbed at national ridicule of Boston. A. Lincoln Filene, leading merchant, wrote in a letter to the Transcript that Boston's reputation was leading to the conclusion that it had lost its vitality and was falling behind more vigorous regions. Even Richard Fuller observed that Bostonians were doing their Christmas book buying in other cities. Henry Shattuck took the lead in the legislature to amend the obscenity law. It took another three years of mobilizing anticensorship forces to change the law, for the Catholic hierarchy had now become the custodian of Boston Puritanism.

Meantime a climax of the absurd came in September 1929 when Mayor Malcolm Nichols banned the playing of Eugene O'Neill's *Strange Interlude* from its scheduled performance in the Hollis Theatre. Hundreds of Theatre Guild subscribers streamed out to Quincy to see the play. The bizarre aspects of censorship had become untenable. The Globe joined the Transcript and Herald in supporting reform; only the Post kept up its defense of cultural deprivation. That winter the legislature amended the law. By then such distinguished sponsors of the Watch and Ward Society as Bishop Lawrence had publicly resigned. Finally in 1931 even its president and long-time defender, Dr. Raymond Calkins, quietly quit the society, which had become a caricature. It had a revival in later decades as a vigorous agency against organized crime. Ultimately the Supreme Court defined the rules on obscenity.

It remained for Elliot Richardson, on becoming Massachusetts attorney general in 1966, to institute a process by which the attorney general determines whether a book is within the law and, if action is indicated, moves against the book rather than the bookseller, who knows from the court decision whether the book is legal merchandise.

Eddie Costello Lands Scoop

The enterprise of a young police reporter gave the Globe a clear beat on one of the great sea tragedies of the 1920's. The newest, finest, safest submarine of the United States, the *S-51,* was rammed and sunk in the dark September 25, 1925, off Block Island by a coastwise steamer, *City of Rome.* The collision was at about 10:30. Saturday morning papers had the bare facts. The *Rome* had picked up three survivors. Thirty-four men were missing. The story opened more questions than it answered: Why only three survivors? Why had the *Rome* left the spot before rescue operations could be organized? What were the chances of the 34 men in the sunken sub?

Another unanswered question, very practical to a Boston newspaper, was whether the *Rome* would put in at New London submarine base with its survivors or come through to Boston on its scheduled run. Frank Sibley was dispatched to New London. Lyons was assigned to stand by in the office.

Uncertainty as to the *Rome* ended about 2 o'clock when it was reported passing Graves Light. So it would soon dock in Boston. But what chance at the story? The Navy would certainly isolate their sailors, and the *Rome*'s captain would withhold his account for the inevitable inquiry.

It looked to the office like a dim prospect. If only a police or fireboat could be had to intercept the *Rome.* That of course was out of the question. But was it? In blew Eddie Costello, brash young Roxbury district man who helped out on the police beat. Eddie jumped at the idea.

Why not? Let's get the fire department boat and go down to meet the *Rome*; interview those sailors before the Navy gets them. Talk to the passengers. Maybe the captain will talk before he freezes up before Navy officials at the dock.

A neat trick if you can do it, a skeptical office told Eddie. But he did it. He found the fire chief, David Sennott, at lunch at Thompson's Spa across the street, and persuaded him. The office put together a crew from the scant Saturday afternoon resources. Lyons and George Noble, an old seadog himself and unterrified of ship masters, Costello, Nat Barrows, a big, enthusiastic office boy at home in boats who had a zest for excitement that later made him a distinguished war correspondent, Alfred Monahan, then working his way through Boston College as a Globe office boy, later city editor, his brother James, the Everett district man, and two top photographers, Eddie Bond and Jim Callahan.

The Monahan brothers had brought to the office an Everett friend, the son of Capt. John H. Diehl of the *Rome,* hoping he could help get access to the story. Young Diehl joined the fireboat party but didn't dare go aboard the *Rome* to face his father.

The fireboat whistled the *Rome,* and only after the ship had slowed to let the Globe men scramble up the fireboat's rope ladder did it announce "press." The captain was furious, but Noble was tough enough. Fascinated passengers helped the Globe men find the sailors, who came on deck in underwear and blankets to be photographed, then went back to their bunks to tell their individual stories to the improvised interviewers. Incredible stories of disaster and survival. Only six men were on duty when the sub was struck. Three were on the deck. All six were lost.

The three survivors had been wakened by the crash and assisted up to the conning tower by the chief signalman, who then stood by to help others. But there were no more. The sea filled the open hatch and the great sub sank in a huge bubble, leaving three sailors awash in the dark as the black mass of the *Rome* plowed past them. "For God's sake, throw us a line." The steamer put out a boat and picked them up, knowing all the others were lost.

The captain, seeing the white forward light of the oncoming sub, had mistaken it for the tail light of a string of fishing boats such as he often passed off Block Island.

At the dock the Navy went aboard and took charge of its sailors. The captain gave the officers a quick summary explanation, George Noble standing by. Then the Globe crew scrambled off amid threats of the captain and maledictions of their frustrated press contemporaries on the dock.

The Sunday front page, besides Sibley's story of the Navy's attempts to reach the sunken sub and Lyons' overall account of the disaster, had three individual survivor stories in three parallel columns across the center of the page: "Survivors Think All Others Died — Three Here on Steamer Recount Tragedy." Their stories, with Noble's and Lyons' filled 12 columns, all authentic eyewitness reports.

Eddie Costello's beat at police headquarters lasted more than 40 years. Seventeen years after the *S-51* went down, Eddie was again the chief prop in the Globe's monumental coverage of the worst disaster in Boston history when a flash fire in the Cocoanut Grove nightclub wiped out 479 lives at the very moment the first edition was going to press on another Saturday night.

No Crime on Monday

In the 1920's sensitive people in Boston were stirred by the constant diet of crime news, by its dominance of the front page. They let the papers know. Church groups, civic groups wrote the editor, even called on the editor, to ask for a more balanced diet.

This was impressive enough to make a difference. For a time the Globe adopted a definite policy of seeking out a positive type of story for Monday morning, ensuring that the paper would not lead off the week with a crime story. It was, in a negative way, backing into one of Joseph Pulitzer's cardinal points for the New York World — that it have a special story for Monday. After Sunday's recess in most public activity, Monday was bound to be a thin news day. Theodore Roosevelt as governor and president had discovered this and learned to take advantage of it with statements and actions aimed at the Monday morning news vacuum. Later this became a cliché of public relations.

But to have a Monday morning story that really had a right to lead the paper took some doing. It was too easy to pick one of the Sunday features to hold back a day, or just jazz up some local event to make it look big — or search out a human interest story that had no special relevance at the moment as news. The Globe did all these things. But it did them by inadvertence. For a time there was a real effort to dig up a "constructive" news story for Monday morning. This meant assigning a good reporter for at least a day or two at the end of the week. Sometimes this worked and the Globe on Monday morning presented news that with consistent energy and imagination could have transformed the paper. But nobody aimed at transformation. They just wanted to appease the crime news critics. Monday morning sufficed, and of course after a time the critics went away and things slipped back as they were. But the experience of seeking out and developing stories had its effect. There was more that was lively and individual in the paper.

On Radio

The advent of radio brought the Globe into a pioneer activity that quickly attracted to it the whole tribe of ham operators and a new cult of do-it-yourself home radio builders.

There were as yet no commercial receivers on the market when WBZ received the first radio station license in Boston September 15, 1921. Those who wanted to receive the new radio programs had to build their own sets. But the Globe had a linotype operator, Lloyd Greene, who had been a radio operator in World War I. Greene was an enthusiastic ham operator who had built his own radio.

He persuaded the Globe to print his instructions and diagrams for building a crystal set. Starting his radio column in the fall of 1921, Greene taught radio enthusiasts how to improve their rudimentary Quaker Oats boxes wrapped in wire into effective receivers. He set up a laboratory in the Globe to which home set builders could bring their problems.

Manufacturers of parts gladly bought space on Greene's radio page to advertise their wares. The Globe printed WBZ's programs and those of other stations as they began to come on the air in 1922. Radio grew from a few thousand sets in 1921 to 14 million by 1930, 44 million by 1940. The Sunday Globe was soon running ten to 12 pages of radio, developed around Greene's instruction, a question and answer column, news of the hams, correspondence about radio, news and features on the new communication.

By 1925 radio shows at the Boston Garden had as much appeal as auto shows. The Globe was a pioneer exhibitor. An annual feature was the Globe's *Radio Call Book,* listing every station in the country and free to everyone attending the show.

In 1926 the Globe began broadcasting. It bought five- and ten-minute spots on all three local radio stations for "talks." Willard DeLue gave the first "talk" September 6, 1926, at 6:25 P.M. over WNAC. He was soon doing a column, "Good Evening Everybody," on the radio page. On February 7, 1927, DeLue gave the first Globe news broadcast from a studio in the Globe building connected with station WEEI. The news was then put on a regular schedule, 12 noon, 4 P.M., 6:35, and 10:05, and each news spot assigned to a member of the copy desk. The first of the newscasters were Donald Willard, Roy Johnson, and Lafayette Marchand. A new column, "What's on the Air," carried radio notes.

On April 20, 1927, the radio column announced that M. E. Hennessy would continue his political talks and that A. J. Philpott, "one of the Globe's pioneer broadcasters," would be back on the air that night. DeLue that day turned in the first radio report of a marathon race (on April 20 because the nineteenth was a Sunday). Clarence DeMar was the winner, as for several seasons. The temperature was 85.

Before the year was out the Globe radio news became a regular assignment, with Howell Cullinan, old Navy man, taken off the news staff for it.

A Globe radio spectacular November 30, 1928, was a special broadcast to Adm. Richard E. Byrd, then wintering near the South Pole. The program carried opera, entertainment by Harry Lauder and Eddie Cantor, talks by the Governor and other notables, and greetings from the families of members of the Byrd expedition. A. J. Philpott was master of ceremonies. It was relayed by short wave out of Boston's station WEEI. Admiral Byrd radioed back that the program came through beautifully and was much appreciated.

Cullinan kept up his Globe broadcasting half a dozen years till he left for commercial broadcasting. Lloyd Greene headed an expanding radio department until radio tubes came in and he moved into manufacturing a tube of his own design in 1936.

By then the pioneer era of radio was over. The Globe ended its news broadcasts in 1934, when the Associated Press instituted a news service to radio stations. That closed a dozen years of agitation among newspaper publishers over radio. Initially many had been hostile to it and worried about it as a competitor. They charged it stole news out of the newspapers and was taking both circulation and advertising from the papers. It did indeed become a serious competitor for advertising. In the depression decade of the 1930's radio increased its share of the advertisers' dollar from three and a half to 20 cents, while the newspapers' share fell from 48 to 36 cents. The magazine share remained unchanged.

But newspapers like the Globe, that had welcomed radio and exploited the popular interest in it, found that their publishing of radio programs stimulated newspaper reading.

When television came in, in 1948, the Globe was again the first paper in Boston to have a television column, conducted by Ray McPartlin, a copy desk editor. After his death, Ted Ashby, then doing a local column, took it on. He was followed by a series of women, Elizabeth Watts Driscoll, Mary Cremmen, and finally Elizabeth Sullivan, who had joined Lloyd Greene's radio department in 1928. Besides editing the daily broadcast schedules, Miss Sullivan edits the Globe's *TV Week,* a 16-page listing of the week's programs inserted in the Sunday magazine. It has its own color cover, and typically a special article by Percy Shain, the television critic, a feature by Miss Sullivan, and other features that she selects. The television listings are arranged by Abbott Lawrence.

Percy Shain was appointed television critic in 1959, to develop a professional critical review of television offerings that soon brought it to a par with the other areas of criticism.

In the early days of broadcasting the Globe missed a chance to get in on the ground floor. In 1939 they had an offer to buy radio station WEEI for $400,000. But the Jordan estate representative on the Globe directors at the time was a leading Boston lawyer, Edward F. McClennen, who insisted that under the terms of Eben Jordan's will his estate could invest in newspaper operations but not in other enterprises, and radio was off limits. The other directors did not put so strict an interpretation on Jordan's will and could have outvoted McClennen. But that wasn't the way they operated. They passed up WEEI.

Nearly 30 years later the Globe did go into broadcasting in a limited way, taking a half interest in Edgar Kaiser's Boston broadcasting, both radio and UHF television, WKBG, Channel 56. But in 1968 they got Kaiser to let them pull out all but ten percent of their interest. In Davis Taylor's view this was wholly an investment against a future that, as his electronics friends told him, might see the newspaper delivered into the home via FM radio. The Globe refrained from exploiting its broadcast interest as a news medium out of conviction that this would divert it from concentration of energy on the newspaper. Principal participation in the 1960's was to broadcast a Sunday television panel interview of Globe reporters with a leading public figure, which created a lively story for Monday morning.

Vermont Flood

It had been raining hard for two days and there was water in suburban cellars the morning of November 4, 1927. When commuters reached their railroad stations to pick up a newspaper they read of a disastrous flood that had struck the narrow valleys of northern Vermont. There had been 11 inches of rain in two days, normally about three months' rainfall.

The Winooski, Lamoille, and White rivers had been turned to raging torrents that engulfed the villages in their paths, swept more than 100 people to death in the night, destroyed most of the covered bridges in the state, and worked untold havoc. Houses and mills were washed away, roads gutted out, 7,000 acres of the most fertile fields buried under rock gravel. Power lines were disrupted, water systems smashed, communication broken with most of the state. Rutland was cut off.

The news was sketchy, details uncertain, but the calamity obviously enormous.

In the Globe office the city editor, George Dimond, a Vermonter himself, pored over timetables and maps. He was ready when the first reporter arrived to send him and a photographer to a train going toward Bellows Falls.

Later in the day, as details of the disaster mounted, the managing editor dispatched half the staff toward Vermont. Some never got there, some got lost. In a couple of days most of them had been called back. For ten days the reporter on Dimond's first assignment wandered about Vermont in as near isolation as one could be in the communications industry. His scrapbook kept a record of that experience.

The train could go only as far as Keene, and it was another day before he crossed the Connecticut afoot on a broken bridge and began the problem of exploring the Vermont flood with his photographer. But there was plenty of work on the New Hampshire side, too. The flood was everywhere in the north country, and though the office didn't realize it for several days, it really made no difference where reporters were sent. All the valleys were drowned out.

But the original assignment was to Rutland. The biggest city in Vermont was cut off. Rumors had untold loss of life and destruction there. In Bellows Falls the Globe pair managed to hire a car and driver, after much persuasion of a reluctant garage owner. It was the first of several cars they abandoned in a broken trail up the state, for they soon ran out of roads — or it was impossible to tell which was the road and which the streambed, till a hidden rock made the question academic so far as that car was concerned.

It was a strange, exciting, confusing journey. All the reporter knew for a week was what he could see or pick up from other travelers or in the stricken isolated villages.

The file of telegrams from the office that he picked up at the few points he could find a telegraph working and for some reason saved make a sort of index of that trip. He filed the second day from White River Junction and asked instructions. Winship had taken over the story by then, and his wire read: "Neary going toward Barre from Woodsville, Batchelder from Burlington to Montpelier, Donovan north from Westfield, Mass., Fiske at Greenfield, Merrill at North Conway. You go to Ludlow unless you have other suggestions."

This told him he had penetrated deeper than the rest and was in virgin territory for reportage.

Then a delayed message from the night city editor: "Glad you have progressed so far. Ludlow, Barre and Montpelier main places with which we have no contact. Some Montpelier details coming through AP. Think your best bet would be Ludlow."

A later message from Harry Poor, the night editor: "We are covered on Montpelier and Rutland but not on Ludlow as yet."

At Ludlow he found relatively little damage. The AP was ahead of him into Montpelier. The AP man, William Chaplin, later a war correspondent, had walked the 40 miles in from Burlington only to find that he had lost the fruits of this energy. The wire had been opened an hour before and dispelled the reports of hundreds dead.

On November 8 the Globe man had reached Burlington and must have queried the office again. A curt wire from Harry Poor: "I have no way of knowing what instructions were sent you, if any. Call Sully in the morning if you are in doubt. Your copy is very late." Next night his wire said: "Better tonight. If you could clear up one half hour earlier it would make things easier all around." And things must have got better, for the wire from Poor on the tenth read: "Thanks. You have all night on the Sunday story."

By November 10 the office knew the score better than their man in Vermont and was aware that he was their only resource there. Sully got into the act with encouraging words: "Your Bolton story this morning was perfectly splendid. Dealing with facts several days old when they are human and appealing makes just as good copy as writing about what happened an hour ago." The Globe pair had begun to record the story of one town and village after another. They were all, as Sully said, human tales of drama, tragedy, heroism, and survival.

There were always choices and perplexing alternatives. The reporter must have asked guidance on one, for Sully wired explicit instructions. The choice was between going on a plane survey of the flooded area with the Red Cross or joining an oxcart relief trek up the Mad River Valley to isolated communities; oxen would make better going than horses where the roads had disappeared. Sully's response:

"Not willing you should take any airplane trip. Oxcart expedition up Mad River Valley sounds very promising. Think you could arrange our Burlington man to get us from Red Cross director results of plane reconnaissance. We are very well covered from St. Albans on conditions north of Burlington. Am sure it is more important for you to make your big effort in territory you are now in. Shall expect Mad River Valley story tomorrow night."

Then another wire from Sully, answering a query:

Please do not use story showing apparent lack of imagination of Gov. Weeks in emergency, as outlined in your telegram. At time of great nervous disturbance and suffering we don't believe it is helpful to public or the paper to seem to be stirring up the discordant note. Perhaps you can write around visit of Secretary Davis, telling what he hopes to accomplish, without leaving bad feeling. Your stories every morning most effective. Your outlined story tonight sounds most interesting. Think it would be well if you come home tomorrow unless you vote against it. I intend to leave it entirely to you.

The Globe man didn't return for several more days, for there were untold stories everywhere. If the two were stuck behind a truck loaded with tanks and pipes, it meant a story ahead of restoring the water system and meantime a dangerous health situation from the flooded mains. If they saw smoke curling from a cabin across a gulch where no bridge was left, the smoke told some village family that relatives over there had survived the flood which had carried away their neighbors.

Globe headlines in the old scrapbook suggest the week's travel:

Vermont Towns Still Isolated
Fate of Several Chief Concern of Neighbors

Sunday of Labor All Over Vermont
Task of Restoring Their State Engages All
Tables Spread in Churches Where Hungry Are Fed

Cavendish Saved by Peddler
Arouses Hamlet as Houses Begin to Slip into Chasm
Homes Disappear in Blackness, but not a Life Lost

Shouted Goodbye as Flood Took Them
Bolton Families in their lighted homes swept to death
28 Lost. Roads are being opened

Citizens Fleeing from Waterbury
Forced Inoculation to Stave off Typhoid
Army men in virtual control of Stricken Vermont Town

Zero Feared at Montpelier
Vermont's Stricken Capital Hit by Winter Weather

First Bridge Put Across Winooski
Supplies Coming In — Cold Weather Helps Keep Down Disease

Save Flood Town from Epidemic
Heroic Work at Waterbury Brings Pure Water into Pipes. Wild Night
    Drive After Chlorine

A wire from Sully said: "I will leave word with Harry Poor so name of New Jersey firm will run in your story tonight." That was the firm, the only chlorinator manufacturer in the northeast, whose truck the Globe pair had followed with its life-saving tanks and apparatus and corps of specialists to handle the chlorination.

It was an extraordinary experience with isolation. Some towns, totally cut off, didn't know there had been a flood in the next town. Some blamed the town above for not having warned them. The state was dissolved by the flood into a multitude of separated little commonwealths, each on its own. Their lives centered on the immediate problems of existence. It did not occur to them that other towns had shared their experience.

In Bellows Falls there was a story that Ludlow was burning. One couldn't communicate with Ludlow from there, but the Globe could and found there had been a small fire in Ludlow. When the men of Stowe responded to Waterbury's call for boats they had to rebuild six bridges between the two towns. It was three months before the Central Vermont Railroad ran a train from St. Albans to White River Junction.

In Montpelier the presses washed out of the Argus office with the back wall. In the hotel they had a paper, brought in from Burlington, chained to a table like a telephone book. There was no food in the hotel and the beds were damp, but they'd let you stay there. The hotel has a bronze tablet, head high, where the water stood in the lobby.

The reporter's scrapbook of the flood closes with this note:

> The enduring fact of that Vermont experience was that the one time I produced copy that attracted the largest response was the one time I was operating in practical isolation, beyond direction from the office and with time to explore the story in the depth it needed. This was and is a rare experience for a reporter. It was luck that on the second day when George Dimond called back all the staffers he could reach, I was out of reach and by the next day the office had realized it might be as well to let me stay there.
>
> It has always been my feeling that among the unnecessary limitations on newspaper reporting are the tight strings to the city desk with their detailed assignments. True, there must be a mobile staff available for the emergencies of disaster and unpredictable events. But for the bulk of the content of the paper, the man on the beat, if he is any good, knows better than any desk can, what is the best use he can make of his time, what situations are worth looking into, where the likeliest stories lie. The desk can fill him in with anything they know that's coming up in his area. But they ought to be asking him, not telling him, most of the time. Half the detailed arbitrary assignments are worth less than the stories the man on the beat lays by till some day when he has time for them, which all too frequently he never does.

Part-Time Office Boy

In 1927 a part-time office boy came on to the night side who later had a larger role in the Globe story.

When John Harris entered Harvard in 1927 he had to get a job to help with three younger children besides pay his way at college. The job as night office boy on the Globe paid $3.50 a night. The Globe had a rule that such extra help could be hired only three nights a week. But in sympathy with John's need, managing editor Sullivan let him work six nights. That made $21 a week. He could do the reading for his courses late at night, when the phones stopped ringing with schoolboy sports and most of the copy had moved from the city desk to the night editor.

Harris' first years on the night side were served under genial Walter McCloskey, who had come on the Globe in 1888 at 16 and served as office boy and Roxbury district man, then for many years as police reporter. He was night city editor from 1922 till his death in 1931. A man of enormous bulk which kept him pretty much to his chair at the city desk, he had an easy way with young reporters that created a relaxed climate after the high tension of William Alcott's regime.

One of Harris' friends of those long nights was Joseph S. Ward, Jr., only five years out of M.I.T. but already the highest paid night staff man at $55 a week. Joe would have stories to tell when he came in from a top assignment that fascinated an eager office boy. Joe's career was to help shape Harris' as was also that of another young reporter, Daniel Lynch. Both soon left the Globe for politics, Lynch to be aid to Leverett Saltonstall, then speaker of the Massachusetts House, Ward as aid to William S. Youngman in his campaign for lieutenant governor in 1928. Their friendship at the State House was a factor in Harris' career.

Harris, on graduation from Harvard in 1930, looked to the Globe for a regular job. The rule was that one started as an office boy regardless. But after the summer John was put on the staff. The salary was $21, just what he had earned as a freshman. The girl John was going to marry was a schoolteacher and earning more than $21. So John decided to be a teacher, but that required a master's degree; and that took four courses, which would be $400. He had $300 and took three courses. With $50 his girl lent him he meant to do two half-courses that summer. But, though the depression was deepening in 1931, Mr. Sullivan told John that he could raise his pay $5, but he mustn't tell anyone. The five dollars turned the trick; Harris never finished his M.A. Working nights on the paper, he added $1,000 a year as assistant clerk of a legislative committee, a job Dan Lynch got for him. He earned extra money covering hearings for the State House news service at $3.50 a hearing. In 1932 he married his school teacher.

He covered fires and murders and trials through the thirties and had a chance at political campaigns, starting with the one in 1932 that found Massachusetts Democrats bitterly divided, all the party leaders for Al Smith except James M. Curley, who rode Roosevelt's coat-tails to an inside track with the New Deal. In 1934 Harris covered Curley's successful campaign for governor and in 1936 was sent to the Democratic national convention with the state delegation. In 1940 he helped managing editor L. L. Winship with the general convention story. Then night city editor Charles Merrill asked him to take on the State House assignment for the morning paper.

At the State House Harris's eager-beaver energy found no resistance from the political editor, John D. Merrill, amiably twirling his elegant mustaches over his Sunday column "Politics and Politicians." He had long left the run of the paper reporting to L. D. G. Bentley, who after a dozen years of pursuing politics was glad of an extra pair of legs. Bent had gone to the State House in 1914 when David I. Walsh became governor. Walsh became Bent's close friend throughout the vigorous reform years of his administrations, and Bent continued the friend and confidant of all governors who followed till his death in 1949. Bent and the Globe enjoyed a special privilege, evidently inherited from General Taylor's staff association with Governor Russell.

The Globe and only the Globe had its own office; other reporters shared a press room. Bent's little office was right over the governor's, and governors used to retire there for a bit of respite, and for a gossip with the entertaining Bentley, whose hobby was dramatics. He was for years actor, stage manager, and often playwright for the Players of Newton, and he was something of a politician himself, serving his home-town for several years as alderman and in 1918, at the request of his friend Gov. Samuel McCall, serving on the local draft board.

But by 1940 Bentley was 64. He had become quite hard of hearing. This and his remoteness from the press room tended to isolate him. Two younger men, the Post's Robert Brady and the Herald's William Mullins, sharing the press room, developed a combination that often made the Globe look laggard. But Harris moved in with new pipelines. His friend Daniel Lynch was now Governor Saltonstall's liaison with the legislature and departments and knew all the ropes; Harris quickly learned them and broke up the combination. What Harris learned about the state government then paid off two decades later.

A Beat on Bank Closing

March 4, 1933, was a benchmark in American history, the day that Franklin Roosevelt became president to inaugurate the New Deal. The depression had reached a crisis point. Bank closings had become epidemic, unemployment had spread its distress through the land. Farmers in Iowa were storming courthouses to prevent foreclosures on their land. The Norris amendment had not yet taken effect. There were still four months and a lame duck congress between election and inauguration. It had been a grim interval of waiting for action against deepening discouragement.

On the night desk of the Globe this proved the most exciting experience in Joseph Levin's 40 years as a night copy editor. At 2 A.M., with the final edition put to bed, the copy desk was released except for one man who stood by till the day side came in — just in case — a parallel stint to the lobster trick* on the news side. Joe had

---

* The lobster trick, or lobster shift, from the last deadline for the morning paper until the day side come on. Its Navy equivalent is the dog watch. Its origin has baffled journalistic research. Even H. L. Mencken, old news man, fails to explain it in his *The American Language.*

the late stint when the final March 4 morning edition had gone in. He kept an eye on the wires. In an emergency there could still be a replate. The composing room and the press room would have a skeleton crew standing by.

Joe watched the wires stutter out a report from Illinois. The Governor had ordered the banks closed next day. Well, that hardly justified a replate in Boston, Joe decided. The midwest banks had proved weak, from the long farm depression.

But presently another story: New York State banks were ordered closed. This was something else. Joe rushed around to the late night city editor. This meant Massachusetts banks would have to be closed. But John Weaver Sherman wasn't impressed. The Massachusetts banks were sound. Joe argued: with the great banking center closed down, Bay State banks would surely be affected. He persuaded Sherman to phone the state bank commissioner. It was 3 A.M. and the commissioner was at a meeting somewhere. Well, this was the answer; so, find the commissioner. The late night reporter was dispatched to the Federal Reserve Bank, to discover it all lit up. That's where the bank commissioner was in all-night conference. He had no statement, he said, but there might be one later.

Joe phoned the day editor, George Gavin, who said he'd come right in and suggested that Joe wake up the managing editor. Joe did and got permission to hold all crews and start copy along for an early evening paper. Then he turned to editing all the bank copy that had come in. When Gavin arrived to take charge at 5 A.M. Joe had copy ready to set. It was 8 A.M. when the announcement came. Governor Ely, in Washington for the inauguration, had been all night in bank crisis huddles that led him to call the Lieutenant Governor to issue a bank holiday proclamation.

The Globe was out on the street with it by the time commuters arrived to work; Saturday was then a working day. An early arriving Globe reporter had the interesting experience of hailing a bank president acquaintance to tell him his bank was closed. The Herald night side hadn't held and the Globe was a couple of hours ahead of the evening Traveler in getting the news on the street. Joe Levin waited up to read George Gavin's extra-early first edition before going home to bed. The banner head was:

> Two-Day Bank Holiday in Bay State
> Ely in Washington Orders Action Conforming With New York
> Acting Gov. Bacon Proclaims Holiday at 8 a.m. Proclamation

Joe had been five years on the night desk then, after five years on Hartford and New Bedford papers. He was to serve another 35 years and become the right hand of a series of night editors. But March 4 at 3 A.M. is what he remembered as the most exciting hour of his career.

It had been a crisis night in Washington. An air of suspense gripped newspaper offices Inauguration Day. As the ceremonies began, the newspapers had no advance text of the President's inaugural. What did that mean? Had he rewritten it after the night's urgent conferences? Had it some ominous disclosures that needed protection from leaking out? The vacuum was filled with the cynical observations of waiting correspondents who talked of Roosevelt as a boy scout or in Alice Longworth's terms as "three-fourths Eleanor and one-fourth mush." He probably had his speech written on his cuffs.

The front page of even the final edition of that evening's Globe showed the unprepared state of the correspondents. Nowhere on the front page was there any reference to what became the most famous line of that inaugural: "The only thing to fear is fear itself." The final headline was: "Roosevelt Tells Plans to Meet the Emergency."

But at the Globe reporters hung on the radio as Americans were doing across the land. One made notes and got two columns into the paper on an inside page. The famous line is there, and that casual story of the way it came over the radio has what the front page didn't have — a reaction to the "clear strong confident tones . . . of new courage for new leadership," what the nation heard and how it heard it.

Roosevelt on Sunday extended the bank holiday through the week and laid down the rules for qualifying banks to reopen.

Between Saturday morning and Monday morning the tone of the front pages and the editorial pages changed drastically. James Morgan's pre-inaugural story carried the headline "Officialdom Fears Roosevelt Economy." It described the gloom in Washington over anticipated heavy slashes in the budget under the new administration's "compelling mandate to reduce the cost of government." Roosevelt had campaigned for a balanced budget.

But on Monday morning Mr. Morgan was describing "the vigorous hand that has grasped the dangling reins of leadership . . . He lost no time in meeting his own call for action. He did not relax his grip even though it was Sunday." A second urgent cabinet meeting on the Sabbath dealt with the urgency.

The Globe March 4 editorial on "The President" said: "Never was the stage better set for the advent of a leader. Never were so many Americans eager to have a President do well. They expect strong sure positive action without delay."

Lindbergh Trial

The Lindbergh kidnapping trial of Bruno Hauptmann in 1935 filled many columns of newspaper space for weeks. The Globe was the only Boston newspaper to cover it with a staff reporter. It was a bizarre and disillusioning assignment. The press descended on Flemington, New Jersey, in such hordes as till then had only been seen at the Scopes trial in Dayton, Tennessee, a decade earlier. The nearly senile rustic judge totally lacked capacity to control the invasion. His court room was a shambles. The sheriff sold press seats, claiming this was to cover the expense of installing a pine board bleacher arrangement; seat space was 16 inches, at ten dollars. He issued three classes of tickets in different colors indicating their relative vantage points. Both prosecution and defense held daily press conferences after court every afternoon to fill in the reporters on their plans for the morrow.

One New York Hearst paper had a staff of 16 at the trial. It was a field day for the cafe society type of gossip writer and for sob sisters of all varieties, who came into court daily to find a new "angle" on the story rather than to report the testimony. It took ingenuity and often imagination to contrive these angles. The working reporters were annoyed to have this flock of trained seals leave before court adjourned each afternoon to take a train that would land them back in New York by the cocktail hour.

But one of the noted reporters of the day, Damon Runyon, sat it out, writing a diligent, fluent longhand account of the endless drama. A young reporter from the New York Herald Tribune established his reputation with his writing from Flemington: Joseph Alsop wrote a daily feature as a "side bar" to the main story that another reporter handled. The dramatis personae abounded in incredible characters, just made for Alsop's descriptive talent. The most eccentric was "Jafsie" Condon, who had become involved through some concept of having a mission to solve the crime. He had been at one phase an apparently innocent go-between, believing he could recover the Lindbergh baby by gaining the confidence of both the law and the kidnapper. "Jafsie" on the witness stand was as unbelievable as the story he had to tell. Joe Alsop dealt with "Jafsie" as Dickens would have.

The trial ended in a great journalistic snafu. In the intense competition to be first with the verdict, all sorts of contrivances were arranged. One wire service persuaded a constable in charge of the jury to accept three press cards which indicated the three possible verdicts: white for acquittal, red for a life sentence, blue for death. He was to pull the appropriate card from his pocket as the jury filed in; flustered, he pulled out the wrong card.

Others set up other signals, such as shifting a handkerchief from one pocket to another. The Globe reporter assumed some of these deals would result in the Globe hearing the verdict flashed before he could report it. But there was still time before first edition and he had a story to write. He plodded along recapitulating the final day, to be ready with all but the lead. The jury filed in around 10:30. Just comfortable time. He relaxed, as telegraph boys began darting around. But his boy sat in the doorway eyeing him in the suspense of the wait through the ritual until the foreman announced the verdict. Then just a raised pencil and a scribbled "flash-guilty-death-lead follows" and the boy was off with it to the wire room in the basement. In a few moments the boy was back with an amazing message from the office: "Congratulations on being first with the news here."

This seemed incredible and was only explained later. Actually the Chicago Tribune man's signals worked correctly and the Trib's New York affiliate, the Daily News, had the story first in New York; being right on a deadline, they got out truckloads of it. Then in came the AP erroneous report and, doubtless from sad experience, the Daily News figured the AP must be right and their story wrong. They pulled back their papers and replated, just in time to be caught with the AP correction. The AP man on the story was fired, an unjust sacrifice to unscrupulous competition. Evidently the first AP report did not get beyond New York before it had to be corrected. Anyway it didn't get to the Globe. Of course that fiasco delayed the AP report longer than if they had just taken the news in stride.

Another spectacular trial, nearer home, afforded another moral for reporting. In Lynn, less than 20 minutes from Boston, a moving picture theater had been held up January 2, 1934, and a bill-poster in the theater shot and killed. Three days later two men were arrested, Clement Molway, 19, and Louis Berrett, 23. Both were Boston taxi drivers, so their photographs were on file with the police. Seven or eight persons had identified them as two of the three men who had held them prisoners in the theater.

The Boston area had had what the newspapers called a crime wave. The crimes followed a pattern, and it looked to the city desk as though these arrested taxi drivers accounted for it. So the trial, at Salem, was staff covered.

The state's case was largely a procession of eight eyewitnesses. They had had a good chance to get an impression of the holdup men, for they had been stuck in the theater manager's office as they came in one by one the next morning, between 8:30 and 10:30, while the holdup men were waiting for the manager so they could force him to open the safe. A mirror on the office wall had provided clear images of the two men on several occasions. The taxi drivers offered an alibi but it sounded very thin; their business had been slow that morning, and the drive to Lynn was short. One alibi witness recalled seeing one of them at the time they needed to prove their absence from Lynn, but the place was an all-night diner where the witness had to admit he was drinking black coffee against a hangover from a hard night. He'd noticed Molway at the other end of the counter. That didn't help much. It looked like a tight case against Molway and Berrett and the Globe reporting indicated this.

Testimony was completed at the end of a day, but next morning Judge Thomas F. Hammond announced that final arguments would be suspended for a day. District Attorney Hugh Cregg mysteriously disappeared.

It was the next evening when court resumed, the jury was summoned back, and the District Attorney recalled his procession of eyewitnesses. They all agreed they could have been mistaken. In 20 minutes the foreman pronounced a "not guilty" verdict. The reporters in the courtroom were briefly mystified — but their offices already knew the answer. The day before, three men had been arrested in a New York hotel, Abraham Faber and Murton and Irving Millen, and the saga of their crimes included the Lynn theater holdup. They were later convicted. The evidence against them was so strong — their bedrooms were arsenals — that their defense was insanity. But this failed to impress the jury. Two years later Berrett and Molway were awarded $2,500 each by the Massachusetts legislature as "compensation." They looked, superficially, very like the Millen brothers.

The Boston American engaged Molway as a reporter in the Millen trial to record his impressions on how it seemed to be on the other side of the dock. The Globe reporter was embarrassed to meet Molway, but the taxi driver was a big, hearty, easy-going fellow. "Your stories would have hanged us for sure," he said. "We said we'd really commit murder if we ever met you outside." It was a sharp lesson that even eyewitnesses are not infallible.

Maine and Vermont for Landon

1936 was the year of the polls, the year that the Literary Digest destroyed itself by depending on a poll of people in telephone books, automobile registries, and such lists that excluded the lower income levels. It was the first time the Globe used the Gallup poll on a presidential campaign.

Dr. George Gallup had turned his attention from market analysis to political polling and interested leading newspapers in publishing his results. Just before Washington's birthday, a Gallup poll showed Gov. Alf Landon of Kansas leading the list of Republican presidential prospects. Lyons was diverted from a planned family ski weekend to fly to Kansas and start a series on the Governor. Topeka seemed deserted that Saturday. No governor, no Republican chairman, nobody to talk to. The reporter left word all around but had to reconcile himself to resorting to clippings for his opening article for Monday. But Sunday afternoon brought a telephone call. The Governor and his highway commissioner would be coming by at four o'clock. They had been horseback riding and came in their riding togs. The first thing Landon said was: "If you write that I was in riding breeches, don't say it was Sunday." The reporter was brought to swift realization of what it meant to be governor of Kansas.

Before the Landon series was finished, the office wired to go on and visit the other Republican candidates: Frank Knox, publisher of the Chicago Daily News, Sen. John Dickinson of Iowa. This would balance things up. Newspapermen were intrigued with one item about publisher Knox. A columnist on his paper, Howard Vincent O'Brien, wrote a piece about his boss to the effect that he was quite the wrong temperament to be president. The word on the News staff was that Knox enjoyed it and took no offense. This tended to warm newspapermen to Knox, who became the vice presidential nominee.

The Globe held to its nonpartisan posture through the 1936 campaign. But the Symposium the Sunday before the election spelled out the issue the Republicans had raised against the new Social Security Act. It quoted Landon that "the Social Security Act is unjust, unworkable, stupidly drafted and wastefully financed . . . Our old people are only too apt to find the cupboard bare" and Roosevelt's succinct rejoinder, "Our workers will not be fooled. To sabotage the Social Security Act is to sabotage labor."

James Morgan's article that day was on "Governor Landon's Problems" and pretty clearly indicated Landon's defeat. "If a Landslide It is FDR" ran the headline. "Landon's only chance if it is close."

Mike Hennessy, who was with Landon, wrote the same day under the headline "Landon Reporters See FDR Win. Feel Governor's Advisers Hold Landon Back." These advisers, Hennessy wrote, "pushed him to hew the standpat line."

The Gallup final poll published that day gave Roosevelt 315 sure electoral votes and counted only Maine, New Hampshire, and Vermont as sure for Landon. It was wrong about New Hampshire.

The Globe explained "Where Literary Digest and Gallup Polls Disagree." The Digest was giving Landon 54 percent of the vote. "Gallup follows the principles of scientific sampling. The Digest draws its names from telephone books, automobile owners . . . Gallup includes all income levels."

The most precise evidence of the landslide came from a poll the Globe made itself in the little Berkshire town of New Ashford, which had achieved note by being the first town in the country to report its returns. A Globe reporter took some ballots and a sealed box and knocked on every door in town, population 96. On the Sunday before election, the Globe gave a whole page to the straw poll in New Ashford. The story began: "President Roosevelt will receive more than double his 1932 strength in this town, according to a straw poll taken by the Globe this past week . . . The battle for New Ashford has increased registration from 36 to 48. It has increased Democratic strength from 8 to 20 of the votes to be counted Tuesday . . . The President will run ahead of the State ticket and get as many Republican votes as Democratic."

The report accounted for every voter and gave Roosevelt 20 to Landon's 28. Since in 1932 this Republican town had given Roosevelt only eight votes to Hoover's 28, a sweeping overturn was clearly indicated. The actual vote in New Ashford came out Roosevelt 19, Landon 26. The Globe in a box proclaimed the accuracy of its prediction.

The "one-party press" first gained currency to describe the extreme onesided political allegiance of newspaper publishers in 1936. In Massachusetts the only daily newspapers supporting Roosevelt were the Berkshire Eagle and the Springfield Evening News, a condition that held through the 1940 and 1944 elections. Each time, Roosevelt carried the state. The publishers were going one way and their readers the other; reporters generally agreed with their readers rather than with their own employers. Even Pulitzer's St. Louis Post-Dispatch supported the Republican candidate against the New Deal. City rooms everywhere told with relish of the notice that managing editor O. K. Bovard put up on the Post-Dispatch bulletin board when Roosevelt carried all states but Maine and Vermont:

Country	46
Country Club	2

The Massachusetts voter's capacity for splitting his ticket was sharply evidenced in the 1936 election. Roosevelt carried the state by 174,000; the Democratic candidate for governor, Charles Hurley, squeaked in by 28,000; but James M. Curley, who had ridden the Roosevelt bandwagon to the governorship in 1934, lost the Senate race by 135,000 to 34-year-old Henry Cabot Lodge in Lodge's first statewide campaign.

Contemporaries and Competition

The depression of the thirties was a long ordeal for the Globe. With all accounts cut down, it lost ground in the intense competitive field — five morning and four evening papers. By the middle of the decade it had fallen to third paper and it only began regaining lost ground at the end of the period with new methods and new men.

The rotund Globe man who had exulted in proclaiming the greatest circulation in New England had been retired from the front page.

The problem was both in the business and in the staff. The Herald, with a new building in 1931, could outprint the Globe, could put out two news sections of 80 pages Sunday to the Globe's 64. This allowed it to display its wares in neat Sunday sections, while the Globe's superior sports department was buried in the news sections and its features spilled through the run of the paper. For the only time in its history even the Sunday Globe lost circulation, though it remained double the Herald, which in its morning and evening had gone 30,000 ahead of the Globe by 1935.

The Globe never went into the red but came very close to it. In the trough of depression, 1936, net earnings for distribution to all the Taylors and Jordan heirs was under $50,000. Doubtless only the close family relations prevented a stockholders' mutiny. Salaries were cut that year. Charles H. Taylor retired in 1937, to relieve the business of one top salary. W. O. Taylor took his son Moseley, then New York advertising representative, off the Globe payroll onto his own.

Forced economy brought publisher and managing editor into daily conference on the news budget, which was held so tight that every out-of-town assignment was an issue for consideration. It was cheaper to buy syndicated matter than to hire staff replacements. Winship bought all the columns and other syndicated features he could get his hands on.

W.O. had so strong a feeling of his role as trustee of the Globe that he would not borrow from a bank. At one point in 1936 his arithmetic on Wednesday showed the Globe would be $60,000 short for Friday's payroll. He called in his circulation manager, Fred O'Neal, and sent him out to ask the news dealers to oversubscribe their Globe account. All O'Neal told them was that the Globe needed the money. They came through with it in a day and a half.

The Globe finally even resorted to contests, which General Taylor had rejected as artificial stimulants 40 years earlier. But its New York advertising agency warned that if it dropped to fourth position national advertisers would lose interest. Contests, however, were not enough. It took long overdue reorganization in 1937 to start turning the tide.

Meantime stringency increased caution. The Globe exhibited less vitality than the other papers in basic treatment of the news. The note of caution had prevailed in the police strike, the Sacco-Vanzetti case, and the book banning era. In the thirties the Globe took a bystander's attitude toward the regime of James M. Curley as mayor and governor. It remained for the Post to take the lead in defeating Curley by supporting young Maurice Tobin for mayor in 1937.

The Globe was doubtless sustained through the hard times by its well-earned reputation for fairness, balance, and impartiality. The Globe management had erected fair dealing to a business principle. But what the staff perceived as the shortcomings of the paper at this period grew from the fact that these sound principles of business also governed the news and editorial policy, spelling caution as total policy. The principle of impartiality often seemed carried to the point of forfeiture of civic responsibility.

There was no stated policy of "don'ts" or "keep-outs." News by its nature offers such a universal and largely unpredictable range that relatively little of its exploration runs against inhibitions. The limits were vague, undefined. One learned them by osmosis or a sharp experience. When a staff reporter in the 1930's wrote a piece for the Nation on Curleyism, Charles Taylor berated him: "You'll lose all your following." When automobile workers in Detroit undertook the first "sit-down" strike in 1937, this was an innovation that commanded national attention. It was a natural subject for a special article or for staff coverage. But the Globe had no appetite to dramatize such a revolutionary development. "Lyons thinks he's going to get to cover the sit-down strike," one knowing editor chuckled to another.

But the more fundamental failure of this simplistic Globe policy was that it ignored the development of its own community. The grandsons of Irish immigrants were going to college and into the professions. They were making their own critical judgments of the arts and of politics. The Globe in the thirties and even later ignored this in its treatment of news, in its definitions of what was news, in the very structure of the organization. It offered no critical guidance in any of the arts, save music, a field least associated with advertising. Any art gallery exhibition received an appreciative notice, nothing that could be called criticism. Plays were reported, not reviewed, and the same was true of movies, the same with books on such intermittent occasions as books received any attention at all. For the most part they did not. The Herald, and the Transcript, had established literary sections. The Globe management accepted the business view that there wasn't enough book advertising to profit another paper entering this field. The same man handled theater reviews who solicited theater advertising. The approach was commercial; and it was equally so in the field of education. At school opening time a special section would be "educational." But this meant featuring the commercial business schools, art schools, secretarial, trade, accounting. There would be nothing in such a section as to how the youngster might find guidance or financial aid in selecting a college or preparing for it — and this right into the time when education was burgeoning as the largest industry in the country, affecting everybody in one way or another, as student, parent, teacher, or taxpayer.

But despite staff chafing at inhibitions and missed opportunities, the Globe remained much the most interesting and satisfying paper to work on. If it preferred human interest stories to investigations, this had its compensations.

It provided opportunity for writing by the younger staff members and the writing improved with better educated staff. The Sunday paper under Winship particularly afforded an outlet. Every new public figure or college president was introduced with a profile in the Sunday paper. It had space for background pieces on the events of the week: Carlyle Holt and Henry Harris on public affairs; Joseph Dinneen, John Barry, and Lyons on the whole kaleidoscope of the passing scene; Donald Willard with a special whimsy of his own; Katherine Bartlett with a penchant for animal stories; and Willard DeLue, indefatigably exploring for one interesting editorial series after another — all were writing in both daily and Sunday papers.

The flexibility of an office that had not become compartmentalized gave the writers a special dimension of variety and interest. Science was becoming news and the depression produced a ferment of labor to organize. Government work projects were launched to cope with spreading unemployment. The office saw no reason to deal with these new fields as specialties. A versatile reporter was expected to move from science to labor to public housing or the financial plight of the cities; for a week or a month or sometimes longer he did indeed specialize, then moved on to another story. Harvard's tercentenary in 1936 brought a new emphasis on science. For 72 days the Globe ran an editorial page series, "The World's Wise Men," brief profiles on the scholars and scientists who were to participate in the exercises at Cambridge.

The fundamental problem of course was that Boston was oversupplied with newspapers; and now in this thinnest period with all advertising budgets drastically cut there were more than there would ever be again. The intensity of local competition is graphically demonstrated in the retail advertising rate, which remained unchanged at 30 cents a line from 1920 to 1950 while the general rate was doubling to 60 cents and the national rising to 70.

Competitive practices led the Globe Sunday editor to withhold from his feature section that went to press Thursday night any notable exclusive or timely story, else he might read it in the Post before Sunday.

In the Boston journalistic spectrum the Globe, independent in politics, was flanked by the Republican Herald and Democratic Post and its competition lay primarily with them. In tempo and tone, the kaleidoscope ran from the idealistic Christian Science Monitor, the sedate Transcript, conservative Herald, and middle-ground Globe in rising decibels of sensationalism to the Traveler, Post, and Hearst's evening American, morning Record, and Sunday Advertiser.

The Post was partisan Democrat, except that it was pro-Coolidge in the twenties and anti-New Deal in the thirties and forties. That pretty well canceled it out in national affairs. But it was influentially Democratic in local affairs and its vigorous managing editor, Clifton Carberry, wrote for the man in the street and the politician in his party caucus in blunt, plain-speaking political editorials that would run on the front page if the issue was hot enough, signed with his pseudonym, John Bantry.

The Sunday Post, ably developed under Charles Wingate, encouraged the individuality of feature writers and gave them liberal space, often a whole page to an article. Kenneth Roberts wrote for the Post from 1909 to 1917. Olin Downes from 1906 to 1924 wrote features, besides serving as music critic, until he left for the New York Times. There he joined Brooks Atkinson, who had left the Transcript for the Times in 1922. That year Bill Cunningham began a 20-year stint on the Post that gave free rein to an unflagging energy and free-wheeling style that ranged from sports to cosmic events.

The Post under E. A. Grozier also took up the kind of campaign the Globe had pushed in its first decade. Publisher Grozier campaigned for free transfers on the street cars and for cheaper gas, and to cut guaranteed dividends of the West End Railway from eight to seven percent. The Post had won a Pulitzer Prize in 1921 exposing a flagrant financial trap for the gullible, manipulated by a slick operator named Ponzi. The Globe had ignored the Ponzi frenzy until General Taylor in impatience ordered that the Globe pick up the Post story.

But E. A. Grozier died in 1924, three years after the death of General Taylor. Unlike the General, Grozier failed to establish a journalistic line. His son Richard, an invalid, rarely entered the Post office and soon placed its management in the hands of a committee of senior executives. The dynamics of the first Grozier deserted the Post. Its circulation had reached some 540,000 by 1918, reputedly the largest in America. This was partly by holding to one cent right through World War I till 1918, while the morning Globe and Herald were two cents. But by 1930 it had fallen to 375,000 daily and below the Globe on Sunday, even though it held the Sunday price to seven cents for nine years after the Globe and Herald had gone to ten cents in 1920. It held its daily two-cent price ten years after the Globe and Herald went to three cents in 1937, and again in 1948 it held back a year behind the others in going to five cents. But undercutting the price did not save it from a gradual decline until bought in the 1950's by a promoter who soon ran it into the ground to expiration in 1956.

The Herald after 1931 had the only modern plant in town. It had become the businessman's paper under the sophisticated editorship of Robert Lincoln O'Brien, who left it in 1928. He had been the Transcript's Washington correspondent and then its editor till 1910. Then Boston financial interests reorganized and refinanced the Herald, which had failed after the long, able tenure of John Holmes ended in 1906; they installed O'Brien as editor. The intellectual appeal of Philip Hale's music

and drama criticism and his extraordinary column lingered even after his retire-
men in 1931.

The Herald's editorial page had a metropolitan tone under the able Frank
Buxton, who won a Pulitzer Prize in 1925 and had as colleague the scholarly
Lauriston Bullard, whose editorial to reopen the Sacco-Vanzetti case received the
Pulitzer award for 1927. But the character of the paper reflected its financial control. A major stockholder, Sidney W. Winslow, was also president of the United
Shoe Machinery Corporation. It was Winslow who recommended to the stockholders in 1928 that they accept an offer of the International Paper & Power Company to buy half the stock. The power company at the same time bought into 14
other newspapers including the Brooklyn Daily Eagle, Chicago News, Knicker-
bocker Press, Albany News, and others from Ithaca to Tampa, for a total investment of eight million dollars. It asserted that its sole interest was to insure a market
for newsprint. But power accounted for 54 percent of its profits to 25 percent from
newsprint.

The Federal Trade Commission opened hearings on this power invasion of journalism in May 1929 and soon broadened the inquiry into propaganda for the power
industry by subsidized newspapers and writers. The Globe, May 1, 1929, reported
some of the testimony. But the Hearst papers exploited it more fully. Super power
systems were extending their empires across the land, obtaining control of local
electric companies to milk their profits by "management services" that escaped state
regulation by their interstate setups. Robert O'Brien by then had resigned from
the Herald. Testifying before the Trade Commission he said his resignation had
nothing to do with the power company connection but resulted from "intervening
ideas and the influence of others." He testified that when he ran an editorial against
government ownership by one F. G. H. Gordon, and letters to the editor on the
same theme by Gordon, he did not know that the writer was on the payroll of
the National Electric Light Association. The publicity to the power company's
purchase of newspaper stock made its role untenable. It divested itself of its Herald
stock, which was put in a voting trust under officers of the First National Bank and
the United Shoe Machinery Company.

The Herald had annexed the Traveler in 1912 to replace the evening Herald and
in 1917 it absorbed the old Journal. The Traveler in a spectacular coup had raided
the Post in 1920 of a whole corps of its feature writers and feature editors and
thereafter competed with the Post and Hearst in sensationalism. In 1935 the morning Herald circulation was 123,000 to the morning Globe's 126,000. On Sunday
the Herald was 142,000 to the Sunday Globe's 304,000. But the Traveler was
170,000 to the evening Globe's 136,000.

With the biggest bank holding half the stock of the Herald-Traveler, those papers
had an inside track on financial advertising and much other business advertising,
inevitably affected by the pervasive influence of the bank as consultant and member of boards of directors. The Herald-Traveler had a combination advertising rate
that gave a bonus for advertising in the Traveler. The Traveler in the late 1930's
built up a "Blue Streak" final edition featuring financial news, put on extra staff
and got it on the street earlier, and took a big lead in the final edition. But the
Sunday Globe was nearly three times the circulation of the Herald, and Globe classified advertising moved ahead on the Globe's policy during World War II paper

Newspaper Row in 1940.

rationing, to treat the small and large advertiser evenly. The Herald restricted classified ads to put space at the disposal of the big stores.

W. O. Taylor and after him Davis Taylor had occasion to keep fending off offers to the Globe. After Robert Choate was made publisher of the Herald-Traveler in 1941, he became convinced that the competitive situation in Boston was uneconomic. From the mid-1940's he was constantly proposing mergers to the Globe, to eliminate one morning and one evening paper. The Taylors would never listen.

In the mid-1950's Samuel Newhouse, acquiring newspapers from one end of the country to the other, made a proposition to acquire the Globe and Herald-Traveler and merge them, a pattern he followed in numerous other cities. The Globe was uninterested and when the offering figure was raised made it plain that they wouldn't be interested at any figure.

Attorney Joseph Welch had called repeatedly on W.O. and on the Globe counsel, Frank Leahy, in the years following World War II to say that Joseph P. Kennedy wanted to buy the Post and the Globe. The answer was always that the Globe was not for sale. "Then there can never be anything for the Post," Welch said, "because Kennedy won't buy the Post without the Globe."

W.O.'s attitude was equally firm against buying another paper. When Richard Johnson came to the end of the road with the Transcript in 1941 he tried to sell it to W. O.

Davis Taylor remembered the meeting and the direct, succinct interview.

"What circulation have you?"

"I can promise you only 8,000."

"How much are you losing a year?"

"Something over $300,000."

"How much do you owe on newsprint?"

"$350,000."

"How much are your Boston taxes in arrears?"

"Almost half a million."

"And how much behind are you on payroll?"

"It is in the thousands."

W.O. concluded the interview with: "The reputation of the Transcript is still a great temptation. But I just don't see marrying it with the evening Globe and taking on your employees. I would rather you tried to sell it somewhere else."

Davis Taylor recalls a similar meeting some ten years later when the Post was failing under trustee management. Chester Steadman of the Post, an old friend of W.O., asked the Globe publisher to a meeting of the three Post trustees at the Parker House.

"We want the Globe to buy the Post for $7,500,000, which we think is a fair figure," Steadman opened.

"Chester," the Globe publisher replied, "I want you to know that I don't want on my conscience putting Boston newspapermen out of their jobs when I think there is a chance for their paper."

Then, "How much did you make last year?"

"We lost half a million."

This disclosed extraordinary weakness in management in a period of small, tight papers.

"You aren't going to like what I'm about to say, Chester," W.O. said. "But if you really want to sell the paper, go out and raise about $3,000,000 on the securities I understand the Post has, for a new building."

Steadman reddened at this rebuff and didn't speak to his old friend for six months. Meantime he tried to sell the Post to the Knights, the Cowles, and the Chicago Tribune and unloaded it finally for about three million dollars on John Fox, the promoter who ran it into bankruptcy in the next few years.

But W.O. was also insistent that the Globe do nothing to hasten the Post's end. He gave strict orders that none of the Post staff were to be hired until the Post was definitely out of business. The result was that the Herald had its pick of Post staffers seeking a haven before the end.

Hearst's American had acquired the old Advertiser for its wire service franchise and used its name on its Sunday edition. In 1921 it had converted the Advertiser's evening appendage, the Record, into a morning tabloid that imported the Walter Winchell column and such other elements of that type of New York journalism as New England could stand. In 1930 the American had a daily circulation of 260,000, the Record some 300,000, and the Sunday Advertiser 467,000.

At the opposite end of the spectrum the Christian Science Monitor, established in 1908, had its special appeal to a small local audience for its first-class foreign news and its idealistic approach to journalism. But, doubtless limited by its name as well as by its inhibitions, it never attained half of even the Transcript's small circulation locally. The Monitor sold more papers in California than New England. Its news treatment became more professional under Erwin Canham, but it was not a competitive factor in the 1930's.

Much the most distinctive of the Boston newspapers was the Transcript. Archaic but intensely individualistic, its special character, like the purple windowpanes of Beacon Street, reflected the atmosphere of old Boston. The Transcript comforted the Brahmin old stock editorially and with a cultural menu that dealt authoritatively with genealogy, grandfather clocks, the departed chestnut tree and the Constitution, which it printed in full for a full page every Wednesday.

Transcript makeup was as changeless as Bulfinch architecture. Vertical headlines persisted to the end, one-column width with as many banks down the column as the weight of the story demanded, and front page ads, also of modest one-column size. One ad of Jay's specialty store, consisting of a silhouette of a woman's profile, was almost a Transcript trademark for many years.

The Transcript offered a special fillip in H. T. Parker's drama criticism and symphony reviews, written with a Carlylean vehemence and vocabulary to match his red-lined military cape and renowned irascibility. H.T.P. was a legend. In William McDonald it had a mature and imaginative writer to come up with a Saturday night feature of substance and literary quality.

Its politics was antediluvian. But it was also committed to accuracy. After valiantly denouncing the Democrats throughout an election campaign, it would publish on the Saturday night before election the forecast of its State political editor, Wendell Howie, that the Democrats would sweep the State on Tuesday — and he'd be right.

In an era before the modern column, the Transcript was fairly efflorescent with special columns: "The Listener," "Nomad," "Saturday Night Thoughts," weekly essays by staff editors for Saturday night, when the price went up from three to five cents for a big weekend paper of reviews and features. The religious editor contributed the Saturday night thoughts. In the twenties and thirties he was the

Reverend Albert Dieffenbach, a liberal Unitarian minister who also had a department, "The Churchman Afield," irreverently dubbed by the staff "The Churchman Afloat." Nobody enjoyed this joshing more than Dieffenbach himself, a cheerful social philosopher whose liberalism was the most pronounced of the Transcript's inconsistencies. Dieff delighted in the Transcript's crotchets and in the extraordinary collection of characters cooped in its loftlike warrens over Dunne's tailor shop; "Editors, one flight up — Reporters, two flights up."

The personality that sustained the Transcript in its special character was George Mandell. He was the last of the founding line, from 1830. He had come into the office right out of Harvard in 1889, had succeeded his father, Samuel Mandell, as publisher in 1914. The vitality of the paper was so much Mandell's that after his death in 1934 it collapsed almost like the one-hoss shay. It survived him with progressive anemia only four years. Yet Mandell had chosen to serve more as moderator than director. He had presided over a loose association of independent departments to influence an almost imperceptible transition to strengthen the features and expand the news. The utopian reformer mugwump Edward Clement had retired as editor in 1903 to be followed by the conservative Robert Lincoln O'Brien. He in 1910 was succeeded by the flamboyant nationalist James T. Williams, followed in 1925 by gentle, scholarly Henry Claus.

But the substance and character of the paper remained essentially unchanged. Joseph Chamberlin, whose Transcript days paralleled Mandell's, described the unique system of autonomous departments as a sort of federated republic. Departmental independence was tolerated even when it resulted in inconsistency in policy. Reporters wrote their own headlines, and selection of front page position was by caucus and debate or who got there first. To any expression of surprise at such a system, George Mandell would say "It works well."

Indeed it did. Transcript prosperity had grown out of all proportion to its small circulation, never much over its 30,359 average of 1935. Advertising rose in volume and value in recognition of the quality of its circulation.

Mandell was a sportsman, master of the hunt of the Myopia Hunt Club. He was a connoisseur of sports news and had the best sports staff in town. He selected the sports pictures himself and saw that they had the space they needed. With the Transcript's superior paper and the clear imprint that its small press run permitted, Transcript pictures had such definition you could almost see the red in the huntsmen's coats and the color of the Marblehead racing sails.

The Transcript and Globe were always friendly. This may have come about in part from absence of close rivalry between the mass circulation paper and the one with a select, small clientele. But also, both were family-owned papers whose roots grew deeper in their community while other papers were changing managements, changing hands. Transcript and Globe managements respected each other's business principles. Only a block apart on Washington Street, their staffs tended to patronize the same lunchrooms, most often the cafeteria Laboratory Kitchen that lay between them. There in the 1920's Globe men met Henry Cabot Lodge, a neophyte among his Transcript colleagues. There in the thirties Globe men came to appreciate the droll humor of Charles Morton, who later put his Transcript days into a book that was a classic account of that paper's idiosyncrasies.

The Transcript had a brief resurrection after 1938. Richard N. Johnson, a New England textile executive, undertook to refinance it and with support of a few old

Boston families, among them Bemises and Lawrences, continued it to 1941. But it was a bizarre anticlimax. Lincoln O'Brien, young publisher of a Cape Cod paper, was brought in as publisher. The price was raised to five cents. The policy was turned inside out, from ultraconservative to New Deal. Comic strips were introduced. All this lost the old readers without gaining new ones. Circulation fell to 8,000 before Johnson gave up trying either to salvage or sell it.

The long depression had made advertisers look harder at their markets. One of the quickest answers to market research was that all readers of the evening Transcript also read either the Herald or morning Globe. The Transcript had become a supplemental paper to an advertiser and so a luxury.

Winship Takes Over

In 1937 the generation gap on the Globe was closed in reorganization of the editorial department. William D. Sullivan, now 75, retired as managing editor. City editor George Dimond, even older, was moved to the Exchange Room.

Laurence Winship came out of the Sunday Room to be managing editor. His classmate Ambler Welch was promoted from the day copy desk to Sunday editor. Charles Merrill, who had joined the paper 25 years before, became city editor, and his Harvard classmate Lucien Thayer was assigned a new role as photographic editor that recognized the arrival of the visual arts. Youth was recognized, too, in the appointment of Alexander Haviland at 33 as night city editor.

This was a whole generation of change, that brought vitality back into the paper and gradually restored it to its earlier position.

Winship left a Sunday paper that, in his 19 years' editorship, had become the main strength of the Globe. Its circulation had passed the Sunday Post and was more than double the Sunday Herald. It had developed its own distinctive character and pattern.

Managing editor now meant what it said for the first time in 40 years. Winship, taking over the news department, kept direction of features and editorials. For the 20 years before he became managing editor, Winship's desk was the point of origin of most moves and major assignments. If a reporter received a telegram, "As soon as you can shake that story W.O. would like to get you to Washington," he learned to read "Winship" for "W.O." But it was all the same. The city desk would receive a parallel note: "W.O. would like . . . put on the Washington story." To a reluctant reporter on one such occasion Winship said, "The Globe ought not to have the same national story as the Haverhill Gazette," that is, the AP report.

The new Sunday editor, Ambler Welch, was responsible for the big feature section on Sunday. The Sunday department was able for the first time to obtain a separate staff of a few writers for the Sunday paper. Till then Sunday features had been written by reporters drafted off the city staff for a week at a time.

Welch, known as "Doc" from school days evidently because his father was the family physician to much of Quincy, went to Thayer Academy in Braintree and on to Harvard, class of 1911, where he and Winship and Gluyas Williams, all W's, fell into the same sections that brought lifelong intimacy.

Welch's first job was in the Old Corner Book Store, but this was tame work and in a few months he found a job on the evening Traveler. He arrived at the Globe by a roundabout route that resulted from a fluke in reporting the Reverend C. V. T. Richeson murder case of 1911. Like other papers, the Traveler assigned a reporter to the jail to keep tabs on developments in the Richeson case pending trial. Welch would telephone in visits or other items, which a rewrite man would take down; he usually had several bits to phone in. One day after he had telephoned several items, defense counsel arrived with the father of Richeson's fiancée for a discussion of defense plans. This indicated that the influential family of his prospective bride was standing by the young minister, accused of poisoning the country choirgirl he had made pregnant. This was much more important than the previous items of the day's grist. But the rewrite man taking Welch's call either stupidly or lazily just added the bigger news on to the end of the earlier reports, instead of making it a new lead. As it happened close to press time, the added copy went right to the composing room. But it was a very tight paper, and the makeup man, having to cut everything down, lopped off the end of the Richeson story. Traveler editors were first aware of the prison visit when they read it in the evening Globe.

Welch was fired on the assumption he didn't know news when he had it in front of him. He had just married; but he found a job with the Brockton Enterprise, and then took hold of a country weekly in Northfield for a few years until his classmate Laurence Winship, by then Sunday editor of the Globe, brought him on as a copy editor. The staff had an affectionate regard for Welch, a man of many idiosyncrasies but a strong sense of community. He had bought a farm in Hingham, which he worked at mornings; he spent many evenings on the school committee and other civic affairs that suggested subjects for a stream of Sunday features.

A source of amusement to the Globe staff was Welch's philosophy of the Sunday paper. Reader surveys had become chronic. Welch studied them assiduously and evolved a formula for Sunday features: a story for men, one for women, and one for children, and an animal story. Somebody was stuck with digging up that animal story every week, come what might.

Welch was also more prudish even than Mark Twain over what should appear in print; so any story that implied a sexual differentiation in the human — or other — species, had to be handled with extreme reticence. This applied especially to photographs in an era of increasing exposure. Welch selected all the pictures himself in daily embarrassment. One of his self-imposed rules was that a female picture must never show what he called "the line" at the center of a woman's bodice. But whether because of or despite Welch's formulas, the Sunday Globe continued to grow at a pace beyond any contemporary.

When Welch died prematurely in 1945 after eight years as Sunday editor, the Sunday paper circulation had increased from 310,000 to 362,000 through a period of depression and then wartime paper rationing that had cut its size from 88 to 66 pages.

When Daniel J. O'Brien followed Welch the transition was natural and easy. O'Brien had started as office boy on the Globe in 1910, out of Medford high school, and had served in the library and as a compositor before going to the Manchester Union, where he was reporter, sports editor, city editor, and managing editor.

Back to the Globe in 1925 he was a copy editor on the day desk for some years, then assistant Sunday editor throughout the Welch period. For the next 17 years he presided over a growing staff and enlarging resources on a Sunday paper that tripled in size and added more than 100,000 to its circulation. On the death of M. E. Hennessy in 1955, O'Brien took over the "Round and About" column in the Sunday paper. An easy boss, a friendly and gregarious man, he presided over most of the journalistic, Irish, and social clubs of Boston in this period. Suffolk University awarded him a doctorate in 1958.

Promotion and Survival

The depression thirties proved a hard school but brought their lessons, starting the Globe on promotion and research. The Globe spent more on research in this period than any other Boston newspaper, beginning with Robert Ahern, who came to the Globe through the Gallup poll. He was Gallup's New England field man in 1936. That was the first year of the Gallup presidential poll and the Globe was one of the first three papers to take it, the Washington Post and New York Herald Tribune the others. So Ahern was in touch with the Globe. Winship assigned Donald Willard to do a feature on the new poll.

A few months later Winship became managing editor. One of his problems was the traditional district notes. They took up a lot of daily space. Did they justify the space in reader response? Winship sent for Ahern to do a study; the result was that district notes were dropped. Then there was another study for Ahern, the Sunday "letters" from country correspondents all over New England. They also were dropped. Times had changed; readers were getting this service in their local papers more fully than in a metropolitan paper. The Globe had other problems for Ahern. From consultant he joined the staff to do market research.

The Globe had undertaken a bit of homegrown promotion some time before Bob Ahern came aboard. The first remembered enterprise was a joint effort of Harry Stanton, statistician in market analysis, and Willard DeLue as writer. They produced a pamphlet that extolled the rich sales potential of the Boston market area and the Globe's thorough coverage of the region.

Ahern provided the statistical background for brochures and sales talks. In early 1940 he was joined by Charles F. Moore, Jr., who had been promotion manager for the Washington Post. Moore was an "idea man" focusing on editorial promotion to convince the advertiser of the solid content of the Globe and its thorough reading. By the end of World War II Ahern was running a promotion department with a staff of six. John I. Taylor, back from the war, joined Ahern and Moore as a team.

John I. Taylor, the fourth of General Taylor's grandsons to join the paper, had come onto the Globe out of Harvard in 1933. The first of this third generation was the third Charles H. Taylor, who in 1918 broke off his Harvard courses to start working on the Globe, as his father had done. He worked in every department from the press room up to become clerk of the corporation in 1921, then successively credit manager, purchasing agent, and for many years assistant treasurer. Moseley, elder son of William O., joined the paper after serving as a fighter pilot in the first world war. A varsity football and crew man in the Harvard 1918 class, he devoted himself to developing sled dog racing and bred Siberian huskies, to become president of the New England Sled Dog Club, 1928–1931. Soon afterward (1935) he became the Globe's New York advertising representative until his death in 1952. His younger brother Davis came into his father's office from Harvard in 1931 to serve as assistant and righthand man of the publisher the next 24 years until he succeeded his father.

John, son of the General's third son of the same name, joined the city staff, covered the Federal Building, assisted Bentley at the State House, put in a year on the copy desk, did rewrite. When the Transcript failed John persuaded the Globe to let him start a book page, once a week. The Transcript had had a strong book department. The Herald did, too, with Alice Dixon Bond as literary editor. But the book industry increasingly felt that one newspaper in a city was all it could support.

John bucked this attitude to try to build up book advertising. He became convinced that the Globe needed a literary "name" to give status to its page. He went to see his friend Robert Linscott at Houghton Mifflin for a suggestion. Dorothy Hillyer, at her editorial desk in the same room, heard the conversation and called over, "I'll take the job, John." Not sure that this was seriously meant, John went on exploring prospects with Linscott. But as he left Mrs. Hillyer offered again, and when he got back to the office she was on the phone to say "I told you I'd take that job, John." She got it and brought a new authority and tone to the page.

By the time John got back from the second world war Moore and Ahern had begun to key the promotion department to the Globe's need to attract young readers, to shake loose from the tag of being a paper for older readers. Winship had been working at appeal to youth since he became managing editor in 1937.

John began writing promotion copy for Moore. They found an opening for their Youth Movement in 1947, when local women's clubs persuaded them to put on a day-long seminar on public affairs. The New York Herald Tribune had been successful in running such a forum. For the Globe seminar, its columnists Dorothy Thompson and Doris Fleeson were brought in; also in the repertoire was a girl who had been doing a "Column for Teens" in New Rochelle. John and Moore set up a tea party at the Ritz Carlton for teen-agers and invited 50 or 60 high schools to send student leaders. They suggested that the student guests report the event for their school papers and offered prizes of $100, $50, and $25 for the best stories. Forty essays were submitted. From this they ran a high school editors' conference twice a year and brought in national figures — Eleanor Roosevelt, Estes Kefauver, Robert Taft, cartoonists, and sports writers. The group grew to 350, to 400.

Science teachers around the state had been running local science fairs but were strapped for funds. They appealed to the Globe to help them organize and fund a statewide science fair. The Globe got M.I.T. to offer the use of its cage. The Globe promoted the Science Fair, which immediately became a notable event and has continued so for more than 20 years.

Drama teachers then wanted help to develop a regional contest for high school plays. The Globe obtained John Hancock Hall and underwrote a weekend of presentation of eight plays and then a banquet for the actors and playwriters. John and Moore started baseball clinics and went on to clinics in football, basketball, and hockey, to pull in the stars of the Red Sox, Celtics, and Bruins.

A key principle in all this was that they never pushed the Globe. They promoted the events with no commercialism. But Charlie Moore came up with a slogan for subway billboards: "Have You Noticed How Many More People Are Reading the Globe These Days?"

And it began to be true. The teen-agers of 1948 were buying the Globe for their own teen-agers 20 years later.

John kept on with promotion after Moore left to become campaign manager for Robert Bradford in 1948, then to serve as governor's secretary, and after that to head public relations for the Ford Motor Company.

Bob Ahern's market surveys had quickly provided welcome ammunition for vital new leadership in the advertising and circulation departments. Jack Reid had become advertising manager in 1938 and Fred O'Neal circulation director in 1940. Both had grown up in the business of selling the Globe.

Jack Reid was graduated from Weymouth High School in 1918. He started college but broke it off to get a newspaper job. He had been selling advertising for the Boston American for six years when he joined the Globe in 1927 as an advertising salesman. Edward Dunbar was coming to the end of his half century on the paper, to be followed as advertising director by Charles Wright for the next ten years. Then Jack Reid took over, in the trough of depression, with an uphill job to build advertising in a competitive situation of four morning, four evening, and four Sunday papers.

Reid had begun his own advertising promotion before Bob Ahern came aboard. His big selling card was that morning and evening Globe circulation could be added together. As the same features and editorials, comics and special departments ran in both, there was obviously little reason for a reader to buy both.

Another advantage he exploited was that the Globe's appearance had improved markedly when ads were taken off the tops of the inside pages in 1936 to let the news headlines show and give some flexibility in makeup.* Reid's story is that William Frye, head of N. W. Ayer & Sons, called on his old friend W. O. Taylor one day when the Ayer newspaper typographical contests were new and told him that when they started choosing the newspapers of best appearance "the first paper we shove under the table is the Boston Globe." To W.O.'s innocent question why, Frye said: "Because it's such a mess — a hodge podge." And he showed him some well laid out newspapers. Reid says W.O. called him in next day and said, "Let's try arranging the ads tomorrow the way other papers do and see how it goes." They never changed back.

It was more than 25 years before ads came off the front page. First political advertising was eliminated; it had reached a point where, the final days before election, political ads reached almost up to the top headlines. To discourage this even the double rate for front page was doubled again, so that political ads were paying ten dollars a line. Then the size for front page ads was limited. But even that couldn't accommodate them all, and advertisers left off complained. It was well into the 1960's before the front page was cleaned of all advertising. Page two was then kept open on Sunday and pages two and three kept for news daily.

Fred O'Neal found his first job out of high school in 1919 as a Globe office

---

* March 4, 1936, was the day the ads came off the tops of the pages. Frye could bait W.O. with the impunity of long friendship; but his criticism of the Globe's typographical anachronism could hardly have been a surprise. W.O.'s son Davis and Sunday editor Laurence Winship had long pleaded with him to drop the ads down and give the news a chance to show.

boy. He was assigned, temporarily, to help Walter Hartwell, who had taken over the circulation department at the end of Tom Downey's 40 years of running it.

In 1919 the paper was still hauled by horse and wagon to the trains that distributed 90 percent of it. But some areas were served all the way by wagon — papers for the South Shore were hauled by wagon to Quincy, where a relay of horses carried them on to Braintree and another change of horses to Whitman and beyond.

For the bigger Sunday papers the four Boston newspapers paid for a special train to the Cape. When the New Haven cut back train service to Hyannis and later Buzzards Bay, the newspapers subsidized seven-day train delivery through the Cape until 1954. Thereafter they used trucks.

The newspapers jointly subsidized a Boston & Maine train to Portland, to split three ways to Rockland, Skowhegan, and Bangor. The Globe had its own special on the Grand Trunk from Portland across to Island Pond, Vermont, until 1945. Another newspaper special ran through Portsmouth to Berlin, New Hampshire, and another via Concord, New Hampshire, to White River Junction. The Globe had its own special train on the Central Vermont to St. Albans and Burlington. Four papers joined to support a train to North Adams, Keene, and Bellows Falls. The Globe then had its own special on the Rutland Railroad from Bellows Falls to Vergennes. Transportation was then the big problem in circulation. Editions went to press to meet railroad schedules.

After O'Neal took charge in 1940, the problem became one of following the commuter into the suburbs to develop home delivery and get the paper out in time for the paper routes. In World War II, with paper rationing, circulation was no problem. The Globe could sell all the papers it could print. Forced economies cut down returns. From an average of 10 percent or more in 1942, returns were cut to less than 1.5 percent for morning editions by 1944 and to 3 percent for evenings. Increased home delivery kept the returns lower after paper rationing ended. In 1969 it was 9 percent morning, 10 percent evening, 5–6 percent Sunday.

The number of evening editions was cut also, from seven before the war to five, and two of those essentially replates. With these war economies, the Globe profited even with fewer and smaller papers.

The severe newsprint rationing in the war brought William O. Taylor's business principles into play. He laid down two rules that were hard to hold and costly to the paper at the time but that paid off later. The restricted space would be allocated to advertisers in proportion to the space they had been using, right across the board, treating every class of advertising the same. Just one exception: "Help Wanted" ads, he said, were part of the war effort, with war plants seeking help. So Help Wanted would not be rationed. But the big store advertisers would be cut in the same proportion as small advertisers. The New York Times followed the same policy. But in Boston the Herald took the opposite tack, as the Herald Tribune did in New York, to give the big store advertisers priority and let the miscellaneous small advertisers take the cuts. The big stores appreciated this and penalized the Globe in apportioning their advertising. But the policy earned the Globe the gratitude of thousands of small advertisers. When newsprint came back such departments as Farm and Garden spurted to new volume, and new circulation grew from this.

The automobile was rapidly removing newspaper readers from the commuting trains and transit system. You don't read a newspaper while driving to work. The

Post had built a huge morning circulation, but it was a headline paper for quick breakfast-table reading. The Post did nothing about home delivery. Advertisers were beginning to study their markets: the paper that went home would be read. The Globe began building up home delivery, sending its road men into the suburbs to sign up customers, then putting delivery boys on the routes. In 1931, 98 percent of all Globes started by train, even to the close-by suburban stations. The shift was soon made to busses as rail lines were cut off, then to the paper's own truck system. Thirty years later less than one percent of the papers went onto trains.

In the early thirties 86,000 daily Globes were sold at intown strategic points: North and South railway stations and the principal subway stations, Park Street, Scollay Square, Copley Square, Bowdoin Square. But this was less than a third of the circulation. To get the paper into homes was the new move. The Post's decline began with the development of home delivery by the Globe and Herald-Traveler. Advertisers soon discovered that ads in these papers yielded more than in the Post. The Globe survived the most intense newspaper competition of any city and weathered the Great Depression of the 1930's that saw the Transcript founder after 110 years in one family, soon to be followed by the Springfield Republican after a century and a quarter, in the fourth Bowles generation.

But now, gradually, the Globe was to broaden its scope and refine its tone from the days when Florence Finch's Beacon Hill friends looked down their noses at it. When the Transcript folded, the formal and elegant Jerome Greene, former Lee Higginson partner and secretary of the Harvard governing boards, said in evident surprise: "You know, the Globe isn't too bad."

The Globe management must instinctively have felt a need to appeal to a different clientele from that of the Herald. Charles Taylor came into the office one day after walking across the Common with A. Lawrence Lowell to demand: "What are you fellows doing with the Globe? President Lowell tells me some of his Harvard friends are now reading it."

One of the Globe's new strengths in the 1930's was Walter Lippmann. Lippmann was editor of Pulitzer's World when it ended in 1931. The Republican Herald Tribune then made a move that was an innovation for its time, to present "the other side" through a column by him which they syndicated. Lippmann's lucid and brilliant style quickly established his column's distinction. Before the end of 1931 the column became a Globe fixture for as long as Lippmann did it. It started as a daily feature, but he soon spaced himself to three pieces a week and always deplored the more usual practice of doing a column a day. It wasn't possible, he held, to do the thinking and preparation for an informed column every day.

In 1936 Dorothy Thompson's column was added to fill in the days between Lippmann's every-other-day. Gradually other columnists were added, Marquis Childs, Alsop, Ralph McGill, a whole galaxy, many of them used only one day a week or less frequently. But the upper righthand two-column space on the editorial page was always, to the office, "the Lippmann column." When Lippmann was on vacation, the managing editor would ask a member of the staff: "Can you do a Lippmann column for tomorrow?" Lippmann for four decades was the philosopher of journalism. He undertook the largest journalistic responsibility. Always writing within the context of his own pattern of world affairs, he used to say the responsibility of the columnist was to write so that his readers would not be surprised at events.

The editorial writers remained the same and did so for another quarter century. Lucien Price, William Packer, and James H. Powers had all come on to the page between 1914 and 1920. Now at their peak, they were an extraordinary team with that amazing, indestructible James Morgan still their coach and guide. Winship kept charge of the editorial page as well as the news department. But he, no less than the editorial writers, was disciple and pupil of Morgan. The Taylors, too, felt secure in the balance and wisdom of the General's trusted editorial adviser. Young Davis Taylor, assisting his publisher father through this period, named his youngest son James Morgan Taylor, an expression both of his fondness for the man and his appreciation of what Mr. Morgan meant to the Globe.

They all clung to Mr. Morgan on his own terms. If he only led the editorial conference once a week, that was an event. Other days he was accessible by phone for any close question, and his ideas continued to stream into the office in brief notes in a hand that only the editorial secretary, Ellen Kaples, could decipher. Mr. Morgan might be in Europe for three months or on a transcontinental jaunt to get the feel of the country; but he would be back to lead the Globe political team to presidential conventions and to contribute intermittent articles on politics to the Sunday editorial page that had as ardent a following as his dispatches from Washington half a century earlier.

To Winship fell the daily task of dealing with the editorial writers. It was up to him to contain their dynamic approach to all the controversial issues of the day. This was a constant chess game: they pressed and he held a line of what was acceptable. They respected his role as the buffer between intellectual urgency and management caution. But where and how to draw the editorial line was a daily debate. The editorial writers knew as well as the editor that the policy of the Globe was constraint and balance. But temperaments clashed. Price could find relief through most of this period, and did, by taking half the year off for his own writing. The managing editor had no such respite. He tried to minimize the editorial conference, which Price tended to ritualize. Winship at one point even tried to operate by having the editorial writers check in with him one at a time to get clearance for their proposals. When a staff friend protested elimination of the conference, the managing editor said, "How would you like to take a beating from those fellows every day?"

The "beating" of course was psychological, the result of having to take a role and hold an unconvinced position. But there was always mutual respect; indeed, the managing editor had a strong pride in the distinction of thought and style of the editorial writers. Price was the finest writer in Boston — and why stop with Boston? That Price also had the most uncompromising mind did not make his editor's role more comfortable. A staff bystander came to realize how much of executive responsibility is being a shock absorber. And beyond that being, besides, the boss, always also the friend. Winship had unique human qualities for filling these divergent roles. He was the balance wheel of the paper. The Taylors knew it, appreciating him only less than they adored James Morgan.

James Morgan and Justice Frankfurter

James Morgan was 73 when he first met Felix Frankfurter, in 1935. An extraordinary friendship that began then lasted the remaining 20 years of Mr. Morgan's life.

Frankfurter had come to admire Morgan's political articles and asked Laurence Winship to arrange a meeting. Frankfurter was a law professor at Harvard, a confidant and adviser to President Roosevelt, when the relation began; from 1939 he was a Supreme Court justice. In the early years Winship, Morgan, and Frankfurter had occasional luncheons together, sometimes at the Locke-Ober Restaurant or the Harvard Faculty Club, at other times with their families at Frankfurter's home or at the Morgans'.

But as the relation ripened, Frankfurter had Morgan to himself for a long talkfest over luncheon several times a year. He was soon confiding to Winship that "since Brandeis' death, James Morgan is the wisest man I know." In 1944 the Justice wrote Mrs. Morgan: "It is easier to tell you than to James's face, what a joy he is to me — and that for me he is the wisest member of the profession. How amateurish even the most serious columnists are by comparison with him."

In a stay at Beth Israel Hospital in 1939, Mrs. Morgan recorded in her diary: "Dr. Herman Blumgart told me Mr. Frankfurter said our home is a haven of spiritual uplift."

Mrs. Morgan's diary records long-distance telephone calls from Frankfurter to Morgan running half or three-quarters of an hour, to discuss a Landon campaign speech of 1936 and Willkie's acceptance speech in 1940. The day of his nomination to the Supreme Court "Mr. Frankfurter called and talked more than half an hour. He had been called to Washington but would be back for our luncheon on Saturday."

Morgan and Winship were at luncheon with Frankfurter February 5, 1937, when a telephone call brought Frankfurter the news of Roosevelt's "court packing" plan. Frankfurter expressed himself as stunned, then outraged by it and poured out his criticism on his journalist guests, whose editorial next morning was guided by the experience.

While on the Court through the war years, Frankfurter was back in Boston for a long luncheon with Morgan at least twice a year. A July luncheon became a fixture. Mrs. Morgan's recording of these events is practically the same each season: 1941 through 1948. "J had luncheon and four hours' steady visiting with Justice Frankfurter" (1942). "J had luncheon and 4½ hours' visit at Locke Ober's with Justice Frankfurter" 1943). "J had luncheon and four hours' talk with Justice Frankfurter at Locke Ober's." "J met Justice Frankfurter and James Powers at Locke Ober's for luncheon and 3 hours' conversation" (1944). "Luncheon at Locke Ober's. Sat at table from 12:30–5" (1945). Mrs. Morgan's record of these luncheon talks runs through 1948, when Mr. Morgan was 87.

Pics

Lucien Thayer's appointment as photographic editor in 1937 was belated recognition of the camera's role. Today the photographer receives equal recognition with the staff writer on a special assignment; the feature article may well start with a double byline, "Story by Robert Taylor, Photography by Gilbert Friedberg." But for more than half the history of news photography the Globe photographer, like his colleagues on other papers, was an anonymous supplement to the reporter.

The Globe had neither an art editor nor a photographic editor. Photographers' assignments were made as afterthoughts on the city desk. "Oh, you'll want to take a photographer," the city editor would say. "Send up a voucher for a photographer to go to Plymouth."

The photographer who hustled down from the cramped attic room two floors above would be whoever was not busy in the darkroom at the moment developing his own pictures. When the photographer's work came through it would sift through the copy desk to be fitted to assigned space. If the story was assigned a two-column head, then the copy editor marked the photograph for a two-column cut, or maybe a one-column if the paper was tight. All the art and much of the detail was thus squeezed out of any picture of quality.

Yet the Globe was served all this time by enterprising and technically proficient cameramen, some with a keen eye for the artistic possibilities of the right picture. The first Globe photographer, John W. Butters, Jr., starting in 1885, was an innovator who explored the town for subjects and topics. By 1905 Butters was in charge of what had become known as the photo-engraving department, with a corps of five staff photographers. Several were exceptional men. But each lived the life of a fireman on call for whatever might turn up. Leonard Small was a Globe photographer from 1910 to 1938. A big, affable, pipe-smoking Englishman, Small took all his assignments in stride. He was never at a loss; he would size up the situation, arrange his subjects, stand off and gauge his distance and angle, note the sun, and then make one picture. Always one picture. If a green reporter who hadn't learned about Small urged another for insurance, Small would say, "I've got it." If he had to deal with fussy women or people who had their own ideas about arranging the picture, Small would appease them by snapping whatever they proposed. "I'd taken the plate out of the camera," he'd explain to the reporter as they left the scene. Frank Colby of the Transcript was of the same breed and persuasion. They knew their trade and they weren't wasting plates.

A contemporary of Small was Edmunds E. Bond, a State of Mainer who'd had his own studio before joining the Globe in 1904 to serve as photographer for 51 years. Nothing fazed Eddie Bond. If he went off on a feature story with a reporter, he'd want to talk all about it on the way. Then he had his plans all made. He knew just what pictures he wanted to illustrate the story. Bond was as inventive as he was enterprising. His first year on the paper brought a notable murder trial, Charles Tucker tried for murdering Mabel Page. Photographs were not allowed in court. But Bond told Butters he thought he could make pictures of the Tucker trial. He constructed a miniature camera in a heavily padded vest. The lens appeared only as an embellishment that might have been a watch charm. The shutter was operated from a bulb in a jacket pocket connected to the camera by a rubber tube under the vest. Bond attended the trial as a sketch artist. He was seated next to the sheriff. When his first picture appeared, showing the defendant, it made a stir. The sheriff told Bond somebody had a hidden camera and he was going to catch him. The sheriff kept a sharp eye out, but Bond's pictures kept appearing. After the trial Bond showed the sheriff how it worked and presented him a picture of himself taken in the courtroom.

Two years later Bond wore his vest camera to the Thaw murder trial in New York. The judge issued strict orders against photographs and announced that any violation of the rule would lead to arrest for contempt. Again Bond found himself next to a deputy sheriff. The photographer worried about a faint click when he snapped the shutter. If the sheriff heard it, Bond might find himself in jail for contempt. He took out a pocket knife and sharpened a pencil, then kept opening and shutting the knife, which clicked each time. When he felt the sheriff was conditioned to his knife clicking, he clicked his camera. Meantime he was busily taking "shorthand" notes of the trial to carry out his camouflage as a reporter. When he had finished a batch of pictures of the chief characters in the trial, he left the New York jurisdiction and the Globe began printing his pictures.

Harvard, under President A. Lawrence Lowell, had a strict rule against cameras at commencement. When James R. Angell became president of Yale in 1921, Harvard awarded Angell an honorary degree. Bond approached President Lowell to ask if he might make his picture. "I never permit pictures," said Lowell severely, and walked away.

Discovering President Angell, Bond told the distinguished visitor he would like to get a photograph of the two presidents together. "Why yes," said Angell. "Dr. Lowell, this photographer would like to get us together." Lowell couldn't very well avoid his visitor's invitation. Disapproving, he stood long enough for Bond to get his picture.

In the later period of Small and Bond younger colleagues, James Callahan, James Jones, Charles McCormick, and Paul Maguire developed into top-ranking news photographers. The advent of Life Magazine in 1930 enhanced the profession of the news photographer. The Sunday magazine cover opened an opportunity for the artist photographer. Arthur Griffin, in charge of rotogravure from 1935, contributed distinctive cover photographs for the Globe throughout the 1940's until magazine work and his own pictorial books on New England drew him away from newspaper work. By then the Globe's own staff included men fully appreciative of photographic art.

These old-time photographers seemed to have iron nerves, or no nerves at all. When the Boston Custom House construction was in the steel girder stage, a girl acrobat announced that she would walk across a plank 400 feet above the street. Leonard Small went to photograph the feat. The photographer quickly discovered that to get the best shot the natural vantage point was to station himself on another plank higher up.

"I felt my head scraping against the sky," Small remembered. But when he laid his picture before city editor William D. Sullivan, Sully shuddered. "Why, it makes me dizzy just to look at it. It would never do to print anything like that."

Small never quite forgave him.

In 1907 a Globe editor chanced upon an 1848 panorama sketch of Boston drawn from the top of the Bunker Hill monument. He thought a matching photograph to show the changes of 60 years would be interesting. Eddie Bond was given the assignment. He took a friend with him and climbed the winding stone steps to the monument's upper room. There the outlook through the narrow windows was disappointingly limited. But repair work was under way; the bars had been taken off the windows and heavy planking lay around. Bond pushed a plank out a window, braced it with another plank, set his friend to keep the rig steady, and slid out over the city on his plank.

"A wonderful view," he reported as, both hands on his camera, he oriented himself and made a series of pictures to complete an arc from the State House around the harbor to the Charlestown Navy Yard.

"You all right?" shouted the worried friend. Bond slid back in, satisfied with his shots that made a page of pictorial history, set against the 1848 print, in the Sunday Globe of July 28, 1907.

Eddie Bond was 20 years older in 1927 when I flew over New England with him after a great flood, in a little two-seater plane. He was hanging half out the window all the time, directing the pilot — "now bank over to your left — get as low as you can" — both hands on the camera, as casual as if looking out his living room window.

The photographer's camera makes him a marked man in a situation where people may be suspicious or resentful of pictures. James L. Callahan had a harrowing experience in the great Lawrence strike of 1912. Strikers had been led to believe that the news photographers were making records for the mill owners to use against them. The sight of Callahan with his camera so enraged one picket that he drew a big knife and charged at the photographer, who ran for his life two blocks to reach a safe place.

Callahan had a closer escape in 1945 when covering a mock invasion by Marines at Carson Beach in South Boston. With Post photographer Moe Fineberg, Callahan was sighting his camera when a mortar burst close by, stunning him. He looked down to find Fineberg dead almost at his feet.

In June 1959 Globe reporter James Hammond and photographer William J. Ennis were covering the police pursuit of two escaped convicts, the Coyle brothers. They suddenly found themselves in a zone of fire as police caught up with their quarry and shot it out with them. As revolvers cracked, Ennis snapped his camera, then hit the dirt. His pictures in the evening Globe of July 17, 1959, received the top award of the Boston Press Photographers competition for that year.

The arbitrary wooden treatment of photographs changed after 1937, when Lucien Thayer brought a keen sense of news and a relish for its flavor and color to the new post of photographic editor. He became an appreciative conductor of the Globe's photographic resources and he had enough status to exert influence on the size of the picture used and the layout of the page. This gradually had its effect on the whole aspect of the paper — makeup, typography, page design.

Thayer was responsible for a photographic innovation that enlivened sports coverage. He introduced the "photo sequence" that showed the development of the winning touchdown or key play in a series of pictures.

Photographers remained in the photo-engraving department almost to the end of the Globe's stay on Washington Street. But their lot improved under the regime of John F. Maguire, who introduced improved equipment for photographers as well

AP Spot News First Prize for 1969: photographed by Tom Landers, August 21, 1969.

as for engraving after he became superintendent of the department in 1923. One of his most appreciated improvements was to install lighter cameras that reduced the photographer's load on a story from 30 to nine pounds. With the move to a modern plant in 1958 photography was given a separate department under a chief photographer, first Charles McCormick (1958–1964), then Paul Maguire, son of John F. Maguire.

By 1966 pictorial development had become so important in all departments that it was coordinated under an executive photographic editor, J. Edward Fitzgerald.

Fitzgerald had been picture editor of the United Press International. The Globe acquired him after Lucien Thayer retired. He brought photography under professional direction and in the next four years recruited a largely new young staff which by 1970 numbered 26 and was winning increasing numbers of photographic awards.

As their many awards indicate, Ted Dully and Paul Connell of the Globe are recognized as New England leaders among this new breed of news photographers.

With Wendell Willkie

The Republican convention of 1940 opened with the European war crisis hanging over the delegates. The isolationist positions of the two front runners, Taft and Dewey, had incited a sudden launching of a campaign for Wendell Willkie, a principled man of great personal charm whose Indiana origins had been overlaid by success in Manhattan — which had brought him into dramatic conflict with the New Deal as counsel for the private power companies in opposition to Roosevelt's great public power program of the TVA. Willkie had a world view that made him acceptable to those who feared the isolationism of Robert Taft and Thomas E. Dewey. A tremendous campaign spearheaded by the Luce publications created a national image of Willkie in the weeks before the convention. He entered the lists with almost no delegate commitments but immense popular demand.

The headlines the week before the convention: June 17, morning: "French Cabinet Falls." Evening: "French Give Up / Britain to Keep up Fight says Churchill."

June 20 evening: "Two Republicans Named to Cabinet / FDR Makes Knox Navy Secretary and Stimson War Secretary."

June 22: "Bulk of French Fleet Taken Over by British / Nazis Hurl Air Might at England."

During the convention a Globe headline: "Walsh Rebukes Navy for Selling Ships" (to allies). Walsh was chairman of the Senate Navy Committee.

At Harvard Class Day: "Harvard Seniors Boo at War Challenge." Mass meetings for and against conscription competed with the commencement exercises. President Conant, a staunch interventionist, was picketed. Secretary of State Cordell Hull, speaking against isolationism, painted a dark picture of war clouds.

Carl Sandburg stood against the war talk. He quoted Lincoln: "If we could first know where we are and whither we are going . . ." Walter Lippmann at Harvard said the American destiny is to become the center of the ultimate liberation and resurrection of the conquered democracies.

Dorothy Thompson's column June 17, "Thoughts on the Fall of France," held that the survival of American democracy depended on the defeat of Hitler. It implied American entry into the war. An avalanche of letters poured in. She pushed on with her argument June 21.

The Globe was printing a dozen or more letters a day and keeping score, to announce June 27 the tally under the head

> Should U.S. Enter the War

The letters ran 79 percent against to 21 percent supporting Dorothy Thompson's position, 443 against to 121 for.

The night before Willkie's nomination the headline on L. L. Winship's story was

> GOP Choice Anybody's Guess

But the headline on the UP story by Lyle Wilson was

> Taft Gains While Willkie Slips

The morning following the nomination, June 29, the Globe carried a front page special:

> Exclusive
> How Willkie Got the News
> Globe Man Says Nominee Couldn't Believe His Ears

When Willkie went ahead of Taft on the third ballot and passed Dewey on the fourth, Winship left the convention to look for the candidate. He found his hotel room door open and walked in as a dozen others had. With Willkie they were clustered around a radio. The candidate kept asking what the score was now. Winship said to him, "I don't know what you're so concerned about, Mr. Willkie. I've just come from the convention and they say it's all over. You've won."

"I hope you're right," said Willkie, but he kept on tabbing one delegation after another. It was incredible to the reporter that he had no staff keeping score for him. When photographers rushed in to ask him, "Raise your hand," Willkie observed: "Of course if this doesn't come out right you won't print it." He kept asking where Taft stood and where he stood until it was over.

In the same edition Joseph F. Dinneen started the life of Wendell Willkie, chapter one.

LETTERS TO THE EDITOR

Leningrad sentences 'incredibly harsh'

The incredibly harsh sentences meted out to the accused in the so-called Leningrad hijacking case have shocked enlightened opinion everywhere. Without a genuinely public trial, 11 Soviet citizens have been found guilty, not of hijacking, but of

Bond to the rescue

Regarding the cabbie murders and robberies:

Why not take a page from James Bond? . . .

All the cabbie would have to do is rig up a couple of canisters of tear gas so that the nozzles are pointed di-

Def

Davi
(Glo
and
state
blam
the i
M.
very

The Church

In the 1920's and 1930's any criticism of any position of the Catholic Church was taboo in most of the Boston press. This was not limited to Boston but was more pronounced there.

Walter Lippmann said of his role as editor of the New York World to 1931 that he never experienced any office constraint on editorials. But he added that, had he been interested in birth control, this would not have been true. In Massachusetts when an amendment to the rigid birth control law was introduced into the legislature in the late thirties the measure had no possibility of passage. But Governor Saltonstall took the occasion to announce his opposition. Oswald Garrison Villard in an article in the Nation described Massachusetts as a Roman Conquest. The Boston newspapers had pulled back from support of the child labor amendment overnight when Cardinal O'Connell announced his opposition. To its opponents it became the "Youth Control Amendment." It never was ratified in Massachusetts. Twenty-eight other states had ratified it by 1938 when the Federal Labor Standards Act regulating the labor of children under 18 made the amendment a dead letter.

One Columbus Day, Lucien Price, weary of the annual ritualistic editorial, wrote a light-hearted piece to the effect that Columbus was the bane of schoolboys who had to remember 1492. This was anathema to the Knights of Columbus, and they complained to the Globe. But such lapses were rare indeed. The paper guarded against them. A veteran member of the copy desk performed his chief function as liaison with the archdiocesan headquarters. He got the word. Even after Al Smith's 1928 manifesto, "The American Catholic," had defined the independence of the Catholic layman in all secular matters, the old inhibitions held in Boston.

The appointment of Richard Cushing as bishop of Boston in 1939 (archbishop 1944 and cardinal 1958) opened a different atmosphere. Long before the ecumenical movement, his own broad sense of community brought a change in the Boston climate. When in 1958 the Cardinal defended the Boston police at a time when lapses in the department were forcing reorganization, the Boston newspapers did not hesitate to refute the Cardinal, whose very human response was, "I guess I was too impulsive." He soon won the respect and even affection of a great part of the large community outside his church.

The election of John F. Kennedy as President in 1960 removed inhibitions about public criticism of positions of the Church. President Kennedy himself rejected the Church position on Federal aid to parochial schools.

By the mid-1960's the churning issue of birth control within the Catholic Church was as much a part of the news as political debate. The unrest among Catholics over Pope Paul's birth control pronouncement made an eight-column banner head in the Globe July 30, 1968: "Pope's Edict Provokes Controversy — Dutch Liberals, Washington Priests Voice Opposition to Birth Control Ban." By 1965 the Globe was editorially pressing for reform of the ancient birth control law of Massachusetts and in early 1970 broke an editorial lance against the ban on abortion.

The Joe Kennedy Story

My role in this history arose from a note that Laurence Winship wrote me in the spring of 1968, asking if I would write out an account of my 1940 interview with Joseph P. Kennedy, to be a chapter in a centennial history of the Globe. I had written it much earlier, in my own memoirs, unpublished. I sent it to him and told him I had a lot of other material that might be useful — profiles of Globe people, accounts of notable Globe stories like the Vermont flood and the Lindbergh kidnapping trial, and so on. As we exchanged notes I became interested in the plans for the history and, finding that they hadn't jelled, offered suggestions, chiefly that most institutional histories were a bore and the Globe's hundred years was entitled to something better.

Then one day a blockbuster from Winship: Will you do it? You'd have through 1970 to get it done. After backing and filling and with misgivings, I took it on. Now I come to the Kennedy interview of November 10, 1940, to puzzle over it. But I see no other way to write it than as I had written it, and as Winship had intended to use it in the Globe history.

Others had written about it in biographies of John F. Kennedy and of Joseph Kennedy, practically always from Joseph Kennedy's side. I had never chosen to comment on these versions. Only one biographer, James MacGregor Burns, had sent me his manuscript to ask me to check it. I had made only one change, that the interview was after, not before, the 1940 election. This, then, is the reporter's own report of the Kennedy interview.

The only trouble with the story is that it blew up.

It set out to be an ordinary Sunday feature story. I had cleaned up my week's assignment for the Sunday and didn't hurry in that Friday morning. I'd had a late Nieman dinner the night before, for I had just taken over the Nieman Fellowship program for newspapermen at Harvard from Archibald MacLeish, who was its first curator, for the one year that I was a Fellow.

Winship had left a note on my desk that Friday morning: "See me. Win." He had seen, as I had, a brief story in the morning papers. Ambassador Joseph P. Kennedy had returned to Boston the night before. There was a short routine press interview at the airport.

Winship said, "We ought to get a Sunday piece on Joe Kennedy."

This was the Friday following the election of 1940. Kennedy had come back from Britain to go through the minimum motions of supporting Roosevelt. I think he had made one speech. Many people questioned whether he'd be returning to England. Kennedy had been close to Chamberlain, had believed in his Munich attempt at "peace in our time," was well known to be out of sympathy with President Roosevelt's ardent interventionism.

I had met Joe Kennedy in the 1936 campaign when the NANA syndicate had asked the Globe to get an interview with him on Roosevelt, who had appointed Kennedy the first chairman of the Securities and Exchange Commission to regulate the stock market. I had gone down to Hyannis and provided a listening post while Kennedy poured it on with his accustomed vehemence most of an afternoon. He was talking like a Dutch uncle to his fellow Wall Streeters, telling them Roosevelt was salvaging capitalism, not undermining it.

The interview ran several columns of very lively copy for the Sunday paper. Its impact was such that to balance things up Mike Hennessy was sent up to New Hampshire to interview Senator Styles Bridges for the Republican side.

Kennedy was tickled with the results of the interview. He bought 100 copies of the paper to circulate, even though the interview was syndicated.

So I felt my only problem that day four years later was to find Joe Kennedy. He was Boston's favorite son, a self-made man who'd married the daughter of Mayor John F. ("Honey Fitz") Fitzgerald and become a financial power whose support of Roosevelt in the circles where it was most needed was rewarded with the ambassadorship to St. James's.

But I couldn't find him all morning. It turned out he was at the Lahey Clinic for a checkup. Fairly desperate by noon, with only the afternoon ahead of me, I telephoned Honey Fitz, who'd been making a play for newspapermen all his life. He had often enough cut in on my efforts to report a banquet speech from the press table, to remind me what he had done as mayor to make "a bigger, better, busier Boston," and he'd keep it up till somebody called on him to sing "Sweet Adeline," his trademark.

I told Fitz he claimed to be a friend of mine and I needed to find his son-in-law for an interview. Fitz promised to help and presently called back to tell me to be at Kennedy's room at the Ritz at one o'clock.

I was there before Kennedy was. While I waited two callers came in. One was a Nieman Fellow from the St. Louis Post-Dispatch, Charles Edmondson. The other was his boss, chief editorial writer Ralph Coghlan, who had been our speaker at the Nieman dinner the night before. Charles was showing his boss around town. They had read that Kennedy was in town and called to pay their respects. They were both intensely committed to isolationism, as was the P-D.

When Kennedy came in I introduced them and they applauded his well-known views about keeping us out of the war. After they'd had their innings I got out my pencil and pad and thanked Kennedy for giving me some time. I told him the Globe wanted to mark his return with a feature story. I hoped the callers would go, but they didn't. They stayed and drank in his rapid flow of talk. It was as though he were making a campaign speech, but not for Roosevelt, rather for his isolationist friend Senator Burt Wheeler of America First. It reminded me of our 1936 interview.

> I'm willing to spend all I've got to keep us out of the war. There's no sense in our getting in. We'd only be holding the bag . . . The war would drain us. It would turn our government into national socialism. Democracy is finished in England. It may be here, because it comes to a question of feeding people. It's all an economic question. It's the loss of our foreign trade that's going to threaten to change our form of government. We haven't felt the pinch of it yet. It's ahead of us . . .
>
> It's all a question of what we do with the next six months. As long as England is in there, we have time to prepare. That's the whole reason for aiding England. It isn't that England is fighting for democracy. That's the bunk. She's fighting for self-preservation, just as we will be if it comes to us

. . . It's a question of how long England can hold out. Hitler has all the ports of Europe. The German submarine bases are nearer the traffic lanes this time. The German Stukas are already over Africa. Keep out of the war and keep the hemisphere out of it. If any of the Latin Americas act up, kick them in the teeth . . .

If we got in, a bureaucracy would take over right off. Everything we hold dear would be gone. They tell me that after 1918 we got it all back. But now there's a different pattern in the world . . .

Lindbergh's not so crazy either. If they want us to go in, how can we send troops over when we haven't got any ships? I say we aren't going in — only over my dead body . . . I supported Roosevelt because he's the only one who can control the groups that have to be brought along.

I asked him about Chamberlain, whose illness had been reported. He told me what it was but quickly admonished, "That's off the record." Two or three more times during an hour and a half of talk, he held up his finger to tell me, "That's off the record." He covered the waterfront with eloquent, at times passionate, talk, the core of it against our getting into the war.

Finally James Landis, who had succeeded Kennedy as chairman of the SEC and whom I knew from his days as dean of the Harvard Law School, came to the door. He'd been handling some of Kennedy's affairs while the ambassador was abroad, and he was there to break it up; Kennedy was going down to Hyannis that night. So it broke up. The P-D men, exclaiming at Kennedy's outspokenness, went off and I went back to the Globe and wrote my story.

It ran Sunday, starting on the front page as one of our Sunday features regularly would. I didn't write it as a political story, but as a straight feature, getting in all the color of Kennedy's personality and vitality and as much about wartime life in London as I had got out of him. But the quotes of course were straight Kennedy, and once I got to them they made the body of the story. I left out what he'd told me to and some other things such as kicking the Latins in the teeth. If I'd had enough more diplomatic caution to leave out a few other things, it would have saved both of us a lot of trouble.

But the dynamite in it that blew him out of his ambassadorship, if it did, was his, not mine.

The eight-column page one headline was "Kennedy Says Democracy Done in Britain, Maybe Here."

Sunday morning the office telephoned. It was Joseph Dinneen, who was sitting on the desk that morning. The Globe had a request from London to cable the Kennedy interview. Dinneen had called Winship, who had told him to call me. Well, I said, go ahead. Evidently the wire services had picked it up, or some of it. I think Dinneen said Winship had suggested he'd better read it over to Kennedy before sending it to London; anyway, Dinneen said he was going to call Kennedy. He soon called back to say Kennedy was just going to church but would talk to him when he got back. Later Dinneen called to report on his Kennedy call: he had read the whole piece and Kennedy had said something like, "Gosh, he certainly got everything in there, didn't he?" but Dinneen said he'd made no objection so he let it go on the cable.

Next day was Armistice Day and I had the holiday off. Some time in the day the United Press phoned to tell me: Joe Kennedy says that interview of yours was sup-

The Boston Sunday Globe

VOL. CXXXVIII — Entered as second class mail matter at Boston, Mass., under the act of March 3, 1879—342 Washington St. — THE BOSTON SUNDAY GLOBE—NOVEMBER 10, 1940—78 PAGES — READ THE ROTOGRAVURE, MAGAZINE AND COLOR SECTIONS (S) — Copyright, 1940, by The Globe Newspaper Co. — PRICE 10 CENTS

MOLOTOFF SEES HITLER NOV. 12

Kennedy Says Democracy All Done in Britain, Maybe Here

Pinch Coming in U.S. Trade Loss

Ambassador Asks Aid to England Be Viewed as "Insurance"; Begs America Wake Up, Give More Power to Mobilize Industry

By LOUIS M. LYONS
(Copyright, 1940, By Boston Globe)

Joseph P. Kennedy was sitting in his shirtsleeves eating apple pie and American cheese in his room at the Ritz-Carlton. His suspenders hung around his hips.

It was the setting for an interview that every American reporter has known 1000 times in interviewing the visiting head of the Elks, or the Rotarians, or the Lions Clubs—as matter-of-fact as the apple pie:

Mr. Kennedy's own words cut sharply across this picture when he lifted the telephone to say, "This is the Ambassador." But his next words brought us back where we were. "O hello Bob, how are y'?"

He and Editor Sees Eye-to-Eye

A journalistic colleague from St. Louis who shared the interview—Ralph Coglan, editor of the St. Louis Post-Dispatch—liked Joe Kennedy from the first look at him. He liked him more every minute and every sentence of the hour and a half that Joe Kennedy poured out to us his views about America and the war in a torrent that flowed with the free, full power and flood of the Mississippi River.

My Missouri friend's eyes flashed in response to Kennedy. He was seeing eye to eye with the American ambassador as he hadn't been able to do with any of the intellectual leaders of Boston and Cambridge he'd seen in

his crowded visit. As these two glowed together in the discussion, it struck me that Joe Kennedy of Boston birth probably comes closer to representing the Mississippi Valley, the great heart of America, than any ambassador at the Court of St. James has had the luck to meet in modern times.

Would Spend All to Keep Out

"I'm willing to spend all I've got left to keep us out of the war." Kennedy flashed toward the end of his talk.

"There's no sense in our getting in. We'd just be holding the bag."

Keep U.S. Out of War
Continued on Page 21

Football

Harvard Ties Penn, 10-10; Eagles Whip Terriers, 21-0

Harvard tied the University of Pennsylvania, 10-10, for the biggest upset in yesterday's hectic football results. Vander Eb's placement goal in the third period gave the Crimson its tie. Minnesota edged Michigan, 7 to 6, in another thriller, and Stanford, heading for the Rose Bowl, belted out the Washington Huskies, 20-10. Boston College ran into stern opposition from the underdog Boston University Terriers, but won out, 21-0. Other scores:

Texas A&M 19 . . . . . So Methodist 7
Cornell 21 . . . . Yale 0
Notre Dame 13 . . . . Navy 7
Lafayette 7 . . . . Rutgers 6
Syracuse 13 . . . . . Penn State 13
Georgetown 41 . . . . . . Maryland 0
Fordham 13 . . . . Purdue 7
Columbia 7 . . . . Wisconsin 6
Mississippi 34 . . . . . Holy Cross 7
Princeton 14 . . . . . . Dartmouth 9
Brown 13 . . . . Army 9
Stanford 20 . . . . . . Washington 10
Temple 28 . . . . Villanova 0
New York U 12 . . . . F & M 0
Northwestern 32 . . . . . Illinois 14
Nebraska 14 . . . . Iowa 6
Rice 14 . . . . Arkansas 7
Auburn 21 . . . . Clemson 7
California 20 . . . . U S C 7

Ex-Convict Taken Outside Jail at East Cambridge
Continued on Page 7

15,000 Italians Face Capture in Mountains

Fascists Trapped Without Food; General Captured

ATHENS, Nov. 9 (AP)—Greek soldiers fighting stubbornly on home ground have halted the most serious Italian thrust so far offered by the invaders—a move down the western coast—and have hopelessly trapped a famed Italian division of perhaps 15,000 men, it was reported here tonight.

Greeks said the Italian Centaur Division—one of the best-known units of the Fascist forces—was so surrounded in t.e Pindus Mountains that its surrender was imminent and that hundreds of the division's men and its commanding General already had been captured.

It was reported the Fascists were without food and their supply lines were cut.

Authoritative circles in Athens could give no details of the report that the Greeks have stopped the Italian drive down the west coast from Albania.

However, they said the Greeks actually were on the offensive on the remainder of the mountainous front and were pushing the Italians back at several points.

Right Wing Attack Halted

A High Command communique said a local attack on the first wing, supported by artillery fire, was repulsed, while 80 prisoners were captured in other local attacks.

15,000 Italians Face
Continued on Page 7

Russo-Germans

Parley in Berlin Hints at Move in East—Turks Say They Won't Yield

BERLIN, Nov. 9 (AP)—Soviet Russia's Premier—Foreign Commissar Vyacheslaff Molotoff was expected tonight to arrive here next Tuesday upon invitation of the German Government "to continue and broaden the constant exchange of opinions" between Germany and Russia.

It was considered certain that Adolf Hitler personally will receive the visiting Minister, who never before has traveled outside Russia, and engage him in a broad discussion of the war and its repercussions since Nazi Foreign Minister Joachim von Ribbentrop visited Moscow in August, 1939, to sign the non-aggression pact between the two countries.

Japan's Role Likely Topic

Observers believed these topics were on the agenda:
1—Effect of the triple military alliance recently signed by Germany, Italy and Japan.
2—Germany's position in Rumania, where it has Nazi troops "guarding oil wells."
3—Italy's attempted drive into Greece.
4—Status of the Balkans and the Near East—both of which now are brought closer to the edge of war by Italy's offensive from Albania.

Strict silence was observed in official circles and the German press concerning the visit. Its announcement was heralded by the official German news agency, D. N. B., as one of importance "in foreign politics."

Molotoff to Confer
Continued on Page 7

State C. I. O. | **Turkey Will Fight,** | *F. D. Victory*

The Joseph Kennedy interview: November 10, 1940.

posed to be all off the record. I hadn't the ready wit to reply that that was a sound diplomatic position for an ambassador to take. It was a shock. He hadn't taken the more conventional line that he was misquoted. One could hardly misquote a man through two or three columns.

That night Winship phoned me. He'd had a call from Archibald MacLeish, who was librarian of Congress and close to Roosevelt. It was obviously an inquiry for the President, about me and the story.

Next day when I got in, Winship asked if I had a Lippmann column in mind. I didn't. A feature maybe? Not especially, why? "We just want to keep your name in the paper."

I ground out something, a book review, I think, for next morning.

The Kennedy office in Boston, I knew later, was demanding my scalp, and also Winship's.

That week Editor & Publisher, the trade paper of the newspaper industry, had a story about the story. I remember the headline: "Globe Defends Lyons." *

* The Globe's refusal to retract anything on the interview cost them many thousands of dollars in advertising for the Scotch whiskies controlled by Kennedy, which was kept out of the Globe for years. It was wholly characteristic of the Globe management under W. O. Taylor that I never heard of this penalty until I came to write the Globe history.

In a day or two William Allen White came to town to speak. He then headed the interventionist organization called the Committee to Defend America by Aiding the Allies. President James B. Conant of Harvard was its vice president. I knew old Will White. He'd been one of our Nieman dinner guests the year before. He had been most kind to me in 1936, when I had to explore Governor Alf Landon of Kansas after he'd zoomed to the top of the Gallup poll as a presidential possibility. White had had me around to his house to dinner even though he had a prior dinner engagement with Governor Reed of Kansas; he couldn't turn away a journalistic stranger in his home state. He warned me in advance that I must leave soon after dinner because he had an evening's work cut out for him to wean Reed away from his sentiments for Senator Borah instead of Landon.

That noon the city desk asked me when I was leaving for the White luncheon. "As soon as I can finish this piece for afternoon, why?" "Davis Taylor wants to walk up with you." That was sweet of him, and characteristic, to show the paper's support publicly. I introduced Davis to White as my boss. "Oh, we just work in the same shop," Dave corrected.

Kennedy's agents, attacking me and the Globe, spread the story that I had made no notes as evidence that I knew it was an off-the-record conversation. Actually I had made notes, though sparsely, but more than in my much longer talk with Calvin Coolidge in 1929 when I was nine years less experienced as a reporter. Kennedy's talk raced ahead of me. But it was the kind of talk that fixes itself indelibly. If you can get quickly to your typewriter afterward you can reconstruct any vivid impression from an outline of notes. Diplomats always do it that way.

The mayor of Boston, Maurice Tobin, later governor and secretary of labor, was a friend of mine. He'd heard the story of my "no notes" and phoned to say he was telling people: "Louis Lyons once interviewed me for two hours on the financial problems of Boston, which were complicated enough, and he never made a note and reported it completely without a figure out of place."

Well, this wasn't quite so, either. I had the city financial report in my pocket. But the more essential thing was to see the problem through the mayor's eyes, to understand what the man who had to meet it felt was the key to the problem and the way to handle it.

To nobody's surprise, Kennedy resigned as ambassador. I always felt that this was in the cards. He'd been a Chamberlain man and could hardly represent Roosevelt to Churchill. Of course the explosive interview precipitated the resignation.

Kennedy and his friends apparently never forgave me. After 20 years the old incident bobbed up again in articles and biographies when John F. Kennedy ran for president.

But there was no carryover of the feud to Jack Kennedy's generation. We shared a radio panel when he was still a young congressman and he was wholly friendly. I saw him as a newspaperman meets politicians of his home state off and on. The season before he announced for the presidency I asked him to come to a Nieman dinner, where the talk is off the record. He couldn't come then but said he'd be up later. He was, in autumn 1959. We had a two-hour session with him over beer and cheese at the Faculty Club and he talked candidly about running for president, which at that time he had not announced. It would have been a good story, but none of the dozen newspapermen there broke our "off-the-record" rule for Nieman sessions. Nobody ever broke that rule, so far as I know, over the 25 years I presided over the sessions.

War News

The Japanese bombs at Pearl Harbor sent shock waves through the Globe, as doubtless all other newspapers. The shock reaction was positive. Winship moved immediately on executive changes that had been in the planning stage. Willard De-Lue, who had served in about every role on the paper but had been as deft as James Morgan in avoiding executive desks, had already been asked to take a new post as night managing editor, with assurance it would be temporary. Victor O. Jones was now asked to break off his Nieman Fellowship at Harvard to come in as night editor, as Earle Edgerton retired. This had been in the cards for Jones, whose executive talent had for some time been counted larger than the sports editor role. It was with such transition in mind that he'd applied for a Nieman Fellowship. DeLue had served on the copy desk in the first World War and had prepared a war lead for the first edition before the Associated Press had got around to it.

John Barry was now assigned to a daily "war diary," which he developed so successfully that he was soon asked to broadcast a nightly radio digest of the war news. This became a major Boston broadcast throughout the war, to convert Barry into a star radio performer of such status that the National Shawmut Bank took over the broadcast in 1945 and John with it as a vice president. This removed one of the most competent newspapermen and sparkling personalities from the Globe. Barry had joined the staff at 19 in 1920, first as a district reporter but soon on the staff, where he attacked any assignment with enthusiastic zest and wrote it with a crackling exuberance that gave fresh individuality to all Barry stories. One of his notable assignments was to cover a tour across Canada by King George VI in 1939. A typical Barry touch enlivened one of these stories, from a mountain resort in western Canada. Out early for a stroll, the reporter was suprised to encounter the King also stretching his legs around the lawn. To a passing greeting, the King asked the reporter where he was from. Boston, Barry responded, and then with a characteristic mischievous impulse, "you know, where they had the tea party, and Bunker Hill, and all that." "Ah yes," the King said. "An historic city."

Winship discovered that Barry followed the whole gamut of news more closely than any other staffer and was most fertile for suggestions for stories. The managing editor came to rely on Barry's news judgment, and in an era of almost no titles on the Globe he became essentially an associate editor, sifting through daily piles of manuscripts, columns, features, suggestions to select the most timely copy from the miscellaneous offerings. Against this background, he took over the daily grist of war copy to digest a daily analysis.

Winship himself edited the front page war news for the evening paper with personal attention to the top headline, in frequent consultation with Barry. One of the managing editor's particular contributions was to distinguish the solid news from the speculative, the propaganda, the rumor, and the indefinite. A boldface underlined "unconfirmed" over a dubious report became a Winship trademark in the evening paper, a warning to the reader that this news might not be so.

The war uncorked the special talents of one of the Globe's latent resources, Carlyle Holt. A veteran of the first world war, Holt had by now been on the Globe nearly 20 years. He was a regular chess mate of Frank Sibley's, equally long and stringy, a laconic listener to Sib's chatterbox. Holt lived in Salem and Sib in Hingham; both were at home with boats, handy for shipwrecks, yacht races, or maritime affairs. Holt had had a rugged youth. He had been to Harvard, class of 1912, but left to drive an ambulance in France in World War I and later to serve in the Yankee Division. He'd been pretty badly shot up in the war and came back somewhat subdued. He had lost a good deal of one hand and had become adept at one-handing a typewriter. Few reporters use more than two fingers, but this is most usually done with two hands, pecking with the forefingers.

Holt was a no-nonsense reporter, sound, skeptical, but he went about his assignments with an air of detachment as though newspapering was tame stuff after war. He'd stick his beaten-up hat on the side of his head and saunter casually off the chess game to a story. But the war opened opportunities that rejuvenated him. He became in effect the military editor.

He toured through American defense plants for a series, "Arsenal of Democracy." A little later he visited the military training camps for a series on the preparation of the American military forces. This led to an interview with Gen. George Marshall that made a notable story, for Holt was one of the first to realize General Marshall's quality and to publicize the impressive character of the man who directed the war effort.

Holt then went overseas with the American Air Force in 1943, the first of a series of Globe war correspondents; he received the European campaign ribbon for "outstanding and conspicuous service with the armed forces under difficult and hazardous conditions." He reported the air cover for the D-Day assault on the coast of France from an air base in Britain.

The black headlines of the battle in Normandy following D-Day pushed to the inside a story headed "Invasion Prelude" that caught the eye of Davis Taylor. It described the tedious dress rehearsals for the D-Day assault by a Coast Guard unit and presented interesting glimpses of their rest interludes in a quiet English town and of the people of the town. Obviously written before D-Day, it had been held back and appeared in the Globe June 13. It carried the byline "By Thomas Winship" (a Coast Guard combat correspondent). Davis knew who Tom Winship was, son of the managing editor. He also knew Winship's feeling about nepotism on the Globe; there was too much of it. But Davis filed Tom's name in the back of his mind. It would keep. As things turned out, on demobilization Tom went to the Washington Post. Soon after, Ben Bradlee joined the Post. For the next 25 years the two kept in touch and swapped ideas. Davis kept an eye on the Post. So did Laurence Winship, for different reasons. He kept up a stream of memos to Tom on the Post's handling of the news. Tom kept them all.

Victor O. Jones.

Victor Jones

The Globe's principal war correspondent was Victor Jones, who left the night editor's desk to go overseas in 1943 and crossed the Rhine with the American forces, to continue throughout the war. The Nazi surrender May 8, 1945, found Jones with the U.S. 9th Army, halted by their orders 30 miles short of Berlin, which the Russians had taken. Jones reported the disappointment of the generals to be balked of their ultimate target, but noted "It is OK with the GI's not to keep on to Berlin." The strategists figured that a final drive on Berlin would have cost another 20,000 casualties.

Jones had come onto the paper in 1928 out of Harvard, where he had been College correspondent. This meant mostly sports. Within five years he was sports editor, presiding over a by-then large staff with many pages to edit. Jones, the staff used to say, introduced English to the sports department. But his own English had verve, vigor and style, and a whimsical touch. In the college era that followed raccoon coats — when undergraduates all seemed to be wearing Oxford gray — Jones reported a stadium response to a touchdown play: "The Harvard stands rose like 10,000 undertakers."

When Jones became sports editor, presiding over a corps of veteran sports writers who had been household names for years, he was 28. James O'Leary was still writing baseball. Mel Webb moved from baseball to football with the season. John Hallahan was the most familiar byline on track events; he was also a popular football referee. William Whitcomb was golf editor. Leonard Fowle had then been yachting editor 23 years and was the best known name in yachting in New England. At his death in 1935 the Eastern Yacht Club established a Leonard Munn Fowle

Memorial Trophy. Dave Egan had a column. Bert Woodlock ranged over the world of schoolboy athletics. Gene Mack's cartoons, a central fixture of the first sports page, dramatized the big game daily. By the time Jones moved out of sports most of these familiar names had gone. Jerry Nason took over with a new generation. One of the new names, that would grow larger, was Harold Kaese, who came over from the Transcript at its end.

The sports world in Jones's period of the 1930's was in transition. New athletic powers were rising to challenge the long dominance of Harvard locally and the Ivy League generally. Jones, though a Harvard man, brought a more contemporary view to the sports scene and pulled the Globe out of its long parochial Harvardiana. Boston College and Boston University came into their share of the top sports headlines.

A most unexcitable temperament, Jones could establish an atmosphere of peace even in the midst of the night's news crisis. Everything was always under control. He always had time to stop and chat or show a visitor around the office. When he became managing editor in 1955, and then the Globe's first executive editor of both papers in 1962, he filled a generation gap between editor Winship and the younger layer of staff. But his health went back on him and he had to give up executive work. This turned him back to writing. His breezy contributions soon established him as a regular columnist to yield for the Globe a light, chatty column that made about the easiest reading in the evening paper until his death in 1970.

Otto Zausmer

Just before the second world war opened in Europe in 1939, the Globe acquired its first European journalist since John O'Callaghan in the 1880's.

Otto Zausmer left his native Vienna when Hitler moved into Austria. Then 31, with a doctorate from the University of Vienna, he was assistant managing editor of the Volks-Zeitung. With his wife, the former Elizabet Fleischmann, he went to London in June 1938, there to wait nine months for their turn in the quota to America.

With only a visitors' visa, the Zausmers could not have had employment in England. They worked on the English language — Zausmer knew only two words of English when he left Vienna, beefsteak and roast beef. Coming to Boston in March 1939, Zausmer began free-lance writing even while acquiring the idiom of English. His wife picked up her medical studies, to specialize in rehabilitation of polio victims, and became later a member of the faculty of Boston University and the staff of Children's Hospital.

A friend introduced Zausmer to managing editor Winship, who said he had nothing for him, but suggested lunch. Zausmer remembered the lunch. For a Boston treat at Patten's, Winship ordered oysters, a strange and horrifying dish to Zausmer, who couldn't have got an oyster down if his life depended on it. But in spite of his embarrassment at having to finesse the oysters, he found Winship interested in his story. The editor took down his address, and two weeks later he phoned. Hitler was making a much heralded speech, at 5 A.M. Boston time. The Globe was going to try to take it down from short wave. Would Zausmer like to come in and help Dorothy Wayman with the translation? That stint finished by nine o'clock. Winship listened to Zausmer's impressions of the speech, then suggested he write it down for the evening paper. Zausmer sweat it out in his half-learned English. He was sure Winship would have to rewrite it. But the editor suggested that if he had an idea for a story. Zausmer should call him. He did, two or three times a week. He also had a chance to write some pieces for the Christian Science Monitor on the European economy.

When the war opened in August the Globe's interest in their Austrian free-lance writer increased. In early 1940 Zausmer suggested that he monitor the war news from Germany and the Balkans by short-wave radio. The Globe ordered a handsome, big console radio for his apartment. But handsome as it was, its short-wave reception was deficient. Davis Taylor, by now general manager under his father, told Zausmer to shop for an adequate radio and tell him the price. It was $700. "Go ahead, get it," said Davis. More than 30 years later Zausmer was still using it. The short wave brought some interesting and important news, which the Globe used at first as by their "Austrian editor," then their "Short Wave editor."

The pace of the war brought increasing chances for Zausmer features, and his grasp of the English idiom grew. Finally Winship suggested he join the staff; but he'd have to give up the Monitor, where he was by now contributing three pieces a week. When Zausmer told Charles Gratke, foreign editor of the Monitor, Gratke was glad for him but said: "The Globe won't want your economic pieces. Can't we use them under a pseudonym?" That was all right with Winship. So Gratke sat down to concoct a pseudonym out of Zausmer's name. He took the last three letters *mer,* then the *z,* but decided to change that to a *k.* Then the last two letters of Otto, *to,* made it Theo, then for good measure he tucked in a von: Theo von Merk, and so Zausmer appeared regularly in the Monitor until, after America's entry into the war, the government sought his linguistic ability and knowledge of the Balkans for its European office of the Office of War Information. He served overseas through the war, then made a dramatic re-entry to the Globe.

At the end of the war, Lyons had gone to Europe to report the disintegration of Germany, had gone with the American occupation forces to Berlin, and then went to witness the restoration of the governments of Denmark and Norway, then to the Potsdam Conference. After that he found himself on a dim morning in London fog, at breakfast in the American mess in Grosvenor Square; he asked a table mate to pass the sugar.

"Louis, what are you doing here?" It was Zausmer, just getting out of his wartime service and rejoining the Globe to go to Vienna, which he hadn't seen since before the war, for his first assignment.

To get to Vienna it was necessary first to move into the orbit of General Patton's Third Army, headquartered at Munich. Zausmer had got hold of a small car. The two drove down across the German countryside and found stories to write in the Third Army area of Bavaria. Then to Vienna, where Zausmer had old acquaintances to look up and their stories of the war to piece together. Lyons found old neighbors in the American occupation group and other stories. The next natural target was Czechoslovakia, in the Russian zone. They waited half a day for a Russian colonel, in Vienna for conference with the Americans, to sign passes. As they made their way to the car the colonel came chasing after them with a blonde interpreter. Could he ride to Prague with them?

The colonel was curious about two things. The first was the American Negro. This made considerable conversation. Then he asked about the American oil pipeline across the Atlantic, a Russian legend Lyons had heard in Berlin: it was the Russian explanation of the swift movement of Patton's tanks across Europe. The colonel quite evidently preferred the myth to the reality. At the zone crossing, they showed their passes to the American guards at one end of the bridge. At the other end, the colonel jumped out, pushed the Russian guard in the chest, and waved the car on.

After calling on the American ambassador, the two reporters looked up the Allied mess for dinner. A Czech functionary asked for credentials. Zausmer had his OWI card, good anywhere. "I haven't got anything," Lyons said. "Yes, you have," insisted Zausmer. "Look in your wallet." Lyons extracted a U.S. treasury card and the head waiter bowed them to a table. "One American card looks like any other to a Czech," said Zausmer.

From his acquaintances in Prague, in a visit that night, they learned the tragedy of the city. Hearing the guns of Patton's army, the Czech resistance rose against the German garrison. But Patton had his orders to keep to his side of the zone line. The Germans destroyed the resistance fighters before the Russian forces arrived a few days later to be hailed as liberators.

The end of the war brought quick disillusion with the Russians. They had been comrades in arms. Their communism had been overlooked in their heroism at Stalingrad, their liberation of Czechoslovakia, their capture of Berlin.

But in Berlin, political and military contact revealed a bellicosity that first baffled, then shocked and incensed the Americans there, notably the American zone commander, Col. Frank Howley. The two correspondents inevitably reflected this. Soon letters to the editor were asking what had happened to Lyons and Zausmer to color their reports anti-Soviet? But their direct contact was only a little ahead of public realization that the wartime comradeship had ended abruptly. The "liberation" of the Balkans quickly became a communist takeover. By 1947 when Winston Churchill at Fulton, Missouri, described an "iron curtain," Americans recognized the description. The communist coup in Czechoslovakia the next year and the death of Jan Mazaryk confirmed the Divided World.

"Count the Bodies"

The Cocoanut Grove fire, November 28, 1942, dealt Boston its most terrible disaster in modern times. A flash fire in a crowded nightclub with flimsy paper decorations and too few exits wiped out 479 lives in a few moments. The Grove had packed in nearly 1,000 patrons that night, many of them gay young people who had stayed in town after an epic football game that saw unbeaten Boston College dethroned in its bowl prospects by an upset victory for Holy Cross.

The football drama was the big story that Saturday night as the early first Sunday edition was going to press at 10:30. Just then the fire alarm rang in the Globe news room. A fire at Cocoanut Grove, a possibility of injuries. Ambulances were being sent. Samuel B. Cutler, the top rewrite man on the night side, dashed off a few paragraphs that just made a spot on an inside page in that edition. Then the alarm rang again, and again and again, five alarms within 20 minutes.

Acting city editor Philip Denvir had sent reporter Nat Kline to the club at the first alarm. Now he looked around the office at his sketchy Saturday night crew, sent out a reporter and photographer to collect any Globe men at nearby restaurants or taverns. One of the first men turned up was photographer William Ennis, who said later, "All I had to do was stand in one place and keep shooting." Nat Kline called in: "My God, Phil, they can't handle the bodies. They're laying them out on the sidewalk." In the office Nye Rosa and a group of photographers and layout men had spent the evening mapping four pages of pictures and stories of the football game. They had stayed on for a card game in the sports department. They were just leaving when Denvir discovered them and bundled them all into a cab. One was Harry Holbrook, a Globe man then in the service. As Holbrook stepped out of the cab someone handed him a body. He laid it carefully in the cab and said "City Hospital." Ennis' first picture was of Holbrook carrying the body. Cabs and cars were drafted to carry bodies to hospitals. Thirteen hospitals and morgues were repositories that night. Whenever bodies were moved to a hospital a Globe reporter followed. Denvir's instructions were the same to all. "Count the bodies. Keep counting. Keep phoning in." Two hundred were taken to City Hospital, where a little later Medical Examiner Timothy Leary pronounced 150 dead. They were moved to the Southern Mortuary; there police reporter Edward Costello followed Leary, who made a deal with the reporter. If Eddie would reinforce the policeman at the door to keep people out so that the medical examiner could do his work, he would share with Costello any identifications he obtained. These Eddie kept phoning in. Denvir then had them checked out through district men who would call back with additional names of those who had been in the same dinner party. Phil Denvir's mobilization of forces that night became a newspaper legend. Phil said Eddie Costello was the architect of the Globe's unmatched service of listing and identifying the dead and injured.

Denvir knew after Nat Kline's first call that there would be 50 or more dead. He reported this to Willard DeLue, night managing editor. DeLue brought together night editor Victor Jones, composing room chief Gus Caesar, and Ray O'Brien, the makeup man, to plan emergency editions, and phoned the circulation manager, Fred O'Neal.

The second edition headline was simply
Scores Dead in Night Club Fire
in 156-point type, five inches high.

By the time the presses stopped at 3:30 the headline had reached 475 dead. The final official figure was 492. By the final city edition Eddie Costello had 65 known dead listed. The list of known injured was longer. A third list of those "missing" was as long as both the others together.

Denvir's staff built up as he reached Globe men by phone and as volunteers heard about the fire and came in. One of the first was Joseph Doherty, Medford district man. Denvir set him to compile lists of dead, alphabetically, with Bob Carr, an office boy, helping. Doherty found 14 of his own friends and neighbors in his listing.

William Tisdall, a day side rewrite man, was one of the volunteers. A psychiatrist friend called him from City Hospital to suggest that families of victims would be thankful to know that most had died painlessly, of fumes. Many bodies were not even scorched. "Noxious gasses," he said. "There'll be one hell of an investigation, Bill. You'll find it centered on flammable decorations and synthetic upholstery." The doctor proved right. The cause of the fire that night was uncertain. A guest's cigarette — a short circuit in the ceiling — . Inquests led to numerous indictments, but only the owner of Cocoanut Grove was convicted and sentenced to 12–15 years in prison on 16 counts of manslaughter.

Lucien Thayer, assistant managing editor, came in at 3:30 to replace Denvir and find relief for exhausted staff. But Eddie Costello stayed through the night at the morgue to finish the listings for Monday. Phil Denvir, DeLue, and Vic Jones left at 8 A.M. for a few hours' sleep, when managing editor Winship and city editor Merrill came in to organize the wrapup of the story for Monday. When Denvir got

The Cocoanut Grove night club fire: November 29, 1942.

The Boston Sunday Globe EXTRA!

VOL. CXLII No. 152 — THE BOSTON SUNDAY GLOBE—NOVEMBER 29, 1942—102 PAGES (6) — PRICE 10 CENTS

400 DEAD IN HUB NIGHT CLUB FIRE

CATHOLIC PRIEST, AT RIGHT, GIVES LAST RITES OF CHURCH TO VICTIM CARRIED OUT BY FIREMAN

Hundreds Hurt in Panic as the Cocoanut Grove Becomes Wild Inferno

By SAMUEL B. CUTLER

The worst disaster in Boston's history last night snuffed out the lives of 399 merrymaking men and women in the blazing inferno of the famous Cocoanut Grove nightclub amid scenes of utter panic and horror.

Crushed, trampled and burned as nearly 1000 patrons, entertainers and employees fought desperately to gain the exits through sheets of flame, scores of victims

List of Known Dead

JEROME ESTES, Coast Guard, address unknown.
GERALD DOWNER, 17 Columbus st. Beverly.
JAMES FITZGERALD, Lake st., Wilmington.
CHARLES DUHAMEL, 19 High st., Millis.
CHARLES HILDRETH JR., 93 Plantation st. Worcester.
VINCENT H. PREZIUSO, 35, 289 Lowell st., Somerville.
HOWARD R. JOHNSON, 40, 52 Burns st. Somerville.
HYMAN STROGOFF, 40 Heatherly road. Brighton, tentatively identified.
WALTER M. KING, 22 Farwell

PHILIP SELETSAY, 45 Rowena road, Waban, and 37 Ferncroft st. Waban.
JACK VIGDOR, 137 Englewood av., Brighton.
CHARLES S. HERTLE, 673 Belmont st., Belmont.
CLYDE C. CLARK, 171 Fort st. Keene, N. H.
ARNOLD M. BAER, 10 Florence st. Dover, N. H.
HARRY J. CONNICK, 66 or 40 Bowdoin st. Boston.
GEORGE T. LOWE, 22 Lynde st. West End.
MARGARET McFARLIN, 52 Mansfield st., Allston.
STEPHEN H. JONES, U. S. N. 4203

COCOANUT GROVE FIRE TIMES

The first alarm was sounded at 10:20 P. M. The "all-out" came at 3:42 A. M.

Frantic Parents Rush to Morgues in Vain Search

By J. MALCOLM BARTER

Frantic relatives, stunned by

Where Bodies Can Be Found

Number of dead as compiled by police at 3:30 a. m. this morning.

Southern Mortuary 166
Northern Mortuary 77
Peter Bent Brigham Hospital. 22
Mass General Hospital........75
St Elizabeth's Hospital........2
St Margaret's Hospital........2
Carney Hospital 2
Cambridge City Hospital......7
Faulkner Hospital 7
Chelsea Naval Hospital........11
U S Marine Hospital, Brighton 7
Beth Israel Hospital............2
Mount Auburn, Cambridge....7

back to the city room he found it full of strangers. "Mr. Winship hired us," they said. Authors, publishers, all kinds of people who knew the town and could write or edit, to help tackle the mound of copy on the city desk that Denvir said was two feet high. Samuel Cutler, who had written the lead story through the several Sunday editions, came back Sunday to sit on the desk and edit Lyons' lead for Monday morning. By the Monday morning edition the Globe had 389 identified dead, listed alphabetically. The staff had assembled 57 individual photographs of victims to go with brief obituaries. In the Monday evening edition the death toll had mounted to 479. They were now listed by cities and towns.

Monday's headlines exploded over the cause and condition of the disaster. "Police Say Busboy's Match Caused Fire / Fire Chief Criticizes Locked Door of Club / Prankishness Real Cause of Tragedy."

The 16-year-old busboy was illegally employed in a liquor establishment. A locked side door could have been an egress for many. The busboy's match was requested to screw in a lightbulb that a customer had loosened to darken his booth. Hatch-like doors to the roof, operated mechanically, couldn't be opened because fuses had been removed to prevent drunken guests tampering with them. Public indignation pressed hard on official inquests to force changes in Boston fire and safety regulations. The statistics of tragedy as the Committee of Public Safety ultimately reported them were 492 dead, 270 injured. An estimated 200 more escaped unhurt. Except for the addition of those whose death was delayed, there was hardly any disparity between the official list and that compiled in the first hours of horror by Denvir, Costello, & Company.

Phil Denvir, then 36, had been 20 years on the paper, from office boy to assistant night city editor. He now became night city editor for another 20 years, then served as suburban editor, and finally as Catholic Church editor to cover Pope Paul's historic visit to the United Nations. When he died in 1968, after 44 years on the paper, managing editor Joseph Dinneen, Jr., wrote of Denvir's marshaling the forces for the Cocoanut Grove coverage that "because of his imagination and ingenuity the Globe was far ahead of its competitors, not only on that day but for weeks and months afterwards."

A lugubrious sequence, to look back into the old files to Sunday, November 29, 1942, to find the four pages of horror story and tragic pictures followed by an equal number of pages and pictures of "the football upset of the year" — the Holy Cross football victory over Boston College, featuring a six-column shot of the hilarious Holy Cross team carrying their beaming coach from the field. But by beating Boston College that afternoon, the Holy Cross men saved their opponents' lives. The one bit of salvage in that night's holocaust was that the reservations made for the Boston College team to celebrate the game were cancelled in defeat.

Frances S. Burns.

"What's This Mean, Mrs. Burns?"

One day in December 1942 a motherly-looking woman came to see the managing editor of the Globe. She wanted a job. "My son is on a submarine and I can't stay home. The only experience I have is the newspaper work I did in Tacoma 25 years ago."

She looked competent, earnest, low-keyed. Then 49, Frances Burns was already a grandmother. One son was a minister, one in the Navy. Her husband was a structural engineer.

Mrs. Burns began handling the news on wartime rationing and gradually expanded her work to cover other of the proliferating alphabetical agencies, especially those concerned with social problems. She proved a thorough reporter and wrote interesting copy. Her comfortable, practical way of going about a story and her keen interest led people to talk freely to her, to give her their confidence. Ordinary stories developed unexpected dimensions with Mrs. Burns, and when they had a human aspect she wrote with feeling. Her work brought her in contact with public health and hospitals.

The great Cocoanut Grove holocaust induced new treatments for burns and brought medicine into the news to stay. Managing editor Winship saw in Mrs. Burns a chance to bridge the gap between medicine and the press, to explore the medical news in the great medical center of Boston. If anyone could break through the tradition that doctors don't talk to the press, Mrs. Burns, with her serious interest and obvious trustworthiness, should be able to do it. She was.

Within a short time she was interviewing Dr. Paul Dudley White on his nationally recognized work in heart disease. She did a series on what the army hospitals were doing to rehabilitate the war wounded. She soon became a familiar of the great hospitals of Boston, a friend of leading physicians. She was too able a reporter to be limited to medicine even after the Globe called her medical editor. She wrote about New England colleges to open a new vein of education reporting. In the fall of 1951 she traveled for a month with Princess Elizabeth in a royal tour across Canada. She proved especially good at biography. Ten months before General Eisenhower's election, the Globe sent her to Abilene and she was ready with a book-length series on the next President. She covered the great Hurricane Carol in 1954, the launching of the first atomic-powered submarine, the *Nautilus*; she reported the reorganization of City Hospital and did a series, "What Causes Heart Failure," in 1955 that brought her an award from the American Heart Association for distinguished reporting. Hers was only the first of a long series of awards for the Globe in medical writing.

Mrs. Burns was on her way to the Eisenhower inaugural in 1953 when the Federal express plowed into Union Station in Washington, a bizarre accident. Coolly she went from the train to the nearest phone and gave the Globe the story well ahead of the wire services. They took it down just as she said it and didn't change a word from her lively description. Standing in the aisle at the moment of the big jolt, "I said: 'What bad driving.'" The story won the New England AP news writing award that year.

Her relations with medical men were such that Paul Dudley White telephoned her when he was called to Denver to treat President Eisenhower for his 1957 heart attack before the word was out from Denver. She grabbed a satchel and followed him. There an Army doctor sat down with her alone and went over Eisenhower's case. Feeling an obligation to press secretary James Hagerty, who was holding off a throng of newspapermen, Mrs. Burns told him about her exclusive interview. "I'm having trouble with my ears, Mrs. Burns," Hagerty said. "I can't hear a thing you say." She had it alone. Later, handling the medical reports, Hagerty asked, "What's this mean, Mrs. Burns?" Frances Burns reported the Nobel Prize discoveries of Dr. John F. Enders and associates at the Harvard Medical School in isolating the polio virus in 1954 and next season attended the announcement of the Salk polio vaccine.

Her most moving story, "Journey Into Surgery," was published anonymously in the Globe November 3, 1957. It was on her own experience on discovering she had cancer, and the emotional and physical ordeal of preparing for the operation and adjusting to life after it. She lived and worked four years after that, covering major stories and interpreting the developments in medical science. On her death February 2, 1961, the director of the Massachusetts General Hospital called her "the best newspaper-science reporter in the United States without any question." Dean George P. Berry of Harvard Medical School said, "I had complete confidence in her and so did all my colleagues. She had the unusual talent of being able to see the meaning of the thing in complete perspective. She could really find the heart of a story and then describe it in accurate terms. Moreover, she had the knack of breathing warmth and life into a complicated story."

Besides being a crackerjack reporter, Mrs. Burns opened up three new channels of news specialization on the Globe, which were now divided among three men, Herbert Black in medicine, Ian Menzies in science, and Ian Forman in education. All three developed these areas further. Menzies went on to become financial editor and managing editor; Forman created a new Globe Sunday magazine; Black, detached from long service as reporter and then copy editor, remained with medicine to establish a reputation and confidence of the medical profession equal to Mrs. Burns's.

The American Cancer Society in 1961 established the Frances Stone Burns Memorial Grant for annual award to a Massachusetts scientist for forwarding cancer research, "in memory of a skilled medical writer who greatly increased public understanding of cancer research."

The Globe set up the Frances Burns Room in the Countways Library at the Harvard Medical School and furnished it with books and journals for the medical press.

United Nations

Back at the office in 1946, Zausmer took over the work John Barry had done assisting the editor until seduced away as vice president of the Shawmut National Bank. A dozen years later the title of associate editor was revived, unused on the Globe for some 70 years, and given to Zausmer. In effect he had become foreign editor. He returned to Europe in 1948 to see the Marshall Plan in operation and made later European trips in 1951, 1955, 1959 and 1960. He visited India in 1955 and Japan in 1960. When Nasser seized the Suez Canal in 1956 and its European investors scoffed that Egypt couldn't operate it, Zausmer got a visa to Egypt and boarded a freighter for a trip through the canal to report that it was operating in full efficiency.

In July 1946 the United States tested the effect of an atom bomb against Navy ships in the sea off Bikini. This was the first atomic bomb test made public and it had a terrific public impact. President Truman sent an evaluation committee that included Senator Saltonstall, President Compton of M.I.T., and Dr. Bradley Dewey, Cambridge industrialist. John Harris went with them to report July 1 on the fourth atom bomb explosion in history and its effect on a "guinea pig" fleet. It capsized one destroyer, sank two transports, and damaged ten other ships. The big ships remained afloat. Admiral Blandy reported the test successful but in a later report said the Navy would have to redesign its ships for the atomic age.

The close of the war found James Morgan and James Powers both at the San Francisco Conference in spring 1945 covering the Allied discussions that shaped the United Nations.

As the United Nations Assembly organized in its first session in London in January 1946, it was quickly agreed that its permanent site would be in the United States; but where? Several cities were candidates. Governor Maurice Tobin of Massachusetts sent a delegation to London to press the claims of Boston. But circumstances in Boston were not much help. The mayor, James M. Curley, was on trial in federal court for using the mails to defraud. In February he was convicted, but he continued as mayor. The same month, while a UN committee was inspecting Boston sites, a local Boston judge, John Swift, supreme knight of the Knights of Columbus, achieved headlines with an attack on the UN. "The UN has banished the very name of God from its deliberations. All the world knows that godless Russia has torn the Atlantic Charter to shreds and enslaved millions of our fellow Catholics."

WEATHER
TUESDAY—Clearing.
Full Report, Page 16.

The Boston Daily Globe
Reg. U. S. Pat. Off.

VOL. CXLVIII   By THE GLOBE NEWSPAPER CO.   BOSTON, TUESDAY MORNING, AUGUST 7, 1945—SIXTEEN PAGES   THREE CENTS in New England 5c Elsewhere

GUIDE TO FEATURES
Burgess ....12 | Editorials .10 | Society 7
Crown Word 8 | Financial ..12 | Sports 11
Dr Crane ..11 | Obituaries 13 | Theatres 4
Culbertson.12 | Radio ....8 | V Forum 7
Deaths ....13 | Serial ......1 | Woman 7
HOME FRONT CALENDAR ... Page 8

ATOM AGE AT HAND

Official Text Tells of High Drama During 1st Bomb Experiment

★ ★ ★

Tech Man Pressed Detonation Button

Harvard President Key Test Figure

Black Desert Flames Like a Bright Day

Clouds Disappeared in Path of Blast

Observers 10,000 Yards Away Felled

More Important Than Electricity

★ ★ ★

WASHINGTON, Aug 6 (AP) —The text of the War Department statement describing the first test of the atomic bomb: (It was also issued locally in New Mexico).

Mankind's successful transition to a new age, the Atomic Age was ushered in July 16, 1945, before the eyes of a tense group of renowned scientists and military men gathered in the desertlands of New Mexico to witness the first real results of their $2,000,000,000 effort.

Here in a remote section of the Alamogordo Air Base 120 miles southeast of Albuquerque the first man-made atomic explosion, outstanding achievement of nuclear science, was achieved at 5:30 a. m. of that day.

Darkening heavens pouring forth rain and lightning immediately up to the zero hour heightened the drama.

Mounted on a steel tower, a revolutionary weapon destined to change war as we know it, or which may even be the instrumentality to end all major wars was set off with an impact which signalized man's entrance into a new physical world.

Success was greater than the most ambitious estimates. A small amount of matter, the product of a chain of huge specially constructed industrial plants, was made to release the energy of the universe locked up within the atom from the beginning of time. A fabulous achievement had been reached. Speculative theory, barely established in pre-war laboratories,

had been projected into practicality.

This phase of the atomic bomb project, which is headed by Maj Gen Leslie R. Groves, was under the direction of Dr. J. R. Oppenheimer, theoretical physicist of the University of California. He is to be credited with achieving the implementation of atomic energy for military purposes.

Tension before the actual detonation was at a tremendous pitch. Failure was an everpresent possibility. Too great a success, overshadowed by some of those present, might have meant an uncontrollable unusable weapon.

Men There Were Prisoners

Final assignment of the atomic bomb began on the night of July 12 in an old ranch house. As various component assemblies arrived from distant points, tension among the scientists mounted apace. Coolest of all was the man charged with the actual assembly of the vital core, Dr. R. F. Bacher in normal times a professor at Cornell University.

The entire cost of the project, representing the erection of whole cities and radically new plants spread over many miles of countryside, plus unprecedented experimentation, was represented in the pilot bomb and its parts. Here was the focal point of the venture. No other country in the world had been capable of such an outlay in brains and technical effort.

The full significance of these closing moments before the final factual test was not lost on these men of science. They fully knew their position as pioneers into another age. They also knew that one false move would blast them and their entire effort into eternity.

Before the assembly started a receipt for the vital matter was signed by Brig Gen Thomas F. Farrell, Gen Groves' deputy.

This symbolized the formal transfer of the irreplaceable material from the scientists back to the Army, which had originally produced it at one of its great separation plants.

During final preliminary assembly, a bad few minutes developed when the assembly of an important section of the bomb was delayed. The entire unit was machine-tooled to the finest measurement. The insertion was partially completed when it apparently needed delicate handling and would go no further.

Dr. Bacher, however, was undismayed and reassured the group that time would solve the problem. In three minutes time, Dr. Bacher's statement was verified and basic assembly was completed without further incident.

Specialty teams, comprised of the top men on specific phases of science, all of which were bound up on the whole, took over their operation after they proved themselves willing to build democracy.

"We shall assist you to rebuild your life on a democratic basis." Eisenhower said in a proclamation to the Germans. The American commander demanded, however, that "there must be no idleness," particularly during and before the coming winter which, he said, would be a hard one.

See IKE   Page 5

Temporary Agreement Ends Bus Strike in Salem Area

As a result of a temporary agreement between union and company officials of the Eastern Mass. Street Railway reached at 1:00 a. m. today normal bus service will be in operation in Salem today. Intervention by three members of the Salem Chamber of Commerce brought about the agreement.

SALEM, Aug 6—Approximately 40,000 persons were left stranded in the rain during the rush hour late today by what Eastern Mass. experts Street Railway officials termed a "surprise strike" by 67 A. F. L. union bus drivers of the Salem division. The was the second week stoppage in less than two months in the Salem area.

See BUS   Page 13

Meanwhile Jap Railroads Stop Running Where First Atomizer Hit

Jap Railroads
Enemy Broadcast Hints Terrific Damage Done

WASHINGTON, Aug. 6 (UP)—The Osaka radio without referring to the atomic bomb dropped on Hiroshima—hinted tonight at the terrific damage it must have caused by announcing that train service in the Hiroshima and other areas had been canceled.

First mention of the bomb itself came in a Japanese Domei Agency dispatch announcing that President Truman and Prime Minister Clement Attlee had disclosed that the new missile had been dropped on Hiroshima, a leading Japanese port of embarkation.

The Osaka radio report of the atomic bomb said this afternoon that the B-29s had begun a campaign against Japanese communication centers and warned that such assaults would be intensified. The broadcast, recorded by United Press in San Francisco, did not mention any unusual form of explosive dropped by B-29s.

New Ultimatum May Give Japs 48 Hours

TOKYO, Aug 7 (Japanese Time)—President Harry Truman and P,ime Minister Clement Attlee are announced simultaneously yesterday. Monday, that American aircraft on Sunday afternoon dropped an 'Atomic bomb' on Hiroshima, according to United Press and Reuters newscasts recorded here.

A Domei dispatch from Osaka recorded in London by BBC more than 24 hours after the raid, reported that damage inflicted in the raid was still under investigation.

See RAILROADS   Page 4

24 Hours After Hit Jap Target Still Hidden in Dust

WASHINGTON, Aug 6 (AP)—Hiroshima, first enemy city to feel the American atomic bomb, was a major military target. Twenty-four hours later, whether it is still anything important could not be determined. Smoke and dust still clouded the place.

See TARGET   Page 4

Ike Grants Germans Right to Form Trade Unions, Parties

BERLIN, Aug 6 (AP)—The United States and Britain today gave the conquered Germans permission to form free, local trade unions and local political parties, but Gen Eisenhower warned the German people they would get full freedom only after they proved themselves

ATOMIC BOMB'S FIRST TARGET—Reconnaissance view of Hiroshima before attack.
(Army Air Forces Wirephoto)

Bomb Can Render Japan Unlivable for 50 Years, Churns Up Earth

By ERNEST BARCELLA
WASHINGTON, Aug 6 (UP)—The most terrifying engine of destruction ever devised by man—an atomic bomb carrying the explosive force of more than 20,000 tons of TNT—was turned loose against Japan Sunday as American airmen opened a "surrender or else" assault against the enemy homeland.

A local scientist told a Globe man that should Japan he hit

See WEAPON   Page 2

La Luce Acclaimed In Debut as Candida

By MARJORY ADAMS
STAMFORD, Conn., Aug. 6—Clare Boothe Luce, Fairfield county's fair representative in Congress, made her debut as a professional actress tonight before the most glittering group of Broadway celebrities that ever came to this city.

See LUCE   Page 8

Bong, Top U. S. Ace, Dies in Coast Crash

Shot Down 40 Jap Craft; Killed in Test Flight of New Jet Plane

BURBANK, Calif., Aug 6 (UP)—Maj Richard Bong, America's greatest air ace, died today in the flaming wreckage of a jet propelled fighter plane which crashed while he was testing it.

Only 24 years old, he wore 26 decorations including the nation's highest honor, the Congressional Medal of Honor. He

MAJ RICHARD BONG

had shot down 40 Japanese planes without a scratch.

The knowledge he gained in those battles was so valuable to risk, so he was brought home to "safe" duty. He was on that "safe" duty today when his P-80 Shooting Star hurdled over a clump of trees and burst like a bomb in a bare field.

See BONG   Page 5

Atom Age
Force in Peacetime Can Alter Civilization

By GEORGE A. ORTON
The new source of energy, released for the first time Sunday as a destructive force against the Japanese empire, has power enough to effect awesome changes in the course of civilization, according to Cambridge scientists.

They predict alterations in politics, economics, sociology, commerce and industry when the death-dealing properties of uranium are harnessed in molding a new world of peace.

At University of Southern California Dr. R. E. Vollrath said that the new atomic bomb is what he believes it to be, "we shall have a power revolution that will eliminate coal and oil as a source of power, and the industrial revolution will become minor in comparison with it."

Long a research worker in atomic energy, Dr. Vollrath predicted the nation or nations having fullest control of atomic power would have control of the world's destiny.

By liberating the power of uranium, man told the Associated Press, man's attempt to reach the moon is brought within the bounds of possibility.

Churchill Tells How Allies Won Atom Death Race

LONDON, Aug. 6 (AP)—Former Prime Minister Churchill said tonight that it was "by God's mercy" American and British, instead of German scientists, discovered the secret of atomic power "long mercifully withheld from man."

Churchill's statement, released by his successor at No. 10 Downing st., Clement Attlee, advised the Japanese in effect to surrender or face utter destruction.

"It is now for Japan to realize, in the glare of the first atomic bomb which has smitten her, what the consequences will be of indefinite continuance of this means of maintaining the rule of law in the world," he asserted.

See CHURCHILL   Page 3

Advance of Mankind

Use of this energy source is even more important to the advancement of mankind than were epoch-making discoveries of past centuries—the invention of the wheel—the discovery that in heat there is power and the translation of that discovery into steam engines; the discovery and development of electricity—the development of the internal combustion engine.

See PEACE   Page 3

Truman to Reach Capital Tomorrow

ABOARD U. S. S. AUGUSTA, Aug. 6 (AP)—The U. S. S. Augusta is headed for an east coast port from which the President will return to the White House. It was announced today. He expects to be in Washington by Wednesday.

The time for his nation-wide radio report on the Big Three meeting has not been set.

How Atom Was Split
Pluto, New Chemical, Unlocked Vast Energy

By JOHN J. O'NEILL
Boston Globe-New York Herald Tribune Science Editor
To produce a superatomic energy source, a new chemical, Pluto, was created by science.

The new element never existed in nature. It was created entirely by artificial processes and was found to have explosive properties even greater than

A Comparison
By the United Press
C. B. S. Correspondent Douglas Edwards reported from London a "single atomic bomb contains more than a fourth of the explosive power of all the bombs the Germans sent against England in five years—about 75,000 tons."

those of "Uranium 235," which was the original source through which tremendous amounts of atomic energy were released from matter—3,000,000 times as much as is released from equal weights of TNT.

Pluto is the newer element now existing in existence. It has an atomic weight of 239, one unit heavier than "Uranium 238" which is the heaviest natural element. It is created by shooting a neutron, a sub-atomic particle of matter, into "Uranium 238."

See NEW CHEMICAL   Page 10

The Russian delegate immediately demanded that Boston be eliminated from consideration. It was.

After the war Carlyle Holt found a new groove when the United Nations began operations in New York. This became his assignment, and the solid work of the UN was his meat. He got as much UN news into the Globe as anybody on a paper outside New York.

In 1947 Holt went to the Moscow Conference of Foreign Ministers with Secretary of State George Marshall and reported from Russia for 50 days. Between UN sessions he would be back on editorials or helping edit the Sunday paper, a regimen he kept up until his death in 1949 at 59.

Henry Harris followed Holt as UN correspondent in 1949 — a happy assignment that fitted his lifelong pacifism. He published a book in 1949, *To Wage Peace,* that expressed his philosophy in a study of the structure and rationale of international accommodation.

Harris came to the Globe in 1920 after selling some Sunday features out of Harvard, where he had been an appreciative student of literature under Charles Townsend Copeland, "Copey." A little later he managed to study law on the side and earn a law degree at Boston University. He never practiced, but added law to his background in literature and his aptitude for politics.

He had a sweet disposition, a warm, natural response to all human situations, an intellectual curiosity, lifelong study habits, an incisive style. He was a maverick scion of a banking family, related to the Websters of Stone & Webster, who had adventured into journalism and taken to it. His family were proud of his attainments in this other world. He was an uninhibited individualist, a natural man, often so preoccupied with his work that he was unconscious of the state of his clothes or hair, and absent-minded even about meals. Colleagues goggled at the number of times a day he would cross the street to Thompson's Spa for a cup of coffee—he had forgotten he'd just had coffee. Breaking off smoking, he acquired a habit of wadding copy paper into his mouth. One day a colleague, reaching for the first take of his editorial, found Henry had chewed it up.

His natural sympathies led him to throw himself into causes. He volunteered research for Senator David I. Walsh in several campaigns, worked for LaFollette's progressive campaign for president in 1924, and was later an ardent New Dealer. Through the thirties and forties he was a feature writer. In World War II he did a daily feature, "The Strategic Slant," on war backgrounds. He often served on the editorial page and became a permanent member, after William Packer's retirement in 1954, until he died in 1965.

Copy Desk versus Composing Room

It was long a legend on the Globe that nobody was ever fired. Like most legends it was not perfect. A man had been fired for cutting the files, an incredible stupidity and as felonious as robbing a man of his memory. Another firing was for stealing a typewriter. But a firing that was applauded throughout the building occurred early in the second world war. The war was responsible for the paper's having to hire anyone it could get to fill the copy desk.

One wartime recruit was a brash and pushing fellow whose manners and language made his desk mates uncomfortable. One night when Joe Levin was in the slot, distributing copy to the men on the rim, the new man kept needling Joe about his handling of copy, calling one of his headlines "stupid." Joe ignored him. But when Joe tossed over some copy to Paul Kennedy, one of the best of desk men, the needler remarked that it was ridiculous to have such a stupe as Joe giving orders to Paul Kennedy. "Yes and I'm giving orders to you too," Joe warned him. "I'm ordering you to shut up." "You goddammed kike. I'm coming around and punch you on your Jew nose," threatened the man. He lunged at Joe. Others leaped to break it up.

Willard DeLue, night managing editor, heard the outburst from his office. He stepped out and beckoned the offender into the office. "You know you have committed the unforgivable thing. Of course you are all through here," DeLue told him. He added that he would give him a reference as an editor if he needed one. "You have a lot of ability. The trouble is that you know it."

DeLue left a memo explaining the firing for managing editor Winship, who sent a note down to the cashier to take the name off the payroll. Later that morning Winship had occasion to go down to see the publisher. W.O. stood up and held out his hand, a gesture so unprecedented that Winship asked, "What's that for?" "For firing that fellow."

The desk in the old building was a real horseshoe, the classic shape of the newspaper copy desk that has been modified to adapt to the space patterns of modern plants.

For the first third of the century, Harry Poor as night editor filled roles that later occupied half a dozen editors. He supervised the editing of everything that went into the paper on a single copy desk. The universal desk continued after Earl Edgerton followed Harry Poor in 1934. Sports news was the first area to receive special treatment. Its volume pressed on the desk.

In 1939 Willard DeLue was appointed to a newly created post, night managing editor. He set up a separate sports desk under Alec Gibson, assisted by William Waldron. Sports was assigned a special room off the desk.

Wartime paper rationing retarded further specialization. The paper was small and space at a premium. "The long story died in the second world war," says Joe Levin, who did his share in killing it off. "The copy desk had to be merciless in cutting."

DeLue introduced copy control to cope with the eternal problem of "overset" copy for which the tight newsprint situation afforded no space. This led to inaugurating a news conference at seven o'clock that brought night city editor, sports editor, and night editor together. The initial purpose was to see that the night editor became aware of the local news prospects in time to give them an adequate share of the tight space. The conference lapsed after the war, to be reinstituted more formally a dozen years later.

The management was persuaded to go into a uniform type face, Cheltenham, to replace the jumble of type varieties that had been going into Globe headlines.

Then came a physical reshaping of the whole editorial floor. The chief objective was to bring the city editor and the desk close enough together to facilitate communication; they had been the depth of the building apart. But also, the rabbit warrens that had housed reporters in rows of cubicles along corridors were eliminated in favor of a central news room. This involved relocating the library and the Sunday department, expanding both by pushing down walls to the old Advertiser Building and the Schrafft Building, with the end result that the Globe fifth floor acquired for the first time a reasonable resemblance to a modern newspaper shop.

With Victor Jones back from the war as night editor, Willard DeLue went to Rome in early 1946 to report a Eucharistic Congress. He stopped in Ireland for what was to be a vacation but, captivated by the Irish spring, he sent back a string of tales of Ireland that the Globe published under the title "Come Back to Eire," in which was "some of the most pleasant reading we have been privileged to publish in a long time," as the paper said in reprinting a selection of tales in a pamphlet.

The Sunday editorship had been unfilled since the death of F. Ambler Welch the year before. DeLue was persuaded to take it on. But he soon found that Daniel O'Brien, who had been filling in, could manage the Sunday department, so he went back to travel and features. Jones continued as night editor for ten years until he became managing editor when Roy Johnson took up the night editorship.

Copy control was the preoccupation of the desk through this period, and it became an intense issue in the late 1950's, when Everett Mitchell followed Johnson as night editor. "Overset" was still the problem. Classified ads could come in until 10 P.M. Until then the composing room could not calculate the news hole within four columns. So the desk had to work on an estimate plus or minus four columns and could only be sure of the shape of the paper after ten o'clock. To set four columns more than could be used was of course wasteful. The composing room blamed the copy desk rather than the advertising department. The night editor battled nightly with the composing room and had to explain daily to the publisher. Against the unionized strength of the composing room and the economic strength of advertising, the copy editors were low men on the totem pole. Finally Mitchell assigned Joe Levin to get rid of overset, giving him three months. Levin went at it with slide rule precision. He got a space estimate on every story and dummied every page.

Within his three-month limit, Levin had the satisfaction of a call from the composing room. "Haven't you any copy? Our machines are idle." Said Levin, "I can't send you any more without being overset." The upshot was that the composing room agreed on a necessary amount of overset as reasonable. With this rigidity removed the desk had a new flexibility to develop and display the worth of a story.

One of DeLue's innovations as night editor was to organize the picture side with a night picture editor. Pictures had been handled casually, partly because the night editor never knew until late in the evening precisely what total space he would have, after the latest ads were in. Edgerton would mark a picture to be made in cuts of three sizes, for two, three, or four columns, and then see which fitted his space. This was wasteful.

After one or two men had briefly handled pictures, DeLue discovered a young library assistant, Nye Rosa, who quickly impressed the desk with his sensitivity to just the right picture and the way to treat it to bring out its full value. Rosa was given a definite space allotment for pictures. All pictures went to his desk, those from the local staff to illustrate local stories and all syndicate and wire photos. He scaled them to precise size, a three-column 75 lines deep — a real guide to the night editor. Rosa's talent for layouts brought him to the day desk in 1953 to edit special sections, and in 1961 to a new "features desk" that edited all the non-news material. Then in 1963 he went to the Sunday department to edit the Sunday sections, and when the new Sunday magazine was created in 1966 he became its picture editor.

Harry Poor's opposite number as day editor all through the Globe's middle period was George Gavin, who came to the paper out of Harvard College in 1896. Two years later he was assigned to the copy desk, ten years later became assistant day editor, and when he died in 1938 had had a full 40 years of processing the news for seven editions of the evening paper, most of the time in full charge of the operation — a job of constant pressure for rapid evaluation and judgment. The day editor sustained his tensions with a wry humorous twist that seemed incompatible with his formal manner and mien. Gavin was an erect, handsome man of considerable elegance, from his trimmed mustache to his hard collar and neatly pressed clothes. In a traditionally shirt-sleeved department, he presided over the desk from the central slot in jacket and tie, which contributed both authority and composure to the atmosphere of deadline chaos.

All the years that George Gavin was day editor until 1938 he oversaw everything on the copy desk himself. It too was a "universal desk," that is, unclassified. He sat in the slot and assigned the copy around the rim, marking the size of headline on each story, writing the top heads himself, planning the front page, changing it for each of the seven evening editions. Between editions he went across the street for coffee at Thompson's Spa.

The day desk in Gavin's time came on at 7 A.M. and got out their first edition by ten o'clock. They got out the final closing stocks at four. Saturdays some stayed on till six to get out a final football edition with summaries of all the major college games in the east.

Gavin had two copy editors who handled sports. The rest took the news as it came. His assistant day editor, William Jones, was makeup man.

When Jones followed Gavin in 1938, he moved his assistant, Ray Finnegan, into the slot and had a separate makeup man. That gave Jones a chance for more perspective. Wartime paper rationing cut down the number of editions and after the war they were held to five. The volume of war news and Washington news led to a separate slot under Herbert Black, with two copy editors. Sports now had its separate place. That left the local news to the general desk. With fewer editions, press time for the first was pushed off till noon.

In 1949 Jones became financial editor and William Waldron took over as day editor, with Black as slot man. With the increase in size of the paper and expansion into the new building in 1958, copy editing became increasingly differentiated. In 1965 when Tom Winship became editor, Waldron was made an assistant managing editor, the day editor was James Keddie, and under him was a slot man, William Meek, with a separate makeup man. Waldron by now was not even sitting on the desk, but had his separate office to plan next day's paper. After the Traveler folded in 1967, the number of evening editions was reduced to three.

All Polls Failed: 1948

More than a decade after the Globe had taken on the Gallup poll on national issues, its trio of promotion men, John Taylor, Charles Moore, and Robert Ahern, initiated a Massachusetts poll that was a drawing card for a year or more. But in the 1948 election, when Gallup and everybody else went wrong, to forecast a Dewey victory over President Truman, the Massachusetts poll also came a cropper.

The Gallup poll on November 1, the day before election, gave Dewey 49.5 percent, Truman 44.5, Henry Wallace 4, and Strom Thurmond 2.

The Globe's Massachusetts poll had picked the Republican Governor, Robert Bradford, over Paul Dever. On September 27 it gave Bradford 54.7 to Dever's 38.1 with 7.2 undecided. On October 24 its final poll showed Bradford 50, Dever 45.5, and 4.5 undecided.

But the Democratic tide that swept the state put Dever in by 300,000, while Truman carried Massachusetts by 200,000. The Democrats captured the legislature for the first time in many years, as well as all the state offices.

The Globe published Gallup's explanation under the headline "What Happened?" Gallup said: "All public opinion polls have underestimated the Democratic strength. President Truman staged a strong upsurge in the closing days to recapture votes previously lost to Henry Wallace. Obviously a substantial number of undecided voters cast their ballots for President Truman."

Messrs. Taylor, Moore, and Ahern offered no explanation. They just quit the Massachusetts poll. Twenty years later the Globe revived it under professional auspices, the Becker Company, and made a big weekly feature of its testing of public opinion on the whole range of state issues.

Gallup was not alone. The Globe's headline the morning after the 1948 election was "Election in Doubt," for the first time since 1916. It was 11:15 the next day that Dewey conceded when California returns were sure.

A birth control referendum to reform the archaic rigid state law against contraceptives lost by 862,000 to 666,000. A series of labor referenda in the general direction of the national Taft-Hartley law to curb unions lost heavily.

Amasa Howe

A "mercy killing" held regional attention in the winter of 1950 and mustered a corps of Globe reporters to the New Hampshire trial of Dr. Hermann N. Sander. He had had a woman patient hopelessly, painfully dying of cancer. The doctor was charged with ending her life by injecting air into her bloodstream.

On January 2, 1950, the Globe had a banner eight-column headline from Candia, New Hampshire:

Town Rises to Aid Doctor
605 of 650 Voters Sign Confidence Testimonial

Amasa Howe.

In Goffstown, home of the patient, 200 signed a petition to the county grand jury to drop the case. A Manchester clergyman, the Reverend Mark Strickland of the First Congregational Church, preached a sermon on the issue: "If this man is guilty, I am guilty. For I have prayed for those who have suffered hopelessly that they be eased into the experience of death." The New Hampshire Academy of Medicine reaffirmed its "confidence in Dr. Sander."

But Attorney General William L. Pillsbury asserted that "the case will be presented forcefully . . . regardless of personalities and theories." On January 4 the 40-year old physician was indicted for murder. Trial began February 20; Amasa Howe wrote the leads for the evening edition, Charles Whipple and Joseph Dinneen, Jr., for morning.

The prosecution had a nurse who saw the doctor inject air and a medical records clerk who heard the doctor describing it. The patient's husband said that if she had been the doctor's wife or mother he couldn't have done more to help or encourage her in her dying months.

The death certificate had described the cause of death only as cancer. The defense put on a physician at the hospital who gave it as his judgment that the patient was dead before Dr. Sander's injection. The jury grasped at this quibble, deciding in less than an hour that the patient had already been dead.

The March 10 Globe headline:

> Sander Cleared of Murder
> Jury's Quick Verdict on First Ballot Hailed by Throng

So the issue of a "mercy murder" was finally bypassed, after providing a season of emotional and philosophical discussion and a plethora of feature articles on the ethics of shortening a painful death.

This was Amasa Howe's last big story. He died a few months later at 43. His coverage of the Sander trial was much admired by his colleagues, for his quick, sure analysis of the essentials of the day's evidence and his rapid, concise recital for the evening paper. Andy Howe had come to the Globe as office boy at 16. Before his life was cut short by leukemia he had reached the status of a senior reporter, known for his instinctive sense of the key to a story, for his clarity in organizing and writing it. He always had time to lend a hand to the newer men, to make suggestions they remembered. The Boston Press Club in his memory set up the annual Amasa Howe award "to encourage high standards of journalism." The first award was made in 1951 to John Harriman of the Globe "for distinguished writing of public significance."

A benchmark in the Globe's financial department was the arrival of John Harriman in 1947. He had had five years in his twenties on the New York Evening World until it folded in 1931. Then he had served several years in an investment house in New York and for a dozen years had free-lanced, writing over a range from fiction to economics, this against a partly European education and his financial experience.

Harriman, a sophisticated, world-traveled, engaging man, then 43, persuaded the Globe he could give a lift to its financial page. By then the paper could hardly have needed persuading, for its financial page was on a par with its drama criticism — a par of zero. It was nothing but a pasteup of stock quotations and wire reports from Wall Street.

Anybody who wanted financial news had to read the Herald. This had always been so. General Taylor, after his one coup that had siphoned Eben Jordan capital into a failing newspaper, had been about as homeopathic on finance as Henry Ford. William O. Taylor, as we have seen in the depression, had followed this with the other precepts of his father, reinforced by a Boston trustee's conservatism. But Davis Taylor and Winship were impressed with John Harriman's obvious quality. He started a column of financial analysis and economic review that immediately installed something to read on the financial page.

In the 14 years to his death in 1961, Harriman established a reputation as an astute student of economics and a readable writer on its complexities; he attracted financial readers to the Globe, whose financial pages, further enlivened and broadened in scope under Ian Menzies in the early sixties, became a new strand of strength to the paper.

Brink's Notebook

On the underside of finance, the great Brink's robbery of January 17, 1950, the first million-dollar holdup, was not only high drama at the time but a continuing story through two decades in the pursuit and gradual capture and trial of the robbers.

It ripened the career of a Globe reporter, Joseph F. Dinneen, who had then been 27 years on the Globe and had become a specialist in crime news. Dinneen, assigned the Brink's case, followed it through the years and made it the core of his extensive book and magazine writing. His "Brink's Notebook" ran intermittently in the Globe as he followed the case on its meandering way.

Sixteen years earlier Dinneen, with his crime reporter colleague Lawrence Goldberg of the Post, had shared a reward by the Massachusetts legislature for cracking the several robberies and murders of the Millen brothers and Faber, whose timely arrest, it will be remembered, saved two taxi drivers from conviction for murder. Dinneen had made a book out of that, *Murder in Massachusetts.*

More than any reporter after Sibley, Dinneen enacted in real life the role of the legendary reporter. His city editor, W. D. Sullivan, used to observe that "Joe never takes his hat off, so you never can tell if he is coming or going." He was going if his antenna told him the city editor was looking for him with a routine assignment. Joe was a man for the big story and he had the qualifications.

A Dorchester boy, born in 1897, he had grown up familiar with the old ward politics; he distilled that early wisdom into a book, *Ward Eight,* recognized as a classic of politics. He had specialized in shorthand at the High School of Commerce and had three years of law school before serving in the first world war. Then he had two years on the old Boston Record before coming to the Globe library as DeLue was reorganizing it in 1922. The next year he was on the copy desk. So when he started reporting, he had an uncommonly full kit of tools for his trade. There were not many shorthand reporters left and law was useful in police work. He had a keen sense of drama, too. When in the trough of depression the small town of Millville, Massachusetts, went bankrupt and was annexed to another town, Joe's lead was: "Millville, Feb. 19 — This dateline dies."

He was assigned to several pilgrimages to Rome with Cardinal O'Connell in the 1930's and out of this background wrote the biographies of two popes, Leo XI and Leo XII.

A magazine article of Joe's about Mayor James M. Curley, "The Kingfish of Massachusetts," so incensed the Mayor that he threatened suit. But out of the ensuing contact, after Curley had inflicted a tirade on Dinneen, charging the press with chronic unfairness in reporting him, Joe offered to wager that he could write a biography of Curley that would be fair. He wrote the biography, *The Purple Shamrock,* in 1949, chronicling the colorful Curley career.

His magazine, book, and broadcasting assignments finally took Dinneen away from the Globe in 1956, the last year of his life. Nine years later, his son, Joseph F. Dinneen, Jr., became managing editor of the evening Globe, and soon developed his own column in the Sunday paper.

A Vice President Is Picked

As State House reporter, John Harris was part of the Globe team to cover national conventions from 1940 on. His close acquaintance with the Massachusetts delegation gave him an inside track at the 1952 convention that yielded a genuine scoop. He was able to report in detail how Richard Nixon came to be chosen to run for vice president on the Eisenhower ticket. His most helpful pipeline was Max Rabb, who was close to Sinclair Weeks; Weeks was one of the chief strategists, with Henry Cabot Lodge, in harpooning Robert Taft's moves to control the convention through several southern delegations which the Eisenhower men successfully challenged in a preliminary battle that Harris covered.

Nixon at 38 had been less than two years in the Senate from California. Senior Californians were Earl Warren, who had the state's 70-delegate vote and a dozen more on the first ballot, and William Knowland, Republican Senate leader much mentioned for vice president. But in the clutch of the balloting California's role proved negative. It was Harold Stassen who switched Minnesota's votes to give Ike the winning margin after the first ballot.

The evening paper headline Friday, July 11, "Ike Nominated," had the subhead "Report Taft to be Ike's Running Mate / Knowland and Warren Also Mentioned."

But Rabb had whispered Nixon's name to Harris. Harris had learned the signals of the Eisenhower floor managers and when he saw Lodge and Weeks, Sherman Adams, Thomas Dewey, and Senator H. Alexander Smith of New Jersey slip away from the convention floor, to be followed by a series of governors, Fine of Pennsylvania, Thornton of Colorado, Langlie of Washington, Summerfield of Michigan, and other key Eisenhower men, he trailed them to the hotel room of Herbert Brownell and from a participant learned what happened there. In the Sunday Globe July 13 he had the full details under the front page headline:

How Leaders Picked Nixon

By Vote in Hotel Room

Harris had the names of most of the 25 or 30 men who participated, with Lodge or Weeks presiding by turns. He reported that Senator Smith first suggested Taft. But it was objected that the administration would need Taft as key to the Senate. Dirksen's name was brought up. But Dirksen had made a savage attack on Tom Dewey on the floor. Governor McKeldin of Maryland and Senators Homer Ferguson of Michigan and Hickenlooper of Iowa were mentioned but none evoked enthusiasm. Finally Wesley Roberts of Kansas proposed Richard Nixon. As a member of the House Un-American Activities Committee Nixon was credited with having broken the Alger Hiss case by his persistence after other members of the committee had given up.

"At his name all hands went up," Harris reported. "Ike happily OK'd the choice." The word was sent down to the convention and Nixon was chosen by acclamation.

James Morgan wrote Harris a congratulatory note to say that in all his years of conventions, that was the most complete account of the picking of a vice president he had ever seen.

McCarthyism

The Globe in the McCarthy hysteria of the early 1950's took the same neutral bystander's stance as earlier on book banning, the Sacco-Vanzetti case, and the Curley regime. The paper was approaching the end of its dimmest period. But this was a dim period for the press generally; it was particularly vulnerable to exploitation by a demagogue, for its tradition of objectivity had been eroded to a timid neutrality of shallow reporting. What a senator said was news, qualified only by "Senator McCarthy today charged that . . ." The press, largely dependent on the wire services, was deficient in technique to explore the allegations. Very exceptional were the New York Times, Washington Post, Baltimore Sun, Milwaukee Journal, and a few more in checking, challenging, and investigating McCarthy's reckless charges. It was only when the Army-McCarthy hearings brought McCarthy into focus before the television cameras that this naked exposure destroyed him. Senate censure soon followed.

The Catholic community, which predominated in Boston, was especially sensitive to any crusade against communism.

The Globe's failure to challenge or even examine McCarthyism had distinguished company. Senator John F. Kennedy justified his silence on McCarthy to Arthur Schlesinger, Jr., as the historian recorded in *A Thousand Days,* with: "Hell, half my voters in Massachusetts look on McCarthy as a hero." Senator Saltonstall resisted White House efforts to have the Army-McCarthy hearings before his Armed Services Committee, according to Robert Donovan's report in his book *Inside the Eisenhower Administration:* "Saltonstall wanted nothing to do with this hot potato. He was facing a fight for re-election in November and he could see nothing but trouble with the Irish Catholic vote if he got entangled with McCarthy."

The Globe shared their constituency.

The climate of the times lent itself to McCarthy's campaign. He had started his attacks on the Truman administration — that it was infiltrated with communists. So reputable a politician as Senator Taft had encouraged these tactics. The country was confused about the extent of the communist threat after the Alger Hiss trial, a noted spy case in Canada, and the shock of the communist takeover in China. World War II had created an illusion about Chiang Kai-shek's regime that took years to dispel. History had not yet revealed how Chiang had divided his limited energies against both the Japanese and the Chinese communists, whose eighth-route army proved the most effective Chinese fighting force and had won the villages both by their protection against the invaders and by their commitment to the peasants against the landlord class that supported Chiang. General Marshall's impossible postwar assignment to unite China and the communists failed in Chiang's collapse. The shock and disillusionment this brought were easy to turn to attacks on Marshall and suspicion of his State Department aides. The warnings some of them had given of Chiang's failure could be twisted into conniving at it. Secretary Dulles complacently weeded out McCarthy victims in the State Department and accepted a corps of McCarthy agents to keep surveillance on the rest. The politically naive businessmen of the Eisenhower administration proved helpless to cope with McCarthy forays, even when these undermined their projects and decimated their personnel. The

more sophisticated, like Attorney General Brownell, seemed at times bent on out-
doing McCarthy in attacks on the loyalty of the Truman administration and even
President Truman himself.

President Eisenhower long held that it was up to Congress to keep its members
within bounds. Detesting McCarthy, he yet refused "to get in the gutter with him"
and held to this stance until McCarthy slandered and humiliated a general of the
Army. Then the commander-in-chief released the counterattack that brought the
Army-McCarthy hearings. Midway in the McCarthy "investigations" the Democratic members of McCarthy's committee withdrew in outrage. This left witnesses
unprotected and McCarthy often the sole authority, after a closed hearing, of what
had gone on. He would announce to reporters the unveiling of just one more communist plot. It was after such one-man charges in hearings on Fort Monmouth that
the New York Times and Washington Post followed up with their own investigations
challenging the charges.

The Globe exhibited, as in New Deal days, the negative decency of not joining
the hysterical pack that abetted the malice and suspicion of McCarthyism. The
paper did nothing to curry favor with the local reactionaries who applauded Mc-
Carthy. The Herald's political columnists were outright McCarthyites. A featured
columnist on the Traveler, when Harvard elected Nathan M. Pusey its president,
called the Senator to get his view of Pusey, and he published it: "I don't think he
really is a Commy, but . . ." To Globe editorial writers such conduct was con-
temptible. But they could express their loathing only in private. The Globe was
just printing the news.

McCarthy's success in exploiting the watered-down "objectivity" of the press
forced newspapers and wire services alike to consider their responsibility for what
they were printing, and to undertake what was called "interpretive" reporting. This
meant simply reporting in more depth — to look below the shallow surface, to
explore, explain, analyze the meaning of an event. Some papers cautiously at first
labeled such fuller reporting "news analysis." But it was soon expected of a competent reporter that he would bring out as far as he could the full meaning of the
news.

The rising competition of television, that could beat the press with the first flush
of news bulletins, soon confirmed this background reporting as a primary role of
the newspaper.

Charles Whipple covered what could have been called the subversives beat during the heyday of McCarthyism in the early 1950's. He followed the investigations,
hearings, exposures, and trials set off by the confessions of ex-communists, exploited
by the McCarthy staff. Whipple says of the McCarthy period: "We tried to express
ourselves between the lines rather than in them."

Whipple came to know the personal history of all the victims in the local universities, as well as of the hard-core communists. He became so intimately informed
about the convoluted tactics, procedures, and involvements of attack and defense
that he could distinguish between what the Supreme Court was to call "exposure
for exposure's sake" and real cases. This produced for the Globe a scoop on the
grand finale of Harvard's handling of its most difficult problem, "the Furry case."
The big black headlines in the evening Globe Tuesday, May 19, 1953, told the
story:

Report Harvard to Keep Three Professors
Corporation Will Spare Those Who Defied Red Probers

Professor Wendell H. Furry, physicist, Assistant Professor Helen D. Markham of the Medical School, and Leon J. Kamin, a teaching fellow, were the three. They all admitted having been communists at an earlier period but refused to testify about associates.

Next morning's papers confirmed Whipple's story with an elaborate statement by Harvard. Furry's was the primary case: a full professor of physics, he had been a communist until 1947. In that period he had given false information to a Senate committee investigator and had later refused to answer committee questions. This Harvard called "grave misconduct." But he had made a clean breast of his history to Harvard's own inquiry. He had left the Communist party six years earlier. He had never attempted to influence the political thinking of his students. There had been no communist slant in his teaching. He was a man of notable integrity, highly respected by his colleagues, indeed, a disillusioned idealist. Furry was indicted for contempt but several years later the indictment was quashed for inadequate evidence.

Harvard's wrestling with the Furry case under intense outside pressure to fire him was an anxious preoccupation for months in a transition period, after President Conant had left to be ambassador to Germany and before President Pusey had taken over. Paul Buck, provost, and Senior Fellow Charles Coolidge, a leading Boston lawyer, labored jointly over it. Between them they arrived at a cutoff date beyond which a man of probity and enough intelligence to be acceptable as a Harvard professor could not have continued under the domination of communism. Furry's case fell just inside the deadline. To the Harvard faculty this was vastly more than a tactical judgment. It was a declaration of the independence of the University and the saving of an honest man. It was the acid test. In the post-mortems on the McCarthy hysteria, Harvard stood as "a strong point in defense of academic freedom."

V New Era

Davis Takes the Lid Off

William O. Taylor's death in 1955 followed by only two months the deaths of James Morgan and M. E. Hennessy. City editor Charles Merrill had died in 1951; Sunday editor Ambler Welch in 1945; A. J. Philpott in 1952; Frank Sibley and Carlyle Holt in 1949. In 1946 John Barry had gone into banking and Louis Lyons had gone full-time to Harvard's Nieman Fellowship program. William Packer had retired in 1954.

So there was quite a generation break as Davis Taylor became publisher. But Davis had grown up in the business, serving under his father since 1931. Winship bridged the generations in the editorial department; nothing disturbed the continuity. But Davis Taylor brought a new dynamic into the paper. It soon became apparent that a new generation in charge in the Globe paralleled the change of generations that John F. Kennedy created in the national leadership.

After the Post died in 1956, competition between the Globe and the Herald sharpened not only in the contest for circulation but in their positions on issues. The Globe that had so long occupied a neutral middle ground now increasingly pushed for change and reform. The Herald, always conservative, became more conspicuously status quo.

The Globe was at this turning point when Harper's Magazine for September 1960 published a scathing report on the deficiencies of the Boston papers: "What the Press Has Done to Boston and Vice Versa," by Peter Braestrup, a New York Herald Tribune reporter who had spent the previous year on a Nieman Fellowship at Harvard.

Braestrup had caught the Globe at its watershed without recognizing it, although he noted that the Globe alone among the Boston papers had gained some circulation — 3,000 in a year. "Almost in spite of itself the Globe has shown increased energy," he reported. But he credited this wholly to

> the initiative of a handful of specialized young reporters. Perhaps their most striking accomplishment was the Globe's campaign for a highly controversial University of Massachusetts faculty pay raise. During the Summer of 1959 a science writer and an education reporter pressed for and obtained approval of a series of reports on the university's plight. Fourteen editorials were written in support of a score of major articles. Despite the opposition of the Herald and its hand-picked candidate for mayor, the legislature reversed itself and the university teachers got their money.

The 14 editorials suggest that the Globe supported reporting enterprise. Braestrup noted with a passing reference John Harris' campaign for a constitutional convention that year, which the Globe also supported editorially, and he reported that the Herald had "played up testimony of those opposed to the measure and labelled the whole idea 'Constitutional confusion' . . . This rivalry tends to cripple and discredit whatever slender influence the papers may have as advocates." This is a curious criticism, that the two papers present sharply differing policies and attitudes; it was a difference that deepened as campaigns for reform became the norm for the Globe.

William Davis Taylor.   John I. Taylor.

Jack Reid, advertising manager, put it succinctly, "W.O. held the Globe together. Davis opened things up and the Globe took off."

Davis took the lid off. The Globe began to take strong editorial positions on civic affairs and public issues. Reporters were uninhibited in exploring and publishing their findings on sensitive situations. It was no accident that in 1965 the Globe won the first Pulitzer gold medal that had come to Boston in 45 years. The same thing was happening in the Los Angeles Times, where the innovations that Otis Chandler brought about when he succeeded his father, Norman Chandler, attracted more national attention. But the generation change was the same. More modern men in tune with their times were changing the tone of their papers, making them a civic force to meet new issues in changed times. The whole society was becoming more open, particularly communications, with television competing in disclosure of events and magazines becoming more journalistically topical; paperbacks permitted book publication on contemporary events almost as fast as the Sunday paper.

When Davis Taylor took over on his father's death in 1955 he found in his cousin John, who had been reporter and promotion manager, a right hand to share in management. John was brought into the publisher's office and elected a director when William O. Taylor fell ill in 1954. The next year John was elected treasurer and in 1963 he became president, with Davis chairman and publisher.

John was a natural liaison between news and management from his long newsside experience and proved a popular figure with the staff. Genial, handsome, a good mixer, he combined the qualities of a thorough journalist, a good businessman, and an effective public speaker — a resource when awards were to be bestowed or received and for talks to advertising clubs. But Globe editors valued him as "a great morale builder," as one of them put it. "He's a walking spreader of good will as he cruises around the news room with that relaxed slouch and a pipe hanging out of his mouth. He has news ideas and is good at personnel problems and he's a great salesman for the Globe."

Davis' son William, graduated from Harvard in 1954, came into the business office in 1956 after two years in the Army, became a director in 1959, and succeeded John as treasurer in 1963.

Taylors of the Globe

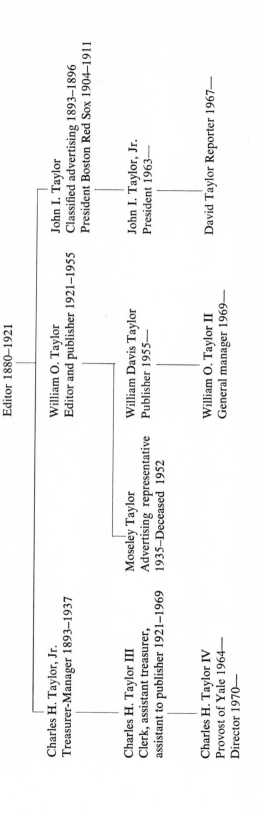

Charles H. Taylor
Publisher 1873–1921
Editor 1880–1921

John I. Taylor
Classified advertising 1893–1896
President Boston Red Sox 1904–1911

William O. Taylor
Editor and publisher 1921–1955

John I. Taylor, Jr.
President 1963—

William Davis Taylor
Publisher 1955—

David Taylor Reporter 1967—

William O. Taylor II
General manager 1969—

Charles H. Taylor, Jr.
Treasurer-Manager 1893–1937

Moseley Taylor
Advertising representative
1935–Deceased 1952

Charles H. Taylor III
Clerk, assistant treasurer,
assistant to publisher 1921–1969

Charles H. Taylor IV
Provost of Yale 1964—
Director 1970—

In 1967 John's son David joined the news staff but within a few months went on the copy desk. His father told him that his one-year hitch on the desk had taught him more about making a newspaper than any other experience.

With the demise of the Post, the Globe took on seven good desk men including Percy Shain to become television critic, Herbert Kenny to become book editor, Edward Doherty, later night editor and managing editor, and Joe Harrington, who moved his humorous "All Sorts" column across the street. The Globe also took over the Post Santa Claus as an annual fund-raising charity.

New Quarters

Davis Taylor's first and major publishing problem was a new building for the paper. He'd been working toward this for several years. Postwar growth found the old Globe buildings on Newspaper Row inadequate. Engineers and architects prowled through them, measuring and testing. But there was no way to add vitally needed new mechanical equipment to modernize operations.

The Herald-Traveler had forged ahead of the Globe after it moved into a new plant on Mason Street in 1931. The Herald had improved its typography, too, while the Globe held to its old-fashioned dress. The Herald for more than two decades was the only Boston paper with a metropolitan appearance. In this period the Herald-Traveler circulation grew by 90,000 while the Globe stood still.

Tom Brown, auditor and business adviser to the publisher, had kept pressing on W.O. the need of a new building. And it was more than the building itself; the site was outgrown. Globe trucks filled narrow Devonshire Street as they backed up to load successive editions. Intown traffic bogged distribution. Davis Taylor had persuaded his father to let him start exploring modern newspaper plants and preparing for a new building. He found the most modern plants in Milwaukee, Philadelphia, St. Louis, and Detroit and sent the composing room superintendent, Francis (Doc) Rooney, the art department superintendent, John F. Maguire, and the plant engineer, Frank Freitas, out to study them.

Then they began the search for a new site outside the congested downtown. They inspected as many as 50 before settling on a space of 11 acres on the Southeast Expressway that afforded ready open highway distribution, access to a railroad siding for newsprint delivery, and parking for the staff. A questionnaire to all the employees showed that nearly 98 percent were driving cars to work. But rapid transit went right by the site. It was 10 minutes by taxi to any Boston hotel.

They timed it and found they could deliver the final closing stocks edition to Park Street in only five minutes more time than from the old plant. The Globe counsel, Francis Leahy, put together 17 parcels of land to assemble the site between 1953 and 1957. Frank Leahy was not only the Globe's lawyer, but a longtime friend and trusted adviser to W. O. Taylor and an increasingly influential director after 1949. He was counted as especially keen in spotting the kind of advertising the Globe could do without, notably the flim-flam financial advertising that some other papers were not too particular to accept. Leahy could also scent libel in time to ward it off.

Globe editors valued his advice, and he was always amiable about their telephone calls at midnight to read him a long story on a marginal case. His response would often go beyond the legal point. "I think you're safe as to libel, but you may want to consider the reaction of a part of your public." He was Globe counsel from 1927 until his death at 81 in 1962.

The Globe bought the land for the new site at 50 cents a foot; ten years later it was worth more than $6.00. The saving on land helped toward the expense of installing foundations for a building with heavy presses on Boston's filled land. This took 1,196 pilings, some of them down 93 feet. Management of the construction was in the hands of Frank Freitas, the Globe plant engineer. He'd been a part of the Globe then for nearly 40 years, stretching and bolstering the old buildings to meet the growing demands on them.

The Globe had acquired Frank Freitas by accident. The accident was to one of the presses one Saturday night, with the big Sunday paper to get out. It was a crisis. The building superintendent, James Flagg, had finally to send out for an emergency repair crew, most of whom were stymied too. But the youngest of the crew, a Portuguese youth who could hardly speak English, proved to know the language of machinery. He quickly discovered and cured the trouble as old Jim Flagg watched in fascination. The press rolled and the Sunday paper came out. The legend of Frank Freitas' magic way with machinery started that night and grew and grew. They even said he could weld two pieces of brass tubing — which just isn't done. On Monday Jim Flagg took him in to see the publisher and got him hired.

This was in 1928. For the next 25 years Frank Freitas was all-round machinist for the presses, the stereotype department, the composing room's linotype machines, and the photo-engraving equipment. In 1953 he was appointed mechanical superintendent and in 1960 became the first plant engineer, this for the new plant he had designed and whose construction he had supervised. He was to have two further firsts in the next few years: in 1962 to become production manager and in 1965 production director. He engineered the transition of the Globe from Washington Street to Dorchester. After 86 years on its original site, the Globe in 1958 was the last newspaper to leave Newspaper Row.

One of the General's habits that the Taylors maintained through three generations was to keep all the managing family in one office. The General had his two sons, manager and business manager, in his own office. After him his sons William O. and Charles always had their two high, roll-top desks backed against each other. Even in a great new building in 1958, with individual offices for numerous editors and specialists, Davis Taylor the publisher and his cousin John the president had their desks in the same office; and when Davis' son William came on the paper in 1956, his office joined the intimate family group.

"The General thought it prevented family quarrels," Davis would explain. It also effectively prevented private talks with either publisher or president. Anyone with a point to take up found himself involved in a family discussion. So the Taylor office naturally became a conversation piece in the office that often occasioned staff amusement.

When the new building was begun in 1956, young William was assigned to it. He lived with its construction for two years, "in the back pocket of the plant engineer," as his father put it. The idea was that one of the family would know every detail of that plant by heart, and Bill did. Being a Taylor on the Globe was never a sinecure.

In the following decade William became business manager and then general manager in 1969. Next year the third Charles H. Taylor retired, after 50 years on the paper his grandfather had launched. On his retirement the Globe was without a Charles H. Taylor for the first time in 95 years. By then the fourth of the name, his son, was the provost of Yale. But six months later this fourth Charles H. Taylor was elected a director of the Globe at a special meeting of stockholders June 17, 1970.

The new building brought the first occasion for outside financing since the Globe's earliest days when the General was straining every credit possibility and selling stock to meet his payrolls. But W. O. Taylor wouldn't borrow from banks through all his 44 years as trustee and publisher. Davis reverted to first principles. His banker's advice was that the big insurance companies offered the likeliest prospect for large financing.

He turned to the John Hancock Life Insurance Company, where he found a hospitable response and secured a loan of $4,500,000 to supplement the Globe's own funds and other loans from the Second Bank-State Street Trust Company and the First National Bank of Boston. Both the Eben D. Jordan Senior and Junior trusts and the Charles H. Taylor trust also put in funds.

Total cost of land, building, and equipment came to about $14,000,000. Construction started in March 1956 and the building was occupied May 11, 1958. The evening of the opening of the new building was a dramatic occasion. With Cardinal Cushing and other community leaders attending, the publishers' "Aunt

The new Globe building (1958), photographed in 1970.

Grace," Mrs. Matthew C. Armstrong, last surviving child of General Taylor, pressed the button that started the new presses rolling. The Globe put out a special edition for Globe employees and guests and a special roto to mark the event.

When the Globe moved in, a white-haired man sat down at one of the new linotype machines and insisted on setting the first line of type. Francis X. ("Doc") Rooney had been superintendent of the composing room for 43 years, but he had been a linotyper longer than that; he had been a member of the typographical union for 59 years. He retired within a few months, in the last year of his life.

Born in Springfield in 1879, he had left school at 14 when his father died, to help support his family. He had learned the printing trade on the old Springfield Republican; then he came down to Boston and worked two nights a week on a linotype on the Post while he attended Tufts Dental School — thus the nickname "Doc." But after two years at dental school, he opted to stay with printing. In 1904 he got a job in the Globe composing room. An ardent union man, he was chairman of the union chapel on the Globe in 1910 for two years. The next year he was promoted to assistant superintendent and in 1915 to superintendent of the composing room.

A tall, handsome, commanding figure, Doc Rooney ran his shop like a commodore on the quarterdeck and would take no nonsense from editors who had their own ideas about type. But he kept abreast of his craft and made do for more than half a century in the limitations of the old Globe building.

In the spit and polish of the modernity of the new composing room, Doc punched out his line of type: "Here's to us. There's too few of us left."

The new building seemed to have every facility that the old one lacked. For one thing, it got rid of the old pneumatic tube that carried copy up two floors to the composing room. In the old cramped quarters the tube had to turn sharp corners and copy was frequently stuck in it; it would take an engineering task force to discover the hangup, and with such treatment the tube often fell apart to spew copy out in the corridors. In the new building the composing room was two floors *below* the editorial department, so gravity would deliver the copy. But nobody had thought of the fact that copy often has to be called back to the desk for changes. The very first day in the building the copy desk was rigging up a string with a weight on the end of it, to drop down and haul back copy by hand, harking back to the primitive beginnings of the paper. This went on until Frank Freitas rigged up a miniature elevator for the sole purpose of retrieving copy. It is a dumbwaiter about 12 by 18 inches that carries a tray up and down when a button is pushed. The desk call it "the bun burner."

With the new building completed, the final touch was added by a Globe employees' Flag Pole Fund, organized by John Harris, that raised $10,000 to plant a tall, handsome white flagpole on the lawn and provide flags for it.

Soon after the move the office developed a theory that the writing had improved under the pleasanter working conditions. When so skeptical a character as Donald Willard opined that this was indeed so, the theory gained an authority that stuck.

In the new building, automation of the mailing department was of key importance with the great increase in volume. Down to the early 1900's the papers were delivered from press room to mailroom by a dumbwaiter type of contrivance, operated by compressed air, and all bundled by hand. Then a wire conveyor system was introduced. The papers were still bundled by hand, tied with ropes, but now delivered

The composing room chiefs in 1958: Henry Roberts and Francis X. Rooney.

to the wagons by a chute. The next development was moving belts to deliver the papers to the trucks. In 1948 wire-tying machines were introduced to eliminate most of the hand-tying.

In 1958, in the new plant, the bundles were automatically fed into the wiring machine and pushed out to chutes to the loading platform. In 1966 the first of ten Cutler-Hammer counter-stackers eliminated manual operation of the conveyors. Papers fed from the press room through the conveyor lines to the counter-stacker were automatically counted, stacked and sent into the machine that put on a bottom wrapper and fed them to the wiring machine.

The new building was equipped with the most up-to-date photo-engraving installations, the newest film processers and high-speed etchers. The Globe has always trained its own apprentices, so it had a staff capable and ready to adapt to the technological advances. Changes included the name, which became the art department. Charles Gibson was in charge when it was installed in the new building. He was followed in 1962 by Gerard Hansen.

The Globe in its new plant in 1958 could outpage the Herald. The Sunday Globe could print 96-page sections to the Herald's 80. This edge in printing capacity lasted only a year and a half until the Herald completed its own new building in South Boston. But this time the Globe was ahead to stay: its daily circulation increased almost 100,000 in the seven years after 1958, and the Sunday that had grown constantly in good times and bad went up 150,000. The Herald-Traveler remained the same daily and on Sunday moved up only 35,000.

The larger press capacity in the new building made it possible to organize the big Sunday paper in orderly sections. But the overcompetitive situation was the key problem. It was a buyer's market: advertisers — the big stores — demanded outside positions. This prevented the Globe having special sections of the Sunday paper, and this retarded the Youth Movement. Old readers had been used to looking for sports through the news section. But new readers expected to be able to pull out a separate sports section. With the new building a separate sports section was set up, its front page cleared of ads. But this proved abortive. In 1965 Sears, Roebuck, opening new stores, brought its advertising pressure to bear for position on the outside of the sports section. For the next three years, editors and many readers pressed to correct this retrogression. Davis Taylor said he would as soon

The night copy desk in the new building, 1958. Victor Jones, scratching head; Warren Dyar, seated left; Joseph Levin in slot.

as business conditions permitted. But the Globe would have to treat the other big advertisers, Jordan's and Filene's the same as Sears. The other sections also must be cleared of ads.

Finally in 1968 he moved on all fronts, all on the same day. With advertising manager Jack Reid, he called on all the big advertisers to convince them that there was more in it for the advertiser to be in a paper with a growing readership than to insist on a preferred position in a declining paper. "What is good for the reader is good for the advertiser." The Globe then became the only metropolitan paper, so far as they knew, with all its Sunday sections opening on pages cleared of ads.

At the end of 1968 the subway billboards featured: "New Easy-to-Pull-Out Sections in the Sunday Globe." The sections, following the first news section, were Metropolitan, National, Foreign, Editorial, Features, Women's, Arts, Travel, Sports; the classified sections were headed Automobile, Real Estate, and Help Wanted. Women's was soon changed to Living, Foreign to World, and Editorial to Focus.

WORLD

JUSTICE HUGO BLACK
. . . solitary view

Why justices split on

Behind th

By S. J. Micciche
Globe Washington Bureau

WASHINGTON — The law at times is neither logical nor just.

The nine Justices of the US Supreme Court say what is legal, and seemingly simple logic surrenders to confusion and disordered reasoning. But it is the law nonetheless, as the court decided last week on 18-year-old voting.

By all that is common sense, it would seem that

the cou
and   c
choice t(
'YES'
youth b(
vote   u
rights
by Cor
NO"
because
its powe
ment to
tion was
the voti
Justic
wrote t
court,

Verdicts delayed

But the problem of advertising interference with makeup was not yet solved. A hangover from the days when the big stores dictated advertising position was their persistent habit to present their ads completely dummied as they should appear in the paper. Full-page ads of course were no problem. Jordan Marsh might have 12 full-page ads on Sunday. An advertising director was not apt to rebuff such an important advertiser if he presented two-thirds of a page on Monday so laid out as to break up the whole page and leave only odd shapes of spaces for news. This thwarted symmetrical makeup. A makeup editor would want to dress the advertising to the right, pyramided up from the bottom, to leave a chance for the broadest headline at the top, to shape the news down the left side of the page. It remained a riddle to editors that high-paid store advertising managers failed to realize that their wares would have more appeal on an attractively designed page than in a hodge-podge. This continued a bitter issue with editors, a daily reminder that advertising still called the tune to frustrate sound journalistic practice. It was a reminder also that journalism is a profession controlled by a business whose economic requirements are determining. The best prospect of winning management to educate advertisers to full acceptance of professional practices appeared to lie in the broadening dimensions of the Globe directorate.

The new building opened with 37 new press units. But this capacity was quickly outgrown and five more were added in 1962, another four in 1967. In 1966 new equipment was added for color printing, data processing and further mechanization of the mailroom. The same year the Globe made its investment in Channel 56.

Early in 1968 the directors approved expansion of the mailroom and further modernization of its equipment for an estimated cost of $5,600,000. Frank Freitas designed this, too, and spent two years, seven days a week, 11 hours a day, overseeing every detail of its construction. The annex was completed in early 1970. That year a new textile material became available for bundle tying and the Globe introduced it to replace the awkward wire.

The move from its original home to the new building suggested a series on the Globe's own history, which Willard DeLue produced. From this he continued research into the Globe's history until his retirement in 1968 and beyond. His thorough record is the basis for the first part of this chronicle. On leaving Newspaper Row the Globe acquired the historic landmark of the Old Corner Book Store for an intown office. DeLue restored its interior, refurbished it with period pieces and wall cases for its book collections. He used as a model the home of the Dorchester Historical Society, of which he was president.

In 1959 reporters' starting minimum pay was $67.50. The minimum after five years was $131.75.

The general advertising rate was $1.10 a line daily and $1.25 Sunday.

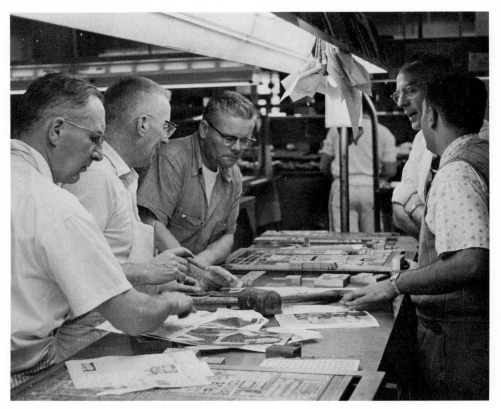

At the forms, about 1960: makeup men and editors.

Another Winship

One of Davis Taylor's early decisions as publisher was that the time had come to bring Tom Winship on to the staff.

"You can, I can't," said Tom's father.

Davis didn't say what the job would be, but Laurence Winship said Washington. They'd bring John Harris back as political editor. John had revived the Washington bureau for three years after Charles Groves's long tenure. Laurence Winship undoubtedly had two things in mind: Tom knew Washington and there wouldn't be two Winships in the office. Laurence had tried to retire the year before.

Tom had had ten years in Washington and had seen the government from inside and out. After a year and a half on the Washington Post he had a chance to become assistant to Senator Leverett Saltonstall, and publisher Phil Graham urged him to do it for the experience. After two years he was back on the Post covering District affairs, equivalent to city hall in any other city.

Tom had gone with the Post political team to the national conventions of 1948 and 1952, then worked on promotion for the paper. He'd written innumerable stories on the Post's campaign for home rule for the District. In 1956 he was assistant city editor.

Tom Winship became the Globe's Washington correspondent in 1956 as Senator

John F. Kennedy began to shape his course for the presidency. Anything a Kennedy did was top news in Boston. Tom "just about lived in Jack Kennedy's office" through 1956 to 1958. He was often the only Washington correspondent to join Kennedy on a speech-making sortie.

In 1956 Tom was in Jack Kennedy's room in the Stock Yards Inn in Chicago with only Ted Sorensen and a policeman, with Kennedy in his shorts just out of the tub, during the critical ballot when Kennedy came within an eyelash of the vice presidential nomination. "I'd better be getting over there," he said. Then came the historic switch of Tennessee to Kefauver and it was all over. But Kennedy got over there to take the platform and move they make it unanimous for Kefauver, a gracious appearance that must have had its carry-over to 1960. Tom had all the action in the hotel room in the morning Globe August 18. He had ridden in a taxi with Kennedy and Sorenson the day before on the way to Kennedy's nominating speech for Adlai Stevenson. He was able to tell the inside story of Stevenson's picking Kennedy for the nominating role, in the evening paper August 17.

In 1958 Davis insisted on bringing Tom into the office. Tom was eager to come. Both he and his wife wanted to get back to New England and Tom wanted to get his hand in on the Globe. It had irked him all the time he was on a prestigious newspaper to hear the Globe talked about as old hat, and Boston as "a journalistic poor farm." His father had followed the Washington Post with a professional eye and had sent Tom a constant stream of memos with observations whose keenness Tom valued. Now Davis was starting to move the Globe and Tom had ideas.

The first that city editor Al Haviland knew of the change was in looking at the assignment book one morning in July 1958, to see that the New England Leather Association had as its luncheon speaker "Thomas Winship, metropolitan editor of the Boston Globe." The leather association had telephoned Davis Taylor for a speaker. He'd pulled the title "metropolitan editor" out of the air. It suggested the suburban area, and it was here that Davis planned to set Tom to work. Boston was losing population to its suburbs at a rising rate; the Globe needed to follow its readers there.

Growth of the daily paper in the fifties and sixties was almost wholly in the morning. Evening circulation declined with both Globe and Traveler. The Globe was selling fewer evening papers in 1965 than in 1925. The Traveler fell from 222,000 in 1945 to 152,000 in 1965 and ceased evening publication two years later to be combined with the Herald. The Globe's only evening gain came from adding 67,000 Traveler readers.

Evening papers were having a thin time everywhere, resulting from the change from train to automobile commuting, the accelerated suburban outthrust, and the outward movement of retail business that provided suburban papers with the sinews of solid advertising. Boston had always been ringed with local suburban dailies, but by 1968 14 of them carried closing stock figures which made them more competitive. The congestion of intown traffic slowed distribution and pushed back deadlines of the Boston evening papers, to put them further behind the news on the commuter's car radio and the television network news at suppertime.

This was of strategic importance to the Globe, for its readership had been shifting from the older ethnic groups of the inner city into the suburbs with their new housing developments, attracting young couples with their new science and technical industries located around the circumferential Route 128, a dozen miles out.

The Globe's more open, liberal stance was shifting the readership also of university professors in Cambridge and environs; this accelerated through the sixties. The outward spread of the paper was chiefly for the morning edition.

Tom studied the question of zoning the paper, of splitting editions. The management decided this wasn't feasible, but they established a suburban desk with an editor and eventually a staff of four for each paper. Tom was contributing ideas for features. In 1960 two assistant managing editor posts were created, Tom for features, Al Haviland for news. This was soon realigned, Tom for the morning paper, Al for the afternoon. Haviland's forte was hard news, the local story, the natural evening paper coverage. Tom was interested in national news, in campaigns, in interpretive writing; and he had an eye for lively, even colloquial headlines to brighten the front page. When Governor Rockefeller pulled out of the presidential race in 1960, the Globe headline was: "Rocky Won't Roll."

Constitutional Reform

When John Harris returned from Washington in 1956, he had five years as political editor that were marked by his campaign for constitutional reform of the state government. Out of earlier experience as State House reporter, he had developed his own concept of the reform and restructure needed.

The two-year term for governor was too short for any program. The executive council was a block on progress with its veto of a governor's appointments, which gave it a chance to block and to trade. County government was obsolete. The legislature was too large; a governor could capture a block of 20 or 30 by patronage or trading and distort the legislative process.

But there was no use trying to get the legislature to abolish the counties; the courthouse ring had over and over again proved too intrenched to be eliminated. The executive council had its lines of support in the legislature. The legislature could not be counted on to abolish the council and free the governor of its veto on key appointments. The legislature pre-empted various executive roles and had a vested interest in keeping the executive weak.

So it would take a constitutional convention, Harris decided. He had to work on the Globe to let him launch such a campaign. It was out of character for the Globe.

But he was able to argue that both Governor Herter, Republican, and Governor Dever, Democrat, had encouraged him. He argued that taxes could be lowered and government made more efficient and more honest. Finally in autumn 1959 Harris was able to launch his campaign for a constitutional convention. He spelled out the need for freeing a governor to perform efficiently, giving the governor a four-year term, restructuring executive departments; for cutting the legislature to a more manageable size; for integrating county functions with the state government; for giving the towns and cities home rule. He had some luck in his timing; Connecticut just then eliminated its county governments; New Hampshire was holding a constitutional convention. Before he was through he had the endorsement of

John Harris, Sunday editor from 1962.

Charles Whipple, editor of the editorial page, photographed in 1970.

political leaders. The League of Women Voters came out for a convention. The Globe itself came out, at the conclusion of the series, in an Uncle Dudley editorial November 18, 1959, wholeheartedly supporting the convention.

The convention plan failed to pass. A major disappointment in the Globe's effort was refusal of the heads of leading banks to take the initiative in setting up a Citizens' Committee for a Constitutional Convention. Some said, candidly, that deficit financing was profitable to banks; generally, they feared to open up the whole issue of taxation. But the planks in Harris' program stuck, and the League of Women Voters stuck with them. Harris came to count the League the most effective agent for reform. The Globe, convinced by the response to its new civic voice, kept on campaigning.

The timing was right to break through the Globe's neutral stance. For in 1960 the State was rocked by the Alfred Worcester case, which disclosed wholesale corruption of legislators and public officials over public works contracts. The case, of an engineer who had had to fake his income tax returns to cover up the kickbacks required of him on highway contracts, was tried before Federal Judge Charles Wyzanski, who closed the trial with a philippic delivered from the bench against the laxity of public morals.

Charles Whipple covered this for the Globe, then wrote an article about it in the Atlantic Monthly, whose title on the cover, "Dirty Money in Boston," had an awakening effect.

A state crime commission's investigations uncovered corruption that led to the conviction and jailing of several members of the executive council and indictment of legislative leaders, present and past.

Dear Mr. President

President Kennedy came to Boston for a birthday banquet when he had been president four months, and the Globe exploited the occasion with an open letter to the President describing the condition of public affairs in his home state. Charles Whipple wrote it after a consensus of editors. It ran May 29, 1961, signed only "The Boston Globe."

Starting on the front page, it was headed "Birthday Letter from Home / Dear Mr. President." Moving inside, it had a whole page, big type, under a banner head

Things are Moving in Massachusetts, Mr. President

The People are Ahead of the Politicians

It described a "network of corruption," MDC contract splitting, closed books of authorities, failure of the legislature. It said:

The people are aroused and angry.

The public has come to distrust too many local politicians.

Constitutional reform has finally become a major issue here.

In 1960 the Worcester case showed large scale payoffs to public officials to get public works contracts.

As 1962 opened, the Globe published a two-page broadside, "A Letter to Our Public Servants: The Challenge Facing State Leaders." It opened with a half-page color photo of the State House.

The Globe urged a whole set of actions: give the governor power to name department heads and reorganize state agencies; abolish the executive council; revise the tax structure — Massachusetts has the highest per capita property tax; reorganize public education on a vast scale.

A Globe series showed need for: an honest crime commission; home rule for Boston; a conflict of interest law and a corrupt practices act; audit of all authorities' books; fair congressional redistricting; support of Edward Logue on urban renewal; modernization of Sunday blue laws; reform of antiquated county government; the barring of political influence in hiring DPW employees; restoration of two-party government; giving minority party leaders the right to appoint minority members of legislative committees.

Within the next three years the powers of the executive council were curbed to remove the veto over executive appointments. Then the governor was given a four-year term and a right to reorganize the departments. Home rule came. The movement to cut the size of the legislature had become a central political issue. When Harris in 1962 became Sunday editor, Robert Healy, succeeding him as political editor, had open sesame to push for reform. The Globe was embarked as a civic force, its momentum gathering as it moved ahead.

Harris brought to the Sunday editorship wide-ranging interests that reflected his own hobbies. As a reporter he had started a column for stamp collectors and also one on gardening later carried on by Earl Banner, whose interests ranged over farming, fishing, forestry, and meteorology. Harris began a column on state politics, later broadened in scope as "The Political Circuit."

THE STAMP HOBBY

Christmas issues still mount in number

By Jay Hatch

Italy produced two gems for the Christmas period. They are both in multicolor which faithfully reproduces the originals. The 25.1 presents in vertical format Filippo Lippi's "The Virgin Adoring the Holy Child" with a background of the manger that seems to include a dove with outspread wings.

The much larger-size 150 1. reproduces Gentile da Fabriano's "The adoration of the Magi" — one of the most celebrated and best-loved renaissance paintings on this subject. Both paintings hang in the fabu-

Austria, for Christmas, released a beautiful,

long step from the days (still attached to some of

On returning from Washington he prepared a tourist's guide to the capital written from memory out of his own tourist enthusiasm that the Globe published as a booklet. He brought into the Sunday paper new departments of antiques and architecture. He eliminated commercial "readers" from the travel section in favor of readable articles. He dropped the routine notes of women's organizations with never a peep of protest. His special sections on New England vacations reflected his own enthusiasm. Harris had in large degree that "perennial curiosity" that Frank Sibley called the essential quality of the journalist.

The Sunday circulation grew by 150,000 from his start in 1962 to 1970. He was soon administering a staff of 20 to edit and illustrate its numerous sections, this besides the separate staff of the magazine and all the writers for the special sections.

Bob Healy Goes to Washington

The new Washington correspondent following Tom Winship in 1958 was Robert Healy. He came on the Globe as a copy boy out of high school in 1942. Next year he was in the Air Force, but he was initiated into reporting when the Cocoanut Grove fire mobilized the whole office. Back from the war in 1946, he was assigned to the night staff and used as a leg man. Night city editor Alexander Haviland had installed a system of rewrite and leg men; but he developed his leg men.

Healy couldn't write, he says now. He enrolled in courses at Boston University. But he credits Al Haviland with teaching him to write, forcing him to write. The night city editor would make him rewrite his stories over and over — but he showed him what was the matter with them. He taught him how to take notes. Healy did some of his leg man duty manning the first Globe mobile car, which tuned in to police radio and sped to the scene of crime or accident or fire, where Healy would phone in the facts for one of the rewrite men to shape up. Haviland applied his discipline to his rewrite men, too, of whom Charles Whipple was one. A Harvard graduate, later editor of the editorial page, Whipple remembers Haviland's discipline, to improve the organization of the story. "He made me rewrite leads over and over," says Whipple.

A disciplinarian, a perfectionist, Haviland had the respect of his staff. He was hard but fair. He taught them something. They had an affection for him as "the old man," though he was still in his forties when, on the death of Charles Merrill, he moved to the day side as executive city editor, later to become executive editor.

Healy developed into a place on Haviland's bank of rewrite men who could shape up a story fast, clearly, accurately, put complexities into simple clear sentences. He was moved to the day side and shifted his Boston University studies to nights; assigned to work with Amasa Howe on a murder case on the Cape, he found another teacher.

Healy was edged into what became his special field of politics, first to help John Harris, State House correspondent, in 1950. He found a byproduct of Al Haviland's discipline: "I never had any problem being tough with politicians." He quickly caught on to their curves. When the 1952 legislative session ended in a scandalous spate of self-serving bills railroaded through in a marathon final weekend session, Healy was assigned to investigate. He diligently unraveled and exposed the mess. Through the early 1950's he was in and out of City Hall, reinforcing a coverage that had grown too soft. He covered the last press conference of James Michael Curley, which ended an era.

In the period of the McCarthy hysteria, Healy covered a series of Boston hearings run by the Wisconsin senator. He reported the state political campaigns and went to New Hampshire for the first primary that launched General Eisenhower's presidential prospects. Healy was growing visibly on the job. Big, hearty, with a durable physique and an appetite for work, a native intelligence and engaging personality, his quality came under the collective eye of the office. The managing editor, Victor O. Jones, had held a Nieman Fellowship at Harvard. He thought he could see what such a year of intellectual exploration and association would do for Healy and persuaded him to try for one. Healy got it and for a year associated with a dozen able young newspaperman from all over the country while he studied government and political history and economics with a great faculty. The year counted in all the ways that Jones had anticipated and more. Healy's growth in confidence and grasp of affairs impressed all his colleagues when he returned from Harvard in June 1956. "And he never stopped growing," said an editor a dozen years later when Healy had become executive editor.

Bob Healy's first big assignment was to lead the Globe team that covered the *Andrea Doria* shipwreck in 1956. He had become a master craftsman by then. The next year he was appointed Washington correspondent when Tom Winship was brought up to the office as metropolitan editor. Healy's five years in Washington — then still a one-man bureau — proved a vital chapter of such investigative political reporting as was new to Boston. His work there came to involve the whole paper and its results to mark a turning point for the Globe as it fought the Herald's politicking to obtain the Channel 5 television license, and in the process learned to fight and discovered its own strength. Healy's can opener reporting spearheaded what was a struggle for survival; for the Herald publisher, Robert Choate, pressing for merger with the Globe, threatened that with the valuable television channel he could put the Globe out of business.

Healy's original assignment in Washington was to dig into the Channel 5 affair as he had dug into the State House mess in 1952. A byproduct of this digging was his uncovering of the "Goldfine story" that forced the resignation of Sherman Adams as the President's chief of staff. He spent a solid year, 1958, on the Goldfine story.

The Senate had set up an Oversight Committee to review the independent agencies. Their counsel was a keen young professor at New York University, Bernard Schwartz, who took his work seriously. Among the agencies investigated were the Federal Trade Commission and the Securities and Exchange Commission. Both had a problem with a Boston industrialist, Bernard Goldfine, trying to get his companies to conform to the law in reporting their financial affairs. This brought about local interest in Goldfine's affairs and brought the committee staff to Boston. Their attention was diverted then to the Federal Communications Commission. Looking into telephone toll slips to trace Goldfine's channels to Washington, they discovered the Boston Herald and a member of the FCC.

The Herald already had a radio station, WHDH. In 1956 it applied for television Channel 5. The FCC chairman was George McConnaughey. A member was Richard A. Mack, later indicted as a result of the Schwartz investigations for peddling political influence in the case of Channel 10 in Miami. The Globe was not an applicant for Channel 5. It had at first been unconcerned about the Herald application because the Boston Post also had an application, and the policy of the FCC had been not to pick one newspaper over a rival but to assign a television channel to a non-newspaper applicant. But the Post was forced out of business in 1956, changing the tactical situation. There were, however, several strong Boston groups applying for Channel 5. The FCC examiner recommended against the Herald and for one of the other applicants. But then the word leaked that the Republican Herald had influence with the FCC to reverse the examiner's report.

Davis Taylor, having neither political connections nor experience with them, telephoned Sherman Adams, a New Hampshireman, to ask if he could talk to him about what he had heard. Adams told him that the White House never intervened with the independent agencies and that it would be embarrassing to him to talk to

POLITICAL CIRCUIT
By ROBERT HEALY

Hanoi boosts
Kennedy image

They speak of the Kennedy mystique. Out of Webster's, mystique is: "a complex or transcendental or somewhat mystical beliefs and attitudes developing around an object."

Taylor about it. "All right, if it embarrasses you, I won't come to the White House," Taylor said and hung up.

Hearing testimony later disclosed that Robert Choate frequently went to the White House to talk to Adams. Also that Choate had been able to arrange two luncheon meetings with Chairman McConnaughey of the FCC when they discussed Channel 5.

Davis Taylor wrote President Eisenhower on January 4, 1957, describing the Channel 5 situation and its relation to the Globe's resistance to Herald pressure for merger "because it felt that the existence of two large Boston papers was healthy for New England." He explained that the Globe had kept its hands off the Channel 5 hearings, counting on the understood FCC policy not to grant television licenses to newspapers when other qualified applicants were available. The examiner's decision had followed this policy, but now the Globe had learned that the decision was to be overturned in favor of the Herald-Traveler. Taylor cited the big profits of television stations; "so you can appreciate why it seems to us extremely unfair to give one of two large New England newspapers this decided financial advantage."

Taylor was answered by the President's special counsel, saying the President never interfered with the regulatory agencies. He sent the letter to the FCC, which did reverse its examiner and awarded Channel 5 to the Herald.

But subsequent protests, revelations, and court suits balked the action. A federal court ordered rehearings by the FCC. A decision in 1960 withdrew the license from the Herald and reopened applications. But meantime the Herald was allowed a temporary license so that it enjoyed the profits of Channel 5 to balance its books through subsequent years. It was finally 1968 when a differently constituted FCC reassigned Channel 5 to a Boston community group. Even then appeals and further litigation put off indefinitely the actual transfer of the channel.

But in 1957 Healy was digging into the FCC and absorbing the investigations of Bernard Schwartz's staff, following leads, reporting hearings.

Davis Taylor and his cousin John followed up the letter to Eisenhower with a trip to Washington to find out if political influence had determined the Channel 5 award and "to do what we could" to have it awarded on its merits, as John Taylor later testified at an FCC hearing February 19, 1959. They made the rounds of the Massachusetts politicians in House, Senate, and cabinet. They were given a runaround. Congressman Joseph Martin told them they'd been "outpoliticked." Speaker McCormack suggested that, now that the Post was gone, they make the Globe a Democratic party paper. Some of the political leaders seemed "not much concerned," John testified.

The Taylors went home angry. They'd been treated like a couple of country boys. It was the first time since their grandfather withdrew from the Massachusetts Democratic State Committee in 1897 that a Taylor had sought any contact with politics. They went home determined to fight.

"It toughened them," Bob Healy said a dozen years later. "It was just what they needed. It was the last time anybody pushed the Globe around." Davis took the lid off the editorial page to take positions. He gave reporters elbow room for investigative work. The Globe moved in on the messes in the state. It began to campaign for reform and has been at it ever since.

Healy had a chance to test this out when they brought him back in 1962 as political editor to succeed John Harris, who had become Sunday editor. Healy was given responsibility for coverage at City Hall, State House, and Washington and to do a column of his own.

He had a new and spunky young reporter, James Doyle, at City Hall, who was making news grow there. He could write, too. Healy was soon giving Jim Doyle a crack at his occasional column "The Political Circuit." The week before Christmas 1962, Doyle produced a column that took some digs at Mayor Collins — "Old Yule Spirit Not at City Hall." It was a rather sophomoric roundup of snafus and muffs: the Mayor had decided to suspend the tradition of mayoral Christmas cards; bulbs for the Christmas lights turned out to be made in Japan and had to be replaced; a needling question at a press conference had led the Mayor to announce the firing of a holdover veteran commissioner, in Christmas week; and more of the same. Mayor Collins was incensed. He demanded an appointment with the publisher, who alerted Healy. "Just promise me one thing, that you won't make any commitment to him," Healy asked. The Mayor came and angrily recited his grievance. Davis Taylor and Healy just listened and said nothing. The Mayor went over it again, with no response. Finally Davis Taylor stood up, shook the Mayor's hand and thanked him "for coming by."

This satisfied Healy that he could feel political editor meant what it said. But Jim Doyle was not long for City Hall. After a year on a Nieman Fellowship he was assigned to Washington, where the one-man bureau was now doubled. In 1967 city editor Richard Stewart, after a Nieman Fellowship year, was assigned to Washington to make a three-man bureau.

"Ask not what your country can do for you . . . ask what you can do for your country."
—President Kennedy in his inaugural address. Jan. 20, 1961.

Color portrait of President on Page 16.

VOL. 184
NO. 146   By GLOBE NEWSPAPER CO.

The Boston Globe

MORNING 🌐 EDITION

Reg. U. S. Pat. Off.

SATURDAY, NOVEMBER 23, 1963

Telephone AV 3-8000

WEATHER
SATURDAY — Partly cloudy, near 70.
SUNDAY- Fair.

High Tide
3:47 a.m.   4:01 p.m.
Sun Rises   Sun Sets
6:44   4:17
Full Report on Page 24.

32 PAGES—10c

SHOCK...DISBELIEF...GRIEF

John Fitzgerald Kennedy, Born in Brookline, Massachusetts—Shot and Killed in Dallas, Texas, at Age of 46

Sniper's Bullet Cuts Down President
Jacqueline Cradles Dying Husband
Johnson Sworn In; McCormack No. 2

By ROBERT L. HEALY
Globe Reporter

WASHINGTON—A sniper's bullet brought death to President John Fitzgerald Kennedy at 2 p.m. Friday, changing with immeasurable impact the history of a shocked, disbelieving world.

The 35th President of the United States and son of Massachusetts became a martyr on a street of Dallas, Tex., to principles he carried to the nation in words and in action.

He answered in death what he said in his own Inaugural: "Ask not what your country can do for you—ask what you can do for your country."

His productive life was ended at 46. Three years ago he was the youngest man ever elected to the presidency.

A rifle bullet, fired into his head from the upper story window of a building at 12:30 p.m. Dallas time, turned an hour of triumph into sudden national disaster.

He never regained consciousness.

Mrs. Jacqueline Kennedy cradled the body of her husband in her arms as the open car sped to Parkland Hospital in Dallas.

John F. Kennedy, the first Catholic President in the history of the nation, died there after he was given the last rites of his church.

Eleven hours after the assassination, police charged a 24-year-old one-time Marine, avowed Marxist and pro-Castroite with the murder. Lee Harvey Oswald, who defected to Russia in 1959, was captured in a theater after slaying a pursuing police officer.

Cardinal Cushing, who performed the marriage of President Kennedy and baptized his children, will celebrate a funeral Mass at noon, Monday, in St. Matthew's Cathedral in Washington.

PRESIDENT Page 2

'Oh, No!'

A Wife's Anguish

By HELEN THOMAS

WASHINGTON (UPI)—The world which had toasted Jacqueline Bouvier Kennedy on many a yesterday wept for her Friday.

This once most fortunate of lovely ladies came home from Dallas, Tex., bearing a burden of grief too heavy for utterance.

At midday she had said gaily to her husband, "You can't say Dallas wasn't friendly to you."

The crowds had been huge, their cheers deafening as they rode side by side through the city.

Moments later she was cradling his wounded body in her arms, crying, "O, no!" Less than an hour later he was dead. They had been married 10 years, 2 months, and 10 days.

Somehow the assassin's hastily fired bullets had missed her, seated inches away on the President's left.

It was the second time in 3½ months that she had seen death strike a loved one while sparing her.

On Aug. 7, 1963, she had given birth prematurely to Patrick Bouvier Kennedy. Two days later he died. She made a brave recovery. On Oct. 1 she left for a two-week recuperative vacation in Greece and the Mediterranean.

JACQUELINE Page 2

Texan Held as Killer

Castroite Accused; How President Was Slain

DALLAS (UPI)—Lee Harvey Oswald, 24, a pro-Castro Marxist who defected to Russia in 1959, was charged Friday night with the assassination of President Kennedy, who was ambushed with a high-powered rifle.

Oswald made no confession and insisted he knew nothing about the assassination of the President or the serious wounding of Texas Gov. John Connally.

Manacled, his face battered in a fight with the police who subdued him in a movie theater less than four miles from the assassination scene, Oswald was taken before Justice of the Peace David Johnson for arraignment.

Police Chief Jesse Curry said he would be brought before a Grand Jury next week.

Police made paraffin tests on Oswald several hours before he was charged formally.

Police also charged the 24-year-old Marine reject with the murder of a Dallas police officer shortly after the President was slain by a sniper firing a military rifle from the window of a building in downtown Dallas.

Capt. Will Fritz of the homicide department said it had been established Oswald was in the building from which the President was killed at the time the shot was fired. Police were making paraffin tests on Oswald's hands for marks of gunpowder.

ASSASSINATION Page 2

SUSPECT OSWALD

IN AN INSTANT—A stunned Mrs. Kennedy seeks to help her dying husband, slumped over beneath her. Secret serviceman leaps on car to give aid. Three shots from sniper's bullet turned cheerful scene into a nightmare. (AP

His Home State Reacts

TRIBUTES—"My heart is broken with grief over his martyrdom"—Cardinal Cushing. This and other eulogies for President Kennedy on page 21.

CANCELLATIONS—Radio and TV cancel programs. Many sports and entertainment events postponed. Page 2, 23.

McCORMACK— Bay State congressman guarded by Secret Service as he becomes next in line to succeed to the Presidency. Page 6.

SCHOOLS—Gov. Peabody urges education officials to omit classes Monday.

. . . As Body Lies in State

PRESIDENT KENNEDY'S BODY will lie in the East Room of the White House Saturday to be viewed by his family and top government officials.

THE BODY WILL BE MOVED to the Capital Rotunda Sunday at 1 p.m. where the public will be permitted to file past the bier until 9 p.m. and again Monday from 8 a.m. to 10 a.m.

CARDINAL CUSHING will sing a Pontifical Requiem Mass at noon Monday at St. Matthew's Cathedral, Washington.

BURIAL expected to be in Holyhood Cemetery, Brookline.

'I'll Do My Best—LBJ'

By DON IRWIN

WASHINGTON—"I will do my best. That is all I can do. I ask for your help and God's."

This was President Johnson's pledge and prayer upon his arrival at 5:58 p.m. Friday at Washington to take over the massive burden that fell to him following President Kennedy's assassination in Dallas, Tex., a scant five hours earlier.

Thirty-five minutes later, Mr. Johnson was back at the White House. He entered immediately upon a series of talks with foreign policy advisers and legislative leaders in a second-floor suite in the executive office building adjoining the White House. Mr.

Johnson has used the suite as his "downtown office" for the past two years.

At his 45-minute meeting with the legislative leaders of both parties in House and Senate, the new President was reported to have said "it is more essential than ever that this country be united." He was assured of bipartisan co-operation.

As the new President worked into the night in his vice presidential office, he talked by telephone with all three of his surviving predecessors, former Presidents Herbert Hoover, Harry E. Truman and Dwight D. Eisenhower.

The 36th President looked grim but self-controlled as he stepped before a bank of microphones and television cameras on the floodlit ramp at Andrews Air Force Base to make a brief statement, his first since he was sworn in at Dallas aboard the blue-and-silver presidential jet that brought him to Andrews.

It was quite a contrast to Aug. 2, 1923, when Calvin Coolidge of Massachusetts was sworn in by the light of a kerosene lamp by his father on a Vermont hillside home.

JOHNSON
Page 3

No More...the Familiar Graceful Figure

By MARY McGRORY

WASHINGTON—It was his last airport arrival.

The field was garishly lit, as it had always been, by landing lights and television lights. A misty quarter moon was rising over Andrews Air Force Base.

There was a crowd as always. At the fence were gathered several hundred people, uniformed men of the Air Force and their families. There

was even a camera or two.

There were high officials of the New Frontier. Undersecretary of State Averill Harriman, face gaunt and drawn, stood at the head of a disconsolant line.

With him were the new Postmaster General Gronouski, H. E. W. Secretary Celebrezze, Undersecretary of Commerce Franklin D. Roosevelt Jr., Supreme Court Justice Arthur Goldberg and his wife.

The leaders of the Senate were there, majority leader Mansfield and his weeping wife, majority whip Humphrey of Minnesota, who told of how the President just before he left for Texas had told an aide he feared for the life of President Betancourt of Venezuela.

McGRORY
Page 4

A NEW PRESIDENT is sworn in by Judge Sarah T. Hughes in cabin of presidential plane before take-off from Love A.F.B., Dallas. Mrs. Johnson and Mrs. Kennedy witness ceremony. (AP Photo)

The Assassination of President Kennedy: November 23, 1963.

"No Deal" on Ted Kennedy

Bob Healy, in early 1962, was still in between assignments in Washington and Boston when he and the Globe became involved in an elaborate negotiation with the White House over a story about Edward M. Kennedy, who had just become a candidate for the United States Senate.

Tom Winship and Healy had probably as close a relation as any pair of newspapermen to President Kennedy. But Winship, like his father, believes that what is common conversation is news — no reason not to print it.

At the Gridiron Dinner in winter 1962, Tom heard politicians and insiders talking about a story that Ted Kennedy had been expelled from Harvard for cheating on an exam. He reported what he'd heard to Victor Jones, managing editor, who agreed this was bound to come out in the campaign. The Globe should not wait to be scooped. Jones put Healy on it. Harvard properly would not disclose its records. While Healy was poking into the story he had a call from Richard Maguire in the Boston office of the Kennedys. What did Healy think of Ted's chances for the Senate? Did he know anything about Ted's record at Harvard? Healy said he did. How widespread was the story? Was it a printable story? Healy assured him it was bound to be printed. Maguire then called Kenneth O'Donnell at the White House, who spoke to the President and asked Healy to come to Washington.

He had three meetings with the President. At the first meeting the President asked what Healy knew about the story. Healy repeated that the story was sure to come out. If the Globe had the full facts it would run the story without the animus of a campaign charge; the Globe would only be interested if it had the full facts, and that meant the cooperation of Harvard. The President wanted to know how the Globe would use the story. He suggested it could be a detail in a profile. Healy checked that with Victor Jones, who said nothing doing. The story would not be buried in a profile.

The conversation ended at that. But three days later Healy was called to the White House again. This time Theodore Sorensen, Kenneth O'Donnell and McGeorge Bundy were with the President. They went all over it again. Healy insisted the Globe would need the full facts but that it would be mutually advantageous to get them out before the campaign. The discussion of the pros and cons went round and round until the President said, "We are having more trouble with this than we did with the Bay of Pigs." "Yes," said Bundy, "and with about the same result." Healy left feeling he had not convinced them.

But then Davis Taylor had a call from the President, to say he was relieved to know that the story would come out in the Globe because he knew it would be fair. This was the first the Globe publisher had heard of it. He called Healy to demand what kind of deal he had been making for the Globe. No deal at all, Healy told him. We get the whole story or nothing.

Healy had a third call from the White House. This time just Kenneth O'Donnell was with the President, who telephoned Bundy to make arrangements with Harvard to release the record to the Globe. He then called the President of the University of Virginia to make sure that Healy could get Ted's law school record there.

The last word from President Kennedy reflected his own early newspaper days.

"Do you think you will play the story above the fold?" Healy thought probably, but that wouldn't be his decision.

The Globe ran the story by Robert Healy on the front page March 30, 1962, under a two-column head, just below the fold:

> Ted Kennedy Tells
> About Harvard
> Examination Incident

The story opened: "Edward M. Kennedy, candidate for the United States Senate, in an interview yesterday, explained the circumstances surrounding his withdrawal from Harvard in 1951 when he was a 19-year-old freshman.

"The story, sometimes distorted, has been making the rounds in the Massachusetts political rumor mill for some time. Kennedy said he wanted to set the record straight."

The affair is then told in direct quotes from Kennedy, of being in trouble in a foreign language course and getting a friend to take the examination for him. The Dean found it out and both of them were required to withdraw with the understanding they could later reapply. Kennedy enlisted in the Army and served two years in Europe, reapplied and was graduated in good standing in 1956.

"What I did was wrong," Kennedy was quoted. "I have regretted it ever since. It was a bitter experience but it has also been a very valuable lesson."

President Kennedy phoned the Globe publisher again to say: "We believe that the Globe in breaking this story for the record presented the facts exactly as they were."

Later, invited to a White House reception, Davis Taylor and his wife were at the end of the receiving line when Robert Kennedy came up to say: "Both the President and I thank you for being fair and factual in the story on Ted's incident and, incidentally, we think it went over very well."

Another delicate story was of the 1964 income tax case of Edward Brooke, attorney general of Massachusetts. The story was all over town among insiders that Brooke, a Republican, was under an income tax investigation that had been under way for 16 months. A good many people believed this was a case of political harassment.

Jim Doyle, then covering the State House, was put on it. He talked Brooke into giving the Globe the whole circumstances. The Globe ran the copyrighted story as told by James Doyle on May 7, 1964, with a banner head:

> Brooke's Tax Returns Probed
> Being Questioned by IRS
> Atty. Gen's. Lawyers Claim Harassment, Needless Delay

The story stated that "there has been no allegation of wrong doing . . . The fact that the attorney general was being investigated by the IRS came to the Globe's attention some time ago. The subject was presented to Brooke and the IRS by the Globe. Brooke asked his attorneys to make available details of the case. The IRS, according to its practice under the law, gave no details." Brooke's lawyers conceded he had understated his income by some $12,000 over three years. This they laid to bookkeeping errors. They had analyzed the case for the IRS and given them full information but had been unable to get a resolution. The IRS investigators had sought out affidavits from more than 20 businessmen with whom Brooke dealt and "with great subtlety called into question the character and trustworthiness of Mr. Brooke," his lawyer charged. "In my opinion someone is out to destroy Mr. Brooke."

Jim Doyle evidently thought so too. He said as much in his column next day: Is IRS Brooke Probe Fair?

"Who stands accused?" Doyle asked. "The attorney general or the IRS?"

No action was ever brought against Brooke. The investigation appears to have been quietly dropped after the Globe disclosed that Brooke's tailor, a department store, the Boston Opera Company, and his college alumni fund had been asked to make affidavit that they actually received the money shown on Brooke's canceled checks. "It has caused friends and clients to further question," Doyle wrote. "Why all the question about Ed Brooke? In the United States each man is entitled to some basic human rights under the Constitution."

A Szep cartoon: new Senator, 1966 — "Of course he's for real — and he's on your team!"

BUD COLLINS

Just a routine year...

While Christmas cards are at the top of everybody's nonreading list this week, the most forgettable a r e those inserts that emulate the Forsyte Saga on one mimeographed p a g e. Everything you didn't want to know about families not nearly as absorbing as Charlie Manson's.

ton' when he comes home for the holidays. He sleeps with his National Rifle Assn. membership card under his pillow and has a Sen. Fulbright dartboard in his room.

"Little Amy's cookie trauma has thankfully just about disappeared. She was frightened out of her appetite by Cookie Monster on Sesame Street, but we found a psychiatrist to fix her up. Dr. Wunderstein — he calls himself the good shrink for little finks — took good care of her, and did you know he has a special shorty couch for 4-year-olds? Now Amy is back into toll house again. This makes us

Bud Collins Comes Aboard

"Bud" Collins was writing a sports column for the Herald when one morning, November 22, 1963 — he remembers the date, for it was the day President Kennedy was shot — his friend Timothy Leland, who was writing science and medicine for the Herald, asked him, "Who's Tom Winship?" Leland had only been in Boston a short time.

"The editor of the Globe."

"Well, why does he want to have lunch with me?"

"Probably wants to offer you a job. Tell him you will only come on a package deal with Bud Collins."

And that's the way it was, according to Bud. It didn't take much sales talk, for Winship had long thought Bud Collins was the funniest man in the newspaper world. In a very few months he had enlarged Bud's assignment from just sports to an op-ed column on "anything." Bud kept his tennis assignment. That was his specialty, his hobby, his first love. It took him around the world for Davis Cup matches and all the rest, and on these travels he mixed tennis with everything else for his column.

Bud Collins brought an inimitable style and crackling humor to sports coverage and much more.

In December 1963 he was in Australia for Davis Cup matches. In 1964 he covered the national tennis championships for NBC. Thereafter his coverage of the national doubles matches at Longwood became a popular summer feature on Boston's educational television Channel 2.

Bud has been a tennis champion himself, won the national mixed doubles title in 1961, and coached college tennis teams at Brandeis for five years. In 1967 the U.S. Tennis Writers Association elected him president.

Bud has other dimensions than humor. On occasion he has turned to pungent satire of public affairs. He decided to drop in on Vietnam in spring 1969, and the article he did for the Sunday magazine May 18, 1969, "The 89th Month," was as grim as anything written on that dismal issue: sardonic, ironical, with ruthless realism, as he quoted the views of the high brass and the politicians he met, and then in savage twists turned to the actuality of misery, dying, destruction, and futility.

Timothy Leland, who came to the Globe in the package with Bud, had a year at Columbia School of Journalism after Harvard, then a short time on the Herald. His first Globe assignment was science writing, but he was soon moved to the State House for exposure to politics and in 1968 was made an assistant city editor with particular responsibility for run-of-the-paper features for Sunday. That year he received an American Political Science Association award for "outstanding public affairs reporting." This was for his last two series at the State House. One in four parts was "The Unfinished Business of Reform in Massachusetts"; the other, in six parts, "The Cheated Voter," described the politics of redistricting the legislature.

Leland spent half of 1970 on a fellowship to England, where he was attached to the Sunday Times of London and studied, among other things, that paper's techniques of investigative reporting. On his return in the fall he was given a new assignment to head up an investigative team, with a hard-digging reporter, Gerard O'Neill, and a young law school graduate, Stephen Kurkjian, as colleagues.

Specialists on Everything

One of the earliest and most conspicuous fruits of the new openness of the paper under the Davis Taylor-Tom Winship regime was the rapid development of a corps of special writers. The news had become more complicated. Specialization was reaching new fields. Its momentum on the Globe was such that in seven years after Mrs. Burns's death in 1961 the number of special writers had increased from three to 19. This did not count critics, political writers, or columnists. By 1965 it was necessary to appoint an assistant managing editor, Joseph Doherty, off the copy desk, to coordinate the work of the specialists and to be a buffer between them and the morning, evening, and Sunday editors who were competing for a share of their production.

This has been an extraordinary group, of immense vitality and commitment. A rough index of one decade of their work is the list of awards that fills some pages of appendix to this book. Calling them specialists follows traditional classification. But their versatility is such that one of them, Ian Menzies, served within four years as science editor, financial editor, and then managing editor. His colleague Ian Forman moved from education editor to recreate the Sunday magazine. Timothy Leland served within five years as science writer, political writer, and assistant city editor. Herbert Black, who took up the medical writing Mrs. Burns had begun, had been a reporter for five years before he was asked to take a stint on the copy desk, which greatly needed fresh eyes; it was 25 years before he could get off the desk. But his handling of national news in World War II led to his being offered the Washington bureau. Not wanting that much politics, Black was asked how about medicine? "Well, I don't know anything about it. But I'll try." That was 1961. By 1969 the list of his awards for medical writing filled a sheet of copy paper, the latter half shared by his later team-mate, Carl Cobb.

They are team workers, these specialists, their association adding dimension to their impact. They plunged into their work with a zest of commitment, to make the public aware of the issues in public health, medical services, quality education, and the advancement of science.

The first team was Menzies, Forman, and Black, joining Mrs. Burns in her final years. Before Sputnik in 1957, Menzies had organized them into a department of science-medicine-education, with a special science page on Sunday. They were self-starters, exploring their fields to discover the public need, then moving in on it with a campaign. Davis Taylor provided the resources. Tom Winship encouraged, often incited, their campaigns. The editorial page gave support.

One of the early and notable services of the Menzies-Forman team was their rescue of the University of Massachusetts, which in 1960 was losing faculty even to Connecticut and Rhode Island under restrictive State House control of its budget and salaries. The university sought financial autonomy, that is, flexibility to apply its legislative appropriations where most needed; the legislative leadership turned it down. At this point Menzies and Forman moved in. Convinced of the vital need of quality public education at a time when rising costs in private colleges were forcing middle-income families to depend on the state university, they disclosed the plight of the university and its need. They investigated what other states were doing and reported that Massachusetts was last in support of higher education. They kept it up until public pressure brought the legislature to reverse itself. The university won fiscal autonomy. Within seven years its enrollment rose from 6,000 to 20,000. A branch of the university was launched in Boston for commuting students and a medical school started. The Globe writers ran interference for this expansion of public education opportunity at every point.

In 1963 Forman turned his attention to the public schools of the Greater Boston area. He did a series of 23 articles — "How Good Are Your Schools?" — exploring the school problems in as many communities. Forman, a Yale graduate, brought to this enterprise both a broad-gauge intelligence and a thorough understanding of the political and economic factors in public education. His articles explored the economic conditions of the towns, their tax problems and political complexion, and the changes that suburbanization and rapid growth had brought. Each piece was an anatomy of the conditions that affected the schools in each community, but in a broad context that presented a profile of the community to itself that must have been instructive to its residents.

This Forman series was an advance in the development of Globe reporting. The Globe took it as a pattern for later series to explore suburbs and city neighborhoods in new depth, sometimes with a task force of as many as a dozen to bring all specialties to focus on the problem. Similarly, the specialists examined the adequacy of the city hospitals, race relations, the attitudes of youth.

In attacking the problem of the state university, Forman and Menzies encountered the weaknesses of public education in the state. This was a curiously disoriented system, rooted in the historic tradition of local autonomy. Local school committees were almost wholly independent of the state board of education, which was insulated from a chance of statewide leadership. The university and each of the state colleges operated on its own, competing for legislative appropriations. The vacuum of state direction in education was paralleled by a near vacuum in state financial aid to public schools. So the schools were as uneven in their quality as in the local degree of affluence to support them: an enormous disparity existed between poor towns and rich suburbs. A Menzies-Forman series on "The Mess in Bay State Education" stimulated reform. State Senator Kevin B. Harrington secured legislation for a study of the whole educational system of the state, headed by Benjamin C. Willis, Chicago school superintendent. It resulted in the Willis-Harrington Report which brought in recommendations that set up a board of education with new authority and staff resources, a board of higher education to correlate the institutions, and a new system of two-year community colleges. Standards were set for local schools, teachers' salaries raised, and financial aid to local schools increased.

Educational reform costs money. The state tax base was inadequate. Massachusetts had a limited income tax, no sales tax, and no graduated income tax. An attempt at a graduated income tax failed on referendum.

At the start of the 1966 legislative session, Timothy Leland, by now at the State House, applied his ex-science-writer focus to the major problems of the state and contributed a signal series, "The State We're In: A Report to the People." It detailed the many unsolved problems of Massachusetts, nearly all related to the lack of an adequate tax base; this put increasing strain on the local property tax, which had to support nearly all public services.

The Globe with the other newspapers had traditionally opposed a sales tax. They were undoubtedly influenced by the retail store advertisers, to whom it was a nuisance and a deterrent to shoppers. To the editorial writers it was, in economic theory, a regressive tax, taking proportionally more of the poor family's purchasing power than the rich. But the Globe came around to a limited sales tax, exempting food, clothing, and medicines, when it became apparent that without it there could be no relief for the burdened property tax or any chance to increase state aid to education. The sales tax fight in the legislature lasted a full year and was nip and tuck, but finally passed. Attorney General Elliot Richardson said that the new weight the Globe brought to the issue tipped the decision.

Science to Ian Menzies is a way of life, not something to be confined to a department on Sunday. When the Russians achieved leadership in space with their Sputnik it made a deep impression on him. Returning from a Nieman Fellowship at Harvard in 1962, he started agitating to bring the financial page into tune with the new tempo of the times. Why doesn't it pick up the revolutionary changes all around us, the new electronics industry, the movement of business out to Route 128? "Why don't you do it?" asked managing editor Tom Winship. Financial editor William Jones was retiring, so Menzies moved in as financial editor and moved science in with him. His own column might take up any economic, social, even political issue. He expanded the scope of the financial pages to approximate the range of public affairs, to write about whatever came naturally, with such an enlivening effect that

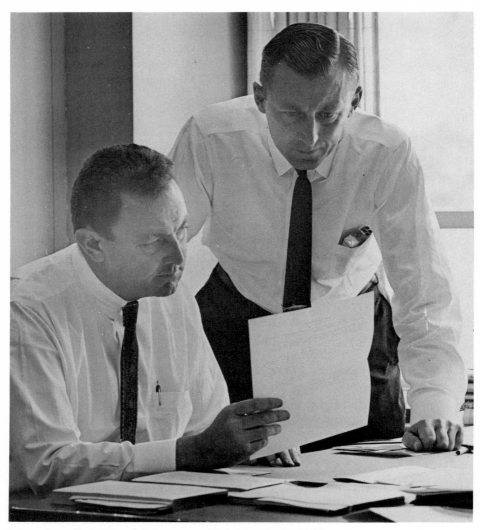

Managing editors Joseph Dinneen and Ian Menzies in 1965.

the Globe for the first time went ahead of the Herald in financial advertising linage. When Tom Winship vacated the managing editor's desk, Menzies, already roving all over the news, was his natural successor.

Ian Menzies, a Scot, was bred on a hard core of reality and educated at the Royal Technical College in Glasgow, where he had worked on the Glasgow Herald; he was 19 when Britain entered the world war. In the Navy he soon had command of a destroyer, and he won the Distinguished Service Cross for action in the Norway, Africa, Sicily, and D-Day landings. He was sent to Hingham, Massachusetts, to supervise the building of a British naval ship. There he married a Hingham girl, then returned to Glasgow and the paper there. But the strict paper rationing frustrated his journalistic instincts. He was given two paragraphs to report Churchill's return to politics, and that finished it. He came to Boston in 1947 and took the first newspaper job open, on the Boston American desk. There he studied the Boston papers and decided on the Globe. City editor Charles Merrill lived in Hingham and introduced Menzies to Laurence Winship, who found a desk spot for him in 1948. He moved from the desk to news, to rewrite, to a stint on the editorial page, then in 1955 to science writing.

Menzies was followed as science writer by Donald White, who in 1962 covered the epic space exploit of Col. John H. Glenn, whose five-hour flight of three orbits of the earth opened a new dimension in America's adventure into space. White followed Menzies as financial editor and Timothy Leland, hired away from the Herald, took up the science beat. When he moved into politics, Sumner Barton became the science writer. His specialty was meteorology — so much so that he left the paper for a couple of years to join the U.S. Weather Bureau, to return as editorial copy editor. Victor McElheny then joined the staff as science writer in December 1966 with wide-ranging experience, the first Globe science writer who could be said to have come with professional training for it. A Harvard graduate, McElheny wrote science for the Charlotte Observer, studied science on a Nieman Fellowship in 1964, then explored the technical aid programs of the United States around the world and became European editor of Science, the publication of the American Association for the Advancement of Science. The expanding space developments fell within McElheny's field in a continuing series of dramatic launchings and orbitings climaxed by the moon landing of 1969.

The specialists reporting to Joe Doherty in summer 1969 were: science, Victor McElheny; health, Herbert Black and Carl Cobb (though Cobb had just been awarded a Nieman Fellowship for the 1969–70 Harvard year); education, Nina McCain (who had come from the New York Herald Tribune at its demise), Alexander Auerbach, and Lawrence Van Dyne (part-time, a member of the Harvard Graduate School of Education), and Robert Levey (who had been handling education and was just back from a Nieman Fellowship year and doing a special column); conservation, James Ayers (he had held a Nieman Fellowship the year before Levey); transportation, Abraham Plotkin; automation, John W. Riley; aviation, Arthur Riley; mental health, Jean Dietz; religion, George Collins and Anne Mary Currier.

A new specialty had just been added: Crocker Snow was assigned to academic affairs, which had become a highly active area with the widespread student eruptions.

A separate group under Alan Lupo specialized on urban affairs, an area of increasing dimension and urgency. Lupo and his staff involved themselves in 1967 in the fight of East Boston residents against expansion of the airport into their residential area. This was a stubbornly fought but losing struggle against the power of eminent domain by the Port Authority to support its claim of public necessity. Lupo's assignment was to cover the inner city neighborhoods, bringing his staff into the whole gamut of issues of displacement of people for urban renewal and highways, the conflicts between community control and city hall, police relations with the black community.

Labor, one of the early specialties, was no longer handled as such. Wilfrid C. Rodgers, former labor editor, continued to handle labor news as assistant city editor.

The conservation department was new as James Ayres had developed it. Lucien Thayer had done a hunting and fishing column 40 years earlier. He was followed by Harold Putnam. Michael Beatrice developed this in the fifties into an outdoors department, until he was moved to the State House for the afternoon paper. William Fripp then had the outdoor column. Ayres took on the newer issues of air and water pollution.

The Globe took a full page in the paper May 20, 1969, to acclaim Ayres's work. The head was:

> For a Breath of Fresh Air
> Follow the Globe's
> Campaign Against Pollution

Of Ayres, it said:

> He doesn't think of himself as simply a conservationist. He calls himself an "environmental writer." His beat is our total environment — the contaminated air, the brackish waters, the precious recreation areas that seem to shrink as our population grows . . . His series on the Charles River won a UPI award in 1964. A Massachusetts Wildlife Federation award went to him in 1965 . . . and in 1966 he received the Scripps-Howard Meeman award for conservation.
>
> Jim Ayres gets solid backing in other sections of the Globe as well. Articles by our outdoors staff — Henry Moore, Barry Cadigan, Bill Fripp, Bill Riviere — each of these men has a vital interest in saving our rivers and marshes and woodlands. And the campaign against pollution is also carried on in Globe editorials . . ."

On January 11, 1970, the front page of the Metropolitan section of the Sunday paper was devoted to "The Dawning of the Age of Ecology." This title in a white spotlight glowed out of a half-page photograph of the city's skyline in a blur of smog.

An eight-column banner head announced "Decade of 70's Fast Becoming Age of Ecology." If this sent Globe readers to their dictionaries, the article under it quickly related ecology to the pronouncements of the President and the Governor, and other governors, that the 1970's must be used to reclaim the purity and safety of air and water. It was written by James B. Ayres, who had written a Globe proposal of December 27, 1969, for a Youth Environment Corps. Ecology and environment were words Globe readers were to become familiar with as the Globe kept the issue of pollution in editorial and news headline.

To practice what it was preaching, the Globe installed on May 29, 1970, a new smokeless and odorless waste disposal "that releases virtually no air pollutants," as the paper reported August 2 after two months' operation.

On July 22, 1968, midway in the schools' summer vacation, Alan Lupo and a staff of eight including education writer Janet Riddell, with four photographers, began a series on Boston's ailing playgrounds that described disrepair and neglect, lack of coordination of parks and schools and other agencies, and failure to involve the neighborhood communities. A new commissioner of parks and recreation, just then appointed, joined in their criticism and presented a program of correction as part of the series.

Joe Doherty's stable of specialists included neither the older specialties of sports, politics, finance, and labor nor such new ones as Dorothy Crandall's food department, Elmer Jones's "Ask the Globe" column in the evening paper, and those specialists on things in general Bud Collins and Victor O. Jones.

Jerry Nason, executive sports editor from 1970.

Harold Kaese.

Peter Greenough, Bruce Davidson, and David Deitch had financial page columns. Harold Kaese and Jerry Nason did daily sports columns. Anne Wyman did travel features. Robert Healy's political domain embraced the reporting and columns of four men in Washington, six at the State House for morning and evening, and four at City Hall.

Nat Kline was doubling in brass as military editor and, since 1964, assistant city editor. Military affairs had been an in-and-out department since the Spanish-American War. Harry Hartley had continued it for two decades chiefly as a Sunday column of notes of the military orders. After him George Noble did it in the 1930's as a part-time chore. In World War II Walter O'Leary did a column "With the Colors" and Harold Putnam a wartime "Victory Forum" that after the war was continued as the "Veterans' Forum," a question and answer service for veterans. Harvey Landers left the Globe for war an office boy to return a general and to become, naturally, the military editor. His Sunday department was then headed "Army, Navy, Air Force." On Landers' retirement in 1956, Nat Kline moved into the department from reporting and activated it. In 1958 he went to the Thule Air Base in Greenland for a story on "The Early Warning System." In 1961 he was in Berlin for the story of "The Wall." He did a war reporting stint in Vietnam in 1964 and followed the development of the Polaris submarine with two underseas tours. After his appointment in 1964 as assistant city editor, he kept up the Sunday column, by now called "Military Affairs."

At the State House the morning Globe in 1969 had a five-man bureau headed by David Wilson; the others were Robert Hanron, Robert Turner, David Ellis, and Carol Liston. The evening paper had Sal Micciche and Michael Beatrice.

At City Hall Gerard O'Neill covered for the morning paper, Fred Pillsbury afternoon. The Globe's veteran City Hall man, Joseph A. Keblinsky, did a column on city politics until his death in early 1970.

⌐Ask the Globe⌐

Q — When the musical "Hair" plays in other countries, is the American flag always burned? Or the flag of the country in which the play appears? — L. N., Brighton.

A — No flags — U.S. or other — are burned in "Hair". The first performances in Boston did use the flag as a dust rag in a brief spoof, but this was a local deviation from the New York production and was dropped after veterans' groups protested. The producer insists that the musical is against war and injustice but not anti-American. The lyrics from one of

The Globe Takes Off

Victor Jones was the last managing editor of both morning and evening papers. The operation was expanding in all dimensions. With the new building and more presses, circulation grew and so did the size of the papers. Specialization of staff proliferated. In 1962 Jones was made executive editor with Tom Winship and Al Haviland both managing editors under him. Jones had a long illness in 1964 that expanded the role of the managing editors.

In 1965 when Laurence Winship "retired" — that is, officially, for he never ceased to be a primary force in the paper — Tom Winship was appointed editor and Haviland executive editor. Jones opted to retire but as he recovered his health soon returned in a welcome new role as columnist in the evening paper.

Two new managing editors were appointed. Ian Menzies, whose innovative vitality had developed first the science coverage and then the financial page, was made managing editor of the morning paper. Joseph Dinneen, Jr., was moved up from city editor of the morning paper to managing editor for the afternoon.

A new title, assistant executive editor, was created for Robert Healy, who also continued as political editor to supervise the local, state, and Washington political coverage and to write his political column. When Haviland retired in 1969, Healy became executive editor and the position of assistant executive editor was dropped.

The larger part of the operation shaped up for the morning paper, for the Globe continued an all-day newspaper. The editorials, columns, comics, women's pages, and other feature fixtures started in the morning paper to run all day. Most special series ran all day. But the evening edition now had a wholly separate staff and, under Dinneen's vigorous leadership, developed as completely individual identity as publishing policy would permit. It gradually developed its own staff at State House and City Hall, its separate sports editor and sports columnist. Jerry Nason became executive sports editor, with Fran Rosa editor for the morning sports pages and Ernie Roberts for the afternoon. Harold Kaese's morning sports column was followed by Nason's in the evening.

Day editor James Keddie would be in at six o'clock to get the copy in shape. Al Monahan, city editor, would be in at seven and Dinneen with assistant managing

ACROSS THE CITY DESK
BY JOSEPH F. DINNEEN JR.

editor Bill Waldron soon after. They'd have a news conference at eight, bringing in suburban editor Bob McLean and sports editor Roberts to lay out the day.

First edition, on the street at 12:30, was their chief focus. This was the day's biggest edition, some 140,000 by 1969. It supplied all home delivery, which had to be in dealers' hands in the farthest suburbs by three o'clock to make the delivery routes. A replate an hour later was small, mostly for intown newsstands. The final was out at 3:30, with some 60,000. The stock market's advance in 1968 to a 2:30 closing gave the staff an extra hour sales time for the final, which had become increasingly important now that a dozen or more suburban papers had their own closing stocks. Commuters could carry home an evening Globe with as late news as the local paper.

When the evening Traveler ceased publication in 1967 the Globe's evening staff hoped and pressed for a completely separate evening paper, with its different editorial and op-editorial pages. This was thoroughly threshed out for three days of conference with publisher, editors, advertising and circulation heads. The decision was finally the publisher's. Davis Taylor decided to keep the Globe an all-day newspaper, with only the news changing as it developed through the day. That kept to the Globe's claim of no duplication between morning and afternoon readership.* Davis made one concession: the afternoon paper could put in a different set of columns on the op-ed page.

Actually and gradually the evening paper changed more than that. The sports staff was divided. The evening news emphasis was naturally more local; it tended also to make a different selection of the specialists' stories available. When a fourth correspondent, Matthew V. Storin, was added to the Washington staff his primary responsibility was the evening paper. The others, James Doyle, Martin Nolan, and Richard Stewart, covered for either paper, depending on what time the story broke. But most national news develops for morning.

Joseph Dinneen, from his experience as general assignment reporter and city editor, had developed a keen judgment on hard news. His equable disposition had no problem with staff morale. With Bill Waldron in charge of the day desk, he had a ready team-mate to develop headline stories and move them against evening deadlines. Between them they improved the makeup and appearance of the evening paper. The editor soon observed that "Joe Dinneen has brought fresh enthusiasm to the evening paper. He's strong on local features. He's developed a better sports department than the morning, that we always thought was tops." This takes some doing, for live sports events break for the morning paper; the afternoon calls for more innovation.

The afternoon paper was also more conventional in news coverage and news

* Duplication of circulation was counted three percent in 1965. A study in early 1971 showed it up to 12 percent. Elimination of the Traveler accounted for some of this, but the Globe management credited more of it to the improved evening paper under Joseph Dinneen.

City editor Al Monahan and reporter Jeremiah Sullivan in about 1960.

treatment. More than willingly was the more sophisticated material left for morning.

The afternoon managing editor, like city editor Al Monahan, had been a crime reporter and trained under the hard news discipline of Al Haviland. And Al Haviland, even as executive editor, was closer to the evening paper. Tom Winship called Al "a bridge between the old Globe and the new."

The editor was not unhappy over the somewhat more conservative tone of the evening paper. It doubtless was more in tune with the intown readers, the old Globe readership. Winship himself had been managing editor of the morning paper; it has his primary attention. And it has the competition of the Herald Traveler.

The management was doubtless glad that a certain balance developed between the morning and evening. Nobody planned it that way. But Al Haviland and Al Monahan knew the attitudes of the readers in the old neighborhoods of Chelsea, Everett, South Boston, Somerville.

Al Haviland, a much-loved figure with the staff, who had mostly grown up under his strict discipline, was known as the best man on detail in the office and the best lawyer. After Frank Leahy's death in 1962, Al handled practically all such problems as libel. He applied his own discipline to himself. In early 1969, the day he became 65, he walked out of the office to stay.

City editor Al Monahan then remained the primary link with the Globe of an earlier time. Al had been working for the Globe since 1922, when as a high school freshman he had helped the Everett district man with the scores of high school games. Two summers later he filled in for district men on their vacations. Then, at Boston College, he served as correspondent four years and was graduated onto the night side in 1929, where much of his work was on crime news.

By 1942 Al was on the night copy desk, where he handled the stories on the Cocoanut Grove disaster. He worked on the sports copy desk until in 1944 he was moved to the early (6 A.M.) day side shift, to cover the whole gamut of early-breaking news. He came to know the town inside out. On election nights Al came in earlier, by 3 or 4 A.M., to pick up the incomplete returns after the last morning edition had gone and wrap it up for afternoon.

This was a jagged job, to pick up the loose ends, check back on an infinite number of questions, nag the AP and the Boston election staff to fill in the holes and find missing precincts. Al became noted for his capacity to smell out errors in compilation, for finding mislaid precincts or mislabeled blocks of votes, and for filling in all the gaps in the late-counted returns for legislature and minor state offices.

He long remembered the early morning reversal in the one race Leverett Saltonstall lost in his long political career, for lieutenant governor in 1936. Saltonstall had led all night, but between 6 and 7 A.M. late returns from Fall River and Brockton put the Democratic candidate Francis "Sweepstakes" Kelly ahead. If this held, and there were only a few precincts still out, it would make the top story for the first afternoon edition. A former Globe reporter, Daniel Lynch, had become Saltonstall's assistant. Al phoned Lynch to suggest they compare notes. The result satisfied Lynch that Salty was licked, and Al turned to write a new story that reversed the morning headline.

The first edition went at 10 A.M. in those days. After World War II there were still five editions, two of them just replates until late in the sixties. After the Traveler dropped out of the evening field in 1967, to leave the Globe without evening competition, the number of editions was cut to three and the second of those was a replate.

By 1969 Al had two assistant city editors, Wilfrid Rodgers and Nat Kline, both veteran reporters; the suburban editor for the evening paper, Robert McLean, had an opposite number, John Burke, for the morning paper. Al's concern was wholly with the evening paper. The morning had its wholly separate staff, some of them even on all day at State House and City Hall.

By the time Dinneen and Monahan left with the final edition put to bed, around 3 P.M., the morning staff would have begun to take over. Night city editor Jack Thomas would be in by two, and Ed Doherty, assistant managing editor for morning, before three. All the morning executives would be in for a five o'clock news conference with Ian Menzies, whose hours ran from about 11 A.M. to 7 P.M.

In 1968 John C. (Jack) Thomas became the youngest city editor the Globe had ever had. A recruit from Northeastern University's cooperative work-study plan, he was a copy boy in 1958 while in college. After a hitch in the Marines he came onto the paper as a reporter in 1963 and proved immediately a hard digging reporter and lively writer. In 1965 he went to Washington to cover a round of hearings on the complications of Channel 5, on which the Herald still had its transient lien. In 1966 he was assigned to the State House. Next year he became assistant night city editor; in 1968, when city editor Claffey moved to the editorial page, Jack Thomas took over as city editor for the morning paper.

The size of the paper peaked at mid-week. If Monday and Friday ran 38 pages, Tuesday, Wednesday, and Thursday might run 60 or even 80 pages. Saturday's size was smaller, for the Sunday paper carried the big advertising for Monday, the big shopping day in Boston. But in the suburbs Saturday was the traditional shopping day; and for food shopping, Friday and Saturday were the big weekend buying days intown or out. The food advertising fattened the Thursday paper. The "news hole," meaning all nonadvertising, would run 135–165 columns. But 100 columns of this would be fixtures, leaving only 35–65 columns for news.

On May 13, 1968, a 60-page evening paper with 480 columns had 327 columns of advertising and 153 columns of news, about a 67–33 ratio of advertising to news.

The Globe at the beginning of 1969 gave up the Saturday evening paper, whose readers on a five-day week had largely given it up earlier. This helped with the problem of setting type for the ever-enlarging Sunday. The morning paper Saturday picked up two-thirds of the afternoon circulation.

By 1968 the Sunday paper, with 276 pages, had doubled its size since 1950. Its price was 35 cents. Its circulation, 560,000, almost doubled the Sunday Herald's 302,000 and was a third above the Sunday Advertiser's 434,000.

The daily paper at 10 cents in 1968 was averaging 49 pages morning, 45 pages evening; its circulation was 230,000 morning and 197,000 evening, a total daily of 427,000 to the Herald Traveler's 215,000. The combined all-day Record-American had 430,000 circulation.

Tom Winship, Editor

When Tom Winship followed his father as the Globe's editor in August 1965, he became the first editor of the Globe in 85 years who had ever worked outside Boston. He came to the staff from ten years in Washington, in 1958, when Davis Taylor had been publisher for three years. So Tom never experienced the earlier inhibitions. He was brought on for innovation and was increasingly given his head. As managing editor from 1963 he had become the pace-setter. There'd been nothing static about the paper in the years of Tom's emergence. A fast tempo created an air of excitement that built its own momentum. Momentum became a favorite word of the editor. He believes a newspaper has to keep doing something new. His lively leadership won the confidence of the staff.

The primary problem of the Globe when Tom Winship became editor, as it had been for a long time, was the need for what he calls "the Youth Movement." The age range of the staff was high. The Globe had had a retirement plan for decades, but it seemed to be largely a voluntary system. People seemed to retire only if they wanted to; even then they were apt to turn from editing to writing or from reporting to doing a column. Circulation and promotion had been working for years to change the "image" of the Globe as an old-fashioned hometown paper. It needed youth, vitality, more sophistication, a staff to be more en rapport with the rapidly

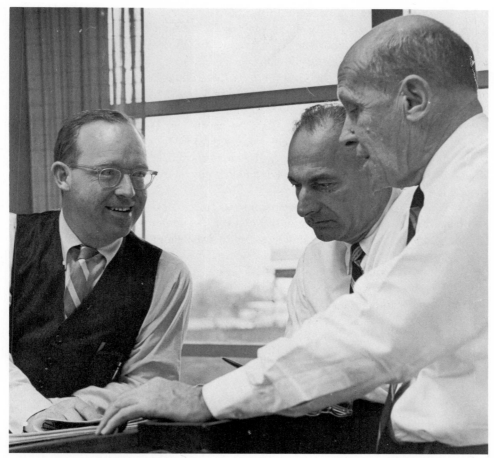

Editor Thomas Winship, associate editor Otto Zausmer, and executive editor Alexander Haviland: photographed in 1968.

changing society, with the youth problem, the race problem, the urban problem. All this in the view of the editor, and management agreed.

In 1963 the Globe introduced a summer in-training program that proved invaluable as a means of channeling able, educated young recruits onto the paper. For summer vacation season the Globe took on a dozen to 16 undergraduates. They came under the training of a veteran newspaperman, Gene Graham, who had won a Pulitzer Prize and a Nieman Fellowship before he became a journalism professor at the University of Illinois. Graham came on summers to organize seminars with editors and public men. The summer recruits worked assisting regular staff reporters, sometimes as a task force to help dig into all aspects of a problem for a series.

Among the students who came for the summer and joined the staff on graduation were James Doyle and Martin Nolan, soon to be Washington correspondents, and Christopher Lydon, who quickly became a top reporter. The Globe began in 1965 paying the summer trainees $100 a week. They aimed at having half of them black as a means of recruiting more Negro staff. Within three years the reputation of the summer program was such that the paper was inundated with applicants.

By 1969 there were 170 student applications for these dozen or so jobs, now at $125 a week. Students aiming at journalism focused on four newspapers whose training programs had found national appeal: New York Times, Washington Post, Los Angeles Times, and Boston Globe.

With this new resource, the Globe upped the standards of its hiring policy. No more leg men were taken on, and no more middle aged people from other papers. The Youth Movement created a new staff and a new staff tone and outlook.

Winship counts one of his early coups the capture of Darius Jhabvala when the Herald Tribune folded. Jhabvala had covered the UN for the Trib. The Globe enlarged its UN coverage but also enlarged Jhabvala's scope to write on international affairs. Sara Davidson was assigned from the city staff to be New York correspondent.

By April 1969, with two correspondents in New York and four in Washington and usually two or three staffers on out-of-town assignments, this outside coverage created its own problem. In its simplest form it was whom to talk to when the correspondent called the office; but it was also who was looking after the interests of the distant correspondent, making the desk aware that he'd have a story coming in, lobbying (the office word) for space for him. In April 1969 Thomas Ryan, who'd been handling national copy on the desk, was appointed national affairs editor, responsible for the outside correspondents.

In January 1967 the editor made a memo for a speech that listed improvements in the paper in 1966:

> Ads off page one
>
> Page two cleared of ads in the daily; pages two and three on Sunday
>
> Increase of 30 percent in letters to the editor
>
> New feature, "Ask the Globe," introduced on page two in the evening
>
> Most exciting political writing staff developed that the Globe ever had
>
> Complete makeover of the Sunday magazine
>
> Darius Jhabvala recruited for UN coverage after Herald Tribune folded; refused offers from Times and Post
>
> Paul Szep, cartoonist, joined staff from Toronto Financial Times; first editorial cartoonist on Globe
>
> Ernie Roberts, Dartmouth publicity chief, rejoined the paper as evening sports editor
>
> Christopher Lydon returned from year as intern with Attorney General Katzenbach
>
> Victor McElheny, new science editor, came on from "Science"
>
> Alan Lupo came from Baltimore Sun, to head up urban affairs team
>
> Recruited Steven Zorn, from San Francisco Chronicle; Janet Riddell, from Columbia Journalism School; Leonard Wheildon and Fred Pillsbury from Herald editorial page; Robert Sales, sports writer, from Herald Tribune
>
> Cleaned up masthead
>
> Expanded and improved arts pages
>
> Introduced Vietnam War Map
>
> Introduced simplified New England weather map
>
> Introduced cities and towns page
>
> Northern New England page for first edition
>
> Stock market finals in evening edition

SPORTS
PAGES
37 to 46

Boston Sunday Globe

New England's 🌐 *Largest Newspaper*

VOL. 193
NO. 182

By GLOBE NEWSPAPER CO.   SUNDAY, JUNE 30, 1968   * *®

SUNNY, SONNY
SUNDAY — Fair and mild.
MONDAY — More of same.
Page 48
High Tide
2:48 a.m.   3:24 p.m.

25 CENTS
(35 cents beyond 30 miles of Boston)

What Is It With These Kids Today

Suburban Boston: Youthful Dilemma—No. 1

Profile: White
And Well-Fed

Metropolitan Boston has a suburban bulge —a layer of white, well-fed affluent and middle-class towns lying between the core city and the country.

Unlike its white, well-fed inhabitants, suburbia is growing younger every year. Some places today you're almost in the minority if you're over 21.

Suburbia is its children—more than 35 percent of its population 19-and-under—and as high as 43 percent youth (Canton) and 42 percent (Hingham) to mention two.

Called pampered and over-protected by some, suburban young people drive more cars, carry more credit cards than some of their parents and have more cash to spend and save from jobs and allowances.

Hard by the greatest concentration of colleges and universities in the nation, they have available the best of educational resources. Per capita school costs in Metropolitan Boston averages close to $600, an all-time high.

Seemingly more articulate than their elders, young suburbia is willing to talk, talk, talk on almost any subject which interests them—The Generation Gap, The War, Drugs, Education, Racism, Their Personal Thing, The Future.

PROFILE Page 12

(Cary Wolinski Photo)

Summer: Search
For Fun, Profit

"I'm opening up a pad on Beacon Hill this Summer with my cousin. Anybody who wants can come and share it with us. I've just got to get away from my father. In this town I've got a reputation as a fag just because I smoke pot. Every time I go downtown, someone wants to beat me up."

This thin, nervous, freckly faced, Woburn 17-year-old is one of many Greater Boston teen-agers who've already begun the Summer migration of suburban youth to the hippy scene of Beacon Hill, Cambridge and the Back Bay.

They say they're escaping the boredom, the dullness, the no-action atmosphere of the suburbs.

"Newton is a dead town in Summer. If you hang around the corner or the park, the cops tell you to move along. But the kids on Boston Common are groovy, just groovy."

The pretty long-blond-haired, 15-year-old Newton girl had just arrived at the corner of Beacon and Charles st., Boston's hippy haven this Summer.

Barefooted, but wearing shorts and a clean white blouse, she wasn't even half-way to the official hip attire.

SUMMER Page 13

The Youth Movement: June 30, 1968.

> Slow improvement in women's and society pages
> Greatly improved rapport between news and production departments; licked "late paper" problem
> Don O'Neill in charge of night production helped overcome production problems

When the Herald-Traveler shortened sail by withdrawing the Traveler from the evening field June 25, 1967, the New York Times reported that "competition from a greatly improved Globe intensified the financial problems of the Traveler."

On June 4, 1968, editor Tom Winship was a speaker at the commencement of the Cambridge School in Weston, on the role of the communications media. He said that as editor of the largest metropolitan newspaper in New England he was spending four-fifths of his time and energy on the problem of communication with two groups, youth and the Negro community.

On Sunday, June 30, what he was talking about began to show in the Globe. Winship spent that weekend in Dublin, New Hampshire, in discussion with spokesmen from varied elements of Boston's Negro community and with other Boston editors on the problem of communication.

The Globe that day devoted the top half of the front page and five pages of its news section to the first chapter of a series, "Suburban Boston: Youthful Dilemma." The front page headline was "What Is It With These Kids Today?" A box inside explained that the articles were a team effort of the suburban desk and editorial department. It named ten reporters, four editors, and a photographer as the team involved.

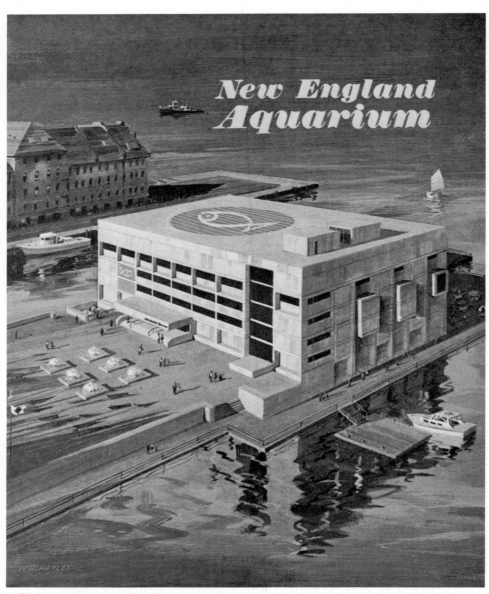

A Globe Sunday Magazine Cover in 1969.

This was the same method used two years earlier in exploring the condition of the various neighborhoods of Boston. Five articles occupied 16 columns, running from the top third of page one through five inside pages. On Monday also, July 1, the top of the front page was devoted to the "Youthful Dilemma." For the following two days a large part of the front page and all the news space in three to five inside pages were devoted to this exploration of the attitudes of youth. Besides its focus on the Youth Movement, this was a journalistic breakthrough: the farthest extension of the new flexibility of the paper to say, in effect, never mind the clichés of what's news. Put the conventional news inside; this is the most important thing we know about. We'll put it up front.

The old-fashioned Sunday magazine was a natural target for a new editor. In this Winship had strategic support; for Philip S. Weld, dynamic publisher of the Gloucester and Newburyport newspapers, had come on to the Globe board of directors in 1963, the first director outside the Taylor family to concern himself with editorial matters. Weld began a vigorous personal campaign to modernize the magazine and section the Sunday paper. By 1966 the combined pressure of Weld and Winship persuaded the publisher.

Ian Forman, the very able education editor, was made magazine editor with three assistant editors, two writers, and a feature photographer, to create a new kind of magazine — contemporary, lively, youth-oriented. Nye Rosa was taken out of the Sunday department and assigned to the layout of the magazine, with Gilbert Frieberg, a star photographer, as feature illustrator. They quickly turned it into an attractive publication with handsomely designed covers and explorative articles, often on the most contemporary and controversial issues. When Forman left the paper in 1968 he left a magazine that had become a substantial element in the Sunday paper.

The magazine covers immediately became items of art. Forman and Rosa would screen through as many as a hundred picture offerings on a projector to select three or four for a month's covers. This continued under William Cardoso, when he was moved from northern New England editor to succeed Forman on the magazine in 1968, and Robert Levey, who became magazine editor in January 1971.

Editing the Sunday magazine was much like editing any big magazine. To handle color required a lead time of four weeks. Text could be put in a week later. This meant planning well ahead of the news.

The television section with its own separate color became an insert in the magazine. This, too, edited by Elizabeth Sullivan, television editor, had to be put up a month ahead. But it contained a box cross-reference to the news section for any late program changes.

In the 1960's Globe reporting grew more sophisticated. An able political staff kept tabs on the legislature, alert to all the changes and chances of bills in the legislative process, putting a finger on the activity of special interest groups, giving the reader the score in terms that meant something.

A classic instance of reader service came in the wrapup of the legislative session of 1968. It closed in the usual frenetic all-night session, catching up breathlessly with important bills that had been left hanging, disposing of whole batches of bills with no time for debate or consideration. A few days before the close the Globe had printed a box score of bills passed, killed, and pending. This not only gave readers a chance to see the pluses and minuses of the session, but gave legislative members themselves a closeup of situations that in the confusion of the final days they might have lost track of. Adjournment came at three o'clock on a Saturday afternoon. In contrast to the 4 A.M. closings of the previous several days, this gave time for an overall review.

Besides the lead story of two columns summarizing the final session and a box score of the fate of major bills, Christopher Lydon reviewed the session in a two-page article, on which all the State House staff must have helped, that analyzed every important piece of legislation, describing what had passed and what failed.

Then he printed the voting record on two major bills that had been defeated. The Globe like other responsible papers had long printed the roll call on major bills. But the final vote is often meaningless. What counts are the amendments that may emasculate a bill, so that anyone could vote for it after all the exceptions have been put in to pull its teeth or protect special interests.

Lydon took two bills that had been proposed by the Consumers Council, one to regulate the new and rapidly expanding Cable Antenna Television, the other to give local authorities a chance to make billboard permits conform to their local zoning. Both had received a favorable vote in the first round but finally failed. In a fore-word to the voting record, Lydon explained: "The decisive voting bloc was not the one on either side of the battle, but the one that switched." He therefore printed the names of the members who had switched from their first favorable vote to help kill the bills.

This was a sophisticated piece of journalism that took close watching through the legislative process. The members who switched were those who failed to stand up to pressure. They could not be counted on in the clutch when the lobbyists got to work. They obviously were the ones for the voter to put on his list to remember in November.

If journalism could be taught by the case method used in law and business schools, this would make a classic case for any book.*

Similarly, in the field of medicine, Carl Cobb was going behind the announce-ments and statements to examine the actual conditions. A situation that particularly needed his exploration was the Boston City Hospital, where deficiencies of equip-ment, staff, money, facilities reached such a sore point that the medical staff brought it to public attention in a strong, candid statement. The Mayor, the trustees, the

* The next year Lydon left the Globe for the New York Times, where he has kept up the same kind of reporting.

Several times while I was at the Nieman Foundation I was consulted about the practicability of a case book for journalism education such as are used in law and business. None ever developed, so far as I know. At one time I started collecting instances for one such enterprise; but I never got beyond three, and two of those were stories by Meyer Berger of the New York Times—his reporting the solar eclipse expeditions in New Hampshire in 1932 and the Unruh murders in Camden that won him the 1949 Pulitzer Prize. The Globe record uncovers a few, notably the Morrissey case, which is the only one I have followed step by step as a "case" would require. But others could be the Titanic story, Cocoanut Grove, the S-51 sinking, Bob Healy's coverage of the Goldfine story. Another would be Martin Gansberg's report in the New York Times, March 27, 1964, of the "38 witnesses" who did nothing about a murder out-side their windows.

Presumably almost any Pulitzer Prize reporting would make a "case" if systematically fol-lowed. But many would require, as with the Goldfine story, perusing a newspaper file for a year. Life is too short and the book would be too long. Probably only a journalism teacher who would patiently collect cases over the years could produce for journalism education the equivalent of James B. Conant's "tactics and strategy of science" that he counted essential to understanding science.

Dexter Eure.

nurses, all rejoined with protective statements in a controversy confusing enough to the public. Cobb dug into the actual conditions with reports that clarified medical and political claims and made the situation understandable to the layman.

In the field of education, Fred Pillsbury, in a series of Sunday articles, took a close look into a number of different kinds of universities to explain how they were handling their problems of rapid growth, expanding curriculum, and student-faculty relationships.

These men required technical proficiency well beyond that of the general reporter that qualified them to examine the problems on fairly equal terms with the professionals they dealt with.

The tempo of editorial zeal in the Globe reached a pitch in December 1968 that found it publishing two major investigations at once in two successive weeks: one week the shortage of doctors and the plight of the cities, the next "A New Deal for New England," an examination of the failure of regional planning for pollution control and power development. At the same time there was an examination of the military-industrial complex that had been strengthened by the Vietnam war.

John Harris' issue of reducing the size of the legislature was revived in 1968 by the League of Women Voters on whom he put so much store. The Globe supported their drive in editorial and cartoon. As the 1969 session opened, Governor Sargent pushed the issue to force a joint legislative session as a constitutional convention. But the Democratic leaders squelched it with a promise to take it up the next year.

The Kerner Report in 1968 with its urgent emphasis on deepening racial conflict brought immediate response in the Globe with a new feature. On June 4, 1968, the op-ed page started a new weekly column, "Tell It Like It Is," by Dexter D. Eure, a black reporter who had handled public relations for the NAACP before coming to the Globe circulation department. Winship, seeking more black staffers, had got circulation to let him have Eure. Editor and reporter between them worked out the plan for the weekly column, to be an interview with someone who had thoughts to communicate on race relations.

Eure's first "Tell It Like It Is" column was an interview with his own minister, Dr. Prentis M. Moore of the Eliot Congregational Church, Roxbury, and secretary of the Greater Boston Ministers Alliance. Eure asked: Do you feel the general public understands the plight of black citizens? What are the churches of this area

DEXTER D. EURE

Affluent talk, but fail to act

If the past 12 months have given any indication as to what to expect from the

vote for the closest liberal pro-NCDF (Newton Community Development Foun-

doing? Dr. Moore's reply was that the problem is one of white racism. The churches are not yet ready or able to deal with it. There is obvious discrimination in employment in the administration staffs and in the calling of ministers for local churches.

That June 18 Eure interviewed Arthur Korn, musician and composer, of Newton. Korn described the musicians' union as divided into white and black, the cream of the jobs going to white members. He saw hopeful signs in more black students, teachers, and musicians. "But improvement will come only with the general economic lifting of the black man as a whole."

Consciousness of race relations permeated all departments of the Globe in the mid-sixties and all departments were actively recruiting Negroes.

Winship and Taylor families both were unquestionably influenced by their children, activists on the campus and beyond. Their response was more to the children than to the Establishment with which they were thoroughly identified. Globe positions had some alienating effects on older members of the staff and of their constituency. The paper lost some circulation in its opposition to Louise Day Hicks for mayor; more in its criticism of the Vietnam war; more still in its positive response to the black community. These temporary losses were submerged in the sweeping advance in momentum of the paper, but they were indicative of reaction to the Globe's attitudes to change.

The Sunday magazine April 21, 1968, was a special issue: "White Racism vs Black Power."

A publishing event of 1968 was a Globe innovation, a "poverty section": 36 pages that catalogued all the agencies, public and private, dealing with the problems of welfare, of the poor, the aged, the sick. It provided a local dictionary on welfare agencies and filled an urgent need.

Joseph Levin, on retiring from 40 years on the night desk in 1967, took up a three-day-a-week column titled "Senior Set," which Frank Harris had run, on the problems of the aged.

With its Saturday evening paper cut off in 1969, the Globe began to develop weekend features. The first was a Friday column, "Let's Eat Out," by Anthony Spinazzola of the Sunday department, who tested and reported on dining spots. On Friday, April 18, "Weekend," an entertainment page, was introduced; it is a guide to what's going on across the board from rock and roll to theater.

Tom Winship sees three main factors in the progress of the past decade. "We gave the Globe a civic voice, a voice for change in the community. We've built an educated young staff that can handle contemporary issues. We've made the paper typographically attractive."

Pulitzer Gold Medal

A Globe headline May 3, 1966, told "The Boston Globe Wins Pulitzer Prize." It was the top Pulitzer award, the gold medal for "meritorious public service," the first time this award had come to a Boston newspaper in 45 years.

Only a few hours earlier the Globe had been presented the Sevellon Brown Memorial Award by the New England Associated Press News Executives Association "for distinguished and meritorious public service."

Both were for the Globe's investigation and campaign that blocked appointment of Francis X. Morrissey to the federal bench.

The May 3 story described a ten-man Globe team, headed by editor Thomas Winship, that had worked on the Morrissey case. "It was an example of perfect teamwork," Winship said. "The issue was the integrity of the federal bench."

The team of staff members was listed. Robert Healy, political editor had the lead part. The others were Charles L. Whipple, editorial page editor; Joseph M. Harvey, court reporter; Joseph Keblinsky, City Hall reporter; James Doyle and Martin Nolan, Washington correspondents; Jeremiah V. Murphy and Richard J. Connolly, staff reporters; and Anson H. Smith, editorial writer.

The Globe's Morrissey campaign was a dramatic episode and an extraordinarily alert and astute journalistic operation.

Robert Healy had learned of the first plan to appoint Morrissey in 1961. Victor Jones, then managing editor, assigned Joseph Harvey at the courthouse to prepare a record on Morrissey which the Globe printed. It showed that after studying at Suffolk Law School he had twice failed the Massachusetts bar exams but in 1933 had enrolled in a law school in Georgia that was later closed, and had been admitted to the Georgia bar on recommendation of the only two members of the staff of that school. He had later been employed in two Massachusetts state departments, had long been of political service to Joseph P. Kennedy, and later was aide to Senator John F. Kennedy, who had secured his appointment to the Boston municipal court in 1958.

This 1961 Globe report raised active criticism of the appointment from lawyers and bar associations. It brought Healy a call from a prominent member of the White House staff, hoping the Globe would be printing nothing more on Morrissey because he was not going to be appointed.

In summer 1965 Healy's Washington pipelines again alerted him that President Johnson had been persuaded to name Morrissey a federal judge.

The Globe broke the story in a dispatch from James Doyle August 27 that "President Johnson is planning to name a friend of the Kennedy family to the Federal bench." The story reviewed the criticisms raised in 1961.

The Globe entered an editorial protest the very next day, titled "The Limits of Friendship." It said: "President Johnson's plan to name Boston Municipal Court Judge Francis X. Morrissey to the Federal bench ought not to be carried through . . . There is room to doubt that Judge Morrissey is professionally equipped to assume this responsibility. The public interest requires a change in Senator Kennedy's stand."

Editor Winship ordered a concerted effort to uncover all pertinent facts on Morrissey and print them as "just deadpan factual stories."

On September 27 Morrissey's nomination was officially announced. The Globe headline:

> Morrissey Named Federal Judge
> Four Years of Controversy Fail To Deter LBJ

Two days later, September 29, a headline:

> Morrissey Furor Mounts
> Wyzanski Opposes

Judge Charles Wyzanski of the federal district court in Boston, to which Morrissey was nominated, had written the Senate committee that "the only discernible ground for the appointment is his service to the Kennedy family . . . He has neither the necessary familiarity with the law nor the industry to learn it . . ." The Globe printed the text of the Wyzanski letter, a column and a half.

The Globe was also printing full reports of the formidable support elicited for the nomination. On October 2:

> Cardinal Urges Senate to Confirm Morrissey

Next day the Massachusetts House passed a resolution in support. Its sponsor called it a rebuttal to Wyzanski.

The New York Herald Tribune and the Washington Post editorially echoed the Globe's position that Morrissey's qualifications were nonexistent. The Post carried the Globe stories daily on its front page, giving them Washington exposure. Senator Edward Kennedy in a Senate speech attacked the press for stories "totally in error and extremely derogatory." Senator Leverett Saltonstall issued an explanation of his "no objection" statement on the nomination: "This has been my customary procedure when I am not personally acquainted with the candidate."

On October 1 a column by Healy headed "Dirksen Key on Morrissey" said that Senate approval was a virtual certainty.

On October 3 the Globe published a detailed biography of Morrissey by Joseph Harvey, who had explored Boston directories and voting lists. Next day it published another editorial, "Judge Morrissey Still Isn't Fit." It called Morrissey "the Kennedy family's political handy man" and said the Senate committee should reject the nomination "and thereby reinforce public faith in the courts."

October 6 brought the headline:

> Hub Bar Votes "No" on Morrissey

The council of the Boston Bar Association had voted 13–9 at a special meeting to put the association on record against the nomination. They wrote the Senate that Morrissey "is entirely lacking in the qualifications necessary to carry out the duties of a Federal judge."

But the Massachusetts Trial Lawyers Association and the Massachusetts Bar Association endorsed the nomination.

On October 10 a Globe headline said:

> Morrissey Approval Expected

On October 12 the Senate committee held an all-day hearing. Speaker McCormack and numerous lawyers, judges, and other Massachusetts figures supported the nomination.

Morrissey himself testified as to his training and career. Among other things, he said he had studied at Boston College Law School. This had been stated in Doyle's August 27 story of the impending appointment. The biographical information on

Morrissey in that story came from Senator Kennedy's office. But the Globe had not found this in its own exploration of his education. The paper now inquired specifically on this point, and the Dean of the Law School told the Globe Morrissey had not attended law courses. In fact, the evening intown extension school that he had attended in 1933 offered no law course.

The Globe's headline Sunday October 17:

B.C. Law School Records Don't Show Morrissey as Student

A committee of the American Bar Association had made its own inquiry on Morrissey. Its chairman testified to the Senate committee that it found no evidence of Morrissey's staying more than a few days in Georgia when he obtained admission to the bar on the basis of a diploma. Morrissey had testified he resided in Georgia nearly a year, from June 1933 well into 1934. Senator Dirksen picked up this discrepancy. The October 13 headline:

Dirksen Not Satisfied: Recall Morrissey

But on October 14:

Senate Committee OK's Morrissey 6 to 3

Dirksen, however, voted against the nomination, and the story reported his cross-examination of Morrissey. "Dirksen brought out that Morrissey's two sponsors required by Georgia law for bar admission were the dean of the diploma mill and its only faculty member."

Next day, October 15, a Globe editorial, "The Morrissey Case," insisted that

> before Morrissey is confirmed his testimony ought to be more fully explored. One question it raises is whether he has enough legal experience to be a Federal judge . . . The other is whether he was less than candid in answering questions as to the length of his stay in Georgia. At one point he said he was there six months after admission to the bar, at another he was in Georgia about a year. Other evidence is he returned to Boston a day or two after admission to the Georgia bar. It is a question the public has a right to have answered before he sits on the Federal bench . . .

But the front page that day had a blockbuster:

Ran Here in 1934

Candidacy Raises New Morrissey Issue

The Globe had had such a break as often comes to a crusading newspaper. A tip. Robert Healy had received a telephone call from a former associate of President Kennedy telling him that Morrissey ran for the legislature in Charlestown in 1934. The requirement of a year's residence overlapped the period Morrissey had testified he was in Georgia. The informant suggested Healy check the records and the conflicting dates. The Globe checked the old election records at the State House.

This really tore it. Senator Dirksen commented, "This gets a little more complicated every day."

That was a Friday. On Sunday, October 17, FBI investigators asked the Boston election commissioner to go to City Hall and open his records to them. They found and photographed a voting register that showed Morrissey had reregistered as a Boston voter July 26, 1933. He had testified that he was a resident of Georgia at that time. Joseph Keblinsky, veteran City Hall reporter, picked up this strategic information in time to report it Monday, October 18.

The same day the Globe carried a column by Robert Healy titled: "Morrissey Hurting Ted Kennedy." "If the nomination goes to the Senate for a vote there is going to be a debate and Kennedy is going to be hurt again . . . The way to avoid this is for Morrissey to withdraw his name."

That day Senator Saltonstall withdrew his "no objection," saying: "Since the committee reported his nomination favorably, various matters have been brought to light that question the accuracy of the judge's testimony . . . I trust the matter will be referred back to the judiciary committee and these uncertainties cleared up."

Senator Kennedy, however, was quoted that he was going to "ride right on through" to push the nomination. On October 19 Attorney General Katzenbach reported that an FBI investigation had confirmed Morrissey's residence in Atlanta November 3, 1933. This was on the basis of a registration card for Staley College of the Spoken Word, in Boston, that gave Atlanta as Morrissey's permanent address. Healy's story pointed out the holes in the FBI report, as he had actually pointed them out in personal confrontation with Katzenbach, telling the Attorney General it was a whitewash job.

Senator Dirksen called the FBI report "avoidance and confession" of shortcomings in the Morrissey record. "We have the votes," the Republican leader declared.

On October 20 James Doyle's story from Washington quoted the Democratic leader, Mike Mansfield, that the Morrissey confirmation was "a tough one" and Senator Dirksen's forecast of "an extended Republican presentation if the nomination comes to the floor." Senator Javits said that new charges published since the committee hearing required the nomination go back to committee and he would so move. But Senator Kennedy was quoted as claiming more votes for the nomination than opposed. Doyle counted Senate noses to report as many as 40 opposed and indications of absenteeism for the vote by embarrassed Democrats running high. Healy's column that day reported the nomination in trouble and indicated it might never come to a vote.

October 21 Senator Mansfield was quoted: "It looks very close, three votes one way or the other." Senator Kennedy got the message. The headline October 22:

Ted Yields: Appointment Shelved

The Globe's editorial that day said "Senator Kennedy's action does him credit."

The sequel came November 5, when Judge Morrissey asked that the President withdraw his name.

Morrissey Bows Out — President Accepts

The Globe editorial called it "a wise and honorable decision."

Tom Winship had been editor just three months when he made the decision to go all out on the Morrissey case. Time Magazine, reporting the Globe's campaign October 29, 1965, quoted Winship: "This is not a personal vendetta. We just think Morrissey is not up to the job. This is not an anti-Ted Kennedy effort. I can't think of a thing of Ted's we haven't supported him on except Morrissey.

"We're in this purely as a matter of principle. This community's been starved for a paper that didn't necessarily say popular things all the time. We decided to join the community and it's been good to us."

Death Catches an Extra

The night Robert Kennedy died, Thursday, June 5, 1968, John S. (Jack) Driscoll, night editor, was nervously watching the wires like every editor across the country. The Wednesday evening headline had been "Kennedy Lives; Condition Critical." Bob Healy's lead for Thursday morning was "Senator Robert Kennedy lay near death Wednesday night."

Driscoll had had an emergency front page made up to replate if the word came. He'd laid out six other pages from copy the office had produced since Kennedy was shot the night before. But there was no change when the last edition left the composing room at 1:55. Two o'clock was the time to say "goodnight" to the desk and all the mechanical crews.

Driscoll phoned the circulation manager for authority to hold another two hours. Still no change, and he phoned again to ask an extension till six o'clock. But this time the answer was no. Before he left he got the press men to put his replate front page on the presses. Then he started to drive home and turned his car radio on. John Burke, assistant night editor, was driving just ahead of him. Just as Burke drove into the tunnel at South Station, Driscoll's radio flashed the word that Kennedy was dead. He had died at 4:44 A.M. EST. Another second and the tunnel would have silenced his radio. He honked Burke to a stop, turned him around to hold anyone still in the office, and raced to a phone to give the word to put things back in motion. The press men and composing room men would be showering and changing before leaving. He might catch some. John Every, head of the press room, was finishing his shower when Driscoll got back. He'd nailed a couple of men in the parking lot. The press foreman, wrapped in his towel, got on the phone to pull in others. "You going to call someone?" he asked Driscoll, meaning an editor or publisher. "No," said Driscoll. "Just push the button."

That started the replate rolling. Driscoll got his other six pages ready for the presses. By 6:30 they had turned out an extra of 60,000 and sold them all downtown and in the close-in suburbs.

The headline was simply

Robert Kennedy is Dead

Extra

U.S. Day of Mourning Proclaimed. Died at 4:44 A.M.

The first 13 pages were all on Kennedy, his murder, his campaign, his family. This was about double the volume of the Kennedy spread in the regular edition that had gone to press four hours earlier.

Eight copy readers and reporters had left the office with Driscoll that night, and every one came back when he heard the radio bulletin of Kennedy's death. One had got almost to the New Hampshire line; one was a sports desk editor; all volunteered to help.

That was the last time it was necessary to wake up the circulation manager to get authority to hold the presses. After that it was arranged that that decision would always rest with someone in the office.

Two months later Tom Winship pulled Jack Driscoll, a man who could get things rolling, off the night desk to be assistant to the editor.

Driscoll had started on the Globe as a sports writer after covering sports in his undergraduate years at Northeastern University. He had tried for a job on the Globe right after high school. Editor Laurence Winship suggested Northeastern to him; its cooperative plan alternated ten weeks on a job with ten weeks at studies. This with summers gave him a good deal of newspaper experience before he was graduated in 1958. Driscoll wrote sports for a year, then was put on the copy desk for three months' training to be assistant to sports editor Jerry Nason. The sports department had its own desk and he was in charge of the department when Nason was away on a story. But Driscoll was more interested in processing the news and in the production of a newspaper.

He got back on the copy desk and in a few years was assistant night editor. He served under Ed Mitchell in the years of crisis with the composing room that led to reinstituting a nightly news conference to get an early shapeup of the paper. At first the conference was at seven o'clock. Then it was backed up to five with the night managing editor, Tom Winship, in charge, and also present the new night editor William Miller, the newly established suburban editor, the night city editor, the picture editor, and the slot man and layout man from the desk. This brought Driscoll to the conference and so into the nightly problems of production. Tom Winship was soon saying that Jack Driscoll was "establishing some communication around here."

The Globe Takes Sides

The editorial page was one of many areas of the Globe that had got along without titles through most of the paper's history. It had traditionally come under the domain of the Sunday editor. When Laurence Winship moved from that post to be managing editor in 1937 and then editor in 1955, he continued his responsibility for the editorial page.

But after Packer retired in 1954, with Price now limiting himself usually to the Sunday Dudley and coming in only for Wednesday luncheons, Henry Harris, then Herbert Kenny, the poet from the Post, and for a time Ian Menzies were added to the page. James Powers' leadership on the page was recognized by the title chief editorial writer. But after 40 years of it all, Powers soon wanted to lighten his load to a four-day week.

In 1962 Charles Whipple was appointed chief editorial writer and two years later editor of the editorial page. Whipple came to the Globe in 1936, after Exeter and Harvard and a year of law school, had several years of reporting, then left to become an organizer for the Newspaper Guild. But he was back on the staff before the second world war, when he joined the Red Cross Field Service to go through the whole European campaign from the Normandy beaches to 1945 and receive a Purple Heart award. He returned to become a top rewrite man. He covered the intricacies of the McCarthy era hysteria. Among other major assignments, he reported the Worcester case in 1960 that disclosed a pattern of corruption in Massachusetts public life. Whipple was 48 when he assumed the editorship of the editorial

A Szep cartoon: Governor Volpe, 1968 — He's the best salesman this state
has ever had . . ."

page: a thoroughly sophisticated reporter, a pronounced liberal, with a strong
commitment to social justice.

The transition on the page under a new generation moved fast in the next few
years, and the tempo of change was raised when Tom Winship became editor of the
Globe in 1965.

The number of editorial writers was increased from three to six; the op-ed page
was developed with the columnists grouped on it; Paul Szep's editorial cartoons
from 1966 brought a trenchant daily dramatization of issues to the center of the
page. New vigor and scope in editorials were reflected in the change in character
and volume of letters to the editor; they dealt with controversial issues of the day
and they piled in — sometimes 100 a day, of which only a tenth could be used,
where a few years before there had been half a dozen.

A sharp symbol of change was the dropping of the Uncle Dudley signature to
the lead editorial on January 5, 1966, after 75 years. This took some doing. The
new editorial writers found the old Uncle name corny. Tom Winship, coming back
to Boston after a dozen years in Washington, wanted to get rid of it. Charles Whipple,
enrolled for an editorial seminar at Columbia, found himself a target of editors
calling the Uncle Dudley signature provincial, country-style. It took Winship and

Whipple several years of pressing against tradition, but finally the issue was settled in a top-level conference with publisher Davis Taylor, editor emeritus Laurence Winship, circulation and advertising managers, Whipple, and Tom Winship. When Davis reluctantly agreed, he ruled they'd just quietly drop it without announcement. If it met too much protest, they could as quietly put it back. The change was hardly noticed. It brought only five letters, two in favor of the change and three against.

Months and years after the name was dropped old readers still spoke familiarly of "today's Dudley," and sometimes they had to be shown that the old Uncle had departed. But his heritage remained. He had imparted a quality, a distinctive flavor and tone, a philosophy, a dimension of character to the page that endured.

The dropping of the "Uncle Dudley" signature was a benchmark of the change that had already come to the editorial page. The three men who had been the composite Uncle Dudley for nearly half a century had departed. Price died in 1964; Harris, who had replaced Packer, died in 1965; Powers was retiring. Herb Kenny, who had served five years on editorials, had been moved to books. With these departures, not only was the stylized format of the full-column Dudley and three shorts loosened up to a more flexible page, but the style that had distinguished the Uncle Dudleys had also changed. The editorials were sharper and generally shorter. Their style was terse and unpretentious. But they spoke out more clearly and urgently on the daily issues. There were more of them, with a larger staff, and they could take up more topics. The new page was more concerned with what it had to say than with the style of saying it. There was no substitute for the distinction of Lucien Price's style. But the new writers did not need to recall the glories of Greek civilization for an oblique allusion to the failures of our democratic process. They could say it bluntly: Senator Kennedy should give us a better judge.

That was roughly the difference. The new men pulled no punches. They gave the Globe a civic voice, which is what Davis Taylor and Tom Winship were committed to. They backed up the political and social campaigns of the special writers for political reform and for meeting social needs. They took on a lagging school committee, the opposition to urban renewal, ineffectual police work, sleazy legislative leadership, an obstructive and superfluous executive council, scandalous mismanagement of the county jail, the outmoded county system.

In 1963 the Globe got solidly behind urban renewal and urged Mayor John Collins to bring Edward Logue to Boston from New Haven, where he had reshaped the city. The Globe put its editorial support behind Logue in his struggles against opposition and intrenched politics to start shaping "the new Boston" that became Mayor Collins' slogan.

The Globe became critical of the Vietnam war policy very early, while this was still very much a minority position. And its editorials were having an effect. Congressman Thomas P. O'Neill changed his position on Vietnam. He heard the opposition from his Cambridge-Somerville constituency, he said.

Vice President Humphrey got hold of editor Tom Winship for a talk on Vietnam. Much of the Globe criticism was sound, Humphrey conceded. But give the President time.

Winship gathered together all the material he could on Vietnam and told Charles Whipple to go off to Vermont for a week and read it, then do a series on Vietnam. Whipple wrote a six-part series, each a full page that ran opposite the editorial page, May 29–June 3, 1967. The Globe reprinted the articles in a booklet, which

The Boston Globe

8   MONDAY, MAY 29, 1967

The War in Vietnam

I – How It All Began

The one word on the lips of everyone these days is Vietnam. This one word alone is enough to start an argument. Seldom in the nation's history have emotions run so high over a single issue.

And the reason is war. Men who were old enough to be sent into the First World War have, in one lifetime, already lived through three American wars, and a fourth one is now going on . . . four wars which have already taken the lives of 588,000 American young men and have wounded, in body or

Stars and Stripes at the side of Ho Chi Minh and his Gen Vo Nguyen Giap when they took over were an American general and major. Those were the days of Rooseveltian anti-colonialism and, despite stormclouds ahead, the Communists were still regarded as our allies.

Ho proclaimed the Democratic Republic of Vietnam on Sept. 2, but back in Paris Gen Charles de Gaulle decided by the year's end to send 70,000 troops to Indochina to re-establish French colonial

Vietnam war editorial: May 29, 1967.

quickly went through several reprintings. Senators Fulbright, Church, and Mc-Govern, the early critics of Vietnam, ordered it by the hundreds to use in answering letters on Vietnam.

Later the Globe stuck its neck out further on Vietnam. In 1968 it introduced a column on Sunday called "Draft Counsellor," advising youths liable to the draft of their rights and alternatives. It was written by David Washburn, who had worked in the resistance movement.

On Friday, March 28, 1969, the whole top half of the editorial page was an airplane photo of an area of Vietnam showing the bomb craters that dot the terrain. It was titled "A Photo Editorial." Under it on one side was a description and location of the cratered landscape, 25 miles northwest of Saigon; on the other side there was a quotation from Gen. David M. Shoup, retired Marine Corps commandant, taken from an article in the April Atlantic: "The U.S. bombing effort in both North and South Vietnam has been one of the most wasteful and expensive hoaxes ever to be put over on the American people."

Only the bottom third of the page was left, for Editorial Points and letters.

The editorial section Sunday, June 22, 1969, devoted an entire page to reprinting from that quarter's Foreign Affairs the article by Clark Clifford on Vietnam in which he urged pulling out all American combat troops by the end of 1970, an article that had rekindled debate on American objectives in Vietnam.

Earlier in the season the full text of Jerome Wiesner's critical analysis of the administration's program to deploy antiballistic missiles was given a whole page. The Globe had never followed the New York Times policy of publishing full texts, but increasingly it was giving full treatment to what it considered vital documents.

Davis Taylor encouraged the reform campaigns and wanted the paper to become involved in the "black revolution." He went to Alabama himself for the march on Selma in 1963 and was only restrained by his own reporters from joining the march. They insisted that as his press card read "publisher" he would lack a reporter's immunity.

The Globe's first clear expression on the ancient birth control law of Massachusetts came in an editorial on July 9, 1965, that supported the recommendations of a special commission for reform of the law. The report was in a legislative committee which had held no hearing on it. "What is happening to the so-called birth control bill?" the editorial asked. "The commission's report was referred on July 1 to the Committee on Public Health for hearing and recommendation . . . The Committee should act promptly on a matter on which there is such wide and general agreement."

The committee did not. The following April 14, 1966, a Globe editorial was titled:

Birth Control: New Chance

Cardinal Cushing says this year's bill contains safeguards not contained in last year's bill . . . This evidently is what the law-makers have been awaiting . . . Last year's effort was killed after the cardinal objected to the lack of these safeguards . . . For Catholics in the legislature and elsewhere there is no doubt now that the prelate bespeaks his deepest conviction when he says that "Catholics do not need to impose by law their moral views on other members of society."

The birth control bill ought to pass. The last excuse for delay and buck passing is gone.

A week later, April 22, an editorial hailed "the near final approach to liberalize our last-in-the-nation birth control law . . . the first time that modern birth control legislation has progressed so far on Beacon Hill. There are still the bitter-enders. For those legislators who support the measure, the words of the cardinal constitute a solid pillar of truth: 'Catholics do not need the support of civil law to be faithful to their own religion.' "

The revised law still restricted birth control to the married. It was four years later that one-man crusader Bill Baird brought that issue to a head. He was convicted for distributing a contraceptive to an unmarried woman. The State Supreme Court in a 4–3 decision upheld the law as a legitimate legislative protection of health. But the Federal Circuit Court of Appeals held it unconstitutional as "conflicting with fundamental human rights."

The Globe editorial July 7, 1970, was headed "We Join the 20th Century." The federal court, it said, "has made Massachusetts at long last a part of the Union . . . All other States except Connecticut had become up to date in this respect many years ago, and Connecticut joined them more recently . . . The Massachusetts birth control law may now join the stocks and ducking stool and scarlet letter in limbo."

When the editor decided to come out for reform of the abortion law in an editorial March 2, 1970, his Catholic associates urged against it as too explosive an issue. The editorial brought one letter of protest.

New York and several other states had just liberalized or repealed their abortion

Boston Sunday Globe

● 1969, Globe Newspaper Co. ●
● VOLUME 196   NO. 41   SUNDAY, AUGUST 10, 1969   ● ●   35 CENTS

The Fight for Equality

WOMEN

Women are on the move.

Today the second sex, the weaker sex, the fairer sex is pressing for "equality" in every phase of American life.

In the home and outside it, in business, in sports, in fashion, women are breaking the traditional barriers, breaking away, breaking down the doors of male dominence.

Some call it "the female revolution." Others call it "Girl Power."

Whatever it is, women are less willing to restrict their lives to a cycle of marriage, child-bearing, house-keeping and general subservience to men.

The Pill, unquestionably, has a great deal to do with this revolution. So have the education explosion, the absorption of women into the work force and the civil rights movement.

Some women are organizing. There are moderate groups picketing for women's rights and there are extremist groups like the Female Liberation Movement, who practice karate to make their points with the opposite sex.

Some women are carrying the banner on their own, fighting the good fight alone.

But whether the action is cautious or crazed, united or solitary, the attitude is the same. Many women are no longer willing to live as an oppressed majority, subject to the whims and wallets of men. (More than half the nation's stockholders are women, by the way.)

Of course many women see no evil in their circumstances. (And plenty of men don't either.) They sense a natural order to their condition as the meek and motherly fragment of the grand design.

But among the young, the new sense of female liberation runs particularly strong, from the stylish equality of short-hair-long-pants Unisex fashion to the gradual elimination of sexual double standards.

Today's Sunday Globe attempts to fathom this phenomenon of the female revolution.

The Movement:
They Act the Part

By ELLEN GOODMAN
Globe Staff

Women: August 10, 1969.

laws. Middlesex Judge Cornelius J. Moynihan had refused to rule on the constitutionality of the Massachusetts law that prohibited abortion except when the mother's health was endangered. The judge said: "If the law is not as responsive to the felt needs as the people believe contemporary life demands, the remedy rests with the Legislature."

A legislative committee was opening hearings on recommendations to revise the law. The Globe said that "statistics make it appear the law clearly is not responsive to needs . . . Illegal abortions are a $120,000 a year business. Cardinal Cushing sees abortion as the taking of human life . . . But it may be that his broad views on birth control should be extended to abortion as well." The paper quoted him: "Forbidding in civil law a practice that can be considered a matter of private morality does not seem reasonable in a pluralistic society."

The editorial then quoted the Reverend Armand Morrisett of Lowell as "one of many Catholic theologians . . . who argues that all abortion laws should be repealed because they are archaic, unjust, hypocritical and a private theological concern of the parents to be." The Globe concluded "With an unenforceable law repealed, the State would be relieved of making decisions which it is ill equipped to make. The decisions to abort or not to abort would be made by the parents and their doctor who are in a far better position to pass on all the attendant circumstances . . ."

In spring 1970, women's liberation militants invaded the Globe with a set of demands that included removal of the labels "male" and "female" from help wanted ads and acceptance of a women's liberation column to be immune from editing. Globe editors rejected these demands. But on August 8, 1970, the Globe editorially urged all Massachusetts members of the House of Representatives to support the women's Equal Rights Amendment, scheduled for vote in the House two days later. They all did, as it was passed 350–15. But it was shelved in the Senate.

The Boston Globe

16

MONDAY, NOVEMBER 6, 1967

Kevin White for mayor

Boston voters elect a mayor on Tuesday. The nonpartisan election is between two Democrats. The term is four years—years that promise both trouble and opportunity. Each must be met by the new mayor.

The problems of the city are real. They are what the businessman, the cabdriver, the waitress, the telephone operator, the policeman, the fireman, are crucial elections, all right." Carl Stokes is a candidate for mayor of Cleveland, Richard G. Hatcher for mayor of Gary, Ind. Both are black.

What the nation thinks and says about Boston is important. It becomes part of the climate for attracting and keeping young people, and drawing new business to the city—the kind of business that means more paychecks form to a stable tax rate. This is a more responsible position. He has not made promises he cannot keep.

He knows that what Boston needs is good business management that can attract bright people, and improved city services that can better the living conditions of the city's residents and reverse the flight out to the suburbs.

The Globe takes sides: November 6, 1967.

The publisher had to be persuaded about taking positions on candidates. Tom Winship and Charles Whipple had pressed this for several years; but they agreed it should be started on a local issue. It wouldn't have mattered much on the presidential campaign of 1964 that was so one-sided. Davis was ready for it in the mayoral race in 1967 when Mrs. Louise Day Hicks, who had blocked desegregation as the chairman of the school committee, ran against Kevin White. To Davis this involved a matter of principle: whether black children were to get a better break. He agreed to break an 86-year tradition, and the Globe came out for Kevin White (November 6, 1967), putting its stand on the matter of principle.

Next year in the presidential race they aimed to treat Gene McCarthy and Robert Kennedy evenly. But in the election they came out for Humphrey against Nixon.

In the 1970 election the Globe endorsed no candidates on the ground that there were no overriding issues in the top contests. But the political columnists expressed strong support for liberal Democrats in the third congressional district where Father Robert Drinan won and in the twelfth where Gerry Studds came close enough to require a recount. Editorially the paper rebuked Vice President Agnew's violent rhetoric against "radical-liberals" and cartoonist Szep was uninhibited in his lampooning of Agnew, Nixon, and Mrs. Louise Day Hicks, who won the congressional seat of retiring Speaker John McCormack.

After the Globe had backed White against Hicks for mayor in 1967, the Harvard Crimson ran a long article about the Globe headed "The Globe Gets a Social Conscience." It quoted Charles Whipple: "I am told that Mrs. Hicks blames the Globe for her defeat. I find that comforting."

The Crimson also quoted Al Haviland, executive editor: "Winship will promote anything aimed at development of the core city"; and managing editor Ian Menzies: "Tom would fill the whole front page with politics if he could."

Winship "has worked to make the old home town paper an instrument for political and social reform," the Crimson discovered. "He has revamped the staff by recruiting younger men and hiring specialists."

A 1969 readership survey found 55 percent of readers saying they read all the editorial page — an extraordinarily high figure, more than any other but page one.

Whipple involved his editorial page deeply in the student eruptions of 1968–69. A notable event of spring 1969 was a spontaneous speech by George Wald, Harvard Nobel Prize professor of biology, at M.I.T.'s day of protest over military research. The Globe gave first currency to what was recognized as a landmark address.

Crocker Snow covered the event. Only the autumn before had he joined the Globe and been assigned a new field, known in the office variously as "the egghead beat" or "ideas editor." Snow was to cover universities and other intellectual centers to follow ideas and trends. One of his first and most fruitful contacts was with Jerome Wiesner, M.I.T. provost, who alerted him at an early stage to the scientists' concern over the antiballistic missile program that soon developed into a commanding issue. Snow, Harvard 1961, had worked first on the Gloucester Times (whose publisher, Philip Weld, was a Globe director), then for Newsweek, then two years at WGBH, the Boston educational television station. One of these years he spent in Germany developing radio tapes. Returning, he enrolled for a year of graduate study in the Fletcher School of Law and Diplomacy. Davis Taylor, alerted by Phil

A Szep cartoon: Cambodia, 1970 — "Here . . . have another one."

Weld, personally recruited Snow for the Globe in September 1968 and dreamed up the new special field for him.

George Wald spoke at M.I.T. extemporaneously. But Crocker Snow felt the impact on the students of Wald's passionate eloquence in his analysis of what was going wrong with America. From his own notes he got the gist of the speech onto the front page of the evening Globe that day, March 4. But he had noticed that WGBH was recording the talks. He told Charles Whipple he could get Wald's full text from the WGBH tapes. An editorial writer, James G. Crowley, had attended the meeting. Crowley and Snow separately told Whipple "I think I've just listened to the most important speech of my lifetime."

Whipple got the text and printed it in full on the op-ed page Saturday, March 8. It was immediately picked up and republished all over. Its impetus launched George Wald on a mission that through the following year carried him the length and breadth of the land to meet the response of students everywhere.

When the explosions reached Harvard the next month, a reader could never have guessed that the Globe's publisher, Davis Taylor, was one of the Harvard overseers attacked by the SDS.

After Harvard called police to remove the students who had occupied University Hall, Whipple gave the op-ed page April 10 to a piece by Richard Goodwin, "The Shame of Harvard." Next day the page was given over to an article by John R. Searle, "Blueprint for a Student Revolt," a penetrating analysis of the pattern of revolt reprinted from Time Magazine of December 28, 1968.

Faculty meetings were traditionally closed sessions at Harvard. But the undergraduate radio station WHRB was permitted to record the April 11 meeting, at which the faculty voted to investigate the cause of the disruption, to determine any discipline, and to explore the question of restructuring the governance of the university. WHRB broadcast the recording to the university community within its limited range through four hours of the following afternoon, a Saturday. The Globe assigned a staff of five to take it off the air and edit it to run through 12 pages of the Sunday paper, so that Globe readers had all that the Harvard community had of this historic and decisive faculty action.

In 1969 the editorial page staff besides Whipple were: Anson Smith (who had come from the Herald in 1964), handling most civil rights and constitutional issues; Beatson Wallace (who had come from the copy desk by way of editing the op-ed page and was a Harvard 1946 graduate), focusing on foreign affairs; James Crowley (a former Detroit reporter recruited from broadcasting), dealing chiefly with national affairs; Charles Claffey, moved onto the page from night city editor in 1968 to deal with local matters; Donald Willard, keeping up the Editorial Points he had done for years, but now contributing light editorials.

Early in 1970 David Wilson joined the page from the State House to add balance and political experience. In the fall Claffey left the page to fill a felt need for a strong general assignments writer on the evening paper and Anne Wyman, completing five years as travel editor, moved to the editorial staff to become the first woman editorial writer on the Globe since Florence Finch in 1884. William A. Davis, a versatile reporter who earlier in the year had been chosen for his style and news judgment to be the first obituary editor, took over as travel editor.

The editorial page now had its own copy editors. Sumner Barton handled the op-ed page. Harold Peters handled the letters to the editor and the page makeup.

That is the present editorial staff. But the chief incitement to the staff and originator of many editorial ideas is the editor. Tom Winship involves himself constantly in editorials. He has a daily talk with Whipple, often passes on an editorial idea before Whipple holds his daily conference with the writers just before lunch. Szep, the editorial cartoonist, usually sits in the conference to pick up a topic for his cartoon, which he then submits in the rough to Whipple. Whipple checks the editorial assignments and the cartoon with Winship. Every few weeks Winship has lunch with the whole editorial staff. There is a continuing flow of ideas.

Metropolitan

On May 1, 1969, managing editor Ian Menzies left the office for six weeks in Europe to explore the new towns of England, Sweden, and Germany. He had in mind also studying the London County Council, expanded in scope to take in the whole area of metropolitan London; this as a suggestive pattern for Boston's urgent problem to adjust its governmental structure to the metropolitan area that had absorbed so much of its population and business.

Menzies' first article had a full page in the Sunday paper, June 1: "London: Fighting Blight With Stream-Lined Government." "There are lessons for Greater Boston in the value of updating cumbersome political machinery in a metropolitan area." Menzies ended his piece, "London has shown that it is possible to change the structure of government.

"The so-called 'political realities' that Boston loves to conjure are just other shibboleths that have to go if Boston, like other major world cities, is going to emerge as a well-governed, well-planned greater community able to contend with the urban afflictions which are choking and stifling so many American cities."

Menzies returned with a series, started June 24, 1969, on "Europe's New Cities: A Lesson for Us."

In the first one he reported:

> Slums are hard to find in Europe's cities today. The American city, not the European, is now the home of the slum, the dirty street, the empty warehouse, the straggling blight of neglect . . . Most impressive is the way Europe has resisted the terrible blight of megalopolis, which now makes the East Coast of the United States an endless labyrinth of aging tenements, dilapidated warehouses, abandoned car dumps, spaced with intermittent suburban towns . . .
>
> Europe seems determined to have green space between one city and the next and this restfulness is an unconscious delight for the traveler, be he foreign or native . . . Although Rotterdam is as big as Boston and the largest port in the world, one feels it has been rebuilt for people, for children, for families, and the rebuilding continues.
>
> If Boston were to move ahead with its downtown pedestrian shopping mall; open up its waterfront to the people (not just luxury apartments); carve out

more parks and playing fields; encourage its restaurateurs to build outdoor cafes; redo its zoo; continue subway improvement; create some spacious boulevards and give perspective to historic sites it would begin, only begin, to catch up with today's European city.

At the end of 1969 Mayor Kevin White proposed a metropolitan regional council, with members from 100 cities and towns of the area, to control regional planning and development. He urged that such a council take over control of the Metropolitan District Commission, the Boston Port Authority, the Massachusetts Bay Transit Authority (MBTA), and the new Pollution Control Board.

The Globe immediately featured and supported the proposal and followed it up in the legislation that the Mayor introduced. The Globe set up its own metropolitan seminar that brought the political and urban writers, the editorial editor, and the environmental specialists together once a week to develop their own information and ideas about metropolitan organization. The Mayor sat through one of these sessions for two hours, answering questions on his proposal.

Gail Perrin.

New Fashion

The Youth Movement had an immediate and impressive impact on the women's department, with the recruitment of two young women in 1965 to enliven the growing number of pages of this important section. Gail Perrin, 26-year-old feature writer of the Washington Daily News, a Wellesley graduate, became women's editor; and Marian Christy, young graduate of Boston University School of Journalism, came from Women's Wear Daily to do a professional, stylish job on fashion. Her column soon became a syndicate and television feature.

For almost half a century Agnes Mahan had run the women's department as household editor, until her retirement in 1953. Dorothy Crandall was then promoted from assistant household editor and was in charge until 1965, when she took on the new assignment of food editor and Sumner Barton, science writer, took charge of the department.

Gail Perrin introduced lively women's features, and Marian Christy quickly brought the paper top national awards for fashion writing. She was abroad as much as three months a year, reporting on the fashion centers of Paris, Rome, Madrid, Dublin. Between 1965 and 1969 she won a full dozen national awards. In 1966 and again in 1968 she won the University of Missouri award as top national fashion writer and in 1967 captured the first Fashion Writers Award of New York.

Her sophisticated writing brought a revolutionary change to the women's pages. The section was assigned a distinctive typeface, Goudy, and its well-illustrated pages designed with a fresh sense of style. They were well filled out with advertising that fattened on Thursday and Friday, the big food advertising days.

The women's department by 1969 had expanded to a staff of 15, three of them men. One of them, Robert Allen, was editor of Confidential Chat. Evolution of the department to a larger compass was confirmed in February 1970 by a change in the title of the section from "Women" to "Living." The new title first appeared in the Sunday section February 15 and was applied to the daily section the next day.

The travel section was given an individuality of its own in 1965 when Anne Wyman was taken off the reporting staff to become travel editor. The travel department had been absorbed in the advertising department since 1957 when Willard DeLue had given over his role as travel writer.

The new magazine introduced a question and answer column for teen-agers, "Ask Beth," run also in the daily paper Thursday; it offered practical counsel on such problems as dating, dress, and behavior. The office soon discovered the identity of Beth as Elizabeth Winship, wife of the editor. "Ask Beth" became syndicated in the spring of 1970.

Ask Beth

—on his toes

—variety

—feet

Dear Beth:

My main love is basketball, but it happens that I'm rather slow and not very agile. I have read that taking ballet would improve my agility, but this brings up several problems.

First, if any of my friends found out that I, a 14-year-old boy, was dancing around in tights, they'd call me a sissy.

Second, I wouldn't know where to find ballet lessons.

JULIA CHILD, THE FRENCH CHEF

Star of the party 1

Tonight at 8, Channel 2 will present the 16th of the new French Chef programs

2½ cups ground fresh raw pork fat (or 1¾ cups goose or chicken fat ground

blender or electric beater until mixture resembles coarse meal. Rapidly blend in the liquid, massing

Society with Smaller s

In the Globe, as in newspapers generally, a quiet revolution overtook society pages in the 1950's. Their gradual democratization was particularly marked in Boston, where the definition of "society" had been especially rigid. Marjorie Sherman, who had been the Globe's file-closer on "society" for many years, proved flexible enough to broaden her perspective. Names that were never in the social register appeared in the society section, which consequently expanded until in the 1960's it spread over as many as ten or 12 pages in the Sunday paper — a community catalogue of weddings and engagements. The name of the section was changed to "Women," and the events chronicled covered a wide range of social activity.

Mrs. Sherman candidly reported the decline of interest and attendance at what had been the high society events. By the time of the debutante season of June 1969, even a nonreader of society pages could not miss the change that Mrs. Sherman's columns recorded. "Few things could have underlined the dropout in the debutante syndrome more than the small group" in the annual presentation line at the Colony Ball. "Instead of 20 to 25 girls, only seven pretty 18-year-olds waited to make their bows."

She noted of a country club dance that it will be "one of the very few big parties this diminished season," and

at the Cotillion the hundred places are far from filled. With no June debut ball in Weston, Salem's assembly, also down to a few this year, will close the shortest June season on record . . . Of the 191 debs the Globe will list on Sunday — nearly 100 names short of last year's list — less than a third will have anything to put down in M. T. Bird's long-time register where it says "debut date and place." Over 90 out of every 100 of these 18-year-olds who once upon a time spent Summers sailing and winters dancing, do volunteer or laboratory jobs all summer and college all winter. It's a different world and they know it.

Ear to Leeward

Weather is always a conversation piece in New England. The range of temperature is about as great as can be found in any area of similar size and the weather is as variable as anywhere. A sea turn in summer that brings an east breeze can dissipate a 100-degree day. A blizzard paralyzes the city and the whole area for a day or two at a time at least a couple of times every winter. Frost may come early or late. It makes all the difference in the Vermont maple syrup crop and Cape Cod cranberries and Nashoba Valley fruit buds, and in home gardens. Indian Summer is a glorious time and the autumn foliage color is Nature's own art form.

The Globe has always given the weather its due. Record temperatures, high or low, make headlines. A weather "ear," long carried at the top righthand corner of the front page, tells the forecast in half a dozen words and refers inside to a half page with a meteorological map, hour temperatures, times of sunrise and sunset and high and low tides, the phase of the moon, and temperatures in all points in the region and foreign capitals, besides a detailed forecast.

In the 1940's Laurence Winship got his summer neighbor Gluyas Williams to draw a series of weather cartoons which the Globe used as stock cuts with its weather ear: for a rainy day, a little boy holding an umbrella; and 15 to 20 variations for appropriate conditions. These ran for several years until Elmer Jones, who handled the weather among other things on the copy desk, thought it was time for a change. He grew bored with picking out a stock cut every night and asked Warren Dyar, in charge of the night desk, to let him try giving a touch of humor to the weather ear.

Jones's innovation began March 14, 1950, when the forecast was fair, with the mercury up a bit. Jones capped it with "Not bad, not bad."

Next day the forecast was fair, clouding for snow at night; Jones's head was "A Speckled Day." April 12 was fair and cool. "An Aloof Day," Jones headed it.

The laconic daily observation on the weather caught on and lasted. When Jones moved on to other chores the weather ear fell to Gene Brackley, who'd been editing sports copy and had been putting a brief punning line across the top of the baseball box score. "I always had a weakness for puns," Gene admits; and for more than a dozen years his penchant for punning had its innings on the weather ear. When

WEATHER
TUESDAY—Warmer.
Thunderstorm. WEDNESDAY—Fair, Cooler.
Full Report, Page 16.

SHOWERS

The B

VOL. CXLVII
NO. 128
Copyright 1945
BY THE GLOBE NEWSPAPER CO.

Gene was moved to the magazine copy desk, Robert Moore was discovered to have a similar weakness, which he too inflicted on the weather to the enjoyment of the staff and evidently most other people.

A frequent trick was to relate the weather to the top news of the day. A storm on income tax day would be "A Taxing Day." With a mild prospect the morning after President Nixon's broadcast on his points for peace in Vietnam in 1969, the weather ear was headed "Peaceful." For a showery April 19 the weather ear head was "The Raincoats are Coming." A bright, sunny election day was "People's Choice," a fair, dry day during a national convention "A Keynoter." Hot, humid weather might be headed "All Steamed Up" or "An Old Soak"; fine summer weather could be "Hammock Time," "A Beacherino," "A Dovish Day." A crisp breezy day was "A Swinger," a day of variable cloudiness "Chancy."

The weather ear is one of innumerable little things that add up to the personality of the paper — a human touch.

In clearing the decks for the moon shot, 1969, the Globe cleaned the ears off the top of the front page and carried both the index and the weather ear in a compact two-column box in the bottom lefthand corner of the page. In autumn 1970 both were moved to page two, but in response to reader protest the weather ear was soon re-installed in its original place, the upper righthand corner of page one, and the index put on the lefthand corner.

JEKYLL & HYDE

THURSDAY — Partly cloudy, hot and showery. **FRIDAY**— Fair & not so humid. (Page 44.)

High Tide
— A.M.   12:12 P.M.

52 PAGES—10c

HAPPINESS IS . . .

FRIDAY—Fair & Hot; High, 75-80.   **SATURDAY** — Cloudy; Showers maybe. (Page 44.)

HIGH TIDE
9:00 A.M.   9:18 P.M.

52 PAGES—10:

ON GOOD BEHAVIOR

WEDNESDAY — Partly cloudy; chance of thundershowers in p.m.; in 80's. **THURSDAY**—Fair, cooler. (Page 40.)

High Tide
— a.m.   12:06 p.m.

50 PAGES—10c

All Opposed

TUESDAY — CHANCE OF SNOW
WEDNESDAY — SNOW LIKELY
HIGH TIDE — 5:54 a.m., 6:18 p.m.
FULL REPORT — PAGE 43.

lephone 288-8000   48 Pages—15c

Help Wanted

"HELP" was the single-word head on the office ad in the lower lefthand corner of the Sunday paper June 23, 1969.

It reported of that year that "in the first five months the Globe had the task of finding people to fill 113,290 positions. That was the number of individual help wanted ads that ran in the Globe — 2,652,547 lines more than the other two Boston papers combined."

That Sunday paper had four sections of classified advertising, 76 pages, two of the sections labeled "Help Wanted."

Classified advertising had been a main strength of the Globe for decades. It had led the Boston papers in this field since 1942 and by the 1960's was fourth paper in the country in its classified linage, led only by the New York Times, Milwaukee Journal, and Los Angeles Times. The swelling volume of classified advertising had become an increasing production problem, finally so critical as to force reorganization of the production process. Only computerized operations made it possible to handle it at all for nearly 600,000 Sunday papers.

Classified was personified in the Globe by Andrew Dazzi, who had managed it for more than 50 years, starting with it as an office boy when all it amounted to was what came out of envelopes mailed in to the Globe office.

Dazzi had finished Everett High School at 16, just crazy about baseball. A Boston Globe compositor, a neighbor, said, "Why don't you get a job with the Globe, Andy? The compositors are through at 3 o'clock, time for the ball game."

That was 1916. Andy hounded the Globe office. Tom Downey, advertising manager and also employment head, kept shaking his head at Andy. One day Andy didn't turn up till afternoon. Downey pounded his desk to demand, "Where have you been?"

"Why I've been in every day."

"Well, I just fired a boy and I need one. What's your name?"

"Andrew Dazzi."

"All right, Andrew Dougherty."

Andy was hired for five dollars a week, and when he lined up at the cashier's window on Friday his pay envelope with his first five-dollar bill was marked "Andrew Dougherty." He was afraid he had the wrong envelope. But big Dan Ahearn, the cashier, straightened it out, not much surprised that old Tom Downey had heard Dazzi as Dougherty. "Tom's a little deaf and he favors the Irish."

Within a month Andy was assigned to the publisher's office, where the General, Charles, and Will had been doing without an office boy. Very soon CH Jr. found a special job for Dazzi, at a tiny desk not much bigger than a checkerboard. There he opened the small want ads that came in by mail with the money for them in the envelopes.

After a little while CH sent him down front to the display advertising desk, where they'd been having trouble. Boys were stealing money from the envelopes. Dazzi straightened that out. Then he was assigned a front window to take classified ads. He had two girls to help him take them through the window and on the phone. One was Ann O'Connell, who retired 50 years later as supervisor of the 100 girls who then handled 18 million lines of classified advertising a year.

Classified was an insignificant department when Dazzi started with it. Its growth was inhibited by CH Jr's rule that no ads could be charged except on a regular account. Dazzi had to convince CH of the handicap that most small ads were telephoned in by people who had no accounts. Finally CH broke down to permit ads to be charged at a transient rate if the advertiser had a telephone. That started the growth of classified and it never stopped growing. William O. Taylor always took a special interest in the classified advertising. In the paper rationing of World War II he made a special allowance for classified advertisers — the little fellow. This won their loyalty to the Globe.

As classified grew, Dazzi organized it with districts assigned to solicitors, 27 of them by 1969, and supervisors for each major department — autos, real estate, help wanted, home and garden. Other classified departments were boats and yachting, schools and colleges, camping and recreation.

As long as the Globe was on Washington Street the telephoned small ads had to come through the one office switchboard, where the callers often had to wait and sometimes tired of waiting. In the new building in 1958 Dazzi was able to install his own automatic telephone signal system: a big board that lights up with each call. The girls took them off in order, left to right, at their ranked desks. He was soon able to boast that no call had to wait more than 30 seconds. Moving belts carried the ads from the receivers' phones to the department's own copy desk, to be edited and sent by tube to the composing room within five minutes of their tele-

Classified ad takers in 1970.

WHAT IS IT?

ITALIAN CONCERTINA

20 Keys . . .

An Arlington man placed this ad in the Globe classified recently. An Italian concertina is an instrument which resembles the accordian, yet it is lighter. It is octagonal in shape, has twenty keys (ten on each side), and is red mother-of-pearl in

phoned transmission. Dazzi retired January 1, 1970, to be succeeded by Lawrence Healy, who had grown up in the advertising department — another case of finding the man for the job at the next desk.

The classified advertising rate when Dazzi began was 12.5 cents per line. A Globe selling point was two lines for a quarter. As circulation grew rates rose, until in the 1960's the rate was increased every year to reach $1.85 a line by 1970.

On Sunday, help wanted filled 35–40 pages, automobiles 12, home and garden 14–15, school and college 4–5, boats and yachting 2.

The minimum size ad was two lines until the 1950's, when Dazzi set it at three lines "and never a squawk." He persuaded the news department to run its daily weather map on the lower half of the first classified page, "good for them and good for us."

W. O. Taylor had always written his own "office" ad, in longhand, to run at the lower lefthand corner of the front page, calling attention to the ads inside. When Laurence Winship became editor he changed this to a small feature, selecting some unusual, often amusing, want ad of each day's grist. Dazzi contributed the stock headline for it: "What Is It?" One day it was old sock darners; another ice cubers; Italian desk; old brass spittoons. A strange-looking ad was Allen Thea Dix Org. The Marblehead woman who placed the ad said she was selling a theater organ that had been in her house for years because she was moving to a smaller house.

Dazzi just grinned at the production problem his vast volume of classified advertising created. It also created revenue. Classified ads always had the right of way. Right into the 1960's he could take them up to 10:30 Saturday night. Till then the night editor wouldn't know what size his news hole was.

Finally the brakes had to be put on. Deadlines that had been pushed back all the way to Wednesday for some Sunday feature sections were pushed back also for advertising. By 1969 the deadline was 5 P.M. for the daily; for Sunday it was 5 P.M. on Friday for some sections, noon on Friday for others.

This was part of the answer, but only part. Production had become the all-important problem of the sixties. Within a few years of occupying the new building it became necessary to start another, an annex just for storing and assembling sections of the huge Sunday paper — nearly 600,000 copies. The dealers could no longer handle it. Advance sections were sent to them Friday and Saturday to put together with the news sections Sunday morning. But the increased size and numbers of the Sunday paper swamped them — they hadn't the space for it.

The Globe would have to subsidize dealers' plants or expand its own. Even as the annex was going up, office conferences considered proposals for satellite printing plants on the edge of the metropolitan district. This would meet distribution as well as production problems, and start the evening paper as well as the Sunday toward the farther suburbs.

Production

Meantime nine new presses stretched capacity to print a Sunday paper whose circulation boomed from 425,000 to 580,000 between 1962 and 1969. The presses were needed for the daily, too; its size kept growing.

Newspaper advertising revenue nationally increased 10 percent the first quarter of 1969 over the same period in 1968. The Globe, dominating the Boston scene, was getting more than that increase. The last week in May 1969 the morning papers were 76 pages Monday, 56 Tuesday, 72 Wednesday, 60 Thursday, 56 Friday, 34 Saturday. The evening paper ran parallel for its five days. This for a total daily circulation of 432,000 (May 1969: 235,000 morning, 197,000 evening). An extra load on the presses came with color for several pages two days a week. On the days that carried color advertising, it was used also on news pictures on the front page and one inside page.

For the morning paper the presses were kept running continually with no breaks between what were still called three editions: the first at midnight for out of state, the second at 1 A.M. for west of Worcester but also the farther suburbs; the third within the metropolitan area that could go as late as 2:30 or 3:30. The mailroom had a capacity to handle 250,000 papers an hour.

Computers were saving the situation. By 1969, 200,000 lines a week were being set by computer. This included daily stock tables, most Sunday features, much of the classified and display advertising, and an increasing amount of daily news. The linotype operators, once they had learned to punch tape on the keyboard for the computer, were setting type seven times as fast as on a linotype machine, the Globe figured.

Computers were also handling payroll, the schedules and billing of 10,000 separate ads for Sunday, and credit checking for classified ads.

But even so, to get copy all set for the big Sunday paper the science and medicine page had to be in by Tuesday, the editorial page Wednesday, most of the rest of the Sunday sections Thursday. Though they had gained time by dropping the Saturday evening edition in January 1969, the demands of the Sunday were so great that Saturday's spot news had to be scamped to what could be set for the Sunday news section. The space problem was acute every day of the week.

Young Bill Taylor, now general manager, gave major attention to the critical problem of production throughout the sixties. As early as 1962 an Arthur D. Little study of the production problem had charted essential long-term planning. This had started the plans for the annex to store and assemble the big Sunday paper. It started consideration of satellite printing plants. It led to a start on computerizing all possible operations.

Edward Sullivan, from the Arthur D. Little organization, joined the Globe as operations engineer for several years to install on-line computers for type setting by 1967. The engineering staff designed a special keyboard to punch impulses into a computer that transmits them to the composing room on tapes. The 1965 union contracts included a computer clause; the unions went along with it.

But production had become too complicated and vital to be left to the traditional autonomy of separate mechanical departments. The Arthur D. Little study had emphasized the need of a production department. Reorganization began and, Globe fashion, was accomplished gradually. In 1962 Frank Freitas, with all his other duties as plant manager, was made production manager, in charge of all mechanical departments. This pulled things together for more streamlined operation. In 1965 Freitas was promoted to production director and David Stanger brought in as production manager. Stanger, whose father had been 50 years a Globe pressman, had served 25 years as a stereotyper, then left to go into industry. But the paper got him back in 1963, first to head the stereotyping department, then to manage all production processes in 1965. This needed to be an around-the-clock operation, and two younger men were taken from the mechanical departments as assistant managers, Donald O'Neill and Paul Woefel.

An important innovation was a daily production conference, parallel to the editorial conference. This brought the heads of the mechanical departments together at 10:30 daily to anticipate the problems of size of paper, volume of advertising, schedules for color ads and special sections. The computer could make a vital con-

The computer room in 1970.

tribution. By feeding it the figures for last year, last month, and last week, they could make close projections at their Friday conference for the size of the news hole each day of the following week.

It began to look as though the century-long warfare between desk and composing room was on the way to resolution. "At least we've got them talking together," Stanger said. The editorial department was represented at the daily production conference by Jack Driscoll, who as head of the night desk had had firsthand encounters with the production dilemma. He had been effective in improving relations between desk and composing room and later in the editorial conference between the news department and the desk. He brought to the production conference editorial problems and suggestions to help improve the appearance of the paper and get it out on time. Many of these didn't wait for conference; Driscoll and Stanger chewed them over at lunch. The production manager introduced realistic deadlines for advertising to give the desk a chance to shape up the paper, and Bill Taylor proved tough enough to make the deadlines stick.

The press room in 1970.

William O. Taylor II.

New Dress

Finally, after long consideration, the management put the paper into a whole new type dress in September 1969. Edmund C. Arnold, type designer, had been working on improved design for the paper for several years. All through the sixties he counseled on page design and makeup, helping the Globe get away from its old-fashioned makeup. Ed Doherty, night editor, had achieved an illusion of a larger, cleaner type by skillful use of leads and an open makeup "to let air into the paper."

The management had long been reluctant to change the appearance of the paper lest it lose its familiar look to readers. But by now its competitive position was so strong that they no longer worried about this.

The primary force to bring about this change was young Bill Taylor. At 37, he had been general manager only a year and a half. Before that for four years as business manager his central concern had been watching the ledger. But the book shelf behind his desk ranged through production, computers, and typography.

"He brought the composing room into the twentieth century" was editor Winship's summary of Bill's activity. The editor had learned to appreciate the reserved young man of few words who had quietly moved to the center of operations. More conservative than his father, his concentration on business had given the editors some concern, and, in the words of one, they "were working on him." A precise man, he was noted as having the cleanest desk in the building. But editors soon found he shared his father's sense of fairness and consideration. To a question whether he had to negotiate with the unions over an operational change, Bill gave a half grin. "No, only have to negotiate with Winship."

Bill decided the time had come to change the type and format. The Globe must have been almost the last big paper to hold to the old Cheltenham for headline type. It now changed to the modern Bodoni — thinner, less black — and increased the size of its body type. From eight point on eight and a half it went up to nine point on a ten point base, which gave more space between the lines. The Herald Traveler had gone up to nine point on ten in 1968.

When the new dress made its debut September 15, the Globe announced it in a front page box: "Today's Globe Sports New Suit." The new Bodoni headline type it described as easier on the eye; the built-in whiteness of the added space between the lines also made the paper easier to read.

Staff response was initially less than enthusiastic, for larger type and more space between lines meant fewer words to a column. With no increase in the size of the paper, this required writing shorter stories or heavier cutting on the copy desk. The reduction in wordage was about 15 percent. It meant tighter writing.

But favorable reader response was indicated in the letters column. On September 24 the Globe printed 16 letters as "the first reaction to the new type." Twelve were in favor, four against. Next day 12 more letters ran 11–1 for the new type.

Herbert Rogalski, type expert in the graphic arts department of the Polaroid Company, had guided the typographical changeover. He now persuaded the Globe to drop its bold face bylines and put the writer's name in the same thin type as the body of the story and carry it flush to the left of the column. This eliminated one type and increased the uniformity and simplicity of makeup.

First reaction of the makeup editors was negative. They generally agreed with Martin Nolan, who complained in an editorial page column December 1 that "too many newspapers have camouflaged themselves in stodgier make-up in the format of a stockholders report or a telephone book, with bylines almost fading from sight."

But when the editor called a conference to reappraise the changes after two months, a survey of office opinions by Jack Driscoll found that the quieter, cleaner design had found general acceptance.

The day copy desk in the news room, 1970.

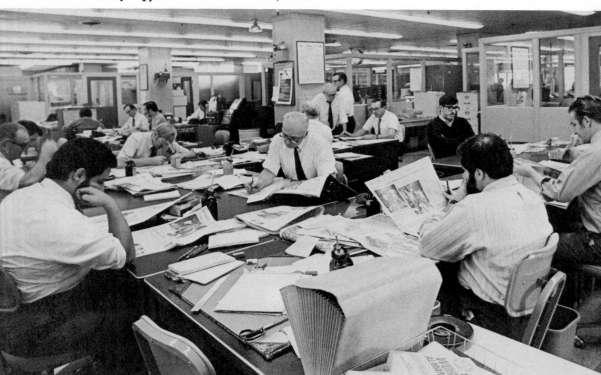

The distinctive Old English italic for the Globe masthead was retained.

With the advent of the computer, the number of typographical errors in the news columns visibly increased. Editors blame the computer. The composing room says it is "dirtier," that is, produces more "bugs" in the type. But the production manager explains that the computer, producing at higher speed, piles up much more copy an hour before press time than can be proofread before the presses roll; the corrections have to be reset on the slower manually operated linotypes.

To cope with this problem, Lee Woods, assistant composing room superintendent, was pulled out to supervise the computer work and concentrate on retraining the converted linotype operators on the job.

By 1969 the Sunday magazine and many whole-page display ads were being set by photocomposition, a cold type process that bypassed the hot metal work of the stereotype department. Some papers were experimenting with eliminating hot metal altogether for offset printing, and the Globe production department was following the experiments closely. Offset gave a sharper, cleaner quality of photograph and type.

By the end of 1969 the use of the new photocomposition process had advanced so far that 16 million lines of the total 64 million of the year's advertising were set that way.

The evolution of a production department appeared to be completed in June 1970, when Frank Freitas was made technical research director; David Stanger became production director; two production managers were appointed, Donald O'Neill for days and Paul Woefel for nights.

Labor

Labor relations have always been a demanding role of the publisher's office. The big city newspaper is highly unionized. The typographical union goes back further than the Globe's hundred years. Stereotypers, pressmen, mailers, and, in the later years editorial staffers, have their separate unions. Charles H. Taylor, Jr., handled labor relations for most of his half century as business manager and then treasurer, until he retired in 1937.

Then for nearly another 20 years negotiating with the unions was the special assignment of the able John D. Bogart, who joined the Globe as assistant publisher in 1934 after many years of managing other newspapers. A 1901 graduate of Yale, Bogart was city editor of Hearst's New York Journal, then its advertising manager, then came to Boston in 1914 as general manager of the Boston American and in 1922 bought the Brockton Times. When his paper was merged with the Brockton Enterprise in 1934, Bogart became the Boston publishers' representative in labor relations. Soon after, he became special assistant to the publisher of the Globe to handle labor affairs.

When Bogart retired he was succeeded by P. J. Flaherty, who also had been the Boston publishers' labor representative. Larry Flaherty became business manager of the Globe and for 11 years pulled a strong oar in the organization, a highly valued right arm for Davis Taylor. He had the respect of labor, too. In 1965, the last year of his life, the Boston Allied Printing Trades and the Graphic Arts Institute of New England joined in giving him the Gutenberg Award "for distinguished service in labor relations." Flaherty had been especially helpful on the Globe's increasingly complicated production problems. He had helped plan the new building.

Young Bill Taylor had worked with Flaherty both on production and in labor relations; he now took over as business manager, with labor relations as a key responsibility.

The business side like the news side was expanding and elaborating. In 1968 Bill became general manager, to pull the business departments together. The Globe found its next business manager in the office: John Giuggio had come up through the ranks of classified advertising salesmen. He had put himself through Boston College and a business school course mostly in night classes. When the Post failed in 1956, Andrew Dazzi persuaded Davis Taylor that the Globe should take over the Post Santa Claus, and Giuggio was assigned to manage it. This became a big business, with contributions of $200,000 at the Christmas season to be accounted for and converted into purchasing, packaging, trucking. The intensive seasonal task revealed Giuggio's executive capacity, and the company turned it to year-round use.

Giuggio then joined Bill Taylor in labor relations, which had become a job for two. It sometimes took a year to complete negotiations for a two-year contract. The printers' contract alone by the end of the 1960's had 136 conditions to work out to agreement. It took 44 sessions for the 1968 contract.

The newspapers conduct joint negotiations with the unions. But each has its

The mailroom in 1970.

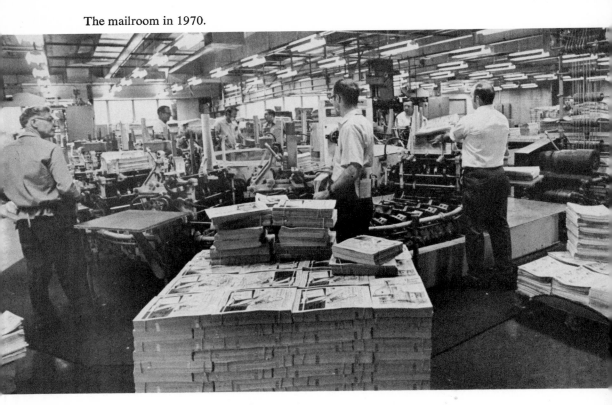

special problems. On the editorial side, for instance, the Herald Traveler is a Guild shop. The Record-American has an AFL union. The Globe has its own employees' association, which succeeded the brief existence of the Globe Newspaper Guild Unit by an election in 1938. It includes news and editorial staffs, and business and clerical workers in the commercial departments and such mechanical departments as are not in the typographical unions. This has proved the least of the labor problems. There never has been a strike on the news side.

There have been three strikes by mechanical unions. In 1957 the mailers' union struck for 19 days. The issue was money. In 1959 the printers struck for eight days, again over money.

In 1966 a strike that involved both printers and mailers lasted five weeks. The federal mediator who worked to settle it called it more complicated than the long New York strike of 1963. It involved pensions and retirement and internal jostling for status between the unions.

Several platoons of the news staff were kept busy broadcasting news on local television stations during the five-week-long 1966 strike. They organized a one-hour program of assorted news, editorials, specials, even comics, to present several times a day on the three commercial stations and the educational television station.

The mechanical union contracts effective July 1, 1970, set these hourly rates: stereotypers, $5.63; compositors, $5.53; pressmen, $5.45; engravers, $5.36. Mailers were at $4.93, truck drivers $4.47. This was for a 35-hour week for stereotypers, 36.25 hours for compositors, 37.5 hours for the other unions. It brought the basic weekly wage for the three big mechanical unions to just over $200 a week, for the engravers with their shorter week just under that. Overtime for all was time and a half and Sunday double time. The night shift received an additional $5 a week and the late night (lobster) shift an additional $7.

For Globe employees other than the mechanical unions the Boston Globe Employees Association has its separate contract, which for the years 1969–70 filled 37 pages of a pocket-size manual, four by five inches, covering wages and salaries, insurance, severance pay, vacations, hours and overtime, and working conditions generally, with a provision for arbitration.

Provisions for minimum wages fill 17 pages covering 31 classified positions from office boys, lumpers, and dictaphone typists to rewrite men and rotogravure editor. For the 12-month period to January 1, 1971, the reporter's minimum for five years' experience was $210 a week, rewrite man $220, desk man $220. The makeup men and slot men on the desk had a $234 minimum, same as the rotogravure editor and travel editor. Head makeup man was at $244. Commercial artists, church editor, real estate editor, and exchange editor were at the same $210 as reporters. Household editor, society editor, automobile editor, assistant librarian, and assistant Sunday editor were all at $211.35. A differential of an additional $7 a week applied to all regular night shift workers.

The number of Globe employees had increased from the 826 when Davis Taylor joined the paper in 1931 to 1,028 when the Globe moved into its new building in 1958; it was 1,900 at the end of 1970. Of this, 350 were editorial staff, 400 in the business offices, and 1,150 in the mechanical departments.

Library

By 1970 the Globe library had grown from the eight boxes of envelopes that Billy Hills had contributed for its start in 1887 to 4,000,000 clippings, 500,000 pictures, and 35,000 metal photographic cuts. Such a mass of identifying reference and background information would be of little use to a newspaper without modern facilities to make it all instantly accessible; for the library is the newspaper's memory. It holds the background for the situation that has suddenly come back into the headlines. It has the material for the obituary, the history of the current issue.

The Globe library has long outgrown the old jargon name of morgue, indicating its earlier limited utility — to identify persons whose names had been in the news and might be expected to recur, with, it was hoped, photographs of them or metal cuts ready to fit into the forms. Its resources had expanded until it was expected to provide relevant information on almost any topic that might come into the news. Every day and every night the newspaper library is besieged by writers and editors demanding the folders and pictures on whatever turns up that calls for news development, explanation, comment, or just fact checking. It all must be instantly accessible to be of use to those working against deadlines.

Every day newspapers must be clipped and new accumulations filed and indexed. Periodically the filing cabinets must be screened for elimination of material that has become dead wood, to make space for ever-expanding live material.

In the spring of 1968 the contents of the library's 65 picture cabinets were transferred into seven electromechanical file units called Lektrievers. Ten feet in height, the new units allow storage of pictures up to the ceiling. The pictures are filed on carriers which rotate at the push of a button. The "Ag" button will bring into reach all the pictures available of Spiro Agnew. The "Br" button will bring into eye view all the pictures of Senator Brooke. The Globe has an estimated 500,000 pictures on file in these units.

That summer the Globe's 35,000 metal cuts were transferred from eight file cabinets into one electromechanical unit called a Kard-Veyer, a smaller unit than the Lektriever with a similar mechanical design.

In the summer of 1969 the library acquired two additional Lektriever units for the purpose of consolidating into the library files all sports and drama pictures, previously filed in those departments. In June 1970 all the 124 eight-drawer metal cabinets that housed the obituaries and other clipping files were replaced with banks of Lektrievers.

The vast bulk and unwieldiness of old newspaper files has been eliminated by putting the paper's back numbers on microfilm. Back issues of the Globe from the first edition of March 4, 1872, are stored on microfilm in the library. Microfilming of the Globe began in the early 1940's and was completed in 1948. The whole century of the newspaper occupies only a few feet of wall space. The film of a month fits into the palm of the hand. By fitting it into one of the microfilm projectors, a reporter or researcher with a few turns of a hand crank can scan the editions for the week of Calvin Coolidge's becoming president, or of Woodrow Wilson's nomination. The Globe donated a duplicate set of its microfilm to the Boston Public Library as a memorial to General Charles H. Taylor.

The library also has the New York Times since 1947 stored on microfilm. Edition numbers of the Globe are microfilmed by a professional microfilming company. Old clippings from the files are microfilmed and indexed on aperture cards by members of the library staff.

Librarian Edward W. Quill in 1970 had a permanent staff of ten, himself included: three indexers, an exchange editor, four library assistants, and a secretarial research assistant. Three Northeastern University students of library management, serving on a rotating system, provided additional assistance.

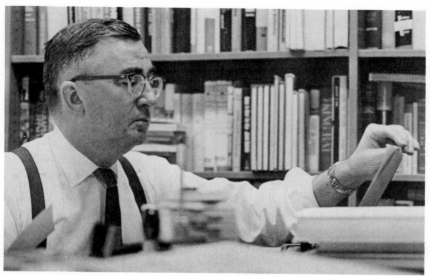

Herbert A. Kenny, book editor.

Critics at Last

The whole area of criticism was the weakest side of the Globe its first 90 years — indeed, practically a vacuum save in music, where Cyrus Durgin performed with distinction for a generation. Durgin died in 1962. He had doubled in brass his later years to include the theater, with Kevin Kelly assisting.

John Taylor's hopes for a Globe book department had to wait 20 years after he brought Dorothy Hillyer onto the Globe in 1941. She contributed a bright book column Sundays for five years but then returned to book publishing. She brought the distinction of individuality and authority to book reviewing, and she knew the book trade as a former member of Houghton Mifflin's editorial staff. When Lillian Smith's *Strange Fruit* shocked prudish sensibilities in 1944, Mrs. Hillyer at once hailed it: "Everyone should read this book . . . the first instance of a white author doing the stream of consciousness of the Negro successfully . . . a novel about a burning issue, the race problem." *Strange Fruit* was banned in Boston but the book and Mrs. Hillyer's judgment on it stood the test of time.

Mrs. Hillyer's title of "editor" meant that she wrote a book column and selected reviewers. Edwin Laycock came off the copy desk to edit the page for Sundays and

THE WORLD OF WRITERS

A unique w

By Herbert A. Kenny, Globe Staff

*THE LIFE AND DESTINY OF
ISAK DINESEN, collected and edited by
Frans Lasson, text by Clara Svendsen
Random House, 227 pp., $15.*

*OUT OF AFRICA, by Isak Dinesen
Random House, 389 pp., $7.95.*

What an extraordinary woman Karen
Blixen was!

When "Seven Gothic Tales" appeared
in 1934, their authorship was as much a
mystery as the identity of B. Traven came
to be. Writing an introduction for them,

a half page Wednesdays; and when Mrs. Hillyer left, Laycock took over until he retired in 1961. By then the demise of the Boston Post had brought Herbert Kenny to the Globe.

Kenny, as night city editor of the Post, had already published two books of verse that won him the Robert Frost Fellowship to the Bread Loaf Writers' Conference in 1956. His first five years at the Globe after a brief period of reporting were on the editorial page.

When Tom Winship became managing editor in 1962 he was determined to build up the status of the Globe's criticism. He moved Herbert Kenny off editorials to take over the book department and made Kevin Kelly drama critic. The other critics in 1962 were Marjorie Adams, movies, and Margo Miller, music.

The Globe began putting new resources into criticism and recruiting new talent. The arts staff was soon doubled: Margo Miller took on dance, Edgar Driscoll was moved from the city staff to art criticism, Gregory McDonald began a new field as pop art critic, and George McKinnon was added as assistant film critic.

Kenny built up the list of book reviewers to 300, all within the region, and started an annual reviewers' cocktail party which became an intellectual event with some 16 college faculties represented among the authors, poets, and journalists. In 1967 Kenny put on his first Book Festival at Suffolk Downs with an attendance of 30,000. The Sunday book page expanded to two pages; there were six more pages for the other critics. Book advertising grew from 25,000 lines to 150,000 in seven years. The Boston Globe-Horn Book Magazine Award was established for best children's books; there were two awards, one for illustrations, one for text, directed by Mrs. Thomas Winship and awarded at the convention of the New England Regional Library Association. She reviewed children's books under her maiden name, Elizabeth Coolidge.

Sound of Music

Then Tom set out to find "the best music critic in America." He had married into a musical family. His wife, Elizabeth Sprague Coolidge, is the granddaughter of the Elizabeth Sprague Coolidge who donated the Coolidge Auditorium in the Library of Congress. Tom's sister-in-law Melba, Mrs. John C. Coolidge, put him onto Michael Steinberg, who had never written music criticism and was then teaching at the Manhattan School of Music. Winship brought Steinberg to Boston in 1965 and things began to jump in the music world. The Boston Symphony Orchestra was practically as sacred as the cod. But Steinberg found much to criticize. The offerings were not contemporary enough, the conductor lacked feeling, the concerts were not innovative enough.

This ruffled tradition and offended classical standards. Symphony-goers wrote letters to the editor. Just who did this Mr. Steinberg think he was? Mr. Steinberg soon found he was taking on the inner core of Boston Establishment. The president of the orchestra was a Cabot — Henry B. Cabot — and it was a proud post for a Proper Bostonian.

When in the 1965 season the Globe music critic complained of Maestro Leinsdorf's conducting of the Beethoven Sixth, and then went on to say of the Handel and Haydn Society's singing of Handel's "Messiah" that the conducting was incompetent, the score used was second-class, and the performance in general was awful, Mr. Cabot blew up.

Michael Steinberg, music critic.

He wrote the Globe:

> Steinberg seems to assume that what he likes is good and what he doesn't like is awful . . . There are many, many examples of this . . . All this would not be very important were it not for the damage which Steinberg can do to the musical situation here in Boston . . . This continued carping may make good reading in the Globe but it certainly is not conducive to a very vigorous outlook in this community.

The Globe printed Mr. Cabot's letter and Mr. Steinberg's reply. The music critic was equally blunt. He challenged Mr. Cabot's view that there was no better orchestra in the country than the Boston Symphony.

> Such complacency is a sure way to let standards slip. There was a time under Koussevitsky when Boston orchestral playing represented, along with that in New York and Philadelphia, the best in America. That is no longer so . . . In orchestral virtuosity, flexibility, precision and tone, I would say that the orchestras in Chicago, Cleveland and Philadelphia fairly consistently play better than the Boston Symphony. I very much want Boston to regain the place it once held . . . It is not my job to engage in public relations work on behalf of the Boston Symphony . . . I cannot afford a parochial point of view. It is my belief that the Boston Globe has engaged me to use whatever resources I have in taste and education to comment on the musical situation in Boston without fear, without prejudice, from the broadest point of view, and with the highest ideals in mind.

Well, Leinsdorf left, Steinberg stayed. Steinberg's music criticism brought him, after two years on the Globe, an honorary degree from the New England Conservatory of Music.

When Leinsdorf was succeeded by William Steinberg with the opening of the 1969 symphony season, the Globe's music critic was initially unimpressed. The opening concert he found unexciting. In the first week two symphony-goers wrote the Globe to protest their critic. "He is too cruel," one woman wrote. "I don't know how anyone wants to accept the position as the conductor of the Boston Symphony Orchestra, let alone play in the orchestra, as long as Mr. Michael Steinberg tears them to pieces so unremittingly."

Bud Collins, in a tongue-in-cheek column October 1, raised the question: "Is there room in Boston for two Steinbergs?" In a ribbing review of his colleague, Collins noted, "After last Friday's opener, he wrote that the Boston Symphony Orchestra was 'soggy . . . undistinguished . . . slow and heavy . . .'" He sounded like a fight writer describing Sonny Liston against Cassius Muhammed Ali Clay."

But before the week was out, Michael Steinberg showed a change of pace. On Saturday, October 4, he said of the Friday concert: "The ladies left too soon — Elgar needs more patience. It is a piece deeply informed by human and musical greatness. It is hard to imagine a performance of it more strongly conceived and more beautifully executed than that given yesterday by William Steinberg and the Boston Symphony Orchestra . . . The performance was very nearly beyond praise . . ."

A month later the issue between critic and orchestra erupted on a broader front. The musicians asked the Symphony trustees "not to welcome Michael Steinberg to our concerts until he apologizes for his insulting and unethical assaults which have gone beyond the scope of musical criticism." This followed sharp criticism by Steinberg of performances under guest conductors in November.

The orchestra manager responded to the players that "the management like the players is offended by the immoderate and unwarranted tone of the Globe critic's writing." The president of the trustees wrote the Globe that Steinberg's "undisciplined and irresponsible" reviews were "doing real injury to the musical life of Boston."

But the musical feud broke open on the Herald Traveler.* A Symphony trustee wrote the publisher complaining that in appointing George Gelles music critic, the paper had "hired one of Michael Steinberg's imitators who has nothing like his knowledge but the same tone of voice." Gelles had, two years before, been Steinberg's assistant on the Globe and had later served as critic of the Record-American. He had joined the Herald Traveler only as the 1969 fall season opened. The Herald Traveler took Gelles off music reviewing. Steinberg went to bat for his younger colleague in letters to music critics in other cities, calling Gelles' dismissal a result of pressure. This brought the controversy to a crisis that resulted in a conference between managements of the Symphony and the Globe, and the critic himself. On December 5 the Globe printed a two-column article, unsigned, that reviewed the controversy under the heading: "The BSO and its Critics." It closed with a statement by editor Thomas Winship that "the Globe, Steinberg and officials of the Symphony are discussing the matter and intend to handle it properly from the point of view of all concerned."

A week later, December 13, the Globe devoted a third of its editorial page to letters on the music issue. Three supported the critic, four objected to his reviews, one criticized the Symphony management. A box noted that the Globe had had 24 letters, 14 supporting, 10 opposing Steinberg.

An editorial that day, "Music Critics and Their Critics," called the controversy "healthy for the musical institutions of Boston . . . A music critic who pleased everybody would not be worth his salt, nor would a critic who pleased no one." Criticism should always be "within the bounds of fairness and good taste. The quality of the performance is what should count. Personalities should play no part." But "above all, the critic's right to criticize must be protected when he comes under attack . . ."

The impression left on a reader was that the Globe had stood by its critic in the clutch but probably had admonished him to tone down his voice.

The other critics, too, were expressing themselves without fear and consequently stepping on toes. Their free-swinging applied even to the critic of Boston's dining spots. When Anthony Spinazzola started his Friday column "Let's Eat Out" in early 1969, he didn't hesitate to observe of one of the prestigious restaurants that the crumbs weren't brushed off the table and the bread tasted as if it had a preservative in it.

But by that time the editor had established a buffer between himself and the

---

* When the Herald-Traveler Corporation dropped the evening Traveler in 1967, the name of the morning Herald was changed to Herald Traveler, but the corporation name remained Herald-Traveler.

LET'S EAT OUT / R

By Anthony Spinazzola
Globe Staff

What is cooking this good doing in a place like this? That's the question you ask yourself after a

It also might be slices of beef with a side order of spaghetti or veal cutlets or honest-to-godness home-made soups like a robust minestrone with pastina, chick peas, baby lima

crisp batter); eggplar (sauteed in a sweetis sauce); Thousand Leav (sort of a wonderfully ligl lasagne with mashed bee peas, tomato sauce ar

feedback from his critics. Herb Kenny, besides editing the book pages, was made editor for the arts, responsible for the whole area of criticism. This didn't include Spinazzola's dining out column, but covered the whole range of criticism in a Sunday section on the arts. At Dave Taylor's urging, a daily book review was added at that time.

Kenny built up the department's own library in the arts with Beatrice Bailey as arts librarian. And with all this enlarging activity, Kenny still had time to publish two more books of poetry and two children's books.

Outside Kenny's department, Percy Shain conducted one of the most recent and most read columns of criticism, a daily television commentary.

Internal Conflict

The crisis over music criticism, although aside from the main stream of reporting, had a parallel in the news department in what some journalists were perceiving as a dilemma for the 1970's. Among the newer generation of reporters, under the influence of Norman Mailer, resistance to the journalistic tradition of objectivity was spreading. They called it ineffectual, timid, neutral, a protective coloration for status quo. They talked of a "journalism of commitment." Objectivity to veteran reporters was the grail of journalism. It meant reporting facts factually, keeping one's subjective biases out of the story — in short, a straight recording of events. But objective reporting had too often been watered down by the rigors of caution to limit "news" to the mere surface of events.

This kind of objectivity had proved fatally vulnerable to the exploitation of Senator Joseph McCarthy in the early 1950's; recognition of that had led to acceptance of "interpretive" reporting, which means reporting in enough depth to show the meaning of the facts. This in turn led, in the more open climate of the 1960's, to freer but sometimes free-wheeling reporting. The once tight distinction between news and advocacy was sometimes blurred. On the Globe, with its Youth Movement, old-school staffers often felt that aspiring young reporters seemed to be writing like columnists. If this made for livelier and sometimes more informing stories, it raised a question of whether the newspaper that departed from the old guidelines of objectivity could establish a new line of equal assurance to the reader.

Another impending question was the authority of the editorial page, a page much outgunned in expertise by the corps of specialists and outshone by the personalities of the columnists. The specialists tended to become advocates of their specialties, which was ordinarily no problem — the editorial page naturally advocated the same causes. But an editorial December 19, 1969, came into direct conflict with a dozen of the specialists on urban, health, and environment issues. The editorial page was doing what came naturally in supporting the views of the transportation editor that took issue with Mayor White's demand for a moratorium on intown highway construction. A. S. Plotkin, a veteran in his field, had long supported highway development.

But the specialists in the newer fields saw ever-expanding highways as destroying neighborhoods, reducing housing, eroding the tax base, increasing pollution from automobile exhaust, and retarding mass transportation. They wanted to challenge the editorial in a letter to the editor that they would all sign. This gave the editor pause. How far to go in unorthodoxy. It would be a less dramatic deviation from the conventional to present both sides of the case on the op-ed page.

His solution came out Sunday, February 1, 1970, in two full pages: the case for a moratorium, signed by Alan Lupo, urban affairs editor; and the case for going forward with Inner Belt and Southwest Expressway by A. S. Plotkin. A box signed "The Editor" explained that "the so-called issue of people versus roads" that had split the community had also split the Globe staff. "For this reason we present these two pages on both sides of the issue." The statement named the dozen specialists who favored Lupo's view and described Plotkin as having been backed by Globe editorials.

But this innovation did not diminish the role of the editorial page as institutional voice of the paper. The editor made this implict in his statement: "Both these pages will be followed by extended editorial page comment on this issue in the near future."

Roads versus people splits the Globe: February 1, 1970.

Roads: the case for a moratorium

By Alan Lupo, Globe Staff

"These roads will take more of our precious land from our use and our tax base. They will merely provide another corridor for people from the suburbs to drive right on through Somerville and into Boston.

"They will create the need for new roads, just as all other roads have done. They will add to the already serious problem of air pollution. They merely postpone facing the real solution . . . developing mass transportation systems through the cities.

"The era of the automobile in the city has passed."

That reads like the rhetoric of a professional highway protestor. In fact, it's an excerpt from the inaugural speech of Rev. S. Lester Ralph, newly elected mayor of Somerville.

The words reflect a growing concern by public officials that highways are not the golden roads to opportunity as billed by chambers of commerce and departments of public works.

They are particularly significant because they deal with Somerville, scheduled for parts of Rte 2, the Inner Belt and Rte. I-93.

Highway advocates often point to Somerville as a community needing such roads to relieve congestion and to promote the development of an industrial park.

Yet Ralph, a man elected by 13,000 votes over his opponent, wants no part of the roads.

"Maybe you could drive in and out of an industrial park at a higher rate of speed with an Inner Belt," Ralph says, "but we already have an access road there. What the highway would do in harm outweighs the benefits. The industrial park will be built and the lack of an Inner Belt won't deter that in any way."

The proposed roads will take 98.7 acres of land in Somerville, the most densely populated community in the state, with 20,954 persons per square mile.

Already, Rte. I-93 construction has removed a minimum of $303,340 in tax revenue from that city. That's 1.5 percent of the tax base in a city with one of the highest tax rates in the state, $143.80 per $1000.

"I don't see how people can argue for roads," Ralph says. "It's plain absurd. This is both a practical and a moral question."

Yet, people do argue and they do so relentlessly. Opponents contend neither the practical nor the moral side of the question has been seriously considered in Massachusetts, despite scores of studies.

The debate sharpens

The conflict between providing decent housing and surroundings for the urban poor as against building highways through and into congested urban areas, has become one of the most basic and sharp social-political issues.

A bill filed by Rep. Michael S. Dukakis (D-Brookline), calling for a moratorium, comes up for a hearing at the State House on Tuesday.

This so-called people-vs.-roads issue has developed into a valid and — at times — quite properly, an emotional issue. The issue has split urban specialists in the universities, in Federal and local government down the middle. So, too, the issue has split thoughtful reporters and editorial writers on the Boston Globe.

For this reason we present these two pages on both side of the issue.

The position on this page—the case for a moratorium on highway construction in Greater Boston — is favored by the following Globe reporters who write urban affairs: Alan Lupo, John Plunkett, Janet Riddell, F. B. Tayler Jr., David Deitch, Crocker Snow Jr., Nina Mcain, James B. Ayres, Thomas Oliphant, Larry Van Dyne, Viola Osgood, Richard Knox.

All the above took issue with a short Globe editorial of Dec. 19. The editorial was prompted by a Mayor Kevin White statement urging a moratorium on all state highway construction in Boston, and also the unfinished portions of the Inner Belt, Southwest Expressway and Rte. I-93.

The case for continuing the highway program as part of a balanced transportation policy is written by Globe Transportation Editor, A. S. Plotkin. He has been backed by Globe editorials and many other Globe political and city specialists.

2000 PERSONS GATHER AT COMMON TO PROTEST INNER BELT

● Highways have been studied "to death." As long as most of them qualify for 90 or 50 percent Federal funds, as long as segments have been or are being built, as long as 80 percent of the Southwest Expressway properties have been taken, why not proceed?

Most studies appear to have been loaded on the side of roads, incomplete, outdated and grossly lacking in community participation.

ing units. Half the households to be eliminated by the Inner Belt and Southwest Expressway alone have incomes of less than $4800 a year.

About 43 percent of the families directly affected by those two roads are financially eligible for public housing. But no public housing is being built, except for a few scattered units for the elderly. Nor is there any provision for replacement housing.

All kinds of neighborhoods are affected by the pro-

They were, two days later, with a long editorial that weighed the pluses and minuses of the demand for a moratorium on highways.

Governor Sargent on February 11 announced a reversal of policy on highway building and halted plans for the Southwest Expressway, the Inner Belt, and extension of Route 2 into the city. These would be restudied to determine not only where and how to build them "but whether to build them at all."

He proposed a "balanced transportation program" as between highways and mass transit and would try to get some of the huge federal highway grants diverted to mass transit.

The Globe hailed this as a constructive program in an editorial February 13 and supported the proposal for federal funds for mass transit.

In its turn, the editorial page rebuked a staff writer for an attack on President Pusey of Harvard upon his 1970 baccalaureate address. The July 2 editorial, "The Record of President Pusey," said: "We take issue with a recent column by Parker Donham printed June 24 on this paper's opinion page. We do so because we believe it was inaccurate in an important way, largely because of what it omitted, and therefore was unfair to the reputation of President Nathan M. Pusey of Harvard." The editorial then proceeded to straighten out the distortions of the Donham article.

Donham, a Harvard graduate of the June before, had in college espoused the radical SDS; on the op-ed page of the Globe he appeared to be following the same line in denigrating President Pusey's historic resistance to McCarthyism.

The editorial on the Donham piece was the culmination of a series of lapses on Harvard that the Globe had fallen into and which then necessitated setting the record straight.

When the Institute of Politics in the Kennedy School of Government was established at Harvard in 1967 for advanced fellowships in government, a traveling British correspondent wrote a sensational story about it for the London Telegraph. In Henry Fairlie's account, Harvard was surrendering control of the Institute to the Kennedy family and it was to become a haven in exile for Kennedy administration men, displaced by the Johnson administration. The Washington Post had rights to material in the Telegraph, and the Fairlie story came to the Globe through the Washington Post-Los Angeles Times syndicate. It appeared in the Globe the same day as in the Washington Post, Sunday, January 15. An eight-column headline asked, "Is Harvard's Institute of Politics a Kennedy Recruiting College?"

The rest of the week the Globe was backtracking on it. January 17 a front page headline: "Harvard Nails 'Prep' Story." Next day: "Shock and Anger at Harvard" and a six-column spread describing the actuality of the Institute under a headline: "Misjudged Kennedy, Underestimated Harvard." Next day: "Harvard Rebukes Critic — Answers Attack of JFK School." This headlined the text of a letter that Dean Don Price of the Kennedy School wrote to the London Telegraph taking Fairlie's fantasy apart line by line. On January 20 the Globe ran an editorial, "Fairlie, Go Home."

Another attack on Harvard with a curious background was by Al Capp; it commanded most of the op-ed page June 25, 1969. It was a commencement address by the cartoonist (whose Li'l Abner is a fixture of the Globe comic pages) delivered two months earlier, April 27, at Franklin Pierce College in New Hampshire. All of it except the last paragraph was abuse of Harvard, its students and faculty, with a detailed attack on Professor Henry Rosovsky. As though in justification, the Globe ran in a center box a letter from Al Capp complaining that the paper had printed two commencement addresses of Professor J. K. Galbraith that referred to Capp but had not reported Capp's address.

Harvard readers blinked at the Capp article, for it had been published in the Washington Post a month before, on May 18. The Post had followed it a week later, May 25, with letters from two Harvard professors denouncing the attack on Rosovsky as unwarranted and untrue and an article by Alan Barth of the Post's editorial page in defense of Professor Rosovsky that showed Capp had, among other things, misrepresented Rosovsky's position.

Capp charged that Rosovsky "gave up the chairmanship of his department and started packing" when militant students invaded University Hall. What Rosovsky had done was to fight against a demand that six black students be added to his special committee planning a Black Studies program. He had carried his resistance to the point of resigning the committee chairmanship when the faculty overruled him. A few weeks later he was elected chairman of the Economics Department.

The Globe's publication of the Capp attack made no reference to its refutations. But the very next day the Globe ran the same protests and defense that the Post had run a month before. This swift juxtaposition made it appear that the Globe had held back the rejoinders and had chosen to publish Capp with no intimation of denial next day. An incredulous inquirer discovered that the Globe editors had been totally unaware of the Post's experience with the Capp article. Naturally, it would be hard for Harvard or Rosovsky to accept this.

Then a sports page agitation over the lack of a stadium for the Boston Patriots football team escalated to front page headlines in January 1970 with the threat that the Patriots would have to leave Boston. Stadium proposals had failed to enlist private financing. Public officials had drawn back from appropriating tax funds. Harvard balked at a request to share its stadium with the professionals.

Bud Collins in a series of columns had savagely attacked and caricatured Harvard and President Pusey over this. When Harvard issued a statement of its position the Globe printed only "excerpts" — about a third of the text. The Herald Traveler ran the full text. That day, January 27, a Bud Collins column was headed "Old Snob Job by Harvard." The university felt the Globe had denied it a fair chance to make its case. The Globe management evidently thought so too, for next day the full text was run. But by then the front page story had receded to the sports section, so the text ran on page 32. The Globe used a picture of President Pusey taken the day of Harvard's refusal of the stadium that caught him with a particularly dour expression; it looked almost like a Grant Wood caricature of an Iowa Puritan.

When President Pusey announced his resignation a few weeks later the same picture was used again. This time the university was further outraged that the story of Mr. Pusey's retirement was written by the same staffer, Parker Donham, whose views of Pusey a Globe editorial was soon after to repudiate.*

The editor of the Globe, on a television panel in spring 1970, remarked:

> The newspaper editor may be going the way of the college president. There's a striking similarity between the job of editor and the college president. Should

---

* Donham soon after left journalism to spend a fallow year on a farm.

the newspaper be the advocate for social and political change? Our brand of Weathermen say "Yes." I say "Yes" too. We've learned an awful lot from our city room Weathermen. We can't any longer be merely observers. We have to be concerned with the under-privileged. But participatory journalism is terribly hazardous. We have got to maintain the integrity of our news columns if we are going to keep our credibility and achieve reform at the same time."

Obviously the staff was divided over "integrity" in the news, militant writers impatient with the "squares" on the copy desk. Winship's Youth Movement of course was responsible for accelerating that militant element he called "city room Weathermen." Sharp differences in cultural judgments were sometimes very visible. Television critic Percy Shain reported a program "For Women Today" as objectionable for its explicit treatment of sex, with particular objection to one four-letter word, the same day that Gregory McDonald was finding hilarity in police attention to a "dirty word song." *

In early 1970 a new column three days a week by George Frazier soon provoked reader reaction to his frequently violent opinions, which recalled his controversial period on the Boston Herald a decade or more earlier. In the 1970 election the Globe withheld a Frazier column attacking Governor Sargent written for the day before election, and ran it the day after election. Editor Winship explained to the columnist that "about the oldest Globe rule is that you abstain from carrying material in the paper during the last 48 hours of a campaign that would logically require a rebuttal."

Al Capp had seemed to bear a charmed life at the Globe — with his increasingly violent attacks on liberals, professors, and critics of the Vietnam war, both in his comic strip and in his platform appearances — until September 25, 1970, when the Globe ran on the op-ed page a column by Garry Wills, a new syndicate writer, on "The Decline of Al Capp." It was an attack on the decline of Capp's art as satirist. "His twitches of wit are galvanic now, vestigial, mere tics of sanity left in him as he tries to outdo Spiro Agnew . . . We must pity him as he becomes ever more despicably ludicrous."

* A breakthrough of sorts for the Globe came in a report of a Harvard sit-in over Laos in the morning paper of February 23, 1971, which quoted explicitly a word that the New York Times had euphemistically edited to "a barnyard epithet" in Anthony Lucas' report of the trial of the "Chicago Seven." That editing incident had gained wide currency when Lucas twitted the Times with the title of his book on the trial, "The Barnyard Epithet." Evidently reporter Thomas Oliphant felt a need to prove a more permissive usage in Boston by his unexpurgated quotation. The copy desk let it stay in.

July 20, 1969

MAN WALKS ON MOON

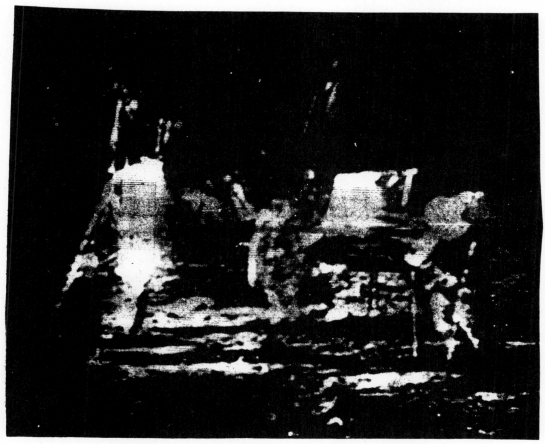

Astronauts Armstrong and Aldrin plant American flag on the moon at 11:46 p.m. (AP)

World Gets Guided Tour: 'Beautiful, Magnificent Desolation'

"OK Houston, I'm on the porch."

★ ★ ★

"I'm at the foot of the ladder."

★ ★ ★

"That's one small step for a man, but one giant leap for mankind."

★ ★ ★

"The surface is fine and powdered, like powdered charcoal to the soles of my boot . . . I can see my footprints of my boot in the fine particles."

"I only go in a fraction of an inch, an eighth of an inch."

★ ★ ★

"Beautiful, beautiful, beautiful. A magnificent desolation."

"It's very interesting. It's a very fine soft surface, but when I dig for the contingency sample, it appears to be very hard cohesive material of the same sort."

Two men from the planet Earth landed on the surface of the Moon at 4.17.45 E.D.T., Sunday, July 20, 1969.

It brought the dawn of a new era in the evolution of man.

The first human imprint on lunar soil was made five hours after the landing by Neil A. Armstrong, a civilian from the United States of America. The time, 10:56.20 p.m., July 20, 1969.

Watching him at the historic moment was Edwin E. Aldrin Jr., an Air Force lieutenant colonel.

"Didn't I say we might see some purple rocks?"

"Did you find purple rocks?"

"Yup."

It took them 109 hours, 8 minutes and 5 seconds to get there.

Orbiting the moon to pick up the two Moon landers was the third member of the historic team, Air Force Lt Col Michael Collins.

The news of the successful landing which was relayed to Earth by TV and radio in play-by-play sequence was hailed by the entire world.

The age of space truly began on this momentous day and throughout the world scientists now await data and samples which will determine heretofore unknown or uncertain facts about our world and ourselves.

"It has a stark beauty all of it's own. Its much like the desert of the United States. It's different but its very pretty out here."

★ ★ ★

"Its quite dark here in the shadow and quite hard for me to see where I'm stepping. . . .

"Looking up at the LM . . . I can see everything quite clearly . . . everything is very clearly visible."

★ ★ ★

"Put it in the pocket . . . got it . . . the sample is in the pocket . . ."

★ ★ ★

"I want to back up and partially close the hatch. Making sure not to lock it on my way out . . ."

Man on the moon: July 21, 1969.

The Moon and a Kennedy

At the time of the epic landing on the moon the Globe, July 21, 1969, gave its whole first section to the moon story and left mundane earth news to separate sections. The front page had the simplest form of headline, "Man Walks On Moon," with the historic date July 20 above it. The headline was in blue type. A page-wide photograph, 12 inches deep, showed the astronauts raising the flag on the moon. The lower part of the page carried selections of the astronauts' first succinct reports, "Eagle Has Landed," and description of the moon surface as it felt underfoot. A centered box at the bottom of the page gave a brief historical account of the event.

Inside, a single picture of the first steps on the moon occupied an entire page. Another page was divided between two pictures.

Victor McElheny led the Globe team of reporters at the launching and at the space center. But even McElheny's story of his greatest assignment was inside. The moon itself took over page one.

But on the day the astronauts had prepared their landing, July 20, the moon story was displaced from the top half of page one by Senator Edward Kennedy's tragic accident on Chappaquiddick Island in which his companion, Mary Jo Kopechne, drowned. He failed to report the accident till the morning after, when his vague statement of his actions and condition during the night proved in his own term "inexplicable."

The Globe's topping the moon story with the Kennedy tragedy was so exceptional, if not unique, as to attract national attention in the news magazines. Managing editor Ian Menzies explained, as quoted in Newsweek: "I knew that Sunday morning would not be important as far as anything happening to Apollo 11. The Kennedys are one of the most important families in history and our coverage was justified."

Menzies was literally correct as to the Apollo 11 story. Only the momentum of the historic flight and public suspense kept it the top headline through the four days from its launching to the landing that Sunday night. The Globe carried ten stories on the Chappaquiddick tragedy Sunday morning and a detailed map of the accident scene.

Kennedy's crisis filled only less news space than the moon shot through the following week. The astronauts returned to earth Thursday, July 24. Kennedy's predicament took over top headlines the next day when he pleaded guilty to leaving the scene of an accident, to receive a two months' suspended sentence, and that night broadcast on all national networks his "explanation," as he put it, to the people of Massachusetts, whose judgment he solicited on whether he should resign. His dilemma filled pages of space in all Sunday papers July 27.

The Globe on Tuesday, July 29, published results of a poll conducted for it by the Becker Research organization. It showed that 78 percent of Massachusetts voters would have him remain in the Senate. This compared with 84 percent who had approved his Senate performance. The Globe gave the poll results the whole top half of the front page. Next day, Wednesday, July 30, the Globe announced it had received 301 letters on the Kennedy issue on Monday and Tuesday. Of these 179

Boston Sunday Globe

SUNDAY, JULY 20, 1969

35 CENTS

Police Seek Leaving-the-Scene Complaint

Ted Kennedy Escapes, Woman Dies As Car Plunges Into Vineyard Pond

CAR SEN. KENNEDY DROVE IS PULLED FROM POND
. . . spectators watch from bridge. (AP)

Senator Wanders In Daze for Hours

By RICHARD POWERS and ALAN LUPO
Staff Writers

EDGARTOWN—Sen. Edward M. Kennedy, the only surviving brother in a family pursued by tragedy, narrowly escaped death early yesterday when his car plunged into a pond on a sparsely inhabited island off the coast of Martha's Vineyard.

A passenger, Mary Jo Kopechne, 28, of Washington, a former campaign worker for the late Sen. Robert F. Kennedy, was drowned.

The car went off a wooden bridge, turned over and sank to the bottom of Poucha Pond.

Police said the accident occurred between midnight and 1 a.m. yesterday on Chappaquiddick Island, where Kennedy was visiting with friends at a small cottage.

Staffers for Robert and Edward Kennedy had been having a reunion there.

Police Chief James Arena said last night that he will go to the Edgartown District Court tomorrow to file an application for a complaint charging Kennedy with leaving the scene of an accident without making himself known.

He said also he would issue a Registry of Motor Vehicles violation citation against Kennedy on the same complaint.

After the accident, Kennedy swam to safety, although he told Edgartown police he could not remember how he got out of the car.

He told police he repeatedly dived into the pond to see if Miss Kopechne was still trapped but that he was unable to do anything.

Police said Kennedy did not go to the station until about 10 a.m.

"I was exhausted and in a state of shock," he told them.

Dr. Robert D. Watt, the Kennedy family physician, on Cape Cod, reported last night that the senator "has a slight concussion at the back of his head."

Watt said he gave the senator a sedative "to help relieve the pain."

Kennedy then retired and was resting comfortably, Watt said.

He plans to see Kennedy again today.

Edgartown Police Chief Dominick J. Arena said the car was first seen about 8 a.m. yesterday by some boys who were going fishing near the narrow wooden bridge.

KENNEDY Page 47

DEAD — MARY JO KOPECHNE

Mother in Shock
Ted First to Call Victim's Father

By KEN O. BOTWRIGHT
Staff Writer

The phone in the home of Mr. and Mrs. Joseph A. Kopechne at Berkeley Heights, N.J., rang about 10 a.m. yesterday. It was Sen. Edward M. Kennedy, calling to tell them their daughter had been killed in an auto accident the night before.

Mary Jo Kopechne, an attractive 28-year-old blonde and former secretary in the office of the late Robert F. Kennedy, drowned when a car the senator was driving plunged into a pond on Martha's Vineyard about midnight.

Her 50-year-old father, an insurance man, said at 4 p.m. yesterday that his wife, Gwen, took the call and lapsed into shock.

MARY JO Page 36

'There's a Car in the Water'

By TIMOTHY LELAND
Staff Writer

CHAPPAQUIDDICK ISLAND—It was Saturday morning, a day of rest for some people, but not for Tony Bettencourt, caretaker of the island dump.

Every day is a work day for Tony in the Summers, even Sundays, because the folk who come down to the island for their vacations make a mess at the dump, and the sea gulls pick the garbage bags apart and spread the refuse all over the place, and Tony has to rake it all up and shovel it back where it belongs.

Chappaquiddick Island doesn't have any stores on it or gas stations. It has a fire station though, big enough for a single fire truck, pride and joy of the seven families who live on the island year around. And it has the dump, which is a pretty big responsibility for Tony Bettencourt, especially in July and August when there are so many Summer folk on the island.

Yesterday morning Tony drove his four-wheel-drive beach jeep down the dirt road to the dike bridge to pick up Johnny Smith, as always.

Johnny, who helps Tony rake up the dump, is 14 years old, son of Rev. David Smith, when Tony drove up to his house at 9 a.m. yesterday he could see the Edgartown police chief's car up ahead, right by the wooden bridge, and Johnny came running down the road toward him, even before he came to a stop.

ISLAND Page 35

All Is Go for Moon Landing Today

By VICTOR K. McELHENY
Staff Writer

SPACE CENTER, Houston—Two men will attempt to make man's first landing on the moon today. An event that should make this date—July 20, 1969—ring down through the ages.

America's Apollo 11 moon-ship entered orbit around the moon at 1:22 p.m. EDT yesterday to begin 24 hours of preparation for today's landing, which is to carry astronauts Neil Armstrong and Edwin Aldrin down to a desolate spot in the Sea of Tranquility.

All portents for the scheduled landing are favorable. The equipment of Apollo 11, fruit of a decade of intense engineering effort, has worked flawlessly since takeoff from Cape Kennedy, Fla., at 9:32 a.m. last Wednesday.

So far the voyage of Armstrong, Aldrin and crewmate Michael Collins has been amazingly smooth, with all indications that the scheduled 4:14 p.m. moonship landing today and Armstrong's first step on the moon at 2:16 a.m. will take place as planned.

The three Americans joined Russia's Luna 15, which was in its third day of orbiting the moon. Its mission never disclosed, Luna changed its course slightly during the day. The Soviets have assured U.S. space officials that Luna will not interfere with Apollo 11.

The astronauts made a vital test of the fragile machine named Eagle that two of them will fly to the surface of the moon today.

Aldrin crawled from the command ship into the small lunar lander called Eagle at 6:58 p.m. to test the equipment.

The Air Force colonel powered up the lunar module for the first time since it was rocketed away from Cape Kennedy four days and 250,000 miles ago.

He also tested the communications systems that will carry word and picture of man's first step on another celestial body.

Collins conducted lunar tracking photography.

He also reported that a small pool of water had formed in one corner of the command module. This occurred in previous Apollo flights and officials said it poses no problem.

Earlier, Armstrong and Aldrin reported sighting some mysterious lunar lights in an area where some scientists believe there are volcanoes.

APOLLO Page 61

Did Luna 15 Make First Scoop?

United Press International

MOSCOW—Russia's mysterious Luna 15 moon ship sent out an unusually long burst of signals yesterday and moved into a slightly higher orbit, causing speculation both in Moscow and at Britain's Jodrell Bank Observatory that some sort of landing might already have been made.

The Soviet government maintained the silence it has maintained since Luna 15 was launched last Sunday but scientific sources have predicted it would scoop up some moon soil ahead of Apollo 11. However, there was no confirmation of speculation that this might have been accomplished by a lunar module.

LUNA Page 54

Rain May Fall

SUNDAY — Cool, possible showers. MONDAY — Chance of showers. (Page 55).

High Tides
3:36 a.m.   4:06 p.m.

Stores Open

Massachusetts merchants, in accord with practices in other retail areas, including New York, Philadelphia and Washington, will be open regular hours on "Moon Day," July 21. Banks will also be open. The stock market will be closed.

Baseball Results

AMERICAN LEAGUE
BOSTON 5, Baltimore 3 (n).
Detroit 10, Cleveland 4.
Chicago 5, Kansas City 4.
Oakland 3, California 2.
Minnesota-Seattle (N).
N w York 4, Washington 0.
Washington 4, New York 0.

NATIONAL LEAGUE
Philadelphia 5, Chicago 3.
Montreal 5, New York 4.
Cincinnati, 10, Houston 9 (11).
Pittsburgh 2, St. Louis 2.
San Diego 6, Atlanta 1.
San Fran. 3, Los Angeles 4.

RED SOX TODAY
Baltimore at Fenway (Cuellar vs. Culp), 2 p.m. TV-Channel 5.

Historical Timetable: From Landing to First Step

United Press International

SPACE CENTER, Houston—The Apollo 11 timetable, based on the revised NASA flight plan. Times are approximate.

TODAY
7:27 a.m. (EDT)—Crew awakens.

9:27 — Aldrin enters Moon lander without his spacesuit.

10:15 — Armstrong enters Moon lander, wearing spacesuit, and starts final check of systems.

9:42 — Aldrin enters lander, puts on spacesuit in command ship and returns to landing craft.

1:42 p.m.—Lunar lander and command ship separate slightly.

10:42 — Aldrin exits lander, drop it into lower Moon orbit and begin the long ride down toward the surface.

3:06 — Astronauts fire descent engine in lunar lander, drop it into lower Moon orbit and begin the long ride down toward the surface.

4:02—Lander's big engine begins final descent.

approach firing, braking ship out of orbit at 50,000-foot altitude on sloping path toward the selected landing site.

4:14 — Lander touches down on lunar Sea of Tranquility.

6:58—Two men begin four-hour rest period prior to leaving Moon lander's cabin.

TOMORROW
2:07 a.m. — Armstrong leaves lander and begins five-minute descent of ladder. He pulls on D-ring, opening equipment stowage area door and allowing television camera a view of surface and foot of ladder.

TIMETABLE Page 61

- A $14.70 Tax Hike Predicted For Boston—Pg. 3
- Nixon Will Offer New Domestic Plan At End Of Trip—Pg. 2

Chappaquiddick: July 20, 1969. For this day, the moon goes to the bottom of the page.

The Boston Globe

Sixteen   TUESDAY, JULY 29, 1969

A good Senator

Only Sen. Edward M. Kennedy can answer whether he should or should not resign from the United States Senate. It is not a matter for a plebiscite. There is far too much emotion attached to the incident on Chappaquiddick Island a week ago

For Massachusetts he worked for such things as greater oil imports to reduce heating bills, and for area cooperation of Federal parks and projects. But, more than that, he has been an effective and diligent representative for the state.

said he should resign and 101 that he should not. Two-thirds of the letters were from out of state, and they ran against Kennedy, 141 to 38. The in-State letters were for him 51 to 38.

The Globe editorially had said the day before his broadcast that his first statement raised more questions than it answered and that he should make a full statement to clear up all questions. On July 29 the Globe editorially found the broadcast statement also inadequate, but said that Kennedy was too valuable a senator to lose; he should continue in the Senate. The editorial was titled "A Good Senator."

That day Senator Kennedy announced his decision to stay in the Senate and run for re-election in 1970, stating that if re-elected he would serve his full six-year term. He thus appeared to remove himself from 1972 presidential consideration.

The Globe had no further comment. It had that morning announced a Gallup poll to be published the following Sunday, August 3, on Kennedy's standing in the nation as compared to an earlier Gallup poll.

It found that those whose view of Kennedy was "extremely favorable" had shrunk from 49 percent in April to 34 percent. Those who took an "extremely unfavorable" view had increased from four to 11 percent.

President Nixon followed the moon shot with a trip around the world, visiting several Asian countries and adding an unprecedented visit to Rumania. The Globe's chief Washington correspondent, James Doyle, covered this tour. Even so brief a glimpse at the conditions of life of the teeming populations of Asia so impressed the young correspondent that he wrote from Lahore: "Perhaps if the Vatican apartments were above Roxas Boulevard in Manila or a bazaar in Delhi or Calcutta, birth control would become a moral imperative instead of an accusation of immorality; perhaps if the Pentagon forced each arms salesman to live in the cities of their clients, the mad escalation of small arms in the third world could be controlled."

Through the first week of August as the Senate reached a vote on deployment of the Safeguard antimissile system, the Globe ran on its editorial page daily chapters from J. K. Galbraith's new book, *How To Control the Military*.

1969: Confrontation

The 1969 fall term on college campuses opened with the radical student attacks on traditional programs increasingly organized and persistent. But some administrations had become more sophisticated in confronting them. This was notably the case at M.I.T., whose large defense research projects had been a primary target of the SDS and their faculty allies. The Globe's science editor Victor McElheny, and its roving observer of the academic scene Crocker Snow, followed closely the confrontations at M.I.T. that focused on the new Cambridge Project, a computer-based research program for the social sciences.

On Sunday, October 5, the Globe explored the issue and the tactics involved in a two-page opening of its feature section: "M.I.T. 1969: Confrontation and Dialog." Most of one page was taken up with a statement by Michael Albert, whose cohesive SDS members had succeeded in electing him, on a minority vote, president of M.I.T.'s student body. McElheny analyzed the attitudes and strategy with which M.I.T. officials had met the radical attack in this first newspaper report of an illuminating confrontation that had been held ten days earlier. Snow described the history of the revolt at M.I.T. against defense-related research.

A side glance at the similar problem of neighboring Harvard was contributed by Robert L. Levey, in an interview with Harvard's new dean, Ernest May.

These two pages gave readers much the closest examination to that date of the issues and tactics of student militants confronting a university and the considered policies and methods of dealing with them.

On the Sunday following the M.I.T. confrontation, the Globe published in a 24-page magazine supplement to its October 12 edition a recapitulation of the "April Crisis at Harvard: An Appraisal of the Confrontation." This was the product of a staff task force exploration of the background of issues and tactics that had reached a climax in the April explosion, its consequences, and its effects on the university. The writing was by Crocker Snow and Parker Donham. Thirty-three illustrations, 12 in color, were contributed by nine staff photographers.

Campus confrontation: October 5, 1969.

Features

	Science, Education, A-32
	World Backgrounds, A-34
	Politics, A-35
	Editorials, A-36
	Columnists, A-37
	Calendar, A-38
	Travel, A-39—A-53

A-31
Sunday Globe
October 5, 1969

MIT 1969:
Confrontation and dialogue

What a campus radical is saying

Last March, the student body at the Massachusetts Institute of Technology elected Mike Albert their undergraduate Association President, the highest elected student office on campus.

Albert ran on a self-described "radical" platform of ending all war-related research at M.I.T., complete acceptance of the demands of the campus Black Student Union, and increased admissions of poor whites. He drew 655 votes to 617 for the

those interests by propping up a fascist, racist, dictatorship with guns and money — perhaps you would be interested in sending your son to South Africa to help defend 'our interests'? Perhaps, Mr. Businessman, you would like to go instead?

Our analysis tells us that imperialism; the war in Vietnam, the ravaging of Latin America and Africa, etc.; serves the needs of a small class of people in this country —people whom we call the capitalists; the

The Boston Globe

Out Now

A moratorium for peace is taking place today on campuses and in communities across the nation. It may be the largest mass demonstration in America for generations. This should be peaceful and prayerful. This day is taking place for one reason: to dramatize the need for withdrawing U.S. men from combat in the Vietnamese civil war as fast as possible.

Almost everyone by now agrees generally on that objective. The question under debate across the land, however, is how to get out, and how soon.

On Sept. 26 President Nixon made perhaps the biggest mistake of his long career.

In discussing opposition to the war on campus and in the nation he said, "Under no circumstances will I be affected whatever" by it. He said it again two days ago. He showed what no leader of a democracy should show, that public opinion will have no effect at all upon public policy.

Rather than discussing what motivated the President's statement it is better to address ourselves to the main issue of our withdrawal from Vietnam.

Those who oppose it and those who favor it can at least agree that we no longer are seeking a total military victory. Mr. Nixon is the second President to say that that is not our aim. But the two sides differ on whether anything can be expected from the negotiations in Paris, now 17 months old, and on several other points.

First, there is President Nixon's position on the war.

He believes the Paris talks can be fruitful — if there is little or no dissent at home. He was elected last November on the basis of a campaign pledge to end the war. He said he had a plan. And while he has not spelled out all of its details, it is clear that it is a flexible one.

The heart of Nixon's policy

The President rules out a cease-fire on grounds it is not relevant in a guerrilla war.

The President is against what he calls abandoning

'Under no circumstances will I be affected whatever by it.' –PRESIDENT NIXON

But under the terms of this treaty, the only obligation under Section 2 was to "Consult," and under Section 1 was to "meet the common danger in accordance with its constitutional processes." Since the Constitution gives only to Congress the power to declare war, those processes were not followed in sending our soldiers to fight in Vietnam.

no danger that those countries would fall to Communism. So does a high government official who has spent many years in that part of the world.

President Nixon has said that all we want is self-determination for South Vietnam "without outside interference." It has apparently never seemed, either to

durance of the enemy, his willingness to absorb punishment, the psychology of the peasant, and the politics of the country. Of these we are largely ignorant. So our structure of careful and rational decisions was built on sand.")

In the last analysis, "Vietnamization" is but the latest in a long line of programs proposed to retrieve a hopeless situation.

Thieu has tied us down

They all have been based on supposed strength, they have been tried for years, and they just haven't worked. The administration is still committed to making Vietnamization work before the Paris talks work, and to make the Paris talks work before we complete our withdrawal.

Finally, there is the emotional appeal, and it is a strong one. It is said that to withdraw unilaterally from Vietnam would mean "walking out" on that country, a wrong thing to do even though we were wrong to go in there in the first place. The term "bugging out" is used. But upon whom would we be walking out? The people of South Vietnam, or a corrupt military government of our own making?

To be sure, it will not be enough to rely upon the National Liberation Front's promise of no reprisals if we withdraw. That is too slender a reed. We do have an obligation to offer a refuge and haven to those South Vietnamese who would otherwise feel themselves in jeopardy. But this should not apply to those with Swiss bank accounts who can be trusted to be first in line at Tan Son Nhut Airport if a collapse seems imminent.

Our support, in any event, must be withdrawn from the corrupt rulers of that ravaged country. For it has become all too clear that President Thieu and Vice President Ky and most of their other generals are on our side for only so long as they can get all they can. Some measure of their devotion can be seen in the fact that only two of the South Vietnamese officers serving as lieutenant-colonels or higher fought for the Vietminh against the French.

President Thieu, for a supposed puppet, has behaved more like Gulliver's army of Lilliputians. He has tied us down. Last Fall he refused to join the Paris peace talks until after the election. Forced by mounting criticism to change his Cabinet, he ignored our appeals for a broader based government and even narrowed it instead.

'One disaster we can end'

Especially offensive, President Thieu recently declared that he will "bill" the U.S. for any troop

---

The "Out Now" moratorium editorial: October 15, 1969.

This was just ten days before the October 15 antiwar moratorium, launched by student groups. The Globe gave the movement full coverage and close scrutiny. This proved sound news judgment, as the momentum of the movement won support of all colleges in the area and then of the Cardinal, the Governor, both Senators, and other political, professional, and community groups. As its dimensions broadened, the character of the planned observance changed from a narrowly based protest to programs of convocation and contemplation, peace vigils and prayer meetings, as various participants variously defined their dedication to peace.

On the day before the moratorium the Globe, in a 48-page paper, carried 25 columns of news about it; nine of those pages had no other news. An editorial page box reported that of 55 letters to the editor 25 supported the moratorium, 24 were opposed, and six were middle of the road.

The Globe chose the moratorium day, October 15, to take a more advanced position on Vietnam. "Out Now" was the title of a forthright editorial that occupied the whole page to call for unilateral withdrawal of American forces "as fast as is logistically possible . . . To extend the withdrawal over a term of years is pointless." It saw no chance of success of the Vietnamization program. "Colonial wars are out of date. A mistake has been made and the only thing to do is to cease making it. The best and indeed the only way to support our boys in Vietnam is to get them out of there."

But it gave the top half its op-ed page to "The Administration's Side on Vietnam," in an interview with Undersecretary of State Elliot Richardson, and carried also a column by David Broder of the Washington Post, "A Misdirected Protest," that deplored the demonstrations and the possibility of so weakening and discrediting the President that he could not lead through his remaining three years.

Szep's cartoon that day showed Nixon, like Gulliver, swarmed over by little people trying to bind him to peace.

The moratorium dramatically brought out the sharp opposition of the Globe and Herald, in both editorial policy and news coverage. The Herald editorially belittled the "breast beating" of the demonstrators and declared that most Americans don't want to replace high-level decision-making by "head counts in the streets or parks." All the letters to the Herald October 15 were hostile to the moratorium. So were the Herald's front page headlines. Its banner head was "Hanoi Note Salutes Dissenters." Another head: "Anti-Protest Swell Moves Across U.S." A front page box featured a proposal for those opposed to the moratorium to keep their car lights on.

The striking opposition of Boston's morning newspapers between liberal and conservative attitudes afforded a reader an alternative that few other cities any longer presented.

In the 1969 municipal elections the Globe carried its political participation an emphatic step beyond its 1967 innovation of an editorial in support of Kevin White for mayor. With no mayoral election in 1969, city council and school committee contests filled the field. In the first-round balloting September 16 that thinned out the candidates' ranks, all incumbents won nomination for the final election.

The school committee chairman, John J. Kerrigan, led in the preliminary vote for that committee. Nine days later the Globe led the paper with a report of its investigation into the handling of school repair work. The headline was "Kerrigan's Friend and School Repairs — Firm Paid $65,000 for No-Bid Work."

The firm had been organized by two Boston firemen after Kerrigan's election to the school committee. One of them was fired the day after the Globe's report, the other had been dropped earlier. Kerrigan denied influencing the assignment of $150,000 of school repairs to the new firm, headed by his close friend, which appeared to have specialized in jobs under $2,000 not requiring competitive bidding. Kerrigan threatened to sue the Globe. But another school committee member called for a finance committee investigation of school repair contracts. The city law department ordered further payments to the firm stopped, pending investigation.

The issue continued to make headlines during the campaign. Mrs. Dorothy Bisbee, a candidate, accused Kerrigan of exploiting the schools in favor of his friends and of undermining moral standards of teaching.

The Globe published attacks on Kerrigan but gave equal space to his attacks on the Globe's "yellow journalism."

After the first week, Kerrigan's controversy with the Globe was somewhat diluted by his need to give attention also to the Herald Traveler, which came in with exposure of his securing appointments of relatives and friends to temporary school department positions that required no qualifications or competitive examinations. His retort to this was that it was accepted practice for the school department to make a certain number of such jobs available to each school committeeman — a practice which till then was not publicly known.

Kerrigan turned his campaign against the Globe and put out a flier attacking the

Boston Evening Globe

®   © 1969, Globe Newspaper Co.   288-8000   THURSDAY, SEPTEMBER 25, 1969   52 PAGES — 10 CENTS

Fin Com School Contracts Probe Asked

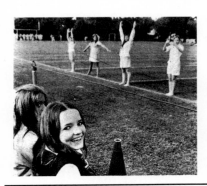

Tierney Presses Issue After Story on Repairs;

Chairman Kerrigan Threatens to Sue the Globe

A full-scale investigation by the Boston Finance Commission into circumstances involved in letting no-bid repair contracts to a personal friend of school board chairman John J. Kerrigan was demanded today by another school committeeman, Paul R. Tierney.

"I will not comment as to whether Mr. Kerrigan abused his public trust as an elected official," said Tierney as he called for a Finance Commission probe with the disclosure by the Globe that R and L Construction Co., Inc., has been the beneficiary of school department contracts to the tune of at least $56,000 since mid-1968.

Kerrigan's immediate reaction to this divulgement and his long-time personal relationship with R and L's treasurer, Michael J. Lombardo, was to

School investigation: September 25, 1969.

paper. On October 31, four days before election, the Globe published the text of Kerrigan's attack and answered it.

Two days before, the city law department had filed suit against the two ex-firemen whose company had obtained so many no-bid school contracts, under the conflict of interest statute, to recover the economic advantage the two had enjoyed from their inside track to school work. The finance commission disclosed that Kerrigan held a second public job, in the Motor Vehicles Department, and raised questions about absences from work on days when he had been checked in as present.

But these things had little effect on Kerrigan's constituency. He again topped the vote for school committee.

An incontrovertible point in Kerrigan's attack on the Globe was that its publishers and editors lived outside Boston. The Globe observed that this was true of most executives of Boston enterprises. It was and long had been a symptom of the civic weakness of Boston. But it undoubtedly diluted the influence of the paper on the inner core residents of the older parts of the city, and they determine local elections.

To them the Boston Record-American was more acceptable reading. Although it had been reduced to a single all-day tabloid with the familiar Hearst aspects, it had developed local news coverage through the 1960's under the able Edward Holland as city editor and then managing editor. By the end of that decade it was more of a competitor than the Herald within the city and afforded an alternative to those put off by the Globe's position on the Vietnam war, its strong concern for civil rights and the black community, and its tolerance of dissenters, students, and others.

On Sunday, November 2, two days before the city elections, Robert Healy and Martin Nolan collaborated in an article on the New York mayoralty campaign, to say: "The election issues here are the same as those in other big cities and the combined results may tell whether the spectre of 'law and order' as a mindless slogan has any future." This slogan was being worked hard by numerous of the Boston candidates for city council and the school committee.

That day the Globe also put out a 24-page magazine on "The Drug Scene," with articles by Herbert Black, Carl Cobb, Richard Knox, Jean Dietz, Phyllis Coons, and Ray Richards of the staff and illustrations by ten Globe photographers.

In November 1969 Richard Connolly, of the city staff, achieved for the Globe a coup in the annals of crime by turning up George Brady, whose six-year disappearance had become a local Judge Crater case. Brady, chairman of the Massachusetts Parking Authority (created to build the Boston Common Garage), had been charged along with others in stealing some $750,000 in the garage construction. He dropped out of sight in 1963, the day before he was to have appeared before a grand jury. Associates were convicted. Six years later Connolly got on Brady's track, followed him from one hideout to another, caught up with him, and directed police to his arrest. Brady was returned to Massachusetts, tried and convicted.

Richard Connolly was one of a very few reporters with such a free-wheeling assignment that he could keep in touch with a George Brady case and follow up any leads, in between more immediate investigations. He had been part of the Globe team that explored every aspect of the Morrissey case in 1965. He dug into the school committee no-bid contracts in the 1969 election. He won the AP award for his coverage of the electric power blackout in 1965 and the national Tom Stokes award for a nine-part series on the regional problem of New England's high electric rates in 1966.

A native of Haverhill, where he had started in newspaper work, Connolly came to the Globe in 1963 after a dozen years on the Post and the Herald.

A few months later another reporter's detective work had the opposite result — to free a man jailed on charge of participation in a $100,000 robbery. The family of Arthur Gautier persuaded the Globe's criminal courts reporter, Robert E. Walsh, that there was a question as to Gautier's identity with the crime. While Gautier remained in jail on double $20,000 surety bonds, Walsh investigated leads that rounded up half a dozen people who could testify to attending a party with Gautier at the time of the robbery. When this was reported to the Suffolk County district attorney, he assigned a detective to check on Walsh's investigation. The district attorney then went before a grand jury with the facts, to obtain a "no bill" verdict. Gautier was freed February 19, 1970, after three weeks in jail.

Titles

A proliferation of titles has marked the Globe's last decade. Titles were scarce 30 years ago. Managing editor, city editor, Sunday editor, day and night editor, night city editor. Hardly anyone else had a title. There was no formal classification, as between reporters and rewrite men, and practically no specialist beyond the traditional political editor and the financial editor. The city staff would specialize as occasion required.

Unionization of the news department started differentiation. Rewrite men came into a top pay scale above reporters — so naturally the top reporters were classified as "rewrite men." The office became more conscious of this function and applied it more. Executives were exempt from union membership; so naturally the management classified as many as possible as executives.

Increased size and complexity of the paper kept calling for more coordination. To call the managing editor "executive editor" was a way of promotion. It also added to the number of executives for decision, judgment, and supervision, and opened the way to recognize the younger men moving into key places. But by 1960 policy was itself a decisive factor in applying titles. As Tom Winship moved in, he felt that responsibility should be definitely indicated and that responsibility for the special areas of news should be recognizable to the reader.

An organization chart became essential to an explorer of the Globe's editorial department. At the opening of 1971 it ran like this:

Editor	Thomas Winship
Executive editor	Robert Healy
Managing editor morning	Edward J. Doherty
Managing editor evening	Joseph Dinneen
Assistant to the editor	John Driscoll
Editor, editorial page	Charles Whipple
Associate editors	Otto Zausmer, Ian Menzies
Sunday editor	John Harris
Assistant managing editor	Crocker Snow, Jr.
Assistant managing editor (day desk)	William Waldron
Assistant managing editor (night desk)	William G. Miller
Day editor	James Keddie
Night editor	Frank Grundstrom
Night city editor	John C. Thomas
Day city editor	Wilfrid C. Rodgers
Magazine editor	Robert Levey
National editor	Tom Ryan
Chief Washington correspondent	Martin Nolan
Assistant managing editor for administration	Joseph Doherty
Suburban editor	John C. Burke

Assistant city editor evening	James Monahan, Gail Perrin, Nat Kline
Assistant city editor morning	Timothy Leland, Bruce McCabe, William Buchanan
Executive sports editor	Jerry Nason
Sports editor	Ernie A. Roberts
Arts editor	Gregory McDonald
Book editor	Herbert Kenny
Financial editor	Donald White
Living editor	Gerald D'Alfonso
Society editor	Marjorie Sherman
Travel editor	William A. Davis
Radio-television editor	Elizabeth Sullivan
Librarian	Edward Quill
Executive picture editor	J. Edward Fitzgerald
Training director	Robert A. McLean

Into the Seventies

The opening of 1970 brought a series of changes in key positions that would affect the tone and direction of the paper through that decade and beyond.

The first changes were in the political bureaus. James Doyle left the Washington bureau at the end of 1969 to join the Washington Star. Martin Nolan became bureau chief and Sal Micciche was moved from the State House to Washington. This kept a four-man staff in Washington. Darius Jhabvala made a fifth when he was reassigned from the United Nations to Washington in the summer of 1970. He would cover the State Department, the first specialization in the bureau.

David Wilson, chief of the State House staff, was moved to the editorial page. He recommended a young Associated Press reporter, Charles David Nyhan, Jr., as the ablest reporter in Boston on state politics. Nyhan had done a notable job covering the 1968 presidential campaign with Senator Muskie. He was appointed chief correspondent at the State House. Nyhan was a 1962 graduate of Harvard, where he'd been a varsity linebacker.

POLITICAL CIRCUIT . . . By DAVID NYHAN

The abortion issue

There was little chance that the incoming Massachusetts Legislature would have voted to liberalize abortion restrictions

Hundreds of Massachusetts women ar consulting various pregnancy counsellin services in the state. Massachusetts Blu

Kenneth Campbell, a Yale man, was moved off the night desk to replace Micciche in the state bureau. Campbell had worked on the Washington Star and in the London bureau of UPI before joining the Globe. Another change was at City Hall. Christopher Wallace was assigned there for the morning paper, joining Gerard O'Neill, whose major effort had been diverted to metropolitan affairs. Wallace was only half a year out of Harvard but had learned reporting there with the undergraduate radio station. O'Neill had come on the paper as an office boy four years earlier, had gone through Boston University's journalism program, and had developed as a digging investigative reporter and writer for the Sunday magazine.

A Nolan column became a regular feature of the Sunday editorial page and Wilson did two columns a week for the daily editorial page.

A month after these shifts a major reorganization brought new men to top editorial positions. Ian Menzies precipitated the moves by a desire to be relieved of the managing editorship for what he called a sabbatical year, to explore in depth the crisis in the cities. The management supported this in terms of a year for travel anywhere in America or abroad, at full salary, to write what he found and to return as a senior editor, a new and as yet undefined post whose definition would be left to the way things developed. Menzies' sabbatical was enriched by his appointment as senior consultant at the Harvard-M.I.T. Joint Center for Urban Studies.

Two things were obvious in Menzies' move. He felt tired after five years of executive work. He believed strongly in rotation of such posts, and he was eager to concentrate on the problems of the cities that had become his central concern. But also he was irked at the organizational structure which had diminished the managing editor's role. Under Laurence Winship the managing editor had run the whole paper, daily and Sunday, morning and evening, news, editorials, and features.

Even after the division of the morning and evening papers, Tom Winship as managing editor for morning had broad authority. But with expansion had come further division. The whole area of politics was outside the managing editor's scope — under the political editor, Robert Healy, now also executive editor. Development of the corps of specialists, critics, and columnists took this large area of talent out of the managing editor's orbit. Menzies, a dynamic journalist, had early been conditioned to command in the British Navy. He drove himself and was demanding of his staff, which in 1970 was less amenable to strict discipline than in Al Haviland's day. He was unquestionably irked at the limits within which his own innovations could be applied.

THE NATION . . . By MARTIN F. NOLAN

The Svengali from Te:

WASHINGTON—"John Connally wants to be President of the United States. He could see that the way things are going in his own party that

If his presence in the Cabinet automatically delivers the 26 electoral votes of Texas, then the presence of two other popular ex-governors —

contri
ment.

Bu
ber o

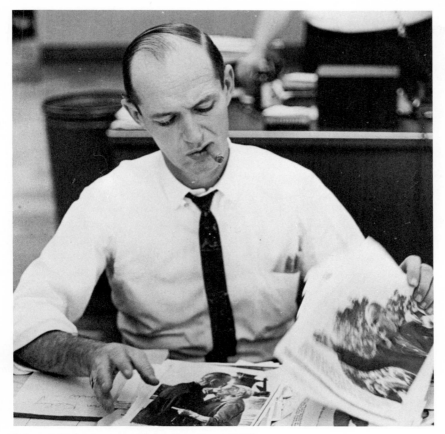

Edward Doherty, managing editor from 1970.

Menzies and Tom Winship were in agreement that the natural successor as managing editor was Edward J. Doherty, who as night editor and assistant managing editor had been shaping the morning paper through most of the sixties.

Now 42, Doherty had come to the Globe at 25 after one year as a reporter on the Post. But he had been shaping up newspapers since his Chelsea High School days as editor of weekly papers first in Chelsea, then in Winthrop. His whole time on the Globe had been on the desk, where he had worked through every position, copy editor, slot man, makeup man, assistant night editor, night editor, then in 1965 assistant managing editor. The night editor was in full charge after the managing editor went home in early evening, so Doherty had already exercised full editorial responsibility. His forte, however, had been in organization of the paper; his talent had long been recognized as an innovator in improving its appearance typographically, in overall design and balance, as well as in news judgment in the selection of page one stories. Also, he had served through the earlier era of warfare between copy desk and composing room and had been influential in working out the cooperative relations that obtained by 1970.

The new assistant managing editor, Crocker Snow, Jr., implied more of a change. Just 29, his appointment at this high level confirmed the editor's commitment to the Youth Movement. Snow was to be a quite different kind of assistant managing

In This Corner

There's Still Only One Pianist Wearing Violet Sequined Suits

editor. Without desk experience, a writer, "an idea man," his role would clearly be in the realm of ideas. Coming to the Globe in 1966 he had covered state politics until in 1968 he'd been given the special assignment to cover the whole university front. At the end of 1969 he had made a tour of Vietnam and Southeast Asia to report on the shape of things in that strategic area. As assistant managing editor, Snow's interests in the intellectual community would supplement Doherty's concern with hard news.

Snow planned to keep up his contact with the universities, to provide more background and analysis of the news, particularly in his own field of foreign affairs. Sunday features would provide the largest opportunity for this, which he hoped to make "more fluid" in relation to news of the week. Within his first fortnight, the Sunday paper of March 1 gave a whole page to assessment of United States foreign policy as defined in the President's State of the World Message. Snow had enlisted five scholars from the local universities to contribute. By April the front page showed the touch of a new hand. Doherty introduced a new light feature story, daily, tucked into the lower righthand corner under a two-column head, "In This Corner."

Other changes in key positions came with the end of the year. Wilfrid C. Rodgers was moved up to city editor of the evening paper as of January 1, 1971. Al Monahan relinquished the city desk to become assistant political editor, a relief for Bob Healy. Arthur Riley retired as aviation editor and James Hammond moved into that spot from the city staff. Robert Levey, who had been education writer and columnist, was appointed editor of the Sunday magazine following William Cardoso who moved on to the morning staff. The aim for the magazine under its new editor was to include a broader range of subjects, to be more oriented to New England, and to have more staff writing.

A reshuffle of the arts department in early 1970 made Gregory McDonald, the op arts critic, arts editor. Herbert Kenny resumed his editorship of the expanding book department. The Herald had just started a new Sunday book section that would step up competition in that department.

McDonald's appointment definitely recognized the newer, changing-frontier forms and attitudes in art. Now 33, he had concentrated on new cultural forms since graduation from Harvard in 1958. He understood the "rock scene," was "the only hip writer on the paper." He had brought op art into the paper and had contributed articles on fringe art forms to the Sunday magazine — one of the elements of appeal to the under-thirty generation that kept the editors in a constant stance of defensive confrontation with the business departments and older executives who could not understand why the magazine had to be full of exotic and ideological jargon they couldn't make head or tail of. The ultimate answer was that the Sunday circulation kept going up. A new generation was tuned in to what looked way out to the business office.

But a concession to conventional views was made on the financial page. David Deitch, whose provocative financial columns challenged orthodox finance, was moved on alternate days to the editorial page, where his ideology would balance off William Buckley. Bruce Davidson, financial editor since 1965, with financial writer Donald White, took on the financial column three days a week.

Another change re-merged the sports departments that had been separated for five years. Ernie A. Roberts' performance as sports editor for the evening paper led to his appointment as sports editor for both papers. Jerry Nason would continue as executive sports editor but freer now for his own column, which with Harold Kaese's had become a primary feature of the sports pages. Roberts brought in David Smith, 32-year-old sports editor from the Miami News, as assistant sports editor for the morning paper, which Smith had soon brought back up to the par that Roberts had established for the evening paper.

The suburban editorships of the two papers were merged under John C. Burke. The other suburban editor, Robert A. McLean, was appointed to a new post as training director. That job would have to evolve, but it was suggestive of a felt need. McLean had had to break in his own suburban reporters, typically new staffers; he had got on well with them and helped develop them. He had a strong feeling about professionalism and was in the office terms "a square" but not rigid. He was president of the New England professional chapter of the journalism society, Sigma Delta Chi, and was himself enrolled in a professional seminar program at the University of Massachusetts, though he'd been nearly 20 years on the Globe.

Crocker Snow's first Sunday Symposium: February 21, 1970.

The Boston Globe　　Saturday, February 21, 1970　　**7**

Three economists present their views ...

One of the most provocative issues of this year and of the forthcoming congressional election is the fight against inflation.

The Administration in Washington is confident it can deal with the rising cost of living and the sliding value of the dollar.

The opposition contends that the President's measures are inadequate.

The public has joined in this big national debate.

The Boston Globe asked three prominent economists to present their views on President Nixon's ability to deal with the menace of inflation. Their opinions are presented on this page.

State of the World message

Can Nixon halt inflation?

PAUL A. SAMUELSON

Must live with creeping inflation

WASHINGTON CIRCUIT
By MATTHEW V. STORIN

What's solution to racial gap?

WASHINGTON — The issue, after this tumultuous week of White House statements and Senate roll calls,

(Paul A. Samuelson is professor of economics at Massachusetts Institute of Technology.)

How can President Nixon end the inflation? Let the answer be given, loud and clear, at the beginning: President Nixon cannot end the current inflation.

All that he can hope to do is (1) keep it from growing worse, and (2) contrive a gradual slowdown of the economy's growth that will bring the 1969 rate of annual price increase of 5 percent down by the end of 1970 to 4 percent.

Then, if his slim margin of Congressional influence should permit it, he might continue his austere program of "blood, sweat and tears" and by the end of 1971 bring the rate of inflation down to

would be simple. The Federal Reserve knows how, as never before, to control the supply of total money; and the President, along with Congress, knows how as never before to engineer fiscal tightness, by raising taxes relative to public expenditures. These two weapons can easily bring down the total of dollar spending. And if, as in the old-fashioned demand-pull case, there were some magic total at which spending becomes excessive and inflationary, the task of the Fed and the Treasury would be a simple one of getting the right dosage:

"To cure simple demand-pull, you just lower total spending until you reach the position of full employment with stable prices and no excessive dollar demand."

Lyndon Johnson's stealthy acceleration of the Vietnam war without daring to raise taxes.

And cost push is the tape worm. If the Fed makes money tight enough to kill off cost push, it will so starve the system of its needed monetary nourishment as to engineer an era of stagnation like that of the Eisenhower years.

Sometimes a gloomy diagnosis calls for desperate surgery. Why not resort to a freeze on wages and prices by law?

Galbraith has long advised this. His "New Industrial State" carries the simple remedy: In war we successfully controlled prices and wages. Peace is no different from war. Ergo the problem is solved by a stroke of the legislative pen.

PROF. SAMUELSON

McLean was to take over the summer training program. He would also be in charge of all recruiting, which had been handled by the editor, managing editors, and city editors. He would have responsibility for the initial training of new staffers. City editors would refer to him staffers who needed help in organizing a story. He'd be playing it by ear. One of his first tasks would be to prepare a new manual of guidelines for Globe style.

McLean had begun as an office boy while a student at Northeastern University under the GI Bill, starting in 1946. The system of alternating periods of study and work had given him two years of part-time work on the Traveler, then two years on the Globe as a student. In 1950 he was graduated onto the Globe staff and under Al Haviland disciplined to the doctrine of fairness, to make sure to give both sides, to keep one's personal bias out of the news. McLean was also impressed with the dynamics of the Globe's young staff.

"Young people are great. They've turned the Globe around the last five years," he said the day after his new appointment. He had no notion of turning them off; "but they can be guided." The way to this he'd have to work out gradually. He is a patient man, and flexible. He hoped that the in-service part of the training program could develop to allow a reporter extra time on some stories, and to give chances for refresher programs such as he had maintained through his summer course and monthly seminars in journalism. He hoped to get the new staffers into professional organizations and involved in professional discussions of journalism. But this would have to work out. He had ready models for neophytes; for such staff craftsmen as Nina McCain, Richard Connolly, and Jeremiah V. Murphy, among others, needed no special license or any appeal to "advocacy" to develop the full dimensions of the story within accepted standards of the news columns.

The Globe's first architecture critic made her debut on the editorial page during a national convention in Boston of the American Institute of Architects in June 1970. Jane Holtz Kay had been contributing for six months to a Sunday column, "Architecture Today," that John Harris had started ten years earlier when Boston began to take urban renewal seriously. A series of architects had contributed to it, but Mrs. Kay's was the first writing from outside the profession.

An honors graduate in history from Radcliffe in 1960, Mrs. Kay had also studied art there and had done her thesis on Lewis Mumford. Starting newspaper work on the Quincy Patriot Ledger, she soon became art critic on the Christian Science Monitor. She then turned from art to the more concrete form of architecture and to free-lance writing in the architectural magazines, where the Globe discovered her work.

The look of the city room was changing. Women were moving out of the special women's departments into the city room and the office was recruiting more black staff.

With the New Year 1970, Otile McManus moved from the Women's Department onto the city staff. Nancy Green, who had been the Globe's first woman sports writer, also joined the news staff. Phyllis Coons came out of the Women's Department to join the education writers, headed by Nina McCain. Mary Sarah King had started a new feature, "Close-up," a weekly profile of a woman of achievement. Elizabeth Jones followed Joyce Dopkeen to be the first Globe women photographers. Virginia Bright and Jane Pierce were doing Sunday features. Sheryl McCarthy,

Mt. Holyoke 1969, joined the staff in January 1970, a short time after Viola Osgood, graduate of the University of Massachusetts; both are black reporters who were in the 1968 training program. Rachelle Patterson was now one of the six suburban reporters. A second fashion writer was added, Sally Robinson, to assist Marian Christy. Mary Meier was shifted from the city staff to Elmer Jones's "Ask the Globe" department. Anne Mary Currier, daughter of a veteran Globe correspondent, covered church news. Carol Liston, first woman reporter in the State House bureau, had been writing politics for several years. Ellen Goodman had won the Women's Press Club top award for 1968.

Other women had become relative veterans. Janet Riddell was a specialist on the urban affairs staff. It was some years since Anne Wyman had become the first woman travel editor, later the first woman editorial writer. Christina Tree was also on travel. Gloria Negri, starting on women's features, had for a decade or more been handling top news assignments. Jean Dietz had filled a variety of assignments over the years before becoming the specialist on mental health.

The Globe still had no full-time women copy editors. They'd managed to hire four women part-time to edit copy certain nights of the week, and Mrs. Margaret Elgin had been holding down a copy desk job two nights a week for four years. But the copy desk appeared to be still the frontier for women in journalism. The Globe already had a black girl on the advertising sales force.

The copy desk now had its first black man, Carl Sims, an experienced copy editor who had come from the Washington Post. Bob McLean alerted the office that he had several "very bright" black students in his summer training program. A new black reporter, Arthur Jones, came on from the Newburyport News.

Other recently recruited male black staff included Thom Shepard and John Robinson, who had come through the summer program from the University of Massachusetts, and Deckle McLean, who came from Ebony Magazine to join the Sunday magazine staff. Robert Jordan had started as a Globe copy boy while a student at Northeastern, then worked a while on the New Haven Register. A native of Roxbury, he'd been a very useful reporter during the 1968 Roxbury riot. Others had come and gone; recruitment had to be continual, for the demand for black talent was brisk in journalism as in other lines.

The Conference

Pulling things together to insure teamwork and coordination in an increasingly complex organization had become a central effort of publishers and editors by 1970. A key to this effort was the conference.

Besides the morning and evening news conferences under the managing editors, and the daily editorial conference, the daily production conference had been instituted. On Monday morning the editor held a conference with the Sunday editor and his top staff to plan the next Sunday paper.

A top-level conference brought publisher, the editor, and key executives together for a breakfast session every other Wednesday. This explored the problems and plans, the difficulties and activities of all departments. Production was always the overwhelming problem, particularly for the big Sunday paper. But the dozen men who came together regularly talked plainly to each other about delays in delivery, bugs in computer operation — all the headaches in publishing that call for attention and action.

The opening conference of January 1970, typical of the fortnightly sessions, brought together Davis Taylor, publisher, John Taylor, president, William O. Taylor, general manager, John Giuggio, business manager, Tom Winship, editor, Jack Reid, advertising manager, Fred O'Neal, circulation director, Frank Freitas, production director, David Stanger, production manager, Robert Ahern, promotion and research director, and John Mullin, assistant controller, sitting in for Albert Holdridge, controller.

At that session John Taylor proposed and all accepted an enlargement of the conference, to include in rotation, two at a time, the second-level executives. These included key men, some of them about to succeed their chiefs, who were approaching retirement. Among them were national advertising manager George McManus, who did become advertising director in June 1970 on Jack Reid's retirement, and John T. Coan, Jr., who became promotion manager at the same time when Robert Ahern took on a newly created post of director of marketing research and planning. Others were Daniel Orr, circulation manager, Richard J. Heyd, computer manager, George L. Hicks, soon to become assistant advertising director, and Richard Ockerbloom, who followed McManus as national advertising manager, Lawrence Healy and Edward Boland in classified, and Charles Bourke in charge of purchasing.

These were men of diverse experience. Dan Orr, now in his forties, had come to Boston from Ireland at 17, had his first job as a Globe office boy for W.O. and Davis Taylor, worked through college in night classes, and grew up in the Globe organization. Jack Coan, Harvard football captain in the class of 1950, a graduate of the Harvard Business School, had come to the Globe in 1959 after six years with the New York advertising agency of McCann-Erickson. Bob Heyd, not yet 40, had come to the Globe with its first computer from the Honeywell organization, seen to its installation, and stayed to manage it.

Charles E. Bourke had come out of the composing room. He was put in charge of the new photocomposition when the Globe started with it, but in the mid-sixties was taken off that to organize the first central purchasing the paper had ever had. Lawrence Healy is a brother of executive editor Robert Healy. Both grew up in the Globe. Their father, John J. Healy, by now 84, had retired in 1969 after 50 years as a Globe mailer — a second career for him that began when he lost his job as a Boston policeman in the 1919 police strike. Albert E. Holdridge became the first Globe controller in 1963. He had been a junior partner in the public accounting firm headed by Thomas J. Brown, Globe auditor for 25 years till his death in 1956. The change in title corresponded to the increased size and complexity of the Globe operation.

Average daily Globe circulation for the six months up to January 1, 1970, was 242,665 morning, 195,227 evening, and 558,931 Sunday.

Increased newspaper prices came with 1970. The Maine dailies went up to 12 cents at the start of the year. The New York Times went up to 15 cents daily and 50 cents Sunday in the spring. In June the Boston Herald Traveler raised its daily price to 15 cents. But the Globe held to ten cents daily, 35 Sunday.

The Globe publisher made a quick calculation: paper at eight cents a pound, four to five pounds in the Sunday paper. "The paper cost of a Sunday Globe is more than the 35 cents we retail it at." The Globe receives 27 cents of the 35-cents Sunday price, 6.8 cents of the ten-cent daily price. In October 1970 the Sunday price was raised to 50 cents, the daily to 15 cents.

The advertising rate was increased an average of ten cents a line January 1, 1970: the general advertising rate rose from $1.70 a line daily and $1.82 Sunday in 1969 to $1.80 daily and $1.92 Sunday.

Advertising linage had increased from a total of 64,115,000 lines in 1968 to 64,790,000 in 1969. Sunday advertising showed the largest increase, up from 21,-176,000 to 22,510,000 lines. The morning paper increase was from 22,570,000 to 22,696,000. But the evening linage was off from 20,369,000 to 19,585,000. Most daily advertising ran both morning and afternoon, but there was clearly a preference for the morning paper with its larger circulation.

The retail rate was lower, $1.30 daily and $1.40 Sunday. Classified advertising was subdivided into a series of rates. The highest was for the largest class, help wanted, $1.85 in 1970; this accounted for 46 percent of all classified. The lowest was for death notices, raised only from 82 to 85 cents a line.

Rates were lower for large-volume contracts, as by department stores and big national advertisers. For over 700,000 lines a year the retail rate of $1.30 daily and $1.40 Sunday was cut to $1.00 daily and $1.07 Sunday. The automobile rate for 200,000 lines was $1.04 instead of $1.60 daily or Sunday. In real estate a contract for 30,000 lines reduced the $1.45 rate to $1.09.

One might expect to multiply total linage by rate and arrive at advertising revenue. But it is more complicated than that. The daily rate is for all day, and most of the linage is duplicated morning and evening. Most national advertising comes through an agency that gets 15 percent commission with two percent more off for cash. So, though the average rate is $1.30 or more a line, the average actual net on advertising the first four months of 1970 was 75.4 cents. This was up from 70.7 cents for all of 1969.

All advertising declined in 1970, as one of the first evidences of recession. The big volume of employment recruitment ads dropped out to reduce total classified linage by 609,000 lines the first half year. In the Sunday paper the reduction in classified was nine percent, but general advertising cut the net loss to one and one-third percent. The Globe's national position actually gained, advancing from fourth to third in classified volume for the half year, according to Media Records.

A Globe reader survey on Wednesday, January 22, 1970, by the Carl J. Nielson Research organization, examined a 54-page morning paper, 58 percent of it advertising, 42 percent editorial and news matter. It found that people liked the improved makeup and that more people were reading deeper into a story than five years before. People were more selective in their reading. The variety of content had its appeal to diverse reading groups. The second section was described as "a real power-house" that had excellent readership: sports, women's news, classified advertising, and comics. The editorial page had "well above average" readership, 42 percent among adults, 10 percent by boys and girls. The impact of the financial page, read by 45 percent of men, 22 percent of women, was "well above average." The op-ed page was described as "a good balance" that had 60 percent reading by men, 59 percent by women, 31 percent by teen-age boys, 38 percent by girls. Its fare that day was Art Buchwald, a cartoon, a humor panel, and columns by political editor Bob Healy, Joseph Alsop, Joseph Kraft, and Evans and Novak. Healy's column had the highest readership.

Sports page readership (73 percent) was just below national average (78 percent) but among boys it had 85 percent to a national average of 75 percent. Harold Kaese's sports column had exceptional readership, 55 percent by men and 58 percent by boys, nearly double the average for a sports column.

Confidential Chat had 60 percent readership, nearly all by women. This compared to 32 percent of men and 41 percent of women who read something in the amusement pages, 27 percent men and 36 percent women who read the radio-television page, 16 percent men and 22 percent women who read the obituaries. Puzzles and games attracted 15 percent men and 17 percent women.

Prominent position in the paper was noted as a factor in readership. The briefs under a page two column, "Names and Faces," had 41 percent men and 48 percent women readers. The weather and the index, both on page one, were read by 29 and 21 percent. But the "Around New England" column, which had been moved further back, had fallen way off to 17 percent men and 14 percent women.

The Globe's 12 comic strips are fewer than the national average of 16. The Smith Family proved most popular with the whole family, but more men read Mutt and Jeff (41 percent to 39 percent for the Smiths). Men proved slightly more addicted to comics than other members of the family. The Smith Family reading was fairly typical: 39 percent men, 34 percent women, 36 percent boys, 38 percent girls.

Cigarettes: Matter of Principle

In the 1950's the Globe, with the media generally, evidenced a nervous reluctance to report the rising agitation over cigarette smoking as a factor in cancer and heart diseases. But as the evidence against the cigarette acquired the authority of government health service studies it forced its way into the news, and by the early 1960's warnings by the Surgeon General were taken in stride, unquestionably news. The evidence was convincing to Davis Taylor, as to many others. It bothered him that advertising to promote cigarette smoking contributed substantially to Globe revenue. When the Federal Communications Commission in early 1969 proposed to ban cigarette advertising from broadcasting, he questioned whether the newspaper had a moral right to profit from a health hazard that might soon be outlawed for television.

On May 1, 1969, a bold face box on the front page stated: "The Boston Globe will cease publication of cigarette advertising when present contracts expire, because accumulated medical evidence has indicated that cigarette smoking is hazardous to health." On March 18, 1970, a front page box announced that no more cigarette advertising would be published.

This was news on the national news wires. When news magazines called up to inquire, they were referred to the publisher. It was perfectly simple to Davis: it's a matter of principle, he said. When they asked what this would cost the Globe in advertising, he was annoyed. You don't measure principles by profits, he said. He expressed to friends a concern over the cynicism of some questioners. "Can't people understand a matter of principle?"

"My father instilled in me a sense of moral responsibility, not only as an individual, but as a publisher," Davis said. "He never joined a church, but he was a man of religious conviction. He would say 'Always tell the truth; then you don't have to remember what you said.'" Davis named his first son, William Osgood Taylor II, for his father.

Davis kept in a desk drawer a number of small slips of paper that his father had had printed at various times when a quotation appealed to him as particularly expressive of the Golden Rule as a way of life. One, undated, is headed "The Globe Principle."

> The Globe policy is to uphold principles and not to tie itself up with personalities, necessarily transient. In fighting men, it would make too many enemies of the measures it advocates day after day, in season and out.
>
> The paper trusts its readers to discern where it stands — for freedom of speech and thought, and against witch hunts and book burners; against turning this into a land of informers, with citizens spying upon one another.
>
> Finally, the Globe perseveres in a good-humored patience with each successive challenger of the American way, in its faith that "they, too, will pass away."

When pushed to defense of principle, Davis would pull out one of these slips and say, "Read that." He would add, "My father was a great man. We forget the restraints on him when he was fighting for the survival of this paper, through years of depression and in intense competition in an overnewspapered town. Now we have a comfortable margin and we can do the things he trained me to believe in."

If electric power interests or public utility commissioners complained to the publisher about Globe criticism of rates and their regulation, Davis would say: "The editorial department stands on its own legs. Take it up with them."

Davis Taylor shares his editor's concern for quality of staff and content of the paper. It was his idea to add a daily book review when only the New York Times and the Herald Tribune had daily book reviews. Winship says that when he proposes a salary offer for a new staffer, Davis is as apt as not to suggest that it ought to be higher.

In the summer of 1969 Davis Taylor enlisted the Globe in a joint program with the Harvard Medical School and the National Health Services on "Medicine for the Ghettos." The three institutions shared the costs of a three-day conference at Wentworth-by-the-Sea, in New Hampshire. They invited 30 participants — medical school deans, leaders in public health, representatives of the black community in Boston, labor and industry figures.

The conference united in recommendations for a national health insurance program and for a national health corps. They urged the federal government to coordinate the efforts of its various health agencies for operation of neighborhood health centers, and that federal subsidies to limit food production be reallocated to a campaign on hunger and malnutrition.

At the opening session Davis Taylor said some might wonder why the Globe should involve itself in a program to bring health services to the poor of the cities. "One reason for our participation is the overwhelming importance of the topic. Another is the fact that whatever solutions are proposed here will require broad public support if they are to be implemented. We believe that the Globe as a sponsor has a role to play, in the process of public education about the significant issues of our time. The public wants to understand the nature and scope of the problem and to realize that something can be done about it."

Colby College, awarding an honorary degree to Davis Taylor June 2, 1968, cited the role of the Globe after a dozen years of his management. The citation read:

> William Davis Taylor: Member of a distinguished newspaper family, you followed two earlier generations by becoming publisher of the Boston Globe 13 years ago.
>
> Under your steady judgment and uncompromising honesty, this newspaper, now nearly a century old, has done much more than simply exist, in itself a formidable task in this difficult age. The Globe has continued to serve its growing metropolitan community with integrity and fairness. Behind every worthy newspaper is a newspaperman who creates this worthiness through devotion to the finest traditions of journalism.
>
> Under your leadership the Globe has fought incompetence, corruption and injustice, as your Pulitzer Prize in 1965 acknowledged. The conscience and quality of the editorial page, the expanded coverage of cultural events demonstrate your vision.
>
> In your long career with the Globe since finishing Harvard in 1931, you have found time to lead a fund-raising campaign for a fine New England secondary school, to serve your own profession by leading a comparable campaign for the Nieman Fellows Program, and to participate in innumerable civic, cultural and social enterprises, including a trip to Selma, Alabama.
>
> Your commitment to society and to your profession is revealed in the journalistic excellence that you have helped the Globe attain.

A matter of principle or a matter of taste made the Globe conspicuous among newspapers on August 9, 1970, when it refrained from using any pictures of the Kennedy families as they took 16-year-old Robert Kennedy, Jr., and his cousin Sargent Shriver, Jr., to Barnstable juvenile court to answer charges of attending a marijuana party. The families had been surrounded, followed, and jostled by a swarm of press and television photographers. The Herald Traveler ran a whole page of the pictures. The New York Times ran two two-column pictures. The Globe made no mention of the absence of pictures in its report; but on the op-ed page it ran a piece by its reporter on the story, Andrew F. Blake, "Newsmen Behaved Badly Toward Kennedys," that scathingly described an "unruly and ill-mannered mob" of pushing, yelling, jostling cameramen harassing the Kennedys in conduct "that far exceeded the bounds of competitive zeal."

Letters to the editor (ten of the 11 letters of August 13) asked the Globe why the stories on the Kennedys should not have been omitted as well as the pictures, and why the names of the other juveniles involved were not printed.

The same week a Senate committee heard testimony that called in question the nutritional value of popular brands of dry breakfast cereals. The big food companies put on expert witnesses to rebut the criticism and defend their products. One was a professor of nutrition at the Harvard School of Public Health who also did a syndicated food column that had its start in the Globe. Under committee questioning, he said that his consulting fees from the cereal companies were considerably less than his Harvard salary and that the $40,000 of annual company contributions to his research had no "strings" attached.

On August 12 in an op-ed column Carl Cobb, medical writer, commented that the circumstances raised doubts as to the professor's impartiality; he deplored the loss to the public of such experts if their impartiality could not be assured. At the instance of Cobb and several of his staff colleagues, the Globe quietly dropped the nutritionist's column.

Spotlight and Self-Examination

The Globe opened 1971 by plunging into three of the most controversial issues: abortion, marijuana, and a national health scheme.

Bills in the legislature for repeal of laws against abortion brought a denunciation by the new Catholic archbishop, Humberto Medeiros, and rejoinders from Protestant and Jewish leaders. The Globe featured letters pro and con and on Sunday, January 10, devoted a full page to "Abortion: The Conflict of Opinion." Religion editor George M. Collins opened the discussion, writing that "Abortion, like birth control, is a political, religious subject in the Bay State." Dr. Robert Nelson Weed, president of the Unitarian Universalist Association, presented the case for repeal and the Reverend James A. O'Donohoe, professor of moral theology at St. John's Seminary, the case against.

The marijuana issue was explored by a team of five medical and science writers for a series of six page-long articles. They found that medical evidence failed to support a physical hazard from marijuana and that young people widely regarded the agitation and harsh penalties as an antiyouth attitude. Their conclusion was that marijuana should be licensed for sale under government control as liquor is in package stores.

In an editorial that followed, on January 11, the Globe stopped short of supporting licensing but backed legislation to remove harsh penalties and to treat possession and use as "minor infractions."

At this point David Taylor, reporter son of the Globe president, aligned himself with the "advocacy" journalists in an op-ed column February 17 that criticized the Globe for failing to support editorially the recommendation of its medical reporters for licensing the sale of marijuana. The editorial statement that the public were not

Wilfrid Rodgers, city editor from 1971.

ready for it was, in Taylor's view, a lame excuse for failing to lead the public in what he felt the Globe investigation had demonstrated to be the sound approach.

The week after the marijuana series Ian Menzies contributed six page-length articles on "The Coming Debate: National Health Service."

The next big issue explored was the President's proposal for federal revenue-sharing with the hard-pressed states and cities. Articles were secured from Governor Nelson Rockefeller, in favor, and Representative Wilbur Mills, against, for the Focus Page of Sunday, January 31. The Globe shared this with the five other papers in the combination called "The Million Market Papers" that for five years had joined in advertising promotion. Their editors held a conference at the end of 1970 and agreed on an exchange of features. This was the Globe's first major contribution; the other papers are the Baltimore Sun, Milwaukee Journal, Philadelphia Bulletin, Detroit News, and St. Louis Globe-Democrat.

Ian Menzies returned from his sabbatical in February 1971 as associate editor for news management. He continued his own specialty with a Thursday column on cities. His larger role was to work on improvements in the paper, and his first assignment was the financial pages — to restore the lively quality that he had introduced as financial editor eight years earlier. Next on his schedule was the sports department, whose opposite problem was that of being too lively and taking a disproportionate amount of the tight space in the paper. Without de-emphasizing the Globe's strong interest in sports, the need was to bring its space demands within bounds.

Menzies' return coincided with a major innovative shift that brought on a woman as assistant city editor and a man in charge of what historically had been a woman's preserve, the Living Section. Gail Perrin was moved into a key role in the city room, to bring a woman's point of view to the news in the evening paper. To replace her in charge of the Living Section, which had developed from the earlier Women's Department, Gerald D'Alfonso was appointed. A talented copy editor, he had shaped the new sections on women's affairs. The move underscored a policy change: the Living Section was to broaden its outlook and content for all the family. On the editorial page, Beatson Wallace was made assistant editor.

Another name change meant to demonstrate an enlarged dimension replaced Education as the title of a new Sunday section with Learning. The section was no longer to deal only with school and college.

"Spotlight," first product of a new investigating team, had its debut Sunday, September 27, 1970, with an investigation of the ten-year monopoly of a Boston Redevelopment Authority parking area in the West End, awarded without bids at a phenomenally low rent. The story opened with the news that Mayor Kevin White, on learning of the Globe's investigation, was demanding that the BRA open the parking lot concession to bids. At the end of the investigation the mayor ordered the parking lot closed. A new city garage would meet the parking need.

On February 11 the Spotlight was turned on suburban Somerville for a two-week series that exposed the mulcting of the city by corrupt relations of politicians with favored contractors. Through the 1960's $4.3 millions had been spent on illegal no-bid purchases from five politically connected contractors — "a classic story of political favoritism in a city where the funneling of public funds to a favored few has become a way of life," as the Globe described it.

A quarter million went to a single plumbing contractor within five years for no-bid purchases. The city was paying retail prices for plumbing supplies of this magnitude, but paying in a steady stream of bills under $1,000, the legal limit for purchases or work without bids.

By the time Somerville voters elected a reform mayor in 1969 the cupboard was bare and the city in debt $6.5 millions, though its tax rate had reached $169; and the city was in frightful physical shape.

Before the Globe series ended, Mayor Ralph fired the city auditor and called a mass meeting of Somerville citizens, who demanded an investigation by the Attorney General. A few days later the Attorney General called a press conference to announce that an investigation was already in process.

Innovations in early 1971 included devoting page two of the Sunday paper entirely to environment — Crocker Snow's idea; adding a full page of Letters to the Editor starting twice a month — David Wilson's proposal; and eliminating engagement pictures and stories from the society pages, to run only a standard list of engagement announcements.

The tight space problem was increased with the recession's effect on advertising. January 1971 saw the average size of the Sunday paper down to 295 from 304 pages of January 1970, and the morning paper cut from 44 to 42 pages.

Figures for the first quarter of 1971 showed the advertising linage further reduced, down 5.8 percent under 1970 figures. Total linage in the first three months was down from 13,862,290 for the 1970 first quarter to 13,056,556 for January–February–March 1971. For the Sunday the decrease was 6.3 percent; for the morning off 7.4 percent; there was less of a drop in the evening, 3.2 percent.

Two women experienced in minority group relations joined the staff at this time. To assist Dexter Eure as community affairs director, Anne Kirchheimer was recruited to work with Spanish speaking groups. She had a master's degree in urban affairs at Boston University, had served in the Peace Corps in Puerto Rico, done social work in South America, taught Spanish at the Martin Luther King School in Roxbury, and served as administrative assistant to the Model Cities organization in Boston.

To replace Alan Lupo, who joined the Boston public television staff, Kay Long-cope, executive director of the Inter-Faith Church Organization in New York, was appointed to head the urban affairs group.

New bylines attracting recognition for the quality of their writing in 1970–71 included Tom Oliphant, Andrew Blake, and David Taylor of the general staff, and in the political field David Nyhan at the State House and Darius Jhabvala at the State Department. The paper found increasing occasion to feature the work of such specialists as Nina McCain in education, Carl Cobb in medicine, and Victor McElheny in science.

When Senator Edmund Muskie traveled to Vietnam, the Middle East, Germany, and Russia in January as preparation for presidential candidacy, Richard Stewart of the Washington bureau went with him. In April Stewart resigned to join Muskie's campaign organization as press chief.

In June the Globe was one of three American newspapers, with the New York Times and Washington Post, engaged in fighting the government through the courts on the right to publish secret Pentagon studies on the American involvement in Vietnam.

The editor had to continue to cope with pressure for advocacy journalism. Early in 1970 a staff delegation urged a "Reporters' Page" where writers could give their own impressions of the news they covered. He rejected this but offered to open the Opinion Page three days a week to columns by younger staffers.

Out of such confrontation came the editor's idea of a three-day "think tank" at the suburban estate of the American Academy of Arts and Sciences. Publishers, editors, and some 100 of the staff joined in workshops to hash over problems and suggestions.

The editor came out of this with four typed pages for "Actions" that were followed through in the following months. One sore point was copy editing, and a new rule was adopted that before changing a story the copy editor was to consult the reporter. To improve communications a standing committee of the staff was set up to bring staff views to the editors: Nina McCain, Ellen Goodman, Tom Oliphant, Richard Connolly, and Dexter Eure.

A monthly luncheon was instituted of editors with staff representatives. A weekly meeting of editors and specialists was initiated. The Sunday feature conference was expanded to all editors, and from it came assignments of all features for the week.

The number one problem was the tight news space. Management could not promise more until business picked up. But five columns of syndicated material were cut to make more space for staff writing. The size of heads was reduced. A more rigorous move was made to exclude business "readers"; any such would require initialing by the assistant to the editor. Op-ed space was pre-empted for a staff column three days a week and a weekly column to be rotated among four black writers.

A committee was appointed for improvement of the Saturday paper. The thin weekend staff was strengthened. One reporter was added to the suburban staff of each paper. Complaints of the multiplying typographical errors and pieing of type led to a summit conference with production and composing room chiefs. The editor said the result was the cleanest paper in ten years. The publisher's contribution to the "Actions" budget was a single line: "Davis Taylor urges the staff to strive for more accuracy in our writing and reporting."

In Perspective

This account of one newspaper has been written in years of crisis challenging historic concepts of journalism, as of all institutions. Its chief problem has been to find perspective for these latest years of change. Instant history loses in perspective what it may claim of contemporaneity.

The Globe has been well in advance of all but a very few newspapers in recognizing and adapting to the dynamics of its times. The dilemma of the editor over "participatory journalism" is suggestive of the issues and problems of the newspaper, both internally and as a civic voice, that will pose questions of the future, both in communications and throughout a society in transition.

Appendixes List of Sources Index

Appendix A   Morgan Letters

Davis Taylor found and sent me these letters from James Morgan, written between ages 86 and 93. The letter to William O. Taylor was written in the last months of both their lives. The two letters to Davis Taylor, one at 86 and one at 90, in similar vein, appreciate the quality of the three publishers in Mr. Morgan's tenure.

HOTEL GREEN
Pasadena 17, California

Eighth of January, 1955

My dear Chief [W.O.T.]: —

On this anniversary of Jackson's victory at the Battle of New Orleans, I salute in honor and affection one whose character is as strong as old hickory.

In turning my mechanized calendar to 1955, I looked backward to New Year's in 1884, when I came on the Globe, and I congratulated myself that, in this world of chance, my lines should have fallen in such pleasant places. In the perspective of those one and seventy years passed in a cloudless association with three generations of your family, I am impressed by the unbroken continuity of the spirit of your father, as the rudder of our good ship has passed from one to another filial hand.

As the builder of the Globe, Charles H. Taylor built himself into its very structure, with his clean nature, his integrity, his sense of honor, tolerance, fair play, with his sympathetic understanding of all sorts and conditions of men gained in his own struggle upward. Those qualities, with his single hearted enthusiasm for the business and the art of newspaper making, inspired and still inspires us of the Globe and the readers as well to look upon it as "our paper." There is the key to its strength after more than four score years. This remains a priceless asset.

Trained by that mastercraftsman, you, my beloved William O., my friend since long, long ago, have communicated to us and the reading public the same feeling of loyalty to the Globe. It is a fitting capstone for your career that you should have reared a son who has won for Davis Taylor the confidence and good will of the entire staff.

Mrs. Morgan and I are gladdened by the good news of you that is relayed to us. I am looking forward on my return to seeing you back in your old familiar corner. [But neither returned — L.M.L.]

With my gratitude and love,

[signed] James Morgan

HOTEL GREEN
PASADENA 15, CALIFORNIA

March 4, 1947.

Dear Davis: —

'Tis sweet to be remembered when far from home. Mrs. Morgan shares my appreciation of your thoughtfulness in writing that note of commendation for the Globe's birthday cake which she helped me concoct. If my penmanship were as good as yours I would not have her type this acknowledgment.

Your remark that you wished the General could read the page gives me a fair chance to get off my chest my first and lasting impression of you. It is that certain qualities of your grandfather have been transmitted to you. Like him, you would rather pat a man on the back than kick him in the pants and you are more interested in getting things in than in keeping things out of the paper. Your mind, like his, is ready for change and for experiment with something different.

Your affirmative temper, like his, was the trait earliest to register with me. This was welcome not to me alone but even more to younger men who were starting their lives with their future and the future of their families bound up in the fortunes of the Globe. It was hailed as a promise that the friendship and leadership of the Taylor management and the progress of the paper would continue in the third generation. Whatever friction there has been was not due, I truly believe, to any personal antagonism but rather to a widespread readjustment of relations between employers and employees.

An affectionate remembrance for you and dear Mrs. Taylor and for your father from both of us.

James Morgan

16 Prescott Road
Lynn Massachusetts

29 July 1952

Dear Davis: I like to infer from your signature on the extra check, which gladdens my Chancellor of the Exchequer as well as me, that you are joining your father in an appreciation of my job. If that inference be correct, and I am sure it is, I prize it as a pat on the back by a third generation of the Taylors. The first was an unexpected mark up of my salary by your grandfather after he and I had sat up days and nights watching the returns from the doubtful election of 1884. (A)

I trust you know how unanimous and warm the verdict is in your favor up stairs.

To a beloved son of a beloved father my gratitude for a friendship that means more to me than checks, handy as they are.

James Morgan

(A) Cleveland won by *1060* plurality in New York!

Appendix B   The Board

In a family corporation families tend over the years either to die out or to proliferate; either way the tendency is to reduce the continuity of control. These aspects of our common mortality account for the rarity of newspapers that have remained more than two generations under the control of the heirs of the founder.

The Boston Globe has had an extraordinary experience of continuity. Stock ownership was almost entirely in the hands of Eben Jordan and General Taylor as long as these men lived. In the early years they usually added to the board of directors their lawyer, some very minor stockholder, and some nominal figure, such as "Uncle Ned" Prescott, Globe cashier. After General Taylor's sons Charles H., Jr., and William O. Taylor came into the business, they assumed places on the board.

In 1895, the year that Eben Jordan died, the directors were Jordan, the three Taylors, and the Jordan counsel. Even as a director Mr. Jordan had, on occasions when the General needed it, given him his proxy. The two men in their wills each provided for three trustees and stipulated that, on the death of one, the two surviving trustees should choose a third, to make each trust self-perpetuating.

After Eben Jordan's death his son of the same name took his place, and when the second Eben Jordan died in 1916 the only change was that his son, Robert Jordan, succeeded. On the death of General Taylor in 1921 the Globe counsel, Frederick E. Snow, was elected to the vacancy. In the following decades the board, usually of five, was made up of William O. and Charles H. Taylor, Robert Jordan until his death in 1932, one other Jordan trustee, and the Globe counsel.

When Charles H. Taylor resigned as Globe treasurer in 1937, William O.'s son Davis was elected in his uncle's place on the board. In 1949 Ralph Lowell, Boston banker and civic leader, was added to the board, joining Sidney W. Davidson, New York lawyer, as trustee of the Jordan estate. In 1954, the year before the death of William O. Taylor, his nephew John I. Taylor was elected treasurer and a director. Francis T. Leahy, Globe counsel, was the sixth member.

On William O.'s death in 1955 the remaining five constituted the board. In 1959 the board was increased to seven with William O. Taylor II and Robert T. H. Davidson added. On Mr. Davidson's resignation in 1960 Neil Leonard, Boston lawyer, Colby College trustee, and civic leader, was elected. Francis Leahy died in 1962 and the next year Philip S. Weld, publisher of newspapers in Gloucester, Newburyport and Beverly, was added to the board — the first newspaperman outside the Taylor family, an addition of a lively, creative journalistic mind.

A further enlargement and enlivening element was the election in 1966 of Hartford Gunn, who as general manager of Boston's educational television station WGBH (Channel 2), had already proved to be one of the most dynamic and successful of educational broadcasters.

On Neil Leonard's death in 1968 Robert Haydock, Jr., Globe counsel, was added to the directors, and in 1969 the board elected Roland D. Grimm of New York, treasurer of Yale, which had benefited from his financial acumen.

Yale Provost Charles H. Taylor, Jr., fourth of the name, was elected to the board in 1970.

Composition of the board was simplified after 1967; for there was no longer occasion to have the General Taylor estate represented. The General Taylor trust was to terminate upon the death of the last child of the General. This was Mrs. Grace Armstrong, who died in 1967. The 16 surviving Taylor family heirs then agreed to set up a voting trust to coincide with termination of the Eben D. Jordan, Sr., trust, 20 years after the death of the only surviving grandchild of Eben D. Jordan.

The Taylor voting stock trustees in 1969 were Davis Taylor, John Taylor, Charles H. Taylor, Alexander Hawes (son-in-law of Mrs. Armstrong), and Evans Pillsbury (son of the late Mrs. Horace Pillsbury, the General's other daughter). Davis and John Taylor represented the Taylor trust on the Globe board.

The Jordan estate trustees in 1969 were Ralph Lowell, Sidney Davidson, and Davis Taylor, all three Globe directors.

MEMBERS OF THE BOARD

The Globe directors over the century span have been the following:

Globe Publishing Company (1872–1878)

February 7, 1872: nine directors elected
 M. M. Ballou
 Lewis Rice
 Eben D. Jordan
 Cyrus Wakefield
 S. R. Niles
 Seman Klous
 M. R. Ballou
 S. A. Carlton
 H. E. Townsend

December 10, 1873: voted that board shall consist of not more than seven nor less than five members

March 3, 1874: six directors elected
 H. E. Townsend
 S. R. Niles
 Lewis Rice
 Eben D. Jordan
 Edwin M. Bacon
 Charles H. Taylor

November 10, 1874: H. E. Townsend resigned

March 2, 1875: five directors elected
 Eben D. Jordan
 S. R. Niles
 Lewis Rice (died 1877)

Edwin H. Bacon
Charles H. Taylor

March 5, 1878: five directors elected
S. R. Niles
Osborne Howes, Jr.
Edwin H. Bacon
Eben D. Jordan
Charles H. Taylor

Globe Newspaper Company (formed 1878)

January 30, 1878: three directors elected
Edward Prescott
Charles H. Taylor
Francis A. Nichols

February 3, 1879: number of directors increased to seven
James McCormick
Edward Prescott
Francis A. Nichols
Charles H. Taylor
Jonas H. French
William Taylor
Abner R. Tucker

February 11, 1884: seven directors elected
Edward Prescott
Prentiss Webster
Jonas H. French
Charles H. Taylor
William Taylor
Francis A. Nichols
Abner R. Tucker

February 9, 1885: seven directors elected
Edward Prescott
Jonas H. French
William Taylor
Charles H. Taylor
Francis A. Nichols
Herbert Dumaresq
James C. Jordan

February 11, 1889: amendment reduced number of directors to five
Charles H. Taylor
Eben D. Jordan

Edward Prescott
Francis A. Nichols
Herbert Dumaresq

February 13, 1893: five directors elected
Eben D. Jordan
Herbert Dumaresq
Francis A. Nichols
Charles H. Taylor
Charles H. Taylor, Jr.

February 19, 1894: five directors elected
Eben D. Jordan
Charles H. Taylor
Herbert Dumaresq
Charles H. Taylor, Jr.
William O. Taylor

November 15, 1895: Eben D. Jordan died

February 10, 1896: five directors elected
Eben D. Jordan (formerly Jr.)
Charles H. Taylor
Henry G. Nichols
Charles H. Taylor, Jr.
William O. Taylor

February 11, 1901: five directors elected
Eben D. Jordan
Charles H. Taylor
R. M. Saltonstall
Charles H. Taylor, Jr.
William O. Taylor

August 1, 1916: Eben D. Jordan died

February 12, 1917: five directors elected
Charles H. Taylor
Richard M. Saltonstall
Charles H. Taylor, Jr.
William O. Taylor
Robert Jordan

June 22, 1921: Charles H. Taylor died; Frederick E. Snow elected July 6 to fill vacancy [Mr. Snow, of Gaston, Snow, & Saltonstall, was Globe counsel throughout his directorship]

April 17, 1922: Richard M. Saltonstall died; W. F. Bentinck-Smith elected June 19 to fill vacancy

August 30, 1924: W. F. Bentinck-Smith died

January 12, 1925: five directors elected
 Charles H. Taylor
 Robert Jordan
 William O. Taylor
 Frederick E. Snow
 Matthew C. Armstrong (resigned April 26, 1925; Edward F. McClennen elected to vacancy)

January 11, 1926: five directors elected
 Charles H. Taylor
 Robert Jordan
 William O. Taylor
 Frederick E. Snow
 Edward F. McClennen

November 2, 1932: Robert Jordan died

March 20, 1933: five directors elected
 Charles H. Taylor
 William O. Taylor
 E. Gerry Chadwick
 Frederick E. Snow
 Edward F. McClennen

April 3, 1935: John C. Rice elected to fill vacancy caused by death of Frederick E. Snow on March 5

September 29, 1937: Charles H. Taylor resigned as treasurer and director

October 8, 1937: at special meeting, William Davis Taylor elected treasurer and director to fill vacancy

January 10, 1938: five directors elected
 Edward F. McClennen
 John C. Rice
 E. Gerry Chadwick (died March 23, 1945)
 William O. Taylor
 William Davis Taylor

January 14, 1946: five directors elected
 Edward F. McClennen
 John C. Rice

William O. Taylor
William Davis Taylor
Katharine F. White

May 6, 1946: Katharine F. White resigned as director; Sidney W. Davidson elected to fill vacancy

July 2, 1948: Edward F. McClennen died

January 10, 1949: amendment decreased number of directors to four
William O. Taylor
Wm. Davis Taylor
Sidney W. Davidson
John C. Rice (died January 27, 1949)

February 7, 1949: Francis T. Leahy elected to vacancy

April 18, 1949: number of directors increased by one; Ralph Lowell elected as fifth

January 9, 1950: five directors elected
William O. Taylor
Wm. Davis Taylor
Sidney W. Davidson
Francis T. Leahy
Ralph Lowell

January 27, 1954: number of directors increased by one; six directors elected
William O. Taylor
Wm. Davis Taylor
Sidney W. Davidson
Ralph Lowell
Francis T. Leahy
John I. Taylor

July 15, 1955: William O. Taylor died

January 23, 1956: five directors elected
Wm. Davis Taylor
Francis T. Leahy
Ralph Lowell
Sidney W. Davidson
John I. Taylor

January 15, 1959: number of directors for ensuing year fixed at seven; seven directors elected
Ralph Lowell
Sidney W. Davidson

Wm. Davis Taylor
Robert T. H. Davidson
Francis T. Leahy
John I. Taylor
William O. Taylor II

May 19, 1960: resignation of Robert T. H. Davidson accepted; Neil Leonard elected to fill vacancy

January 9, 1961: seven directors elected
Ralph Lowell
Sidney W. Davidson
Wm. Davis Taylor
Neil Leonard
Francis T. Leahy
John I. Taylor
William O. Taylor II

February 13, 1962: Francis T. Leahy died

January 17, 1963: number of directors fixed at six for ensuing year; six directors elected
Ralph Lowell
Sidney W. Davidson
Wm. Davis Taylor
John I. Taylor
Neil Leonard
Philip S. Weld

June 29, 1966: special meeting; voted to increase number of directors to serve for the remainder of 1966 from six to seven; Hartford Gunn elected seventh

January 19, 1967: seven directors elected
Ralph Lowell
Sidney W. Davidson
Wm. Davis Taylor
John I. Taylor
Neil Leonard
Philip S. Weld
Hartford Gunn

September 15, 1968: Neil Leonard died; Robert Haydock, Jr., elected September 18 to fill vacancy

January 15, 1969: number of directors fixed at not less than three, nor more than eight; eight directors elected
Wm. Davis Taylor
John I. Taylor

Sidney W. Davidson
Philip S. Weld
Ralph Lowell
Hartford Gunn
Robert Haydock, Jr.
Roland D. Grimm

June 17, 1970: at special meeting of stockholders, Charles H. Taylor, Jr. (fourth of the name) elected a director

Appendix C   Editors and Publishers

Globe publishers, editors, and key executives since 1872 are listed in chronological order under each position.

Publishers

Charles H. Taylor	1873–1921
William O. Taylor	1921–1955
William Davis Taylor	1955—

Presidents

Charles H. Taylor	1873–1921
William O. Taylor	1921–1955
William Davis Taylor	1955–1963
John I. Taylor	1963—

Treasurers

Charles H. Taylor	1878–1892
Charles H. Taylor, Jr.	1892–1937
William Davis Taylor	1937–1955
John I. Taylor	1955–1963
William O. Taylor II	1963—

Editors

Maturin Ballou	1872–1873
Edwin M. Bacon	1873–1878
Edwin C. Bailey	1878–1880
Charles H. Taylor	1880–1921
William O. Taylor	1921–1955
Laurence L. Winship	1955–1965
Thomas Winship	1965—

General Managers

William Davis Taylor	1941–1955
William O. Taylor II	1969—

Business Managers

Charles H. Taylor, Jr.	1892–1910
William O. Taylor	1910–1921
Charles H. Taylor	1921–1937
William Davis Taylor	1937–1941
Patrick J. Flaherty	1954–1965
William O. Taylor II	1965–1969
John P. Giuggio	1969—

Advertising Managers

Edward F. Dunbar	1905–1928

Charles Wright   1929–1938
John F. Reid, Sr.   1938–1970
George McManus   1970—

Circulation Managers
Thomas Downey   1878–1918
Walter Hartwell   1918–1925
Frank Perkins   1925–1935
Robert McCance   1935–1940
Frederick J. O'Neal   1940—   (director 1964—   )
Daniel Orr   1964—

Controller
Albert E. Holdridge   1963—

Promotion Managers
Harold J. Stanton   1937–1939
Andrew Carmichael   1939–1941
Charles F. Morse, Jr.   1941–1948
John I. Taylor   1948–1955
R. L. M. Ahern   1955–1970
John T. Coan, Jr.   1970—

Director of Marketing Research and Planning
R. L. M. Ahern   1970—

Executive Editors
Victor O. Jones   1962–1965
Alexander J. Haviland   1965–1969
Robert Healy   1969—

Managing Editors
Clarence S. Wason   1873–1878
Edmund Hudson, Jr.   1878
Leonard B. Brown   1878
Benjamin P. Palmer   1878–1884
A. A. Fowle   1884–1926
William D. Sullivan   1926–1937
Laurence L. Winship   1937–1955
Victor O. Jones   1955–1962
Thomas Winship   1962–1965
Alexander J. Haviland   1962–1965 (evening)
Ian Menzies   1965–1970
Joseph Dinneen, Jr.   1965—   (evening)
Edward J. Doherty   1970—   (morning)

Night Managing Editors
Willard DeLue   1939–1946
Victor O. Jones   1946–1955

*Editorial Page Editors**

Michael Curran	1881–1883
Allen Kelly	1884–1885
James W. Clarke	1885–1892
James Morgan	1892–1926
Laurence L. Winship	1926–1959
James H. Powers	1959–1962
Charles Whipple	1962—

Associate Editors

Clement H. Hammond	1885–1888
Otto Zausmer	1958—
Ian Menzies	1971—

Editorial Pointers

William H. Hills	1902–1928
Carlyle Holt	1928–1937
Frank P. Sibley	1937–1944
Donald B. Willard	1944—

City Editors

Clarence S. Wason	1872–1873
Edward S. Sears	1873–1878
Charles W. Dyar	1879–1881
James P. Frost	1881–1886
Charles H. Montague	1886–1889
William D. Sullivan	1889–1926
George Dimond	1926–1937
Charles A. Merrill	1937–1951
Alexander J. Haviland	1951–1962
Joseph Dinneen, Jr.	1962–1965
Richard Stewart	1965–1967 (morning)
Alfred Monahan	1951–1971 (evening)
Charles Claffey	1967–1968 (morning)
John C. Thomas†	1968— (morning)
Wilfrid C. Rodgers‡	1971 (evening)

Night Editors

Almy Aldrich	1873–1874
Michael Curran	1875–1877
Charles M. Vincent	1877–1879
George B. Perry	1880
Clement H. Hammond	1881
Marshall H. Cushing	1883
Byron A. Somes	1883–1884
William Taylor, Jr.	1887
John N. Taylor	1891

* This title was not used in the Morgan-Winship period.
† On leave for Stanford University journalism fellowship 1971–72
‡ Metropolitan editor 1971— (evening)

Harry Poor	1895–1934
Earle Edgerton	1934–1942
Victor O. Jones	1945–1955
Roy Johnson	1955–1958
Everett Mitchell	1958–1961
Edward Doherty*	1961–1965
John Driscoll	1965–1969
William G. Miller†	1969–1970
Frank Grundstrom	1970—

Day Editors

Byron A. Somes	1883–1884
Edson White	1885–1888
W. F. Kenney	1888–1918
George Gavin	1918–1938
William Jones	1938–1949
Ray Finnegan	1949–1955
William Waldron‡	1955–1965
James Keddie	1965—

Sunday Editors

Michael F. Curran	1877–1883
James Morgan	1883–1895
Edward F. Burns	1895–1914
Thaddeus DeFrieze	1914–1918
Laurence L. Winship	1918–1937
F. Ambler Welch	1937–1945
Willard DeLue	1945–1946
Daniel O'Brien	1946–1962
John Harris	1962—

Washington Correspondents

Edgar H. Luther	1878–1881
James Morgan	1886–1888
Maurice Low	1888–1914
Charles A. Groves	1914–1948
John Harris	1948–1963
Thomas A. Winship	1956–1958
Robert Healy	1958–1962
Wilfrid C. Rodgers	1963–1965
James Doyle	1965–1969
Martin Nolan	1964—
Richard Stewart	1967—
Matthew V. Storin§	1969–1971

* Assistant managing editor 1965–1970
† Assistant managing editor 1970—
‡ Assistant managing editor 1965—
§ Metropolitan editor 1971— (morning)

| Sal Micciche | 1970— |
| Darius S. Jhabvala | 1970— |

Sports Editors

A. A. Fowle	1883–1884
William D. Sullivan	1884–1889
John N. Taylor	1889–1891
Walter S. Barnes, Jr.	1914–1933
Victor O. Jones	1933–1941
Paul Edward (Jerry) Nason*	1941–1970
Ernest A. Roberts	1970—

Women's† Editors

Georgia Hamlen	1877–1879
Florence Finch	1881–1884
Estelle Hatch	1884–1908
Agnes Mahan	1908–1953
Dorothy Crandall	1953–1963
Sumner Barton	1963–1965
Gail Perrin	1965–1971
Gerald D'Alfonso	1971—

Arts Editors

| Herbert Kenny | 1965–1970 |
| Gregory McDonald | 1970— |

Librarians

Henry M. Jarrett	1887–1890
Edson W. White	1890–1894
Laurence E. Boyle	1894–1908
Frank A. Wilson	1908–1911
Esther C. Tomelius	1911–1922
William Alcott	1922–1950
Esther C. Tomelius	1950–1952
Eugene J. Elliott	1952–1959
Mary H. Welch	1959–1966
Edward W. Quill	1966—

Photo-Engraving Department

Morgan Sweeney	1885–1893
John W. Butters	1893–1923
John F. Maguire	1923–1954
Charles W. Gibson	1954–1962
Gerard Hansen	1962—

* Nason continued executive sports editor
† Changed to *Living,* 1968

Production Directors
Frank Freitas	1966–1970
David Stanger	1970—

Production Managers
Frank Freitas	1963–1966
David Stanger	1966—

Plant Engineers
Frank Freitas	1960–1967
Ralph Cataloni	1967—

Composing Room Superintendents
H. Kemble Oliver	1872–1873
Robert P. Boss	1873–1905
Charles Rolfe	1905–1915
Francis X. Rooney	1915–1958
Fred Costello	1958–1970
Joseph Orne	1970—

Press Room Superintendents
J. H. Moody	1872–1898
G. E. Holt	1898–1917
F. F. Flagg	1917–1936
F. L. Fowler	1937–1943
J. O'Brien	1943–1953
J. F. Flagg, Jr.	1953–1964
Frank Duffin	1964—

Stereotype Superintendents
James H. Moody	1872–1898
George E. Holt	1898–1917
Willis B. Chase	1917–1925
Frank O. Bigelow	1930–1947
Elmer O. Hunt	1947–1959
Henry W. Nelson	1959–1962
John D. Fahey	1963–1964
David Stanger	1964–1965
Edward O. Wall	1965—

Mailroom Superintendents
George J. Kelley*	1872–1874
Charles E. Wadleigh*	1874–1926
Patrick Sullivan	1926–1938
Daniel F. O'Brien	1938–1959
Charles E. Greene	1959–1970

* Kelley and Wadleigh overlapped. Both began as part-time mailing clerks, part-time reporters. Kelley moved to full time on news, Wadleigh moved the other way.

Melvin McIntyre   1970
Paul F. McCoy   1970—

Delivery Department Superintendents
Joseph F. Howley, Sr.*   1937–1953
Calvin A. Marble   1953–1967
Arthur F. Rourke   1967–1971
Edward Sullivan   1971—

* Mr. Howley was with the Wilson, Tisdale Company that handled Globe delivery until 1953 when the Globe started its own delivery system.

Appendix D   Awards

The Globe's specialization and its campaigns on public issues have brought it awards in practically every field of journalism in recent years. The Pulitzer gold medal in 1966 was the highest distinction. But the paper has been cited in eight other awards for its day-to-day news coverage, its editorials, and its public service.

In 1958 the paper began keeping a record of awards. In the next ten years it received over 100 editorial awards, more than 80 of them first prizes. Its photographic staff have won over 300 awards, more than 100 of them first prizes.

Each year the Globe received the Sevellon Brown award for public service, six times first prize. The Amasa Howe award went to Globe members five times, the Rudolph Elie award four.

For medical writing Herbert Black and Carl Cobb between them won ten awards in ten years. Paul Connell was named photographer of the year three times in five years by the Boston Press Photographers Association. Marian Christy won ten fashion writing awards in her first three years on the Globe, 1965–1968, several of them major national awards.

The Associated Press has made more than 25 awards to the Globe, a dozen of them first prizes. The United Press International has awarded its first prize to the Globe ten times, besides giving the paper other awards. A special UPI award in 1958 was for the number of series on public affairs the Globe ran in one year; six staff members were cited.

The major awards are listed by years.

AWARDS	RECIPIENTS
Editorial Awards 1958	
UPI Newspaper Editors of Massachusetts (special citation)	The Boston Globe for the number of series within a year on a variety of subjects; six staffers cited
New England Associated Press Managing Editors Association Big City Series	Frances Burns and Ian Menzies for series on public health in Massachusetts
UPI's News Writing Contest	Ian Forman and Ian Menzies
New England Women's Press Association (second place medal)	Marjorie Sherman for reporting the America's Cup Races
National Foundation for Highway Safety (citation)	The Globe for its Sunday roto series on highway safety
Editorial Awards 1959	
Boston Press Club's Rudolph Elie award	Ian Forman and Ian Menzies for series on the University of Massachusetts
UPI Newspaper Editors of Massachusetts	Ian Forman and Ian Menzies for series on the University of Massachusetts

NEAPMEA's Sevellon Brown Memorial Public Service award

The Globe for the most meritorious and distinguished public service

NEAPNEA's Big City Series

The Globe for its coverage of the Coyle brothers manhunt

Boston Business and Professional Women's Club Woman of Achievement award

Frances Burns for medical reporting

Strebig Doblen award by Trans World Airlines

Arthur A. Riley for distinguished aviation reporting

Henry D. Chadwick award of Massachusetts Tuberculosis and Health League

Ian Menzies for special feature story on James Gray

National Defense Transportation Association, New England Chapter (tribute of appreciation

Nat Kline for meritorious achievement

Editorial Awards 1960

UPI Newspaper Editors of Massachusetts

Thomas Winship for editorial on Boston redevelopment

Lincoln National Life Foundation award

"Uncle Dudley" for "most timely Lincoln editorial on 'The Man Alone' "

Boston Press Club's Rudolph Elie award

Twelve-man Globe team for 11-part series on Massachusetts legislature

National Headliners award

Otto Zausmer for 1959 articles from Europe on immigrants to U.S. who contributed to homelands, "The Natives Return"

U.S. Olympic Association (certificate of appreciation)

Jerry Nason for support of U.S. Olympic team

Editorial Awards 1961

Associated Press Managing Editors Association

The Globe for outsanding day-to-day news coverage

Boston Press Club's Amasa Howe award

Mark Feinberg for story on Kimble Berry

NEAPMEA Best News Story

Mark Feinberg for story on Kimble Berry

Massachusetts Mental Health Association Mental Health Bell award

Herbert Black for perceptive reporting in field of mental health

Boston Press Club (special honorable mention)

The Globe for 46-page entry, "Spotlight on Massachusetts in 1961"

Editorial Awards 1962

UPI Newspaper Editors of Massachusetts (news writing contest)	Edward G. McGrath for coverage of integration riots in Mississippi
Boston Press Club's Amasa Howe award	Edward G. McGrath for coverage of integration riots at the University of Mississippi
NEAPMEA Best News Story	Robert Healy for story on President Kennedy and Adlai Stevenson
National Safety Council	Herbert Black and Robert Carr

Editorial Awards 1963

Rudolph Elie award	Ian Forman for series on schools in Boston and New England

Editorial Awards 1964

Yankee Quill award (Sigma Delta Chi)	Laurence L. Winship for his editorship
Amasa Howe award (best spot news series)	Gloria Negri for "Mrs. Peabody's Trip to Florida"
UPI News Writing	Robert Levey for "Dilemma of Boston Schools"
American Medical Association (special commendation)	Herbert Black for several articles

Editorial Awards 1965

Pulitzer Prize gold medal (public service)	Tom Winship, Bob Healy, and team for Morrissey case
Sevellon Brown award	Tom Winship, Bob Healy, and team for Morrissey case
UPI Contest (distinguished service award)	Tom Winship, Bob Healy, and team for Morrissey case
Education Writers Association	Ian Forman for "The Massachusetts Master Plan for Education"
Massachusetts Psychological Association (for "contributions to public education, human welfare, and development of psychology as a 'profession' ")	Jean Dietz for articles of 1965
Herreshoff trophy	Leonard Fowle, yachting
Sigma Delta Chi (Boston University School of Journalism chapter)	Ed McGrath for series on Selma

American Medical Association (special commendation: category, valuable contribution to better understanding of medicine and health)	Herbert Black for several stories
UPI Contest (spot news class, citation)	Herbert Black for in-depth series on LSD
Massachusetts Business and Professional Women's Club	Marian Christy for "Woman of Achievement"
Associated Press News Writing Contest (enterprise classification; news classification)	William Buchanan; Richard Connolly
National Council of Senior Citizens (annual award of merit)	Frank Harris for "Senior Set" columns
American Institute of Men's and Boys' Wear	Marian Christy

Editorial Awards 1966

Rudolph Elie Memorial award	Joseph Dinneen, Jr., for column "Death of a Youth Strikes Home"
Sevellon Brown award (AP: special citation for "Architects")	Globe staff
Allan B. Rogers UPI Memorial award for editorial excellence	Anson Smith for "Must Tracy Die?"
Thomas Stokes (National Conservation) award	Richard Connolly for series on New England Power
AP Best Written Story	James Stack for "Miracle of Guest House"
AP Best Sports Story	Bud Collins for story on playground facilities in Roxbury
Special UPI News Writing award	James Stack for "Miracle of Guest House"
Massachusetts Association of Mental Health	Jean Dietz for outstanding public service leading to increased public understanding and action on behalf of the mentally ill
Education Writers Association	Robert Levey for series on six New England universities
J. C. Penney-University of Missouri Journalism award	Marian Christy: named country's top fashion writer

National Shoe Institute of New York	Marian Christy for excellence in press coverage of shoe fashion
Boston Business and Professional Women's Club Woman of Achievement award	Marian Christy for entirety, depth, and dedication displayed in her work
American Institute of Men's and Boys' Wear (for men's fashion writing)	Marian Christy for best coverage of men's fashions

Editorial Awards 1967

Lasker award (for best medical story of the year)	Carl Cobb for series on Mississippi medicine
Sevellon Brown award (AP)	Ray Richards for series on Bridgewater State Prison
American Medical Association Special Commendation award (for most valuable contribution to better understanding of medicine and health)	Herbert Black and Carl Cobb (won by Black 1964, 1965, 1967)
UPI Writing Contest (special team writing award)	Alan Lupo and John Burke for neighborhood series
Amasa Howe award (for news writing)	Robert Turner, Alan Lupo, and William Cardoso for coverage of cog railway crash on Mt. Washington, N.H.
FRANY. Fashion Writers Award of New York (First Prize First Time award, from Mayor Lindsay and the New York Couture Business Council)	Marian Christy for outstanding coverage of New York fashion scene
National Shoe Institute of New York	Marian Christy for excellence in press coverage of shoe fashion
American Institute of Men's and Boys' Wear (for men's fashion writing)	Marian Christy for best coverage of men's fashions

Editorial Awards 1968

Yankee Quill award (Sigma Delta Chi)	Alexander J. Haviland for his editorship
Rudolph Elie award	Carl Cobb
Sevellon Brown award (AP)	Ray Richards
UPI News Awards: Allan B. Rogers Memorial award (for best editorial of 1968)	Charles Whipple
UPI Feature Story	Bud Collins

National Medical Committee for Human Rights, "In recognition of the outstanding Medical Journalism of 1968" (special citation)	Herbert Black and Carl Cobb
American Cancer Society, Massachusetts Division (for outstanding service in cancer control and general excellence in medical writing	Herbert Black
Massachusetts Heart Association (for outstanding medical writing)	Herbert Black
American Medical Association (for general excellence in journalism contributing to better understanding of medicine and health in the U.S.)	Herbert Black and Carl Cobb
New England Women's Press Club Woman of the Year	Ellen Goodman
Women's Press Association special award, first time (for courage in reporting)	Marjorie Sherman
John B. Gillooly award (1968 sports writer of the year)	Jerry Nason
Knox College Sang Prize for Critics of the Fine Arts	Michael Steinberg (co-winner)
J. C. Penney-University of Missouri Journalism award	Marian Christy
National Shoe Institute Lulu award	Marian Christy
American Institute of Men's and Boys' Wear (for men's fashion writing)	Marian Christy
New England Associated Press Executives' Association special award	The Globe for sharing with world AP member newspapers exclusive story on assassination of Robert Kennedy

Editorial Awards 1969

Sevellon Brown Memorial award (AP)	Richard J. Connolly for search for George Brady
Community Service award (UPI)	Gerard M. O'Neill for series on politics and cronyism
UPI Spot News	Richard J. Connolly for search for George Brady
Robert T. Morse award (for major contribution to understanding of psychiatry)	Jean Dietz

Massachusetts Heart Association	Herbert Black
American Cancer Society	Herbert Black
American Society of Abdominal Surgeons	Herbert Black
John F. Kennedy symposium award (for analysis and interpretation in medicine and science)	Herbert Black and Carl Cobb
Boston Tuberculosis and Respiratory Disease Association (for contributions to improvement of the environment)	James Ayres
Ente Italiano Della Moda (international award for fashion writing, second prize)	Marian Christy
Society of Technical Writers, Boston chapter (for distinction in writing)	Arthur Riley
International Association of Firefighters (for outstanding coverage of fire fighting)	Frank Mahoney
International Association of Firefighters (for policy of sustained fire reporting and "innovative handling of every dimension of the fire story")	The Globe

Editorial Awards 1970 *

Audubon Society Award (for outstanding environmental coverage)	Boston Globe
UPI Civic Service Award (for investigation of School Committeeman John Kerrigan's relations with contractors)	Gerard O'Neill
American Bar Association Certificate of Merit (for a distinguished series on the new law school graduates' concern for the underprivileged)	Alan Lupo
Sports Writer of the Year, by Massachusetts Sports Writers	Tom Fitzgerald
J. C. Penney-University of Missouri Journalism Award	Marian Christy
Silver Slipper Award by National Footwear Institute	Marian Christy

Photographic Awards 1958

Boston Press Photographers	
Feature	Paul Connell

* 1970 list is incomplete. Awards are made in the following year.

Series	Joe Runci
UPI Photo Contest	Harry Holbrook
Special awards	
Boston Garden Hockey	Charles Carey
Massachusetts Bankers Association	Paul Connell

Photographic Awards 1959

Boston Press Photographers	
Series	William Ennis
Feature	John Sheahan
Sequence	Paul Maguire
Special awards	
Boston Garden Hockey	Charles Carey
	John Hurley

Photographic Awards 1960

Boston Press Photographers	
Spot News	Phil Preston
Best of Show	Phil Preston
Sports	John Sheahan
Series	Joe Runci
Boston Firefighters	Edmund Kelley
American Airlines	Paul Connell

Photographic Awards 1961

Boston Press Photographers	
Sports Feature	Paul Maguire
Sports	Paul Maguire
Pictorial	Paul Connell
Picture Story	John Sheahan
UPI Photo Contest	
Feature	Harry Holbrook
News Picture	Ollie Noonan, Jr.
Sports	Paul Maguire
New England Chapter, National Press Photographers Association	
New England Press Photographer of the Year	Paul Connell
American Airlines	
Outstanding Aviation Picture	Jack O'Connell, Jr.

Photographic Awards 1962

Boston Press Photographers	
Best of Show	John Sheahan
Press Photographer of the Year	Bob Dean
Spot News	Bob Dean

Picture Story	Bob Dean
Personality	John Sheahan
General News	Edmund Kelley
Special Award for Hockey Shot	Dan Goshtigian

Photographic Awards 1963

Boston Press Photographers
    Press Photographer of the Year   Paul Connell
                                              Joseph Dennehy

AP Contest
    Four awards   Paul Connell

Photographic Awards 1964

Boston Press Photographers
    Press Photographer of the Year   Paul Connell
    Best of Show   Daniel Sheehan
    Picture Story   Paul Connell
    Spot News   Daniel Sheehan
    Personality   Paul Connell
UPI Contest
    News   Paul Connell
    Feature   Paul Connell
    Sports   Charles Carey

Photographic Awards 1965

Boston Press Photographers
    General News   Paul Connell
    Sports   Dan Goshtigian (two)
    Sequence   Paul Maguire
    Sports Feature   Paul Maguire
    Pictorial   Joe Runci
    Bruins Hockey   Dan Goshtigian
UPI Photo Contest
    Citation for Excellence   Paul Connell
    Feature   Joe Runci
    Sports   Dan Goshtigian

Photographic Awards 1966

Boston Press Photographers
    Spot News   Joseph Dennehy
    General News   Frank O'Brien
    Sports   Dan Goshtigian
    Pictorial   Oliver Noonan
    Picture Story   Joseph Dennehy
    Sports Feature   Bob Dean
    Personality   Bill Brett

| Bruins Hockey | Dan Goshtigian |
| Boston Fire | Richard Fallon |

New England AP News Executive Association

Spot News	Bill Brett
Sports	Dan Goshtigian
Personality	Paul Connell

Photographic Awards 1967

Boston Press Photographers

News Photographer of the Year	Paul Connell
Picture Story	Bill Brett
Sports Feature	Paul Connell
Spot News	Bill Brett
General News	Bob Dean
Sports	Frank O'Brien
Personality	Paul Connell
Animal	Joe Dennehy
Pictorial	Joe Dennehy
Bruins Hockey	Dan Goshtigian
Best of Show	Bill Brett

UPI Photo Contest

Spot News	Bill Brett
Personality	Joyce Dopkeen
Sports	Dan Goshtigian
Sports Sequence	Paul Connell
Feature	Joyce Dopkeen

Boston Press Photographers Awards

| Press Photographer of the Year | Paul Connell |

Photographic Awards 1968

Boston Press Photographers

News Photographer of the Year	Paul Connell
Animal	Paul Connell
Picture Story	Paul Connell
General News	Joe Dennehy
Pictorial	Ted Dully

UPI

Spot News Sequences	Tom Landers
Sports	Dan Goshtigian
Sports Sequences	Paul Connell
Personality	Ted Dully

Photographic Awards 1969

Boston Press Photographers

| Bruins Hockey (best sports picture) | Dan Goshtigian |

Color News	Bob Dean
General News	Paul Connell
Animal	Joe Dennehy
Color Feature	Bill Potter
Edwin T. Ramsdell Memorial trophy (first in spot news)	Edison Farrand

Globe Staff Members Awarded Nieman Fellowships

Louis M. Lyons	1938–39
Victor O. Jones	1941–42
William H. Clark	1944–45
Robert Healy	1955–56
Wilfrid C. Rodgers	1958–59
Ian Menzies	1961–62
James S. Doyle	1964–65
Richard H. Stewart	1966–67
James B. Ayres	1967–68
Robert L. Levey	1968–69
Carl Cobb	1969–70
Carol Liston	1971–72

Nieman Fellows Who Joined the Globe

Fred Pillsbury	1956–57
Victor K. McElheny	1962–63

List of Sources

I Another Newspaper

Ballou's Globe: Venture in Bankruptcy
Willard DeLue manuscript, "Materials for a History of the Boston Globe"
E. M. Bacon, *Dictionary of Boston,* 1886
Joseph E. Chamberlain, *The Boston Transcript,* Houghton Mifflin, 1930
James Morgan, *Charles H. Taylor,* privately printed, 1923
A. A. Fowle manuscript, "Fifty Years with the Boston Globe," 1926
Frank Luther Mott, *American Journalism: A History,* Macmillan, 1941
Emery and Smith, *The Press in America,* Prentice-Hall, 1954
"Edwin Percy Whipple," DAB
Charles H. Taylor, "The Middlesex Club" (interview with Taylor, Boston Herald, January 5, 1919)
Harvard Class Reports
James B. Cullen, *The Story of the Irish in Boston,* James B. Cullen & Co., 1889

By Foot and Horsecar
A. A. Fowle manuscript
Willard DeLue manuscript
James Morgan, *Charles H. Taylor*

Beecher Trial
DeLue manuscript

First Telephone Story
DeLue manuscript

Eben Jordan Saves the Globe
DeLue manuscript

II A Different Newspaper

Chas. H. Taylor's New Globe
Willard DeLue manuscript

A New World to Florence Finch
DeLue manuscript
Florence Finch Kelly, *Flowing Stream,* E. P. Dutton & Co., 1939

Chas. Taylor Finds James Morgan
James Morgan, *Charles H. Taylor*
Don C. Seitz, *Joseph Pulitzer: His Life and Letters,* Simon & Schuster, 1924
William H. Hill manuscript, "Reminiscences"

The Irish
DeLue manuscript
Cullen, *Story of the Irish in Boston*

A Poem from Dr. Holmes
DeLue manuscript
Morgan, *Charles H. Taylor*

Mugwumps and Democrats
DeLue manuscript
Cullen, *Story of the Irish in Boston*
Geoffrey Blodgett, *The Gentle Reformers,* Harvard University Press, 1966
Arthur Stanley Pease, *Sequestered Vales of Life,* Harvard University Press, 1946

Women Are People — and Readers
DeLue manuscript
William Hill manuscript

Harvard Invasion
DeLue manuscript
Hill manuscript
Harvard Class Reports

The First 100,000
DeLue manuscript
Seitz, *Joseph Pulitzer*

New Building
DeLue manuscript
Mott, *American Journalism*

Transit and "Corruption"
DeLue manuscript
Blodgett, *Gentle Reformers*
Barbara M. Solomon, *Ancestors and Immigrants,* Harvard University, 1956
Charles Allen Madison, *Critics and Crusaders,* Henry Holt, 1947

General Taylor and Uncle Dudley
DeLue manuscript
Morgan, *Charles H. Taylor*
Harry T. Morgan manuscript, "Fragments of an Uncompleted Biography of James Morgan," 1953

News Enterprise, 1890
DeLue manuscript
Louis Stark, "The Press and Labor News," in *Annals of the Academy of Political and Social Science,* vol. 219, January 1942

The Globe and Lizzie Borden
DeLue manuscript
Victoria Lincoln, *A Private Disgrace: Lizzie Borden by Daylight,* G. P. Putnam's Sons, 1967

Color, Contests, and Comics
DeLue manuscript

Globe Wins on Elections
DeLue manuscript
"William E. Russell," DAB

Family Business
DeLue manuscript

Confidential Chat
DeLue manuscript

Bryan Upsets Gold Bugs — and the Globe
DeLue manuscript
Morgan, *Charles H. Taylor*
"William E. Russell" and "George Fred Williams," DAB

Harvard and Other Sports
DeLue manuscript

Dewey's War
DeLue manuscript
"Finley Peter Dunne," DAB
Chamberlain, *Boston Transcript*

Advertisers and Contemporaries, 1899
Addison Archer, *Interviews Regarding the Character, Circulation and Advertising Value
    of the Boston Newspapers,* pamphlet, March 1899

III   New Century — No Change

1900
Willard DeLue manuscript

"That Mad Man" President
Margaret Leech, *In the Days of McKinley,* Harper, 1959

The Auto Arrives
M. E. Hennessy, *Massachusetts Politics,* Norwood Press, 1935

Patent Medicines and Other Ads
Arthur & Lila Weinberg, *The Muckrakers,* Simon & Schuster, 1961
"Mark Sullivan on Patent Medicine," Collier's, November 4, 1905
Samuel Hopkins Adams, "The Great American Fraud," Collier's, October 28, 1905

Steffens' Boston
Lincoln Steffens, *Autobiography,* The Literary Guild, 1931
——— *The Shame of the Cities,* McClure, Phillips, 1904
"Edward A. Filene," DAB
M. E. Hennessy, *Massachusetts Politics*
Francis Russell, *The Great Interlude,* McGraw-Hill, 1964
Arthur & Lila Weinberg, *Muckrakers*
Joseph F. Dinneen, *Ward Eight,* Harper & Bros., 1936

Two for the North Pole
"Robert Peary" and "Frederick A. Cook," DAB

History Day by Day
James Morgan, *Charles H. Taylor*

Uncle Dudley Joins the Globe
"Dr. Elwood Worcester," DAB
"Frank P. Sibley" and "Lucien Price," Harvard Class Reports
Lucien Price, "Message to the Middle Class," Atlantic Monthly, July 1914
———— *Dialogues of Alfred North Whitehead,* Little, Brown, 1954
———— *Immortal Youth,* Beacon Press, 1945

Long Count of 1916
Letters of Franklin K. Lane, ed. Anne W. Lane and Louise H. Wall, Houghton Mifflin, 1922

Sibley to France
DeLue manuscript
Frank P. Sibley, *With the Yankee Division in France,* Little, Brown, 1919

IV   Struggle and Survival

Police Strike
Calvin Coolidge, *Autobiography of Calvin Coolidge,* Cosmopolitan Book Corporation, 1931
Claude M. Fuess, *Calvin Coolidge,* Little, Brown, 1940
William Allen White, *A Puritan in Babylon,* Macmillan, 1938
Coolidge, *Have Faith in Massachusetts,* Houghton Mifflin, 1919

All Souls
Lucien Price, *A Litany of All Souls,* Beacon Press, 1945
W. Raymond McClure, *Prometheus: A Memoir of Lucien Price, January 6, 1866–March 30, 1964,* Cambridge University Press, 1965
Letters of Franklin K. Lane, ed. Lane and Wall

Transition: CH Jr. and W.O.
Oswald Garrison Villard, *The Disappearing Daily,* Alfred A. Knopf, 1944
Hutchins Commission Report: A Free and Responsible Press, University of Chicago Press, 1947
Peter Braestrup, "What the Press Has Done to Boston," Harper's, October 1960
Louis M. Lyons, *Reporting the News,* Harvard University Press, 1965

Trustee Publisher
Lyons, *Reporting the News*

Sacco-Vanzetti
Francis Russell, *Tragedy in Dedham,* McGraw-Hill, 1962
Felix Frankfurter, *The Case of Sacco and Vanzetti,* Little, Brown, 1927
Letters of Felix Frankfurter and John H. Wigmore, Boston Transcript, April 21, May 2–11, 1927

City Editor
James W. Barrett, *Joseph Pulitzer and His World,* Vanguard Press, 1941

Gardner Jackson
"Gardner Jackson Reminiscences," *Columbia Oral History,* 1959

Banned in Boston

American Mercury, September 1925; April 1926

Paul S. Boyer, *Purity in Print,* Charles Scribner's Sons, 1968

Extracts from editorials of Boston Herald on "The Strange Interlude," September 18, 1929

Richard F. Fuller, "How Boston Handles Problem" Publishers' Weekly, May 26, 1923

Maine and Vermont for Landon

Robert Shaplen, *Ivar Kreuger: Genius and Swindler,* Alfred A. Knopf, 1960

Contemporaries and Competition

Dale Kramer, *Heywood Broun,* A. A. Wyn, 1949

Louis M. Lyons, "Boston—A Study in Inertia," in *Our Fair City,* Robert Allen, ed., Vanguard Press, 1947

The Joe Kennedy Story

James MacGregor Burns, *John Kennedy: A Political Profile,* Harcourt, Brace, 1960

Joseph F. Dinneen, *The Kennedy Family,* Little, Brown, 1960

Richard J. Whalen, *The Founding Father: The Story of Joseph P. Kennedy,* New American Library, 1964

Joe McCarthy, *The Remarkable Kennedys,* Dial Press, 1960

United Nations

Henry Harris, *To Wage Peace,* Excelsior Press, 1949

Brink's Notebook

Joseph F. Dinneen, *The Purple Shamrock,* W. W. Norton, 1949

McCarthyism

Arthur M. Schlesinger, Jr., *A Thousand Days,* Houghton Mifflin, 1965

Robert J. Donovan, *Eisenhower: The Inside Story,* Harper & Bros., 1956

V   New Era

Another Winship

Charles Whipple, "Dirty Money in Boston," Atlantic Monthly, March 1961

Index